STRATEGIC MANAGEMENT

VALUE CREATION, SUSTAINABILITY, AND PERFORMANCE

G. Page West III

STRATEGIC MANAGEMENT

VALUE CREATION, SUSTAINABILITY, AND PERFORMANCE

Seventh Edition

© 2013, 2014, 2016, 2018, 2020, 2021, 2022 by G. Page West III. ALL RIGHTS RESERVED. No part of this work covered by the copyright hereon may be reproduced or used in any form or by any means whatsoever – graphic, electronic, or mechanical, including photocopying, recording, taping, Web distribution, information storage and retrieval systems, or in any other manner – without written permission.

For permission to use material from this text, submit all requests to:
Riderwood Publishing, 3109 Allerton Lake Drive, Winston Salem, NC, 27106, USA.
Permissions questions can be emailed to strategytext@gmail.com.

eBook ISBN: 978-1733174435
Print ISBN: 978-1733174442

Riderwood Publishing
3109 Allerton Lake Drive
Winston Salem, North Carolina, 27106, USA

About the cover to the 7th Edition

The book's cover design reflects themes discussed throughout the text: new versus old, new technology and industries, and competition in a global environment. Continuing from earlier editions of Strategic Management, we again allude to changes in the auto industry. Customers now shop online for cars and take delivery just like delivered food orders. EV charging stations will soon blanket the country as manufacturers devote capacity to this growing segment. But personal flight vehicles are on the horizon, such as the Jobian Aviation eVTOL. In 1971 Intel's 4004 microprocessor was the first programmable chip, calculated 92K operations per second with 2300 transistors. Apple introduced the M1 Pro in 2021, with 33 billion transistors calculating 11 trillion operations per second. We have now moved way past the "advanced" Blackberry 6710 from 2002. Also included are logos for companies that have changed the way we live our lives: Spotify, Instagram, Square, Apple Airtag, and HBO Max. Each of these operates in a highly-competitive global environment. All images are © their respective companies, and are used herein only to illustrate competition in today's global markets.

Dedication

To my wife Linda and to our five children. Their constant support for my work has kept me going. They have each inspired me with their curiosity, their humor, their intuition, their thoughtful approaches, and especially their hopes for a better world. They also keep me on my toes, up to date with new music and apps, and aware how new trends shape our collective experience.

This page is intentionally left blank.

Preface for Students

If you are a student, no doubt you're starting to read this textbook because your professor has assigned it for your Strategic Management course. No doubt you've also read many textbooks during your time in school. So have I, and these are some conclusions I draw about many of them:

- Often relatively dry, long-winded, hard to hold your attention.
- Heavy on concepts, and light on examples that you can easily relate to.
- Difficult to put to practical use.
- And unbelievably expensive!

No wonder so many students recommend "get rid of the textbook" in end-of-semester course evaluations! I spent 20 years in industry practicing strategy, and I've been teaching strategy for about 30 years. Until I wrote and started using this book in my classes I never failed to receive this comment at the end of the term. I tried changing textbooks now and then, but my feedback on the books never really changed. So I wrote my own.

OK, so what's different here? First, let me start with the last point I made above about expense. Since you're reading this version, you already know it didn't break your college budget. You may have noticed on the dedication page that I have five children, which represents 20 years of college textbook bills to pay (actually 21, since one of my kids did the "5-year" plan). Ouch! The costs of textbooks alone during these years was just shocking. Over time I've seen textbook prices getting totally out of control! In fact the Bureau of Labor Statistics reports that college textbook prices have inflated more than any other category over the last 35-40 years! Today new printed textbooks can cost well over $250. Even their digital counterparts through the big publishing companies can cost $75 to "rent" for 4-6 months. My book overcomes this huge burden. Assuming you're now reading the digital version, you know that it did not break the bank.

I'm also trying to solve the other problems I mentioned above. Using a comfortable writing style with contemporary examples about companies you know, it will hold your interest. I know this because we have classroom-tested it over and over again. And we get remarkably positive feedback from faculty who have used it.

No textbook would be any good, though, if it didn't have quality impact. So here you will read about cutting edge ideas in strategy, and I will explain complicated ideas in ways that you can easily understand.

Our strategy "theories" are only helpful if you can actually put them to use in situations you will soon encounter. You will discover here a step-by-step process to show you how to apply the ideas.

No other strategy textbook puts all this together. I think you'll appreciate the approach.

I hope you will send me feedback on this text, so that I can continue to make improvements. If you find a typo, let me know! Let me know what you like and what you don't like. Tell me where you think something is confusing, tell me when you read something that you enjoyed or gave you new insight.

Preface for Instructors

If you have already been using a previous edition of my textbook, I am grateful for your support. You no doubt chose the book originally for many of the reasons I outline in this section. But since you probably already understand these advantages, you can skip to the last subsection in this Preface to find out what is new in this seventh edition. If you have not yet used my book in your course, please read on.

As a strategy professor or instructor, you're probably saying to yourself, "There are so many strategic management texts. What makes this textbook unique in a crowded field? Why should I give up the book I already know and prep a new text?" Good questions. Even as the question of "competitive advantage" is fundamental to the field of Strategic Management, it is also important in the selection of a textbook to use in your strategy class.

So here's my pitch. When I first developed this text, I wanted to create something special for professors. I wanted to create a text that was sure to enable every instructor to teach strategy more effectively. This is accomplished through a text that truly engages students with easily-understood theory, useful examples from practice, and really current information. To do so I have incorporated several key innovations into the book:

- The content is the most current of all strategy textbooks. The copyright for this 7th edition is 2022. This means you will find examples and company data right up into 2022, not ending in some years past.

- Integrating content across chapters throughout the book, relying on
  - Two strategic imperatives: value creation imperative, and opportunity recognition imperative.
  - Two strategy concepts as integrating mechanisms: value chain, resource based advantage.

- Devoting a full chapter to performance.

- Providing guidance on practical application of important strategy concepts (e.g., steps to conduct an industry analysis, how to conduct a resources analysis).

- Adopting a writing style that is student-friendly and accessible.

This approach has been successful. Since 2019 Strategic Management is one of the fastest growing texts in our field in new adoptions and sales volume. Faculty adopters have expressed appreciation for the crystal clear presentation and unpacking of theory and frameworks. Students engage with a familiar writing style. Both groups appreciate the low cost and fresh content of the text, unparalleled in other books. I briefly explore these advantages below.

2022 actually means 2022

The beauty of this digitally-published textbook is that the lag time between finishing the updated manuscript and publishing the edition is, literally, only days. This 7th edition is copyright 2022. You will find that the company examples used as illustrations have updated performance numbers through the latest fiscal year and into 2022. When students open this text for your course, everything is fresh.

I challenge you to compare this to any other strategy text. Printed textbooks from legacy publishers are already dated by the time they come out. This is because of how long it takes for the publishers to do their physical print-production thing. Manuscripts for legacy publisher texts with 2022 copyrights were likely completed in 2020. By the time students get the book, the data is already at least 2 years old. Compare this text to other traditional texts, and you will see for yourself how dated other material is.

By the way, don't be fooled by texts published in 2022 with 2023 copyright dates! This is simply a marketing trick used by large publishers to make the book appear more current. The manuscript was still completed earlier and the material is likely to be dated.

Integration Across Chapters

One of the problems I grappled with over my years in teaching is that we must cover a great deal of material in a typical strategic management course. Students often view the course as a series of almost stand-alone frameworks – industry analysis, then value chain, generic strategies, etc. – that are not well integrated with each other or with more complicated material later on in the course such as M&A, global strategy, structuring, or implementation. I address the integration problem in this book.

First, to lay the groundwork for students, I explicitly introduce two strategic imperatives in Chapter 1. These include the *value creation imperative* and the *opportunity recognition imperative*. I position strategic management today as occurring in a constantly changing context, so a real challenge has to do with superior performance both now and in the future. These two imperatives are revisited and touched upon in virtually every chapter, because they are central to every dimension of managing strategically. This helps to consistently draw the chapters together.

For you as instructor, the textbook uses "value chain" and "resource based advantage" as core integrating strategy concepts. As you build the foundation for strategic management, the combination of these integrating concepts requires students to consider how firms achieve superior *performance* by creating *value* on a *sustainable* basis. Note the italicized words are the subtitle for the book.

This approach offers several advantages. First, the concept of value facilitates the discussion of industry entry as well as the discussion of how value is created in different ways at different stages of an industry's or company's evolution. Importantly, the issue of value creation is seen as a critical ongoing strategic challenge in industries characterized by evolutionary and revolutionary change. Therefore, the tension that exists between mandates for change versus the need for continuity can be highlighted.

But these more contemporary ideas cannot exist in isolation from the essential *sustainability* goal of superior performance. I strongly emphasize the importance of coordinating mechanisms across the value chain, routines, and other intangible dimensions as extraordinary strategic resources. In turn, these help make the discussion of resource-based advantage more practical and more understandable.

Finally, the value chain integration focus enables a broader discussion of organizational stakeholders, corporate social responsibility, and organizational goals. Economic value and social value are each perceived as legitimate organizational goals by students today, and therefore *value* embraces a wide range of organizations including not-for-profits and those with social goals. The relevance of the strategic management course to these sectors, where student interest is rapidly growing, becomes more transparent.

Throughout the text you will find that we regularly refer back to these integrating aspects. Conclusions from industry analysis can be evaluated in the context of value adding activities and resource-based capabilities, as can business level strategies, competitive dynamics, diversification, organizational structuring, and internal control. I believe that this integrative approach makes the field of strategic management more understandable to students, from beginning to end. And it allows instructors to more easily draw on the critical foundations all the way through the semester.

Chapter on Performance

This text emphasizes – in fact spotlights – *performance* as a key outcome of strategic management by treating this dimension in its own stand-alone chapter. Few other strategy textbooks do this. I encourage the perspective that strategic management demands an ability to move with facility back and forth between the conceptual and the practical, including the performance that results from best laid plans. Students need to recognize early on that strategic decisions and actions ultimately translate to financial effects. With this understanding, case discussions and other class interactions can easily move deeper than merely "I think the company should do….." to "I think the company should do…..and this is the estimated performance impact."

Faculty want students to conduct financial analyses of companies for class discussions and projects, yet texts do not usually provide sufficient content to assist in this effort (other than the usual appendix containing financial ratios – we have one of those, too, by the way). By addressing this important topic early in the book in Chapter 2, instructors will have an easier time in drawing upon financial analysis throughout the course and in asking students to consider performance implications in class discussions. Performance becomes front and center. We know this works based on classroom tests and surveys we have done among users of this text.

Theory to Practice

This book is strongly grounded in foundational strategic management theory. I draw upon the most contemporary thinking in strategy, from both academic publications and industry experience. The manuscript for this book has been reviewed by other strategy professors like you (see list that follows), and went through a rigorous "revise and resubmit" process. It received overwhelmingly favorable ratings on content and writing style.

But it also has a very practical bent. I want students to be able to take these ideas and use them, easily. So you will find that many chapters provide guidance on actually putting the ideas to use (e.g., steps to conduct an industry analysis, how to do a resource analysis, how to conduct a value chain analysis) along with examples of how to do so. Resource-based theory? It's complex! How many other texts provide *practical* advice on how to use this important theory?

Students are increasingly being pushed to translate their education into useful, growth-oriented and value-creating efforts within the companies that recruit them. Today's job search process often involves phone or virtual interviews on the front end. In this environment, to the extent that your students can adeptly apply strategy ideas to real situations and problems they are asked about, they will outperform others. Making the ideas practically useful becomes their competitive advantage.

Engaging Style

Finally, this book overcomes an enduring complaint by students about so many textbooks: they are dry and uninteresting to read. The writing for this book strikes a balance between providing well-explained theory and a style that is engaging for students. I make liberal use of companies and industries that students can relate to in order to provide good translation of ideas to practice (e.g., music industry, Xbox and the gaming industry, cell phones, PCs, Starbucks). In fact, one reviewer commented "bang – hits the spot!" when an example from a video game illustrated a point about industry analysis in Chapter 4.

I also use the first person plural "we." I view learning about strategic management as a journey we faculty are embarking on alongside our students, rolling up our sleeves and working hard together to understand this fascinating field.

How do I know this style of writing works? Before the first edition was ever published, I classroom tested this textbook for years. Students responded favorably. Now in 2022 the book is being used by thousands of students across dozens and dozens of universities.

Since using this book in my own classes at Wake Forest University and in other venues, I receive positive comments in the anonymous end-of-semester course surveys about the instructional materials. And this is the honest truth: not once since using this text have I ever again received the student comment "get rid of the text"!

One Last Important Item: The Price

In my remarks to students above, I mentioned the significant cost benefits of using this digital textbook. This is very real for students and their parents. The cost of textbooks has risen 1041% in the past 30+ years (U.S. Bureau of Labor Statistics). That's *more* than increases in healthcare costs, housing prices, and college tuition, all of which have risen faster than the pre-2022 rate of inflation.

Estimates suggest a student should budget $1,500 annually for books and supplies at public four-year colleges. Why is this? First, the $9 billion textbook publishing industry is highly concentrated, where 80% of college textbooks are accounted for by just three publishers (McGraw Hill, Cengage, and Pearson). As strategists, we know what the effect of market concentration is. But how much publishers can charge for textbooks depends on students' ability to pay. Enter the federal government student aid programs, which have nearly doubled over the last twenty years. The ballooned level of federal student loan debt includes billions of dollars for textbook purchases that went directly to big publishers over the years. Millions of students still owe thousands of dollars for books they used for only four months. This is really saddening, and maddening.

Buying or renting this digital book does not break the bank! Your adoption of this text makes a real difference in more ways than one!

What's New in the 7th Edition?

Below are new enhancements in this 7th Edition.

- **2022 actually means 2022**. I repeat this from above, because having a "fresh" book is so important to faculty and students. The beauty of this digitally-published textbook is that the lag time between finishing the manuscript and publishing the edition is, literally, only days. This 7th edition is copyright 2022. You will find throughout the book that company and industry examples have updated performance numbers through the latest fiscal year and into 2022. When students open this text for your course, everything is fresh. Printed textbooks from legacy publishers are dated by the time they come out, because of how long it takes for the publishers to do their thing. Compare this text to examples in other traditional texts, and you will see for yourself how dated some of their material is. And, again, don't be fooled by texts introduced in 2021-2022 with a 2023 copyright date; this is a marketing trick used by some large publishers to make the book appear to be fresh.

- **Updated Strategic Management Model.** In Chapter 1 we present a roadmap for the remainder of the textbook. See the revised Figure 1.6. This has been revised and updated. The Implementation and Evaluation section now includes three separate chapters positioned as alternative ways for a company to grow its business: innovation, corporate strategy diversification, expand internationally. Previously, innovation and international strategy were included in one chapter as growth alternatives following a discussion of organizational life cycles. These two areas now appear in their own separate chapters.

- **New Chapter 9, Managing Innovation.** This edition moves the major section on Managing Innovation into its own chapter. Chapter 9 follows the discussion of life cycle stages and issues related to growth. This chapter first unpacks forms and degrees of innovation. Here we add a novel dimension to the customary incremental–disruptive–radical typology by including "Amplifying" innovation that draws on leveraging and extending existing value chain practices and resources. It represents a middle ground between incremental and radical, which companies practically are often seeking to accomplish. The section moves on to a detailed discussion of opportunity recognition and evaluation, and concludes with useful ideas for managing an innovation effort.

- **New Chapter 11, International Strategy.** This edition also moves the major section on International Strategy into its own chapter. Chapter 11 follows the discussion of corporate strategy and diversification. Here we review the historical importance of global trade, as well as both traditional and emerging motivations for expanding abroad. We also tackle: Porter's fit model, accounting for country-level factors and conditions; the CAGE distance model to help qualify decisions on global expansion; different modes of entry; and political and economic risk considerations.

- **New section on Strategy During Crisis.** Chapter 8 is now dedicated exclusively to strategy during stages of industry evolution and in differing organizational life cycle stages. Here we add a new section that draws upon recent McKinsey research on response during crisis. We discuss both tactical and strategic steps to accelerate decision making and intervene in normal process as response styles. This new section can work nicely with news reports about companies during the pandemic and other unpredictable events.

- **New sections within Competitive Dynamics, Chapter 12.**
    - We enhance the predicting competitive moves discussion by including new material on the Awareness-Motivation-Capabilities framework that has appeared in Academy of Management publications. This is a novel perspective that aids in identifying direct and indirect competitors most likely to stage a competitive attack.
    - The continuum list of tactical responses has been revised, to clarify distinctions between tactics and strategy and to show where they overlap.

The above build on previously-described 6th edition enhancements:

- **"Managing in Markets: Questions for Class Discussion."** Periodically appearing are call-out boxes that challenge student thinking about how they will actually manage companies. "Why are you studying business?" "Do you think government should intrude in industries?" "Should you outsource when your competitors do?" The questions in these call-outs present markets-related, often ethical, challenges that take students out of the safety of a straightforward strategic management text into how ideas are practically applied. For several years I have been drawing my students out with the sorts of pivotal questions that strategic leaders face, related to the chapter content. The class discussions that result have been very provocative, and very rewarding. These discussions help elevate the entire strategy class experience into something very special.

- **Section titled "Why Business?" in Chapter 1.** Reflecting the evolution of thinking within the discipline of Strategic Management (e.g. "civic wealth creation"), it is incumbent on us as instructors to help our students see a bigger picture – to the extent we can. Strategy is the capstone, of course. But there are larger reasons why students major or minor in business and take this course. This short section opens up a topic that resonates with students and can lead to very interesting and reflective class discussions.

- **Industry Analysis Rating Method, Chapter 4.** Over the years I have found that student conclusions from industry analysis tend to be a bit more "eyeball" and subjective than I would like. I developed and tested a simple rating system for students to use to help them quantify conclusions from their five forces analysis. We introduce this in Chapter 4 and provide a detailed example of how it works. The method sharpens student thinking and forces them to make clear assessments with accompanying rationale.

- **Enhanced value chain discussion and example, Chapter 5.** An emphasis in the value chain chapter has always been the intangibles that are behind the scenes. How do companies achieve coordination across the value chain? More importantly, how do they achieve amplification where an action taken in one area enhances the actions taken in other areas? Chapter 5 now provides an illustrative example and discussion of this important aspect of the value chain. These coordinating mechanisms lead right into the subsequent discussion in Chapter 6 on resource based advantage.

- **Enhanced M&A examples with graphics, Chapter 10.** Three examples help illustrate important concepts in this chapter on corporate strategy. Recent pharmaceutical combinations demonstrate a "bandwagon" effect in market entry. Recent changes in United Technologies help illustrate the types of fit and synergies possible among their various SBUs and headquarters. And an example drawing on Meredith Corp. provides a nice example illustrating the BCG Matrix.

- **Partnership with Capstone strategy simulation software.** This text is the Strategic Management textbook partner with Capsim, the leading strategy simulation software program, for both their Capstone 2.0 and CapsimGlobal simulations. If you are interested in a bundle of a text and a simulation, then visit our website for more information:
  http://www.strategicmanagement.org

Acknowledgements

I would like to acknowledge many people who have contributed to this effort through reviewing the text and commenting on material in its various development stages. My thanks to:

Terry R. Adler, New Mexico State University
Brent Allred, College of William & Mary
Joe S. Anderson, Northern Arizona University
Phil Anderson, Wake Forest University
Sonny Ariss, University of Toledo
Nachiket Bhawe, North Carolina State University
Turanay Caner, North Carolina State University
John Ceneviva, University of North Carolina at Greensboro
Yang Cheng, North Carolina State University
Amod Choudhary, City University of New York
Samuel DeMarie, Iowa State University
Pat H. Dickson, Wake Forest University
Thomas J. Douglas, Southern Illinois University
Scott E. Elston, Iowa State University
Robert E. Ettl, Stony Brook University
Dr. Charles R. Fenner, SUNY – Canton
Robert Gemmell, Georgia Institute of Technology
Debora J. Gilliard, Metropolitan State College
Ari Ginsberg, New York University
Barbara A. Good, Ursuline College
Marcellina Hamilton, SUNY - Canton
Jay J. Janney, University of Dayton
Sal Kukalis, California State University Long Beach
Joseph W. Leonard, Miami University
Paul Mallette, Colorado State University
Gideon Markman, Colorado State University
James Randall Martin, Florida International University
Elouise Mintz, Saint Louis University
Michael L. Monahan, Frostburg State University
J. L. Morrow, Jr., Birmingham - Southern College
Fred P. Newby, Sullivan University
Daewoo Park, Xavier University
Ralph W. Parrish, University of Central Oklahoma
John K. Ross III, Texas State University
Amit Shah, Frostburg State University
Bren Varner, Wake Forest University
Paula S. Weber, Saint Cloud State University

About the Author

Page West, Ph.D.

Dr. Page West is Professor of Strategy and Entrepreneurship, Emeritus, at Wake Forest University. He earned his B.A. in Economics at Hamilton College, an MBA at The Amos Tuck School of Business Administration at Dartmouth College, and a Ph.D. in Strategic Management at the University of Colorado at Boulder. Prior to earning his Ph.D. he held positions in new business development at consumer packaged goods companies including General Mills and Celestial Seasonings, and consulted with Westinghouse and other technology companies. He also started up a food manufacturing company, raised venture capital, and expanded the business to a national level.

At Wake Forest he has taught undergraduate and graduate classes in Strategic Management, Entrepreneurship, International Entrepreneurship, Global Capitalism, Capitalism and Free Markets, and Shakespeare on Management. He has taught strategic management in London UK, Vienna Austria and Venice Italy, and he has been a regular visiting management faculty member of École de Management in Bordeaux, France. He has won awards for innovative teaching multiple times, and has more than once been named as the most influential professor by Wake Forest business school alumni.

His research focuses primarily on strategy and strategic resource evolution in new ventures, and secondarily on the contributions that new business can make to economic development. He has published articles in *Journal of Management, Journal of Management Studies, Journal of Business Venturing, Entrepreneurship Theory and Practice, Academy of Management Learning and Education, Journal of Technology Transfer, Journal of Small Business Management, Management Research Review, Strategic Direction*, and *International Journal of Organizational Analysis*. He has also co-authored or co-edited three books: on entrepreneurial leadership, on business education, and on challenges presented by the 2008 financial crisis.

Page is married to his college sweetheart Linda. They have five children and six grandchildren. In his spare time he enjoys hiking in the Colorado high country, international travel, and researching family genealogy.

This page is intentionally left blank.

TABLE OF CONTENTS

Preface 5

Section A: Strategy Foundations 19

1 The Need for Strategy 21

    Today's Strategic Imperatives 24
    What Is Strategy? 26
    History of the Field of Strategy 36
    Vision, Ethics, Leadership 41
    Strategic Management Process 43
    Why Business? 47

2 Strategy and Performance 57

    Focus on Performance 59
    Financial Performance and Competitive Advantage 65
    Insights from Detailed Financial Analysis 69
    Economic Logic and Operating Characteristics 75
    Strategy Planning 77
    Appendix 85

3 Vision, Mission, Values 89

    Strategic Direction 90
    Vision and Vision Statements 94
    Mission Statements 98
    Principles and Values 107
    Communicating Vision, Mission, Principles 110

Section B: Formulation – Analysis Fundamentals, Strategy Types, Adaptations 119

4 Industry and Competitive Analysis 123

    The Nature of Markets and Opportunity for Competitive Advantage 125
    Structure - Conduct – Performance 128
    Defining an Industry 130
    STEEPG – General Environment 133
    Five-Forces Analysis 137
    Conclusions from Five Forces Analysis 150
    Extending Industry Analysis: Strategy Maps and Strategic Groups 157

5 Value Chain Analysis 169

    Internal Analysis Versus External Analysis 171
    SWOT 173
    Value Chain 179
    Value Chain and Competitive Advantage 185
    Conducting a Value Chain Analysis 191

6 Resource-Based Competitive Advantage 201

    The Characteristics of Resources 202
    Resources and Capabilities 214
    Conducting a Resource Analysis 216

7 Business-Level Strategy 229

    Logic of Business-Level Strategies 231
    Low Cost Strategy 238
    Differentiation Strategy 244
    Other Strategic Approaches 251
    Outsourcing, Strategy, and the Value Chain 255

8 Adapting Strategy to Industry and Life Cycle Stages 265

    Industry Life Cycles 267
    Fragmented and Consolidated Industries 274
    Organizational Life Cycles 277
    Strategy Issues in Stages 282
    Strategy During Crisis 286

Section C: Implementation – Growth Alternatives, and Competition 297

9 Managing Innovation 299

    Forms of Innovation 301
    Degrees of Innovation 303
    Opportunity Recognition and Evaluation 307
    Managing the Process 309

10 Corporate Strategy 317

    Corporate Strategy Versus Business Strategy 319
    Historical Perspectives 320
    Motivations for Diversification 325
    Types of Diversification 332

Diversification Performance 339
Managing the Corporate Portfolio 347

11 Developing an International Strategy 363

Historical Perspectives on Global Trade 365
Motivations to Expand Internationally 367
Leveraging Value Chain and Resources 370
Assessing Strategic Fit with Country 373
Practical Dimensions of International Expansion 395

12 Competitive Dynamics, Tactics, and Cooperation 383

Competitor Intelligence 385
Industry Characteristics and Trajectories 385
Predicting Competitive Moves 390
Tactical Responses 400
Cooperation 403

Section D: Implementation – Structure, Control, and Strategic Leadership 415

13 Strategy and Structure 417

Aligning Strategy and Structure 419
Understanding the Structuring Imperative 420
Key Organizational Components 423
Coordinating Mechanisms 426
Types of Organizational Structure 431

14 Implementation, Internal Control, and Strategic Leadership 447

Keys to Implementation 448
Control Leads to Performance 450
Metrics 451
Developing an Implementation Plan 460
Strategic Leadership 473

Index 481

This page is intentionally left blank.

Section A: Strategy Foundations

Look around you. Read the headlines in today's *Wall Street Journal*. Some companies succeed wildly, others fail miserably, and most fall somewhere in between. Why is this? Why do some companies perform better than others in the same industry? Why do some companies achieve superior performance over long periods of time? These questions are what this book is about.

Whatever sort of organization you plan to work for – whether it be a large company, small business or family business, law firm or accounting firm, not-for-profit, government agency, or school – you should be interested in understanding how your organization can excel. It will excel by creating value in unique ways, doing this better than its competition, and sustaining that superiority over time. The sense of accomplishment and personal happiness you will feel by being part of a successful endeavor such as this, as well as any financial reward you might gain, are worth preparing for. The principles and ideas in this book should help you succeed in this agenda!

Recent world events, including the 2020-22 Covid-19 pandemic, have caused many leaders and managers to think and act with a short term view. This is dangerous. Interruptions in the normal course of affairs, unique events, and – yes – even globally impactful crises have now become "normal" in the sense that something like this occurs regularly. Just in the last twenty-two years in the United States we have experienced the September 11, 2001, terrorist attacks, the Iraq war, the great recession from 2008 until 2012, vitriolic political strife that has impacted labor and regulation, interruptive social movements and attacks on capitalism, and most recently the global coronavirus pandemic. Managers have worried about how their organizations should respond to each of these. But we cannot afford to put everything on hold and wait out one major event after another. A continuous focus on the strategic foundation of any organization will enable it to succeed in the long run while at the same time weathering short term disruptions. More than ever before, strategy is necessary and important!

OK, so here's how we start the journey. This first section of this book covers both the beginning and the ending of Strategy. "Strategy" is a word used all the time, but in our context it has a very specific meaning. Chapter 1 will tell you about Strategy itself and then provide a roadmap for where the book will take you during the course. Strategy is different in interesting and important ways from other business functions and related courses. And the "need for strategy" has become super-important over the last few years.

Then Chapter 2 drills down into Performance, which is what senior managers (and everyone else in the organization) should be working toward. Superior company performance is THE outcome we are looking toward, the end-result of great strategy. Although performance is a goal or an endpoint, I put this ending right up front precisely because it is so important. Performance is more than just the numbers, and we will explore this. But, the numbers have to work, or else all the other desirable performance dimensions are for nothing!

Then in Chapter 3 we return to an important foundation. Here you'll read about crafting the strategic vision, the mission, and the principles for how to get where you want to go (hint: Performance).

Each chapter throughout this first section and the rest of the book will begin with two standard dimensions. First is a short list of "Learning Objectives" that outline what the chapter will help you understand. Each chapter also begins with a short story about a business to help you see that the subject of the chapter is really relevant and important. After you have finished reading each chapter, the Chapter Summary section provides a review of the learning objectives.

Occasionally throughout the text you will also encounter a boxed-in provocative question titled "Managing in Markets: Question for Class Discussion." Strategy is about leading your company to consistently-excellent performance. But it is also about leading your company in a challenging environment, where questions may arise about whether a company should take certain actions or adopt a certain public stance. These call-outs in the text pose challenging questions that are great to think about and discuss.

I look forward to working with you collaboratively to better understand Strategy.

Chapter 1: The Need for Strategy

LEARNING OBJECTIVES:

1. Identify and discuss the two strategic imperatives facing every company today.
2. Define the term "Strategy" and describe the five critical questions encompassing what we study in strategy
3. Explain the evolution of the field of strategy and why it is so important today.
4. Connect the concept of strategy with leadership and ethics.
5. Describe the process for developing and implementing strategy.

Fierce Competition: Walmart vs Amazon[1]

If you had spent $1650 to buy 100 shares of Walmart stock when the company went public in 1969, in 2022 your shares would be worth nearly $30 million. And you would also collect over $450,000 each year in dividend income. If you had spent $1,800 to buy 100 shares of Amazon stock when it went public in 1997, in 2022 your shares would be worth almost $3 million.

Walmart and Amazon arose from completely different circumstances, at completely different times, in completely different industries, with completely different goals. Sam Walton started up Walmart to help people "save money, live better" by offering the lowest prices possible on everyday merchandise in large stores competing in the discount retailing industry. Jeff Bezos started up Cadabra in 1995 (later named Amazon) to sell books, one of five categories of products that lent themselves most easily to online sales. Despite these differences, these two companies are now locked in a fierce competitive battle for the future of retailing.

Emerging from humble origins in Arkansas, by 1985 Walmart reached $8 billion in sales from stores located largely in the southern U.S. As it expanded into new states, it outperformed Kmart, Sears, Montgomery Ward, and other retailers, some of whom had been in existence for over 100 years. To grow further Walmart started Sam's Club in the warehouse club retail segment. It entered the grocery business to compete with supermarkets and stocked more toys to compete with toy retailers. In 2022 it is the largest supermarket and the largest toy retailer in the world. The company also grew by expanding outside the U.S. into the Americas, Europe, Asia and Africa – sometimes acquiring local chains, sometime joint-venturing with them, and sometimes starting up its own stores from scratch. In 2016 Walmart acquired Jet.com and other companies (like Moosejaw and ShoeBuy) in order to extend its presence into the online environment. By the end of 2021 the company reached over $559 billion in annual revenue; it is the world's largest company by annual revenue and the 19th largest by market capitalization.

Amazon also came from humble origins. Jeff Bezos operated out of his garage at first, relying on publishers' warehouses to inventory books the company sold. It took the company over two years to acquire its first 1 million customers, but then only 6 months more to double that. Bezos wanted to go beyond books, and he guided the company into being "the place where people can come to find and discover anything they might want to buy online." They added music, toys, videos, electronics, tools, hardware, and more. It took ten years for Amazon to achieve $8 billion in annual sales. Its phenomenal growth damaged Barnes & Noble, Walden Books, Books-a-Million and other bookstore retailers. The company moved overseas, establishing sites in Germany, the UK, and elsewhere. It made acquisitions that enhanced its online retailing presence (like Zappos and Audible). It moved into technology devices, with the Kindle reader in 2011 leading to a commanding presence in eBooks, and then with Echo and the Alexa digital assistant in 2014 to compete for the home entertainment space. It creates content for film and television to compete with Netflix and Disney, amped up its cloud services for business and streaming, and added groceries to its online retailing business. In 2017 it unexpectedly acquired Whole Foods Market, moving into physical store retailing with 400+ retail stores and a well-developed food supplier network. With annualized revenue exceeding $450 billion by 2022, Amazon is the world's 5th largest company in market capitalization, exceeding even Walmart.

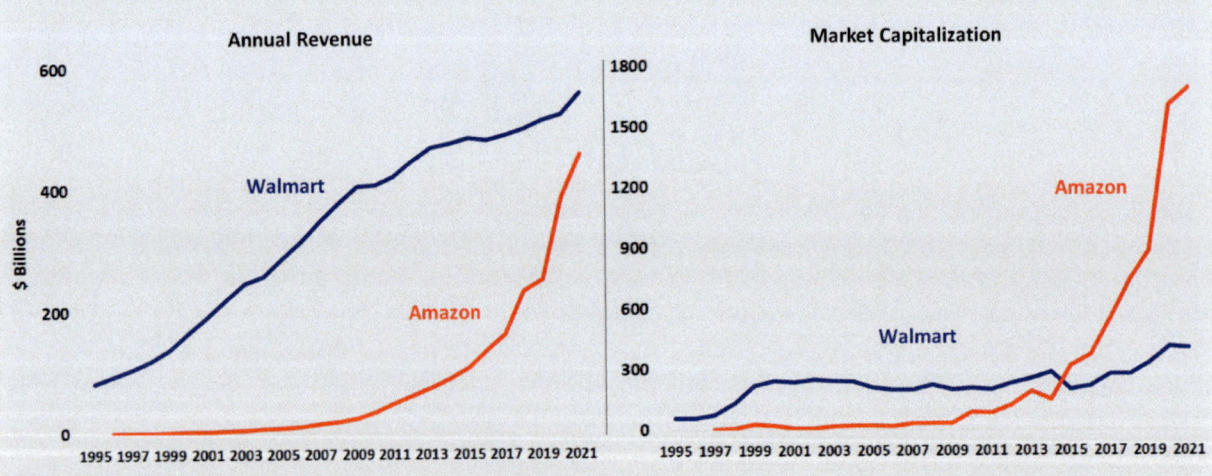

The retailing industry is brutally competitive, and many sectors in the industry have experienced serious upheaval over the last few years. Traditional department stores have shut down store locations. Sears, founded in 1893, encountered such losses in customer traffic and cash flow problems that it declared bankruptcy in 2019. In business since 1848, Macy's saw same-store sales declines from 2014 until 2018 and has suffered during the recent pandemic. Saks Fifth Avenue was sold in 2013; poor performance at Neiman Marcus led to management shakeups. Staples, unable to survive as a public company in office supplies, sold itself to a private equity firm in 2017. In electronics Circuit City and HH Gregg are long gone; Toys 'R' Us filed for bankruptcy. The Whole Foods acquisition by Amazon in 2017 was telling. Its original point of differentiation – fresh organics – was so successful that other food retailers (including Walmart) started imitating it. Price pressures from these more efficient competitors contributed to a steady loss of customers and a tumbling stock price.

Despite these trends, both Walmart and Amazon have prospered. Each has taken actions and made investments over many years to create fully-integrated organizations that create value in ways competitors find hard to imitate. Each company has invested billions of dollars in sophisticated warehouse and logistics systems, tied end-to-end (from supplier to customer) with cutting edge technology and information systems. Each company has unparalleled supplier relationships and networks spanning the globe, rapidly responsive to local needs. Each company achieves a high level of coordination of effort internally among tens of thousands of employees worldwide. Each company has demonstrated foresight in moving opportunistically into new markets and new ways of competing.

The competition between Walmart and Amazon is intensifying, as each company confronts the other's business. Online shopping is projected to grow by 44% between 2021 and 2024 while physical store sales project to eke out only 3.7% growth. Walmart's acquisitions and investments are squarely aimed at reducing Amazon's dominance. In 2017 Walmart also instructed its partnering technology companies to no longer use Amazon's AWS cloud services. It created a program for low-income families to receive online shipping benefits at lower prices. Amazon responded by making Prime benefits available at reduced prices to low-income families, a core Walmart shopper group. Its acquisition of Whole Foods was a direct assault on one of Walmart's core retail segments. By 2021 both companies were pursuing virtual consumer healthcare services.

Despite success, each company confronts significant issues related to their business. Walmart's e-commerce efforts have taken a long time to come to fruition. It has a reputation for paying less than a living wage and gender bias in promotion and pay. Amazon's forays into "bricks and mortar" stores have also not all fared well; it's tough to succeed in physical retailing. It has been sharply criticized for harsh working conditions and for unethical and illegal merchandise sold on its site through third-party sellers.

Walmart is over 50 years old, Amazon is about 25. How do you think the competition will look by the year 2030? How can you assess which company is better poised to succeed on a sustainable basis? Which company's stock would you buy today? This story raises many other questions that arc ticd to strategy.

QUESTIONS

1. What elements constitute an effective strategy, and how do you measure its outcome?

2. Over what time horizon does strategy play itself out? How does management measure progress toward the accomplishment of outcomes over long periods of time?

3. What is the value of a vision and a mission in achieving coordination across the company?

4. How do you define your industry? Who is your competition? How do changes in competition and evolving technologies affect strategy?

5. Is every industry equally attractive to expand into?

6. When does it make sense for a company to acquire another company?

7. Why should a company move internationally? To what country? Should it acquire a local company, do a joint venture, or start up from scratch there?

8. What are your options when another company assails your business by coming directly after your customers?

9. Should companies engage in socially-desirable behavior that reduces financial performance and possibly shareholder returns?

10. Who should be involved in setting strategic direction and making key strategic decisions?

TODAY'S STRATEGIC IMPERATIVES

Once upon a time, long before the 2000s, companies sought to achieve superior performance amidst fairly stable markets. Back then, markets were fairly well defined (e.g. a phone company provided phones and voice telephone service), barriers to entry to many markets were fairly robust, competitors basically understood one another, respected each other's turf, disruptive innovations occurred infrequently, and people working in business kept fairly sane work hours.

Today, the game has changed and the rules are very different. Advances in technology occur rapidly and make even the smallest competitor a nuisance to the large, incumbent firm. It's hard to know how to accurately define an industry (e.g. a phone, provided by a company that doesn't even offer telephone service, is a camera is an e-mail device is a portable music player is a web browser). The pace of work has escalated because we are now in a global environment. Although the financial markets close in New York at the end of the workday, they are open 24/7 because of the Tokyo, Hong Kong, Johannesburg, London and other exchanges. When you attend a trade show in Chicago, a visitor to your booth uses her cell phone to snap a picture of the new product that your company is proudly displaying. Within forty-eight hours, halfway around the world, a possible competitor has "dummied up" a similar new product in its low-cost manufacturing facility and added the item to its price list.

Globalization and the relative ease of forging alliances create conditions where even geographically remote firms can compete in your own backyard for your most prized customers.[2] Customers have come to expect more from all companies, pushing out the essential value frontier of ever more features and ever greater customization at ever lower prices. The need for speed seems to dominate transactions and competition: faster delivery of complex orders, setting up regional operations to be super-responsive, and using digital technology internally to automate everything.[3] The combination of big data, artificial intelligence, robotics, analytics, and the internet are changing the way businesses compete. Along the way companies must now account for a wider range of stakeholders affecting many aspects of their business, instead of just stockholders.

On top of these trends interruptions in the normal course of affairs, unique events, and globally impactful crises have now become "normal." Just in the last twenty-five years in the United States we have experienced the September 11, 2001, terrorist attacks, the Iraq war, the great recession from 2008 until 2012, a presidency marked by vitriolic political strife, the antifa and Black Lives Matter movements, and most recently the global coronavirus pandemic.

Strategy professor Richard D' Aveni coined the term *hypercompetition* to describe today's competitive environment.[4] In this disruptive world "blitzscaling" has become paramount – where speed, size and growth overshadow all else.[5] Jack Welch, former CEO of General Electric, described "white knuckle" competition and said future decades would be even worse. Those decades are now here. According to former Siemens CEO Joe Kaeser:

"The information comes faster and is more accessible than ever before....It has become harder to set priorities correctly because...by the time you get the numbers it's too late already, the numbers only reflect what happened in the past. It's much more important to understand...how do we recognize early indicators of a changing world."[6]

These ideas about intense competition amidst rapidly changing and evolving circumstances have tremendous implications for strategic management today. We believe that every aspect of the practice of strategy today – analysis, formulation, implementation, and evaluation – must embrace two imperatives in light of this new dynamic and disruptive competitive context:

1. *Value creation imperative*

2. *Opportunity recognition imperative*

These two imperatives are the cornerstones of this textbook, and should be the lens through which you examine various aspects of the field and how companies are performing. Creating and maintaining a successful business in the face of ever-changing industry and competitive contexts brings to light the value creation imperative. Successful companies are like machines: once they figure out how to do something well, they refine the process and "institutionalize" it so they become better and better at it. Value creation is a central theme in this book, and we will unpack it more carefully in Chapter 5. As we shall see, however, value creation embraces many stakeholders in a company, not just customers. Therefore, many opportunities are presented to create unique value, which is the foundation of sustainably superior performance.

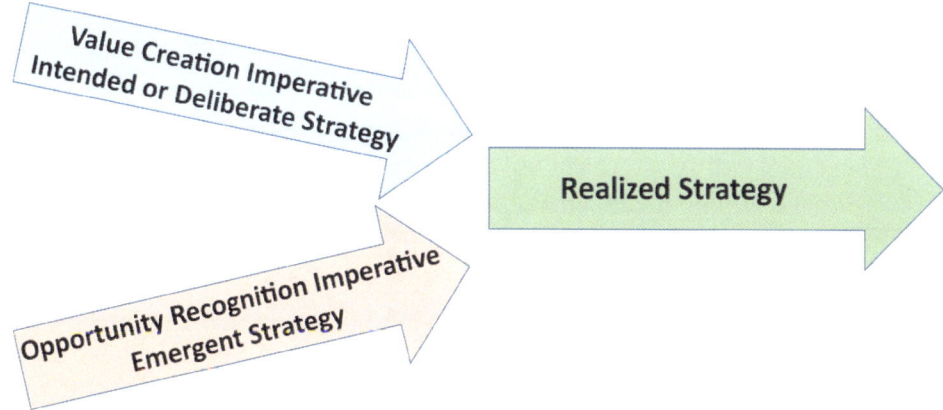

But now along comes a new type of business direction that requires value to be created in fundamentally different ways, challenging the status quo (and likely upsetting a lot of people who made the company so successful under the old ways of doing things). Because industries, technology, globalization, and competition evolve so rapidly, every company must also excel at opportunity recognition – the critical need to identify and exploit where the market is heading. In this environment, companies must constantly position themselves to search for, identify, and embrace new opportunities that may ultimately replace their existing business. Rapid change tends to make every new product or service obsolete much faster than in the past. Few companies can rest on the laurels of what they accomplished five years ago or even last year, because hungry new competitors – both small and large – will seek to imitate what made them so successful. Just look at how the new, encroaching competition from Amazon has affected Walmart in a few short years!

The problem that many successful companies have is they become set in their ways of doing things and looking at things. They become complacent. This is in part because "conformity, defined as adhering to conventional wisdom, which gets leaders to the top too often disqualifies them from grasping the scale and nature of disruption."[7] The downside of rapid technological advances, the ability to partner with other firms to gain complementary capabilities, and the fluidity of international financial institutions is that competitors now have the tools to go after lethargic companies whose management is rewarding itself for past performance by basking in the sun at a villa on Turks and Caicos. The upside is that change produces many new opportunities that are ripe for pursuit by you and your company. The challenge for management, then, is to build an organization and a process that will also encourage a corporate entrepreneurial orientation: proactively searching out new opportunities, bringing them to the table, and embracing experimentation on brand new products or services.[8] The constant tension between managing the existing business and pursuing valuable new business opportunities requires exceptional management talent.

Companies must recognize that, as markets change, the process of creating perceived value will also change. This means that every company must become adept at both value creation and opportunity recognition on an ongoing basis. It's not just a one-time shot! Companies today must understand who their new customers are going to be, what new values these new customers will increasingly appreciate, and how to make money creating and delivering those new values.

Sounds Really Big Picture, So How Does This Relate to Me?

This is a great question to ask, right here at the beginning of a course in strategy. Soon after you graduate the likelihood that you will soon become a senior exec at Spotify, Disney, Toyota, or any of the other companies we will mention throughout this book is slim. Yet strategy is not something that is decided upon or occurs at only the very top of the organization. Strategy permeates every aspect of an organization. In fact, every part of an organization is a reflection of its strategy. And people throughout every level are involved essentially in strategy. Larry Culp, CEO of GE, believes that "all workers should understand the company's strategy and how their role can contribute to it, enabling feedback and improvement to come up from lower levels."[9] Take a look again at the Walmart versus Amazon story that began this chapter. Logistics and technology development, supplier relationships, customer marketing, finance, international relations: both separately and in combination, each of these functional areas is central to a company's effective market entry and successful performance. No matter where you go to work or in what function you work, you will be involved with company strategy.

Perhaps you will not go to work in a large corporation, but instead find employment in a small business or your family's business. After all, 99.7% of all business organizations in the United States in 2022 are small businesses (defined as having fewer than 500 employees), and they employ roughly 48% of the U.S. workforce. These types of companies generate two-thirds of job growth in the United States because they are responsible for the lion's share of new technological innovation, export, and 44% of GDP.[10] The person who understands strategy in a sophisticated manner is better prepared to succeed in the small business environment.

Who do you think is better able to recognize new opportunities coming along? Who do you think is more flexible to embrace and learn about them as possibilities for new value creation? Hint: it's usually not Pops! Young people are far more capable here! This strategy book is for you.

WHAT IS STRATEGY?

Strategy may be one of the most overused and misused terms in society today. Everyone has a "strategy" for so many aspects of their lives. These range from those that might truly contain legitimate elements of a strategic decision to those that are fairly mundane and inaccurate uses of the term. Here are a few representative examples of how we often see the word strategy used:

- A strategy for getting to work in the morning. Brittany faces a tough commute each day because of the traffic snarls and construction around her house. Each morning she listens to the traffic reports before leaving and uses one of more than a half-dozen routes that she has mapped out to get her to the office.

- A strategy for achieving a career goal. Realizing that often those individuals with "line" management experience appear to obtain the top spots in her company, Jennifer requests a transfer from her "staff" analyst position into a lower level line position in one of the plants where she will have "profit and loss" responsibility. Her hope is to develop her operational and P&L skills and increase her prospects for promotion into senior roles.

- A strategy for waking up on time. Primarily because he has missed his 8:00 class four times this semester, Jesse decided to set two alarm clocks. On his bedside table is a normal buzzer alarm clock. Across the room his Android phone automatically cranks up a music set-list starting with The Weeknd's "Blinding Lights."

- A strategy for developing an innovative product. Realizing that their new battery and miniaturization technique for employing GPS technology might have many uses, Derek and Morgan – the founders of FindemNow LLC – decide to evaluate each potential market before employing an engineering design firm to adapt the technology into a marketable product configuration.

- A strategy to be #1. Jack Welch, CEO of General Electric for 20 years, had a strategy for every GE division to be #1 or #2 in its industry or to leave it.

A term that describes almost anything can describe nothing very well. Strategy is much more than a simple set of activities or some immediate actions. It is also not the outcome or desired end such as Jack Welch's #1 position above. The ownership of "first place" in an industry offers no particular insight about the ways in which the company intends to operate.

So let's first talk about what strategy is generally, then we will define it in more specific terms. In general terms you can think of strategy as "the overall concept for how a company organizes itself and all its activities in order to conduct business successfully, outperform competitors, and deliver superior returns to its shareholders." As the earlier retailing story illustrates, a company's strategy has implications for every functional area across a company. That is, the efforts in each functional area (marketing, operations, finance, etc.) should reflect and support the central idea about how a company intends to conduct business and compete. But the concept of strategy is more than just how a business coordinates all its activities; it is also about performing *better* than competitors and delivering superior returns. Some companies may be well-coordinated across their functional areas, but are beat up by competitors in the marketplace and earn only average or below-average returns. We are interested in how to achieve superior performance when we talk about strategy.

Five Key Questions That Define Strategy

This general description of strategy and strategic management is helpful only up to a point. We need to get more specific and detailed. So here we define strategy as an area that deals specifically with the following five critical questions:[11]

1. **Why do some firms perform better than others?** Strategy is about the creation of a position of advantage over other companies in a competitive marketplace, resulting in superior performance.

2. **How are competitive and performance differences sustained?** Strategy is focused on sustaining a superior position in the market and superior performance over an extended period of time.

3. **What is the nature of strategy in a multi-business firm?** Questions 1 and 2 are fundamentally about a *single* line of business. Today, however, many companies are diversified, owning and operating many different kinds of businesses. The top execs at headquarters cannot possibly know every detail about all the different lines. So what kinds of issues do they deal with and what kinds of decisions do they need to make?

4. **How is strategic effectiveness measured?** Examining summary financial performance measures is the most frequently used method of assessing strategy. However, many executives understand that strategy must also consider other stakeholders, and that both qualitative and quantitative measures are required.

5. **What is special about strategic decisions?** Strategy deals with types of decisions that rise above specific functional concerns, and that have a unique character to them.

Why Do Some Firms Perform Better? Creating Competitive Advantage

Conventional economic theory about "perfect competition" assumes that any advantage for one firm can be quickly imitated by its competitors and thus neutralized or negated by natural market forces. The result of this process is that all firms in an industry will eventually look and act alike. And yet the reality, that there are many different types of firms in any industry, is obvious to us all. Why do some firms perform better, then, given what we know about economic theory?

Strategy describes the specialized approach a company takes to the market that places it in a superior position relative to its competitors. It is fundamentally about developing a dominant logic for how the company can create value uniquely, focusing its attention and investments on that unique model, and ensuring that all parts of the organization are working consistently in support of that model. A sound strategy is one that creates value appreciated by various stakeholders, and that makes it difficult for competitors to do the same. When companies create value in unique and compelling ways, then markets respond and the results for the company will often include higher market share and profits.

Consider the commercial banking industry and its challenges during the financial crisis and ensuing recession. Chances are, if your family lives east of the Mississippi or in Texas, you   are probably familiar with Truist Financial (formerly BB&T).[12] Between 2009 and 2021 this bank grew from 15th to 6th largest bank in the country (now with $499 billion in assets), and it outperformed many of its competitors. How? While many competitors moved outside their traditional areas of expertise and took on added risk during the credit crisis period, Truist stayed focused on its strategy as a community bank lender to local businesses and homeowners. The former CEO John Allison had for years personally emphasized the company's mission, vision and values to employees at all levels, especially to those out in the branches interfacing on a daily basis with customers. Together with strong internal reporting systems and close attention paid to operating practices across its various departments, the bank maintained a tight strategic focus in the face of incredible challenges in the financial markets. By 2012 Truist's performance exceeded nearly all its competitors on net interest margin and return on equity, while maintaining significantly lower volatility (beta).

Excellence in strategy involves several factors. First, it involves clear choice. To create value uniquely a company must decide not only what it *will* do, but also what it *will not* do. Many banks by 2007 had decided to get involved with exotic new financial innovations, or to broaden out their loan portfolios to higher risk clienteles. Truist stayed focused on its core mission, practices and customers (even though they were tempted to go for quick profits and higher returns like their competitors!). Second, to create value uniquely requires a sustained, systematic approach in developing capabilities that set a company apart from its competitors in a way that is compelling to both its suppliers and customers. One of Truist's unique resources is its culture and internal practices for ensuring consistency of its strategic approach across all functions, and from the boardroom to the branch lobby. In later chapters we will more carefully discuss these ideas about strategic choice and building resources.

We have already mentioned value creation several times in these first few pages. One of the central concepts of this book is a focus on value creation and the value chain - "a systematic way of examining all the activities a firm performs and how they interact" in order to find a basis for competitive advantage.[13] Later on we will also be discussing how to uniquely create value and how this can contribute to superior performance.

How Are Performance Differences Sustained? Long-Term Orientation

It is nice to get an A on an exam, better yet to earn an A for an entire course, but best of all to graduate with close to a 4.0 GPA after several years of coursework! Strategy is not just about current position and performance; it is also about performing well into the future. In business this involves mapping out a direction for the longer term, which takes into account an always-evolving market and smart competitors. When we understand that strategy is about ensuring the longer term, we come to realize that many everyday uses of the word strategy are inappropriate, because they often refer only to short-term actions or short-term results.

Strategy is therefore about the *sustainability* of competitive advantage and superior performance over a period of time. In today's global marketplace we are often witness to rapid changes in technology, economic conditions, and competitive actions. Under these circumstances when so much is constantly in flux, how is it possible to have a long-term orientation? An essential component of strategy is therefore the vision the company develops. We also seek to understand the context and anticipated future moves of competitors, customers, suppliers, and other known and anticipated stakeholders. While today's incredibly disruptive competitive environment might seem to be one in which a longer-term approach is of little value, the simple fact is that the *need for strategy* (the title of this chapter!) is even greater as a consequence of these rapidly evolving marketplace conditions. Otherwise, companies will find themselves bouncing along haphazardly, based on decision-making that responds mainly to immediate circumstances. Strategy is the rudder to navigate choppy, even turbulent waters.

Truist is a great example of sustained performance differences. In the aftermath of the financial crisis, it was one of few large banks

Bank Performance Comparisons 5 Years, 2016-2020		
	Truist	Top Four Banks
Net income %	21.9	20.2
Return on assets %	1.1	0.8
Return on equity %	8.4	8.8
Volatility (beta)	1.27	1.43

which did not need bailout funds from the Federal Reserve Bank. Compared to the four largest U.S. banks, ten years further on into 2020 it continued to produce higher margins, superior return on assets, comparable return on equity, while exposing shareholders to lower volatility.

Distinguishing between longer-view strategy and shorter-view tactics is critical. Imagine an NCAA Final Four basketball tournament in which the national championship is decided by only one point at game's end. What enables one team to win at that moment, in that game, is how they and their coach *tactically* deal with the other team's plays and players. Tactics refer to how to match up resources and strengths in the short run with competitive challenges and opportunities. The *strategy* for the winning team, however, was determined much earlier when the coach's vision for how this group of players could compete effectively was put into practice. The combination of years of experience in a competitive arena, complete knowledge of the competitors, experience in recruiting new high school players, hiring coaches with specific skills and understanding, and thorough training regimens. These strategic dimensions are what puts a team in a position to win.

Figure 1.1 captures the sense of these first two important dimensions of strategy.

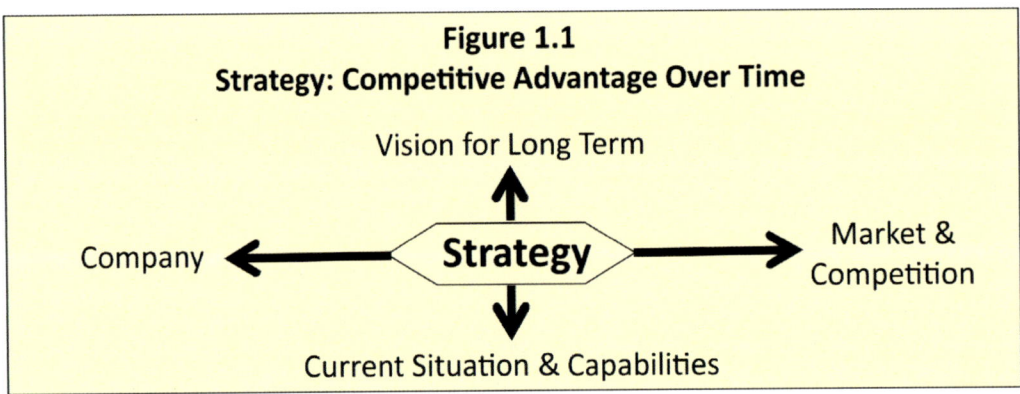

What Is the Nature of Strategy in a Multi-Business Firm?

A completely unique issue in strategy involves corporate strategy, that is, the efforts involved in companies that operate multiple business units under the same corporate banner. Corporate-level strategy is fundamentally concerned with acquiring, managing, and divesting various business units in an effort to create a portfolio that achieves economic returns in excess of what the individual business units could produce on their own. This is done primarily through resource sharing and efforts to achieve economies of scale and scope within the organization. Corporate-level strategy is often discussed today in the context of the relatedness of a company's diversification efforts. 3M Corporation (formerly Minnesota Mining & Manufacturing Company) was founded in 1902 by a group of businessmen to exploit abrasive mineral deposits. On the basis of several successful product launches in the 1920s, 3M began to acquire other promising businesses with the help of a set of wealthy investors. In 2022 the 3M company has 95,000 employees worldwide, revenues of $35 billion, and draws upon 51 technology platforms for 23 operating  companies in 4 different strategic segments: Consumer; Safety and Industrial; Transportation and Electronics; and Health Care. 3M management oversees the entire operation from St. Paul, Minnesota, and regularly acquires and divests various components within the different business segments. In its recent annual report CEO Mike Roman highlighted how important managing the "corporate portfolio" is in achieving superior results:

> "Our first priority is Portfolio. The ongoing review and reshaping of our portfolio is critical to maximizing value for our customers and shareholders. We've taken significant actions over the last several years, including realigning from 40 businesses

to 23, and completing both acquisitions and divestitures. Yet there is more we must do to stay relevant to the fast-moving needs of our customers and the marketplace."[14] Corporate-level strategy will be covered in great detail in Chapter 10.

How Is Strategic Effectiveness Measured?

Because the nature of strategic decisions focuses attention on the performance of the company, companies must employ metrics. These can be qualitative and quantitative measures that allow the firm to measure the effectiveness of its strategy. The customary manner in which the effectiveness of strategy is assessed is by financial performance metrics. Included here are measures such as return on equity (ROE) or one of its constituent components.

Figure 1.2 a
Performance in Retail Grocery Store Industry

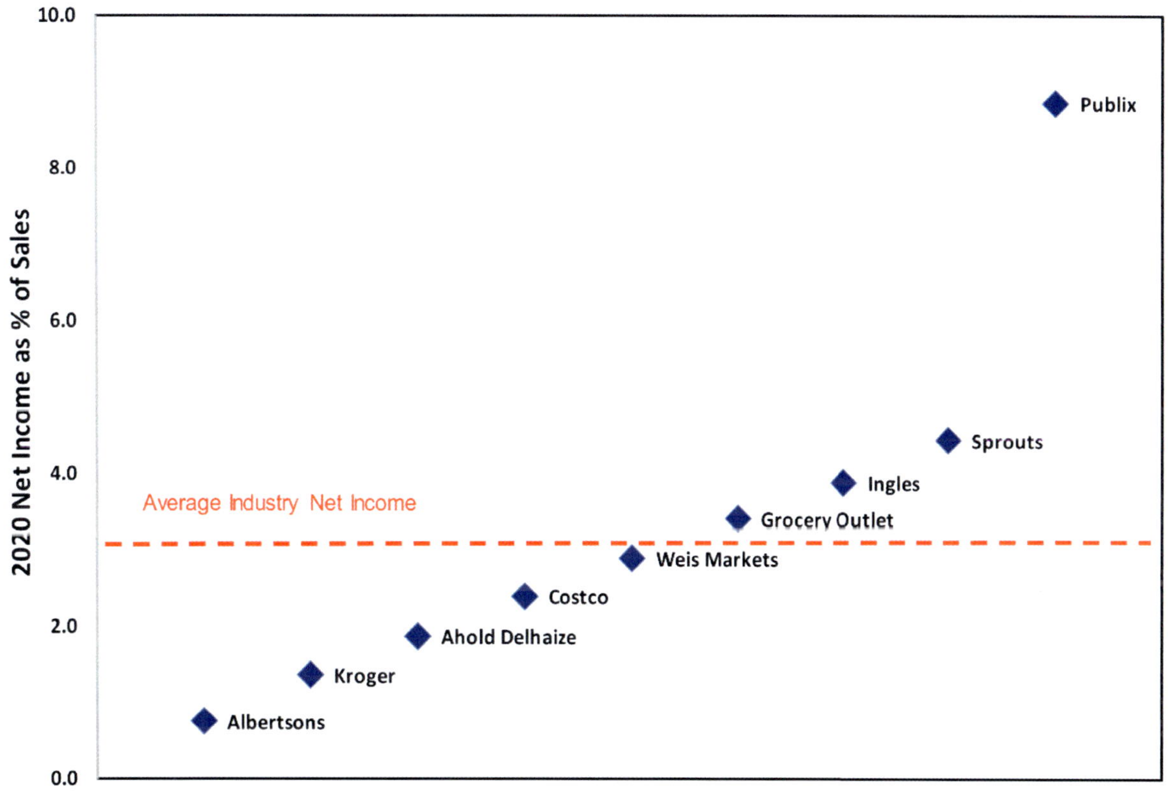

Even more important than isolated return measures, the assessment of strategic effectiveness usually involves a measure or set of measures that compare how well a company did *relative* to its competitors in the industry. Figure 1.2a shows recent performance, defined by a profitability metric (net income divided by sales revenue) for key competitors in the retail grocery store industry in 2020. The average for the entire industry during the period was just 3.0%; this "thin margin" results from intense competition among traditional players, the advent of Walmart and Costco, and international companies extending into U.S. markets. Publix exceeds the industry average smartly, while Albertson's and Kroger each fall below the industry average. Publix is an example of a strategically high-performing company partially because it is by definition delivering "above-average profitability" through its business model. An above-average profitability metric means that Publix may be more attractive to financial markets; it most likely has superior cash flows enabling it to reinvest back in its business to further enhance its position and growth.

But wait! Recall that strategy is about impact over the long run and about longer-term results. Figure 1.2a shows that Kroger performed below average on the profitability metric during 2020. But longer term measurements of Kroger's performance provides a more nuanced view. In Figure 1.2b are listed the 5-year average return on equity (ROE) and the change in stock price from 2016-2020 for each of the companies. Here we see that Kroger exceeds Publix and others in how well it provides returns to equity investors. We also note that in spite of average profitability, Weis Markets' ROE appears below average and its stock price has not grown as much during this same period.

There are several customary types of financial metrics used to gauge effective strategic performance, such as ROA and ROE. A CEO often pays close attention to the financial markets' response to the company's performance, since stock prices and debt ratings can significantly impact how and when a company can raise capital. Increasingly, corporate executives also consider how well their companies create value for other stakeholders beyond those with purely financial interests in their companies. In Chapter 2 we will further explore dimensions of performance, including financial and nonfinancial measures.

Figure 1.2 b
5-Year Performance, 2016-2020

	% Return on Equity	% Change in Stock Price
Kroger	31.6	114.2
Sprouts	26.9	56.1
Costco	23.8	251.4
Casey's	17.4	83.4
Publix	15.7	65.4
Ingles	15.1	245.4
Ahold Delhaize	10.4	93.1
Weis Markets	8.5	53.6
Grocery Outlet	5.7	*
Albertson's	3.9	*

* Stock not previously traded

The essential goal of strategy is the development of competitive advantage that can be refined and sustained, so that the company will achieve superior performance over time. Superior performance refers to outcomes that exceed the average for the industry in which the company competes. Firms whose performance are average or below average are less attractive. This kind of relative evaluation approach asks the firm to compare its most important measures of performance against those of its direct competitors. This approach in turn emphasizes an evaluative system that rewards moving the organization consistently beyond the average expectations in the industry. In Chapter 4 we will further discuss the nature of above-average returns.

Competition in Commercial Aircraft Manufacturing[15]

In 2006, Boeing rolled its last 717 model off the aircraft assembly line in Long Beach, California. The Boeing 717 and its predecessors were 100-seat models designed for regional transportation between cities that did not require large capacity aircraft. The Long Beach factory opened in 1941 and produced almost 10,000 airplanes for the World War II effort. After the war it converted to commercial airplane construction. Even though airplanes had only been mass-produced for a few years by the time this factory opened, Boeing built a factory that then lasted 65 years. Do you think Boeing contemplated a 65-year run at that time?

During 2006 Boeing faced critical decisions that would affect its rivalry for decades into the future with its chief competitor Airbus Industries. Boeing needed to decide whether to ratchet up the schedule for its 787 model (The Dreamliner) in order to preempt the new Airbus 350 model that was in development. And whether to create a "stretch" version of the 787 to better compete with the huge Airbus A380 scheduled to roll out the next year. Ratcheting up the schedule to get into production sooner might put significant pressure on its suppliers, thereby raising costs, causing shortages and cutting profitability. Developing a stretch 787 would cost more in the short run, but might also blunt Airbus should the market for jumbo-jet 500-seat planes grow quickly.

For its part Airbus had to decide whether to significantly redesign its A350 model to better compete with the 787, already taking an enormous share of the midsize 200-300 seat market in pre-orders. The A350 was already two years behind schedule, and delays had more than tripled its development price from $4 billion to $15 billion.

Boeing's 787 was the most expensive development program in company history, with an estimated total cost of $32 billion. This represented roughly 12 times the annual net income for the company, and the 787 was just one of many R&D projects across Boeing's many divisions. It represented more than just a financial "bet;" it was also a technological bet and a market bet. The airplane incorporated technologies never before used in commercial aviation – composite materials for the fuselage, and mostly electronics for flight control systems. Because of the long development cycle and the length of years that new models are in service, in the airline business "such strategic moves usually occur only once or twice in a decade."[16]

Boeing was also betting on how the entire commercial aviation market would unfold in decades to come. The Airbus A380 targeted at carrying 500+ passengers on very long hauls between only major "hub" markets. The smaller Dreamliner 787 was to provide greater flexibility for airlines to fly modest numbers on long hauls between moderate-sized cities, so that passengers need not catch connections. Only time would tell which way the industry would develop.

Plans for Airbus's A380 had been announced 16 years earlier in 1990, development started in 2000, and the plane flew for its first customer in 2007. But because the huge capacity long haul market never fully materialized, in 2021 Airbus discontinued the plane. The A380 lasted only 14 years. In contrast the Boeing 747, introduced in 1969, was manufactured until 2022 – a lifespan of 53 years!

This short story richly illustrates important dimensions of strategy: the long-lasting effects that strategic decisions can have, and how decisions made early on can lead to significant differences between competitors. The Boeing 717 model flew for forty years. In 2006 both Boeing and Airbus made huge commitments to stake out competitive positions for decades into the future through the development of new classes of planes.

Do you think Google, Microsoft, Facebook, or Apple will be able to sustain competitive advantage for another 40-50 years?

What Makes Strategic Decisions Special?

The four previous questions and this commercial aircraft manufacturing story bring us to the fifth critical dimension that describes strategy. We want to separate the kinds of decisions and actions that are truly strategic from those that are not. Deciding how to get up in the morning or get to work on time may be important, but those decisions and plans are not strategic, in part because they are not fundamentally dealing with the questions of competitive advantage, sustainability or long-term outcomes. Additionally they are also not strategic because they do not exhibit the critical characteristics that define a strategic decision.[17] Strategic decisions are different from other types of decisions in that they:

1. Are ill-structured and non-routine.
2. Significantly affect the subsequent actions of functions and departments across the entire organization.
3. Involve a significant commitment of resources (broadly defined).
4. Are difficult to reverse both economically and politically.
5. Involve making a clear choice among competing alternatives.
6. Are easily identified with the success or failure of the organization.

Ill-structured and non-routine situations. Though companies are continuously reviewing their strategy, executing it, and monitoring their strategic progress, decisions on major new strategic initiatives are not made on a regular basis. Making a significant decision on strategy is unlike the decision a brand manager at Procter & Gamble might make regarding a new advertising campaign, and unlike the decision a company makes to raise capital by issuing new bonds. Corporations regularly raise capital by issuing bonds. The design and execution of new ad campaigns occurs with some regularity in a packaged goods company and there is a generally prescribed method for managing and implementing these efforts.

This is simply not true for major strategic decisions. Here we are talking about the need to confront unique and changing market conditions, and competitive circumstances for which there is often no historical record of similar types of decisions. Furthermore, beyond generic advice, company executives find that there is little off-the-shelf information readily available. Strategic decision making deals with a level of ambiguity not only about conditions in the present but also about how decisions made today will affect the company years down the road. This is actually what makes the practice of strategy so exciting and interesting: the opportunity for the decision maker to use intuition, creativity, and analysis – a combination of art and science.

Affects subsequent actions. Strategy is also unique in the field of management because effective strategy requires that all of the functional areas of a business (marketing, finance, operations, accounting, sales, etc.) act in ways that consistently support the overall approach to the market. A company's strategy may, for example, involve continuous innovation and new product development. Nevertheless should the finance function not support the investment spending in R&D, or if the production department refuses to allow for adequate test production runs in the factory, or if sales fails to place sufficient emphasis on new products in their customer calls, then the overall approach is likely to fail. Strategy requires internal consistency across all functions in a company. Indeed, a clear statement (mission and/or vision) and understanding about the strategy of the company is one of the most important means of ensuring that all functional areas consistently support one another in the implementation of strategic direction in all of their individual activities.

Significant commitment of resources. Because outstanding accomplishments rarely come from limited efforts or small initiatives, strategic decisions most often involve significant commitments of resources. To create unique competitive differences that are well valued in the marketplace, as well as to sustain those differences over time, a company must commit itself to a challenging path. When Amazon first started up, it relied upon publishers to warehouse and ship books that Amazon customers were ordering online. As the volume of business increased, however, shipping times and quality control suffered. It became clear to CEO Jeff Bezos that publishers did not share his view of what constituted quality customer service. Amazon was positioning itself on customer service, information, and rapid results. Amazon made the decision to build and operate its own regional distribution warehouses, fully stocked with best-selling books. We think of Amazon as a "digital" company, but look at the physical assets carried on its balance sheet. In 2022 the company carries over $211 billion in gross property, plant, and equipment on its balance sheet; this is more than *twice* what industrial auto manufacturer General Motors reports! The consistency of its infrastructure investment over time has ensured the quality of service Amazon promised, distanced itself from its competitors, and helped launch the company on an unparalleled growth trajectory.

Difficult to reverse. Suggested by the discussion earlier about long-term sustainability, strategic decisions have a long-lasting impact on the company and the competition in the market. Strategy is not like riding a bicycle, where you know immediately if you have erred because you fall down and scrape your knee. Strategy is more like navigating a high-speed oil supertanker far out at sea: you turn the rudder to change direction, but because of the inertia and the size of the ship, the turn may take many miles to complete. You cannot "turn on a dime." Decisions made today to move forward with strategic investments will not usually manifest themselves in results until some years down the road.

This dimension is actually of significant concern to leaders, who want to know as time goes by whether or not positive progress is being made on strategic initiatives. We will discuss methods for keeping track of strategy progress in Chapter 14.

Making a clear choice. We mentioned earlier that strategy is about deciding what a company will do and what it will not do. It involves making a choice. We will read later on about companies trying to be "all things to all people" by going in multiple directions, and thus winding up "stuck in the middle" (a dangerous place to be). But think about what we have just said above about strategy: affects the entire organization, involves significant commitment of resources, difficult to reverse. These characteristics of strategy and strategic decision-making suggest that companies must not try to go simultaneously down different paths. It's too expensive, it can result in mediocre results in several areas rather than superior results in a distinctive domain, and it can create organizational schizophrenia!

Identified with success or failure. It is for the reasons just described that strategic decisions have the greatest impact on a company's performance. They involve huge commitments of resources over long periods of time. They focus attention on specific opportunities, meaning that other possible opportunities are passed up. These focused commitments are designed to create a unique and sustainable competitive position. Strategy sets the goals of the overall organization as well as establishes how all the functional areas will work both individually and in concert. This is not to say that functional area issues and decisions are unimportant. Quite the contrary, when a problem occurs within a functional area, it is because it can affect strategy for the company – and therefore all the other functions that must be seamlessly integrated – that overall company performance may be put at risk.

HISTORY OF THE FIELD OF STRATEGY

How did the area of strategy get to this point, where it is defined by the five questions just discussed, and where both value creation and opportunity recognition are absolutely imperative for any company? While there might be some disagreement regarding the roots of the field, it has an intellectual foundation some 2,500 years ago with the writings of Sun Tzu, general and military strategist, in *The Art of War*. Thirteen chapters in this succinct text helped codify many of the fundamental concepts of strategy that are still important today. These include:

1. A complete understanding of the nature of the competitive marketplace is the first step in a winning campaign.

2. A deep understanding of the mindset of your competitors and how they might react to various moves enables you to anticipate competitive challenges.

3. The realization that preparation, understanding, and a deep commitment to excellence allows one to preempt competition. An organization that is focused on its business, that is constantly refining and improving its ability to compete with attention to the finer details, and that is on the cutting edge of best practices in its arena may actually prevent others from even attempting to compete. Therefore victory (in its most pure form) is defined as never having to enter battle.

4. An evaluation of the resources and capabilities of the organization will point toward the best ways to compete and win.

Reading Sun Tzu through the lens of business provides many insights about the most basic nature of strategy analysis, formulation, and implementation. An illustration some of the chapters of Sun Tzu's book is included in Figure 1.3.

Figure 1.3
Strategy Excerpts from *The Art of War* (Sun Tzu, 500 B.C.)

Chapter & Title	Quotation and Interesting Strategy Points
1 Estimations	"Warfare is a great matter to a nation; it is the ground of death and of life; it is the way of survival and of destruction, and must be examined." • Calculation and rational thought are keys to success. • Important factors to evaluate include moral influence, leadership, competitive arena, and plans. • Example: In contrast to other commercial banks, Truist avoided significant credit risk by rational analysis and objective evaluation of its loan applications.

2 Waging War	"When doing battle, seek a quick victory. A protracted battle will blunt weapons and dampen ardor…. If the army is exposed to a prolonged campaign, the nation's resources will not suffice."	
	• Continuous battling depletes resources and makes you vulnerable.	
	• Example: When Microsoft decided to compete in the internet browsing business against Netscape, it offered its Internet Explorer software for free, seeking to drive Netscape out of business quickly.	
3 Planning	"To gain a hundred victories in a hundred battles is not the highest excellence; to subjugate the enemy's army without doing battle is the highest of excellence. Therefore, the best warfare strategy is to attack the enemy's plans, next is to attack alliances, next is to attack the army…."	
	• Example: After September 11, 2001, the United States initiated a series of security policies designed to detain suspected terrorists and ferret out terrorist plans before they could be implemented.	
6 Vacuity & Substance	"In order to prevent the enemy from coming forth, show them the potential harm. In order to cause the enemy to come of their own volition, extend some apparent profit."	
	• Erect barriers to entry to keep potential competitors away.	
	• Form alliances or joint ventures with competitors to achieve shared goals.	
	• Examples: Pharmaceutical companies seek patent protection on new drugs to prevent competitors from invading their product space. The Star Alliance network of competing airlines was established to save on logistics, marketing and ticketing costs. It includes Air New Zealand, United, Lufthansa, Singapore Airlines, and others.	
7 Military Combat	"Accordingly, if the army does not have baggage and heavy equipment it will be lost; if it does not have provisions it will be lost; if it does not have stores it will be lost."	
	• Failure is guaranteed without the right resources, effectively organized.	
	• Examples: Atari pretty much invented the video game category in the 1970s, but failed because it lacked sophisticated game programmers in the 1980s. A&P supermarkets failed in 2015 because it lacked financial resources needed to scale up to compete with other lower cost food chains.	
9 Maneuvering the Army	"If orders are consistently implemented to instruct the people, then the people will submit."	
	• Communication of mission drives coordinated effort.	
	• Example: Walt Disney's mission "to produce unparalleled entertainment experiences" is known and practiced daily by its thousands of employees. It	

	so epitomizes excellence in customer service that other companies visit the company to learn how they, too, can improve.
11 Nine Terrains	"When the soldiers and officers have penetrated deeply into [enemy territory], they will cling together. When there is no alternative, they will fight." • Where exit barriers exist, competitors will retaliate and fight viciously. • Example: When auto sales flattened out in the 2008-2011 recession, auto manufacturers offered steep discounting, rebates and 0% financing for 72 months. Companies are willing to lose money on a sale to keep from shutting down plants and hurting ROA.
13 Spies	"The means by which enlightened rulers and sagacious generals moved and conquered others, that their achievements surpassed the masses, was advance knowledge." • Importance of prospective information that guides the future. • Example: When Staples opened its first stores in Boston, it collected detailed data on customers, their locations and spending, allowing the company to learn what neighborhoods were successful for their stores. This enabled them to quickly expand down the eastern seaboard, pre-empting Office Depot

Sun Tzu never actually used the term "strategy." The seeds of strategy in business were only sown about one hundred years ago, as economies moved out of the industrial revolution and into an era of big business. The development of large industrial giants such as Standard Oil of New Jersey led to antitrust legislation in the United States that aimed to ensure free market competition. New labor legislation was also passed to protect the rights of workers in what were becoming huge factories where the work was distant from the head office. As legislation sought to create a level playing field in competitive markets, large companies began to look internally for sources of advantage over competitors. In the early 1900s, Frederick Taylor conducted "science of work" time-and-motion studies that helped identify more efficient production processes and ideas about structure and hierarchy. These studies contributed to more effective structure and organization in progressively larger companies. Mass production came into being in the 1930s, relying on Henry Ford's moving assembly line innovation, and was thus nicknamed "Fordism." It contributed to even greater efficiencies and a lowering of costs in manufacturing.

In 1962 Harvard professor Alfred Chandler catalogued the growth and administrative changes which had occurred over the previous fifty years at four giant pillars of industry at the turn of the twentieth century (General Motors, Sears, Standard Oil, and DuPont).[18] As these companies grew, top executives found that they were increasingly removed from day-to-day business activities. The complexity of their businesses and the sheer number of activities made it virtually impossible to manage in the same ways that business owners had in the past. Chandler explained how senior managers discovered new roles for themselves making long-term decisions about the direction of their diverse enterprises. They made investments and modified organizational structures to increase the efficiency and generate higher returns. Chandler called these long-term plans "strategy," the first time the term was used to describe business processes.

The term derives from two Greek root words, *strat* and *egos*, meaning "general of the army," or more directly from the combined ancient Greek word *strategos*, meaning "art of the general."

The popular model for strategy in the 1960s and 1970s included the concepts of "policy" and "long-range planning." Policies were simply guidelines within which managers could make decisions. Long-range planning came to be very popular; almost every firm instituted an annual long-range planning exercise. The mainstay of this exercise was the budget process, where programmed activities essentially remained the same, but new updated numbers were plugged in for the next year. Consequently, long-range planning became more of an extrapolation of the past than a real look to the future. This complacent business approach and a belief that the U.S. economy defied all models ran headlong into a strong group of rising global businesses headquartered outside of the United States.

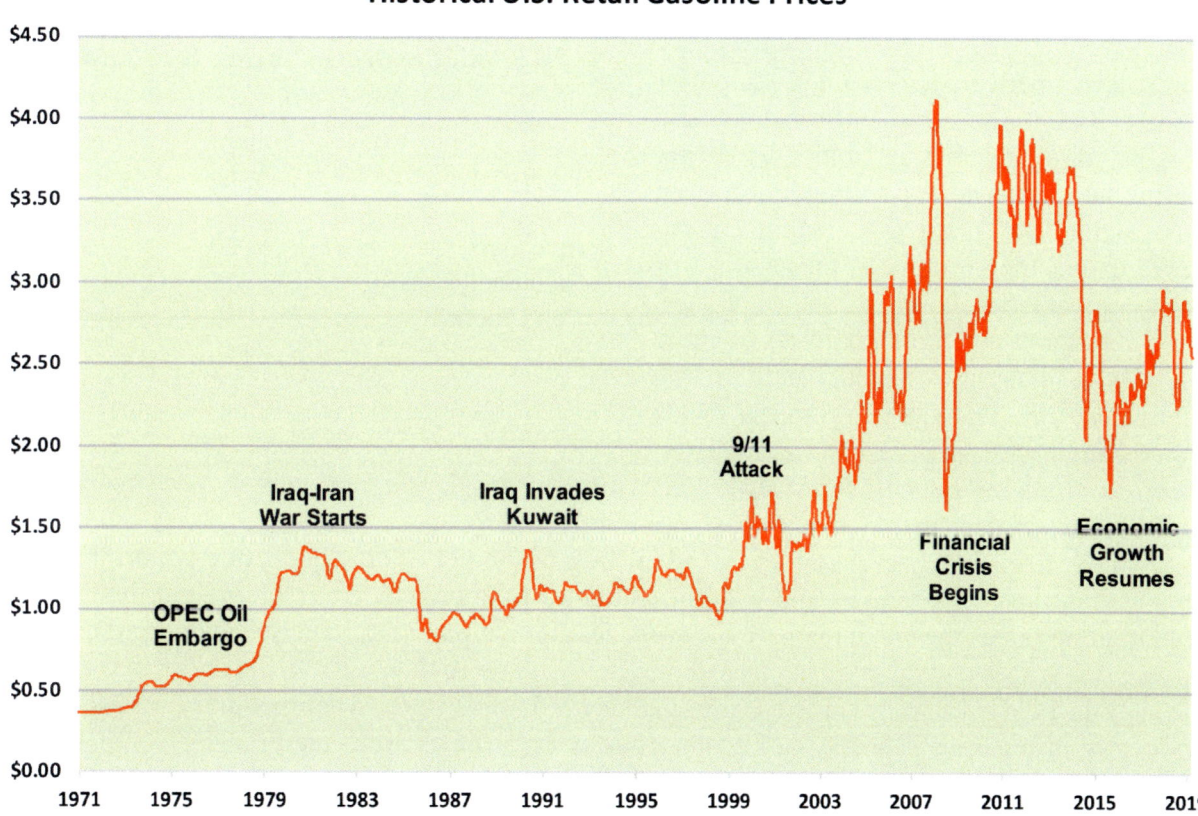

**Figure 1.4
Historical U.S. Retail Gasoline Prices**

Beginning in the early 1970s American industry suffered a number of significant macro-economic jolts, which forever changed the way businesses plan. The first of these was the 1973 Arab oil embargo, which resulted in gas prices increasing roughly 35 percent overnight, from under 40¢ per gallon to 55¢ per gallon on average nationwide (Figure 1.4). Significant shortages and prices over $1 per gallon occurred in many local areas, and people recall 1-2 hour waiting lines at gas stations because gas was so scarce. It had taken over forty years for gas prices to rise from 21¢ to 38¢ per gallon, but only five more years before average prices topped $1 nationwide in 1979. Americans started questioning the wisdom of buying large, gas-guzzling automobiles, opening the door for a host of foreign competitors who were already trying to enter the market with smaller fuel-efficient cars. Honda, Toyota, Datsun (now Nissan), and other international car companies aggressively sought a foothold in the U.S. market. In 1973 foreign companies had a tiny percentage of the U.S. auto market, but within ten years their market share increased to over 35 percent. U.S. auto manufacturers never foresaw this as a possibility, because they had simply been extrapolating past trends into the future. They never really considered a situation where competitive conditions might change so dramatically and so rapidly. Moreover, it took five years to bring a new automobile model to market since U.S. companies had been trying to maximize the "life" of their previous models. So any sort of rapid response to the new competitive threats was virtually impossible. These developments had an enormous cascading impact, as well, in other industries (steel, rubber, parts, and other industries). The intense competition and stumbling in the U.S. automobile industry caused a significant rethinking by American business about how to sustain superior performance in a new global environment.

At the same time, a fundamental shift was occurring in the sources of industrial growth during the 1970s. There was movement toward a more service and technology-based economy that shifted the emphasis away from manufacturing. Consumer tastes increasingly appreciated better quality and superior service. Easy access to information and markets diminished the value of being nearby, and made foreign competition even more viable. An aging U.S. manufacturing infrastructure compromised the ability of many companies to deliver these new values, while foreign competitors could do so more easily with their newer plants built in the aftermath of World War II. From the 1970s until the mid-1980s in industry after industry, American firms lost out competitively to international firms. During this period, more than half of all U.S. industry categories lost market share (Figure 1.5).[19]

Figure 1.5
U.S. Industry Gains & Losses, 1978-1985

Industry type	Share Gains	Share Losses
Raw materials	27	23
Manufacturing	18	28
Consumption	38	46
	83	97

U.S. firms had been like the proverbial frog in the pot of slowly heating water: they had been content in their positions and had not recognized the change going on around them or the need to jump out as the water temperature rose. Traditional planning largely downplayed external competitive forces and most often consisted of doing no more than what had worked in the past.

The field of strategy as we know it today was thus born, when people in industry and professors in business schools realized that newer approaches were required for companies to achieve sustainable competitive advantage and deliver superior performance. A number of important books and articles published during the 1970s began to articulate the kinds of ideas we now teach in strategy, ideas that might have helped American companies avoid their declines in the previous decade.[20] In his seminal 1980 book *Competitive Strategy,* Michael Porter described competitive strategy as "positioning a business to maximize the value of the capabilities that distinguish it from its competitors."[21]

The need for strategy is even more important in 2022. Look once more at Figure 1.4 to see what has happened to fuel prices over the last few years since the 2008 financial crisis and ensuing recession. When the crisis began, prices for crude oil and refined petroleum products dropped precipitously. A result of supply and demand, when world financial markets seized up, demand for oil dropped and so did prices. Then things returned to "normal" with gas prices rising back up to nearly $4 per gallon. But since 2015 the price of oil has plummeted, and gas prices followed.

Supply and demand again: the slowing China economy had ripple effects across the globe, decreasing demand for fuel. The Mideast oil cartels have continued to pump oil and the United States (through fracking) had for a time become the world's largest exporter, creating excess world supply.

These are positive events for companies who rely on fuel as a major cost element. Commercial airlines and automobiles are great examples. Airlines were more profitable before the 2020 Covid-19 pandemic than they had been in two decades. From 2016-2018 auto manufacturers set records for new auto sales (+7.3% compound annual growth over 9 years), especially SUVs and pickups. Buyers didn't mind buying "big" since gas cost less. On the other hand, imagine how difficult strategic planning and execution is for companies when raw materials costs are so volatile, such as what we have witnessed since the pandemic struck. It has taken awhile, but in 2016 the major oil drilling and exploration companies began to shut down many operations, which couldn't be economically justified at such low market prices. Do you think low-priced oil and gas will last? For how long? In 2021 excess supply over demand caused gas prices to again rise precipitously. What if it rises as sharply in 2023 as it dropped in 2015? The need for sharp, long term strategic thinking is even greater today than ever before!

VISION, ETHICS, LEADERSHIP

We cannot talk about or teach strategy today without simultaneously considering issues of vision, ethics, and leadership. Where the goal of effective strategy is superior competitive performance and superior financial performance, these other dimensions of strategic management are always lurking just beneath the surface. That is to say, these dimensions are not always discussed explicitly when we talk about a particular aspect of strategy, however they are always implicit in the conversation. It's smart to be aware that they are relevant and important as we move along in this book, and as you move along in your careers.

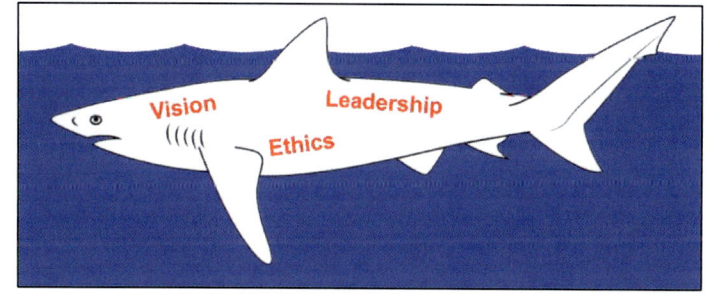

We will actually have a lot more to say about vision shortly – in fact, a whole chapter (Chapter 3). Suffice it to say here, though, that part of the problems encountered by U.S. companies in the 1970s was a lack of vision. Mere extrapolations from the past, combined with a sort of complacent attitude about what changes the future might bring, led to the situation described earlier. The contemporary view of strategy that has since emerged now emphasizes the need to sustain competitive differences over time. A longer-term view is called for to help guide the company and its employees in the right direction. The importance for today's strategic imperatives of value creation and opportunity recognition demand that companies be forward-looking, anticipating dynamic changes in the business environment while simultaneously leveraging what they do best. As we will describe later, articulating vision (and mission) is one effective means for helping to bridge between the present and the future.

Recent headlines have screamed about unethical behavior at companies such as Volkswagen, Enron and Tyco. In 2015 Volkswagen admitted that mid-level engineers installed software in engines over several years so that its cars could pass lab emissions tests. Is it possible they did this on their own, without their superiors knowing? How far up the hierarchy did knowledge about this misleading practice go? Although senior management first claimed it was unaware of the deception, the CEO resigned, former executives have since paid €288 million in fines for "breaches of due diligence," and the company has also paid fines. It is abundantly clear that a culture which allowed unethical behavior to prosper is one where leadership is sorely needed. In 2019 the CEO and former CEO of Volkswagen were indicted for misleading shareholders about emissions cheating, and in 2021 he was indicted for lying to the German parliament.[22] This is evidence that ethical lapses can have long term consequences. The 2008 financial markets crisis was fueled by factors such as unusual mortgage lending activity and baffling financial instruments. These events trigger cries about the ethical behavior of senior executives, and in fact 2020 U.S. Presidential candidates Bernie Sanders and Elizabeth Warren made this a centerpiece of their populist campaigns.

But ethics in strategy covers a far broader range of behaviors than strange accounting techniques or mysterious financial innovations. Externally, managers need to carefully consider decisions such as advertising to children, manufacturing in offshore locations where sweatshops are prevalent, or how "green" a company should be in its business practices. Internally, we need to carefully consider decisions such as how fairly employees are treated and provided opportunities, communicate and enforce zero tolerance for forms of harassment, and ensure that privacy and personal data is secured. Many strategic decisions concern initiatives or actions that may be technically legal and highly effective from a competitive point of view, but which may be morally challenged. Throughout this book you will encounter a discussion of strategy where ethical dimensions surface, and you will need to balance these factors in decision situations.

Strategic leadership is crucial at all levels of a company, and will be important to you as you start your career. No doubt you have already encountered in other courses some dimensions of leadership – such as setting direction, establishing goals, making decisions and allocating resources, building culture, engaging in symbolic behavior. Articulating vision and establishing ethical guidelines are also part of the responsibility of strategic managers.

However, there is also an interesting contradiction about strategy. Senior management, who we usually think of as in charge of strategy, often knows *less* about what is really working (or falling apart) in their company than do people further down in the organization. The closer you get to dealing with competition, the closer you get to dealing with customers, the closer you get to the actual operations in your company, the more aware you will become of the two strategic imperatives mentioned earlier: value creation and opportunity recognition. Because you will be closer to "the action," you will notice details and nuances that senior management cannot possibly comprehend from 30,000 feet. In fact, in 2019 General Electric CEO Larry Culp started rolling out a Japanese strategic planning process called *Hoshin Kanri*. This process holds that "all workers should understand the company's strategy and how their role can contribute to it, enabling feedback and improvement to come up from lower levels."[23] You will have a strategic responsibility to feed this information up the line when and where you see the company doing exceptionally well or poorly, and when and where you see new opportunities emerge that the company can pursue. You will be on the "firing line," where the balance often plays itself out in real terms between ethical behavior and actions that further increase competitive advantage or financial performance. You can exert strategic leadership, even at a lower level, to help others articulate and further develop these ideas. Today, every employee in an organization has a strategic leadership role to play.

STRATEGIC MANAGEMENT PROCESS

So far we have briefly reviewed the history of strategy in business and why it became so important. We have also described the characteristics and chief concerns of strategic decisions, and how these are very different from other areas of management that you may have studied already. Now let's talk about the *management* of strategy.

Strategic management is the process through which strategy is developed, implemented, and evaluated. The strategic management process is what the rest of this book is about – a concise and practical guide to analyzing, formulating, implementing, and evaluating strategy. Figure 1.6 provides a blueprint of how the rest of the book is organized to present the topics critical to strategic management.

**Figure 1.6
Strategic Management Model**

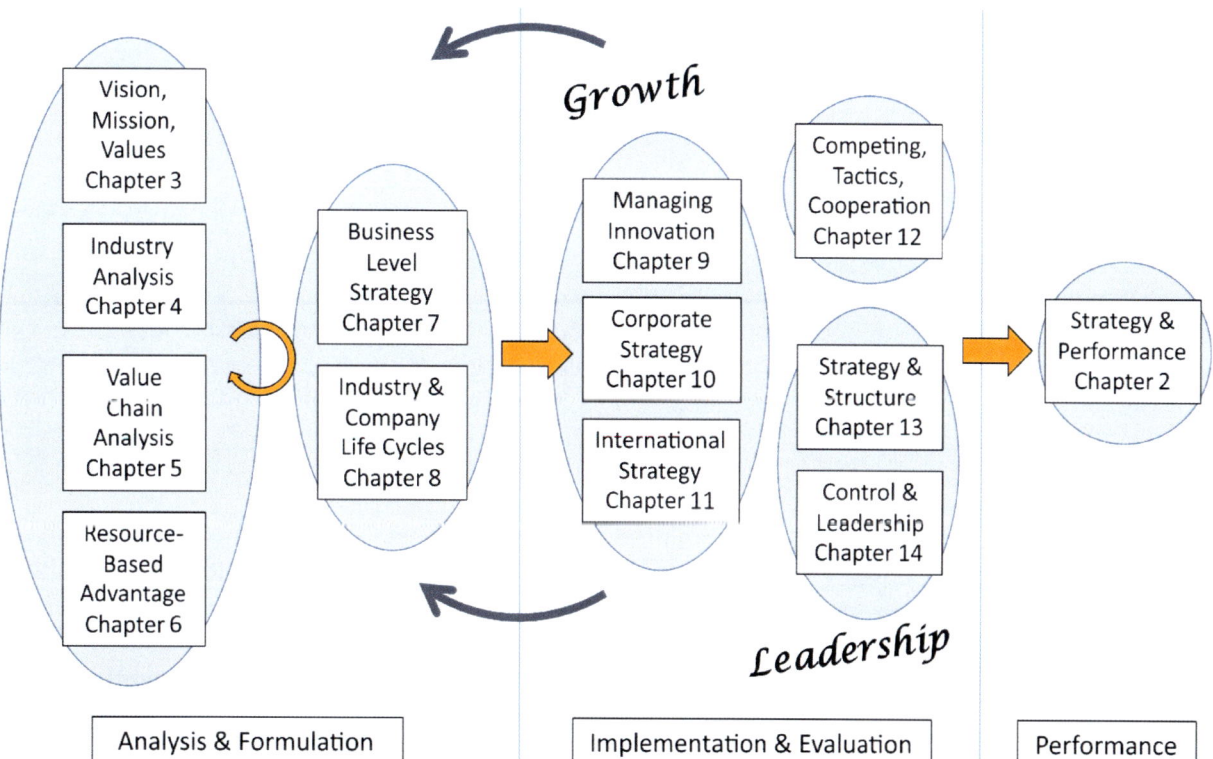

There are typically four stages of the strategic management process: analysis, formulation, implementation, and evaluation.

- *Analysis* includes examining and understanding the industry in which you want to compete, and looking carefully inside the company to understand what its unique competitive strengths are and how it organizes its activities to create and deliver value. It is through the analysis process that companies often discover new opportunities or threats, and begin to realize how they can organize or reorganize to create new value.
- *Formulation* is the stage in which management articulates its vision and mission, outlines its goals and objectives, and decides upon a particular type of strategic approach to take. Of course, formulation depends on good, strong analysis.

- *Implementation* is where the rubber hits the road. In this stage, the formulated strategy is put into practice through the decisions that companies make about how to allocate resources, how to structure the organization and motivate employees, and which types of tactics, programs, and activities the company actually engages in. Strong implementation efforts call for consistency of effort across all the functional areas of a company.
- The fourth part of the strategic management process is *evaluation*, an activity that actually occurs throughout each of the first three stages. By creating a system of evaluation that operates continuously, management is able to rethink and respond more rapidly when actual results begin to diverge from what they had expected in the analysis, formulation, and implementation stages.

Within each of these four stages are a set of well-grounded approaches and analytical frameworks that can be applied in a variety of business settings. More on this below.

What you might notice first about Figure 1.6 is that the next Chapter 2 is on the *right* side of the figure, traditionally indicating the end. You might be asking yourself, why would the authors begin the book at the end? We do so to emphasize the need for keeping our eye on the ball. The "ball" is superior performance, the fundamental goal of strategic management. So to emphasize superior performance as the ultimate goal, we concentrate on it in our very next chapter, before we describe in more specific detail in the subsequent chapters how to achieve it.

After considering performance, we move into the processes of analysis and formulation (Chapters 3 - 8). But as the circular arrow in the center of this block of chapters suggests, there should be a constant cycling back and forth between analysis and formulation. It is an iterative process, not "one and done." The remaining sections of the book (Chapters 9 - 14) explore topics that contextualize strategy in the process of its implementation and evaluation. Here we will cover practical methods for how to grow the business, how to organize, and how to evaluate whether a strategy will ultimately lead to the desired outcome of superior performance.

Analysis and Formulation

The process of analysis and formulation is not really linear. For instance, even though a high degree of analysis might be required before a company's vision and mission can be solidly established, a company needs to formulate a vision and mission statement to guide its analytical efforts. Therefore, before getting into a discussion of the analysis process (Chapters 4 - 6), mission and vision are covered in Chapter 3. This chapter describes the necessity of establishing a vision that guides the company into the future, a mission statement that enhances day-to-day consistency and coordination of activities in support of the vision, and objectives that represent tangible targets for a company and its employees to work toward. We also cover the establishment of principles and values that help guide employee and corporate conduct.

The analysis chapters yield a more detailed understanding of what works in a particular competitive environment and why, while helping us understand how well our company's activities and resources are suited to the competitive environment. Often, the industry a company competes in or how a company competes is a reflection of an earlier choice that management made about its long-term direction.

Types of analysis. Every attempt to grapple with strategy formulation and implementation relies upon a strong foundation of analysis. The analysis process described will begin with an "external analysis" at the industry level, and then drill down into the company of interest. A detailed analysis of industries and competitors (Chapter 4) builds a solid understanding of the competitive context, how it is evolving, and what competitive dimensions appear to be growing in importance. This analysis also offers insight into the intentions of key competitors. Probing this broader industry and competitive context contributes to a better understanding of how a particular company will be able to effectively compete.

The "internal analysis" of the company encompasses two perspectives. The first is the value chain (Chapter 5), because value creation is a central theme in this book. Value chain analysis takes into account two sets of activities that create value and offer the potential for competitive advantage: 1) activities by people and departments within the walls of the company, and 2) activities transacted between the company and its suppliers and customers. It will be pointed out that companies themselves are merely an organization of a set of activities in a chain of value-adding activity across an industry. We will also learn that products and services produced by a company are simply a manifestation of sets of activities that occur within the company. Therefore, if we are interested in the source of competitive advantage in a market, we need to carefully examine how value is created by a company through what people actually do. We will also examine when it makes strategic sense for a company to outsource important activities instead of performing them in house.

The second internal analysis method is resource-based analysis (Chapter 6). This is an exciting and relatively new area of study for strategy that offers the opportunity to better understand how to develop *sustainable* competitive advantage. While the value-chain perspective in Chapter 5 helps answer the first key question about strategy (Why so some companies perform better?), the resource-based perspective in Chapter 6 helps answer the second question (How are competitive differences sustained?).

One final comment on the analysis chapters: Recall from the earlier discussion that strategic decisions are special for a variety of reasons. The nature of strategy (dealing with ill-structured situations, uncertainty, and making decisions for the long term) will necessarily require decision makers to "make bets." Strategists must make decisions and investments today for payoffs that are often far down the road; it's simply the nature of this area of management. When a strategic decision is made, the decision maker is essentially building on a logic that he or she has developed about cause and effect in the marketplace, saying "If we do X now and over time, then Y will occur in the future." The best way to build that logic is through strong, foundational analysis. This enables decisions to be made, based not upon "I hope this will work," but based upon "I have developed a sufficient case to believe that this will work for my company."

Strategy choices. In Chapter 7, we consider business-level strategic approaches to the marketplace and competition, focusing especially on "low-cost" and "differentiation" approaches. Having analyzed the industry and a company's internal resources and value-creating activities, and taking into account its long-term vision, we are now in a position to formulate a precise and actionable approach to building a business, engage competition, and produce superior returns.

Chapter 8 outlines interesting strategy issues that occur in different stages of the life cycle of both companies and industries. The resources, activities, and strategic approach of a young company are likely to be very different from those of an established competitor in the same industry. In fact, there are specific market entry strategy issues faced by new ventures and young companies that existing companies need not worry about. Similarly, there are differences in strategic approaches that depend on the nature of the industry itself. What works in a young, growing industry may not work well at all when that same industry begins to mature. What works in fragmented industries may not be appropriate for consolidated industries. This chapter tackles what to do when the industry or the company enters a mature stage. Here we explore ways to redefine the value chain as a way of uncovering new growth opportunities. And finally, we offer perspective on how to handle strategy during times of crisis.

Implementation

Will all of the effort put into analysis and formulation be successful for the company in developing sustainable competitive advantage? The answer you will often hear is "It depends." What does effective strategic performance depend on? It depends on precisely these evolving contexts in the marketplace that confront the company.

Growth. Once a company has been in the marketplace competing for a period of time, it will need to find ways to grow its business. No company can just stand pat. Industries change, technology advances, new competitors come along, customers' expectations and desired values tend to escalate. There are four basic methods for any company to achieve growth. The first and most obvious method, drawing on its developed understanding and expertise, is simply to sell more of its existing products and services in its existing markets. Encouraging existing customers to buy more frequently and attracting new customers in its domestic markets are the usual approaches. Still, there is often a limit to how much growth such efforts can generate over time.

Chapter 9 explores the second method, which involves opportunity recognition and new value creation through innovation. There are different forms that innovation can take (product and process) and different degrees of innovation, from incremental to radical. Each has implications for the company's value creation methods and strategic capabilities. This chapter breaks these dimensions down and reveals how to manage the innovation process.

Chapter 10 concerns itself with a different avenue for growth, specifically growth achieved by buying or merging with other companies. This is a chapter on corporate strategy, that is, the strategic management of a company that owns and operates more than one type of business. Mergers and acquisitions (or their "divestitures" counterpart) are often front-page news in the *Wall Street Journal*. It is important to understand what motivates this approach to growth, critical dimensions of the acquisition process, and how to manage a diversified company.

One especially important area for potential growth may be international expansion, and so in Chapter 11 we look at the unique challenges presented by this fourth method of growth. Moving beyond the domestic borders is not at all like expanding domestically. The way to expand internationally again depends on appropriate value creation capabilities. But it also calls for an understanding of potential fit with other countries' economies and cultures.

Competitive dynamics. What do you do when your competitors start taking actions in response to your strategic moves? Chapter 12 explores many possibilities of competitive dynamics. For those students who enjoy gaming and sports, there are some very interesting parallels here to your out-of-class activities. Cooperation has recently become of great interest to companies (remember what Sun Tzu said), so here we also examine when it makes sense to cooperate instead of compete.

Evaluation

The missing piece in so many discussions of strategy is the practical internal implementation of the plan and its ongoing evaluation. A well-developed strategy involves the coordination of a tremendous number of areas within the organization, including its structure and systems. Chapter 13 walks us through different ways to coordinate important value-creating activities, their relationship to the sort of strategic approach adopted by the company, and the various organizational structures that are then appropriate.

Ensuring the success of strategy entails setting up internal control procedures and establishing a system to keep track of key performance metrics. Chapter 14 tackles this agenda. The chapter concludes by revisiting comments we have made here in Chapter 1 about the critical importance of strategic leadership and principled decision making.

Iterative Processes

The model in Figure 1.6 makes the strategy process appear to be linear and sequential, where one step logically follows another and where one cannot take a step until others before it have been completed. This isn't really the case in practice, though. For the purposes of studying strategic management, particularly for the first-time student, it is easier to lay the process out as we have done in Figure 1.6. However, note that there are arrows feeding from the Implementation and Evaluation sections back to Analysis and Formulation. This is a visual way of suggesting that there is a "continuous dialogue" that occurs among portions of this process. As we read earlier in this chapter on strategic imperatives, the nature of markets today requires the strategy process to be synthetic and integrative across all the areas pictured in the diagram. Therefore, the creation of strategy is both intentional and emergent. We conduct analyses, draw conclusions, lay plans, and implement those plans with programs and actions. Yet the nature of markets and competition will change the context in which we did our planning and require us to make modifications as we go along. At the same time, if we are prepared, we will recognize new opportunities that changing markets expose, and we will elect to make modifications in our plans to take advantage of them.

WHY BUSINESS?

We close this first chapter by posing an important question. Why do we study Strategic Management, or more generally why do we study business? Usually the strategy course in business school falls near the end of the curriculum, as a "capstone" course or experience. Students are required to take it, so it counts toward graduation and helps qualify for a job. But we hope that this instrumental view of strategy – and of an entire business degree – is trumped by something much more profound, much more substantive.

Both at home and abroad, our society today is characterized by many sorts of problems that are really tough to solve. Some may call these "wicked" problems because they are complex and involve many moving parts. We might count problems like poverty, disease, health, education, lack of opportunity, welfare and overall life happiness among them. Many people we know do not experience these problems, but many we do not know do.

What's the best way to solve wicked problems? Typically, the problems are so vast and so complex that the default solution is to let government handle it. But many would argue that big government and big bureaucracy is not particularly effective. For example, the "war on poverty" was started by the U.S. government in the 1960s, and since then trillions of dollars have been spent to combat it. But by 2022 poverty is as rampant as ever in America.

So a new school of thought suggests, instead, that business can play a pivotal role in "civic wealth creation." This is where "positive societal change happens when community members, supporters, and entrepreneurially-minded agents come together to aggregate resources and build new capabilities."[24] Many believe it possible that through their efforts companies can make the world a better place while simultaneously achieving positive returns to their shareholders. We will return to this very idea in the next chapter on Strategy and Performance.

Figure 1.7
The Moral Architecture of Business

- Humane and Just Society
- Political and Economic Institutions
- Market Economy
- Honorable Business
- Personal Purpose and Productive Value

But the idea runs deeper than explicit social responsibility efforts of businesses to try to address specific problems. As a major force in society business can be a rewarding profession in which to engage. A few pages ago we mentioned how ethics in decision making covers a broad range of the facets of conducting business and decision-making. Honorably conducted, the efforts of business can contribute to a smoother functioning economy, strengthen political and economic institutions, and lead to the sort of humane and just society that we all hope and strive for. In fact, in the 2021 Edelman Trust Survey 68% of respondents believe that business should step in to fill the void left by governments. This causal chain reflects the upward-directing arrow in Figure 1.7. Now consider the downward-directing arrow. It is important to realize that the same honorable conduct of business can lead you to the accomplishment of personal purpose, and enable you to create productive value that makes the world a better place. Even as we get caught up in the immediate challenges facing us in our everyday lives, calling up from memory this moral architecture of business can keep us centered.[25]

Managing in Markets: Question for Class Discussion

Recent Edelman Trust Barometer studies reported that among the general population in 28 countries surveyed:
- ➢ only 61% trust business
- ➢ only 48% believe information from a CEO is credible
- ➢ 56% believe business leaders purposely try to mislead
- ➢ 56% believe that free markets as they exist today do more harm than good in the world

Do you find this disconcerting? Why do you study business? Can business make a difference in the community and the world? Can you make a difference by studying business? How?

CHAPTER SUMMARY

We began this chapter with a discussion of the real meaning of strategy. The area of strategy is generally defined as addressing five critical questions in business:

1. Why are firms different?
2. How are competitive differences sustained?
3. What is the nature of strategy in a multi-business firm?
4. How is strategic performance measured?
5. What is special about strategic decisions?

A review of the history of strategy from its earliest foundations with Sun Tzu to its emergence following the 1970s demonstrated that firms needed to think more clearly about how to create and sustain valuable differences versus their competition. Doing so can lead to superior performance. The need for strategy is even greater in the twenty-first century with the advent of technology, globalization, ease of access to financial markets, and other macro-economic trends. As a result of these forces, strategy must increasingly concern itself with two imperatives:

1. *Value creation imperative*
2. *Opportunity recognition imperative*

Sustained superior performance depends upon these capabilities. The structure of this book follows a model for strategic planning. We recognize that strategy planning and implementation requires continuous monitoring of the competitive environment and constant reevaluation and adjustment of plans.

Learning Objectives Review

1. *Identify and discuss the two strategic imperatives facing every company today.*

- **Opportunity recognition.** Identifying and exploiting where the market is heading.
- **Value creation.** Understanding and delivering new values appreciated by both existing and new customers and other stakeholders.

2. *Define the term "Strategy" and describe the five critical questions encompassing what we study in strategy.*

- **Strategy.** The overall concept for how a company organizes itself and all its activities in order to conduct business successfully, out-perform competitors, and deliver superior returns to its shareholders.
- **Questions defining what we study in strategy.**

    1. Why are firms different? Why do some firms perform better than others?
    2. How are competitive differences sustained?
    3. What is the province of strategy in multi-business firms?

4. How is strategic effectiveness measured?

5. What is special about strategic decisions?

3. *Explain the evolution of the field of strategy and why it is important today.*

- **Sun Tzu**. Author of *The Art of War*, an ancient Chinese book on military strategy.

- **Frederick Taylor**. Father of the "science of work" time and motion studies that helped identify more efficient processes and ideas about structure and hierarchy.

- **Long-range planning**. A traditional approach to planning used before 1980 that often extrapolated into the future what the company had done well in the past.

- **1970s-1980s**. Macro-economic shocks to U.S. industries and technological advances led to foreign competition, share losses in many important industries, and the realization that long-range planning was insufficient.

- **Michael Porter**. Leading proponent of the move from long-range planning to strategy. His two early books on the subject, *Competitive Strategy* and *Competitive Advantage*, described competitive strategy as "positioning a business to maximize the value of the capabilities that distinguish it from its competitors."

- **Importance today**. Strategy is the glue that binds different parts of an organization together into a consistent approach to the marketplace. Strategy enables companies to create value and meet the growing desires of customers and other stakeholders. Strategy delivers superior performance to owners of companies. Strategy encourages explicit consideration of ethics in decision making and corporate behavior.

4. *Connect the concept of strategy with leadership and ethics.*

- Every aspect of strategy and the strategic management process depends on effective leadership. Articulating vision and establishing ethical guidelines are part of the responsibility of both leaders. However, senior management often knows less about what is really going on in their company than do people further down in the organization. Employees closer to the action notice details and nuances, see where the company is doing well or poorly, notice new opportunities emerging, and see where ethical behavior and actions impact performance. You can exert strategic leadership, even at your lower level, to help others articulate and further develop these ideas. Today, every employee in an organization has a strategic leadership role to play.

5. *Describe the process for developing and implementing strategy.*

- **Analysis**. Careful "external analysis" of an industry and "internal analysis" of a company's strengths, resources and ways of creating value.

- **Formulation**. Articulating vision, mission, goals, and a type of strategic approach to adopt.

- **Implementation**. Putting strategy into effect by allocating resources, choosing appropriate paths for growth, responding to competitive dynamics, structuring the organization, and motivating employees.

- **Evaluation**. Ensuring strategy-consistent actions across departments, and establishing performance metrics to ensure that progress is being made toward long term goals.

Key Terms

Corporate strategy - The strategy involved in managing multiple business units under the same corporate banner.

Entrepreneurial orientation - An embedded set of managerial attitudes supporting a sustained pattern of innovative and proactive company behaviors leading to entry into new markets and new businesses.

Frederick Taylor - Father of the "science of work" time and motion studies that helped identify more efficient production processes and ideas about structure and hierarchy.

Hoshin Kanri – A Japanese strategic planning process which holds that all workers should understand the company's strategy and how their role can contribute to it, enabling feedback and improvement to come up from lower levels.

Long-range planning - A traditional approach to planning used before 1980 that often simply extrapolated into the future what the company had done well in the past.

Metrics - Qualitative and quantitative measures that allow the firm to measure the effectiveness of its business strategy.

Michael Porter - Leading proponent of the move from long-range planning to strategy. His two early books on the subject, *Competitive Strategy* and *Competitive Advantage*, described competitive strategy as "positioning a business to maximize the value of the capabilities that distinguish it from its competitors.

Opportunity recognition - the critical need in business to identify and exploit where the market is heading.

Resource-based analysis - A method that examines the extent to which a company possesses resources that will allow it to achieve sustainable competitive advantage.

Strategic decisions - Strategic decisions exhibit five characteristics: 1) are relevant to ill-structured and non-routine situations; 2) significantly affect the subsequent actions of the entire organization; 3) involve a significant commitment of resources; 4) are difficult to reverse both economically and politically; and 5) are easily identified with the success or failure of the organization.

Strategic management - The process through which strategy is developed, executed, and evaluated. There are typically four stages of the strategic management process: analysis, formulation, implementation, and evaluation.

Strategy - The overall concept for how a company organizes itself and all its activities in order to conduct business successfully, outperform competitors and deliver superior returns to its shareholders.

Sun Tzu - Author of *The Art of War*, an ancient Chinese book on military strategy.

Superior performance - As used in the field of strategy, refers to performance outcomes that exceed the average for the industry in which the company competes.

Value chain - Provides a systematic way of examining all the activities a firm performs and how those activities interact with each other to find a basis for competitive advantage.

Value creation - The primary goal of strategy. The value created is widely accounted for by all the stakeholders of the company.

Short Answer Review Questions

1. Imagine that you have arrived back home from your first class in strategy and you receive a call from your parent asking you about your class. How would you explain what strategy is?
2. How was strategy operationalized during the early part of the 1900s?
3. How has strategy evolved over the past forty years?
4. If you were asked for some advice about how strategy can help a business develop and grow, what are the areas in which you would suggest that strategy could make a difference?
5. Who are Sun Tzu, Michael Porter, and Frederick Taylor?
6. What do you expect to be able to do after you finish this course in strategy?
7. How might your understanding of other areas of your business studies (finance, accounting, marketing, management, and information systems) be affected by your ability to apply the concepts of strategy?
8. Why is being better than average in an industry an important strategy concept?
9. Who uses strategy in a typical company?
10. What elements help distinguish a strategic decision from one that is tactical?
11. What are some measures of an effective strategy?
12. Why is opportunity recognition such an important concept in strategy?
13. What strategic concept encompasses a detailed understanding of the processes within an organization?
14. Describe five types of strategy decisions in which ethical concerns must also be accounted for. Search the Internet for a business article that discusses this type of decision for a real company.

Group Review Exercises

1. Hewlett-Packard is facing a significant strategic dilemma. Consumers can buy personal computers from any one of a number of companies, and they are all pretty much identical to each other. Form a group of three to five people and answer the following questions:

   a. How is HP different from Dell, Lenovo, Acer, Apple and many other brands?

   b. How might you create new value in this industry and make it the centerpiece of how the company does business?

   c. How should HP measure its success?

2. Oil prices significantly affect many businesses. Businesses that were highly profitable when gas prices were higher have unexpectedly experienced disruption by lower gas prices: lower costs allow competitors to lower prices. Form a group of three to five people and address the following:

   a. Are some businesses not affected by the price of oil?

   b. How would airlines cope if super-high fuel prices come back? Are there alternatives to simply raising ticket prices?

   c. What would you suggest as a sustainable strategy for firms operating in the trucking industry?

3. Netflix out-competed Blockbuster in the DVD and movie rental business, effectively driving it out of business. In your group discuss the following:

   a. What was the strategic approach and resources that made Netflix successful in the past?

   b. Now discuss the challenges confronting Netflix as it faces competition from video streaming sources such as Disney, Hulu, Amazon, HBO Max and others.

   c. How have its past strategy and its resources assisted and/or constrained the company's approach to the market?

Investor Relations Sites for Companies Mentioned in This Chapter

Airbus Industries: https://www.airbus.com/en/investors
Amazon: https://ir.aboutamazon.com/overview/default.aspx
Boeing: https://investors.boeing.com/investors/overview/default.aspx
General Electric: https://www.ge.com/investor-relations
Kroger: https://ir.kroger.com/home/default.aspx
Publix: https://www.publixstockholder.com/
Siemens: https://new.siemens.com/global/en/company/investor-relations.html
3M: https://investors.3m.com/ir-home/default.aspx
Truist (formerly BB&T): https://ir.truist.com/
Volkswagen: https://www.volkswagenag.com/en/InvestorRelations.html
Walmart: https://stock.walmart.com/investors/default.aspx

References

[1] Financial data from corporate 10K reports and Morningstar. J. Greene & L. Stevens, 2017, "Wal-Mart to vendors: Get off Amazon's cloud, Wall Street Journal, June 21. J. Jacobo, 2019, "Walmart to limit sales of guns, ammunition in wake of horrific shootings," ABC News, September 3. S. Kapner, 2017, "Store closings accelerate," Wall Street Journal, April 22, A1. S. Kapner, 2017, "To the worsening troubles at Sears, add skittish suppliers," Wall Street Journal, Novermber 6, A8. S. Kapner & D. Cimilluca, 2017, "Neiman Marcus goes on sale," Wall Street Journal, March 15, A2. D. Mattioloi & D. FitzGerald, 2017, "Sycamore agrees to purchase Staples," Wall Street Journal, June 29, B1. L. Matsakis, 2019, "Social issues raised by Amazon investors aren't going away," Wired, May 22. D. Mattioli, S. Kapner, & D. Benoit, 2017, "Saks owner Hudson's Bay makes takeover approach to Macy's," Wall Street Journal, February 16, B1. S. Nassauer, 2019, "US says bias likely in Walmart's pay," Wall Street Journal, September 18, B3. S. Nassauer, 2019, "Walmart's Bonobos lays off workers," Wall Street Journal, October 8, B3. S. Nassauer & P. Rudegeair, 2021, "Walmart, with eyes on Amazon, tried to build a finetch startup," Wall Street Journal, October 16, B1. S. Nassauer & L. Stevens, 2017, "Black Friday crowds thin," Wall Street Journal, November 27, A1. S. Nassauer & R. Winkler, 2021, "Walmart buys health provider MeMD in push into virtual care," Wall Street Journal, May 7, B3. J. Scheck & J. Emont, 2019, "Amazon sells clothes from factories other retailers shun as dangerous," Wall Street Journal, October 23, B1. L. Stevens & A. Gasparro, 2017, "Amazon to buy Whole Foods for $13.7 billion," Wall Street Journal, June 17, A1. L. Stevens & H. Haddon, 2017, "Amazon acts first on food prices," Wall Street Journal, August 29, B3. "Wal-Mart takes aim at Amazon," Wall Street Journal, 2017, October 24, B2. "Wal-Mart works to narrow gap between itself, Amazon," Associated Press, 2017, May 30.

[2] See for example M. A. Hitt, B. W. Keats, & S. M. DeMarie, 1998, "Navigating in the new competitive landscape: Building strategic flexibility and competitive advantage in the 21st century," Academy of Management Executive, 12: 22-42.

[3] https://www.mckinsey.com/business-functions/strategy-and-corporate-finance/our-insights/five-fifty-the-need-for-speed.

[4] R. A. D'Aveni, 1994, *Hypercompetition*, Free Press: New York.

[5] The Economist, 2019, "Herd instincts," April 20, 23-26.

[6] D. Gross, 2017, "Siemens CEO Joe Kaeser on the Next Industrial Revolution," Strategy+Business, February.

[7] N. Gowing & C. Langdon, 2018, "Be prepared for disruption: Thinking the unthinkable," Strategy+Business, October.

[8] J. G. Covin & W. J. Wales, 2019, "Crafting high-impact entrepreneurial orientation research: Some suggested guidelines," Entrepreneurship Theory and Practice, 43 (1), 3-18.

[9] Gryta, T., 2019, "CEO's plan for GE: A fix, not a reinvention," Wall Street Journal, October 8, A10.

[10] U.S. Small Business Administration, 2019, "Small businesses generate 44 percent of U.S. economic activity," Release No. 19-1 ADV, January 30. S. Venkatraman, 2004, "Regional transformation through technological entrepreneurship," Journal of Business Venturing, 19 (1): 153 – 167. G. P. West & C. E. Bamford, 2005, "Creating a technology-based entrepreneurial economy: A resource-based theory perspective," Journal of Technology Transfer, 30 (4): 433 - 451.

[11] R. P. Rumelt, D. E. Schendel, & D. J. Teece (eds.), 1994, *Fundamental Issues in Strategy*, Boston: Harvard Business School Press.

[12] In 2019 BB&T merged with SunTrust, and the bank's new name became Truist Financial.

[13] M. E. Porter, 1985, *Competitive Advantage: Creating and Sustaining Superior Performance*, Free Press, 33.

[14] 3M Corporation Annual Report 2018, 2.

[15] E. Basu, 2014, "Boeing 787 and Airbus A350: A tale of two planes," Motley Fool, August 31. M. E. Babej, 2014, "Airbus A380 vs. Boring 787 revisited," Forbes, December. D. Michaels, 2013, "Airbus A380 is jumbo shrimp," Wall Street Journal, January 16, B3. P. Sanders, 2009, Boeing sets deal to buy Dreamliner plant," Wall Street Journal, July 8, B3. G. Topham, 2013, "Battle for the future of the skies: Boeing 787 Dreamliner v Airbus A380," The Guardian, December 29. R. Wall, 2016, "Airbus pulls back as clouds gather," Wall Street Journal, December 28, B1.

[16] D. Michaels & J. L. Lunsford, "Jet makers reach crossroads," Wall Street Journal, May 12, 2006, A4.

[17] Schwenk, C.R. 1988, *The Essence of Strategic Decision Making*, Lexington Books, New York, NY.

[18] A. D. Chandler, 1962, *Strategy and Structure*, Cambridge, MA: MIT Press.

[19] Data abstracted from M. E. Porter, 1990, *The Competitive Advantage of Nations*, New York: Free Press, 534.

[20] K. R. Andrews, 1971, *The Concept of Corporate Strategy*, Homewood, IL: Irwin. C. W. Hofer & D. Schendel, 1978, *Strategy Formulation: Analytic Concepts*, New York: West Publishing. R. E. Miles & C. C. Snow, 1978,

Organizational Strategy, Structure, and Process, New York: McGraw-Hill. H. Mintzberg, 1977, "The strategy concept I: Five P's for strategy," California Management Review, Fall: 11 – 24. H. Mintzberg, 1978, "Patterns in strategy formation," Management Science, 24 (9): 934 – 948. R. P. Rumelt, 1974, *Strategy, Structure, and Economic Performance*, Cambridge, MA: Harvard University Press.

[21] M. E. Porter, 1980, *Competitive Strategy: Techniques for Analyzing Industries and Competitors*, Free Press, 47.

[22] L. Alderman, 2021, "A former VW chief will pay the automaker $13.7 million over its emission scandal," New York Times, June 9. W. Boston, 2019, "Volkswagen CEO faces charges from scandal," Wall Street Journal, September 25, A1.

[23] T. Gryta, 2019, "CEO's plan for GE: A fix, not a reinvention," Wall Street Journal, October 8, A1.

[24] Lumpkin G.T. and Bacq S., 2019, "Civic wealth creation: A new view of stakeholder engagement and societal impact," Academy of Management Perspectives, 33 (4), 383-404.

[25] Figure 1.7 was developed in collaboration with James Otteson of Wake Forest University.

This page is intentionally left blank.

Chapter 2: Strategy and Performance

> LEARNING OBJECTIVES:
>
> 1. Explain the value of using both financial and nonfinancial performance dimensions to measure strategy effectiveness.
> 2. Describe the relationship between financial performance and a sustainable competitive advantage.
> 3. Use financial analysis to examine company strategy.
> 4. Explain the economic logic of industries and companies.
> 5. Examine and explain the interaction between strategy formulation and financial analysis.

Buckle Up: Rollercoaster in the Un-Friendly Skies[1]

When the Covid-19 pandemic spread around the world, the airline industry suffered. The global airline industry lost $190 billion in 2020-21 because people stopped flying. But this is just another down in a series of ups and downs over the last 50 years in this industry.

Since it was deregulated in 1978, the financial performance of the domestic airline industry has been feast or famine, and mostly famine. By 2009 the industry had cumulatively lost $59 billion. Large carriers had routinely dropped ticket prices to attract customers, but were slow to tailor their huge asset bases (planes, maintenance facilities, airport gates) to the size of their business. Recessions during 2001-02 and 2009-11 resulted in less demand for air travel and continued financial woes. According to one airline CEO, it was "tough" and "sloppy" for U.S. airlines and for the traveling public. By 2012 five of the "legacy" airline carriers had gone through Chapter 11 bankruptcy (American, Delta, Northwest, United, and US Airways). Balance sheets were in disarray and shareholders were not earning positive returns on equity. Financial markets had beaten down stock prices to uncomfortably low levels.

Amidst this backdrop, mergers dominated headlines. US Airways merged with America West in 2005, then bid to acquire Delta in an attempt to grow larger and improve operating efficiency. The offer was rejected. But in 2015 the airline merged with American. Northwest was acquired by Delta in 2008, United consummated a 2010 deal with Continental, and in 2016 Alaska Air acquired Virgin. These mergers were an attempt to create larger, more efficient carriers by taking out competitors, controlling routes, and reducing excess capacity.

The traveling public experienced headaches while (and maybe because) the airlines were constantly in trouble. Most airlines instituted fees for checked-bags and pre-assigned seat reservations to generate revenue offsetting their costs. New security procedures involving full-body scans and the banning of carry-on liquids created long lines and short tempers at airports. Since new security prompted customers to check more bags, lost baggage plagued many airlines. In 2008 system wide mishandled baggage reports had increased 37% over 2004. Overbooking by airlines resulted in a 14% increase in passenger "bumping" off flights.

But then the airlines started flying in the clear by about 2013. With emergence from the financial crisis passenger traffic picked up. Refraining from adding capacity as demand grew, the industry-wide "load factor" grew from 70% in the early 2000s to over 85% by 2019.[2] Jet fuel costs declined for two years, and airlines began replacing aging jets with more fuel-efficient equipment.

2019 Selected Domestic Airline Financial Performance					
	American	Delta	JetBlue	Southwest	United
Revenue (millions)	$ 45,770	$ 47,007	$ 7,953	$ 22,428	$ 43,259
Net Income (millions)	$ 1,690	$ 4,767	$ 440	$ 2,300	$ 3,009
Net Income %	3.7 %	10.1 %	5.5 %	10.3 %	7.0 %
Stock Change / Year (5-Year)	- 9.8 %	4.0 %	3.8 %	5.8 %	6.7 %
Stock Volatility (5-Year Beta)	1.7	1.2	0.9	1.5	1.2
4-Year Return On Assets	3.5 %	7.3 %	6.3 %	10.5 %	5.3 %
4-Year Return on Equity	n/a*	30.3 %	14.0 %	27.1 %	24.4 %
* Negative shareholder equity previous two years					

By 2019 the financial performance story had changed. In a traditionally commoditized business known for its low margins, net income now ranged between 6-10% of sales. Stock prices had risen in the face of strong customer demand, lower costs, and discipline to avoid fare discounts. Airline operations had also become more efficient. Mishandled bag reports dropped 21% since 2014, on-time arrivals increased 2% to 78%, and denied boarding due to overbooking decreased.

2019 Selected Domestic Airline Operating Performance					
	American	Delta	JetBlue	Southwest	United
ASMs (available seat miles, millions)	151,465	130,931	43,779	152,791	116,996
Load Factor	86.0 %	87.2 %	85.3 %	84.1 %	86.1 %
Cost Per ASM (cents)	17.1	15.1	10.3	11.4	14.4
On-Time Arrival	76 %	85 %	71 %	78 %	1 %
Bags Mishandled (per 1,000)	9.0	4.8	5.5	4.9	7.2

Yet headwinds also reappeared. Although demand had increased, inflation-adjusted ticket prices had actually declined -3.4% since 2009. This reflects the commoditization of the flying experience, where once you are in your seat it is hard to tell exactly which airline you are on. Even with rising demand, the airlines have kept low prices in order to increase their load factor. Fuel prices started to creep up again. And operational problems remained among large legacy airlines, especially American due to its size, as they still seek to fully digest their acquisitions they made and gain the much sought-after "synergies." Morningstar claimed that the cost structure of the core airline business would prevent some carriers from earning competitive returns to shareholders.

Enter the Covid-19 pandemic. With customer demand at only 40% of pre-pandemic levels, domestic airlines were hard-pressed to make productive use of their assets. Sicknesses among pilots and ground crew caused delays and cancellations, especially during the 2021 holiday season. The result has been sharp reductions in revenue, losses, and negative returns to shareholders.

2021 Selected Domestic Airline Financial Performance					
	American	Delta	JetBlue	Southwest	United
Revenue (TTM, millions)	$ 24,480	$ 24,402	$ 4,203	$ 12,752	$ 19,854
Net Income (TTM, millions)	- $ 3,240	- $ 67	- $ 53	$ 1,000	- $ 3,215
Net Income %	- 13.2 %	- 0.3 %	- 1.3 %	7.8 %	- 16.2 %
Stock Price 12/31/21	$ 17.96	$ 39.08	$ 14.24	$ 42.84	$ 43.78
Return On Equity	n/a*	- 2.6 %	- 1.3 %	9.8 %	- 59.2 %
* Negative shareholder equity last four years					

QUESTIONS

1. Since all domestic airlines confront identical industry conditions, why did certain airlines enjoy superior financial performance in 2019?

2. How was Southwest able to report the highest 4-year return on assets (ROA) in 2019 despite having the lowest load factor?

3. Southwest was the only carrier to earn positive return on equity (ROE) during 2021. Why?

FOCUS ON PERFORMANCE

In the first chapter we highlighted the need for strategy in today's competitive and ever-changing world, and we discussed several critical questions that help us understand dimensions that define what strategy is actually about. Throughout that discussion we often used terms or expressions that referred to performance. These included phrases such as "superior performance," "substantial positive return," and "above average profitability." This is because performance is one of the key outcomes of interest for students studying strategy and for managers who are responsible for formulating and implementing a company's strategy. Remember Figure 1.6 in the first chapter, where performance is both the culmination of the strategy model and a starting point for its continual refinement. In fact, such importance is placed on performance that we locate this chapter on performance right here near the beginning of this book.

Sound strategy helps to create a position of sustainable competitive advantage in the marketplace, the results of which should be superior performance. Recall that strategic decisions involve *non-routine situations* calling for a *significant commitment of resources and effort* that affect the *entire organization* over the *long run*. When managers are called upon to make such decisions, they must be able to reason that the company's subsequent performance will justify their resource investments and spending commitments. A consistent pattern of decision making that doesn't result in superior performance is often a signal that it is time to replace those making such impactful decisions. In 2019 hedge fund Elliott Management sought to dislodge management, shed assets, and effect changes in the strategy of AT&T, after the latter company's acquisition of Time Warner led to loss of focus and a huge debt burden.[3] So as you study strategy this semester by examining company cases and situations, you should always be considering the performance implications of strategic moves and actions. By discussing performance early in the study of strategy, we have learned that students can be far more insightful about and discriminating in their company evaluations.

Customary Performance Dimensions

There are three aspects of performance that are important to consider from a strategy point of view (Figure 2.1). First, since strategic decisions and actions involve virtually the entire organization, the types of performance measures we pay the greatest attention to are those that reflect the company's achievement as a whole. A marketing department may be interested in market share gains or advertising effectiveness as key performance outcomes, and a finance department might work toward an optimal capital structure or lowering the company's cost of capital as an outcome. However, at the strategic

Figure 2.1
Key Strategy Performance Dimensions

Summary performance
Relative to competition
Over the long run

level we are interested in summary accomplishments of the entire company that roll up and include these functional area effects, as well as the performance in other functional areas. Since strategy requires consistency and coordination across all functions, the key performance measures of interest should be those that reflect the impact of integrated efforts across the entire company.

Second, the kinds of performance measures we will pay the greatest attention to are those that can be compared to other companies. As mentioned in the first chapter, the goal of strategy is to produce *superior* performance, and so strategists are by definition relativists. Reporting that net income per employee increased by 3 percent over last year is interesting; however, realizing that the comparative average in the industry was up only 1 percent makes the result remarkable and indicates a significantly better approach. In Figure 1.2 in the last chapter we saw that, although its 3.9% profitability did not by itself appear astounding, Sprouts exceeded the retail grocery store industry average by 30% and bested most of its competitors. Relative to competition, the company was doing very well. Therefore, it is especially helpful to consider key performance measures that can be easily compared to other companies.

Finally, since the nature of strategy is about commitment and sustainability, the kind of performance measures we pay the greatest attention to are those that reflect the company's long-term commitment. Although many public companies are scrutinized carefully every quarter with the release of their financial updates, a long-term strategic orientation leads to superior performance for revenue and earnings, investment, market capitalization and job creation. Kenneth Frazier, former CEO of pharmaceutical company Merck, said his job was to "ensure that our decisions don't make sense only for the short term. Otherwise we'll be borrowing value from the future…which would be a mistake." [4]

A more complete view of strategic performance, therefore, would require assessing whether a company is delivering superior returns over time. There is normally a long lead time between strategic investments and the outcomes of those investments. Imagine, for example, the decision made in 2014 by Microsoft CEO Satya Nadella to fundamentally move the company away from its Windows operating system, which had been the company's "cornerstone" and  "foundation" and "primary growth engine" for decades. Moving into server software and Azure cloud services, artificial intelligence, gaming, and making acquisitions (e.g. LinkedIn) required time and commitment. This included a complete management reorganization, new ways of cooperatively innovating internally and with external developers, the creation of new internal capabilities, and a significant change in the culture across the company. Five years following his appointment as CEO, Microsoft's stock surged in 2019 and it became the world's largest company in market capitalization, retaining a 2nd place position in market capitalization by 2022.[5] So it may be misleading to evaluate performance over a short time frame, simply because the time between a strategic investment and its performance impact can be substantial.

Using performance measures that implicitly or explicitly incorporate dimensions of a company's long-term commitments are usually more insightful. Better than using statistics from a single year, then, are measures which calculate firm performance over longer periods. Look back at the first table in the airline story which began this chapter. Here you will see both 4-year ROA and 4-year ROE, each presenting views of how well the airlines performed at a summary level over a longer period. Note that Southwest and Delta exceeded other competitors on these dimensions. As importantly, also note that American was unable to report ROE, since in some of the 4 years it reported losses, and actually had negative stockholder equity accounts.

Emerging Stakeholder Performance Dimensions

Despite examples that emphasize financial measures of performance, effective strategy also demands consideration of other more qualitative dimensions of the strategic performance question. Whole Foods created more than just economic value for its shareholders early on. The company created markets for organic and natural foods that were previously underdeveloped. This effort served to legitimize producers of these foodstuffs such that even Walmart is now offering organic products in their superstores. In this way the company helped create value upstream for its suppliers. There is also a social benefit to communities in which Whole Foods stores are located, as consumers in these areas are provided with shopping choices previously unavailable to them. Since the company sponsors cooking and health and cooking seminars as part of its operations, noneconomic benefits accrue to communities in which the company located stores.

One of the more recent moves by companies that benefit both society and the organization is the effort at becoming "green." Many businesses now design and occupy office buildings which are LEED-certified (Leadership in Energy and Environmental Design). Using natural light, installing natural power generation, reducing the use of water and eliminating waste, such businesses present a more attractive work environment for their employees and  communities. Selling products that are made in a sustainable way lead to significant benefits for society and are rapidly being seen as a means of competitive advantage for companies.[6]

These ideas emphasize that strategy is about value creation which can take many forms – economic, cultural, community, social, and knowledge-based – and which are not just for the benefit of those with formal economic claims on a company. Businesses are sometimes perceived as having a purely economic transactional view of their relationships, with a focus on enhancing profitability for shareholders to the exclusion of other goals. This approach has occasionally been associated with what we now consider abuses of the public good, such as the belching smokestacks in heavy industry, the use of child labor for clothing manufacturing in emerging nations, untreated animal farm runoff in the Southeast, or the tearing down of a neighborhood health clinic to make room for a parking garage for corporate executives in the skyscraper next door.

But today a more holistic view of business exists, a view recognizing that business operates in both a competitive *and* social context. In this more emergent view, firms consider performance with respect to a broader range of stakeholders. Stakeholders are those individuals or groups who have an interest in or an influence on the business and operations of a company. They generally fall into two categories, internal and external stakeholders (Figure 2.2).

Figure 2.2
Stakeholders

Internal	External	
Employees	Suppliers	Governments
Managers & Officers	Unions	Communities
Board of Directors	Creditors	Interest Groups
Stockholders	Customers	

As awareness of stakeholder issues has become more prevalent over the last few years, a vibrant debate has sprung up as to whether firm performance should be focused purely on financial measures or on a broader selection of measures that account for stakeholder interests. This debate implies that profitability and stakeholder performance may be at odds with each other. However, some companies find that addressing broad stakeholder goals may also further their financial goals.[7] For instance, Toyota's groundbreaking efforts on the Prius hybrid automobile not only responded to society's concerns about the impact of automobile exhaust on global warming, but also catapulted the company to the forefront of the industry as gas prices rose and a more fuel-efficient car was sought. Microsoft embarked on a drive to enhance information technology education in community colleges across America. This effort provided much-needed resources to schools in a time of constrained state spending, and also responded to the company's long-term need to hire a large number of new advanced-trained IT graduates.

Taking into consideration the interests of a range of stakeholders is consistent with the two strategic imperatives we discussed in the first chapter: the value creation imperative, and the opportunity recognition imperative. Supporting the more enlightened view that business organizations and society are mutually dependent on each other, new trends becoming prevalent in society and industry can represent opportunities for both existing and new businesses. Some new companies actually start 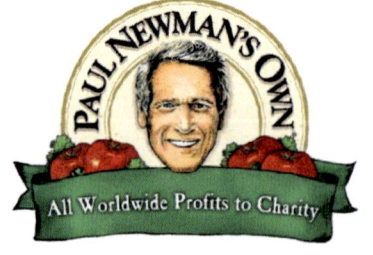  up with social objectives stated explicitly, in addition to ordinary corporate profitability objectives, and by doing so create a valued connection with consumers that goes beyond merely the benefits of the products they sell. Newman's Own started in 1982 with the goal of selling a few bottles of salad dressing and donating whatever profits they might earn to charity. The company attracted considerable consumer attention and has grown dramatically. Since its founding it has made over 22,000 grants in excess of $550 million to charities worldwide. Ben & Jerry's similarly attracted a broad following and achieved phenomenal economic performance by combining an economic mission ("sustainable financial growth") with a social mission ("innovative ways to make the world a better place"). Acquired by multinational Unilever two decades ago, the business continues to seek value creation in multiple ways:

"We have a progressive, nonpartisan social mission that seeks to meet human needs and eliminate injustices in our local, national and international communities by integrating these concerns into our day-to-day business activities. Our focus is on children and families, the environment and sustainable agriculture on family farms.
- We strive to create economic opportunities for those who have been denied them and to advance new models of economic justice that are sustainable and replicable.
- By definition, the manufacturing of products creates waste. We strive to minimize our negative impact on the environment.
- We support sustainable and safe methods of food production that reduce environmental degradation, maintain the productivity of the land over time, and support the economic viability of family farms and rural communities....
- We strive to show a deep respect for human beings inside and outside our company and for the communities in which they live."[8]

The integration of corporate financial performance and corporate social performance goes beyond simply attracting like-minded customers. Increasingly, companies are finding ways to make a difference in socially important issues as they go about the day-to-day activities that have to do with their core business. In Walmart's South African division, Massmart helps to preserve small-scale farming by sourcing raw materials for its produce sections from local sources, while Sysco's reliance on small family farms in the U.S. also ensures the provisioning of fresh, locally grown produce for their foodservice and restaurant supply operations. Marriott provides job training for chronically unemployed workers, which helps the communities in which Marriott does business and also aids the company in its recruitment of entry-level workers.[9] Known for its industrial climate and security technologies, Ingersoll Rand leveraged its capabilities and collaborated with local firms to develop a sustainable new business in affordable refrigeration addressing a vast need among poor families in India who are living at the "bottom of the pyramid."

Corporate social performance has now become proactive, stretching beyond the customary activities of companies. In 2016 legislation was passed in North Carolina which had the effect of limiting gay and transgender rights. Alcoa, Dow Chemical, and Northrop Grumman all waded into the public debate, condemning these measures and lobbying elected officials for change. In 2019, in response to mass shooting incidents in the U.S., retailers Walmart, Kroger, Dick's Sporting Goods and others announced they would no longer sell handguns and ammo. This reflects a new reality that companies are often *expected* to take stands on issues important to the communities in which they operate. 78% of Americans support corporate political engagement on social issues.[10]

Although this sort of corporate activity can have a beneficial effect in communities and with their stakeholders, it also presents challenges for strategic leaders. Expending corporate resources on issues unrelated to the core business may not be wise, and taking positions on social issues – even when consistent with espoused corporate values – may be controversial. Although there is some recent evidence that corporate social responsibility activities can enhance company performance, there is also evidence that CEOs who engage in such activity are more likely to be fired if their companies' financial performance is poor.[11] So social stakeholder performance is valuable only if it does not detract from firm financial performance.

Managing in Markets: Question for Class Discussion

In 2021 Georgia legislators passed a law that many viewed as restricting voting rights of Blacks, while others viewed it as protecting voting process integrity. Delta Airlines, headquartered in Atlanta and the state's largest employer, made general statements in support of voting rights but declined to take a position on the legislation. Its muted response drew fierce criticism, protests at Atlanta's airport, and calls for a boycott. In response, Delta CEO Ed Bastian made a stark reversal, announcing the bill was "unacceptable." Delta lost goodwill among protesters by avoiding the issue before being pressured, and Delta customers who favored the legislation were unhappy with the corporate announcement.

Do you think CEOs and companies should weigh in on public issues?

Reflecting these newer orientations of many for-profit companies, over the last few years the concept of the triple bottom line has emerged. Companies that embrace the triple bottom line concept measure their performance in economic, social and ecological (or environmental) terms. They develop internal processes and measures to ensure that they are making progress on each of these performance dimensions over the long run (see Chapter 14 for monitoring progress on key strategic performance dimensions). Often these companies also provide significant disclosure – on their websites and in their annual reports – about the progress they are making. Marks and Spencer, for example, is a leading UK-based retailer of fashion clothing, home products, and food. In 2007 they launched "Plan A," involving 180 environmental and social commitments. They update their progress on this strategic initiative regularly, and have extended their goals to 2025.[12]

Triple Bottom Line

Economic performance
Social performance
Ecological performance

Finally, the increasing application of strategic management principles in the nonprofit sector and in government has also heightened attention to nonfinancial measures of performance. Since by definition these organizations do not produce profits and do not have shareholders, we must deal with important questions about how to measure their performance. In both these instances the key to measuring performance is to focus on the critical values created for and appreciated by the organization's various stakeholders. Profits in ordinary businesses are an outcome measure reflecting successful value creation. Similarly, measurement for nonprofits and governments should begin with how well stakeholders are being served. Some nonprofits have very focused missions, in which case the summary performance measures that report how well the entire organization has functioned are relatively easy to describe and measure. Feeding America, the largest national charitable food donation network, collects and distributes food to people in need at community kitchens, food pantries, homeless shelters, Kids Cafe, senior centers, soup kitchens, and youth programs. Their performance is measured by tonnage of distribution, and by the proportion of cash donations received which are devoted to programs rather than to administration (the "charitable commitment rating"). Figure 2.3 illustrates performance measures for valued stakeholders for this relatively focused nonprofit organization.[13]

**Figure 2.3
Feeding America, 2021 Performance**

- ✓ Rescued 4.7 billion pounds of food from waste, a 34% increase over 2018
- ✓ Served 6.6 billion meals, a 53% increase over 2018
- ✓ Raised $380 million in donations, a 133% increase over 2018
- ✓ 98.5% charitable commitment rating (% of raised funds to programs)

In contrast, other nonprofits and government engage in missions that are more difficult to measure. The mission of Partners in Health is to reduce starvation in developing countries like Haiti and Sierra Leone. But this is a broad mission, and they face competition from other charities to raise funding. So they set and measure performance indicators to show investors the impact of their efforts, and to enable their own workers to evaluate their success. They collect data using electronic health records, and share this data with investors and local governments.[14] Nonprofit think tank American Enterprise Institute measures the percentage of congressional testimonies it participates in and how often its op-ed editorials are published in major newspapers. Government entities are likely to have far more complex networks of stakeholders – citizens, interest groups, businesses, arts and entertainment organizations, schools, municipal employees, etc. – so that gauging performance would likely require an array of measures.

Managing in Markets: Question for Class Discussion

Economist and Nobel Prize winner Milton Friedman claimed that the only business of business is to earn a profit for its shareholders. Bill Gates, founder of Microsoft, advocated for corporations to practice "creative capitalism," where they use their capabilities to "do good" while not sacrificing "doing well" for shareholders. The public outcry for corporate social responsibility is great. Should corporations focus only on economic performance for shareholders, or should they also address broader social and community concerns in their day-to-day activities and goals?

FINANCIAL PERFORMANCE AND COMPETITIVE ADVANTAGE

Having made the case that strategy should be assessed by a balance of both customary financial and emerging nonfinancial measures, we turn back now to more carefully examine aspects of financial performance and their relationship with strategy. Once again we begin with the premise that effective strategy is connected with *superior* financial performance – that is, something *more* than what the average competitor achieves. When people invest in a company and become shareholders, their expectation is that the return they will earn through their investment is at least equal to the kind of return they could earn on average by investing elsewhere in the marketplace at the same level of risk. Otherwise, why would they invest in this company?

The answer to this question lies in the conceptual differences between normal profit and superior returns. Normal profit may be viewed as the minimum return earned by a company that is necessary to attract and secure the owners' inputs. Long ago, however, economist Alfred Marshall distinguished economic profit from normal profit.[15] Economic profit represents the *residual income* above and beyond normal profit that accrues to owners, deriving from the prowess of management in planning, supervision, and control (i.e. from effective strategic management). Residual income associated with economic profit occurs when a company's return on equity (ROE) is greater than its cost of equity capital.[16] This is precisely the logic behind the focus of CEOs (and strategy students) on ROE as one of the key strategy performance indicators. If a company produces higher ROE than the average in the marketplace, without incurring any additional risk, then the company is earning economic profit – or as we usually refer to it in strategy, above-average profitability.

In turn, we must now ask, in practical terms, how can strategy impact a company's return on equity? To partially answer this question, we can break ROE down into its component parts: profitability, asset productivity, and financial leverage. This is called a "DuPont Analysis" because it originated in the 1920s with that company. When these three ratios are calculated and then multiplied together, the resulting product is the return on equity percentage for the company. The three ratios provide the insight that there are different ways in which superior returns can be created, either through a focus on one area or through some combination of areas within the company. As your grandmother may have said, "there is more than one way to skin a cat." Illustrating this, Figure 2.4 breaks down ROE in 2019 for three airlines profiled earlier in this chapter. Here we see why JetBlue's 9.2 % ROE in that year was lower than that of either Southwest or United: the combination of lower profitability, lower asset productivity and less financial leverage all contribute toward this performance difference.

Figure 2.4 **DuPont Analysis: Decomposing 2019 Return On Equity (ROE)**				
Component:	Profitability	Asset Productivity	Financial Leverage	ROE
Calculation:	$\frac{\text{Net Income}}{\text{Sales}}$	$\frac{\text{Sales}}{\text{Assets}}$	$\frac{\text{Assets}}{\text{Shareholder Equity}}$	$\frac{\text{Net Income}}{\text{Shareholder Equity}}$
JetBlue	5.5 %	0.67	2.48	9.2 %
Southwest	10.3 %	0.87	2.63	23.4 %
United	7.0 %	0.82	4.56	26.1 %

The decomposition of ROE into its component ratios can be extended to provide greater ammunition for the strategist. In Figure 2.4 we observe that Southwest's profitability is higher than JetBlue's, despite having a higher cost per available seat mile and a lower load factor in 2019 (see earlier table). So Southwest must be doing something else much better than JetBlue to generate stronger profitability. Can we break this down further to better understand how this is possible? Yes! There are other financial ratios that can be used to develop an even more refined view of the sources of advantage within each of the three components. Figure 2.5 lists many such subcomponent ratios that are helpful in assessing company performance, identifying advantages that can be leveraged, and calling out areas that might require management attention. Remembering that performance evaluation should be relative to our competitors' performance, we may see that one company's profitability is lower than that of its competitors. Closer examination may reveal that the sources of that inferior position can be traced back to its higher cost of goods sold, higher selling general and administrative costs (SG&A), or some other non-operating characteristics of the business such as interest paid to carry higher inventories. These areas might then receive greater focus by management to improve profitability and overall return on equity. The Appendix to this chapter reviews financial ratios that are helpful in analyzing companies and performance. Use these ratios when you examine cases and companies in your strategy course.

Figure 2.5
Financial Ratios Providing Strategic Insight

Return on Equity

Profitability	Asset Productivity	Financial Leverage
Cost of goods sold / sales Gross profit / sales SG&A / sales Operating income / sales Non-operating gains & losses / sales EBIT / sales Taxes / sales	Current asset turnover Working capital turnover Accounts receivable turnover Inventory turnover Accounts payable turnover Days' receivables Days' inventory PP&E turnover	Current ratio Quick ratio Cash ratio Operating cash ratio Liabilities / equity Debt / equity Debt / capital Interest coverage ratio

Strategy performance is gauged "over the long term," however, as we mentioned earlier in this chapter. So we need to be careful about looking at just one year's performance. Figure 2.4 derives ROE for the three airlines for just 2019. However, viewing a longer time period provides a better measure of the sustainability of superior performance. The ten years leading up through 2012 was a brutal period that included both economic expansion and contraction in the economy. Southwest's ROE was 6.2 percent while JetBlue's was only 3.5 percent at that time. This is because Southwest managed to stay profitable during the post-September 11 decline in airline traffic and following the 2008 recession. JetBlue was unprofitable during some of this period. An excellent question to ask here is, why was Southwest able to sustain its performance while JetBlue and other airlines were not? To understand Southwest's strategy and the sources of its superior performance, we will have to dig deeper into the company using ideas coming up in the next few chapters.

So far the measure return on equity has been highlighted as being particularly important, because of its direct relationship to the strategy goal of superior performance. However, there are other market-based measures of performance that are also used by CEOs, analysts, and strategy students to quantitatively assess how well companies are performing. While there are a variety of other such measures, four seem to be used most frequently: sales revenue growth, returns to common stock, some measure of a company's market value such as market capitalization, and return on invested capital (ROIC).[17]

Sales revenue growth is generally of great interest to the senior executives of most companies. The ability to grow a company's revenue demonstrates that the company continues to develop relationships with existing and new customers, is able to expand into new geographic territories, and is staying relevant to the marketplace. Unfortunately, revenue growth often occurs at the expense of profitability, since the factors that generally drive up sales (e.g., more advertising, investment in new product development, building a more effective sales force, adding new manufacturing capacity) often add expenses that diminish the bottom line. So there is a certain yin and yang quality to sales growth and ROE (which depends on the profitability ratio). Senior managers who can increase both sales *and* profitability simultaneously are highly regarded, since in practice this does not happen very often (only 9 out of 1,077 companies in a recent McKinsey survey achieved this feat).[18]

Common stock returns and market capitalization are two other measures of firm performance that are commonly mentioned. Common stock returns take into account both the dividends paid by a company to its shareholders as well as increases in the price of the shares. Abnormally high returns, relative to common stock returns for competing companies, are desirable and indicative of high-performing companies. A well-known and popular business book, *Good to Great*, used abnormally high returns as the starting point for examining the strategic moves of "great" companies. The eleven companies (out of 1,435 analyzed) that formed the basis of the book were identified by examining this type of performance metric over long periods of time.[19]

Market capitalization, defined as the market value of outstanding shares of stock, also depends on stock price and characterizes the total value of the company. While both these measures provide perspective on the performance of a company, they also mirror investors' anticipation of future performance and assume that all available information is reflected in the stock price. Investors partially base their evaluations of companies on traditional metrics such as ROE and revenue growth rates. Yet we have recently witnessed times when an "irrational exuberance" (an unaccountable and unsupported opinion that things will keep getting better and better) among investors drives stock prices so high that they bear absolutely no relationship to a company's fundamental economics (e.g., the "dot bomb" era). Similarly, stock price declines also occur when companies fail to meet analysts' expectations in the short run. Since a purely market-based evaluation of a company's performance might be misleading, it is always important to evaluate companies using several measures.

Lately there has been interest in return on invested capital (ROIC) as an alternative to, or enhancement of, ROE. This is a metric which measures how efficient a company is in earning cash flow from its strategic investments of invested equity capital and debt. Says former General Motors CFO Chuck Stevens: "ROIC provides the clearest picture of how we are managing our capital and our business. It's really starting to become part of the DNA of our decisions."[20] Since higher levels of ROIC are correlated with superior performance versus rival companies, increasingly executive long-term bonuses are being tied to this measure.

INSIGHTS FROM DETAILED FINANCIAL ANALYSIS

Although companies often make public statements about their strategies and discuss broad strategic initiatives in shareholder meetings or analysts' conference calls, they generally do not "publish" great detail about their strategies. This is because they don't really want to reveal their deepest, most critical thinking to competitors. Strategy should be articulated to and understood by important external constituents, but not so much revealed that it can be easily imitated. So then how can we determine what a company's strategy really is, what is really at the core?

Financial analysis of companies and competitors is a tool that should be used in parallel to the forthcoming strategy frameworks you will read about in this textbook. This is because, as companies implement their strategies, their implementation results in patterns of investments, asset allocations, and sets of interrelated activities that ultimately manifest themselves in financial results. The key to utilizing strategic financial analysis is that the patterns revealed by the numbers demonstrate what companies are really doing and how they are actually operating in the marketplace, regardless of what they *say* they are doing. In combination with the strategy frameworks we will be developing in later chapters, we can then induce what their intended and actual strategies really are. Another way of thinking about this is that a company may state what its overall strategic approach will be, but the numbers show what they are actually doing. It should come as no great surprise to anyone that Walmart pursues a low-cost  strategy; we hear about it all the time, from them in their ads as well as from others. But you can really understand how the company makes this an effective strategic approach by carefully examining its financial statements. Here is where we can see what they are actually doing.

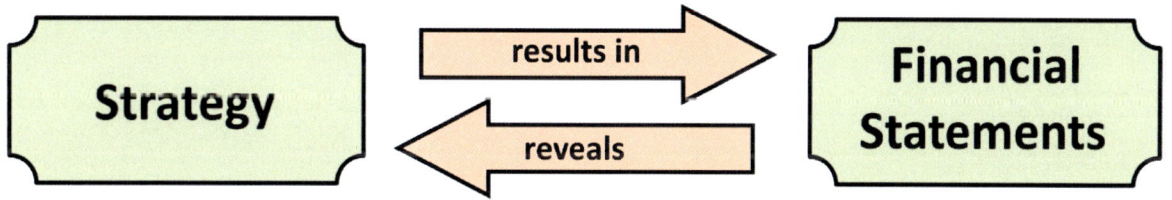

This graphic captures what we mean, and you should keep this in mind as you read through the examples coming up. It bears repeating: the best way to understand what a company's strategy really is involves examining their financial statements in detail. The company is not going to tell you in detail what their strategy is. But its financial statement patterns reveal what investments they are making and how they are really operating. We will repeat this graphic toward the end of this chapter.

Current Financial Statements

Financial statements paint a picture about how companies are operating. A quick example can illustrate this quite easily. Figure 2.6 (a) provides recent income statement and balance sheet information for three well-known national retail chains – a supermarket, a drug store, and a department store. Without telling you their names (the three chains are labeled A, B, and C), we can examine the financial detail to determine which is which. The financials show us that each type of retailer operates very differently, and will reveal dimensions of their strategies to us.

Figure 2.6 (a)
Financial Data For Three Retail Chains (millions)

Income Statement	Chain A	Chain B	Chain C
Revenues	$ 25,641	$ 122,662	$ 184,786
Cost of goods sold	15,181	95,662	153,448
Gross profit	10,460	27,000	31,338
Selling, general & admin (SG&A)	8,954	21,952	18,809
Depreciation & amortization	0	2,436	181
Other expense / income	-358	0	2,810
Operating income	1,864	2,612	9,538
Interest expense	321	601	1,062
Taxes	-39	-405	1,637
Misc. after-tax expense	27	509	217
Net income	**1,555**	**1,907**	**6,622**

At the outset we can make a couple of obvious comments and draw preliminary inferences. Chain A produces more than 50% of the net income of Chain B on only about 25% the sales revenue. It accomplishes this while using an asset base that is roughly 50% that of Chain B. Apparently size or scale is less important for the industry in which Chain A competes, since it is quite profitable on a much lower revenue base. At the same time, Chain C is producing 350% of the net income of Chain B on a revenue base that is only 50% higher. So it appears as if Chain B is conducting business in a low-margin industry, is experiencing significant operational issues that cost more, or is facing strong competition that forces B to keep its pricing low.

Balance Sheet	Chain A	Chain B	Chain C
Assets			
Cash & short term investments	$ 1,455	$ 1,508	$ 1,807
Receivables	363	1,637	13,181
Inventories	5,178	6,533	15,296
Property, plant, equipment (net)	6,672	21,071	10,292
Other assets	5,915	6,448	54,555
Total Assets	19,583	37,197	95,131
Liabilities & Shareholder Equity			
Accounts payable	$ 3,271	$ 5,858	$ 8,863
Other current liabilities	1,908	8,339	21,785
Long term debt	5,861	12,029	22,181
Other liabilities	2,810	4,040	4,611
Equity & retained earnings	5,733	6,931	37,691
Total Liabilities & Equity	19,583	37,197	95,131

All three companies carry considerable inventories and have significant investments in physical infrastructure (property, plant, and equipment) that are financed by varying combinations of long-term debt and equity. Chain C, however, has a far higher level of receivables than the other two chains. This suggests that it relies much more on credit to effect its transactions.

It is difficult to get a clear picture when comparing companies of different sizes. So a more useful view can be developed by converting financial statements to common-sized statements. This is done for income statements by setting revenue for each company equal to 100 percent, and for balance sheets by setting each side of the balance sheet to 100 percent. Figure 2.6 (b) shows the common-sized statements for the three retail chains.

Figure 2.6 (b)
Common Sized Data For Three Retail Chains (%)

Income Statement	Chain A	Chain B	Chain C
Revenues	100.0 %	100.0 %	100.0 %
Cost of goods sold	59.2	78.0	83.0
Gross profit	40.8	22.0	17.0
Selling, general & admin (SG&A)	34.9	17.9	10.2
Depreciation & amortization	0.0	2.0	0.1
Other expense / income	-1.4	0.0	1.5
Operating income	7.3	2.1	5.2
Interest expense	1.3	0.5	0.6
Taxes	-0.2	-0.3	0.9
Misc. after-tax expense	0.1	0.4	0.1
Net income	6.1	1.6	3.6

It can now be observed that Chain C has the highest cost of goods sold as a percentage of sales, but makes up for this through its lower SG&A expense. Its receivables represent fully 14%

Balance Sheet	Chain A	Chain B	Chain C
Assets			
Cash & short term investments	7	4	2
Receivables	2	4	14
Inventories	26	18	16
Property, plant & equipment	34	57	11
Other assets	30	17	57
Total Assets	100 %	100 %	100 %
Liabilities & Shareholder Equity			
Accounts payable	17	16	9
Other current liabilities	10	22	23
Long term debt	30	32	23
Other liabilities	14	11	5
Equity & retained earnings	29	19	40
Total Liabilities & Equity	100 %	100 %	100 %

of its assets, significantly higher than the other two retailers. Its "other assets" represent a whopping 57% of the total. Its property, plant and equipment is much smaller in percentage terms than A or B. This sounds like a chain operating in smaller buildings with less distribution infrastructure or could be leasing store, sells expensive merchandise, and whose customers take time to pay for their purchases.

Chain B has the largest portion of its assets in property, and produces a razor thin 1.6% net income with little margin for error (literally). This sounds like a business that is primarily distribution-focused, an asset-intensive operation selling high volumes of low margin goods. Compare sales, general and administrative (GS&A) expenses across the three chains. A spends considerably more than both B and C. This seems to be a retailer that is dealing with administrative complexity and must advertise regularly to bring customers through the doors.

Selected Financial Ratios	Chain A	Chain B	Chain C
Current assets / current liabilities	1.48	0.78	1.02
Inventory turnover (x per year)	2.93	14.64	10.03
Receivables collection (days)	5.17	4.87	26.04
Total debt / total assets	0.71	0.81	0.60
Net income / sales (Profitability)	6.1 %	1.6 %	3.6 %
Sales / assets (Asset productivity)	1.31	3.30	1.94
Assets / equity (Financial leverage)	3.42	5.37	2.52
Net income / equity (ROE)	27.1 %	27.5 %	17.6 %

Selected financial ratios provide further insight into who is who. Chain B turns its inventory over almost 15 times each year. What kind of merchandise would we hope and expect to be turning more frequently – clothing, drugs and sundries, or food? There are also very different receivables collection periods for the three companies. Chains A and B average collection periods are under 6 days; these are almost a pure cash or immediate transaction business. On the other hand, Chain C's collection period is 26 days, suggesting that it relies on extending credit to customers.

We can start drawing conclusions about these observed differences: Chain C with smaller stores and expensive cost of goods that turns slowly, versus Chain B with large investment in property and low value inventory that turns over rapidly. These differences, in fact, describe the differing operating characteristics that we should expect to see across three types of retail chains:

Chain A - Department store chain (Macy's)
- large stores with basic display furnishings
- carries a vast array of moderately priced merchandise
- requirement for variety in styles and sizes produces low inventory turnover
- must advertise in order to compete with other retailers and online shopping
- some use of store credit card increases receivables collection versus pure cash and third party bank credit cards

Chain B - Supermarket chain (Kroger)
- large stores with sophisticated furnishings (freezers, coolers, bakery) and heavy investment in warehousing and transportation logistics

- lower priced, everyday merchandise that sells through quickly
- largely a cash, debit card, or bank credit card business
- competition with other chains ensures low prices and thin margins

Chain C - Drug chain (CVS Health)
- smaller stores than supermarkets or department stores, often leased
- higher priced merchandise because of carrying costs of expensive medications
- reimbursement from insurance companies for medications sold takes a long time
- high asset value in "other" assets due to capitalizing intangibles from acquisitions and the value of long term medication supply contracts

Interestingly, although the supermarket develops half the net income percentage of the drug chain and less than half the net income percentage of the department store chain, its ROE is the greatest of these companies. This is because B also has superior asset productivity (3.30) and superior financial leverage (5.37); in combination its ROE is competitive with other retailers.

Trend Analysis

In the preceding example we have examined three companies at a point in time, using the financial data from one year's performance. The observed differences illustrate different approaches to the marketplace. It can also be helpful to evaluate the financial statements of a company over a series of years. Figure 2.7 provides five years of historical financial data, from 1997 through 2001, for a company you probably know quite well – Amazon. These five years are when Amazon really took off. The financial trends here provide insight into what the company was doing strategically as it grew from small online retailer into a larger internet powerhouse.

Figure 2.7
Selected Financial Data For Amazon (millions)

Income Statement	2001	2000	1999	1998	1997
Revenues	3,122	2,762	1,640	610	148
Cost of goods sold	2,323	2,106	1,349	476	119
Gross profit	799	656	291	134	29
Selling, general & admin (GS&A)					
Fulfillment & marketing	512	594	413	133	40
Technology	241	269	160	46	13
All other	457	657	323	64	8
Operating income (loss)	(412)	(864)	(606)	(109)	(33)
Interest expense (income)	139	131	85	27	0
Net income	(567)	(1,411)	(720)	(125)	(31)

We could spend considerable time picking apart these statements, as you should when you conduct your own strategic analysis of a company. But let's highlight a couple key areas that go to the heart of this company's successful growth trajectory. First we observe that the company's gross profit increased from 19.5% in 1997 to 25.6% by 2001. This might mean that the company had been able to raise its prices to consumers during this time, or that it was receiving more favorable prices from its suppliers. We know that the retail book business is pretty competitive and that Amazon was seeking to drive more buyer volume to its website. So it is not likely it was raising its prices. Instead, the much greater volume of business they were doing by 2001 ($3 billion in sales versus $148 million only five years earlier) suggests they struck agreements with suppliers (likely facilitated by a higher volume of business). Efficient scale achieved through greater volume is also evident when we calculate that "Fulfilment & marketing" had decreased to only 16% of revenues in 2001, compared to 27% in 1997.

How did the company manage to grow so quickly? The statements tell us they were making massive investments in fulfillment and marketing, technology, and administrative support. These investments helped make their website especially attractive and easy to use, helped drive consumers to their website, and made sure there was sufficient staff and infrastructure to support the added business. In 1999 and 2000 the company's balance sheet intangibles increased considerably, indicating it was purchasing other companies and/or booking significant technological innovations onto its balance sheet.

Balance Sheet	2001	2000	1999	1998	1997
Assets					
Cash & marketable securities	997	1,100	706	373	125
Inventories	144	175	221	30	9
Fixed assets	272	366	318	30	9
Goodwill & intangibles	80	255	730	179	0
Other assets	145	238	496	37	5
Total Assets	**1,638**	**2,135**	**2,472**	**648**	**149**
Liabilities & Shareholder Equity					
Accounts payable	445	485	463	113	33
Other liabilities	476	490	276	49	11
Long term debt	2,156	2,127	1,466	348	76
Equity & paid-in capital	1,467	1,342	1,199	302	65
Other equity	(45)	(16)	(51)	(1)	(2)
Retained earnings	(2,861)	(2,293)	(882)	(162)	(34)
Total Liabilities & Equity	**1,638**	**2,135**	**2,472**	**648**	**149**

A closer look at the balance sheet data reveals startling increases during this period of time in a number of categories. As the company's business volume grew, it began to build its own inventory and distribution warehouses to make sure that ordering customers received their books quickly. So we see that fixed assets skyrocketed in one year from $30 million to over $300 million. How could the company afford to make such large investments in warehousing, marketing, and technology? It had been losing money throughout this period, as illustrated by its net loss of hundreds of millions of dollars each year! Its growth was financed by both long-term debt and the sale of additional shares of stock (paid in capital); both categories combined to provide the company $2.8 billion in cash between 1998 and 2000. At the time this was going on many people wondered why anyone would invest in shares of a company that was losing so much money every year, a company that had not produced positive ROE at any time in its history and wasn't likely to for the foreseeable future? Hindsight is wonderful, but back in 1998-99 no one knew what the future held! The company's success – and the investor's return – would depend critically on the market and the company's strategy in that market. These are areas we will be tackling in the next few chapters. Stay tuned!

The preceding examples have illustrated two key points about how strategy and financial performance mirror each other:

1. Strategy is implemented by taking actions and operating in the marketplace in certain ways, which result in certain financial performance characteristics we can see in the financial statements; and

2. Financial performance characteristics reveal the way in which a company is operating in the market, which follows from the company's strategic direction and decisions.

Analyzing a company's operations and financial performance provides evidence about its strategy (the coordinating pattern of decisions and investments affecting the entire company over a long time period). It also provides insight into whether the company is actually pursuing the strategy that it claims to be. Strategy is not just words and intentions; it is about action and the commitment of resources. A stated strategy that is not backed by sufficient investment and supportive actions is not a strategy at all.

ECONOMIC LOGIC AND OPERATING CHARACTERISTICS

If you step back from a detailed analysis of financial statements, you can often discover that there is a core economic logic that helps in understanding a successful company's strategic thinking and operational execution. Economic logic is sort of a "recipe" by which the successful company seeks to generate a return that is greater than what competitors earn and greater than its cost of capital.[21] The economic logic for warehouse club retailing, such as Costco stores, can be described as being "pile it high, mark it down, and move vast quantities." Successful retailers

whose strategies embrace this logic are likely to develop healthy ROE by increasing the asset productivity component as a consequence of sales throughput. In contrast Saks Fifth Avenue's approach might be characterized as "merchandise beautifully, pamper the clientele, and charge premium prices." Such operations are relatively less interested in asset productivity and more interested in profitability as a route to superior ROE. Although Costco and Saks Fifth Avenue compete in different industry segments, in some industries sufficient strategic variety exists that we might witness very different economic logics being used by different competitors. In grocery retailing, Wegman's and Whole Foods have a very different economic logic in mind (premium quality, wide variety of selection, higher prices) when compared to Food Lion (commonly needed household foods priced to sell).

In other industries conditions may exist where a single core economic logic drives all competitors to a great extent. For example, commercial banks historically earned profits by focusing on "net interest margin," the difference between interest rates they pay to borrow capital and the interest rates they charge to lend that capital out. Online discount stock brokers such as E*Trade and online auctions such as eBay earn extremely small fees on each of their transactions, and therefore seek to drive up the sheer volume of transactions. This is a low-margin, high-volume economic logic. In several technology-based industries (e.g., inkjet printers, gaming, computer operating systems), the logic for competing often involves establishing a broad "installed base" of users while earning little in the process of doing so. Having established the installed user base, returns are then earned   through future transactions that users must engage in (e.g., replacement ink cartridges, buying additional games for the game platform). In 2021 HP Inc. – which makes laptops, desktops, and printers – realized $63 billion in revenue and $5.3 billion operating earnings. The printer division, which largely generates earnings from replacement toner cartridges, produced only 32% of total company sales but a whopping 69% of its operating earnings! Once you own the printer, you must buy the ink! The business of making computers and printers is high volume and low margin, but the business of supplying replacement cartridges is high volume and high margin. None of these overarching economic logics dictates exactly what actions and investments any individual competitor in an industry must follow or how they are to operate. Yet once we understand the economic logic that tends to operate in an industry, we have a better chance of accurately diagnosing the strategy of a particular company in which we are interested.

Along with the core economic logic that helps to frame an approach in an industry, strategy analysis should also pay close attention to important operating characteristics that describe how well the company addresses the economic logic at play. In the commercial airline industry, which was profiled at the beginning of this chapter, the economic logic reflects an industry that has become commoditized. This is where the combination of low costs and high passenger volume might be the key to success. What drives profitability for every carrier are low costs per available seat mile flown, in combination with passenger load factors. These two operating characteristics  are closely watched by financial analysts, because they are so critical to airline profitability, and thus they command great attention from senior managers in charge of strategy. Referring back to the tables in the opening story of the chapter, Southwest Airlines has a lower load factor than the other airlines listed, yet it also has the lowest cost per available seat mile of any of its major competitors. Though the low-cost-high-volume economic logic generally applies to every carrier in the industry, it does not dictate a particular set of strategic actions and behaviors. In this case Southwest achieves its low-cost position through a combination of fast gate turnarounds at airports, use of identical aircraft to save on maintenance costs, crew training, crew availability and downtime, routes that take passengers to less expensive airports near major cities, and other unique investments the company has made. In Chapters 5 through 7 we will learn more about designing unique and sustainable strategic approaches, such as those developed by Southwest.

Every industry has combinations of operating characteristics that provide insight on how well competitors are faring. Important operating characteristics in retailing include, among others, sales per square foot of retail space and same-store sales increases (for stores open at least one year). Wholesaling and distribution companies are interested in metrics such as warehouse turns and percent of complete orders shipped/received on time. The cable TV industry pays close attention to net subscriber additions, churn (the tendency of subscribers to drop out quickly), average revenue per subscriber, cash costs per subscriber, and average minutes of use per subscriber. Your analysis of companies and industries will be aided by researching important operating characteristics that are consistent with the economic logics you have identified. This might include standard measures of performance as well as measures that are unique to the strategy they are pursuing.

STRATEGY PLANNING

The important connection we have made in this chapter between strategy and performance is that it is a two-way street. Financial statements can be revealing about strategy, while a type of strategy should result in certain patterns in financial statements (Figure 2.8). The student of strategy should strive to develop a comfort level in going back and forth between a strategy and its financial outcomes.

Figure 2.8
Relationship Between Strategy and Financial Statements

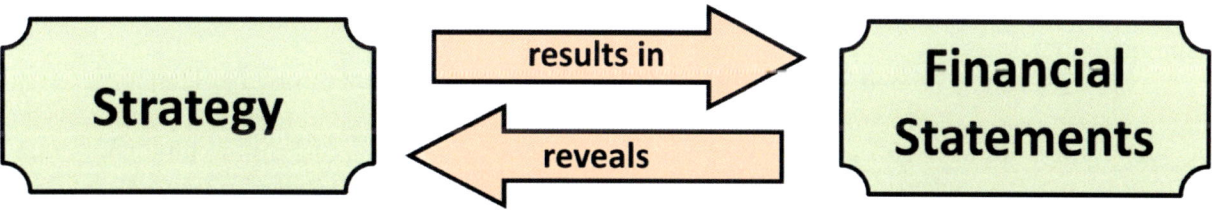

Most of what we have just covered illustrates how the analysis of financial statements can reveal dimensions of important strategic behavior. This is because, as we mentioned earlier in this chapter, strategy really involves a pattern of asset allocations and inter-related activities that ultimately manifest themselves in financial results. It is nice to have a statement of the company's strategy that the financial media and analyst communities can consume. However, a company's strategy is given real force when the company *acts* - when it organizes itself to support its pronouncements, when it pursues a segment of a particular industry that matches its investments, and when it commits resources to specific projects and initiatives. The allocation of resources and the activities that people in the company engage in are often below the radar of competitors and the financial community in specific terms, but ultimately reveal themselves in financial statements. So understanding a company's strategy through financial statement analysis is sort of like what baseball great Yogi Berra once said: "You can observe a lot by watching."

At the same time, we want to emphasize that excellence in strategy *formulation* also requires excellence in financial analysis. When you are the architect of a new strategy for your company, it means that the company will need to act in new ways in organizing itself and allocating human, physical, and financial resources. Every strong strategic plan projects out what these new activities and resource allocations will look like financially. In addition, every strong strategic plan ensures that desired outcome of "above-average profitability" or "superior performance" will be the financial outcome realized. Remember, though, that the financial outcome of superior performance will often involve longer time horizons.

CHAPTER SUMMARY

Performance (both quantitative and qualitative) is the key outcome of interest for those studying and managing strategy. Three dimensions of performance are important: 1) summary measures that reflect the impact of integrated efforts across the entire company, 2) measures that can be compared to competitors, and 3) measures that account for longer periods of time. Return on equity (ROE) is the most common performance measure used by executives. ROE can be broken down into three component ratios in the DuPont Analysis that provide insight on company profitability, asset productivity, and financial leverage. Each of these components may be further broken down into additional financial and operating ratios to provide more specific information about sources of strengths and weaknesses.

Other financial dimensions are also used frequently to assess performance resulting from strategy (stockholder returns, market capitalization, sales revenue growth, ROIC). Nonfinancial performance dimensions account for two other important considerations: 1) the realizations that companies may create social, cultural, and knowledge value as well as economic value; and 2) the emerging view that there are a variety of stakeholders (internal and external) who have interests in a company. Whereas debates have existed in the past as to whether companies should be single-mindedly focused on providing returns to shareholders, an emerging view suggests that attention to stakeholders can create profitable new growth opportunities for companies and simultaneously strengthen their existing franchises.

Insight can be gained about company strategy through three methods: 1) detailed financial statement analysis, often using common-sized statements to compare competitors; 2) identifying the economic logic (s) that may operate within an industry as a means of framing how companies operate; and 3) identifying and evaluating important operational characteristics that portray how well companies appear to be addressing economic logics. Together, these techniques can provide a better understanding of the nature of a company's strategy.

Learning Objectives Review

1. Explain the value of using both financial and nonfinancial performance dimensions to measure strategy effectiveness.

- **Stockholders**. For-profit companies are expected to produce positive financial returns for investors who buy their stock. A company's stock will be more attractive to investors if it produces above-average returns, without requiring investors to accept greater risk. This is consistent with the goal of strategy. Certain financial measures of performance (ROE, sales growth, common stock returns, market capitalization, ROIC) are indicative of strategic performance when considered over a longer time horizon.

- **Stakeholders**. Many corporations today create value for other stakeholders, and thus embrace the idea of triple bottom line performance measurement. Non-financial measures of performance (e.g. "green" environmental benefits, supplier relationships, employee satisfaction, positive company culture) can lead to a stronger business and enhanced opportunity to accomplish strategic goals.

- **Non-profits and governments**. Strategy is equally important in the management and administration of non-profits and governments that have important long term goals. Non-financial measures that relate to each organization's value-creation model are important to develop in evaluating progress.

2. *Describe the relationship between financial performance and a sustainable competitive advantage.*

- **Above average profitability**. The goal of strategy is superior competitive performance. This should translate to above-average profitability and other superior measures of financial performance.

- **Long run performance**. Strategy involves directions and investments that produce superior competitive position and superior performance over the long run. Corporations are challenged to maintain competitive performance in the short run, while developing superior performance in the long run. A company may produce slightly more or less financial return in any given year, however its long run financial performance relative to competitors is of greater interest.

3. *Use financial analysis to examine company strategy.*

- **Return on equity (ROE)**. This is the primary measure used to assess strategic management effectiveness.

- **Composition of ROE**. ROE is composed of three ratios: profitability, asset productivity, financial leverage. Companies may achieve superior ROE by excelling in any one ratio, or by some combination of ratios. Each ratio may be further decomposed into contributing dimensions that reveal sources of performance differences versus competitors.

- **Current financial statement analysis**. A strategy involves a pattern of investments, asset allocations, and sets of activities in pursuit of a specific direction. These are manifested in financial statements, examination of which can reveal what companies are actually doing in the conduct of their business. It is helpful to develop "common sized" financial statements to compare competitors of different sizes.

- **Trended financial statement analysis**. Evaluating a company's financial statements over time is like watching a movie of its strategy in action (i.e. its unfolding pattern of investments, asset allocations, and sets of activities). It can reveal areas of activity where the company is moving very quickly, and can help determine whether its strategic objectives are being accomplished.

4. *Explain the economic logic of industries and companies.*

- **Economic logic**. This is a general description, or a "recipe," for how a successful company seeks to earn superior economic returns in its industry. You can identify the recipe by stepping back from the specific detailed activities that a company engages in, to describe in broad terms what it is trying to do. Example in retailing: "pile it high, mark it down, move vast quantities." There can often exist more than one workable economic logic in an industry.

- **Operating characteristics**. Usually there exist key operational metrics that companies must pay attention to, given the economic logic they employ. These metrics tend to reveal which companies will do well financially, and which will struggle. Example in airline industry: cost per available seat mile.

5. *Examine and explain the interaction between strategy formulation and financial analysis.*

- A formulated strategy indicates long term direction for a company and calls for a pattern of investments, asset allocations, and sets of activities. Strategists must project out the financial implications of these investments, allocations, and activities, and develop proforma financial statements that will be the result.

- Financial statement analysis can reveal what actions a company is actually taking. These may be consistent with its articulated strategy. If the actions revealed by financial statement analysis are inconsistent with the company's articulated strategy, then it provides an opportunity for the company to take corrective action.

Key Terms

Common-sized statements - A method of financial analysis that facilitates comparisons between different size companies. For income statements set revenue for each company equal to 100 percent, and for balance sheets set each side of the balance sheet to 100 percent.

Common stock returns - Takes into account both the dividends paid by a company to its shareholders as well as increases in the price of its shares.

Economic logic - A "recipe" by which the successful company seeks to generate a return that is greater than what competitors earn and greater than its cost of capital. A broad description of the way the company will operate in its industry.

Economic profit - The residual income above and beyond normal profit that accrues to owners, deriving from the prowess of management in planning, supervision, and control.

Market capitalization - The market value of outstanding shares of stock. Stock price multiplied by all outstanding shares.

Normal profit - The minimum return earned by a company that is necessary to attract and secure the owners' inputs. Generally defined as the cost of equity capital multiplied by the amount of shareholder equity.

Return on invested capital (ROIC) – A performance measure similar to return on equity, but which focuses on cash deployment. It is calculated through dividing after-tax cash flow by total capital available less cash equivalents.

Sales revenue growth – A measure often referred to by analysts, it reports the experience of a company in growing its business through new markets, new customers, and additional purchasing by existing customers.

Stakeholders - Individuals or groups who have an interest in or an influence on the business and operations of a company. They fall into two categories: internal stakeholders and external stakeholders.

Triple bottom line - Measuring performance in economic, social and ecological (or environmental) terms.

Short Answer Review Questions

1. What three dimensions of performance are most critical?
2. What is the most common performance measure used by executive management? Why? What components make this particular measure so useful?
3. What are non-financial performance measures?
4. What three methods of performance analysis provide the greatest insight into company strategy?
5. Explain the performance considerations necessary when we involve stakeholder's desired outcomes.
6. How do financial ratios provide insight into a company's true strategy?
7. Why is revenue growth such a critical performance measure?
8. How would you determine what strategic approach a company is actually pursuing?

Group Review Exercises

1. Examine the last five years of annual financial statements from a public company that you think you already know fairly well from your own personal experiences (for example, Starbucks or Apple).

- Identify patterns in the income statements and balance sheets, and discuss their possible meanings.
- Use the financial ratios in Appendix A to compare the company to its closest competitor.

- What differences do you now observe about the company's strategic approach to the market, as compared to observations from your personal experiences or ideas you hear about the company in the news media?
- Do you believe this company is achieving superior performance? Why or why not?

2. Choose a nonprofit organization that you are interested in. Examine its publications and documents to determine how it measures its performance.

3. In 2018 Exxon Mobil (XOM) came under public scrutiny. Its 2017 reported net income of $19.7 billion represented 8.3% of revenue, but the company paid no federal taxes and had not done so since 2015. Its return on equity was 11%. But gas prices by mid-2018 were rising to nearly $3 per gallon for the American public, up 50¢ over the last year. Some politicians were recommending a tax on oil company profits. Discuss whether you think it would be prudent for government to place additional financial regulation on oil companies.

4. Many of the financial ratios for companies in a given industry (e.g. retailing) exhibit a wide range across companies. But ROE stays within a narrower range. Why do you suppose this would be the case? Why wouldn't we see greater variability in ROE? Discuss this with other members of your class. We will explore the answer to this question in the upcoming chapter on Industry and Competitive Analysis.

5. In the supermarket industry Kroger is experimenting with advanced technology that can calculate checkout bills as items are put into or taken out of the shopping cart. Choose an industry and discuss how advanced technology and data-driven initiatives might create new operating characteristics that are important to measure.

Investor Relations Sites for Companies Mentioned in This Chapter

AT&T: https://investors.att.com/
Amazon: https://ir.aboutamazon.com/overview/default.aspx
American Airlines: https://americanairlines.gcs-web.com/
Ben & Jerry's (Unilever) https://www.unilever.com/investors/
Costco: https://investor.costco.com/
CVS Health: https://investors.cvshealth.com/investors/default.aspx
Delta Air Lines: https://ir.delta.com/home/default.aspx
Feeding America: https://www.feedingamerica.org/about-us/financials
HP: https://investor.hp.com/home/default.aspx
Ingersoll Rand: https://investors.irco.com/home/default.aspx
JetBlue: http://blueir.investproductions.com/investor-relations
Kroger: https://ir.kroger.com/home/default.aspx
Macy's: https://www.macysinc.com/investors
Marks & Spencer: https://corporate.marksandspencer.com/investors
Marriott International: https://marriott.gcs-web.com/
Merck: https://www.merck.com/investor-relations/
Microsoft: https://www.microsoft.com/en-us/investor
Newman's Own: https://newmansownfoundation.org/financials/

Partners in Health: https://www.pih.org/annual-report
Saks Fifth Avenue (Hudson's Bay Company): https://www.hbc.com/
Southwest Airlines: https://www.southwestairlinesinvestorrelations.com/
Sysco: https://investors.sysco.com/
Toyota Motor Co.: https://global.toyota/en/ir/
United Airlines Holdings: https://ir.united.com/
Walmart: https://stock.walmart.com/investors/default.aspx

References

[1] Several sources were used for this summary. S. Carey, 2017, "Big airlines offset rising costs," Wall Street Journal, October 27, B3. S. McCartney, 2007, "A report card on the nation's airlines," Wall Street Journal, February 6: D1. S. Sindreu, 2019, "Delta bets against global alliances," Wall Street Journal, October 2, B14. A. Tangel & A. Sider, 2018, "Airlines cash in on loyalty credit cards," Wall Street Journal, August 27. M. Trottman, 2006, "Airline CEO's novel strategy: No bankruptcy," Wall Street Journal, April 17: B1. R. Wall, 2019, "Rising costs, tensions hit airlines," Wall Street Journal, June 3, B3. K. Wingfield, 2007, "A dogfight in business class," Wall Street Journal, January 25. M. Young, 2019, "American streamlining operations in the face of a softening yield environment," Morningstar, August 19. "Economic report of the airline industry," 2017, International Airline Transport Association. U.S. Department of Transportation. Morningstar. Financials reflect TTM performance through 2017.

[2] Load factor is calculated by dividing the number of revenue passenger miles flown by the number of available seat miles.

[3] D. FitzGerald, 2019, "Elliott Management discloses AT&T stake and calls for shakeup," Wall Street Journal, September 9, A1.

[4] D. Barton, J. Manyika, T. Koller, R. Palter, J. Godsall, & J. Zoffer, 2017, "Where companies with a long-term view outperform their peers," McKinsey Global Institute report, February. Ignatius, A. 2018, "Businesses exist to deliver value to society," *Harvard Business Review*, March-April, 82-87.

[5] K. Favaro, 2019, "Strategy talk: How long should a long-term strategy be?" Strategy+Business, March 21. N. Levy & T. Bishop, 2019, "Windows no longer a 'cornerstone' for Microsoft, as company changes how it describes its business," GeekWire, August 2. R. Miller, 2019, "After 5 years, Microsoft CEO Satya Nadella has transformed more than the stock price," TechCrunch, February 4, https://tcrn.ch/2Sq6H1v.

[6] E. L. Plambeck, 2007, "The greening of Walmart's supply chain," Supply Chain Management Review, July 1.

[7] M. E. Porter & M. R. Kramer, 2011, "Creating shared value," Harvard Business Review, 90 (1): 62-77.

[8] https://www.unileverusa.com/brands/food-and-drink/ben-and-jerrys.html

[9] Porter & Kramer, op. cit.

[10] M. Peters & R. E. Silverman, 2016, "Big business speaks up on social issues," Wall Street Journal, April 16, B1.

[11] C. Flammer, B. Hong & D. Minor, 2019, "Corporate governance and the rise of integrating corporate social responsibility criteria in executive compensation: Effectiveness and implications for firm outcomes," Strategic Management Journal, 40, 1097-1122. T. D. Hubbard, D. M. Christensen, & S. D. Graffin, 2017, "Higher highs and lower lows: The role of corporate social responsibility in CEO dismissal," Strategic Management Journal, 38, 2255-2265.

[12] https://corporate.marksandspencer.com/plan-a/our-approach.

[13] http://www.feedingamerica.org/.

[14] B. McKay, 2017, "How one nonprofit tries to show donors their money is well-spent," Wall Street Journal, October 29.

[15] A. Marshall, 1890, *Principles of Economics*, London: Macmillan Press.

[16] Using the capital asset pricing model, the cost of equity capital for a company depends on the company's sensitivity to market risk (which is captured by the company's ß). When we discuss economic profit, we refer to the ability of a company to earn above-average returns without requiring shareholders to assume enhanced risk (higher ß). In this case the company earning economic profit produces an ROE that is greater than the expected return using the capital asset pricing model.

[17] B. S. Chakravarthy, 1986, "Measuring strategic performance," Strategic Management Journal, 7: 437 – 458. G. G. Dess & R. B. Robinson Jr., 1984, "Measuring organizational performance in the absence of objective measures: The case of the privately held firm and conglomerate business unit," Strategic Management Journal, 5: 265 – 273. M.

Lubatkin & R. E. Shrieves, 1986, "Towards a reconciliation of market performance measures to strategic management research," Academy of Management Review, 11 (3): 497 – 512.

[18] J. Devan, M. B. Klusas, & T. W. Ruefli, 2007, "The elusive goal of corporate outperformance," The McKinsey Quarterly, May. V. Gupta, T. Koller, & P. Stumpner, 2021, "Which metrics really drive total returns to shareholders?" The McKinsey Quarterly, October.

[19] J. Collins, 2001, *Good to Great*, New York: HarperCollins Publishers.

[20] D. Benoit, 2016, "Finance's hot new metric: ROIC," Wall Street Journal, May 3, C1.

[21] D. C. Hambrick & J. W. Fredrickson, 2001, "Are you sure you have a strategy?" Academy of Management Executive, 15 (4): 48 - 59.

APPENDIX

Financial Ratios Useful in Strategy Analysis

PROFITABILITY

Measure	How to calculate it	What it means
Return on equity (ROE)	Profitability x Asset productivity x Financial leverage	Profitability of shareholder investment
Profitability	Net income / Sales	Profitability per dollar of sale
Asset productivity	Sales / Assets	Sales generated per dollar of assets
Financial leverage	Assets / Shareholder equity	Assets in place per dollar of equity investment
Return on assets (ROA)	Net income / Assets	Profitability of assets employed by the company
Return on invested capital (ROIC)	EBIT x (1 – tax rate) / [(Debt + Equity) - (Cash + Equivalents)]	How much new cash is generated from capital investments
Gross profit margin	Gross profit / Sales	Gross profit % per dollar of sales
Operating profit margin	Operating profit / Sales	Profitability % of ongoing company operations
Economic value added (EVA)	Operating profit after tax – (Capital invested x Weighted average cost of capital)	Measures returns in excess of the firm's cost of capital

LIQUIDITY – SHORT TERM

Measure	How to calculate it	What it means
Current ratio	Current assets / Current liabilities	Ability to meet current obligations
Quick ratio	(Current assets – inventories) / Current liabilities	Ability to meet current obligations without having to sell inventory
Cash ratio	Cash / Current liabilities	Ability to meet current obligations relying only on existing cash
Inventory to working capital	Inventory / (Current assets – Current liabilities)	How much working capital is tied up in inventory

LIQUIDITY – LONG TERM

Measure	How to calculate it	What it means
Total debt ratio	(Assets – Shareholder equity) / Assets	Reveals percentage of balance sheet tied up in debt
Debt-to-assets ratio	Total debt / Assets	Reveals percentage of assets financed by debt
Debt-to-equity ratio	Total debt / Shareholder equity	Ratio of borrowed funds to funds provided by shareholders
Long-term debt to equity	Long-term debt / Shareholder equity	Ratio of long-term borrowings to equity contributions
Times interest earned (coverage ratio)	EBIT / Interest	Ability to meet interest payments
Cash coverage ratio	(EBIT + Depreciation) / Interest	Ability to meet interest payments using operating cash

ACTIVITY RATIOS

Measure	How to calculate it	What it means
Inventory turnover	Cost of Goods Sold / Inventory	Number of times a firm sells its inventory each year
Asset productivity	Sales / Assets	Sales generated per dollar of assets
Fixed asset turnover	Sales / Fixed assets	Sales generated per dollar of fixed assets
Capital intensity	Assets / Sales	Dollar investment in assets needed to generate each dollar in sales (the inverse of Asset Productivity ratio)
Accounts receivable turnover	Annual credit sales / Accounts receivable	Number of times each year a company collects on credit sales
Receivables collection period (days)	Accounts receivable / Average daily sales	How long it takes for the company to collect payment for sales

SHAREHOLDER RETURNS		
Measure	**How to calculate it**	**What it means**
Dividend yield	Dividend per share / Current market price per share	Return to common stockholders through dividends
Dividend payout ratio	Dividend per share / Net income per share	Approximation of profits returned to investors versus those kept to reinvest in the business
Price-to-earnings ratio PE	Current market price per share / Earnings per share	How much investors are willing to pay per dollar of current earnings
Market capitalization	Current market price per share x Total shares outstanding	Total value of all the company's stock at current stock market prices
Enterprise value	Market capitalization + Total debt + – Cash – Investments	Valuation of a firm as a whole enterprise, taking into account its debt and liquid assets

This page is intentionally left blank.

Chapter 3: Vision, Mission, Values

LEARNING OBJECTIVES

1. Examine how vision and mission statements provide effective direction for a firm.
2. Describe the process of developing a vision statement.
3. Explain the steps involved in developing an effective mission statement.
4. Name five techniques for communicating vision and mission.
5. Explain how principles and values can lead to superior performance.

Alphabet Soup?[1]

The Google division of Alphabet is a high growth, high margin company. 150,600 employees produce annual sales of $239 billion, or $1.6 million per worker. Operating cash flow exceeds $596,000 per worker per year, far above the average worker annual pay of $133,000. The typical Google worker possesses a very high IQ, and about half of their employees hold advanced degrees in science or engineering, most from elite universities.

Alphabet was created as the holding company in 2015, but its mission is unclear. Google's original mission was – and still is - "to organize the world's information and make it universally accessible and useful." But Alphabet is "a collection of companies…that aren't very related." It engages in enterprises "far afield": glucose-sensing contact lenses, smartphones, laptops, driverless car technology, biotech on aging, think tank on global challenges, and more. The Alphabet holding company structure recognized the complexity of managing units whose daily work and direction were so different from each other.

Laser Focused

The National Oceanic and Atmospheric Administration (NOAA), a division within the U.S. Department of Commerce, is a far cry from Google. As a government agency it generates no revenue, but it has a $6.9 billion budget in 2022. Of only 12,000 employees, nearly 7,000 are scientists and engineers with advanced degrees – often Ph.D.'s.

NOAA is laser focused. Its everyday mission is "To understand and predict changes in climate, weather, oceans, and coasts; to share that knowledge and information with others; to conserve and manage coastal and marine ecosystems and resources." To do so they relentlessly focus their limited resources (budget allocations from Congress) on nine areas in which its work can deliver against its mission and its longer term vision.

Though incredibly different, Google and NOAA are each successful in their own very different ways. But the two have the following in common:

- Each organization has a simple mission. These organizations know who they are. As they diversify into new areas, they still know who they are. In fact, their missions determine how far afield they each might branch out.
- The brand and the mission statement of each are aligned. Picture Google and NOAA in your mind. There's no confusion about what these organizations do. Neither is there confusion for their employees.
- Each organization's offerings are simple to understand and to appreciate. Hurricane and tornado warnings emanate from NOAA's research and facilities, as do new policies to protect the environment and the coastlines. Most of us use Google daily for practical ideas and advice, though the search engine behind the curtain is the product of a prodigious intellectual feat.

Principles, What Principles?

In 2008 Volkswagen announced its "Strategy 2018" plan: "…make Volkswagen the most successful, fascinating and sustainable automaker in the world….Our particular focus is on the environmentally friendly orientation and profitability of our vehicle projects…." In 2013 the company reiterated its principles to "offer attractive, safe and environmentally sound vehicles." In 2015 it came to light that it had been installing software in engines so they passed laboratory emissions tests but belched out dangerous nitrogen oxides when on the road. They had been doing this for years in 11 million vehicles sold. Although CEO Martin Winterkorn said "I am endlessly sorry that we have betrayed that trust," in 2016 it was discovered that he knew about the cheating scandal more than a year before it was admitted. In late 2017 VW environmental office head Oliver Schmidt was sentenced in U.S courts to seven years in prison for conspiracy to deceive government officials and customers. While admitting responsibility, he maintained he was following orders from superiors and was "coached" to lie. Principles and values run deep in companies, and those at the top can set clear examples for acceptable behavior to those down the line.

STRATEGIC DIRECTION

We will learn in the chapters to come that for any organization to achieve superior and sustainable returns, it is imperative to have a deep understanding of the competitive environment, the company's position in that environment, and how it may profit from that position. But at the same time we face these complicated challenges, we must understand that *where* we compete and *how* we intend to compete must also be consistent with the *direction* we choose to take for our company. We have to make sure that whether everyone in the company is pulling in unison in that direction. We must find a way to develop tight coordination and internal consistency of activities across the company. The coherence that results from coordinating all the activities is critical.

Getting all the individuals in a corporation to move in the same direction is as difficult as "herding cats." Without a true understanding of a company's guiding purpose, people – like cats – will tend to wander wherever each thinks it is best to go. A mission statement helps because it is a brief statement that summarizes how and where the firm will compete in the present. A vision statement also provides guidance because it presents a compelling image of the organization in the future that motivates employees to focus actions toward a common reference point.

Students and managers often get mission and vision confused. Mission statements have a significantly more bounded close-in nature than broader, longer-term vision statements. Think about it this way. In the 2017 Star Wars movie "The Last Jedi" a conversation took place between Luke and Rey as she sought to recruit him for the immediate battle against the growing menace of the Empire. But Luke wanted her to recognize the power of the Force, a much more infinite phenomenon. Their conversation goes something like this:

Luke: "Breathe. Just breathe. Now reach out. What do you see?"
Rey: "Light. Darkness. A balance."
Luke: "It's so much bigger."

Mission is about the here and now, what we see and what we do in our immediate circumstances in order to accomplish our goals. Vision is about the longer term horizon, which is much more encompassing of both the present and an unfolding future.

A statement of principles (or values) is also important in today's environment. Because companies often have employees dispersed around the country or the world, espoused principles help guide acceptable versus unacceptable behavior when management may not be in the immediate vicinity. As the above Volkswagen example illustrates, a principles vacuum at the top – or a principles policy that is only words with no substance – can lead to inappropriate behavior way down inside the organization. Statements espousing principles are also important in recruiting, since young people today are especially interested in matching personal goals and ethics with those of prospective employers.

The combination of a vision statement, mission statement, and statement of principles provides fundamental guidance by laying out the unique purpose of the organization and its defining approach.[2] But defining the mission and vision for a business are two of the most difficult, yet equally most critical, elements in any company's long-term success. In fact, some have referred to the creation of vision and mission statements as a "wicked problem" because the problem is ill-formulated, the process can involve many people with conflicting values, and the result has ramifications for the whole business system.[3] What constitutes a good mission and vision statement? How can these statements be developed? What impact will an effective set of statements have on the overall strategy and performance of the business? We will try to unpack these questions in this chapter.

Business involves coordinated action among many people. However, studies have demonstrated that significant differences of opinion exist among senior-level executives about both strategic goals and the means to accomplish them.[4] Disagreement with others' goals, or even mere consent about goals and the means by which to achieve them, can have a cascading negative effect on employee behavior across the company. Employees left without clear corporate direction will intuitively and explicitly try to guess what their bosses really want them to do.

A sobering question for senior management is: "Do you have confidence that what employees are doing on a day-to-day basis is consistent with your overarching goals for the organization?" Evidence from industry suggests that the resounding answer to this question in many cases is *NO!* In fact, fully 25% of the world's largest companies have no written statement at all that would serve to guide their organizations. Only about half of the Fortune 500 companies have developed and published comprehensive mission statements. Of these, some have added lists of superfluous elements, hoping to satisfy as many stakeholders without upsetting others. Roughly 5% of the Fortune 500 has no mission or vision statement, but they do have written values or principles. The result is that many companies fail to provide this sort of over-arching guidance.[5]

In the last two years we have witnessed a global pandemic, a global recession, unprecedented government actions, turbulent elections, and deeply felt social and racial injustice. This has caused many companies to become self-reflective about their roles in society. In 2022 corporate "statements of purpose" have gained great visibility in the media. This is because many corporations increasingly feel the need to be seen as proactively addressing "stakeholder" needs (versus just stockholders), and to appear more attractive to both existing and prospective employees amidst the "great resignation" of 2021. As we shall read below, framing a corporate statement of mission or purpose takes time and hard work. But companies driven to quickly cranking out new statements of purpose are "waffling on the challenge…and adopting language without much action behind it."[6]

Providing Direction and Purpose

Before we proceed to the details of developing effective mission and vision statements, let's consider a larger question first: Why does it even matter whether a company has a defined mission or vision statement? Think about where you will go to work after you graduate. You will likely go to your job every day with the intention of working hard, doing something of real value for your company, and finding both a personal and professional sense of accomplishment. What will truly motivate you to do your work? It is unrealistic to believe that a paycheck is your primary motivation. The mission, vision, and principles *are* the glue that binds employees' collective actions into a consistent and unified effort for the company.

Why is any company in business? To some this may sound like a foolish question, but as we pointed out in Chapter 1, companies are certainly *not* in business just to make money. Imagine a company's mission statement:

Company X Mission

We strive to make the most money possible within the legal constraints of the countries within which we do business, because our fiduciary responsibility is to maximize shareholder value.

No doubt this mission would energize employees in the firm in their daily tasks. They would explain to customers, suppliers, and fellow employees that since the organization must make as much money as possible, it is why they must: 1) charge more for the same value or provide less for the same price, 2) require pay, benefit, or work condition concessions, 3) demand reduced prices for raw materials, etc. Furthermore, since any type of technically legal business activity is acceptable within this mission, employees may find it okay to pursue all kinds of directions.

A company's mission is *not* to meet its "fiduciary responsibility to maximize shareholder value." This provides no direction for the company's employees and therefore provides no unifying reason for its existence. Profitability and shareholder value are the *results* of a strategically focused organization, not its reason for being.

The reason that companies are in business is to provide a product or service that creates value for customers, who in free exchange are willing to profitably compensate them for their efforts. This idea is the essential starting point for mission and vision statements.

An organization exists to create and deliver value in ways that an individual cannot accomplish alone in free-market transactions. We call a company an "organization" because everything it does involves the organization of the efforts of more than one individual. The most pressing issue that develops as the company grows is one of coordination and consistency of effort toward a common purpose. Pointed out many years ago by Henry Mintzberg in his definitive book *The Structuring of Organizations*, the issue of coordination is the continuous struggle to get more and more of employees' efforts focused on the mission of the organization.[7]

Employees have routines they use and actions they take to handle situations on a day-to-day basis. These should be guided by the set of objectives that reflect each employee's job within her or his department. In turn these objectives are a subset of the strategic plans of the organization, which are a reflection of the mission that company wishes to accomplish. A mission statement, then, provides clear guidance on what the company does in the present. It also helps distill down overall company direction into actionable components at the departmental and employee level. Vision initiates the whole process by laying out the compelling, overarching focal image guiding everyone in the organization in a long term direction. Therefore, mission and vision statements help to answer two basic questions for every employee in an organization:

1. What am I expected to be doing today? Answer: Mission statement, which characterizes how the company competes in today's market.

2. Why are my co-workers and I expected to act this way? Answer: Vision statement, because this is what we want the company to become.

Figure 3.1
Strategy Planning Hierarchy

Figure 3.1 illustrates the relationship between vision, mission, and activities. The organization and its employees should have an under-girding foundation of principles and values.

VISION AND VISION STATEMENTS

Whereas the mission defines specifically what the organization does in the present, the vision is the desired future state of the organization. What is the organization's ultimate objective and why should anyone who works for the organization care? The vision helps define the long-term future for the company, which management guru Peter Drucker described as "what should our business be."[8] Figure 3.2 lists the elements that characterize effective vision statements.

> **Figure 3.2**
> **Effective Vision Statement Elements**
>
> Incorporates foresight
> Provides event horizon
> Connects with current capabilities
> Incorporates enduring values
> Is short
> Is memorable

The benefits of a shared vision can be remarkable. Employees not only engage more easily with collective understanding of where they are headed, but they can also better imagine how they will be rewarded through the accomplishment of the vision. When people see how their individual efforts can work toward a grand future, collective effort can make a powerful difference. In 1995 South Africa hosted the World Cup rugby tournament. On the heels of the end of apartheid and the election of Nelson Mandela as president, incredible animosity still existed in the country among people of different ethnicities. Mandela encouraged the Springboks rugby team, traditionally a poor performer, to win the world title against all odds. Before the championship match against the New Zealand All-Blacks, the team visited the island where Mandela had been imprisoned for 27 years. Team captain François Pienaar shared with the team the *Invictus* poem that had given Mandela strength during those awful years: "…I am the master of my fate: I am the captain of my soul." The implanted vision, that victory and great accomplishment can be borne out of desperation and misery, inspired the team to win the title on behalf of their country.[9]

> **Figure 3.3**
> **Henry V's Speech at Agincourt, 1415**
>
> "That he which hath no stomach to this fight,
> Let him depart; his passport shall be made
> And crowns for convoy put into his purse:
> We would not die in that man's company
> That fears his fellowship to die with us.
> This day is called the feast of Crispian:
> He that outlives this day, and comes safe home,
> Will stand a tip-toe when the day is named,
> And rouse him at the name of Crispian.
> He that shall live this day, and see old age,
> Will yearly on the vigil feast his neighbours,
> And say 'To-morrow is Saint Crispian:'
> Then will he strip his sleeve and show his scars.
> And say 'These wounds I had on Crispin's day.'
> Old men forget: yet all shall be forgot,
> But he'll remember with advantages
> What feats he did that day: then shall our names
> Familiar in his mouth as household words
> Harry the king, Bedford and Exeter,
> Warwick and Talbot, Salisbury and Gloucester,
> Be in their flowing cups freshly remember'd.
> This story shall the good man teach his son;
> And Crispin Crispian shall ne'er go by,
> From this day to the ending of the world,
> But we in it shall be remember'd;
> We few, we happy few, we band of brothers;
> For he today that sheds his blood with me
> Shall be my brother; be he ne'er so vile,
> This day shall gentle his condition:
> And gentlemen in England now a-bed
> Shall think themselves accursed they were not here,
> And hold their manhoods cheap whiles any speaks
> That fought with us upon Saint Crispin's day."

A more compelling example of how vision motivates occurred on October 15, 1415, when King Henry V of England confronted the French army in Agincourt, France. With only 5-6,000 soldiers confronting an estimated 20,000 French soldiers, the odds were against the English. Henry delivered his visionary "band of brothers" message to his troops, later immortalized by Shakespeare (Figure 3.3), and his troops went on to defeat the French in what is regarded as the most lopsided military victory in world history.[10] Henry's vision inspired his troops to imagine themselves years later as old men, when others would still recount their heroism in victory at Agincourt. It worked! Over 600 years later, we are still recounting this story!

Designing a vision is an exercise that balances foresight with a deep understanding of the company's present resources. On the one hand, senior management wishes to establish long-term direction that will require the company to grow significantly beyond its present position and capabilities. On the other hand, the vision cannot afford to imagine a future that is simply unattainable, given current capabilities and position.

Through this process the vision should establish an event horizon that guides current practices within the company. There should be a specific and discernible endpoint in mind – for example the championship, living to old age, etc. – that is at the horizon but is not further than the eye can see. So, the vision statement encourages the organization to significantly stretch its strategic capabilities, in order to achieve a valuable and secure position in an unfolding future. The event horizon presents a motivational, attainable goal that is true to the vision statement. The former CEO of Rubbermaid articulated the vision for the company as being able to go into any supermarket and walk down an "aisle of Rubbermaid." Can you imagine an entire aisle of Rubbermaid products in a store!? It sounds a bit funny to us, but to employees it crystallized in their minds what they wanted the company to become, and it led to significant and effective innovation and new product introductions over the next few years.

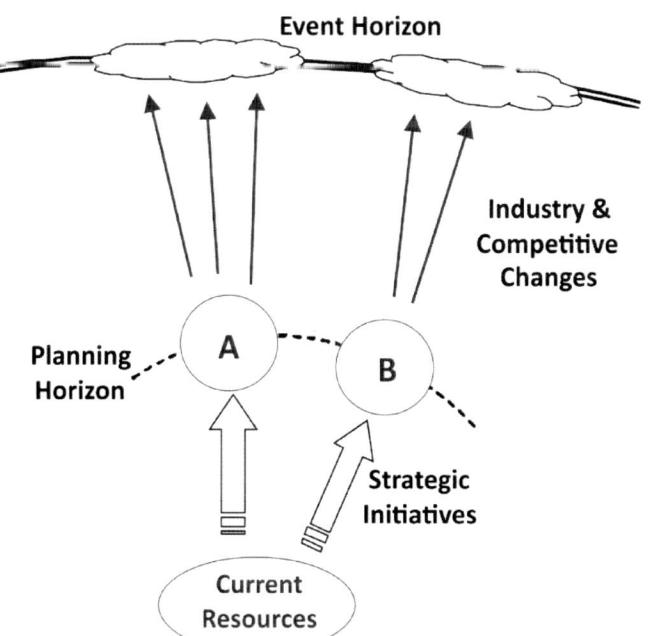

**Figure 3.4
Horizon for Vision**

Typically the time horizon for a vision statement will be something close to a decade. This makes sense when we think about the fulfillment time required for ongoing strategic initiatives, which can often take a few years to pan out (recall the character of strategic decisions discussed in Chapter 1). This means that the event horizon is beyond a more immediate boundary marking the longer-term outcomes of current strategic initiatives, and is in all likelihood beyond what can be accomplished with just existing capabilities. Setting an event horizon thus requires management to consider carefully not only how external forces will shape competitive markets, but also how current capabilities may be enhanced or supplemented to develop a portfolio of possibilities. Figure 3.4 captures the sense of this discussion. Here a company builds on two of its resource positions as it engages in strategic initiatives that are estimated to have A and B as outcomes. The horizon for the company's vision, however, extends well beyond outcomes A and B, to fuzzy sets of possibilities that might build further on A or B and the resource positions that led to them.

Examples of successful visioning such as this can further illustrate the nature of longer-term horizons. President John F. Kennedy propelled NASA in the 1960s with his very clear and well-articulated vision of putting a man on the moon and returning him safely to earth within the decade. In his speech to Congress on May 21, 1961, he resolutely laid out his stretch goals for the United States while recognizing its current technological capabilities. He asked us to imagine how proud we would all feel in such an accomplishment (Figure 3.5). Management author Jim Collins referred to this type of statement as a "*BHAG*," that is, a Big, Hairy, Audacious Goal.[11]

**Figure 3.5
John F. Kennedy's 1961 Speech**

"Finally, if we are to win the battle that is now going on around the world between freedom and tyranny, the dramatic achievements in space which occurred in recent weeks should have made clear to us all...the impact of this adventure on the minds of men everywhere, who are attempting to make a determination of which road they should take.... Now it is time to take longer strides – time for a great new American enterprise – time for this nation to take a clearly leading role in space achievement, which in many ways may hold the key to our future on earth. I believe we possess all the resources and talents necessary.... I believe that this nation should commit itself to achieving the goal, before this decade is out, of landing a man on the moon and returning him safely to the earth.... But in a very real sense, it will not be one man going to the moon – if we make this judgment affirmatively, it will be an entire nation. For all of us must work to put him there."

A more recent example of vision is the case of Amazon, which started as a new business in 1995. As an internet startup in the dawn of the internet age, the original vision espoused by founder Jeff Bezos was to be the "biggest bookstore" – quite a stretch for a small technology company that relied on book distributors for its merchandise. After the company's business took off in the late 1990s, Bezos updated the vision to "earth's most customer-centric company ... a place where people can come to find and discover anything they might want to buy online."[12] Since then, Amazon has been reinvesting in technology to deliver superior online selling performance, as well as establishing relationships with providers of a tremendous variety of merchandise.

As suggested earlier, vision statements should be memorable and inspiring to everyone throughout the organization. Though politicians and Shakespeare are accustomed to using "words, words, words"[13] in their inspirational passages, vision statements for organizations should be short. Whirlpool Corporation has a simple, but compelling vision: "Every home... Everywhere... with Pride, Passion, and Performance." This sets forth an event horizon that can easily be used as a guidepost for current activities and tactics. Other useful examples are presented in Figure 3.6.

Figure 3.6
Examples of Vision Statements

Company	Vision
Alzheimer's Association	A world without Alzheimer's disease.
Charles Schwab	Helping investors help themselves.
Wikipedia	Imagine a world in which every single person is given free access to the sum of all human knowledge.
Kodak (in 1880)	To make photography as simple as using a pencil.
Progressive Insurance	To reduce the human trauma and economic costs associated with automobile accidents.
Cornerstone Health Care	To be the model for physician-led health care in America.

Developing the Vision

Developing a vision for the organization is a process that can be full of ambiguity. There is no one way to develop an effective vision statement, although there are clearly methods that seem to assist in the process. Gaining buy-in from the entire organization is crucial in the initial development process, however. This is not to say that everyone in the company has a great sense of what the vision should be, but it is to suggest that everyone should have input on the ideas that are ultimately reflected in the long-term direction. As Jim Collins suggests, leaders at the top cannot "set" or "install" organizational values; values can only be discovered.[14] This can sometimes be approached through a solicitation to the whole organization for direct input, yet in large companies with many employees this process may result in a deluge of communication that becomes difficult to sift through for meaningful content.

Instead, another more effective method used to come together on core values, present capabilities, and desired future states is to compose a small team of five to seven people who embody the deeply held values of employees. If employees are asked to nominate members of the team, often the result is a group of individuals who employees look up to because they stand as exemplars for the company's important values and knowledge. Together with top management, the group should consider several critical questions to generate a compelling vision:

1. What do we hold to be "true" and meaningful in our business, factors that should never change as we go forward?

2. What does it mean to work in this organization? After ten more years what would I want to look back upon and be proud of for having worked in this organization?

3. At the core, what are we particularly good at doing? What is our core competence, and what extraordinary resources do we possess?

4. What are the compelling changes and opportunities in the competitive environment that we should be taking advantage of?

5. Where should our company be in ten years? Are there interim milestones that we can use to more concretely guide us forward?

These questions spur the development of a vision statement that can be used by every individual in the course of his or her daily interactions. The actual writing of the statement is an iterative process, attempting to capture the richness of a company in a statement that is short, memorable, and inspiring.

MISSION STATEMENTS

The firm's mission helps the corporation by focusing its current efforts in specific arenas and on specific opportunities. No business can or should attempt to serve up all things to all people. Instead, the business needs to concentrate on those areas where it possesses extraordinary resources and creates value in ways that competitors cannot. Research has shown that corporate performance improves as firms focus their resources and capabilities on a narrower, not broader, set of activities.[15] The firm's mission helps the business achieve this because it specifies what the company does best right now. In a wonderfully related manner, a well-developed mission statement also helps the business *stay away from* areas that opportunistically sound promising, but which actually take the business away from its principal strengths. Note that as a business diversifies into other areas of competition, what comprises its core may become muddied or muddled. If that fragmentation occurs, there may be singularly focused companies in any market that are ready to capitalize on it.

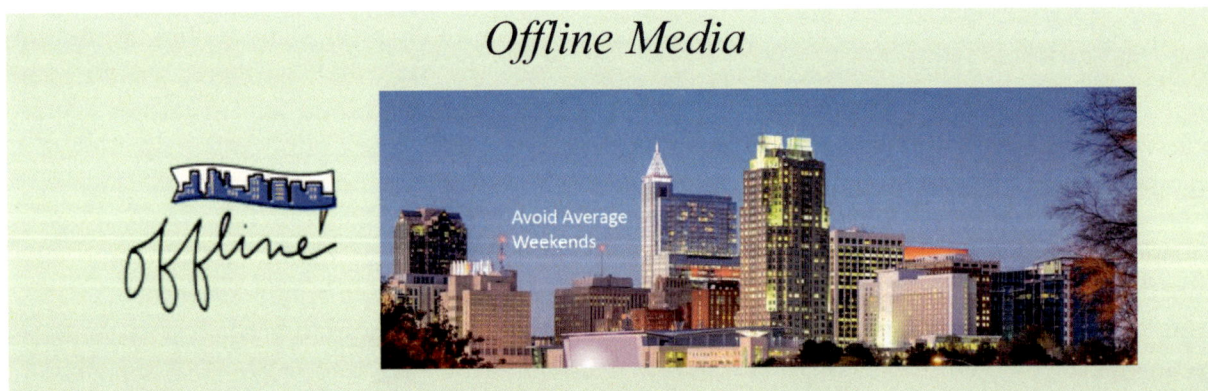

Offline Media started up in 2012, when a small group of college graduates with little business experience had an idea about a new way for people to meet up to have fun. Three founders, led by David Shaner, wanted social media tools to enable users to learn online what was going on in their cities, and then go offline to meet friends at places and events they had read about.

Shaner brought in students as "interns" to do programming and marketing development. But the startup progress can be slow. Two of the founders lost interest in the business and left. Interns floated in and out over the next two years. Shaner hired a computer science grad to become chief technology officer and a partner.

The company started offering its service in Raleigh, NC, and developed a small following instantly. But like so many startups, aspects of the business remained unclear: how to grow the user base; how to efficiently develop content for its site; when and how to expand to other cities; whether they could continue to raise sufficient venture capital; and more.

Part of the challenge presented by these questions had to do with the fundamental purpose of the business. Were they simply a new social media version of established competitor Yelp? Was the business more for the online users, or was it more for the restaurants and venues in the city that wanted to attract new customers? Offline was in business, but its mission was unclear.

Shaner oversaw efforts to articulate a statement of its mission that would guide and direct future efforts. Through casual conversations during the day, Saturday brain-storming sessions, and scheduled offsite meetings with investors and customers, they developed and refined a mission statement: "*help people rediscover and reconnect with the world around them.*" This mission statement has focused their entrepreneurial efforts in very productive ways. At the core of their enterprise is a new set of algorithms to automate the process of identifying and curating local events. They create greater value by making this content more engaging for both visitors to their site and the event locations in the city. For example, restaurant menu items and local area events become "stories" and "experiences" that are attractive to their millennial target audience. Having a focused understanding of their capabilities and market approaches has enabled them to more easily expand to other cities. And their uniquely-defined focus has attracted additional venture capital, strategic partnerships, and enabled them to develop a successful revenue model. In 2019 the company for the first time developed positive annual cash flow.

Developing a Mission Statement

The mission statement is the vehicle that captures the immediate direction and focus of the company and its unique way of going in that direction. The process of developing an effective mission statement calls for management to align five key criteria (Figure 3.7). These criteria can be further described as follows:

1. Short. Does it fit on a coffee mug?

2. Simple. It has to be something that can be easily learned and understood.

3. Company-Specific. A mission should tell everyone exactly what the company does (and by definition what the company does not do).

4. Actionable. It has to be able to guide every individual each and every day.

5. Measurable. The company should be able to develop a measurable metric for each part of the statement.

Figure 3.7
Elements OF Effective Mission Statements

Short
Simple
Company specific
Actionable
Measurable

These criteria are what an effective mission statement should try to achieve. Let's look at each in more detail.

Keep It Short

There are two schools of thought about the length of mission statements: keeping them short and succinct, or using them to summarize desirable elements of what a company is all about. We prefer keeping them short, since such statements are more easily remembered and therefore more easily relied upon for day-to-day actions and decisions.

Some guides suggest that a long list of items be included in order to create a comprehensive statement. Such a list may include many or all of the following elements:[16]

1. Customers
2. Products/Services
3. Geographic Markets
4. Technology
5. Concern for Survival/Growth
6. Philosophy
7. Public Image
8. Employees
9. Distinctive Competence
10. Communities

As you may imagine, the effect of this approach is to create a list so inclusive that the statement will be relevant to a broad variety of stakeholders inside and outside of the company. As a result, some company mission statements have become multi-sentence or even multi-paragraph tomes that are geared to avoid conflict rather than guide employees. They cannot be easily recalled, unless an individual has a photographic memory, and therefore cannot be easily acted upon. An all-encompassing mission statement that cannot be recalled and used by employees is an exercise in frustration, expense, and occasionally outright derision by employees.

Does it fit on a coffee mug? This may be the most important element of a well-crafted mission statement. It is not an essay that describes everything a company has done or might do, such that the organization can cover every single avenue of potential profit. An effective mission statement is best described as a short, direct statement that precisely encapsulates what approach the organization takes as it seeks to accomplish its purpose.

One of the truly outstanding companies in the United States is Caterpillar. Unfortunately, this manufacturer of enormous earthmoving equipment used to have a mission that failed every tenet of effective statement development. Consider the following:

Caterpillar (older). *Caterpillar will be the leader in providing the best value in machines, engines and support services for customers dedicated to building the world's infrastructure and developing and transporting its resources. We provide the best value to customers. Caterpillar people will increase shareholder value by aggressively pursuing growth and profit opportunities that leverage our engineering, manufacturing, distribution, information management and financial services expertise. We grow profitably. Caterpillar will provide its worldwide workforce with an environment that stimulates diversity, innovation, teamwork, continuous learning and improvement and rewards individual performance. We develop and reward people. Caterpillar is dedicated to improving the quality of life while sustaining the quality of our earth. We encourage social responsibility.*

This statement encompasses many potential stakeholders in the business. It has the look and feel of a checklist with a series of ideas that, while not objectionable, are not going to be remembered by anyone in the organization. An effective mission statement does not explain in detail how the mission will be done. However, it does state the purpose of the company and the basic approach the company will use to accomplish that purpose. An improvement on the Caterpillar mission might look something like this:

Caterpillar (newer). *We strive for economic growth through infrastructure and energy development while providing solutions that support communities and protect the planet.*

It simply states the mission of the organization. It is easily recalled, leaving the detailed means of attainment up to the experts within the organization. Unfortunately, this newer statement still leaves it unclear exactly what business the company is in.

Another unclear example that an excellent company formerly used is as follows:

Halliburton Company (older). *The world needs energy resources and commercial and industrial facilities to fulfill the need of its communities in a safe and environmentally sound manner. Halliburton Company is dedicated to leading the way in meeting this need through demonstrated excellence in providing a broad spectrum of services and products for finding and developing energy resources; designing, constructing, operating and maintaining facilities; and protecting the environment. We will afford our employees opportunities to contribute to our Company's success. Through their skills and abilities, we will continuously improve the quality of services and products we supply our customers. We will provide a fair return for our shareholders and good opportunities for our business partners and suppliers, and be good citizens of our communities.*

Reading carefully, we can see that this statement contains a smorgasbord of ideas. While no one can really find anything they would disagree with here, neither would most employees be able to remember or execute against this lengthy statement. What might be the alternative? The company recently retooled its mission statement to the following:

Halliburton Company (newer). *Our mission is to achieve superior growth and returns for our shareholders by delivering technology and services that*

> *improve efficiency,*
> *increase recovery and*
> *maximize production for our customers.*

Keep It Simple

A well-designed mission statement has to be something that everyone in the organization can learn and understand. A mission statement that does not incorporate shared language and meaning for all employees has little value to the organization. Learning and understanding require that the statement be relatively simple. The senior management team needs to ensure that the words and concepts employed in the statement are straightforward and have a clear meaning to all who hear or read them. If you saw the movie *Pirates of the Caribbean*, you may recall the entertaining language at play when Captain Barbossa replied tongue-in-cheek to his upper class captive, "I'm disinclined to acquiesce to your request," pauses for moment, and turns back to his captive and says, "Means NO!" Simplicity!

Consider the following corporate mission statement from a very focused and successful company, which certainly meets the first criteria of keeping it short but fails on the dimension of simplicity:

Waste Management (older). *To maximize shareholder value, while adhering to the laws of the jurisdictions within which it operates and observing the highest of ethical standards.*

Try to imagine the army of trash truck drivers being told to use this mission statement in the course of their daily pickups. The terms "adhering," "jurisdictions," and "ethical standards" are all fine concepts and yet are of little practical value in advising on day-to-day activities to most employees. Why is Waste Management in business? Why would a customer want to use them?

What are their resource-based capabilities? Where do they attain extraordinary returns in their value chain? Don't all corporations (or should we say, *shouldn't* all corporations) adhere to the laws? What exactly is useful for employees to take from this? Would any corporation seriously suggest that it will *minimize* shareholder value?

We're being a tad facetious here to make an important point. It is not to suggest that Waste Management isn't a fine organization; it is simply to suggest that the true mission of the organization is not what is stated here, and its poor focus does not help the organization move consistently toward a goal in a unified fashion. The use of terms that have no meaning to employees, suppliers, customers, or the investing community provides inadequate direction. It opens up the possibility of both an unfocused future and a group of employees who will "interpret" the mission of the organization in different and possibly creative ways.

>**Waste Management (newer).** *To maximize resource value, while minimizing - and even eliminating - environmental impact so that both our economy and our environment can thrive.*

Okay, this newer one come closer to the mark of what Waste Management employees actually do. Yet it is still not clear that the company is America's leading provider of comprehensive waste management environmental services.

The ability to learn and understand a mission statement requires that it be written in such a manner that everyone can get meaning from it and knows how to apply it. Look at the following short, simple, and effective mission statement:

>**Parker Hannifin.** *Enabling Engineering Breakthroughs that Lead to a Better Tomorrow. As the global leader in motion and control technologies, Parker plays a pivotal role in applications that have a positive impact on the world.*

Keep It Company-Specific

There are occasions where a short and simple mission can also miss the mark of being company-specific:

>**J.P. Morgan Chase (older).** *To create exceptional value for our clients, employees and investors by delivering our deep, broad and integrated capabilities.*

We hesitate to guess what the result of this statement would be if it were used to make daily decisions. The ideas are so vague that few could understand what the company does or how employees are to conduct themselves for the company to achieve its goals. This mission is not company-specific. This could be a statement about virtually any company! Perhaps reflecting this sort of ambivalence, by 2022 J.P. Morgan publishes no specific mission statement for its company. Maybe CEO Jamie Dimon assumes that everyone knows who J.P. Morgan is and what they do. We think that's a risky assumption. And we note that in their 2021 annual report they spend several pages discussing their "purpose." Few will probably spend the time to read all those pages!

Mission statements that stay at too general a level are like the mass mailings from aspiring political candidates that show up in your mailbox. They seek to curry favor with the entire population. Everything seems so agreeable; who could disagree? Just as the mailings provide no precise definition of the candidates or even what political parties they actually belong to, these types of statements provide no clear definition of the company in question. A mission statement that is not specific to the company invites questions about purpose and direction.

The GM Financial AmeriCredit division is a leading company in subprime (individuals with less than stellar credit records) automobile lending. It used to have a mission that prevented employees and others from learning or understanding what the company sought to achieve:

GM Financial. *To create value for our stakeholders by constantly improving our services, investing in innovative solutions and information-based strategies, and promoting a culture of teamwork, excellence and integrity.*

Upon a first reading one would be inclined to believe that they had read the statement of a software company or a web-based business. You could easily take this statement and apply it to almost any organization, anywhere in the world. Because it was so generic, it was relatively useless in guiding specific actions and behavior specifically in the auto finance business. In the last few years they have revised the mission statement to provide much greater clarity:

GM Financial
- *Help GM sell more vehicles throughout the world.*
- *Build relationships with auto dealers and their customers in order to optimize customer experience, loyalty and retention.*
- *Provide the means to help people purchase or lease a vehicle.*

It is not difficult to find other well-known and respected companies that may suffer from ineffective writing.

Albertson's (older). *Guided by relentless focus on our five imperatives, we will constantly strive to implement the critical initiatives required to achieve our vision. In doing this, we will deliver operational excellence in every corner of the Company and meet or exceed our commitments to the many constituencies we serve. All of our long-term strategies and short-term actions will be molded by a set of core values that are shared by each and every associate.*

If all you had in front of you was this mission statement, how might you know what the company actually does? Can you tell that Albertson's is a supermarket? How might the statement help anyone in the organization to make decisions? The statement could be interchangeably attached to any company. There appears to be nothing outside of its "opportunity space." In fact, it is not unusual to read comments from corporate executives stating that one of their goals is remain open to any opportunity. So when mission statements stay at a general level reflecting this sort of thinking, employees may act in ways that lead companies to stray from their core strengths.

Interestingly, Albertson's was acquired a few years ago by an investor group that combined it with other supermarkets around the U.S. In the process they retooled the mission statement, to a much more focused business:

Albertson's (newer). *We want to run really great stores and provide great customer service.*

One of the primary goals of an effective mission statement is, therefore, its ability to allow (and empower) employees at all levels to use their discretion and judgment as they execute their daily responsibilities. Employees are constantly faced with decisions that may have both an immediate and cumulative strategic impact. An effective mission statement tells everyone exactly what to "DO" and therefore, by omission, what "NOT TO DO." The focus within the mission statement must go beyond a laundry list of areas covered in the business; instead it should be narrowly articulate "an organization's unique and enduring purpose...."[17] Consider the following mission statement:

Autoliv. *To create, manufacture & sell state-of-the-art automotive safety systems.*

Every employee, customer, and supplier knows exactly what Autoliv does and does not do. If an employee is approached by a vendor with an interesting new product that might improve the sound quality within an automobile, the employee knows instantly that this product is outside the stated purview of the company. Management has made the decision to focus their time, energy, and resources upon the creation, manufacture, and sale of state-of-the-art automotive safety systems. This focus prevents the company from wasting valuable time and resources pursuing areas outside of its core competence.

Keep It Actionable

A fourth criteria exhibited by a high-quality mission statement is its ability to practically guide behavior. It takes extraordinary care to develop a statement that can provide overall guidance for the entire organization while at the same time help guide every employee in daily tasks and decisions. Imagine an employee who talks to customers calling in with concerns and complaints. If the mission statement of the organization is a long, multi-paragraph affair that essentially says "we do it all," or if it is like so many statements and simply extols the employees to "maximize shareholder value," then how is the customer service employee to act? What is most likely to happen is that they will simply do the best they can (or are allowed to do), given some mixture of their own common sense along with advice from and admonishments by their immediate superiors.

An effective statement helps employees make decisions in the moment without always having to refer up the chain of command. One that comes fairly close to simultaneously achieving all of the components that we have thus far discussed is from Southwest Airlines.

Southwest Airlines. *Connect people to what's important in their lives through friendly, reliable, and low-cost air travel.*

Reading this mission statement, no one could argue that it could be applied generically to just about any organization. Southwest is an airline company. Every aspect of the activities performed by employees on a day-to-day basis are focused on providing exceptional service to the company's customers.

Keep It Measurable

The final dimension of an effective mission statement involves a bit more complexity than the previous four. The mission statement is only as valuable as it is practical. And it is only of practical value if we have confidence that it works in guiding actions to be consistent with direction. So while corporations have sets of metrics used to evaluate the organization as a whole (Chapter 2), developing a mission statement also requires us to think through how we can measure its effectiveness.

Mission statements often exhibit one of three types of performance dimensions: 1) "feel-good" goals, 2) general financial or vague market goals, or 3) specific financial goals. Feel-good goals, such as "provide employees with meaningful work and advancement opportunities," tend to be ineffective. This is because they focus on qualitative dimensions that cannot be easily measured on a regular basis. It's just too easy to eyeball a soft concept like this, and then conclude that "we do this" even if data is unavailable. If a portion of a statement cannot be measured, it is of little help in providing direction for the company.

This idea applies to general goals as well. General financial goals or vague market goals are not very helpful in connecting mission statements to performance. This is because it is difficult to connect specific actions and practices to such fuzzy goals.

In contrast, highly specified financial goals appear to lock management and employees into definitive targets, potentially compromising long run performance in the rush to accomplish short term goals. Financial performance goals are ethically neutral, and therefore may lead to a distortion in the activities of employees by possibly encouraging short-termism. This is not unlike the challenges faced by public companies in managing toward short-term earnings targets.

Studies suggest, instead, that alignment between a mission statement and the firm's performance evaluation system helps to magnify the impact on performance of the mission statement.[18] Since mission statements guide actions at the individual level, some metrics should presumably be tied to the firm's personnel performance evaluation system. For example, since innovation is central to the mission of 3M Corporation, each employee is encouraged and expected to devote a percentage of their workweek to investigating new business ideas. The actual time percentage spent by each employee in this area can be captured on an individual basis, and then aggregated to a departmental, divisional, or corporate level.

A great check on the quality of a statement is to determine whether metrics can be designed to measure each part of the mission. Consider the following:

New York Times. *Enhance society by creating, collecting and distributing high quality news, information and entertainment.*

This well-designed statement allows for the development of metrics that can be used to assess its practical value and utility. *The New York Times* aims to do three things (create, collect, and distribute) across three areas (high-quality news, high-quality information, and high-quality entertainment) in order to accomplish one goal (enhance society). All of these can then be translated into a mix of qualitative and quantitative metrics given the top management's interpretation about what constitutes high quality. Examples might be:

1. Number of high-quality news articles written by *NY Times* staff writers divided by the total number of news articles appearing in the *NY Times*. This could be measured daily.

2. Perception of the quality of articles in *NY Times*.

3. Number of *NY Times* articles that are picked up by other news sources.

The metrics designed for the *NY Times* will be unique to that organization and truly measure how it is succeeding in its mission.

Evaluate the following mission statement from an office products manufacturer:

Steelcase. *Our mission is to provide the world's best office environment products, services, systems, and intelligence ... designed to help people in offices work more effectively.*

Steelcase does one thing ("provide," which can be defined as producing, outsourcing, or simply purchasing for resale) across four areas of expertise (products, services, systems, and intelligence) aimed at one arena (office environments) with one goal (helping people work more effectively). The specificity of the items appearing in the statement focuses employees on sets of activities, and also provides substantial opportunity for the development of measurable metrics.

Well-Designed Mission Statements

Combining all of these qualities into an effective mission statement is both an art and a science. Figure 3.8 shows several examples of well written mission statements.

No mission statement is ever perfect, and everyone in the organization will have their own ideas of how the five concepts presented might best be articulated. However, the effort made to design a quality mission statement can have a payoff for the business that undertakes its creation.

Figure 3.8
Examples of Mission Statements

Company	Mission
Best Buy	Enrich lives through technology.
British Sugar	Creating a thriving homegrown sugar industry.
Collins & Aikman	To be recognized as a leading-edge automotive systems supplier and an innovator of world-class NVH (noise, vibration, harshness) and acoustic technologies.
CVS Pharmacy	We will be the easiest pharmacy retailer for customers to use.
Host Marriot	To be the premier hospitality real estate company.
Ikea	Offer a wide range of well-designed functional home furnishing products at prices so low that as many people as possible will be able to afford them.
Mars Wrigley	Creating better moments to make the world smile.
Merck	We invent for a more hopeful future.
MGM Mirage	To design and operate an unmatched collection of resort-casinos and provide unsurpassed service and amenities to our guests.

Mission Creep[19]

Everyone knows Facebook, which was started in 2004 by Mark Zuckerberg. The business has grown phenomenally, and now attracts nearly 3 billion monthly users worldwide. In 2012 the company went public at $38 per share. By 2022 its annual revenue exceeds $110 billion, its stock price had risen to $328 per share, and its market capitalization was over $900 billion.

Facebook's mission statement has evolved considerably over time, as its user base and its articulated purpose broadened:

2004: Connect people through social networks at colleges.
2006: Connect people through social networks at schools.
2007: Connects you with people around you.
2008: Helps you connect and share with people in your life.

2009: Gives people the power to share and make the world more open and connected.

2012: To make the world more open and connected.

But the company encountered significant headwinds during 2017. The proliferation of fake news, claims about Russian influence in the U.S. presidential election, the presence of bad actors on its pages, and a live video platform used to broadcast murder and suicide: the company came under fire. Mark Zuckerberg wrote that these features of its business have contributed to a "decline in community." So in 2017 he announced a new mission statement for the company:

"Give people the power to build community and bring the world closer together."

By 2019 change was again under way. Zuckerberg announced that the company would pivot to a "privacy-focused platform," while admitting that "we don't have a strong reputation for building privacy." The fundamental change in direction prompted long-time execs to leave the company.

Then in 2021 the company announced it was changing its name to Meta Platforms. This time Mark Zuckerberg claimed "Connection is evolving and so are we…. The metaverse is the next evolution of social connection. Our company's vision is to help bring the metaverse to life, so we are changing our name to reflect our commitment to this future." Apparently, the evolving technologies will become quite a large part of how the company will provide "immersive all-day experience." However, for now its mission statement remains the same as in 2017.

QUESTIONS

1. How often should a company modify or change its mission statement? Why?

2. How did the 2017 mission statement change affect people inside Facebook?

3. How will the "metaverse" concept change the mission statement?

PRINCIPLES AND VALUES

We have spent most of this chapter discussing the importance of vision and mission statements for achieving coherence across the company and guiding employee behavior. But if you now refer back to Figure 3.1, you will remember that vision, mission, objectives, and the activities of any company rest on a foundation of principles and values. In the aftermath of corporate scandals such as Volkswagen, Enron, Tyco, and the BP Gulf oil spill during the first decade of the 2000s, and of the 2008 financial crisis, it has become increasingly fashionable for major corporations to publicize a set of principles or values that they purport to live by. In the aftermath of social unrest during 2020-21 this seems to have taken on added importance lately.

If you evaluate values espoused by companies on the Fortune 500, you would often see listed ideas such as social responsibility, diversity, honesty, trust, and more. In fact, three words – integrity, respect, and innovation – occur most frequently in the principles and values statements of these companies. These sound great, don't they? But here's the problem. First, they all sound the same, offering no clarity regarding what is unique and special about a particular organization. If all companies sport "integrity," then how is calling this out supposed to indicate that this company is different and better? More importantly, what company would ever assert that "integrity" is *not* one of its principles?

So the more fundamental question is whether or not corporations actually use and apply such principles in the day-to-day conduct of their business. Such lofty ideas only become meaningful if senior management communicates their importance regularly, serves as a role model for their importance, and aligns performance incentives with them.

Crushed: Actions Speak Louder Than Words[20]

Activision Blizzard is the game company that produces "Call of Duty," World of Warcraft," and "Candy Crush Saga." The company is included in ESG funds (Environmental, Social, and Governance) by BlackRock, Vanguard, and Fidelity. In its own 2020 ESG annual report Activision claims it is "working to create the most diverse games in the world by creating innovative tools, training, and practices to ensure our players see themselves reflected in our games, including through characters of color, characters from the LGBTQ+ community, characters of differing abilities, and non-binary characters." Activision boasts that 20% of its directors are women and 20% are underrepresented minorities, and that it enjoys a 100% rating on the Human Rights Campaign 2020 Corporate Equality Index. Sounds good, right?

In 2021, however, the company has drawn complaints from employees and regulators about sexual misconduct, retaliation and discrimination. Charges allege that "women were subjected to constant sexual harassment, including groping, comments, and advances," that the company's execs and HR department knew of the harassment and failed to take steps to prevent the conduct, and that they instead retaliated against women who complained. The EEOC made a public complaint, State of California agencies are investigating, and the SEC is looking into whether complaints were properly disclosed in financial filings.

It was reported that CEO Bobby Kotick failed to fully inform the board of directors about complaints of sexual misconduct, including a female employee's rape accusation. 20% of the company's 10,000 employees signed a petition to have him removed. Board governance oversight committees failed to pick up on what was going on behind the scenes. In 2022 it was revealed that the company had so far fired 37 employees and disciplined 44 others for "bad behavior."

QUESTIONS

1. What steps should be taken to ensure that espoused principles are followed?
2. Are any of the other ESG claims made by the company to be believed?

Some corporations develop statements of values and principles because it is in vogue. It is "expected" of them and provides a defense if and when they encounter trouble rooted in unethical behavior. Some corporations develop these statements because senior management believes this approach will hopefully keep the company out of trouble while possibly also enhancing performance. But some corporations do this because senior management actually believes such principles are vital for corporate success and personal employee happiness.

The challenge in developing statements of principles is that, while they are espoused by the corporation, the values extolled must be internalized by employees to be effective. It's one thing to say we have integrity; it's quite another for every employee to act regularly with integrity. Part of the problem here is definition: if you ask ten employees what integrity means, you will get a variety of different responses. So in developing statements of principles and values, management must take two essential steps. First, each principle or value must be defined and explained so that every employee has the same understanding of what it is and how it can contribute to the company's mission. Second, management must regularly and continuously reinforce the espoused principles so that they become living, breathing dimensions of how work is performed in the company.

Ernst & Young publicizes three principles for employee behavior, and discusses these with prospective employees as part of the hiring process:
- People who demonstrate integrity, respect, and teaming.
- People with energy, enthusiasm, and the courage to lead.
- People who build relationships based on doing the right thing.

Coming in to E&Y one understands that these are the foundational principles upon which both personal and professional success depend. And it is rewarding to newly-hired employees to realize that E&Y ascribes these values to them as one of the reasons they are hired.

We briefly mentioned Truist Financial Bank (formerly BB&T) in Chapter 1 as one such corporation which embraced principled decision making. The bank published a booklet for all its employees titled "The BB&T Philosophy," in which were listed ten critical values:

1. Reality (fact-based) - the foundation for quality decision making.
2. Reason - thinking through the facts logically to objectively make the best decisions.
3. Independent thinking - each employee is responsible.
4. Productivity - creativity, productivity, and turning thoughts into action improve economic well-being.
5. Honesty - say what we mean, mean what we say.
6. Integrity - always acting consistent with our principles.
7. Justice (fairness) - individuals are evaluated and rewarded based upon contributions toward the mission.
8. Pride - performing work in a manner to be justly proud.
9. Self-esteem - self-motivation leads to goals accomplishment.
10. Teamwork - respect for fellow employees while acting in a mutually supportive manner.

In addition to publishing the principles internally on a regular basis, including them in annual reports and listing them on the company's website, former CEO John Allison spent years visiting offices and far-flung branches of the bank to meet employees and reiterate these ideas. The application of these ideas to the bank's business during the 2000s prompted loan officers to refrain from extensive sub-prime and Alt-A mortgage lending that crippled other large national bank competitors. During the 2008 financial markets crisis and ensuing years, Truist outperformed many of its competitors and continued to grow its deposits base.

Managing in Markets: Question for Class Discussion

Corporate statements of principles are often indistinguishable from one another, because so many use the very same words or terms. Many also claim that such statements are not useful because employees' moral framework and sense of right and wrong are already deeply embedded from their upbringing. So is it worth the time, energy, and resources for corporations to develop and promote such statements of principles? Or is this sort of effort "virtue signaling" and merely designed to create a positive image of the company by outsiders?

COMMUNICATING VISION, MISSION, PRINCIPLES

The strategy department of Thyssenkrupp, a German industrial company with 155,000 employees, conducted an electronic survey in 2015 to learn how well the company's mission and vision statements were understood by the workforce. The results were underwhelming: roughly 50% of the company's employees had no clue what was the mission of the company![21]

The computer manufacturer Dell wanted to retool its code of principles a few years ago. The goal of the company's Chief Ethics and Compliance Officer was to get employees to be "believers" rather than mere "obeyers," and felt achieving such a goal would require employee engagement. Dell created a game challenging employees to work through an ethics scenario. Within the first few days after the game's introduction, over 5,000 Dell employees participated. A subsequent voluntary survey about the game generated over 30,000 employee responses.[22]

The best statements are of little value if they are not communicated to all employees on a regular basis.[23] Because employees learn in different ways, communications should embrace many forms and styles. An organization's culture and means of interacting are not uniform throughout and so the means of communicating can be tailored. The goal is to increase coherence across the organization. This can be done in a number of ways:

1. Creating Narratives. One of the newer means of embedding the vision and mission in an organization is the use of storytelling, one of the oldest communication techniques known to humankind. Telling stories that point to the understanding and use of the vision and mission is an effective method of relaying important, actionable concepts. A story allows the listener or reader to visualize the situation and the result. Individuals have a much higher recall level with good stories than they do with bulleted items, lists, or verbal presentations.[24] When Sony was developing the first music CD in 1982, at a time when cassette tapes and albums dominated, they took a prototype CD to Stevie Wonder at his Los Angeles home. He was enamored with the sound quality and excited about its possibilities for sound reproduction. This story was repeated throughout Sony, inspiring further commitment to the new direction. In an earlier case, Sony founder Akio Morita said "I'll leave Sony if we don't do the Walkman," a story that was repeatedly told throughout the company, which mobilized the entire organization to become the first mover in the portable listening device field.[25]

The biggest benefit of storytelling is that it can create a more vibrant picture of the future than the shorter statements of mission and vision afford. The elements of great stories[26] as powerful metaphors that inspire understanding and commitment include:
- Hero/heroine
- Quest/purpose
- Obstacles/enemies
- Helpers/Magic
- Resolution/fulfillment

2. Role Models. Management has a profound ability to affect the actions of their employees by serving as a role model in the embodiment of the vision and mission. When top management demonstrates that the vision and mission are the measures by which they evaluate their own actions, it provides direct and compelling evidence of its importance to all employees. The president of a prestigious U.S. university is regularly observed picking up litter as she walks across campus. Chinese president Xi Jinping has forgone luxury class accommodations as he travels. Lower-level Chinese government officials are now following his lead, saving the government tens of millions of RMB as the country's economic growth slows down.

3. Specific Short-Term Objectives. Translating the loftier and more general direction provided by the vision and mission into specific, short-term objectives clarifies the actions expected of individual employees and provides a quick reinforcement that employees are headed in the right direction. Simplicity and focus are crucial. General Mills (Big G cereals, Betty Crocker desserts) says its mission is "building leading brands that our consumers trust around the world." This provides guidance for employees to focus on great tasting products made with superior quality, and acting in ways that enhance the company's image.

4. Personalizing the Vision and Mission. Employees are encouraged to develop their own vision and mission that are consistent with the ones developed for the organization. The ability to personalize the vision and mission for themselves not only has the effect of internalizing what is needed, it also acts as an effective check to ensure that senior management has developed a set of statements that resonate with employees. Whole Foods includes the following in its mission statement: "to satisfy and delight our customers – and to support Team Member happiness and excellence." The company seeks employees who share a similar vision and mission, believing this consonance is a source of strategic superiority.

5. Create Objects that Display the Vision and Mission. Placing the vision and mission on a coffee mug and distributing one to every employee has been used as a communication device to set the stage for constant reinforcement of the company's approach to business. Printing the vision and mission on posters, banners, and/or plaques that can be prominently displayed helps reinforce their importance to the future of the organization. Pepsico CEO and Chairman Steve Reinemund carried in his wallet a card that listed the mission statement and values of the company. Every employee was provided the same card.

Here's a story to remember. Medtronic is a leading medical device company that specializes in cardiac and spinal products. Its mission statement reads: "To contribute to human welfare by application of biomedical engineering in the research, design, manufacture, and sale of instruments or appliances that alleviate pain, restore health, and extend life." To this end, one of the founders of the company had a medallion cast with the image of a patient rising from the operating table. Every new employee, when he or she is hired, is presented a medallion by a member of

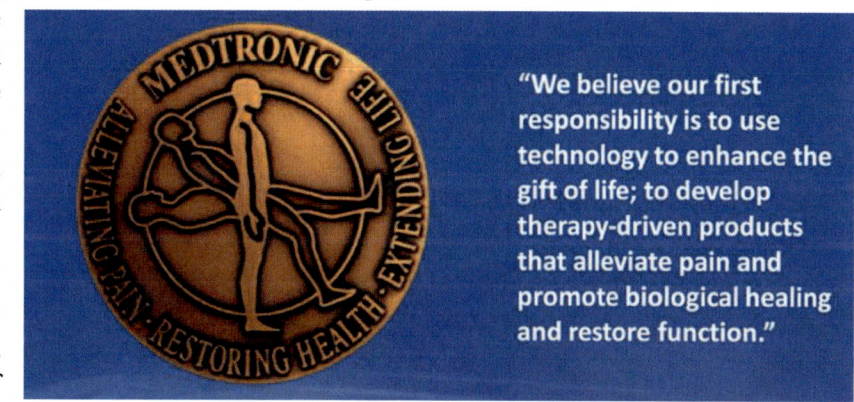

the senior management team at a ceremony. Employees are encouraged to keep the medallion at their desk to remind them of the goal of the organization.[27] The organization celebrates its ability to accomplish this mission with events throughout the year and honors employees who exemplify their approach to this business. It is part of what separates them in a very competitive field.

CHAPTER SUMMARY

This chapter has focused on: 1) Understanding the importance of effective vision, mission, and principles for an organization; 2) Developing the criteria for evaluating and writing the statements; and 3) Understanding the process of developing them. Truly great companies have developed a vision and mission that provides direction and accountability for their businesses. As in much of strategy, the process, evaluation, and use of both a vision and a mission statement is a combination of both art and science. Increasingly, companies are also beginning to develop statements of values and principles. Like mission statements, the effectiveness of statements of principles depends on their communication throughout the company and on substantive support from senior leadership.

Effective vision statements incorporate six elements: 1) Incorporate foresight; 2) Provide an event horizon; 3) Connect with current capabilities of the organization; 4) Incorporate enduring core values; 5) Be short; and 6) Be memorable.

Effective mission statements incorporate five criteria in their design. They can be evaluated by their simultaneous accomplishment of the following characteristics: 1) Be short; 2) Be simple; 3) Be company-specific; 4) Be actionable; and 5) Be measurable.

Statements of principles become effective when management finds ways to personalize expressed values with every employee, and when management behavior serves as an exemplar of principled conduct.

Learning Objectives Review

1. *Examine how vision and mission statements can be used to provide effective direction for a firm.*

- **Provides direction and purpose.** Establishing a vision for a company provides every employee (and suppliers and customers) with a view to the long term direction the company wishes to take.

- **Defines immediate approach.** Establishing a mission statement provides fundamental guidance for how employees should act in the present toward more immediate goals. The mission statement helps distill an overall strategic approach in the market into a more actionable guideline for day-to-day behavior.

- **Complements strategy.** Strategy plans are often developed and usually endorsed by senior management, far removed from employees at lower levels. Vision and mission statements help overcome the coordination problem that exists in large, complex organizations.

2. *Describe the process of developing a vision statement.*

- **Assemble a small team.** The team of five to seven employees should represent key employee groups and understand deeply held values of the company.

- **Consider important questions.** What are we particularly good at doing now? What are the compelling changes and opportunities in the competitive environment that will leverage these capabilities, or require us to develop new ones? What is meaningful in our business that should never change? Where should we be in ten years? What should we look back on and be proud of after ten years?

- **Establish an event horizon.** Where will we be if we establish stretch goals for our strategy?

3. *Explain the steps involved in developing an effective mission statement.*

- **Short.** This makes it memorable.

- **Simple.** This makes it easily learned and understood.

- **Company-Specific.** This makes it relevant.

- **Actionable.** This provides day-to-day guidance.

- **Measurable.** This provides feedback on how consistent employee actions are with strategy and direction.

4. *Name five techniques for communicating vision and mission.*

- **Creating Narratives.** Telling stories makes it memorable.

- **Acting as Role Models.** "Walking the walk" demonstrates the ideas in action.

- **Establishing Specific Short-Term Objectives.** Clarifies actions expected of employees.

- **Personalizing.** Encourages employees to internalize company values.

- **Creating Objects that Display.** Keeps the message visible.

5. *Explain how principles and values can lead to superior performance.*

- **Establishes trust.** Employees, suppliers, and customers will trust the company and its actions. Helps to communicate the pursuit of business *as* a moral undertaking.

- **Provides ethical boundaries of action.** Helps employees understand moral obligations and ethical basis of decision-making.

- **Leads to positive outcomes, and avoids unhealthy outcomes.** Positive outcomes gained through ethical practices are personally rewarding for employees and perceived as positive by markets.

- **Establishes distinctive platform compared with many competitors.**

Key Terms

Mission statement - A brief statement that summarizes how and where the firm will compete in the present.

Vision statement - More compelling and overarching than the mission statement, an image of the organization in the future that motivates employees to focus their actions toward a common point.

Statement of Principles – A statement that articulates important values and principles, intended to guide employee and corporate behavior when confronting ethical, moral, social or legal issues.

Short Answer Review Questions

1. How is a vision statement used in organizations?
2. What criteria should be kept in mind for writing an effective vision statement?
3. Why is it important to keep a mission statement short?
4. How are vision and mission statements best communicated to employees in an organization?
5. What is a BHAG?
6. How would you evaluate a mission statement?
7. How can you make a mission statement actionable?
8. How would you suggest a company create narratives for its vision and mission statements?
9. How does a company's sustainable competitive advantage guide its vision and mission?
10. Describe how a mission statement can encourage ethical behavior in a company.

Group Review Exercises

1. Using the information presented in this chapter, create a vision statement for your business school.

    a. How well did the process work?
    b. Who else would you include on your team if you were to do this again?
    c. What might you do differently if you were to try this again?
    d. How accurately does your vision statement present the school and its future?

2. Have your team agree on five large, publically traded companies. Using the internet, try to locate the vision and/or mission statement for each.

    a. How many were you able to find?
    b. Evaluate each vision/mission on how well it meets the criteria laid out in the chapter.

c. Do you have any excellent statements? Any horrible ones? Which are they and why did you evaluate them as such?

d. In what part of their websites did you locate the statements? Why do you suppose the statements are there? Do they mention if they communicate the statements to employees?

3. Look at the following list of mission statements. Match them to the company listed in the table that follows. For answers, see footnotes.[28]

Company # 1 - One team, one plan, one goal. People working together as a lean, global enterprise for automotive leadership, as measured by: customer, employee, dealer, investor, supplier, union/council, and community satisfaction.

Company # 2 - Use our pioneering spirit to responsibly deliver energy to the world.

Company # 3 - To be the most creative, innovative and efficient company in high-quality interactive entertainment experiences across a range of genres.

Company # 4 - To be a leader in the distribution and merchandising of food, health, personal care, and related consumable products and services.

Company # 5 - To be one of the world's leading producers and providers of entertainment and information. Using our portfolio of brands to differentiate our content, services and consumer products, we seek to develop the most creative, innovative and profitable entertainment experiences and related products in the world.

Company # 6 - To continually provide our members with quality goods and services at the lowest possible prices.

Company # 7 - We seek to be Earth's most customer-centric company for four primary customer sets: consumers, sellers, enterprises, and content creators.

Company # 8 - We will become the world's most valued company to patients, customers, colleagues, investors, business partners, and the communities where we work and live.

Possible Answers	
Amazon.com	Pfizer
Conoco Phillips	Safeway
Costco	Sam's Club
ExxonMobil	Take Two Interactive
Ford	Toyota
GlaxoSmithKline	Walt Disney
Kroger	Wells Fargo

[23]

115

Investor Relations Sites for Companies Mentioned in This Chapter

Activision Blizzard: https://investor.activision.com/
Albertson's: https://investor.albertsonscompanies.com/corporate-profile/default.aspx
Alphabet: https://abc.xyz/investor/
Amazon: https://ir.aboutamazon.com/overview/default.aspx
Autoliv: https://www.autoliv.com/investors
Caterpillar: https://investors.caterpillar.com/overview/default.aspx
Dell Technologies: https://investors.delltechnologies.com/
Ernst & Young: https://www.ey.com/en_us
Facebook: https://investor.fb.com/home/default.aspx
General Mills: https://investors.generalmills.com/home/default.aspx
GM Financial: https://www.gmfinancial.com/en-us/investor-center.html
Halliburton: https://ir.halliburton.com/
J. P. Morgan Chase: https://www.jpmorganchase.com/ir
Medtronic: https://investorrelations.medtronic.com/
New York Times: https://www.nytco.com/investors/investor-relations/
NOAA: https://www.noaa.gov/budget-finance-performance
Offline Media: https://letsgetoffline.com/about-us/
Parker Hannifin: https://investors.parker.com/
Pepsico: https://www.pepsico.com/investors/investor-contacts
Rubbermaid (Newell Brands): https://ir.newellbrands.com/
Sony: https://www.sony.com/en/SonyInfo/IR/
Southwest Airlines: https://www.southwestairlinesinvestorrelations.com/
Steelcase: https://ir.steelcase.com/home/default.aspx
Thyssenkrupp: https://www.thyssenkrupp.com/en/investors
Truist (formerly BB&T): https://ir.truist.com/
Volkswagen: https://www.volkswagenag.com/en/InvestorRelations.html
Waste Management: https://investors.wm.com/
Whirlpool: https://investors.whirlpoolcorp.com/home/default.aspx

References

[1] W. Boston & S. Sloat, 2015, "Volkswagen emissions scandal relates to 11 million cars," Wall Street Journal, September 22: A1. C. Bryant & R. Milne, 2015, "Boardroom politics at heart of VW scandal," Financial Times, October 4: 1. R. Karlgaard, 2005, "YingYang, Big Bang," Forbes, March 14, 175 (5): 33. P. Knapp, 2015, "Alphabet might appease shareholders but has it lost its vision?" The Guardian, August 14: 1. J. Nicas, 2017, "Google weighs reunion with Nest Labs, maker of devices for the home," Wall Street Journal, December 1, B4. NOAA website, http://www.noaa.gov/.

[2] J. A. Pearce & F. David, 1987, "Corporate mission statements: The bottom line," Academy of Management Executive, 1 (2): 109 - 116.

[3] J. E. Conklin & W. Weil, 1997. *Wicked Problems: Naming the Pain in Organizations*. Washington, DC: Group Decision Support Systems Inc.

[4] For perspectives on top management team disagreement see the following. Bourgeois, 1980, "Performance and consensus," Strategic Management Journal, 1: 227 – 248. Eisenhardt, Kahwajy, & Bourgeois, 1997, "How management teams can have a good fight," Harvard Business Review, 75 (4): 77 - 85.

[5] Many of the largest corporations in the world are highly diversified in unrelated businesses. It may be that these corporations refrain from offering a corporate mission statement because such statements should be focused.

Evidence suggests, however, that many operating divisions of such diversified corporations still do not have mission statements.

[6] A. Bryant, 2021, "The purpose of "purpose," Strategy+Business, December 1.

[7] H. Mintzberg, 1978, *The Structuring of Organizations*, Prentice Hall.

[8] P. Drucker, 1974, *Management: Tasks, Responsibilities, Practices*, New York: Harper & Row.

[9] C. Carlin, 2009, *Playing the Enemy: Nelson Mandela and the Game That Made a Nation*, London: Penguin. W. E. Henley, 1888, *Invictus*.

[10] J. Barker, 2006, *Agincourt: Henry V and the Battle That Made England*. New York: Little, Brown.

[11] J. Collins, 2001. *Good to Great*. New York: HarperBusiness.

[12] Amazon.com investor relations (http://phx.corporate-ir.net/phoenix.zhtml?c=97664&p=irol-faq).

[13] W. Shakespeare, *Hamlet*, act 2, scene 2.

[14] J. Collins, 1996, "Aligning actions and values," Leader to Leader, 1: 19 - 24.

[15] L. E. Palich, L. B. Cardinal, & C. C. Miller, 2000, "Curvilinearity in the diversification- performance linkage: An examination of over three decades of research," Strategic Management Journal, 21: 155 - 174.

[16] F. R. David & F. R. David, 2003, "It's time to redraft your mission statement," Journal of Business Strategy, 24 (1): 11 – 14. R. D. Ireland & M. A. Hitt, 1992, "Mission statements: Importance, challenge, and recommendations for development," Business Horizons, 35 (3): 34 – 42. J. A. Pearce & F. R. David, 1987, "Corporate mission statements: The bottom line," Academy of Management Executive, 1 (2): 109 - 116.

[17] C. K. Bart & M. C. Baetz, 1998, "The relationship between mission statements and firm performance: An exploratory study," Journal of Management Studies, 35 (6): 823 - 854.

[18] Ibid.

[19] K. Chaykowski, 2017, "Mark Zuckerberg gives Facebook a new mission," Forbes, June 22. J. Constine, 2017, "Facebook changes mission statement to 'bring the world closer together'," TechCrunch, posted June 22, www.techcrunch.com. The Economist, 2019, "Facebook's third act," March 9, 58. J. Horwitz, 2019, "Facebook plans new emphasis on private communications," Wall Street Journal, May 7, A1. J. Horwitz & G. Wells, 2019, "Facebook executives exit after shift in strategy," Wall Street Journal, March 15, A1. A. Kessler, 2021, "The metaverse is already here," Wall Street Journal, December 27, B1. C. Newton, 2017, "Facebook just changed its mission, because the old one was broken," The Verge, posted February 16, www.theverge.com. G. Reagan, 2009, "The evolution of Facebook's mission statement," The Observer, posted July 13, www.observer.com.

[20] A. Finley, 2021, "How did Activision pass the ESG test?" Wall Street Journal, November 26, B3. K. Grind, 2022, "Dozens of Activision staff out over misconduct allegations," Wall Street Journal, January 18, A1.

[21] P. West, 2016, Field research on mission and vision.

[22] B. DiPietro, 2014, "Turning employees into ethics believers," Risk and Compliance Journal, September 26, http://on.wsj.com/1sxyzic.

[23] For example, see A. M. Carton, 2017, " 'I'm not mopping the floors, I'm putting a man on the moon': How NASA leaders enhanced the meaningfulness of work by changing the meaning of work," Administrative Science Quarterly, 63 (2), 323-369.

[24] R. Goffee & B. Jones, 1996, "What holds the modern company together?" Harvard Business Review, November - December 1996: 133 - 148.

[25] J. C. Collins & J. I. Porras, 1991, "Organization vision and visionary organizations," California Management Review, Fall: 30 - 52. G. Shaw, R. Brown, & P. Bromily, 1998, "Strategic stories: How 3M is rewriting business planning," Harvard Business Review, May/June.

[26] https://www.nigelbarlow.com/-Why-Stories-Are-Better-Than-Vision-Statements

[27] S. A. Buckler & K. A. Zien, 1996, "The spirituality of innovation: Learning from stories," Journal of Product Innovation Management, 13 (5): 391 - 405.

[28] 1 = Ford, 2 = Conoco Phillips, 3 = Take Two Interactive, 4 = Kroger, 5 = Walt Disney, 6 = Costco, 7 = Amazon.com, 8 = Pfizer.

This page is intentionally left blank.

Section B: Formulation – Analysis Fundamentals, Strategy Types, Adaptations

In the first three chapters of this book we laid a foundation for understanding strategic management. The first chapter outlined the nature of strategy as the direction for the firm reflected in an ongoing stream of decisions impacting all areas of the company. Through its strategy the firm seeks to achieve a level of performance that is superior to competing firms in the short term, and offers the potential to sustain performance differences over time. We also discussed the two fundamental imperatives that impact every strategic management process today. Rapidly-evolving markets and aggressive competitors make it exceedingly difficult to sustain superior levels of performance. So the imperatives of "value creation" and "opportunity recognition" become absolutely critical. This context makes developing and executing strategy complex, challenging, exciting, and fun!

Chapters 2 and 3 provided a set of "bookends" for the strategic management process. In the beginning management needs to develop a vision for the direction the company is heading, a mission that describes how it is going to get there, and principles that help guide decisions and behavior. The result that strategy seeks to achieve is superior performance, and we discussed ways in which the performance of companies can be evaluated.

Strategic Management Model

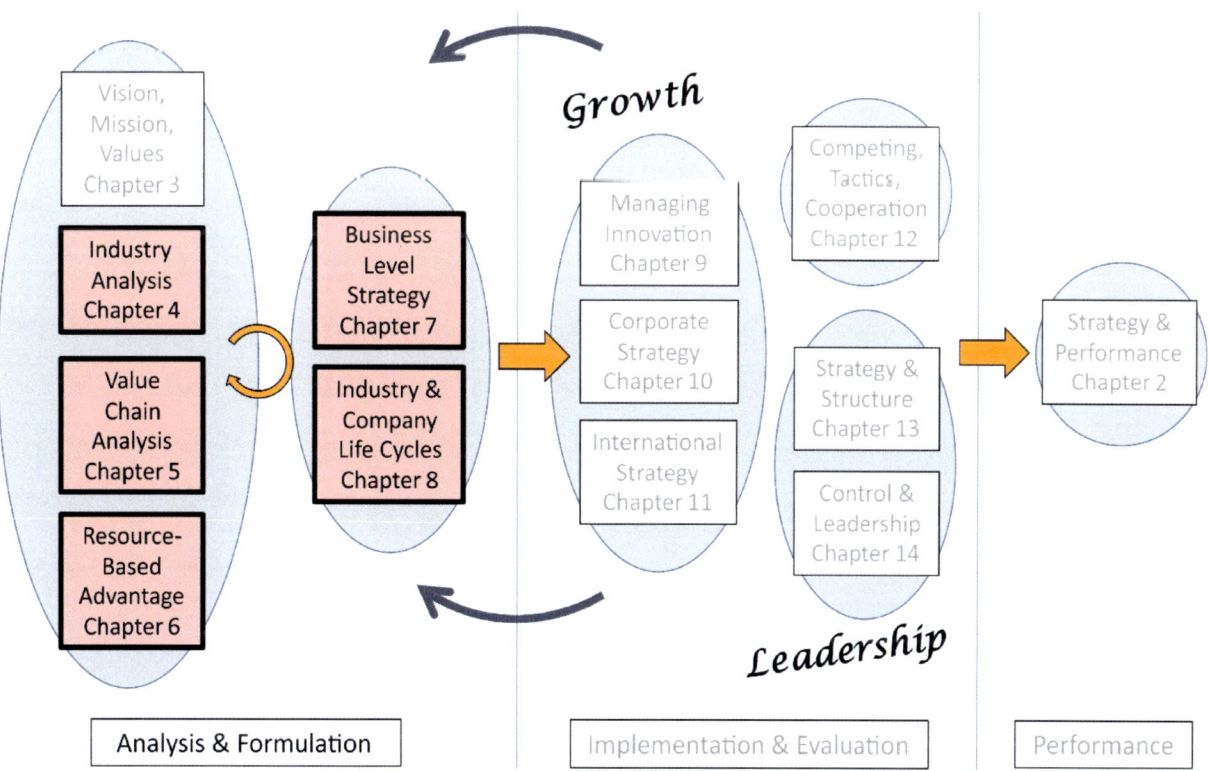

Given this, you are probably still asking yourself "What is strategy, really? What the book has done so far is provide an outline, but it hasn't really described it in detail." So let's get specific.

The next five chapters of the book take up the challenge of how to formulate strategy to achieve sustainable competitive advantage. Before we can formulate the strategy, we must do some strategy analysis.

Two basic analytical approaches aid in the formulation of company strategy: 1) externally, analyze the industry and competitors to develop a deep understanding of the market and how your firm must operate within it in order to be successful; 2) internally, examine your own company to develop a list of activities and capabilities that provide a foundation for competitive advantage.

EXTERNAL ANALYSIS OF INDUSTRY

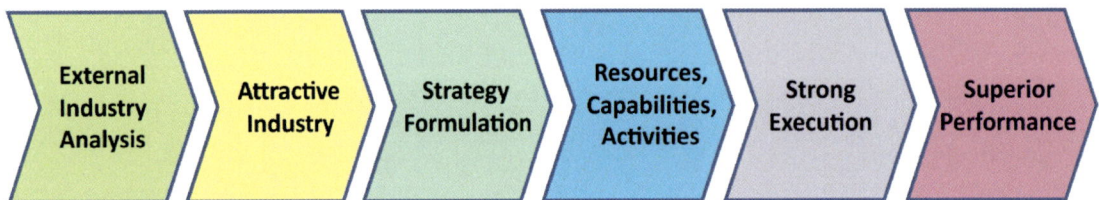

This model originates from a branch of Economics called Industrial Organizational Economics, and focuses on the economic structure of an industry. Attractive industries are those where the conditions are favorable for a company to earn above-average returns. An industry's attractiveness as a place to do business is largely determined by industry characteristics outside the company. Analyzing these characteristics leads us to identify "key success factors" that any strategic approach should address. In turn the strategic approach requires the company to assemble or develop certain kinds of capabilities and resources. According to this approach, effective execution of the strategy using these capabilities and resources would then lead to superior performance.

Here's a quick example of this approach. Before mp3 music and players were available, the only way musicians like Bruce Springsteen could grow to make it big beyond playing in local clubs was to get a contract with an established music label. The music label companies would then provide studio time to record, schedule the artist on tours, and provide marketing and promotional support. The "barriers to entry" to this industry were significant. Then along came digital. First, compressed files and file-sharing platforms like Napster, then Apple's iTunes made distribution of music much easier. Subsequently social media platforms like Facebook and YouTube, and then music sharing services like Spotify and Google Play, made it inexpensive for musicians to gain visibility. At the same time, easier entry to this industry created widespread competition. Now artists must find ways to promote themselves, and getting concert gigs is much more difficult. The rules of the game have changed! So successful companies in the industry have now completely re-engineered their strategy approaches and capabilities, in light of the new industry context.

The Industry Analysis methodology is covered in Chapter 4, along with several means of analyzing specific competitors.

INTERNAL ANALYSIS OF COMPANY

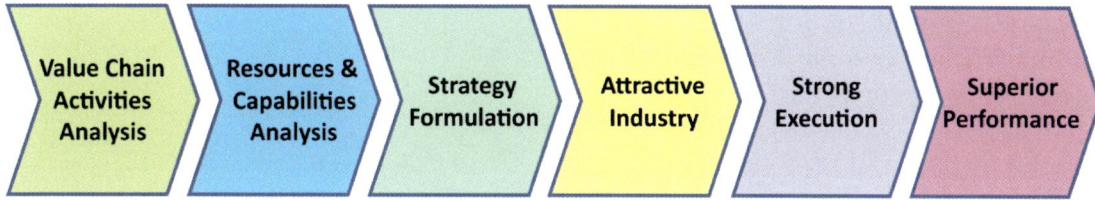

The second approach begins with a detailed internal examination of the company. This model begins with what we call value chain analysis. Here our analysis identifies value-creating activities across a company and determines whether the set of activities are coordinated and reinforcing. Then we examine the company's current resources and capabilities, and from that determine which resources and value-adding activities are truly extraordinary providing a foundation for sustainable advantage. The result of this analysis will suggest a type of strategic approach that can leverage these valuable resources and activities. This in turn suggests the kinds of industries where it would be attractive to compete in (where existing capabilities can make a difference). Successfully implementing this approach in such circumstances can lead to superior returns for the company.

Another quick example to illustrate. GoPro, the manufacturer of action cameras often used in extreme-action videography and part of the connected sport movement, started up in 2002. Founder Nick Woodman was first mover into an untapped market, and his company developed moderate quality wearable video capture technology. The company's activities and capabilities centered on unique designs and making inroads into action sports to generate sales. But as the industry grew and competitors entered the market, GoPro's activities and capabilities became less unique and relevant. Competitors introduced higher quality technology that was cheaper, and were out-maneuvering the company in ways to sell technology through retail distribution and online. The competitive dynamic of the industry had shifted, but GoPro had 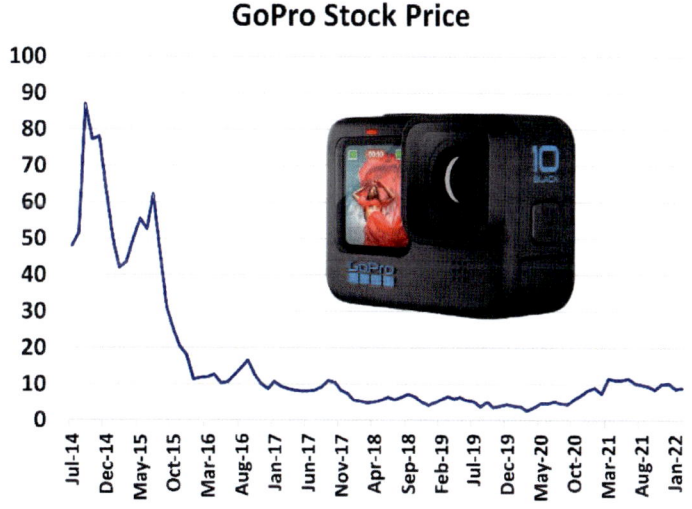 failed to keep up. The company went public in 2014, but by early 2016 its revenue was down 49% versus a year earlier, and in 2019 revenue was still 26% below what it had reached five years earlier. In 2019 the company lost $31 million, and its stock price of only $3.61 was WAY below its peak price of $86.97 per share. By early 2022 its revenue remained below its peak years, and its stock has traded between $8-10 per share. Value creating activities and capabilities are only important if they are relevant in the industry!

Chapter 5 covers the Value Chain and its associated analysis techniques, while Chapter 6 explores Resources and the associated application of a resource-based analysis.

FORMULATING A STRATEGIC APPROACH

In practice most companies do external industry analysis and internal company analysis simultaneously, and on a continuous basis. They must! Industries are dynamic, and so ongoing attention to emerging competitors is critical. But companies are also not static. They get better and better at some things they have done for a while. This sort of improvement can present new opportunity in the market. But along the way they may also discover new things they can become particularly adept at. Effective strategy blends all these perspectives together. Remember the balance that is needed between the two imperatives: value creation and opportunity recognition.

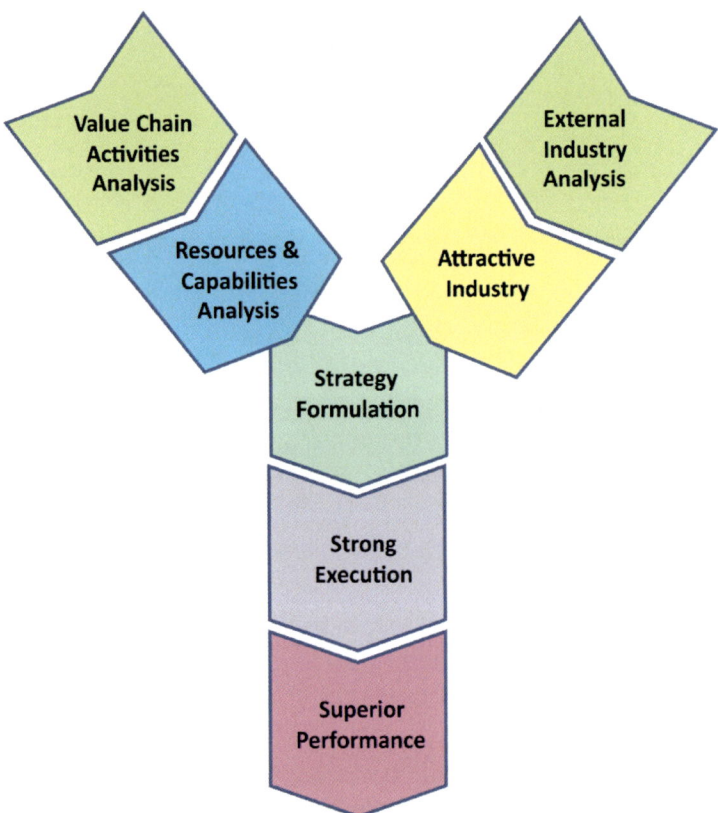

Chapter 7 puts these chapters together in a discussion of Business-Level Strategy as a way to approach the marketplace. Specific strategic approaches must respond to the requirements dictated by industry conditions, but must also build on sets of activities or resources and capabilities that enable a company to create and deliver value in a superior fashion. At the same time, managers must have a sense of trajectory that accounts for anticipated dynamic changes in the industry and competition, but that also builds and follows a vision for the company.

Companies face continuously changing sets of circumstances. Competing can be like getting onto a rollercoaster – moving from slow to fast very quickly, with rapid rises and possibly precipitous descents. When dynamic changes occur in the marketplace in the form of an evolving industry, they have an impact on types of value creation that can be successful and on the need to continuously embrace new opportunities for future growth. Companies also evolve through stages, and must address unique strategic challenges that parallel their evolution. There are implications for building resources and for configuring the company's value chain in order to succeed. Chapter 8 adds this context to the preceding analyses and strategy formulation material. Here we will explore how industry life cycles and company life cycles offer context and insight for the formulation and implementation of strategy.

Chapter 4: Industry and Competitive Analysis

LEARNING OBJECTIVES

1. Explain how the phrase "competitive advantage" is connected to company strategy and performance.

2. Describe how an industry definition can affect conclusions drawn from an industry analysis.

3. Explain the impact that forces other than competition can have on company strategy and performance.

4. Employ strategy mapping techniques to identify strategic groups in an industry.

5. Explain how an industry is shaped by driving forces.

6. Explain how dynamic changes in industries and competitive positions will impact a company's strategy.

Afraid of Concentration in Office Supplies Industry

In 1996 Staples and Office Depot announced plans to merge their two chains of office supply stores. Combined operations would exceed 1,100 stores, generating $10 billion in revenue.

The potential merger between two intense competitors raised immediate concerns about dominating market power. Many feared that the nearest competitor – Office Max with 425 stores and $3.3 billion in revenue – would be left "in the dustbin." Suppliers, competitors, and customers filed comments with the Federal Trade Commission (FTC) advising against merger approval.

In response Thomas Sternburg, founder and CEO of Staples, said that office products are sold in a fragmented $185 billion market in which the merged firm would have a meager 6 percent market share. He claimed they were in competition not only with traditional office supply stores, but also with other large outlets such as Walmart and Best Buy who also sold office machines, paper, pens and pencils. Furthermore, with larger operations the combined company would achieve efficiencies, eliminate redundancies, and develop greater buying power with its suppliers. These would lead to price reductions and bigger savings for both business and individual customers.

The FTC disagreed with Sternburg and announced that it would seek an injunction against the merger. It entertained a much narrower definition of the market, composed only of the "one-stop-shop" office supply stores. In this narrower market definition, the merged company would have a 70 percent market share. FTC research determined that there were higher retail prices for office supplies in markets where there was high industry concentration of office supply stores. Under pressure from the FTC, the merger never went through.

Fast forward 17 years. In 2013 Office Depot and Office Max merged in a $1.2 billion stock deal, producing a combined market share of 42 percent compared to Staples' 35 percent share. The FTC remained silent.

In 2015 Amazon launched Amazon Business to cater to corporate customer needs for office supplies, and its online business took off. So in 2015 Staples and Office Depot once again announced their intention to merge into a combined entity with a 75% market share and $39 billion sales. Retail office supplies industry sales had declined by 38% since 8 years earlier, and each chain had experienced rough going. Staples and Office Depot again argued that competition in the industry was vibrant, especially now with Amazon in the fray. The FTC again disagreed. In April 2016 a federal judge upheld the FTC's case, and the two companies gave up (again) on their plans.

In 2017 the Wall Street Journal reported "the digital transformation of workplaces...has permanently depressed the market for things like printer paper and filing cabinets." Reflecting precisely what Staples had contended all along, its same-store sales (of stores opened at least one year) declined 6% versus 2016. In June 2017 Staples agreed to sell itself to private-equity firm Sycamore Partners at a stock price 61% below its all-time high a few years earlier.

By 2021 Amazon's office supplies division, particularly strong in the B-to-B segment, enjoyed a 50% market share. RBC Capital predicted Amazon Business' sales would reach $31 billion by 2023, with the business expanding faster than Amazon's Retail and AWS segments.

In 2021 Staples again proposed to acquire Office Depot's retail division. The proposed tie-up intends to generate significant cost savings by eliminating duplicate operations and closing overlapping stores. The FTC has not commented. Will the 3rd time be a charm?

Forces Make for Tough Startup for Championship Chili

Traditionally the food manufacturing industry has experienced a very high level of entrepreneurial activity. This is because the barriers to entry have been fairly low. Nearly everyone's grandma has passed down a special food recipe, so coming up with a unique and tasty food product idea has never been a problem. In addition, everyone has access to a "manufacturing plant" to try out new concoctions. It's called your kitchen at home with a sink, refrigerator, stove, and ingredients easily accessible.

Championship Foods started off exactly this way, with a recipe for prepared chili that twice won the Texas State Championship and other national chili cook-offs. The company intended to sell its chili in supermarkets, shelved next to Hormel and other canned products. Championship Chili was made with fresh ingredients and high-quality beef, and it was packed in glass jars to exude homemade quality. Who would buy gross canned chili when Championship was available?

The company encountered industry forces that made it exceedingly difficult to earn profits. While food ingredients are readily available from a variety of suppliers, glass and manufacturing capacity are not. Glass manufacturing is heavily concentrated. Glass suppliers charged exorbitant prices for their products sold in smaller quantities to smaller firms, and Championship had no recourse. Manufacturing chili that contained beef required USDA-inspected plants, and these plants tended to be huge in size compared to small startup companies. As a small startup, the company had no opportunity to negotiate for better prices or terms from its contracted producer.

On the other end of the spectrum, the supermarket buyers were fairly concentrated. Championship started business in a city where only three supermarket chains controlled 85 percent of the market. Supermarket buyers entertained many possible new products to place in their stores. They required manufacturers to pay up-front fees called "slotting allowances" to gain initial shelf space, and to buy special advertising and display programs. This concentration of buyers, with no mass market alternatives, made it unprofitable for small manufacturers.

The food industry is characterized by intense rivalry. Notice the ads on TV every day, and the volume of coupons that appear in local newspapers or online each week. To create consumer awareness and trial, Championship had to play the game where rules were set by the likes of Kraft, General Mills, and other large food manufacturers. Hormel and other incumbent chili brands engaged in competitive retaliation when Championship's products first appeared on store shelves.

THE NATURE OF MARKETS AND OPPORTUNITY FOR COMPETITIVE ADVANTAGE

We continue our discussion of strategic management with a chapter on the external analysis of markets. Why do we begin here? First, every company exists in a market of some sort, and as the chapter's opening stories illustrate there are varying market forces exerting influences on companies. These forces pressure every company to behave in certain ways in order to be successful, and to not behave in other ways. Second, when we think about achieving "competitive advantage," which is the goal of strategic management, we must accept there are many companies that may be competitively close to our business. Sets of competitors, in fact, help to define markets. Abraham Lincoln once said, "If we can know where we are and something about how we got there, we might see where we are trending – and if the outcomes which lie naturally in our course are unacceptable, to make timely change."[1] Understanding the market in which a company competes will be helpful in guiding the company in its strategic direction and choices.

But let's first step back in time a bit earlier than Lincoln, to the eighteenth century and economist Adam Smith. You will probably recall from one of your first economics courses that in 1776 he published *Wealth of Nations*. To Adam Smith what created the successful functioning of an economy was the pursuit by each individual of self-interest:

> "… and by directing industry in such a manner as its produce may be of greatest value, he intends only his own gain and he is in this, as in many other cases, led by an invisible hand to promote an end which was no part of his intention. By pursuing his own interest he frequently promotes that of society more effectually…."[2]

Here and elsewhere in his book we find Smith arguing that there is an efficiency in markets that is guided by the aggregated pursuits of individuals. Resources are efficiently allocated, and the demands and needs of the marketplace are met.

If it is true that markets can efficiently allocate resources and meet demand through the actions of individuals, then why do business organizations even exist? Why shouldn't commerce be conducted by individuals merely transacting on their own? The answer, of course, is that businesses can do a number of things that individuals cannot. They can achieve administrative efficiency and more easily organize the specialization of labor. They can gain access to significant capital and therefore have the ability to construct large facilities to achieve economies of scale and scope that individuals cannot. In today's world business firms can also shield managers and employees from some of the legal liabilities of the business itself as well as from the risks taken on by the firm's investors. So the existence of business organizations opens up a much wider range of possible transactions and approaches in a market.

In Chapter 1 we pointed out that strategy concerns itself with five basic questions, two of which are particularly relevant here: 1) why do some firms perform better than others; and 2) how are those differences between successful and unsuccessful firms sustained over time? The slight deviation we have taken here into Adam Smith and the nature of markets provides us with a very important starting point for exploring these questions. Adam Smith and two centuries of economists have focused on the efficiency of markets in allocating resources and meeting demands, with perfect competition as an elegant concept that illuminates this efficiency. In contrast, the ability of firms to create sustainable performance differences versus other firms is only possible because of the *failure* of perfectly competitive markets.

Let's explain this carefully. Recall from your economics courses the characteristics that describe perfectly competitive markets: all firms are identical, produce exactly the same products, and no firm earns any profits at all. This is because in this type of market every firm enjoys perfect information about what is going on in the industry, there are no costs associated with making adjustments in how or what a firm produces, and there are no costs for new firms to enter the

industry. If Billy Bob's Barbeque somehow figures out how to make a better sauce and starts generating more business as a result, in a perfectly competitive market all the other barbecue joints would see this change instantaneously and just as instantaneously imitate it exactly. Why wouldn't they? Why would they allow Billy Bob to generate more business and more profit, if they can produce exactly the same award-winning sauce? As soon as any firm has figured out how to make more money, in a perfectly competitive market all the other firms will immediately imitate that recipe for success. In addition, there are no costs to enter the industry. So if Jake and Aubrey on the outside observe that the barbecue sauce companies are making money while they are not, then they will enter the industry to participate in the profit-making. This process will continue until all the profits have been competed away. As economists say, the market equilibrates at the point where once again all firms are virtually identical and no firm is making any profit.[3]

Perfect competition is on one end of a continuum of types of markets. Commodities markets, like soybeans and airline seats, are examples of markets that closely resemble perfect competition. The other end of the continuum is the exact opposite of perfect competition. Instead of lots of firms all selling identical goods or services and none of which is earning a profit, on the other end there is just one firm and it earns all the profits. This is called a monopoly (Figure 4.1). Here one company owns all of the business in an industry. Without the policing effect of an efficient market populated by competitors, the monopoly firm can usually charge what it wants for its products or services. Because it is the only game in town, it can likely extract economic concessions from its suppliers that lower its costs and raise its profits even further.

Because government regulators believe the public interest is usually not well-served by monopolies, it seeks to prevent them from being created or to rein them in when they naturally occur. In 2022 a federal judge ruled that Meta Platform's Facebook unit is "abusing a monopoly position in social media...and willfully maintained it through anticompetitive conduct."[4] Along with Google it has also been targeted by the European Union for its monopolistic position and the aggressive business practices it engages in with the market power it exerts.[5]

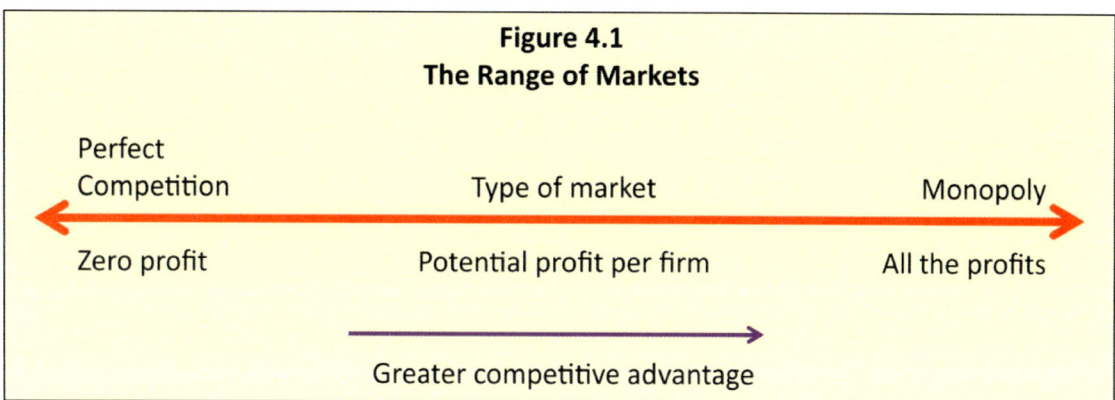

Monopoly companies are sometimes protected from new firms entering the industry and from substitute products or services taking away their customers. Local gas and electricity utility companies and cable TV providers are examples of monopolies that have been historically protected through government regulation that keeps competitors at bay.

Competitive advantage is therefore possible when there is a *failure* of perfectly competitive markets. In a perfectly competitive market, no firm has or can gain a competitive advantage and no firm earns profits. In a monopoly market, one firm exerts market power and one firm earns all of the profits. If we think about the goal of strategy as being the creation of sustainable differences between companies that result in higher profits, then we see that the possibility for competitive advantage and higher profits are more likely when our company exists in a market that is at a point on the continuum further away from perfect competition and closer to the monopoly position.

At the beginning of this chapter we profiled the possible mergers between Staples and Office Depot in the office supplies industry. The Federal Trade Commission has twice prevented the merger from going through, because the combined company would have been too far to the right in Figure 4.1 and would have possessed too much market power. The FTC came into existence in the early years of the twentieth century in order to regulate and prevent precisely this type of powerful business combination. To do so they often examine the *structure* of industries and how industry structure can increase or reduce competition.

In the 1970s Harvard Business School professor Michael Porter proposed that instead of using principles of industry structure analysis to prevent monopolies from developing, the very same principles could be productively used by companies to guide them in the development of strategies that will create and sustain positions of advantage.[6] The great insight of the industry analysis view is that a firm can generate competitive advantage and earn above-average profits if it uses tactics to move the market away from perfect competition.

How do companies do this? In Chapters 5 through 7 we will explore how companies can develop specific types of activities and resources to create value uniquely. The strategic approaches that depend on these activities and resources will often involve consciously creating "barriers to entry" to prevent new companies from entering the industry, as well as "barriers to mobility" that make it difficult for other companies already in the industry to imitate what the company is doing. By creating these kinds of barriers, the company makes the industry less perfectly competitive. Sustainable competitive advantage is then possible when companies figure out how to take advantage of this type of imperfect market.[7]

So what had changed by 2015 that made it possible for Office Depot and Office Max to consummate a merger while Staples was denied its move? This is a complicated question which this chapter will help shed light on. Step back for a second and think about where your parents went shopping for office supplies when you were a kid, and where you might first look for these items today. Retailing has changed dramatically in a number of industries, in large part thanks to Amazon. Regulatory examiners at the FTC are just as likely themselves to be shopping via the internet as to visit an office supplies retail store. So the sort of industry fragmentation that CEO Sternburg argued for many years ago is now recognized as more prevalent in the retail landscape. On the other hand, the FTC believed that allowing the 2015 merger proposal to go through would have resulted in an uncomfortable – and possibly damaging – level of industry concentration moving too far to the right in Figure 4.1. The lesson here is that industries may change over time, but a chief concern remains the competitiveness of industries as a function of their structure.

STRUCTURE – CONDUCT – PERFORMANCE

The structural analysis of an industry will allow us to develop clear insight about characteristics of the industry that are helpful to a company in developing and executing its strategic approach. Through industry analysis we can:
1) determine how attractive an industry is, and
2) identify key success factors that provide guidance on how to earn above-average profits.

Industry Attractiveness: Potential for Above-Average Profits
Industry analysis is a means by which we examine whether the nature of competitive forces makes an industry attractive or unattractive. In industries that are less perfectly competitive, the potential is greater for a company to earn superior returns.

At the outset one might ask, "Why is this important, since my company is already in an industry? Whatever that industry is, we just have to deal with it." The answer is that companies often make strategic choices to participate in an industry, or not. Today most large companies operate in several industries, and companies often engage in acquisitions that further diversify their operations into new industries (we will discuss this in depth in Chapter 10).

But not every industry is equally profitable; see Figure 4.2 for example.[8] Firms in the cable TV industry earned 19.2% return on equity over this 5-year period. These firms consider many options to grow their business including internal R&D, geographic expansion, and acquiring other companies. Cable TV companies might be attracted to other media companies. And yet during the same period publishing and newspaper firms produced -3.8% ROE, far below the U.S. average. So in looking for growth cable firms may shy away from an industry sector in which economic returns are tough to produce. If your grandfather took you fishing, he may have told you that "it's best to fish where the fish are," and that's why he bushwhacked his way into that remote stream or pond that was not over-fished. In this case it is generally better to participate in industries where there is a stronger likelihood of earning profits rather than in industries where the average profitability presents a challenge at the outset.

Figure 4.2
Selected Industries ROE, 2017-2021

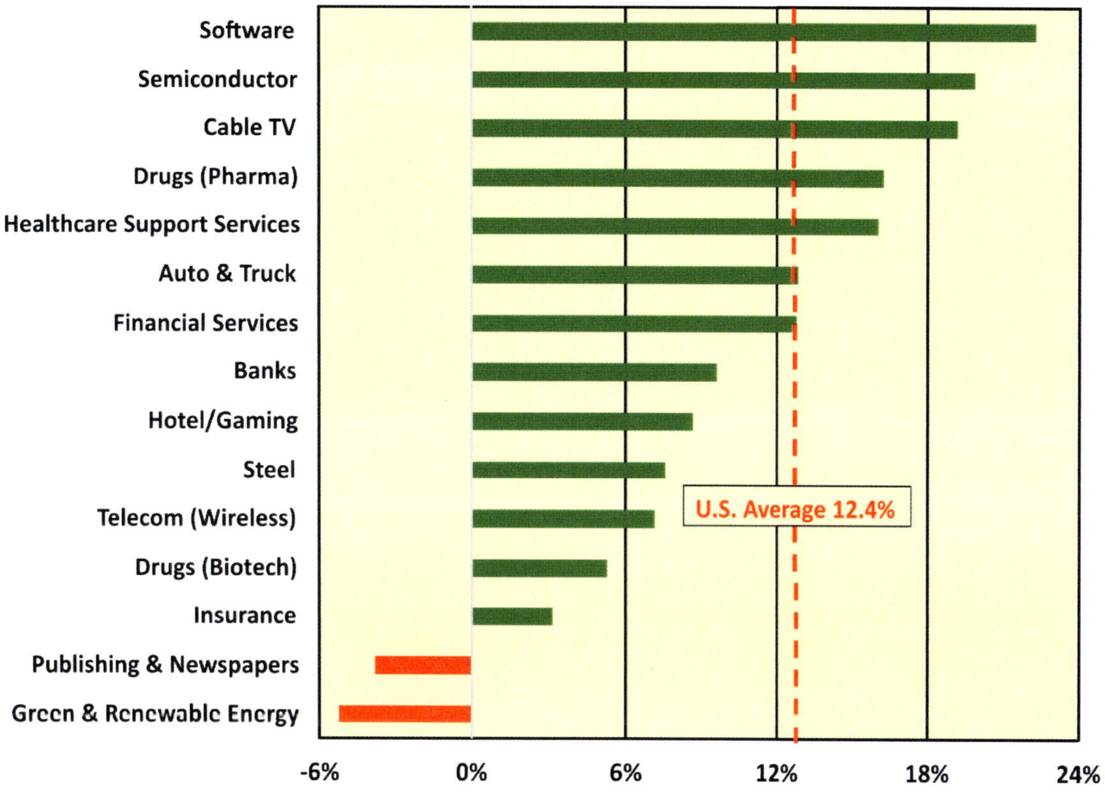

Industry	ROE
Software	~23%
Semiconductor	~19%
Cable TV	~19%
Drugs (Pharma)	~16%
Healthcare Support Services	~16%
Auto & Truck	~13%
Financial Services	~13%
Banks	~10%
Hotel/Gaming	~8%
Steel	~7%
Telecom (Wireless)	~7%
Drugs (Biotech)	~5%
Insurance	~3%
Publishing & Newspapers	~-2%
Green & Renewable Energy	~-4%

U.S. Average 12.4%

Key Success Factors

If your company is going to participate in an industry, industry analysis can provide guidance on how it should be done. The structure of every industry imposes constraints on and defines options for firms competing in it. For example, an agricultural business operating in the wheat market could not charge higher prices than the current market rate for wheat. This is because wheat is bought and sold as a commodity with a virtually identical product readily available from many competitors. A company manufacturing PCs and laptops cannot afford to forgo innovation and product line upgrades, because its suppliers push new technology and its customers demand continual progress. In any industry there will always be a small number of key factors that characterize how to navigate the challenges that the industry presents. These key success factors (KSFs) are "rules of thumb" for operating that reflect the structural conditions of the industry. The KSFs identify the aspects of business that each company must pay attention to – and make strategic investments in – if it is to be successful in the industry.

> **Strategy Acronym: KSF**
>
> The "rules" of an industry
>
> K Key
> S Success
> F Factors

Think about an industry in the same way you might think about a video game such as *Call of Duty: Black Ops Cold War*. The cross-platform multiplayer online video game was released by Activision Blizzard in late 2020, becoming the best-selling videogame of the year in 2021.[9] Players can select single player Campaign or different multiplayer modes. Within each there is an overall mission objective to be accomplished. Along the way toward the objective players can engage in side missions and earn trophies. Some trophies help progress through the overall plot of the game, while others may not. Side missions can be entertaining, but pursuing them can increase the player's risk and distract from accomplishing the primary mission. Completing primary missions will earn experience points, prestige, <u>and</u> move the player to deeper levels. Similarly, focusing on the key success factors in an industry – the industry's "rules of thumb" – also increases the odds of success for the company.

We now see that the potential to earn superior returns in an industry partially results from the structure of the industry. We also see that the structure of an industry will suggest that there are certain fundamental rules, which are referred to as key success factors. These ideas help explain what is commonly known as the Structure-Conduct-Performance (SCP) paradigm in strategic management. SCP has now become one of the foundations in strategic management for understanding how to improve company performance.[10] The SCP perspective tells us that the structure of an industry helps determine rules for competing, forcing companies to conduct their business according to the rules. The company's conduct refers to its strategic approach and the types of strategic investments it makes that support its approach (like manufacturing infrastructure or field sales force development). If the conduct of the company aligns with the KSFs suggested by the structure of the industry, and presuming the company is effective in its execution, then the company's performance should be enhanced.

> **Strategy Acronym: SCP**
>
> Connecting industry analysis and firm performance
>
> S   Structure
> C   Conduct
> P   Performance

DEFINING AN INDUSTRY

Before we move on to conducting an industry analysis, we need to be clear what we mean by "industry." An industry can generally be defined as a group of productive, profit-making, or value-creating enterprises[11] that draw upon related suppliers of various sorts, develop different kinds of customers, and compete with each other. Economists like to further narrow this definition by focusing on two types of possible substitutions: 1) substitutions for the consumption of a company's output, and 2) substitutions in supply/inputs to the company's production process.[12] A firm is included as a competitor in an industry if its products or services present alternatives for other companies' products or services in the eyes of customers. If a price rise in another company's product would cause someone to buy your company's product instead, then the other company is considered a competitor (Figure 4.3). This is usually how we think about competition.

However, competitors may also exist on the supply side of what a company does. Imagine a high-tech firm located in Silicon Valley, for example, that is seeking to expand its business and needs to hire well-trained programmers. This is precisely what has been going on in 2022 as Meta Platforms has poached Microsoft employees with experience in developing augmented-reality headsets.[13] In 2019 Netflix was blocked by a federal court from recruiting Twentieth Century Fox Film executives to bolster its film production business.[14] So a firm is also included as a competitor in an industry if it uses similar raw materials or employs similar production methods as other companies, even if the final products produced are not entirely similar for consumers. In this case, since the company already competes with other companies for production inputs, it might then easily compete for customer business by producing similar products if the lure of potential profits is great enough.

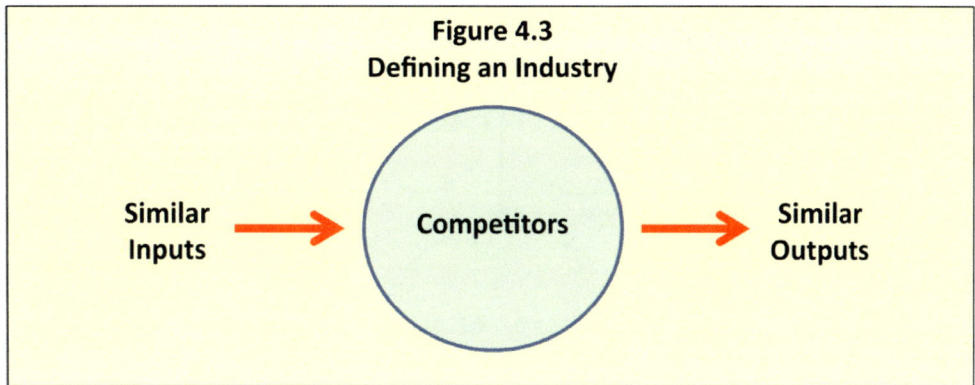

It is important to recognize that industries can be defined differently, depending on who's doing the talking. We saw earlier in this chapter that Staples and Office Depot sought to describe the office supplies market as encompassing competitors as diverse as Best Buy (who largely sells audio and video equipment) and Walmart (who largely sells general merchandise and food). On the other hand, the FTC defined the industry very narrowly, including only "one-stop-shop" office supply stores like Office Max and the local mom-and-pop shops that traditionally sold these goods. The narrowest industry definitions ordinarily involve the group of competitors who produce similar outputs *and* utilize similar inputs.

Sometimes industry definitions can be very confusing. For example, what industry classification do cell phones exist in? Until the early 2000s it seemed very clear that cell phone manufacturers and cell phone service providers competed in the telephone industry, that is, in local and long distance calling. But consider the nature of cell phone capabilities just a few years later, serving multiple functions competing with products and services in multiple industries (Figure 4.4).[15] By 2019 actually *talking* on the phone was the least popular way to communicate, with only 45% of phone users reporting doing it.[16] If a company is in the cell phone business today (equipment or service), it is not entirely clear how it might draw the boundaries around its industry. Here's another example: consider the "home entertainment" industry. Not long ago this industry included manufacturers of various kinds of equipment such as stereos, TVs, VCRs, and DVD players. But within the last few years technology has now enabled a host of new types of firms to go after the consumer home entertainment dollar. These include new equipment manufacturers as well as content providers: video game manufacturers, internet-based gaming sites, downloadable music, and video on demand from cable and other services. How to define the boundaries of an industry can be complicated. How you define the industry you are interested in analyzing will affect the kinds of conclusions drawn from the industry analysis.

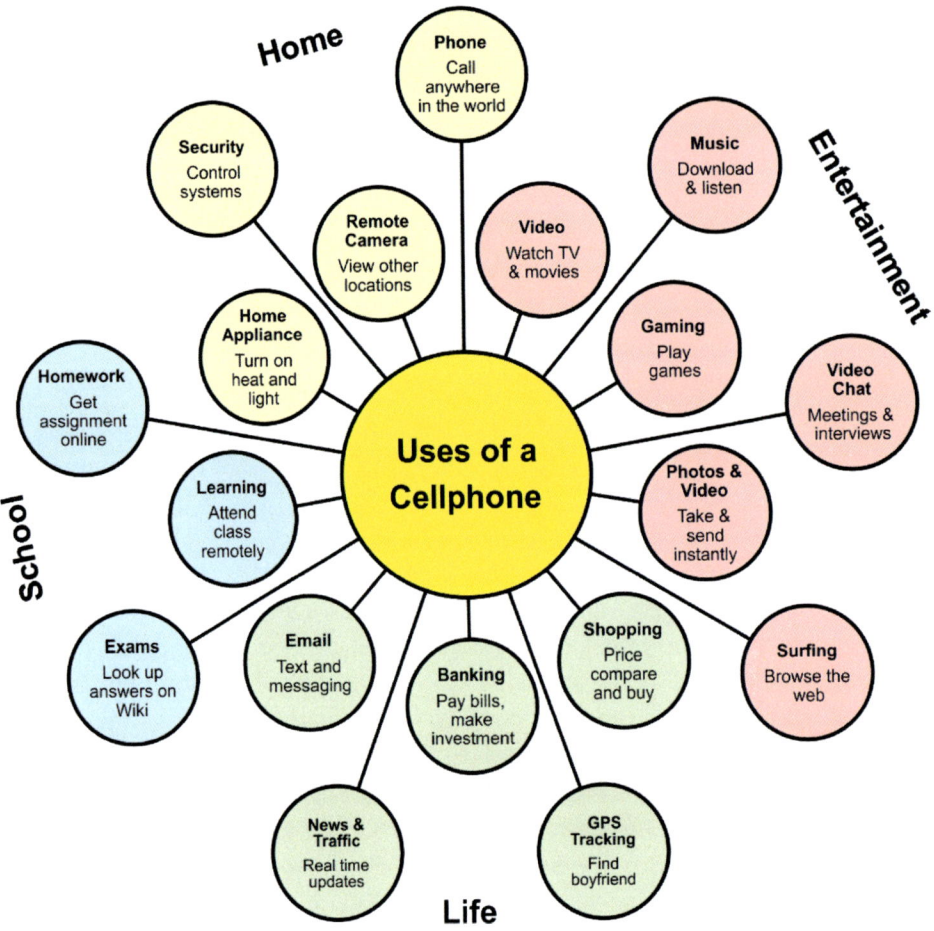

Figure 4.4
Industries May Be Hard to Define

As we shall see, an industry definition is very important to come to grips with. Broadly defined industries will usually require companies to engage in a variety of value-creating activities that depend upon developing broad and deep resource positions in order to be successful. Broadly defined industries usually encounter international competition or require international development, which of course place additional demands on companies. Narrowly defined industries, in contrast, allow companies to focus their efforts and resource investments more carefully. So the definition of the industry has real implications for the boundaries of the firm, the kinds of capabilities it has to develop, and the competitors it will encounter.

Basic information on virtually any industry can be obtained from the internet, library, or data search engines. Start with locating the NAICS code (North American Industry Classification System) for the industry. An NAICS code (formerly known as a SIC or Standard Industrial Classification Code) is generated by the U.S. government in an effort to

\	Figure 4.5
	NAICS Codes for Office Supplies Industry
Code	Classification
45	Retail trade
453	Miscellaneous store retailers
4532	Office supplies, stationery, gift stores
45321	*Office supplies & stationery stores*
45322	Gift, novelty & souvenir stores

132

gather, track, and publish data on specific industries. The code can vary from two to seven digits; the more digits, the more specific the industry classification. Figure 4.5 illustrates the NAICS classifications in which the office supplies industry (code 45321) is found, where Office Depot and Staples compete.

There are two relatively simple means available to properly identify industries using this system. The first is to consult the list of NAICS codes available from the U.S. government.[17] The second is to locate either your company or a public company that might be a direct competitor to your business (e.g. via *Dun & Bradstreet,* or *Nexis*) and then use their NAICS code to look up overall data on the industry.

At an aggregated national level the data gathered on a firm's industry has some value; however, it is the rare business that draws customers equally from all parts of the United States. Most of the data available will be on a national basis, but provides little understanding of the local, regional, or territory-specific competitive environment. The national industry may be doing very poorly while in a local area there may be few competitors or the industry is doing very well. For example, across the U.S. there is an average of one coffee shop for every 10,107 people; but in San Francisco there is one coffee shop for every 2,297 people. California is caffeined out! So effective analysis requires a definition of the industry that is broad enough to be inclusive of all potential competitors, but not so broad as to negate effective evaluation. Ferreting out important details like this is one part of the art of strategic management.

STEEPG – THE GENERAL ENVIRONMENT

It is important to recognize that every industry is surrounded by an array of outside forces in the general environment that can impact the growth of the industry and the nature of competition. These driving forces are conditions and trends in the general environment that no company can change, but that every company must incorporate into its planning. Driving forces can have a variety of significant effects on an industry and the competition within it:
- Increase or decrease demand
- Increase or decrease supply or supply alternatives
- Create opportunity to provide greater value to customers
- Create higher costs for suppliers or buyers
- Create higher costs for rivals
- Lower barriers to entry and elevate the threat of new entrants
- Create a wider pool of potential substitutes

These possible effects need to be figured into your analysis, because they suggest ways in which the nature of the industry may change over time.

Consider driving forces as equivalent to trying to drive on a really steep slope in a car or a four-wheel drive vehicle. No matter where you're trying to go, the grade is so steep that it will affect your direction and your speed, and if it is steep enough you may not get where you're trying to go. Therefore an easy way to remember these forces is by using the acronym STEEPG, which is the combination of the first letters of each of the driving forces: social, technological, economic, environmental, political/legal, and global. Figure 4.6 provides a detailed list that categorizes types of driving forces in the general environment, with key dimensions

Strategy Acronym: STEEPG

Driving Forces

S   Social
T   Technological
E   Economic
E   Environmental
P   Political
G   Global

for each category. While a comprehensive study of the various dimensions of these forces could take up an entire book by itself, we will highlight a few of these more carefully below to provide a sense of how powerful they may be.

Figure 4.6
STEEPG: Driving Forces in the External Environment

Social
Demographic
- population size & trends
- age structure
- geographic distribution
- ethnic composition & segment growth
- income distribution

Psychographic & cultural
- lifestyle
- entertainment
- convenience
- women in workforce
- work/home balance

Technology
- discoveries in basic science
- governmental support for R&D
- broader availability of new technologies

Environmental
- increasing pressure for sustainable approaches
- increasing attention to externalities of pollution
- greater scrutiny about accessing natural resources

Economic
- inflation & interest rates
- general economic conditions—growth vs. recession
- capital market availability
- unemployment rates
- exchange rates for currency translations

Political / Legal
- antitrust laws & philosophy of enforcement
- tax laws
- legislation on corporate governance and financial regulation
- SEC regulations
- labor issues—minimum wage, health insurance, pension coverage
- patent laws & changes
- social expectations that can lead to political and legal initiatives

Global
- political events
- consolidating institutions—OPEC, European Economic Community
- emerging markets—consumption, supply, finance
- cultural sensitivities—moderating vs. escalating
- terrorism and security issues

Social. Social driving forces are of two varieties: 1) demographic, and 2) psychographic, or cultural. Basic demographic structure and changes can have a dramatic impact on the nature of competition within industries. The clearest example of this impact is illustrated by the often-discussed "baby boomers," which refers to U.S. citizens born in the years 1946-1964 (Figure 4.7a). During this time U.S. birth rates spiked, creating a large new demographic segment defined by age. As this segment has aged through the decades, it has dramatically affected demand in an array of industries, including baby food, soft drinks, education, real estate, vacation homes, automobiles, investments, and now retirement planning. Now examine panel (b) of Figure 4.7. Although boomers have demographically dominated the workforce for decades, look at the rapidly-rising impact of the millennial generation in the marketplace.[18] How do you think this will impact the provisions of goods and services in the years to come?

Basic demography tells an important story, but it is the *combination* of demographics and the "psychographic," or cultural, factors that have affected industry growth, decline, and competition. For example, the first minivan was introduced by Chrysler in the 1980s, just as baby boomers were entering the lifestyle years of having their own families with young children. In contrast to many other automobile manufacturers, Chrysler sensed the opportunity for a new kind of passenger vehicle after conducting psychographic customer research rather than traditional demographic studies. They identified lifestyle needs of potential buyers.[19] During the last decade the changing combination of demo- and psycho-graphics has led to the proliferation of app-driven services and new ways of reaching customers.

Other major cultural factors are worth mentioning. 56 percent of women in America are in the workforce by 2021. Where this has resulted in a family with two working adults, it has had an economic effect in the form of higher disposable income per family and has led to the dramatic changes in industries as diverse as daycare and luxury vacations. On the other hand 32% of all U.S. children (and 57% of African-American children) live in single-parent homes,[20] which considerably impacts available income and time for a range of economic activities.

Technology. In the example mentioned earlier about the home entertainment industry, technology advances *outside* an industry can considerably impact companies and competition *in* the industry. Microchip design, fiber optics, file compression algorithms, and many

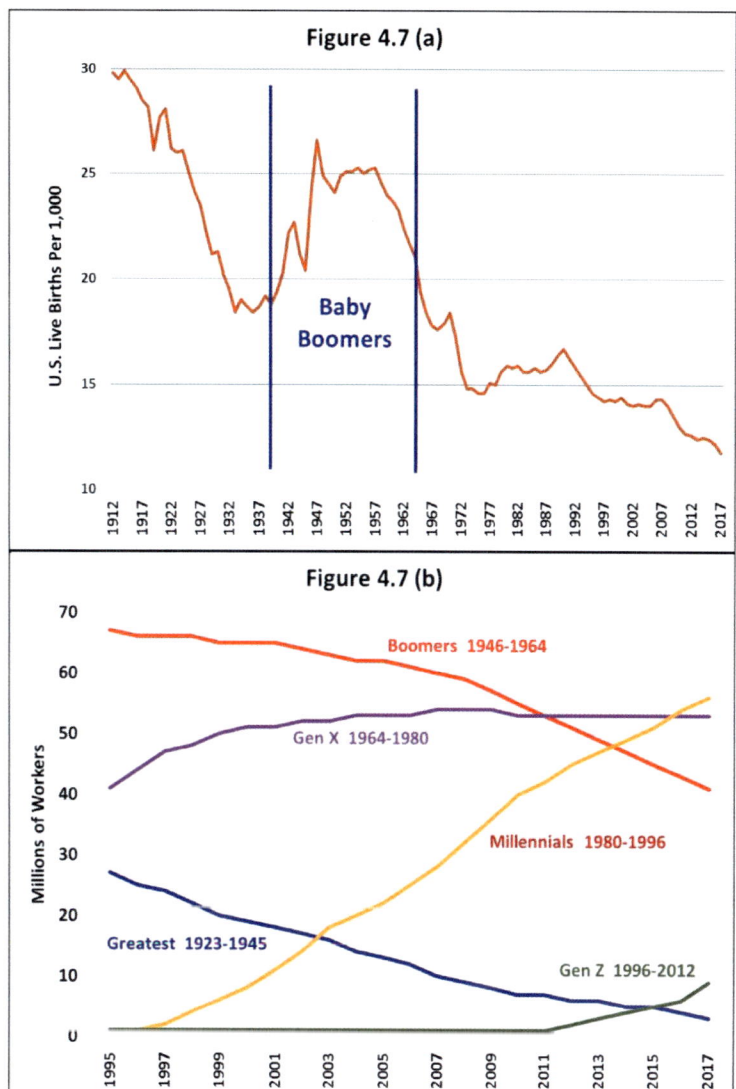

other developments have enabled new companies to begin competing with the traditional equipment manufacturers. These types of technological developments most often originate in other firms outside the industry or are discoveries made in science and research laboratories. Yet the new developments will diffuse throughout the economy and be used productively within many different industries. This can change the nature of competition.

Environmental. Environmental factors are increasingly seen as driving forces in many industries today. It might seem that these effects would be most pronounced in basic manufacturing and in the kinds of suppliers that manufacturers rely upon for raw materials. So we read about pollution control equipment requirements on smokestacks and in runoff from factories that use large amounts of water. However, environmental concerns are expressed in ways that affect us in our daily lives, as well. For example, Hewlett Packard and other companies that provide toner cartridges now include recycling instructions and mail-back envelopes in every package they sell. Hotels which have embraced water-saving practices (low pressure shower heads, re-usable towels) are in greater demand. The Environmental Protection Agency recently issued a report clearing the way for lawn mowers, watercraft, and other small gas-powered engines below 50 horsepower to meet tougher emissions standards.[21] Engineering these more stringent standards into small engines will raise the cost of manufacturing these products and we will likely see higher prices in stores. On the plus side, of course, our back yards and lakes will have much cleaner air as a result!

Political. Political and legal forces can come and go, and that uncertainty can present challenges. During the 1990s there was relatively less attention on antitrust issues than has been the case at other times. On the other hand, a high level of mergers and acquisitions by U.S. firms during the same decade led to the issuance of new Financial Accounting and Standards Boards (FASB) regulations in 2001 that eliminated "pooling of interests" as an acceptable method of accounting for business combinations. When this method had been used, investors often had difficulty telling who was buying whom or determining how to evaluate the transactions. Instead, FASB favored the "purchase method" of accounting for mergers. With the purchase method, one company is identified as the buyer and records the assets of the company being acquired on its books at the price it actually paid. This led to greater transparency for investors. Other more comprehensive, frame-breaking pieces of legislation directly affecting business practices include the Sarbanes-Oxley Act (SOX) in 2002 and Dodd-Frank in 2010 following the financial markets crisis. The SOX legislative initiative responded to violations of financial reporting and imposed stiff new demands on companies and their auditors to ensure that published financial statements are accurate. Dodd-Frank added reams of additional regulation on financial services companies. In 2018 President Trump imposed tariffs on imported washers, dryers, and solar gear. This prompted an immediate response by foreign manufacturer LG to lift its prices, making a more price-competitive U.S. market. The President announced further steep tariffs on imported steel, aluminum, and other goods, largely to level the playing field with Chinese competitors exporting to the U.S. Many economists believe such political moves have decreased GDP growth and thereby negatively affected corporate investment.

In addition to explicit political and legal forces, we add a final dimension to this category that has been increasingly important for companies to pay attention to: social expectations that could become political and legal initiatives. SOX is an example of a social concern about business that was institutionalized into a body of law, largely because companies were often perceived as acting in ways detrimental to their shareholders. There is an entire class of social issues that falls into this gray area, such as environmental concerns, offshoring jobs to countries with lower wage rates, or privacy and data protection issues. A survey by *McKinsey Quarterly* found an overwhelming majority of readers felt that corporations needed to take on a wider role in dealing with these issues, something that goes beyond simply producing returns for their investors.[22] The implied social contract that businesses have today with the communities and societies within which they exist has become a standard that is embraced by the public and it can result in greater regulation that affects how industries function.

Managing in Markets: Question for Class Discussion

In 2010 Live Nation merged with Ticketmaster, becoming vertically-integrated from concert promotion to ticket sales. By 2017 the four largest concert promoters accounted for 67% of the business. In 2019 the Justice Department pressed Live Nation into a "consent decree" agreement that prevents the company from forcing venues to use Ticketmaster for the concerts it promotes. What do you think? Should government intrude in markets to dictate corporate behavior?

FIVE-FORCES ANALYSIS

An analysis of the industry is possible once the industry has been defined and we gain a better understanding of the STEEPG driving forces in the general environment. Five forces analysis and competitive mapping are then the most useful techniques to analyze any industry.

Figure 4.8
Five Forces of Industry Structure

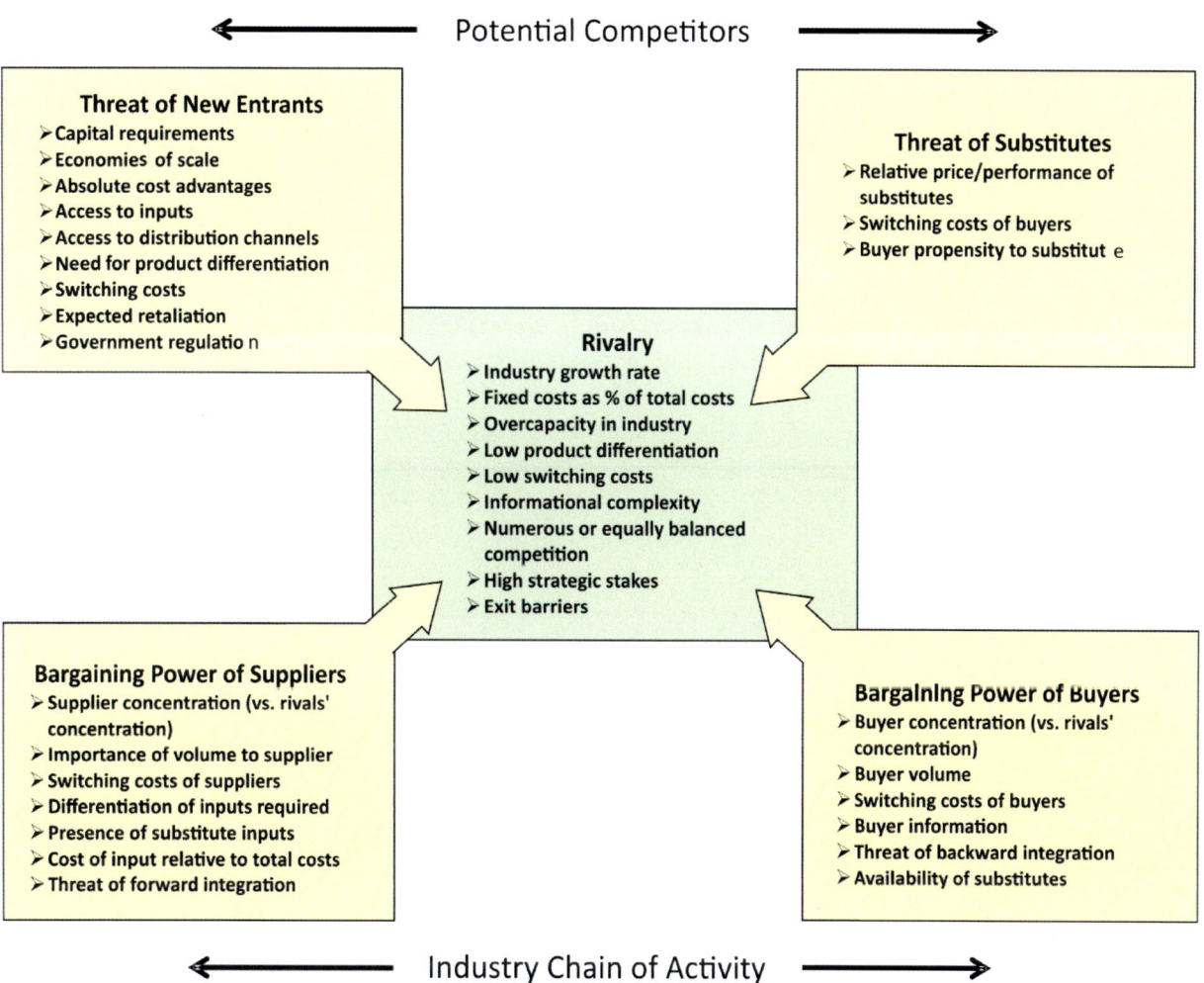

The Harvard Business School professor we mentioned earlier, Michael Porter, developed the five-forces model in the 1970s to examine the five main structural elements in any industry; Figure 4.8 provides a summary of these forces. This model expands the way we think about competition. To the untrained eye, one might view only direct competitors as the primary dimension affecting the economic performance of a company. However, the five-forces model explicitly acknowledges the roles that new entrants, substitutes, suppliers, and buyers also play in this equation, in addition to rivalry. In the process of considering all five forces, every effort should be made to evaluate how each force influences the industry to be either more or less profitable. This is because when each of these five forces is strong, it will tend to reduce the profitability in the industry. Five-forces analysis is also used to understand how one industry compares to another regarding the opportunity to earn above-average profits.

Threat of New Entrants

Industries that tend to be profitable are attractive to companies outside the industry because they see the possibility of entering the industry and participating in the profit-making. New entrants may take the form of either startup companies going into business for the first time, or existing companies that decide to grow by acquiring their way in to the industry. Existing companies are the most challenging new competitors when they enter an industry since they may already possess a set of capabilities and financial resources that allow them to enter in a big way.

Regardless of whether they are a start-up or an existing company, new entrants will tend to do two things that can hurt the profitability of incumbent firms: expand capacity and steal their customers. New firms often expand industry capacity as they seek to sell goods and services to the same customers. Expanded capacity has the tendency to lead to downward pricing pressure on industry competitors for two reasons: 1) each company wants to ensure that its existing capacity continues to be fully utilized; and 2) greater availability generally leads buyers to compare products and look for bargains. Competition for the same customers will lead to higher levels of marketing, sales, and promotional expenses by all competitors as the requirements for differentiation continually increase (i.e., the "why should I buy from you?" question). So unless new entrants to an industry can significantly expand overall industry revenue, the profit pool that is available in any given year will be spread across a greater number of competitors, on average reducing the potential profits available to any one company. Therefore, the combination of a greater number of competitors, lower prices, and increased expenses diminish the potential for the existing firms in the industry to generate revenue and profits.

Figure 4.9
Threat of New Entrants

➢ Capital requirements
➢ Economies of scale
➢ Absolute cost advantages
➢ Access to inputs
➢ Access to distribution channels
➢ Need for product differentiation
➢ Switching costs
➢ Expected retaliation
➢ Government regulation

This threat of new entrants is considerably reduced if substantive barriers to entry can be erected. Existing competitors attempt to reduce the threat of new entrants by building entry barriers to raise the costs of entering the industry. Higher entry costs then prompt potential entrants to question whether they can afford to enter the industry, or make sufficient profits once they have entered. On the flip side, current competitors must balance the cost of erecting barriers against the potential downside of additional competitors. There are several varieties of barriers to entry that affect the threat of new entrants (Figure 4.9), and we discuss each of these next.

Capital requirements. Starting up a new business in an industry generally involves a significant commitment of capital. For example, in a manufacturing industry a new entrant would need to invest in a manufacturing facility, production assembly line, tools and dies, as well as build inventories of raw materials and finished goods. Depending on the industry, this can involve a huge outlay. The restaurant industry experiences a very high level of new entrants, and yet establishing even one restaurant location can be costly. A typical stand-alone

Chick-Fil-A outlet might cost as much as $2 million or more to build out and equip. By the beginning of 2022 Best Buy had 1,159 stores worldwide, with an average gross investment in each store of $10 million in property and $4.8 million in inventory. If a company competes against Best Buy in the home electronics retailing industry, the initial investment for just one store is huge! In our experience, students often believe that it would be fairly easy to set up an internet business by developing a web site fairly quickly. However, the kinds of web-based businesses that promise the potential for sustainable advantage will usually involve making an initial investment in excess of $750,000 to develop a sophisticated web site, back-end database, and the programming that smoothly integrates the two.

Economies of scale. In some industries the ability to compete will depend on whether a company can produce its product or service at a cost that is low enough to offer low competitive prices. Low costs are sometimes achieved because companies produce on a large scale where the benefits of volume translate directly to unit production cost reductions. Economies of scale characterize many industries, including automobiles, packaged consumer products, and computer manufacturing. They are often achieved as a direct result of huge investments in physical infrastructure, which raises the initial capital requirements (e.g., barrier to entry) mentioned above.

Absolute cost advantages. New entrants may be deterred from entering an industry if the incumbent firms in the industry enjoy a cost advantage that comes from having been in the industry for a while. The usual type of absolute cost advantage derives from what is known as the experience curve. Here cost reductions per unit produced are based upon cumulative production over time (in contrast to economies of scale, in which unit cost reductions are associated with volume during a fixed time interval). With greater experience the company learns about subtle and not-so-subtle new procedures that can contribute to cost reductions. Figure 4.10 diagrams a classic experience curve relationship. It is important to note that the entry barrier of experience holds only if the learning that comes through experience cannot be appropriated easily by new entrants. Hiring away a competitor's employees, purchasing machinery or equipment that incorporates the refined production practices, or somehow copying what the competitor is doing can help a competitor to overcome a low cost advantage.

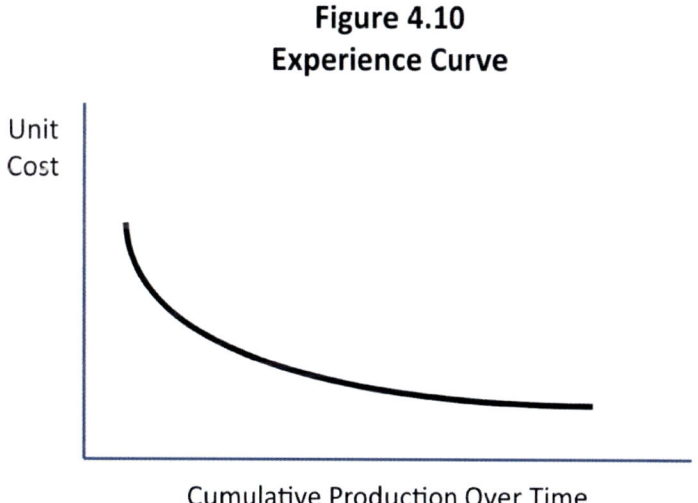

**Figure 4.10
Experience Curve**

Cumulative Production Over Time

A second type of absolute cost advantage occurs when an existing competitor has developed a unique and proprietary design for a product or manufacturing process that may be obvious to others, but which is protected through patents. Here a new entrant would have to invent a new way to produce a particular product, and this will involve significantly greater expense.

Access to inputs. Barriers to entry exist when raw materials or important inputs are not available to potential new entrants. A group wishing to start a new hamburger restaurant needs a good-quality, high-traffic location. However, the best street corner locations in your community may already be occupied by other businesses (or by McDonald's itself!). Once these prime corner locations are occupied, then there are simply no more available. Moving from the mundane to the sublime, the De Beers Company has nearly exclusive access to South African diamond mines, making it exceedingly difficult for any other potential competitor to gain access to the raw materials. Over the next decade electric vehicle manufacturers will require increasing amounts of lithium for their batteries. But anxiety is growing about lithium supply because its production is dominated by only a handful of companies worldwide: Albemarle, Sociedad Química y Minera de Chile (SQM), and Chinese companies Tianqi Lithium and Ganfeng Lithium. Some Chinese auto manufacturers, with support from the Chinese government, have been in discussions to buy stakes in suppliers in order to ensure future supply. In 2021 Australian mining company Orocobre merged with its rival Galaxy Resources to create Allkem, the fifth largest lithium miner in the world and ensure its long term raw material supply.

Access to distribution channels. Companies that desire to enter an industry may discover that they are unable to easily gain access to customers. If a new company wanted to introduce a cola or lemon-flavored soda into the soft drink industry, for example, it would need to find a bottler to mix its concentrate with water and CO_2, can it, and distribute it. However, the major bottlers are contractually locked into long-term deals with existing soft drink competitors and are prevented from bottling competing cola or lemon soda products. In other cases, access to distribution may be difficult because prospective customers simply place limits on the number of companies with whom they do business. In the food business, supermarkets have limited shelf space and are only interested in carrying proven products that will sell quickly. Therefore, supermarkets charge exorbitant fees ("slotting allowances") to manufacturers who seek to sell place their new products on the store's shelves. For Championship Chili, mentioned at the beginning of this chapter, this was a key barriers to entry problem in its startup. In the financial industry, companies often provide a limited set of mutual fund alternatives to employees for investing through their retirement programs, so other firms seeking to offer new mutual funds may be excluded from consideration.

Switching costs. Customer resistance to new entrants may also arise due to the costs to switch to the new competitor's product or service (both real and perceived). The costs involved in changing buying habits include the real costs of time, price, new buying patterns, inventory turnover, and customer service.

Real switching costs can take many forms. For instance, those individuals who live near and fly out of Atlanta often fly on Delta, and by doing so accumulate mileage under Delta's miles program. This program encourages customers to remain loyal to the airline, and creates real switching costs for those customers when they consider flying on another airline. A Platinum traveler on Delta has priority boarding, a high chance for upgrading to first class on many flights, and a reduced membership fee for the Delta Room Club. Each of these items has a real, tangible value that would have to be overcome by a competitor for a traveler to switch to another airline.

Perceived costs are important, too – including reputation, history, market image, and comfort. Many folks who began using personal computers in the early 1980s were forced to learn a continuing series of newer word processing, spreadsheet, and systems packages throughout the years. Switching from Edline to WordStar to VolksWriter Deluxe to WordPerfect to Microsoft Word was a painful, slow process. Today it is difficult to convince many people to switch to using

Google docs or other online shared programs, as both the real and perceived costs to switch from Word appear enormous.

Consider the switching costs related to changing soft drinks. There are no real switching costs involved. Consumers do not have to learn how to open the can or bottle in a new way, swallowing is unchanged, the purchase price is virtually identical, and availability is not an issue. For the retailer who stocks soft drinks, the same size cans and bottles require no new handling in their warehouses or stores, and promotional displays are built the same way as before. However, there are enormous *perceived* switching costs involved in convincing a Coke drinker to move to Pepsi or vice versa. Take a look at a typical advertisement by these two rivals. The ads focus exclusively on perceptions and lifestyle, not on quality ingredients or packaging. Similarly, for most retailers the strength of long-term supply relationships with Coca-Cola and Pepsi may make it difficult to switch out one or the other to stock some other new concoction instead. Or if you have your entire music library on iTunes, imagine your angst in being forced to convert it over to the android platform after you have dropped and cracked your iPhone.

Need for product differentiation. In most industries, existing competitors have carefully crafted a brand image and reputation that helps generate a continuing customer base. One of the key elements of strategy is the positioning of the business in a way that differentiates it in the mind of customers relative to the businesses' competitors. Similarly, in established industries new entrants most often find they must effectively differentiate each of their products or services. Often this will involve major marketing and sales expenditures on advertising, promotion, sales force development, and penetration in order to create a unique positioning in the minds of customers.[23]

Government regulation. "Big Brother" – in the form of federal, state, and local government – can have an enormous effect on the propensity for new firms to enter an industry. In order to enter the food manufacturing industry, every new entrant must at a minimum be in compliance with FDA rules; it may also be required to have all its products, packaging, and processes approved in advance and regularly inspected by USDA. Getting a cosmetologist or barber license in the State of North Carolina in 2022 requires 1500+ hours of training and then a licensing exam. In starting a restaurant the new business must meet all state and local health regulations, submit to regular inspections, and post those results in the public view. All of this takes significant time and expense. Every industry has its own unique set of regulations, required licenses, and personnel to ensure compliance. If the costs of starting a new business are onerous, then the rate of new entrants will be dramatically reduced. Despite the enormous efficiency that nuclear power can provide, new power stations in the United States have been at a standstill since the late 1970s. The primary reason has been government regulation and compliance. Those wishing to build, operate, acquire fuel rods, and then dispose of the rods must overcome an almost Herculean set of regulations. The impact of the government regulation has crushed the growth of this and other industries in the United States.

When new start-up companies are possible new entrants, regulation by various countries' governments can be a significant constraining force. Whereas in the United States you can organize and start up a new LLC in minutes for only a couple hundred dollars, government regulations in some other countries are onerous and can significantly impede foreign new-venture competition. For example, in Greece new companies must complete fifteen separate steps that take thirty-eight days on average, at a cost of nearly 25% of average personal income.

Expected retaliation. New entrants in any established industry should not expect existing competitors to sit idly by and watch another company suddenly show up and start competing for their customers. Retaliation by existing competitors is increased when the following conditions exist: 1) there is a history of such retaliation in the industry; 2) the existing competitors have deep pockets and plenty of resources to devote to more intense competition; 3) the existing competitors have already sunk significant costs in building infrastructure or establishing a market position, and a loss of business would create financial pressures; and 4) the industry is not growing quickly, meaning that any business for a new entrant must come from an existing competitor. In April 2006, low-cost carrier JetBlue Airlines announced that they would begin daily nonstop service from Charlotte to New York City's LaGuardia Airport. Tickets went on sale for the equivalent of half the current market price of the major airlines flying out of Charlotte. Within two weeks all of the major airlines announced dramatic fare reductions to NYC in a bid to retain their customers. When Tiger Woods broke into the professional golf circuit and started winning tournaments by out-driving other pros off the tee and showing pinpoint short-club accuracy, what did the other pros do? They increased their physical training regimens and began spending longer hours in practice. His entry changed the game.

Threat of Substitutes

Substitutes are products or services that perform the same function or meet the same need as the products or services in the industry under study, but which are produced using different raw materials and inputs. The classic example that economists use is coffee, tea, milk, and sodas. The competitors to Starbucks or Folgers would be other brands of coffee, whereas Lipton tea and Coca-Cola would be viewed as substitutes. Over the last twenty years bottled water, as a substitute, has significantly impacted the traditional soft-drink industry. In 2005 carbonated soft drinks experienced its first volume decline in U.S. sales in since the 1980s.[24] Between 2013-19 per capita consumption of bottled water increased by 38%, while that of soft drinks declined 12%.[25]

The availability of substitutes can have two impacts on industry competition and profitability. First, they establish a price ceiling for products and services in the industry; exceeding the ceiling would prompt customers to take flight to the substitute products that are available. Second, substitutes can prompt the competitors in an industry to ramp up their marketing and promotional efforts to stem the outflow of customers. Together these put pressure on competitors in the industry to keep prices low enough, enhance the performance of their products, and to spend more to attract and retain customers – all of which can reduce revenue or profits.

Three factors determine how strong the threat of substitutes will be for an industry. These include: 1) the relative price/performance of the substitute products; 2) the switching costs for the buyer to obtain and use the substitute; and 3) buyers' propensity to try substitute products or services. Substitution tends to increase when the substitute's price is equal to or lower than prices of incumbents *and* the value to the buyer is equal to or greater. In this case the value to buyers can sometimes be satisfied more economically by turning to the substitute-providing companies outside the industry. If the switching costs for buyers to move to substitutes are also fairly low, then even greater pressure is exerted on the competitors' ability to generate sales, as buyers then have even less reason to remain loyal. Think about the growth of tablets versus laptops computers recently. Although tablet users sacrifice some performance (e.g. ease of printing), the overall combination of price and performance has made these extremely attractive substitutes to an industry narrowly defined as "PCs and laptops."

Finally, although many buyers and consumers maintain loyalty to companies and brands, today there is a greater willingness to experiment and try alternatives. This may arise from a diminished relationship between companies and their customers, going far beyond product characteristics. Figure 4.11 offers some examples of increasing substitution.

Whereas the threat of new entrants will usually depend on the attractiveness of the industry, an increase in the threat of substitutes depends on the dynamics of *other* industries. Competitors should watch for warning signals that pressure from substitutes may be increasing. For example, in the early 1990s the soft-drink aisle in supermarkets contained beverages on one side and snacks and chips on the other side. By the late 1990s the aisle had become the "beverage" aisle, with soft drinks on one side and bottled waters on the other. It was obvious that consumers were flocking to bottled waters. Major soft-drink companies all made the move to add bottled water to their product offerings. Warning signs that companies in substitute product industries might be getting more aggressive include production capacity increases, significant accumulations of cash, merger and acquisition activity, as well as significant technological changes. The addition of production capacity signals that substitute producers might want to get more aggressive in pricing and marketing in order to fully utilize available capacity. In addition when profits are growing, such companies might consider investing additional marketing dollars to broaden their customer base.

Figure 4.11
Threat of Substitutes

Factors Increasing Substitution	Examples
Better relative price and performance combination	Making airline reservations online, compared to using a travel agency.
	Listening flexibility using Spotify, versus your fixed purchased list on iTunes.
Low switching costs	Consumers buy electricity for their homes from wind farms, by merely signing a form with their power company.
Propensity to try new alternatives	Relying on Uber or Lyft, compared to owning and maintaining your own car.

Bargaining Power of Buyers

Buyers affect the profitability of the industry's competitors with their purchase choices. The profitability levels in any industry are determined by the bargaining power that buyers have in purchasing goods and services offered. Buyers may affect profitability by demanding that competitors spend money to deliver additional valued dimensions such as enhanced product quality, extended payment terms, promotional support, and other services. Buyers will often pit competitors against one another in order to negotiate the best terms possible. The ability of buyers to extract various economic concessions depends on the variety of factors shown in Figure 4.12.

Figure 4.12
Bargaining Power of Buyers

- Buyer concentration (vs. rivals' concentration)
- Buyer volume
- Switching costs of buyers
- Buyer information
- Threat of backward integration
- Availability of substitutes

Buyer concentration. It is important to remember that an industry analysis is an examination of the *structure* of the entire industry. This reminder is very important when we talk about the bargaining power of buyers that may result from buyer concentration. Here we are not discussing the bargaining power that any one buyer (such as Walmart) may have with its suppliers; instead we are referring to the structure of buyers as an entire group. A high level of buyer concentration means that there are just a few major buyers in an industry, and each one on average commands a significant share of the market. Under these circumstances competitors have few meaningful alternative places to sell their products. Furthermore, the loss of any one buyer to a competitor would create a dramatic shift in the industry: the company would lose significant sales and market share, which could be entirely taken up by a direct competitor. These conditions make it likely that buyers would be able to exert significant pressure on the companies in this industry to either reduce prices or provide additional services, or both.

Buyer concentration can be measured in one of a couple ways (Figure 4.13). A simplistic measure of concentration is the concentration ratio, calculated as the percentage of market share in the industry owned by the largest buyer firms. The U.S. government often looks closely at the concentration ratio of the largest four firms, known as CR4. If this measure is less than 40 percent, then it suggests the industry is very competitive, with no buyer owning a very large market position.

Concentration ratios are the "quick and dirty" method for determining concentration, but the measure is incomplete because it captures only the largest firms in the industry. Instead, the Herfindahl-Hirschman Index (HHI) is often used, because it provides a more complete portrayal of industry concentration. The HHI uses the market shares of *all* the firms in an industry to calculate a measure that can range from 0 to 10,000. The FTC uses HHI as a guideline for evaluating mergers. An HHI between 1,000 and 1,800 signals moderate concentration, while an HHI exceeding 1,800 reflects an industry that is highly concentrated. In the opening story of this chapter, the merger of Staples and Office Depot would have produced an HHI greater than 5,000, while in the second story the HHI for the supermarket buyers in the city where Championship Chili started up was greater than 2,600. In these two cases, companies selling to these highly concentrated groups would be subject to intense bargaining power of buyers.

**Figure 4.13
Calculating Industry Concentration**

Concentration Ratio

The concentration ratio uses the formula:

$$CR_m = s_1 + s_2 + s_3 + \ldots + s_m$$

where m is the number of firms to be included, and s_j is the market share of the jth firm.

Evaluation of CR_4:
  < 40   very competitive industry
  40-70   moderately concentrated
  > 70   highly concentrated

Herfindahl-Hirschman Index (HHI)

The HHI uses the formula:

$$HHI = s_1^2 + s_2^2 + s_3^2 + \ldots + s_n^2$$

where n is the number of firms in the industry, and s_j is the market share of the jth firm.

Evaluation of HHI:
  < 1000   very competitive industry
  1001-1800   moderately concentrated
  > 1800   highly concentrated

Increases in HHI by more than 100-200 raise serious anti-trust concerns in markets where HHI is greater than 1800.

The impact of concentration is best evaluated on a relative basis. When buyers as a group are significantly more concentrated than are firms in the industry you are studying, then concentration can surely impact the attractiveness of the industry. So when the HHI for supermarkets is 2600 but the HHI for food manufacturers might be only 750, the buyers as a group can make demands and cause the food manufacturing industry to be less profitable, and therefore less attractive. But if the relative concentration is balanced – for example, where both buyers and producers have "highly concentrated" HHI levels of 2100 – the relative bargaining power between the two groups is balanced.

Buyer volume. Similar to buyer concentration, if buyers purchase a high percentage of goods and services produced by companies in the industry, it means that the producing companies cannot afford to lose that business. Under these circumstances buyers have the potential to demand additional services, changes, and/or price concessions. 63% of appliance manufacturer sales are to retailers, and among retailers only three chains account for roughly 72% of this volume. Not only is appliance retailing concentrated, but they also account for a critically large share of the manufacturers' business.

Switching costs of buyers. In a similar manner to the earlier discussion about switching costs under the "Threat of New Entrants" section, as switching costs (both real and perceived) go down, the relative power of the buyers is increased. With lower switching costs there is less to keep buyers loyal to incumbent producers. Switching costs tend to decline as the standardization of an industry's products or services increases. For this reason producers in many industries seek novel improvements in their offerings.

A cautionary note is in order here. Remember once again that this is a discussion about *industry* structure. So when we discuss a dimension like switching costs, keep in mind we are not referring to the ability of just one buyer to switch. We are referring to the ability of a significant block of buyers to switch. This then becomes a *structural* condition of the producer-buyer relationship which enables a critical mass of buyers to seek more from the producers. This puts pressure on all rival producers to lower their prices, develop new doohickeys that will satisfy customers, provide them with extra services to complement the existing business, etc. All of these efforts cost the rival producers, and thus lower the profits they are able to make.

Buyer information. The advance of technology has dramatically increased the power of buyers. Whereas most buyers were previously limited in their knowledge of competitive pricing, product availability, and comparisons of the features of competitive products, the advent of technology has created an empowered buyer. Until the mid-1980s, for example, food manufacturers used to conduct their own research on product sales and market shares in supermarkets using third-party research firms like A. C. Nielsen, and would then present their  findings to supermarket buyers. With the advent of UPC scanning technology and personal computers, supermarket buyers now capture data instantaneously about sales in their stores, and have more information than do manufacturers. The rollout of enhanced technology (such as RFID) allows even greater information about sales, inventory levels, product locations, and more. Information asymmetry refers to a situation where either buyers or sellers have more complete information. If buyers are in this position, their bargaining power can increase.

Threat of backward integration. Buyers may decide to simply produce the product or service that was previously being purchased from someone in the industry. Frustration with the unwillingness of rivals in the industry to provide further concessions, an excess amount of buyer cash, desire to control the whole process, ego, and a host of other factors may encourage certain buyers to integrate its business backward by developing or acquiring their own production capacity in the industry. This is particularly true if buying organizations observe that the competitive rivals in an industry are earning attractive levels of profits and returns. This is one reason why many supermarket chains now manufacture and stock their own "private label" food products. After failing to wring lower prices from their milk supplier Dean Foods, in 2018 Walmart opened its own milk processing plant. Kroger had earlier done the same thing, then Food Lion followed suit. With volume sown significantly, Dean Foods declared bankruptcy in 2020.[26]

Bargaining Power of Suppliers

Similar to buyers, suppliers can exert their own power upon the competitors in an industry. This power manifests itself in price pressures, availability issues, services provided, and speed of technological advancement. Figure 4.14 presents a list of factors impacting supplier power.

Supplier concentration. The same methods of analysis (HHI and CR4) are performed for supplier concentration as they are for the buyer concentration. As supply becomes more concentrated in just a few businesses, the more they will be able to control the interactions between themselves and the producers. Intel and AMD, for example, have manufactured a majority of the computer chips used as the "brain" in personal computers for the past three decades. This power has allowed them to set the pricing, availability, and features available to the many manufacturers of personal computers. In the same industry Microsoft's Windows operating system powers 89% of PCs and laptops worldwide. Because this supplier force of operating systems is so concentrated, with few real alternatives, it is no surprise that Microsoft can charge PC manufacturers much more for each licensed copy of Windows installed on PCs.

**Figure 4.14
Bargaining Power of Suppliers**

➢Supplier concentration (vs. rivals' concentration)
➢Importance of volume to supplier
➢Switching costs of suppliers
➢Differentiation of inputs required
➢Presence of substitute inputs
➢Cost of input relative to total costs
➢Threat of forward integration

Importance of volume to supplier. As the volume of material that businesses buy from the suppliers increases, the importance of the suppliers to the businesses increases. A common theme in the business press is one of reducing the number of suppliers and forging long-term relationships with just a few suppliers. While this does provide an element of control to the process, those suppliers are also in an increasingly powerful role relative to the company they supply.

Presence of substitute inputs. Businesses work very hard to develop their products with particular inputs going into the final product. In cases of supply disruption, raw material shortages, or supplier efforts to raise prices, the presence of effective substitutes will dampen the impact of that supplier's power. In 2019, for example, UPS announced that it would add more than 6,000 natural gas trucks to its delivery fleet. Natural gas provides that important combination of price and performance, and thus reduces the company's sole dependence on gasoline suppliers.

Cost of input relative to total costs. The power of suppliers increases as the cost of the input increases relative to the total cost of the product or service produced. If the suppliers' input represents 25% of the value of the total product produced, then suppliers will have significantly more leverage compared to an industry where the suppliers' part is worth only 1% of the final value of the product. This is especially true if substitutes for the input are not available.

Switching costs of suppliers. Once again, the cost to switch (both real and perceived) to other customers can be factored into the power of the supplier. When suppliers have customers across many industries to whom they can sell their inputs and raw materials, then it costs them less to forgo any one company buyer who becomes particularly demanding of pricing, terms or other dimensions. The more rivals in an industry tie their operations to certain types of supplies or highly specified inputs, the more power such suppliers have with these companies. In today's competitive environment, many companies are tying their operations very closely with select suppliers in order to get guaranteed just-in-time deliveries, advanced access to new technology, more favorable pricing, guaranteed prices, and first options on raw materials. Supplier management is a two-edged sword, though. The higher degree to which producers lock themselves in to suppliers, the greater leverage such suppliers will then have to exact economic concessions from the producers.

Threat of forward integration. Just as buyers have the ability to integrate backward to replace their rivals as suppliers, suppliers have the ability to integrate forward and become a competitor to the businesses that they may still supply. For years Honda produced small engines for many kinds of power equipment. Now they have integrated forward, also selling their own Honda-branded lines of lawn maintenance equipment and portable generators. In 2020 rappers Travis Scott, Yo Gotti, and Kendrick Lamar are all on the verge of gaining ownership of their masters from their record labels, and then establishing their own labels to stream their hits. They are able to pull this off because the "concentration" of wildly-successful rappers is high and there are few substitutes for their music.

Intensity of Rivalry

The intensity of competition among rivals varies from industry to industry. Although we often read that many organizations believe they are in a chaotic, intense, cost-conscious, highly competitive industry, the fact remains that not all industries experience the same level of intensity. Each industry should be evaluated with a set of criteria (Figure 4.15) that may then be used to understand the intensity of competition. Recall that it is important to first define the industry and the rivals in it. The most important rivals are those companies who are in direct competition with a company for its customers and for the

**Figure 4.15
Intensity of Rivalry**

➤ Industry growth rate
➤ Fixed costs as % of total costs
➤ Overcapacity in industry
➤ Low product differentiation
➤ Low switching costs
➤ Informational complexity
➤ Numerous or equally balanced competition
➤ High strategic stakes
➤ Exit barriers

same types of supplies or inputs to production. This may or may not be the industry as defined by the government or the popular press.

Industry growth rate. Industry growth rates range from negative to explosively positive. In growth markets all companies may grow and prosper, but in a stagnant or declining market companies will become extremely aggressive in either trying to grow their business or prevent declines. The simple fact is that slowing or negative industry growth rates lead to destructive patterns of corporate behavior and dramatically increase rivalry. Consider the emerging battle between the world's two largest internet companies, Alibaba and Tencent, both headquartered in China. As the growth in online users slowed in 2018, rivalry sharpened as each competed head-to-head in finance, payments, cloud computing, entertainment, bike sharing, meal delivery, and the convergence between online and offline retail sales.[27]

In contrast, "a rising tide lifts all boats." When an industry is enjoying fast growth in revenue dollars and units shipped, then an individual company may also increase sales without necessarily having to take it from a competitor.

Industry capacity. The sheer capacity of the industry has a significant effect upon industry rivalry. Throughout the 1980s, many cable and telecom firms spent billions laying fiber optic cable in a bid to take advantage of the cutting-edge needs of an expanding internet. Within several years the bubble burst as cable supply far outstripped demand. By 2001, utilization rates ran around 40 percent and prices dropped almost 80 percent. Cable operators needed competitively low rates in order to generate enough business to pay back the investment they made in laying the fiber optics.[28] The same dynamic is true in the auto industry. Here excess plant capacity as well as fixed union contracts represent huge financial burdens. So whenever there is a glitch in the economy, U.S. manufacturers repeatedly turn to intensely competitive "dealer rebate" and "72-month 0% financing" schemes in order to generate sales, keep the plants up and running, and maintaining employment of union workers.

Why is running at full capacity so important for every company? Recall from Chapter 2 how ROE is calculated. ROE depends on strong asset productivity, measured by how much revenue is generated using the existing set of corporate assets. There is nothing worse for a plant manager than dead silence on the factory floor!

Industries with too little capacity to meet the buying desires of customers will find that there is less intense rivalry relative to an industry where there is overcapacity. Where industry demand exceeds industry capacity, rivals do not need to turn to intensely competitive tactics. If we were to examine the narrow industry sub-segment of electric cars, for example, we would find that consumer demand far exceeds industry supply. Ten years ago while Ford was discounting F-150 pickups trucks and General Motors was discounting Impala four-door sedans, Toyota did not discount the Prius which sold close to MSRP (manufacturer's suggested retail price).[29] Now that Ford, GM, and others have increased manufacturing capacity to produce hybrid vehicles, the intensity of rivalry has increased in this segment.

Numerous or equally balanced rivals. Another means for evaluating the competitive intensity in the industry is to examine the source of sales in the industry. A widely fragmented market with lots of competitors leads to practices that are detrimental to the success of any one company. Dry cleaners appear on many corners of populated areas in the United States. Price changes and competitive moves to differentiate oneself in this industry are quickly copied by all the other companies in the immediate area. Similarly, rivalry can become intense even in fairly concentrated industries with only a few major players, such as the personal computer manufacturing industry. Here price changes and moves to differentiate one's self are also quickly copied by competitors in an effort to maintain market share. The key point here is that relative equality among competitors – whether in a fragmented or concentrated industry – tends to make them fight against each other to a greater extent as each seeks to develop a superior position.

Product or service differentiation. The degree of separation between the offerings of different companies has a significant impact upon the intensity of rivalry. In industries where competitors have been able to establish a significant level of differentiation among their products, the intensity of rivalry is sharply reduced. But where differentiation is not present, each company competes very hard to acquire and retain members.

Take a look at the streaming business in 2022. There are numerous competitors vying for this space – Netflix, Amazon, Disney+, HBO Max, Paramount+, Hulu, Apple, and other services. Most all have relationships with major movie studios to secure content, and most also now produce their own content. All have easy-to-use apps that can be downloaded to a phone, tablet, smart TV, or connected device. Lacking substantive differentiation in their activity sets, "the cost to build, the cost to market and the cost to retain customers will all be going up in a competitive market."[30]

Switching costs. Similar to each of the other four competitive threats, switching costs have an impact on the intensity of rivalry. When products or services are nearly identical and switching costs to buyers are low, competitors fight fiercely to keep their existing customers and attract new customers. This leads to rivals expending significant resources in marketing, promotions, price concessions, innovation, and other costly initiatives that reduce their profitability.

Exit barriers. High costs to exit a business cause competitors to behave in ways that are often counterproductive to both company and industry performance. Exit barriers can exist in the form of fixed manufacturing plants, long-term contracts, costly infrastructure, ownership of basic inputs, governmental limitations, or specialized and unique assets. These may all sometimes be complicated by declining markets in which there are simply no buyers. Rather than write off millions of dollars of manufacturing assets, companies will often continue to operate plants at less than capacity and lose money.

However, exit barriers can also be perceived, and perceived barriers can be just as compelling. These include a long history in the industry, prior decisions or statements by senior management that would look questionable in the face of exit, nostalgia, a desire to protect a community and the employees, as well as a stubborn desire to prove that the business is still viable. The combination of real and perceived exit barriers causes competitors to fight very hard to maintain their business. Eastern Airlines fought a losing battle in a post-regulated world in the 1980s. The major airlines have extremely high fixed costs and a strong need to fill seats on each plane that takes off. As new, low-cost carriers entered the market and other established airlines were able to negotiate cost-effective contracts with their workers, Eastern suffered with a pre-deregulation high cost structure, a debilitating inability to work with their labor unions, and a series of highly publicized crashes. Despite all this, the airline continued to fly unprofitably until 1991 before it was finally forced to cease operations. High exit barriers impacted the business decisions and were a significant influencing factor in the industry.

CONCLUSIONS FROM FIVE FORCES ANALYSIS

Having gone carefully through each of the five forces, it is now possible to develop conclusions from your observations and to put those conclusions to practical use. Recall that there are two types of conclusions that should be drawn from this analysis: 1) the attractiveness of the industry, and 2) the identification of key success factors.

Industry Attractiveness

To draw conclusions about industry attractiveness, we first seek to summarize our findings from the five forces analysis. Then we will use a simple rating system to formalize our findings.

Five forces summary. Each of the five forces will exert an influence on an industry that either enhances or detracts from the potential for any company to earn above-average profits. Summarizing the effect of all of the five forces at one time provides a clearer picture of the industry. The "Five-Forces Analysis Checklist" in Figure 4.16 provides a convenient means to create this summary. Every item within each force should be evaluated as to whether its effect is strong or weak on that force. Having profiled each of the items, this checklist then provides a summary for making an informed judgment about whether each of the five forces is strong or weak.

Developing judgments about the impact of the five forces allows for drawing conclusions about the attractiveness of the industry as a whole. The industry appears attractive when the five forces are weak, helping to insulate the profit-making potential of participating companies. It looks much less attractive when the five forces are strong. This indicates that potential profits for rivals in the industry are being siphoned off to suppliers, buyers, new entrants,

Figure 4.16
Five Forces Analysis Checklist

	Strong	Weak
Threat of new entrants is low when		
Capital requirements	★	
Economies of scale	★	
Absolute cost advantages	★	
Access to inputs		★
Access to distribution		★
Need for differentiation	★	
Switching costs for buyers	★	
Government regulation	★	
Expected retaliation	★	
Threat of substitutes is low when		
Relative price/performance		★
Switching costs of buyers	★	
Buyer bargaining power is low when		
Buyer concentration		★
Buyer volume		★
Switching costs of buyers	★	
Buyer information		★
Availability of substitutes		★
Threat of backward integration		★
Supplier bargaining power is low when		
Supplier concentration		★
Importance of volume to supplier		★
Presence of substitute inputs		★
Differentiation of inputs required		★
Cost of input relative to total costs		★
Switching costs of suppliers	★	
Threat of forward integration		★
Intensity of rivalry is low when		
Industry growth rate	★	
Overcapacity in industry		★
Fixed costs as % of total costs		★
Product differentiation	★	
Informational complexity	★	
Switching costs of buyers	★	
Numerous or equally balanced competitors		★
Strategic stakes		★
Exit barriers		★

and substitutes, or possibly because the intense rivalry among competitors causes all of the companies in the industry to spend at much higher levels or commit additional resources in order to compete (Figure 4.17).

Industry Analysis Ratings. Having made judgments about each of the five forces, now the strength of each force can be quantified and we can draw conclusions about the industry as a whole. We employ a simple, straightforward rating system to do so. First, assign a rating to each of the five forces using the 3-tier range in Figure 4.18a. Then add the ratings for each of the five forces, in order to develop a summary rating for the entire industry. The summary rating for an industry can range from 5 (a 1 rating for each of the five forces) to 15 (a 3 rating for all the forces). Figure 4.18b provides guidance for interpreting the summary number. A low range of 5-7 indicates a reasonably attractive industry, where there is the potential to earn superior profits. This is because none of the five forces is particularly strong or has the potential to siphon off profitability. A high range of 12-15 suggests just the opposite. In this scenario many of the five forces are strong, making the industry environment a challenging one in order to perform in a superior fashion. In the midrange of 8-11 companies must be cautious when competing in the industry, or when considering entering into it through acquisition or internal expansion. Careful attention should be paid to those forces with higher ratings, in order to better understand whether these forces might be particularly challenging.

Figure 4.17
Potential to earn superior returns in industry

Five Forces	Good Potential	Poor Potential
Threat of new entrants	Low	High
Threat of substitutes	Low	High
Bargaining power of buyers	Low	High
Bargaining power of suppliers	Low	High
Intensity of rivalry	Low	High

Figure 4.18a
Industry Analysis Rating Scale

Strength of Each Force	Rating
Very high, significant	3
Moderate	2
Low	1

Figure 4.18b
Industry Attractiveness

Conclusion	Sum of Five Forces Ratings
Very attractive	5 – 7
Moderately attractive	8 – 11
Extremely competitive, not very attractive	12 - 15

Identifying key success factors. We mentioned earlier in this chapter that key success factors (KSFs) are like the "rules" of the industry. They are indicative of the kinds of activities that every company needs to focus upon in order to succeed. Unlike external driving forces, which affect an entire industry and which no company can impact, the KSF-related activities are dimensions that companies can affect through their own strategic investments. The extent to which companies pay attention to KSFs and succeed in addressing them will distinguish the winners from the losers in an industry.

Every industry will have its own unique set of KSFs, and in each industry there are likely to be no more than four to six such factors. While there are a vast number of competitive factors within any industry, KSFs are those that are the *most* critical to success. Because the KSFs are a "short list," it is important to understand that not every company in an industry will be forced to compete in exactly the same way in order to succeed. In fact, one of the most challenging and interesting aspects of strategic management is that strategic variety not only exists within most industries, but also that there is equifinality – the idea that there are many routes to achieve success. That is, despite the fact that there are only a limited number of KSFs, companies compete quite successfully for industry profits in many different ways. KSFs provide guidance for being strategically competitive, but do not dictate specific actions that companies must take. In ancient history it used to be said that "all roads lead to Rome." Here in the twenty-first century, the roads are the KSFs: they guide companies to the destination of superior performance. Companies vary in the roads they may take, the chariots and horses they use, the training of the charioteers, and the speed or deliberation in their journeys.

Having conducted a five-forces analysis, identifying KSFs becomes a more straightforward exercise. There are two key questions to answer in this identification process (Figure 4.19):

1. *How is value created for customers in this industry?* In the five-forces analysis we considered the conditions under which customer bargaining power is increased, with the result being that concentrated customer power may actually diminish the profitability of competitors in the industry. Though this structural power of customers can negatively impact industry profitability, it is important to remember that customers are individually the fundamental source of revenue and profit for companies. Customers in any industry will prize certain product or service features and characteristics over others. They will also value a certain type of relationship with a company that provides them with products or services. Carefully defining the values that are most appreciated by customers will lead a company to take actions to deliver those critical values. Earlier, for example, we mentioned that consumers increasingly demand that cutting-edge technology be incorporated into the PCs and laptops they use. To deliver on this value, PC and laptop manufacturers must engage in continuous innovation. In the fast food industry consumers value convenience, which has led companies like McDonald's and Burger King to develop expertise in real estate site selection for new restaurants. This ensures that each new restaurant is centrally located and easily accessible to their customers.

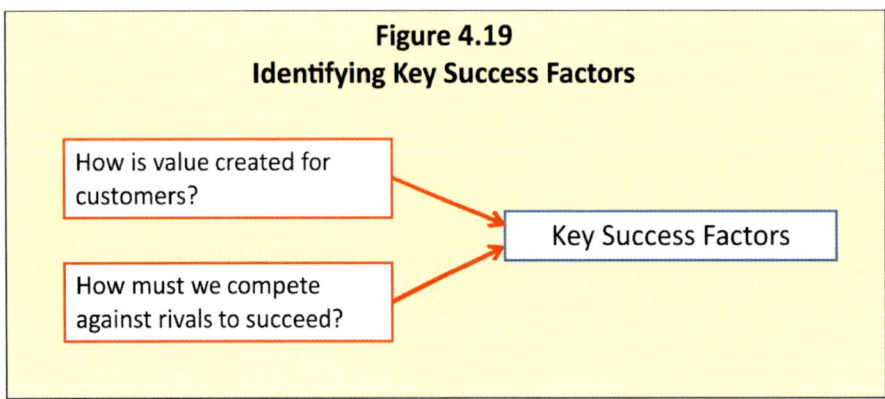

2. *How must we compete against rivals to succeed? What are the critical dimensions of rivalry that enable a company to successfully compete in delivering values to customers?* This question should be addressed as a multifaceted problem to be solved with the best combination of approaches. What is it that the company will have to do in order to compete effectively and survive in the industry? The other way to phrase the question is "what are the factors that will cause the company to fail if we do not attend to them?" Five-forces analysis goes a long way toward addressing these questions. The threat of new entrants often prompts existing competitors to either create or increase economic barriers to entry or to establish stronger brand reputations that will differentiate their products. This might lead existing competitors to build

larger manufacturing facilities or to increase the amount they spend on advertising and image development. The pressure on costs from suppliers as well as on prices from buyers, and the presence of potential substitutes, generally cause companies to seek ways to develop a low cost structure so that they can offer more competitive pricing.

Answering these questions completely often requires thinking through the reasons that lie beneath surface dimensions that might be initially identified. We have already noted that in the PC industry customers value the opportunity to shop for cutting-edge technology, which in turn means that PC manufacturers must focus on innovation as a fundamental KSF. However, the customer desire for innovation is balanced by the desire to have technology that is also manufactured around a commonly accepted standard. Standardized product offerings allow customers to comparison shop more easily among competing models, instill confidence that the technology will work well, and ensure the customer that the product can be repaired easily if something goes wrong. There are two implications derived from the parallel need for innovation and standardization in the PC industry. First, companies must find ways to produce standardized models inexpensively. Their competitors will be producing to the same standards, and when standardization occurs then price competition will likely be fierce. This suggests that *cost control* is an important KSF in this industry. Second, companies must seek to move their models incorporating new technology standards into the marketplace quickly, suggesting that *speed to market* is also a KSF.

A "Quick & Dirty" Illustration: PC Industry

So far in this discussion we have mentioned the personal computer (PC) industry a few times to help illustrate some of the ideas about industry analysis. Let's briefly take a closer look at this industry, employing the techniques we have so far covered.

First, let's define the industry narrowly, in this case as just PCs and laptops. In this narrow definition, therefore, we exclude other devices and machines that can perform some similar functions but which may not have full PC/laptop functionality. So here we are not including tablets like the Kindle, the iPad, Samsung's and others' tablets. In our analysis these alternative devices present attractive performance/price combinations, and so we will consider them as substitutes.

Next we might consider a few relevant STEEPG conditions. This is a "quick & dirty" illustration, so we will not consider all that might impact this industry. But a couple important ideas are worth mentioning. Business and technology is moving to cloud servers and apps, and so local computing power is less relevant today than previously. This trend is buttressed by the growth of tele-commuting especially during 2019-21, shared office arrangements, distance learning, etc., where connections to central computing are increasingly important to transact affairs. Demographically and socially, the new generation of workers are more comfortable working with alternative – or substitute – devices. So although during the 2020-21 pandemic years PC shipments jumped 12-13% per year, reversing a long term trend, in 2022 these trends are projected to result once again in declining or flat sales of PCs and laptops.

Briefly consider the strength of each of the five forces. The threat of new entrants is not particularly strong, since it would be brutally expensive to enter this industry. The threat of substitutes, as alluded to, is quite strong and growing. We also mentioned earlier the bargaining power that suppliers like Intel and Microsoft exert in this industry. PC and laptop manufacturers must purchase their chips and software, else they simply will not be competitive. They have no real choices here. On the other hand a number of supply side inputs to computers are commodity-like (plastic, wiring), and here suppliers have no bargaining power. If we consider the retail buying scene, it is fairly concentrated among a small number of large chains. Switching costs for retailers are very low, since computers are standardized and every PC manufacturer will be offering similar models. Recent HHI calculations for suppliers, buyers, and rival are as follows:

    Chip suppliers   6,575   Electronics retailers   2,006
    Operating system suppliers   7,316   PC / laptop manufacturers   865

Rivalry among PC/laptop manufacturers is fairly intense. They compete in similar ways on a number of fronts: same customers, same technology, quality, reputation, etc. The total size of the industry exceeds $230 billion per year, which makes each percentage point of market share worth over $2 billion, extremely valuable to protect. In a flat or declining market, competitors will fight tooth and nail to protect their market shares and sales base.

We can now summarize and rate the strength of each of the five forces, as seen below. Adding the ratings of all five forces yields a summary industry rating of 12-13. This indicates the industry is extremely competitive and not very attractive. In fact, further analysis of the annual reports of the major PC manufacturers during this analysis period shows that the top four averaged only 1.8% in 2019 net income. It is not particularly profitable to sell high-tech boxes!

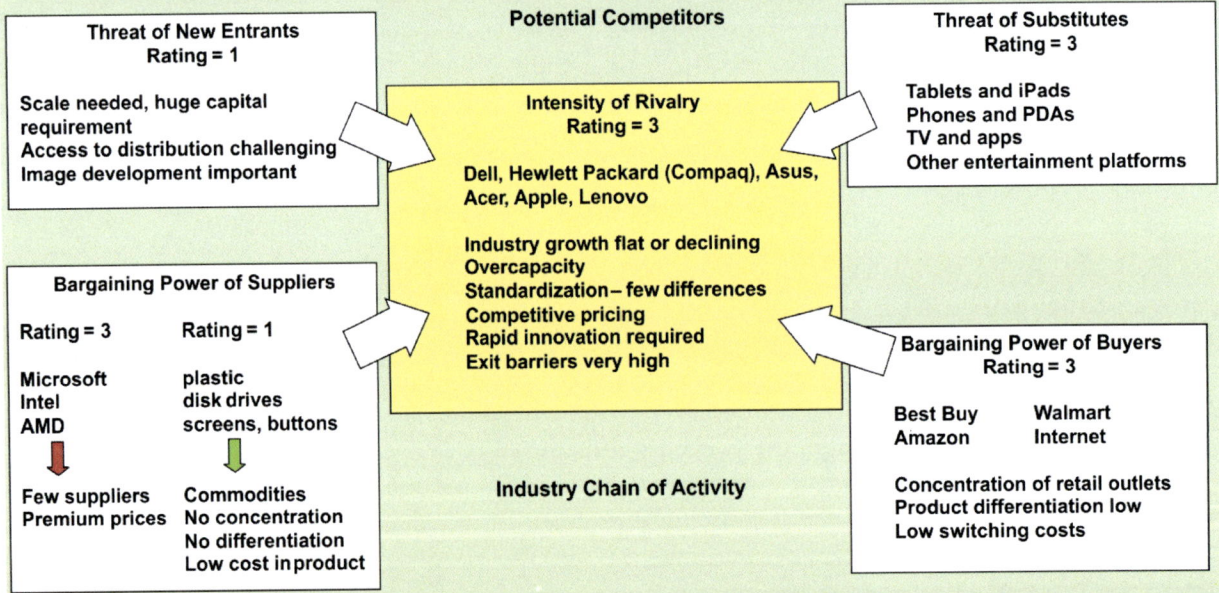

What are the key success factors in this industry? How is value created for customers, and on what dimensions must companies compete in order to be successful? A preliminary list of KSFs for the PC industry would appear to be as follows. Each company will need to make strategic investments in, and initiate company-wide actions, to address these KSFs.

Customer Values	Compete Against Rivals	Resulting KSF
Compatible technology		Innovation
New tech advances		Speed
	Competitive prices	Cost control
Quality	Brand image	Reputation

Changes in key success factors. By answering the two questions posed earlier, we should be able to identify a short list of KSFs for any industry. Before moving on, however, we want to emphasize that industries do change over time. Therefore the important KSFs might also change. This is especially true as an industry matures and its growth rate of new customers or revenues begins to flatten out, or as the presence of viable substitutes becomes increasingly important. The U.S. automobile industry has seen a continuous evolution of KSFs over the last seventy-five years, moving from purely low cost and basic functionality, to style and design, to quality and performance, and now to economic performance. General Motors and its unionized workforce remained so mired in a model of business dating back to the 1960s and 1970s that the company failed to recognize a fundamental shift in the kinds of KSFs that were emerging in the 1980s and 1990s. Poor anticipation of major shifts that generate new sets of KSFs led many of the U.S. automakers into "critical condition" during the mid-2000s. General Motors was forced into cutting jobs and costs, was forced into a government-mandated bailout, and then went through bankruptcy.[31] Therefore, the ability to identify changing and emerging KSFs helps a company to better anticipate possible threats to its existing business.

By the same token, a company can recognize opportunities for new value creation through efforts to anticipate changes in KSFs that its industry will be experiencing. Recall that in Chapter 1 we discussed "opportunity recognition" as one of two key strategic imperatives. By answering slightly reworded questions in Figure 4.19, a company can potentially develop insight about new opportunities before its competitors do. The questions now become

"What kinds of value *should* be created for customers in the future?" and

"How *will* we need to compete against rivals to succeed?"

Companies that develop activities and routines to regularly ask and answer these questions can do a better job of scoping out significant opportunities and threats.

Competitive KSF Analysis

Identifying key success factors that are currently important in the industry is an important step that allows for a critical evaluation of each primary competitor. This is accomplished by looking at how well each competitor addresses the KSFs that distinguish between success and failure in the industry. A comparison of competitors on each KSF dimension highlights the relative positions of strength in the marketplace. This is important on many levels, not the least of which is that companies need to be careful about attacking a competitor's position of strength. You will recall from Chapter 1, where we paraphrased the ancient writings of Sun Tzu, that this was one of the lessons he taught. Attacking the strength of a competitor is an attempt to win based upon the competitor's strengths and experience rather than based upon the unique capabilities of the company doing the attacking. Comparative analysis can also reveal relative positions of weakness and thus possible areas of exploitation through strategic moves. This sort of comparative analysis was central to Sun Tzu's beliefs about how to succeed.

**Figure 4.20
Competitive KSF analysis table**

	Key Success Factors			
	KSF #1	KSF #2	KSF #3	KSF #4
Firm A				
Firm B				
Firm C				
Firm D				

The goal of a competitive KSF analysis is to produce a table that resembles that in Figure 4.20. Here the KSFs we have just identified are listed across the top, and the chief competitors in the industry are listed down the side. In evaluating each firm it is important not to "guesstimate" or simply "eyeball" how well or how poorly the competitor does on a particular dimension. This analysis should be based upon hard facts and data, not simply on opinions and subjective evaluations. Since the KSFs are the critical dimensions that distinguish success from failure in the industry, basing strategic decisions on factual evidence will be particularly helpful. In contrast, basing important strategic decisions on estimates and opinions may lead a company to under or over-estimate a particular competitor.

Here is another illustration. We earlier suggested that innovation is a KSF in the PC industry. The question, then, is how innovative are competitors in this industry? We need to measure innovation somehow, and there are several ways we might consider:

- Dollars of R&D spending each year
- R&D spending as a percentage of revenue
- Number of new models introduced each year
- Degree of improvement in performance characteristics of new models

Dollars spent on R&D each year is an industry standard means of assessing the level of commitment that companies are putting into discovery and innovation. However, there is a wide variation in company size in this industry. Some companies are significantly larger than others, and therefore simply have more dollars available to spend on discovery. In fact, in fiscal year 2021 Apple spent $21.9 billion on R&D, while HP spent only $1.9 billion and Lenovo spent $1.5 billion. It looks like Apple is outspending its competitors by a ratio of roughly 12-to-1. But another way of evaluating innovation is to "common-size" R&D spending by looking at it as a percentage of sales revenue. A different picture emerges: during 2021 Apple spent 6.0% of sales on R&D, HP spent 3.0%, and Lenovo spent 2.4% – so the relative difference is not as great.

It is likely that the R&D spending for each company is spread across multiple product lines: Mac computers, iPhones, iPads, Apple Watch for Apple; HP is focused on computer and printers; and Lenovo has a broad line of electronics in its portfolio. However, we are particularly concerned here with how innovation impacts the PC industry. So perhaps a more salient metric to evaluate, and one that would be more relevant for customers like Best Buy or for competitors, is the number of new PC models each firm introduces in a given period of time. While R&D information is generally available on the internet by accessing an annual report, data on models introduced is not as easy to identify. This is data that requires careful investigation, such as interviewing purchasing managers at Best Buy or finding and reviewing historical price lists of the companies.

Still, in the PC industry Lenovo and HP are significantly larger than Apple. One might expect that larger companies with broader lines would tend to introduce a larger number of new models during any given period. So a fourth possible measure for innovation is one of relative degree. That is, how much have new models improved in computing performance over existing models? Here one might examine specific operating characteristics of new PCs such as increases in speed, capacity, or size relative to power.

This brief discussion illustrates that selecting the best metrics to evaluate companies on KSF dimensions involves choosing among a range of options. The best choices will usually be the type of measures that best align the needs and desires of the core customers with the resources and capabilities of the company.

EXTENDING INDUSTRY ANALYSIS: STRATEGY MAPS AND STRATEGIC GROUPS

We can take the analysis of competition one step further by using KSFs to provide greater insight on strategic positions within an industry. "Mapping" the position of competitors in an industry allows for the identification of important strategic groups. A strategic group is a collection of companies that tend to behave in much the same way strategically because they are making investments on the same subsets of KSFs. They therefore occupy positions in an industry that are close enough to each other that they become primary competitors with each other. A competitive KSF analysis (Figure 4.20) can help identify companies that are very similar to each other on key competitive dimensions. However, a strategy map is a visual tool that takes this one step further by revealing competitors' relative positions. A strategy map is created by using a pair of the identified KSFs as axes in a graph, and then plotting the companies on the graph according to their measures for each of the KSFs.

Constructing strategy maps. Let's use the PC manufacturing industry once again to illustrate the creation of strategy maps and the identification of strategic groups. There are several steps in the process:

1. Identify the KSFs in the industry and measure each competitor on these dimensions as objectively as possible. Choose two of the KSFs and plot the competitors in the industry in a graph using these dimensions as the axes (Figure 4.21). Earlier, for instance, we identified that two of the KSFs in the industry are innovation and cost control. By convention we put the "desirable" condition for each KSF toward the outer end of each axis. So in this case "Low" for Unit Cost (one objective measurement of the cost KSF) is toward the right end of the horizontal axis, and "high" for Innovation is toward the top of the vertical axis. This makes the upper-right portion of each graph the most desirable part of the graph to be, in this case the combination of low unit cost and highly innovative. Note that no company currently occupies that position in "strategic space." It can be

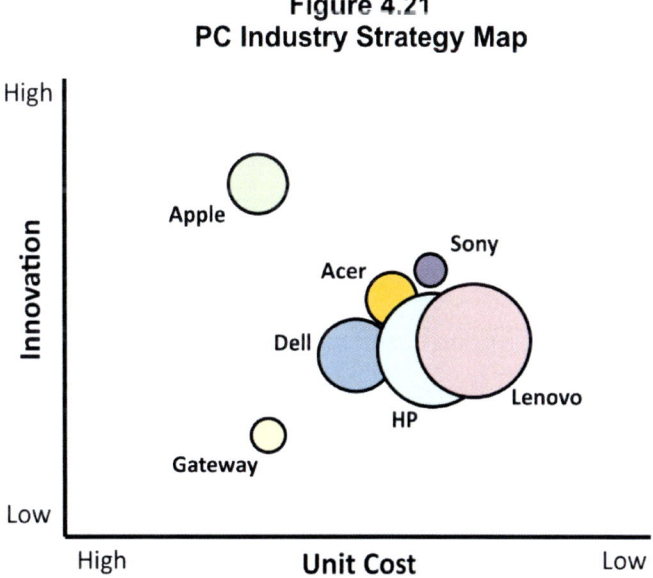

**Figure 4.21
PC Industry Strategy Map**

seen that Dell and others have pushed the frontier of low-cost production with an average level of innovation, while Apple is significantly higher on the innovation dimension but less advanced in unit cost manufacturing.

2. At the point where competitors are located on the graph, draw circles for each competitor. The size of the circle should represent the relative size of the competitor, in either market share

of the industry or annual revenue. In Figure 4.21, for instance, PC manufacturers are represented by circles whose size approximates market share for each company; thus HP is larger than Dell and three to four times the size of Apple.

3. Assess the presence of strategic groups. In this example, Dell, Acer, Lenovo, HP, and Sony make up a strategic group because they are extremely close to each other on these two critical strategic dimensions in the industry. Sony should be most concerned about the way in which HP and Lenovo will be competing in the marketplace, because they tend to create value for customers in much the same way and represents a greater threat to take its business away. These are the competitors that threaten it the most. Dell would be much less concerned about Apple, who appears to compete more on the dimension of innovation and less on the cost/price dimension.

4. Use other combinations of KSFs to draw additional maps. With four KSFs identified in an industry, there will be six possible graphs to draw using combinations of any two KSFs. Other graph combinations can also be revealing about industry competition. In the PC industry a graph showing Unit Cost versus Speed to Market might also portray a strategic group made up of Lenovo, Dell, and HP. This finding should elevate the attention paid by any one of those competitors to the other two, because it reinforces the relationship seen in Figure 4.21.

5. Make sure that KSFs provide unique information. Sometimes industry KSFs turn out to be highly correlated with each other. Figure 4.22 is a strategic map of the fast food industry in which Food Quality and Low Costs had been identified as KSFs. The alignment of all the companies along the downward sloping diagonal indicates that there is a high degree of correlation between food quality and unit costs: the lower the unit costs, the lower the food quality. Therefore the addition of Food Quality to the list of industry KSFs does not impart any new information that is not already captured by the Low Cost KSF. If Food Quality similarly aligns with other KSFs identified in the industry analysis, then it should be removed from the list of KSFs, because it does not distinguish between success and failure any better than the other KSFs do.

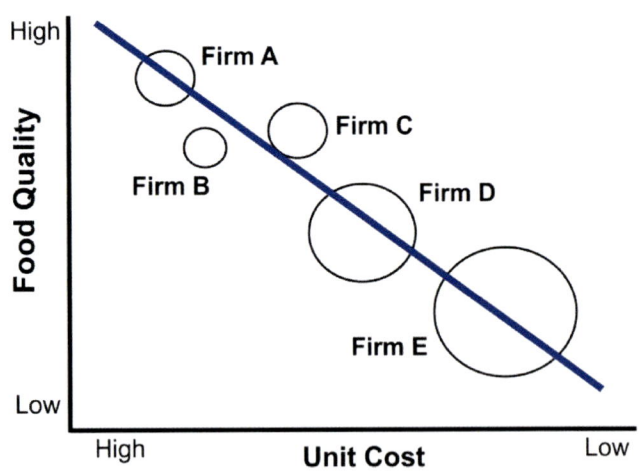

**Figure 4.22
Fast Food Industry Strategy Map**

Identifying strategic trajectories. Another advantage of strategy maps is that they can be used to illustrate the trajectories of strategy development that have occurred in an industry. A single strategy map is similar to a photo: it is a static view that is a representation of the industry at a point in time. A series of strategy maps developed over time would be like a movie, showing the dynamic character of the industry over a period of time. This type of dynamic view would help illuminate the historical trajectories that competitors have taken throughout this period of time.

Building further on the PC industry strategy map developed earlier, Figure 4.23 now provides a dynamic view of the changes in strategic position over time for two key competitors in the industry. Apple has always been an innovative company since its founding in the 1970s. A few years ago Dell was superior to Apple on the Unit Cost KSF, but was inferior to Apple on the Innovation KSF. Over time Dell has worked diligently to continue lowering its unit cost structure, and its trajectory from the past to its present-day position illustrates its accomplishments. At the same time, it has only marginally improved its Innovation position since it relies heavily upon Intel, Microsoft, and other suppliers of subassemblies for its basic PC models. In contrast, Apple has continued to push an innovation agenda, evidenced by its introduction of the iMac with Retina display, Mac Book and Mac mini, Mac OS Monterey, and more. Apple has also recognized the need to become more price competitive, which has caused it to make substantial improvements in its unit cost dimension. The solid arrows in Figure 4.23 illustrate the trajectories each company has followed over the last few years.

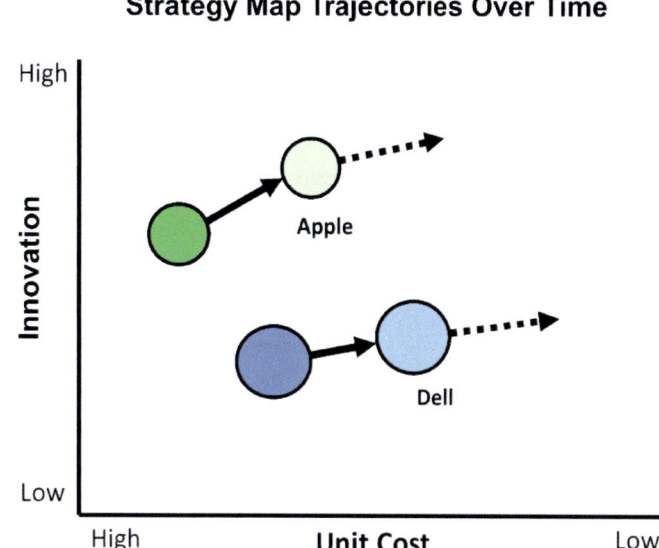

**Figure 4.23
Strategy Map Trajectories Over Time**

These historical trajectories are manifestations of the strategic approach each company has taken in the marketplace in order to improve its competitive position. To pursue these trajectories each company has made strategic investments in certain resources and activities that allow it to make significant progress. In Chapter 6 we will discuss in some detail the nature of these types of resource investments and how they can lead to competitive advantage. The point that should be emphasized here is that such investments are major commitments by a company and, like most strategic decisions, are not easily reversed. They are "sticky," meaning that once you build a capability for innovation, that capability will stick with you for a long period of time.

Past strategic intentions are indicators of future strategic direction. Because the strategic investments made by each company are sticky, it is reasonable to expect that each company will continue to move in a similar direction. In Figure 4.23 the dotted-line arrows suggest the direction that each company will move in the near future, assuming each will continue to build on past strategic investments. Anticipating the direction in which one of your competitors will move can be extremely helpful. To achieve further reductions in unit cost, for instance, Dell can expect that Apple will be evaluating a range of options that will help fulfill this intention. Since PC manufacturing costs have been well-connected with economies of scale, one option that Apple may consider would be a way to make their PCs more attractive to a wider audience. It should come as no surprise, then, that in 2006 Apple developed its own software enabling users to run Windows and Windows-based software on its Apple computers. It has expanded Apple Stores to 516 worldwide by 2022, and now sells its machines through Best Buy and other popular retailers.[32] This instantly makes the Apple computing platform a viable and highly-available option for tens of millions of computer users. Breadth of availability combined with a more attractive user interface helped to ramp up Apple's overall volume.

Identifying strategic opportunities. The strategy map can also be a useful tool for identifying new opportunities for strategic distinction. In Figure 4.21 Acer appears to be competing directly with several larger companies in the PC business. Direct competition seldom has positive results for smaller companies, simply because the smaller company has fewer resources at its disposal to fight the good fight (another lesson from Sun Tzu). This is one of the reasons why competitors frequently score goals in lacrosse or ice hockey when a player has to sit out in the penalty box. Additional resources generally lead to higher performance. So what options are available for Acer to compete, while at the same time trying to remove itself from a battle of attrition? The map in Figure 4.21 suggests an opportunity for Acer may lie in the space toward the upper-right corner. The anticipated trajectories Lenovo and HP appear to be taking are primarily to the right, as they pursue an agenda of unit cost reductions. Therefore, Acer might consider making new strategic investments in innovation capabilities, which would create strategic separation from Lenovo and HP and allow them to move into a currently unoccupied part of the "strategic space."

What about Sony in this highly-competitive industry? Sony faced the same challenge as Acer. The company found the industry to be unattractive in the present. The investments and resources required to become more competitive in the future would be extraordinary. In part because of this sort of analysis, in 2014 Sony decided to exit the PC industry and refocus in other industries.[33]

Effect of industry definitions. Earlier in this chapter we discussed the difficulty that can arise in defining the precise boundaries of an industry. Similarly, industry boundary definitions can make a difference in how strategy maps are interpreted. Let's assume that we are conducting an industry analysis of the pizza industry, and that two of the KSFs that have been identified are Quality and Convenience. Figure 4.24 portrays a hypothetical strategy map of the industry. Pizza Hut, Domino's, and Papa John's dominate the industry and constitute a strategic group of companies that court the consumer in much the same way. Brick Oven is a sit-down restaurant that produces high quality pizzas, while Pizza Spinners is the local late-night place that students call only if everything else is closed. We also plug in DiGiorno's Pizza, which is purchased in supermarket frozen food sections, simply to acknowledge that this brand is also a competitor of delivery and restaurant pizzas.

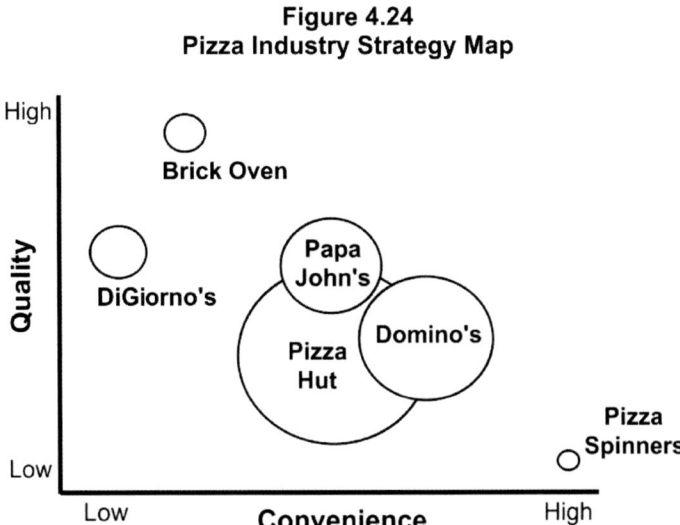

Figure 4.24
Pizza Industry Strategy Map

A broader industry definition can lead to a very different view of the main competitive strategic group. In fact, consumers often choose pizza instead of some other type of fast food, and vice versa. So if the industry analysis is broadened to account for the wider variety and values that consumers seek when they make choices, a different strategy map emerges. Figure 4.25 illustrates the strategy map when the industry definition is broadened to "fast food." In this instance we observe that McDonald's and Burger King have been added to the map, and they appear to compete for the consumer in precisely the same manner as do the popular delivery pizza restaurants. Consequently, Domino's must worry about not only the competitive efforts of Papa John's in producing moderate quality pizzas and delivering them in a timely fashion. They must also worry about McDonald's efforts to deliver the same values to consumers – convenience and moderate quality – available through their drive-up windows and their newly-developed online order capabilities. Presumably the broader definition of the industry would also have implications for relative strengths on other KSFs, such as Price/Value.

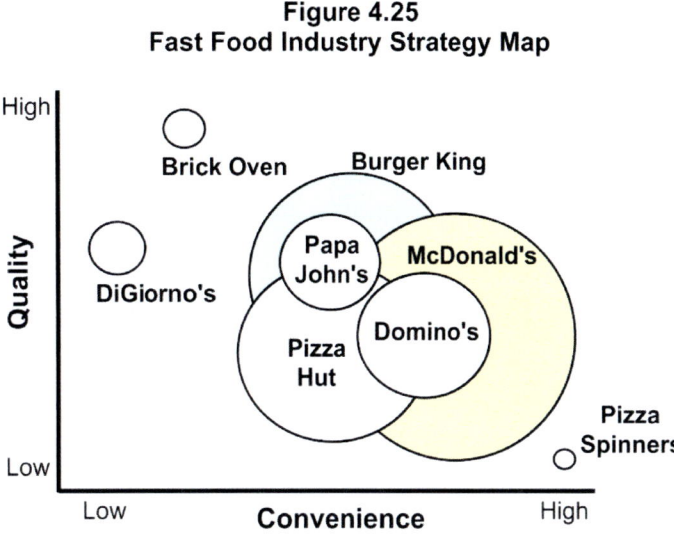

Figure 4.25
Fast Food Industry Strategy Map

CHAPTER SUMMARY

Industry analysis is a tool that provides an evidence-based evaluation of where an industry stands on a continuum that ranges from a perfectly competitive market to one that is a monopoly. In perfectly competitive markets (which are rare), it is difficult for any company to earn superior profits. Imperfect markets are characterized by the potential to sustain differences between companies, which can lead to superior profits. The examination of five structural forces of an industry provides insight on the extent to which there is potential for companies to earn profits. These five forces include the threat of new entrants, threat of substitutes, bargaining power of buyers, bargaining power of suppliers, and the intensity of rivalry among competitors. The stronger each of these forces is, the lower the potential for the any company in the industry to earn superior returns. Using an industry analysis rating scale, a quantitative assessment can be developed for the attractiveness of the industry.

Inferences may be drawn about the critical strategic dimensions of competition that distinguish between successful and unsuccessful companies. These are referred to as key success factors (KSFs). KSFs can be used to evaluate the relative strengths and weaknesses of competitors in the industry as well as to construct visual strategy maps, which may reveal groups of companies that compete in very similar ways.

Industry analysis involves the following steps:

1. Define the industry of interest. Narrow industry definitions involve companies whose inputs are very similar, whose geographic markets are similar, and whose customers are very similar.

2. Examine the general environment for driving forces that will affect the industry and every company in it. These STEEPG forces include social, technological, economic, environmental, political/legal, and global forces.

3. Examine the five forces in the industry to understand how the structure of the industry affects the potential to earn profits. Each force is evaluated through a series of characteristics that will indicate whether profits for competitors are insulated or may be drawn off.

4. Complete the five-forces analysis checklist. Draw conclusions about the attractiveness of the industry for earning profits.

5. Assess industry attractiveness (potential to earn superior profits) using the industry analysis rating system.

6. Identify key success factors by answering two pivotal questions: 1) how is value created for customers; and 2) how must we compete in order to succeed?

7. Determine the appropriate way to measure companies in the industry on each of the KSFs.

8. Complete the competitive KSF analysis table, in order to easily compare companies on the KSF dimensions.

9. Draw strategy maps using paired combinations of KSFs. Identify strategic groups of closely competing companies. Identify historical trajectories of competitors, as well as anticipated direction of future development.

10. Change the industry definition used, and re-examine KSFs and strategy maps for new insights on the nature of competition.

11. Anticipate how KSFs in the industry might change in the future, based upon your earlier driving forces analysis.

Learning Objectives Review

1. Explain how the phrase "competitive advantage" is connected to company strategy and performance.

- Competitive advantage can be achieved in an industry that is not perfectly competitive, where there are differences among companies. In this environment some companies can earn higher profits than others. Strategy is about the sets of decisions and investments that result in a position of "above average profits."

2. Describe how an industry definition can affect conclusions drawn from an industry analysis.

- Different industry definitions will result in different sets of competitors, and in different key success factors.

- Broadly-defined industries usually require companies to engage in a wider variety of value-creating activities that depend on developing broad and deep resource positions. Broadly-defined industries usually encounter international competition or require international development.

- Narrowly-defined industries allow companies to focus their resource investments and efforts more carefully.

3. *Explain the impact that forces other than competition can have on company strategy and performance.*

- There are four forces internal to an industry, in addition to competition, that affect company strategy and performance: threat of new entrants, threat of substitutes, bargaining power of suppliers, bargaining power of buyers. When any one of these four other forces is strong, it prompts incumbent competitors to spend more to prevent other companies from entering the industry, to develop new products or meet escalating demands, or to lower prices to remain more competitive. Each such effort reduces the profitability of incumbents.

- Customers are stolen away by new entrants and by substitute products and services, resulting in lower revenue to incumbent competitors.

- External STEEPG driving forces can have either beneficial effects on an industry (e.g. increasing target population) or detrimental effects (e.g. more government regulation; technology that obsoletes products).

4. *Employ strategy mapping techniques to identify strategic groups in an industry.*

- Identify key success factors in the industry. Plot the location of competitors on a graph using objective measures for two of the KSFs.

- Draw a circle for each competitor at its plot location, where the size of the circle represents the size of the company.

- Repeat these steps using other pairs of KSFs. Identify groups of competitors that are close to each other on the sets of graphs.

5. *Explain how an industry is shaped by external driving forces.*

- External driving forces can have either beneficial effects on an industry (e.g. increasing target population) or detrimental effects (e.g. more government regulation; technology that obsoletes products).

6. *Explain how dynamic changes in industries and competitive positions will impact a company's strategy.*

- Driving forces can produce changes in industries over time. This may lead to newly emerging key success factors that companies will need to invest in. External driving forces can also lead to the emergence of new industries whose products and services increasingly serve as substitutes to existing products and services.

- Understanding changes in the positions of competitors can lead companies to pay more attention to some competitors and less attention to others.

Key Terms

Concentration ratio - The percentage of market share in the industry owned by the largest firms.

Dodd-Frank - The legislative initiative enacted in 2010, following the 2008-09 economic crisis, imposing significant new regulations on financial institutions.

Driving forces - Forces outside the control of the company, but which the company must pay attention to.

Economies of scale - Low unit costs that result from producing on a large scale.

Equifinality - There are multiple paths to achieve success.

Experience curve - Reductions in cost per unit that are achieved through the learning that occurs in cumulative production over time (in contrast to economies of scale, in which unit cost reductions are associated with volume during a fixed time interval).

Five-forces model - A model originally identified by Michael Porter as a means to examine the aspects of an industry's competitive environment. The model consists of the threat of new entrants, substitutes, suppliers, buyers, and rivalry.

Incumbent firms - Established firms in the industry.

Industry analysis - Method through which the examination of competitive determines whether an industry is attractive or unattractive, i.e. whether there is an opportunity for a company to earn above average profits.

Key success factors (KSF) - Rules of thumb for doing business in an industry that reflect the structural conditions of the industry.

Monopoly - An industry where a single firm constitutes the entire industry and earns all the profits.

NAICS (North American Industry Classification System) - A U. S. government coding method to gather, track, and publish data on industries. See
    (http://www.census.gov/epcd/www/naics.html).

Perfect competition - A marketplace in which there is perfect information, zero transactions costs and costless entry, so that all firms become virtually identical and no firm earns any profit.

Profit pool - Generally, the amount of profit available in the industry in a particular period of time.

Sarbanes-Oxley Act (SOX) - The legislative initiative enacted in 2002 that imposes stiff new demands on companies and their auditors to ensure that published financial statements are accurate.

Social contract - Implied relationship between businesses and the communities in which they operate.

Strategic group - A group of companies competing in the same manner.

Strategy map - A two-dimensional map showing the positions of competitors using a quantitatively defined set of criteria.

Substitutes - Products or services that perform the same function or meet the same need as the products or services in the industry under study, but which are produced using different raw materials and inputs.

Short Answer Review Questions

1. What did Adam Smith have to say about efficient markets?
2. How do key success factors (KSF) inform us about a particular market?
3. What elements help us define an industry?
4. How are NAICS codes utilized in industry analysis?
5. How can we use the five-forces model to examine industries?
6. What criticisms do you have of the five-forces model? What does it not explain that you believe is important in competitive strategy?
7. What factors help limit the entry of new competitors into an industry?
8. What are the types of cost advantage, and how do they impact the five forces?
9. What are perceived switching costs?
10. Provide examples of real switching costs.
11. How do substitutes affect an industry's attractiveness? What are appropriate responses by competitors when possible substitutes emerge?
12. What are the three factors that determine how strong the threat of substitutes will be for an industry?
13. How would you explain buyer concentration?
14. In what ways do suppliers impact the attractiveness of an industry?
15. Name the elements that affect the attractiveness of an industry and explain their impact.
16. The general environment impacts industries and companies. Explain how the internet has affected competitive rivalry and the attractiveness of the airline industry.

Group Exercises

1. Classifying a company is the first step in analyzing an industry. Take two businesses that are close to the university and use the NAICS classification system to classify them. Try to get the code as specific as possible.

    a. How difficult was it to get the classification code to five digits?

b. What other businesses fall under the same classification code?

c. What insights does this classification provide you in your analysis of a particular company?

2. Take one of the businesses that you used in Exercise #1 and develop a five-forces analysis for the industry in which it competes.

a. What conclusions can you reach about the competitiveness of the industry?

b. What areas of the industry concern you most?

c. What aspects of the industry appear to provide the best opportunities for those already in the industry?

d. What conclusions have you reached about the general competitiveness of this industry?

3. Take the same business for which you developed a five-forces analysis in Exercise #2 and create a strategic map for the industry in which it competes.

a. What conclusions can you reach about the industry's KSFs?

b. What recommendations would you provide a company that wished to enter this industry?

Investor Relations Sites for Companies Mentioned in This Chapter

Activision Blizzard: https://investor.activision.com/
Allkem: https://www.allkem.co/investors
Alphabet: https://abc.xyz/investor/
Apple: https://investor.apple.com/investor-relations/default.aspx
Best Buy: https://investors.bestbuy.com/investor-relations/overview/default.aspx
Chick-Fil-A: https://www.chick-fil-a.com/about/who-we-are
Dell Technologies: https://investors.delltechnologies.com/
Delta: https://ir.delta.com/home/default.aspx
Domino's: https://ir.dominos.com/
Facebook (Meta Platforms): https://investor.fb.com/home/default.aspx
Ford: https://shareholder.ford.com/investors/overview/default.aspx
General Motors: https://investor.gm.com/
HP Inc: https://investor.hp.com/home/default.aspx
JetBlue: http://blueir.investproductions.com/investor-relations
Lenovo: https://investor.lenovo.com/en/publications/reports.php
McDonald's: h https://corporate.mcdonalds.com/corpmcd/investors.html
Microsoft: https://www.microsoft.com/en-us/investor
Office Depot (The ODP Corporation): https://investor.theodpcorp.com/
Papa John's: https://ir.papajohns.com/
Sony: https://www.sony.com/en/SonyInfo/IR/
Staples (Sycamore Partners): http://sycamorepartners.com/Investment
Stellantis: https://www.stellantis.com/en/investors/investor-dashboard
UPS: https://investors.ups.com/
Whirlpool: https://investors.whirlpoolcorp.com/home/default.aspx

References

[1] Basler, R. P. (ed.). 1953. *Collected works of Abraham Lincoln*. Piscataway, NJ: Rutgers University Press.

[2] Smith, A. 1977. *An inquiry into the nature and causes of the wealth of nations*. New York: Dutton.

[3] Technically, the economists would say that the market equilibrates when the firm's marginal revenue equals its marginal cost. Since every firm is identical, this means that no firm is earning a profit. At this point there would be no inducement for firms to change what they are doing or for other firms to enter the industry.

[4] Kendall, B., 2022, "FTC case against Facebook to proceed," Wall Street Journal, January 12, A3.

[5] Haget, K. & V. Ngo, 2019, "How Google edged out rivals and built the world's dominant ad machine," Wall Street Journal, November 8, A6. Stevis-Gridneff, M., 2019, "EU's new digital czar: 'Most powerful regulator of big tech on the planet'," New York Times, September 11, 12.

[6] Porter, M. E. 1980. *Competitive strategy*. New York: Free Press.

[7] Goodman, R. A. & M. W. Lawless. 1994. *Technology and strategy: Conceptual models and diagnostics*. New York: Oxford University Press.

[8] Chart derived from author's calculations using data from Damodaran Online Data Archives, http://pages.stern.nyu.edu/~adamodar/New_Home_Page/dataarchived.html#returns.

[9] NPD, 2021. https://www.npd.com/news/entertainment-top-10/2021/top-10-video-games/.

[10] Saloner, G., A. Shepard, & J. Podolny. 2001. *Strategic management*. New York: John Wiley.

[11] We distinguish between profit-making and value-creating enterprises for the moment. Value-creating enterprises might include for-profit companies that produce economic value, but a broader view will include nonprofits as well because they create social value. Nonprofits also exist in industries, and compete with other firms for resources and customers.

[12] Scherer, F. M., & D. Ross. 1990. *Industrial market structure and economic performance* (3rd ed.). Boston: Houghton Mifflin.

[13] Tilley, A., 2022, "Microsoft talent poached in race to build metaverse'" Wall Street Journal, January 11, A1.

[14] Flint J., 2019, "Netflix recruiting blocked," Wall Street Journal, December 13, B4.

[15] Lewis, P. 2004. "Broadband wonderland." Fortune. September 20: 191 - 198.

[16] Bindley, K., 2019, "The phone call isn't dead, it's evolving," Wall Street Journal, October 19, B4.

[17] See http://www.census.gov/eos/www/naics.

[18] Fry, R., 2018, " Millennials are the largest generation in the U.S. labor force," Pew Research Center, April 11, https://www.pewresearch.org/fact-tank/2018/04/11/millennials-largest-generation-us-labor-force/.

[19] West, G. P., III & J. O. DeCastro, 2001, "The Achilles heel of firm strategy: Resource weaknesses and distinctive inadequacies," *Journal of Management Studies* 38(3): 417 - 442.

[20] Pew Research Center. http://www.pewresearch.org.

[21] EPA. 2006. Cleaner small engines are safe. March. http://yosemite.epa.gov/opa/admpress.nsf/a8f952395381d3968525701c005e65b5/db1ecd1d6a793d51852571340069 45e0!OpenDocument.

[22] Bonini, S. M., L. T. Mendonca, & J. M. Oppenheim, 2006, "When social issues become strategic," *McKinsey Quarterly* (2): 20 - 32.

[23] Ries, A., & J. Trout. 2000. *Positioning: The battle for your mind* (3rd ed.). New York: McGraw Hill.

[24] Terhune, C., 2006, "Coke attempts to paint it 'black'," Wall Street Journal. April 1: A2.

[25] https://www-statista-com.

[26] Bunge, J. & J. Kang, 2020, "Grocers bottle their own milk and shake up dairy industry," Wall Street Journal, July 28, A1.

[27] Yuan, L., 2017, "Alibaba, Tencent go to war over Chinese web," Wall Street Journal, December 22, B4.

[28] Kalla, S, 2001, "Fiber glut: It's real," Network Fusion News. September 10.

[29] See http://www.edmunds.com.

[30] Mullin, B. and D. Narcelis, 2022, "Streamers struggle to keep subscribers drawn by one hit," Wall Street Journal, February 1, A1.

[31] Loomis, C. J., 2006, "The tragedy of General Motors," Fortune. February 20: 59 - 75.

[32] Mossberg, W. S., 2006, "Boot camp turns your Mac into a reliable Windows PC," Wall Street Journal. April 6: B1.

[33] Arthur, C., 2014, "Sony's exit from the PC market will not be the last," The Guardian, February 14.

This page is intentionally left blank.

Chapter 5: Value Chain Analysis

LEARNING OBJECTIVES

1. Explain the differences between internal analysis and external analysis.
2. Explain the benefits and drawbacks of using SWOT analysis.
3. Describe how value is created through a firm's internal sets of activities (value chain).
4. Assess how the value chain perspective provides insight on sources of competitive advantage.
5. Perform a value chain analysis.

Apple iPhone X Introduction[1]

The mobile phone industry is intensely competitive. Since the Apple iPhone came to market in 2007, the smartphone industry has skyrocketed to over $500 billion worldwide. This means that each percentage point of market share is worth over $5 billion! In 2021 Apple had a 16% market share of units shipped globally, and increase over the last two years. But since the iPhone is priced higher than competitors, Apple's share of industry profits generated was 75%. Samsung's market share has been declining in the face of lower-cost competitors from the far east.

Apple's iPhone franchise is the core of the company, in 2021 representing fully 52% of its corporate revenue. The iPhone is one of the most successful commercial introductions of all time among consumer products (Figure 5.1). Apple regularly upgrades its line with new models, often leap-frogging competing technology. This affords Apple the opportunity to create value its competitors find difficult to imitate easily. And upgrades continue to foster Apple's image as cutting edge.

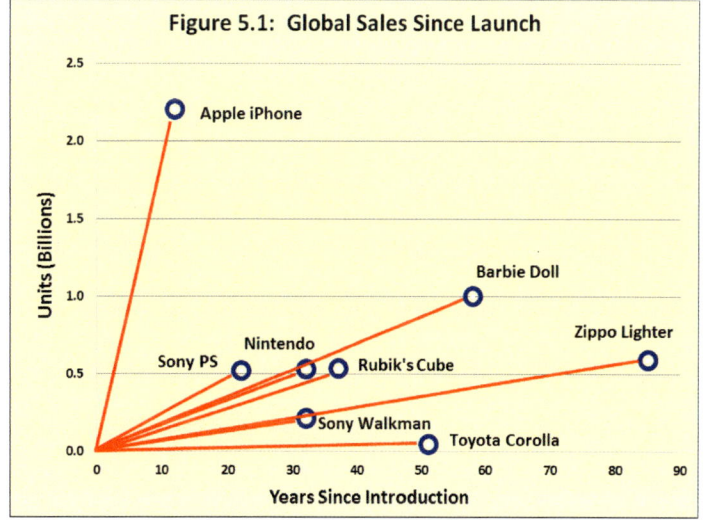

In 2017 Apple introduced the iPhone X. This was an incredibly complex undertaking for so many technical reasons. In development for years, the X featured facial recognition software using vertical-cavity surface-emitting lasers, an organic light emitting diode (OLED) super retinal display screen, advanced true-depth camera and image capture sensing systems, and more. As a complete remake of the iPhone line, the X developers pushed the envelope on how the integration of software and hardware came together in an elegant design.

But once design was complete, Apple needed to work a complicated supply chain to manufacture components, assemble them, and ship them expediently to hungry consumers around the world. The facial recognition system incorporated a "Romeo" laser projection component manufactured by LG Innotek (South Korea) and Sharp (Japan), married to a "Juliet" sensing component manufactured by Lumentum Holdings (Taiwan) and Finisair (Texas). OLED screens were made by competitor Samsung Electronics (South Korea). The phone's antenna came from Murata (Japan) and Career Tech (Taipei), and its main processor was produced by TSMC in Taiwan The entire phone, with components from these and other manufactured parts from 200 suppliers, is finally assembled in China by Hon Hai Precision Industry (Foxconn).

With rival brands like Samsung and Xiaomi becoming increasingly adept at working with suppliers, Apple's design-build system using outside manufacturers has been critical in its success. "Apple has shone as a beacon of how to discover and develop unique materials, coerce and cajole suppliers, and churn out millions of units all without owning any factories," writes Bloomberg tech analyst Tim Culpan. This coordinating capability has also been a facet which competitors have been unable to imitate easily. In developing this process Apple also receives praise for pioneering the elimination of harmful PVCs and brominated flame retardants.

The journey continues past the coordination of assembly, though! Assembled iPhones are loaded onto pallets and taken to the nearby Zhengzhou airport. Apple maintains distribution centers around the world in Australia, China, the Czech Republic, Japan, Singapore, and the U.K. For the U.S. the pallets are put on board Boeing 747 freight planes and flown to a logistics center in Kentucky (after a refueling stop in Anchorage). Pallets are transferred to other carriers, destined for the distribution centers of major retailers (e.g. Best Buy, Verizon, Costco). And Apple arranges to have cartons of phones expressed to each of its nearly 272 domestic retail stores.

This entire process began anew each year from 2019-21 with the new iPhone 11, 12, and 13 models. In 2021 it has reworked its value chain to source chips and OLED screen from new suppliers, so that it can rely less on competitor Samsung and then bargain for lower input costs.

Figure 5.2
Value Chain for Apple iPhones X, 11, 12, and 13

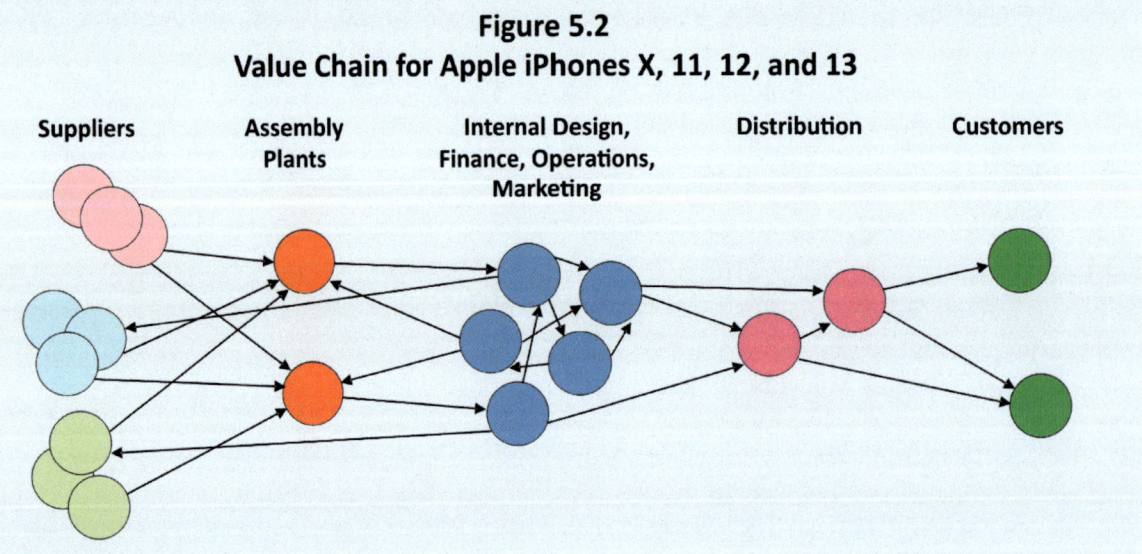

QUESTIONS
1. How does Apple create value?

2. What activities does Apple perform particularly well, and how do they affect the company's position in the mobile phone industry?

3. What is it that Apple does which competitors cannot easily imitate?

INTERNAL ANALYSIS VERSUS EXTERNAL ANALYSIS

In the last chapter we had a chance to explore the impact of industry structure on the strategies of firms and their ability to earn profits. Out of the analysis of the five industry forces, we are able to draw conclusions about industry attractiveness, key success factors (KSFs), and STEEPG driving forces. These factors and forces partially determine how firms must act if they are to succeed. Key success factors can also be used to plot the locations of competitors on a strategic map, determine if there are groups of companies that seek to compete in similar ways, provide insight on the trajectories that companies are following strategically, and identify both potential threats and opportunities.

Figure 5.3
Selected Pharmaceutical Company ROE Percent, 2017-2021

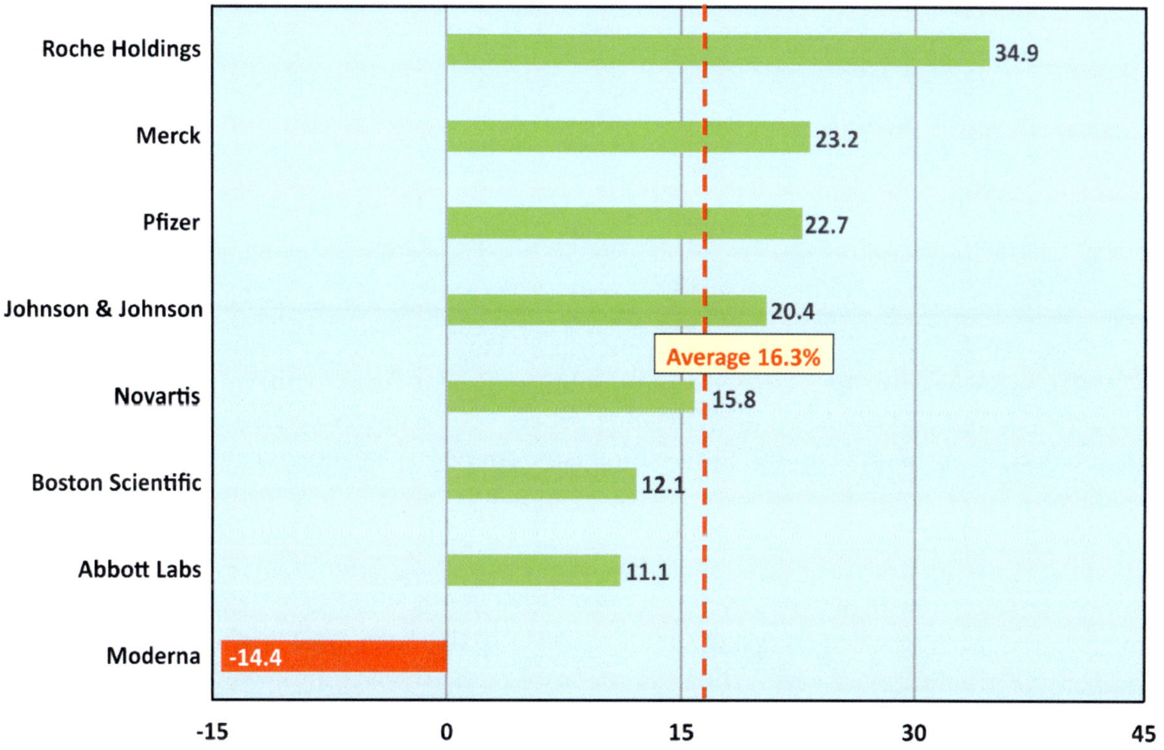

Company	ROE %
Roche Holdings	34.9
Merck	23.2
Pfizer	22.7
Johnson & Johnson	20.4
Novartis	15.8
Boston Scientific	12.1
Abbott Labs	11.1
Moderna	-14.4

Average 16.3%

Despite the insight gained about competitors and firm strategy through industry analysis, understanding strategy requires us to go to a much deeper level. As you may recall from the last chapter, different industries exhibit very different levels of profitability. Industry analysis helps us understand why some industries tend to be more profitable than others. However, this is only part of the picture. The pharmaceutical industry enjoyed one of the highest average levels of returns between 2017 and 2021. However, we see in Figure 5.3 that there is tremendous variation in the performance of companies within this one industry. Roche Holdings earned stellar returns, Merck and Pfizer earned strong returns, while Boston Scientific and Abbott Labs earned below the average for the industry; Moderna produced negative returns. Figure 5.4 demonstrates that variations in performance also hold true in a super-competitive industry characterized by low returns, such as the steel manufacturing industry.

Figure 5.4
Selected Steel Company ROE Percent, 2017-2021

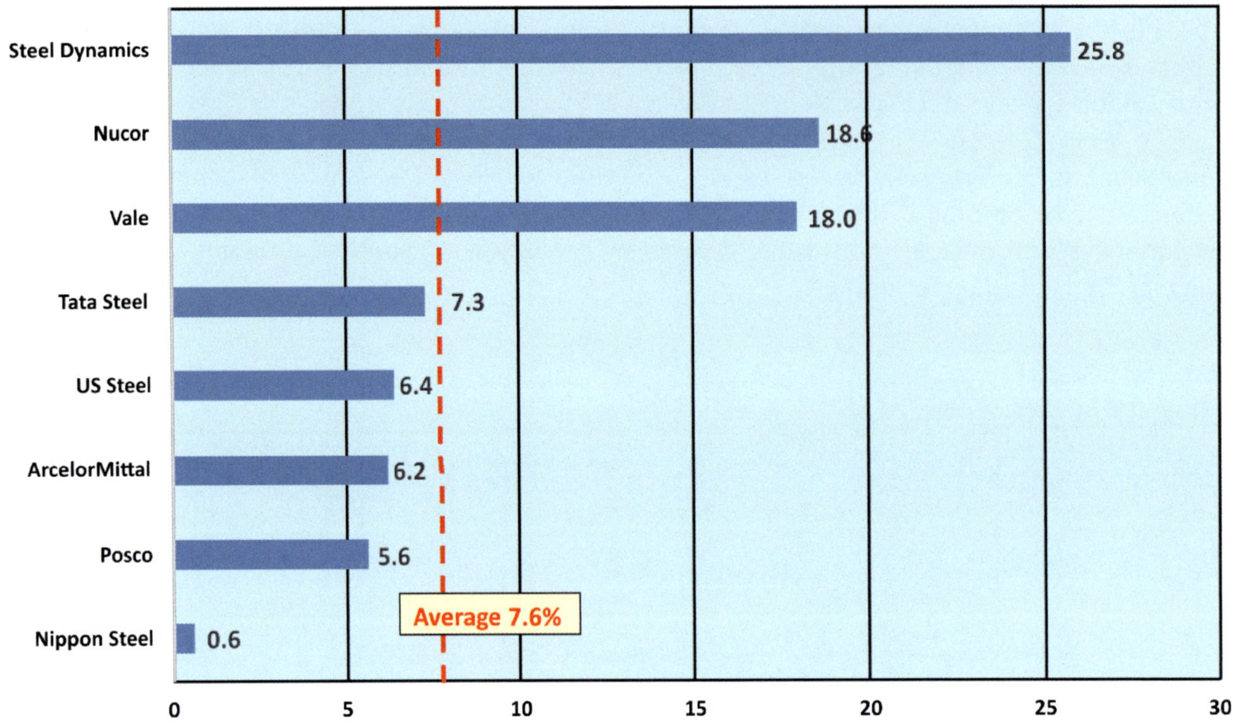

Company	ROE %
Steel Dynamics	25.8
Nucor	18.6
Vale	18.0
Tata Steel	7.3
US Steel	6.4
ArcelorMittal	6.2
Posco	5.6
Nippon Steel	0.6

Average 7.6%

Sophisticated strategy research has demonstrated that industry structure and conditions can only explain a portion of the variance in the performance of firms within an industry. In fact, somewhere between 20-40 percent of the differences in performance among firms within an industry can be explained using the tools of industry analysis.[2] While that insight is critical and important as a starting point for strategy analysis and planning efforts, it is simply not enough! As strategic managers we need to develop more than 1-in-5 odds of understanding the marketplace. Much more of the performance differences between companies in an industry can be understood by looking *inside* companies to examine what they do, what they fail to do, and how they operate. Through "internal analysis" of companies it is possible to gain much greater insight into the sources of competitive advantage that enable them to occupy leading (or lagging) positions in an industry, and to better understand what strategic paths they will follow based on their activities and resource investments. This can be accomplished by delving deeply into companies in order to better answer the key questions we posed in Chapter 1: why do some firms perform better than others, and why are those differences sustainable over a long period of time? It's to the internal analysis of firms that we now turn our attention.

There are three basic methods for conducting an internal analysis that will provide insight into a company's strategic potential: resource-based analysis, SWOT analysis, and value chain analysis. Resource-based analysis is a very popular topic among many strategy professors and professionals; it deserves separate focus as a technique. So the next chapter of this book (Chapter 6) takes up resource-based analysis, since it builds upon ideas in this chapter about the value chain.

The focus of this chapter is on SWOT and value chain. There is a big distinction between these two internal analysis methods. SWOT provides a snapshot of what a company *is*, while the value chain provides perspective on what a company *does*. When asked what music you are listening to today, you share information that is both momentary and dependent upon your mood that day. That music choice describes you at a point in time, just as a SWOT approach attempts to summarize the perception of a company's situation at a moment in time. But when we look at your playlist we can see how many times you listen to different songs and get a pretty good idea on the type of music you listen to the most over time. It is the *patterns* of behavior over time, leading to your present state and suggesting a future path of development, which the Value Chain idea seeks to capture. So you might think about the differences between the methods like the differences between a photograph and a movie: SWOT is a static view of a company at a point in time, and value chain is a dynamic view over time. Each has its uses and benefits, but each also has inherent drawbacks.

SWOT

There is hardly a firm of any size or age that is unfamiliar with the concept of SWOT, and so it is important for you to be familiar with it as well. SWOT consists of four categories: strengths, weaknesses, opportunities, and threats. SWOT analysis has been taught in business schools for over forty years. Almost without exception, every large corporation will go through an annual or biannual strategic planning process. SWOT analysis is usually on the front end of that process in nearly every case. Like fireworks on the 4th of July, it is a familiar – and therefore comfortable – process to anyone involved in strategic planning. As testimony to its ubiquitous nature, a simple Google search in 2022 for the term "SWOT" turns up 123 million hits! Wow!

Strategy Acronym: SWOT

S   Strengths
W   Weaknesses
O   Opportunities
T   Threats

SWOT is usually conducted by a team. Several individuals representing various functions in a company will convene to discuss and agree upon the strengths and weaknesses inherent in their company, and to identify the opportunities and threats that the company faces. The initial conversations are designed to identify these characteristics and can happen at different levels of management. Sometimes senior management will participate, while in other circumstances a middle management team will do the initial work and then present their ideas to senior management for approval. The result of a SWOT analysis is usually a list of factors that the team agrees on as being most important for management to consider. This is a very early first step in the formulation and adjustment of their strategic plans.

Strengths and weaknesses are ordinarily thought of as characteristics of the company. Opportunities or threats are ordinarily construed as either elements of the competitive environment or outside factors, such as the driving forces discussed in the last chapter. In fact, the output of the KSF analysis and strategic mapping exercises done in an industry and competitive analysis (Chapter 4) can be an important input into the process of identifying areas of potential threat (e.g., encroaching competitors on a particular KSF or in a strategic group) and opportunity (e.g., uncontested space in a strategy map). Figure 5.5 shows a typical SWOT analysis, in this case for a manufacturing company that is adding an online sales channel to supplement its traditional physical distribution process.

Figure 5.5
Manufacturing Company SWOT Analysis

Strengths	Opportunities
• Product quality and reliability. • Superior product performance. • Flexible manufacturing capacity. • Staff with end-user experience & perspective. • Possess lists of heavy-user customers. • Strong innovation capability for new products. • Achieved superior industry certifications. • Good information systems support. • Experienced management team.	• New products desired by customers. • Few competitors in international markets. • Suppliers are generally unhappy with manufacturers. • New Capabilities enabled by advances in technology.
Weaknesses	**Threats**
• Customer service unproven. • Products do not cover full range. • Small size relative to competition. • No direct marketing experience. • Limited distribution capacity for all markets. • Sales force thin. • Limited access to outside financing. • Poor long term planning; greatest attention on short term needs	• Pending legislation on safety and standards. • Unclear if recent market growth reflects fad or long term trend. • Possible cannibalizing core business. • Retention of management and staff. • Vulnerable to reactive attack by major competitors.

SWOT Benefits

Easy to understand and use. One of several benefits that arise to companies that use SWOT analysis is that it is a fairly simplistic method of internal analysis that nearly everyone can understand with little formal training. For this reason it is easy for management to involve a broad cross-section of departments and employees in the process. Although companies ordinarily do not extend SWOT involvement to the lowest levels of a company's hierarchy – such as production line workers, salespeople, and customer service reps – the simplicity of the method does at least offer this potential. This may actually be a missed opportunity for many companies because these employees on the "firing line" are often the first to observe how well or how poorly certain company initiatives are faring, or how customers might react. Therefore they tend to have early, first-hand knowledge about potential strengths and weaknesses.

Alignment. Matching up items that are identified in a SWOT analysis can be helpful in determining whether a company is prepared for and properly aligned to deal with looming threats and opportunities. Here the management team compares each of the elements with the other three to make judgments of the following kinds:

- Will our strengths play into emerging opportunities?
- Are there emerging threats that might marginalize our existing strengths?
- Do our weaknesses seriously compromise the company, even though it has strengths?
- Can our strengths overcome looming threats?

As an illustration, let's take a brief look at 3M. 3M is widely recognized as being an innovative company, because they have institutionalized innovation throughout their business practices. Reflecting "research and development which remains the heartbeat of our enterprise,"[3] the company has historically sought to develop 40 percent of its sales from new products introduced within the last four years. In fact, they encourage all employees to take 15 percent of their time – nearly one full day each work week – to experiment with new ideas. So innovation has become a virtue for the company, but it has implications for the nature of opportunities they are realistically able to pursue. In its 2021 10-k the company reported $32.2 billion in worldwide revenue. So achieving the 40 percent new business goal sets a target of $12.9 billion in revenue per year in the next four years from products that do not exist today. Hold on! Did you know this is larger than the annual revenue of more than half the companies in the S&P 500? With this goal in mind, 3M can pursue only large business opportunities. Smaller opportunities (like its original Post-It Notes product line) are likely to be passed over, because the company would need to start up dozens of such small businesses in order to reach the revenue goals. This example illustrates that matching strength to opportunity can reveal appropriate development direction.

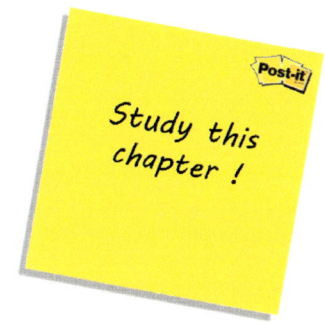

Suggests overall direction. Occasionally management teams will use the matching process to develop overall guidance for the direction of the company. This is accomplished through the use of a TOWS matrix (just SWOT spelled backwards!). Figure 5.6 shows a TOWS matrix that provides general guidance for what direction a company might take. When new opportunities present themselves, for example, the company may decide to expend efforts to overcome existing weaknesses instead of leveraging its current strengths. If threats are looming, the company may focus greater attention on defensive actions to protect the downside from some combination of threat and apparent weakness. In the example above, we saw that its large size prevents 3M from pursuing smaller new business opportunities. One possible way to overcome a weakness associated with large size would be to spin off a new product development group into a separate operation that is unconstrained by size. Hewlett-Packard did this in the 1980s with its printer division. Freed from the corporate policies, constraints, and focus on their main sources of revenue at that time (instruments, calculators, and other tech products), the new division became very successful with new printer technology. In 2021 printers are part of HP Inc., which was spun out of Hewlett-Packard. Printers accounted for 32% of HP's annual revenue but a whopping 69% of its operating earnings. Not bad!

Figure 5.6
TOWS Matrix

	Opportunities	Threats
Strengths	Use strengths to take advantage of opportunities	Use strengths to avoid threats
Weaknesses	Take advantage of opportunities by overcoming weaknesses	Defensive measures to minimize weaknesses and avoid threats

Competitive analysis. With SWOT, the management team may also begin to make comparisons between its company and competitors. This would involve a process similar to the Key Success Factor competitive comparisons discussed in the previous chapter. Having identified a list of strengths and weaknesses, the team would need to decide how to accurately measure each of its own and its competitors' SWOT items using accessible data and information. In this way an objective analysis would reveal the relative strengths and weaknesses of the company versus its competition. Comparisons such as these might lead to decisions to further invest in strength-building initiatives, or to find ways to minimize areas of weakness that competitors might take advantage of.

Strong starting point. Perhaps the greatest value gained by identifying the SWOT components is that the process provides a really good starting point for in-depth discussion and analysis of company strategy and competitive position. Preparing a SWOT list is a first step to focus attention on critical components. Then management needs to engage in a deeper conversation about the nature of its business and its competitive environment.

Potential SWOT Drawbacks

Results in a laundry list. One of the key dangers in a SWOT analysis is that the list of items identified across the four categories becomes very large. This can often occur because the items on the list are usually based upon the opinions of the team members, without supporting data or critical analysis. Since teams are ordinarily composed of managers from different functions in the company, each functional area would like to see its own critical issues included in the list. Other team members may not have sufficient expertise to judge whether function-specific issues outside their areas of expertise are important enough. So inclusion of ideas tends to occur more than exclusion. The result is that a SWOT list can include an immense number of items. For instance a SWOT analysis done for the City of Wilmington, Delaware, produced 95 items in the four categories,[4] while a Columbus State University SWOT analysis contains 70 items.[5] Figure 5.5 shows a more typical list of items generated by a manufacturing company that is considering starting up an online presence for sales directly to competitors. When the list becomes even this long, it becomes very difficult to use in practice. Try to imagine the challenge for 6-7 key team managers from different departments in a company trying to substantively address up to 25 important issues each year as part of the planning process, while at the same time taking care of their ongoing daily departmental management responsibilities.[6] With long lists it is hard to know where to focus.

Over simplification. The items that are listed in SWOT often tend to sound fairly general, lacking the kind of specificity that creates meaning. Where "new product development capability" is listed as a strength, for instance, the generality of the item tends to disguise whether this is really a successful business practice, and if so what is behind it. Is the company strong in this dimension because they are excellent at sourcing new ideas, excellent at translating ideas from concept to actual product, able to move through the process very quickly, or adept in their marketing and sales methods for introducing new products to the market? A manufacturing company in North Carolina listed "new product development capability" as one of their strengths even though sales from products introduced in the past four years accounted for less than 1% of sales. General descriptions often hide more than they reveal. In addition, the guidance provided by the use of the TOWS matrix also tends to be fairly general, not focusing on specific products, services, or operations. Finally, the method provides little guidance on the appropriate balance of effort that should be devoted to different cells in the TOWS matrix.

Definitions may vary. In many cases it is not clear to management whether a particular item represents a strength or a weakness, or perhaps both. 3M's size clearly presents a strength for the company because size confers market power, better access to financial markets, and other advantages. However size also represents a weakness since the company is unable to pursue the smaller business opportunities that once made it successful, and is not particularly agile in responding to sudden competitive moves. If size is both a strength and a weakness simultaneously, the management implications may be difficult to determine. Here's another example. General Electric CEO Jeffrey Immelt took over the company in 2002 and was widely hailed as one of the strongest corporate leaders in the world. He led the company through multiple industry cycles, the 9/11 tragedy, recessions, and the global financial crisis. And yet by 2020 he has been roundly criticized for GE's poor long term performance relative to the S&P 500, largely arising from his penchant for burying bad news and only focusing on positives.[7] Was his leadership truly strength or weakness, or possibly both? Hard to tell.

Are they relevant? Simply because a company has a particular strength does not mean it can effectively compete in its industry. If a company's strengths or weaknesses have relevance for the key success factors in the industry, then attention devoted to them can be important. However business history is rife with examples of companies which developed amazing strengths that were incredibly irrelevant for their industries. Sharper Image, which finally went bankrupt in 2008, originally thrived on its knack and pizzazz in sourcing and presenting high-tech personal gadgets such as ion air purifiers, jogging watches, and nose hair trimmers (!). Unfortunately, the kind of creative force that was the foundation of the business became irrelevant to consumers and retailing in the 2000s.

Figure 5.7
Strengths in Successive SWOT Analyses

Year 1	Year 3
A ──────→	A
B ──────→	B
C ──────→	C*
D ──────•	
──────→	E
F ──────→	F
──────→	G

Static view. The most discouraging part of SWOT is that the list developed during each planning cycle only provides a picture of the company at a fixed point in time. Remember that we said SWOT is like a snapshot. From one planning cycle to the next it is not uncommon to find new strengths appear and previously held strengths disappear. A company conducts its strategic planning biannually, and in successive plans has identified the strengths pictured in Figure 5.7. Items A, B, and F remain strengths consistently over this period, but C has morphed into something slightly different as C*. Meanwhile new strengths E and G have appeared and D has for some reason dropped off the list. As time goes by and companies encounter changing market conditions with evolving competition, it is not unusual to witness these kinds of changes in perceived strengths taking place. In the process of creating the list there is little attention devoted to understanding why or how a company came to possess a certain strength or develop a certain weakness to begin with. Without developing an understanding of cause-and-effect, management is not provided with guidance on what kinds of steps to take going forward.

A dynamic view of a company's strategic potential is more appropriate and more useful. As strategic managers we are interested in understanding not only that strengths and weaknesses may exist, but also what it is that creates strengths and prevents weaknesses from developing. Do you recall the quotation from Abraham Lincoln in Chapter 1? If we understand how actions and activities undertaken in the past result in our current strategic position, then we can make better judgments about the effects that our current actions and activities will have going forward. This is the vital distinction between SWOT and the value chain perspective, to which we turn below.

The Greenbrier Resort[8]

The Greenbrier resort has stood in the mountains of West Virginia for more than two hundred years. Founded as a haven for those seeking the healing powers of the nearby White Sulphur Springs, the resort really came into being as more than a hotel when the C&O Railroad purchased the property in 1910. Today the enormous property has more than 700 rooms, 10 lobbies and a complete conference center. The resort boasts five championship golf courses, tennis courts, a spa, and more than 6,500 acres of land. Twenty-seven U.S. Presidents have stayed there, and the U.S. Congress regularly sojourns there to discuss policy and upcoming legislative agendas. Among the more interesting features of the resort is the vast underground bunker built to house the President and Congress in the event of a national emergency. While not easy to travel to, one of the real appeals to the resort is its relative proximity to major cities in the eastern United States.

As the 2008 recession wore on, the Greenbrier reported a sharp drop in hotel stays. The recession had accelerated a trend in declining traffic due to competition from a wide variety of resorts. Other resorts were more appealing to younger generations and could be reached easily and inexpensively by air. In March 2009 the resort filed for bankruptcy, having lost $168 million in 2008. It listed debt of $500 million and assets of only $100 million.

QUESTIONS

1. What are the Strengths and Weaknesses of the resort?
2. What are the Opportunities and Threats for the resort?
3. How would you suggest they take advantage of their Strengths and minimize their Weaknesses?
4. How would you suggest they take advantage of their Opportunities and minimize their Threats?

VALUE CHAIN

Much like SWOT, the concept of the value chain was first explored in strategic management a little over thirty years ago, when management scholars started thinking about the sets of activities that are combined by a company to form a successful "business system." The value chain provides "a systematic way of examining all the activities a firm performs and how they interact ..." in order to find a basis for competitive advantage.[9] In the first chapter of this textbook, we stressed that value creation is one of the core concepts at the heart of effective strategic management. As a method of internal analysis, exploring the value chain requires us to go significantly deeper into a company than does the SWOT approach. The basic rationale of the value chain is that some types of activities are observed when a company competes one way, while other sets of activities are observed when another company competes in a different way. Therefore through the value chain we move below summary ideas about a company's strong or weak points; instead, we examine the nature of activities performed in or by the company, and we estimate how such activities are able to uniquely create value in the industry vis-à-vis competitors.

Industry and Company Value Chains

The value chain concept recognizes that a company is one of many entities that participate in an entire chain of value-adding activity within any given industry (see Figure 5.8).

Figure 5.8
Chain of Industry Value-Adding Activities

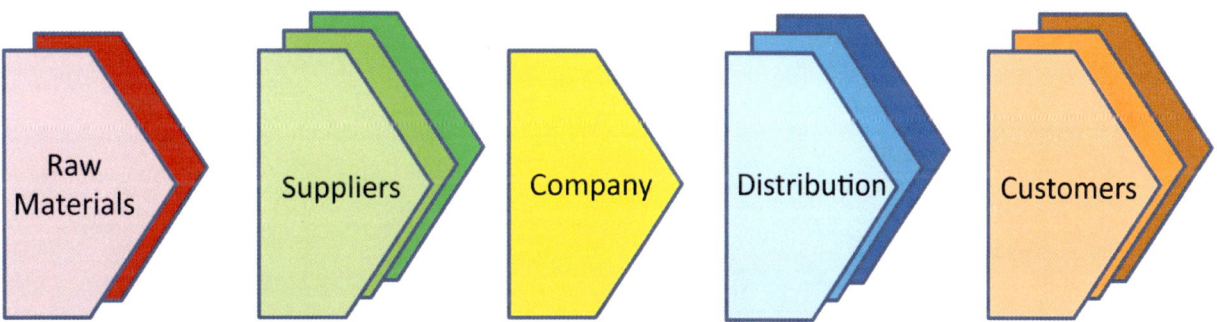

When you open up a can of La Croix flavored seltzer at home, it is because a complex array of integrated activities has taken place across an industry or industries that provide you this enjoyment. The chain of activities starts with basic raw materials and extends all the way to the finished product in your hand. Consider just the aluminum can itself: from mining bauxite ore, to the smelter, to mixing aluminum with manganese and magnesium, to mixing in recycled content, to extruding and roll casting aluminum sheets. Then in the production facility sheets are cut and formed into cans, filled with a beverage mixture on a high-speed production line (that in itself is a complicated process involving multiple parts of an industry), packed in 12-can cartons, and loaded onto pallets. These are shipped in semi-trucks and then finally distributed to your supermarket. The iPhone story at the beginning of this chapter also illustrates some of the sophisticated array of activities across an industry value chain that manifests a new phone in your pocket.

In addition to value chain activities across a single industry or multiple industries, there are value chain activities *within* each company competing in the industry. Although we may tend to think about competing companies in terms of the products or services that we see them providing, the value chain concept instead focuses on the different sets of activities that ultimately lead to the production of their products or services. This is the great insight about strategy that the value chain perspective provides: *a company is nothing more than a set of organized activities, and their products or services are simply the outcomes of the activities that have led to their creation.* When we refer to a company as an organization, occasionally we might be referring to an organization of people, such as through departmental structure and hierarchy. However, at a very foundational level a company is structured so that employees *act* in certain ways. It is their *activities* that describe how a company actually conducts its business and produces products or services.

It is relatively easy to observe examples of how different activity sets define the differences between competitors and their approaches in an industry. In the photo finishing business Kodak was known for its focus on producing high-quality paper that was used by camera shops to print pictures. With the advent of digital photography, Canon (known for its strengths in plain paper copiers and printers) entered the camera market and encouraged end users to print pictures on Canon printers. In response Kodak developed the Easy-Share camera-printer dock, and rapidly expanded its photo kiosks in drug stores and other retail locations nationwide. In book retailing the activity sets that distinguish Amazon.com from "bricks and mortar" based Barnes & Noble are quite dramatic. Figure 5.9 provides other examples that illustrate how competitors' strategic approaches are characterized by different activity sets.[10]

**Figure 5.9
Company Value Chains Differ**

Industry	Company & value chain activity	Company & value chain activity
Used car sales	Carmax used car lots physical inspection	Carvana online previewing delivery to your home
Business education	Harvard real professors in physical classrooms	University of Phoenix directed self-education diplomas by mail
Personal computers	Dell, HP modular design mass customization JIT manufacturing	Apple proprietary design limited model selection
Movie rental	Redbox neighborhood kiosks	Netflix access by mail & streaming
Steel	Arcelor-Mittal blast furnaces large volume from iron ore	Nucor electric arc furnaces mini-mills using scrap
Food retailing	Whole Foods exceptional quality organics & naturals	Food Lion average quality wide selection

Primary and Support Activities

Looking carefully within any company, we can differentiate between two kinds of important value-adding activities. When we mention "Toyota," most people will think of Celicas, Prius's, 4Runners and other cars and trucks; when we say "Starbucks," it calls to mind something like a "vente latte double shot no whip skim extra hot" (yikes!). If we mention "Priceline," we tend to think of the inexpensive ticket we were able to get on their website. That is, most people naturally tend to associate companies with their products and types of services.

But we need to develop a more complex view. Figure 5.10 presents a customary value chain diagram.[11] Along the bottom are "primary activities." These are the activities engaged in to tangibly produce the products and services that come to mind when a company's name is mentioned. If we walked into a Pepsi facility, we would expect to see these activities on the bottom of the figure taking place: ingredients and packaging materials coming in the back warehouse door, the high-speed lines queuing and filling cans, preparing the finished goods for shipping, and so on. We also regularly observe the Pepsi trucks delivering product to local stores, and we see their ads on TV with their most current "hip" pitch person.

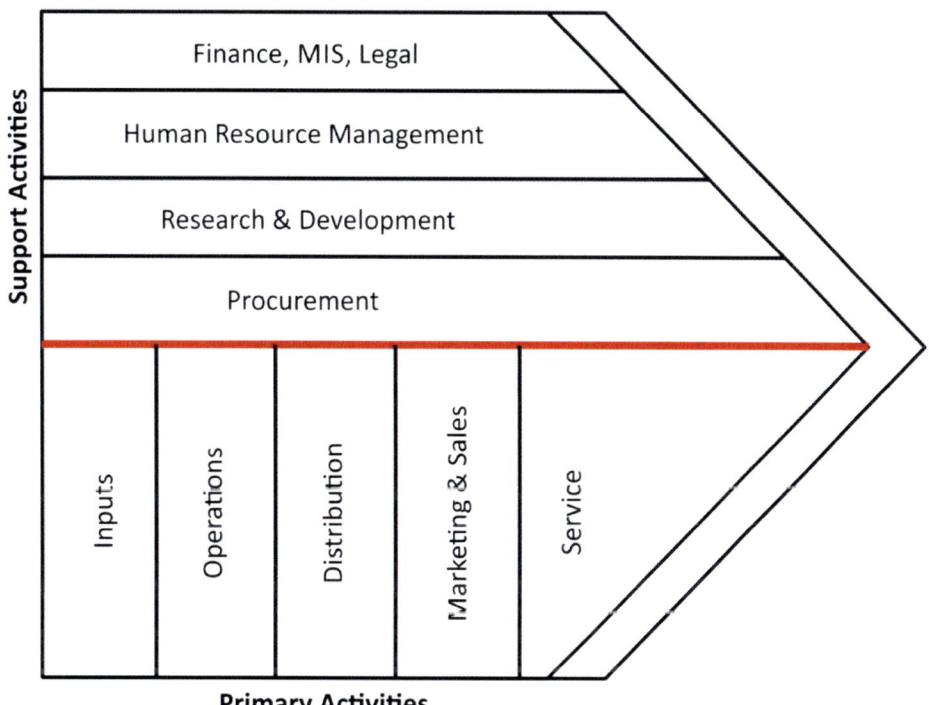

**Figure 5.10
Company Value Chain**

In contrast, in the top half of Figure 5.10 are what have been called "support activities." These include much of the white collar work done in companies such as finance, information systems, human resources, legal work, research and development, and purchasing efforts. When we consider any type of company and its products or services, we generally do not think too much about the people performing these so-called support functions despite the fact that those jobs are usually more coveted by new college graduates. When we step into the Pepsi plant, we are struck with the furious production activity going on before our eyes, not with what the person in the cubicle upstairs is working on.

Which type of activities – primary or support – do you think are more important from the standpoint of strategic management? One perspective on this comes from a study on employment in the United States conducted a few years ago, examining the importance of both manufacturing and service jobs in America. Whereas manufacturing jobs involve handling physical objects, service jobs involve "anything … that could not be dropped on your foot."[12] Service activities include such areas as finance, HR, purchasing, research, design, engineering, administration, and legal, even in traditional manufacturing companies. By the beginning of the 21st century manufacturing activities constituted less than 20 percent of U.S. employment while service activities represented more than 75 percent. Service activities, which include all the activities in the top half of the company value chain in Figure 5.10, are where employment is concentrated. Here, and in the coordination that must occur between support activities and primary activities, is where significant strategic value is truly added.[13]

Figure 5.11 provides an example of a value chain, in this case for a restaurant that intended to serve its customers within 60 seconds of their order. The restaurant's approach to the market and competition is based on a "differentiation" strategy (we will read more about this in Chapter 7). Guided by its mission "saving people time," the company engages in speed-supporting activities in virtually every cell of its value chain. Moreover, it works to ensure that activities and investments it makes in one part of its value chain are consistent with or amplify activities in other parts of its value chain. The connecting lines in the figure, for example, illustrate how its investment in research on cooking technology and kitchen layout impact speedy store operations. Its purchasing department identifies suppliers who can rapidly provide pre-cut and pre-cooked ingredients, which makes food preparation much faster. Its development of a food ordering app allows it to target market to busy customers on the go.

Figure 5.11
Value Chain of Speedy Fast Food Restaurant

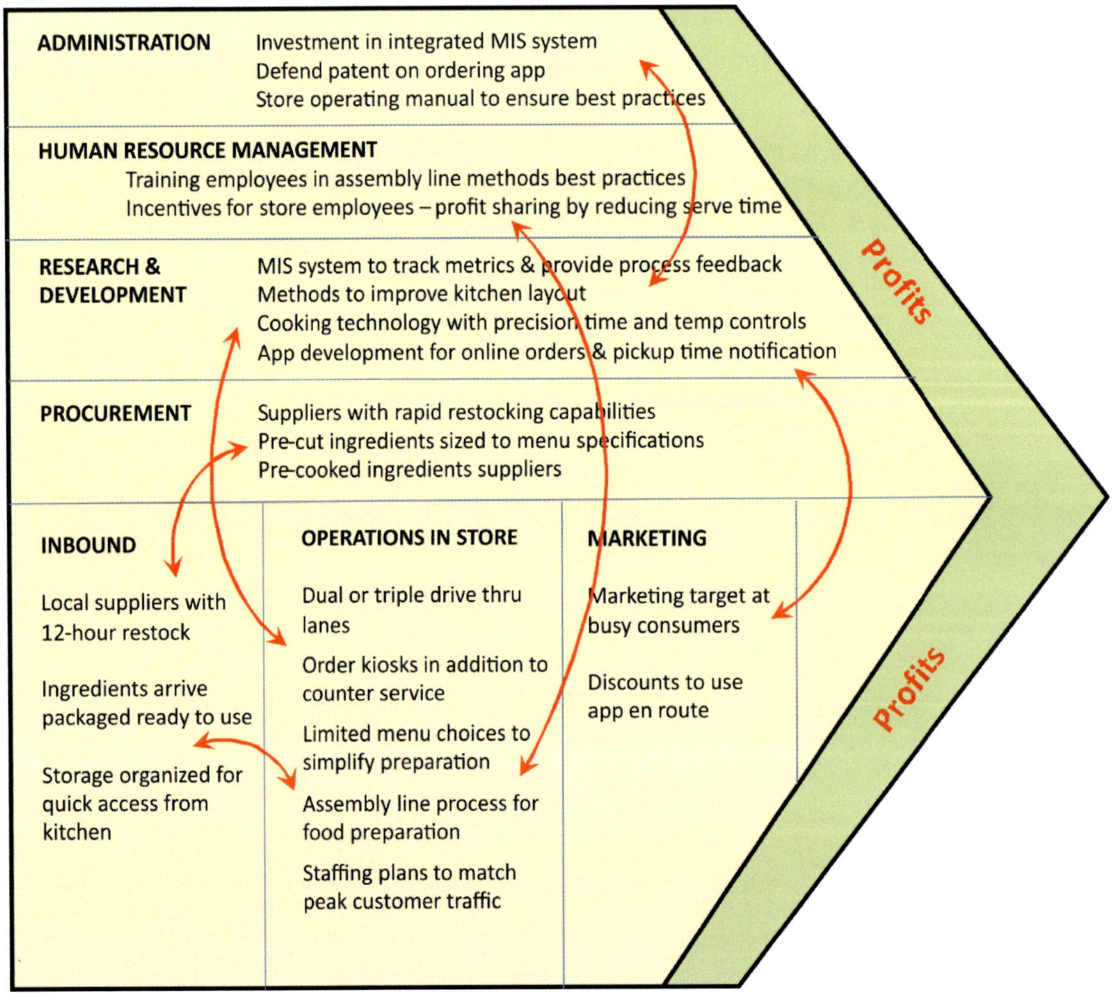

ADMINISTRATION
- Investment in integrated MIS system
- Defend patent on ordering app
- Store operating manual to ensure best practices

HUMAN RESOURCE MANAGEMENT
- Training employees in assembly line methods best practices
- Incentives for store employees – profit sharing by reducing serve time

RESEARCH & DEVELOPMENT
- MIS system to track metrics & provide process feedback
- Methods to improve kitchen layout
- Cooking technology with precision time and temp controls
- App development for online orders & pickup time notification

PROCUREMENT
- Suppliers with rapid restocking capabilities
- Pre-cut ingredients sized to menu specifications
- Pre-cooked ingredients suppliers

INBOUND
- Local suppliers with 12-hour restock
- Ingredients arrive packaged ready to use
- Storage organized for quick access from kitchen

OPERATIONS IN STORE
- Dual or triple drive thru lanes
- Order kiosks in addition to counter service
- Limited menu choices to simplify preparation
- Assembly line process for food preparation
- Staffing plans to match peak customer traffic

MARKETING
- Marketing target at busy consumers
- Discounts to use app en route

Profits

Value Chain Benefits

Illustrates derivation of strengths and weaknesses. We pointed out earlier that the list of strengths and weaknesses is likely to change over time, but that SWOT does not substantively explore the reasons behind such changes. The value chain perspective can answer these questions because it is the activities that a company undertakes that lead to positions of superiority (strength) or contribute to positions of weakness. Examining the activities therefore focuses attention on the causes of internal strengths and weaknesses. For example, "we are particularly strong in new products because of how well our marketing research and R&D staff works together to move new ideas rapidly into development and production." A position of strength is the result of activities.

Dynamic. The activities that take place within companies are often routines – organized and systemized ways of conducting affairs. When companies are successful, like a well-oiled machine they seek to reproduce and fine-tune the actions they took that made them successful. For these reasons the activities that lead to success tend to persist over periods of time. If companies are not successful, then they try to change the ways they conduct business in order to find more effective methods. When weaknesses that have developed remain stubbornly persistent, it is likely because a company's actions are perpetuating them. So a focus on the activities, which reflect patterns of behavior over a period of time, has a dynamic quality to it that the static SWOT approach invariably misses.

More predictable path of development. When the analysis focuses on how patterns of activities result in performance, it becomes much easier to predict what future developments will take place for a company. If it is true that examining activities helps develop a cause-and-effect understanding of successes and failures, then that same logic can be used productively to look ahead. Since managing strategically involves setting goals and objectives for the future, an understanding of the effects of actions and behaviors can guide goal setting. This understanding can also reveal gaps that exist between goals that have been set and the predicted results of activities the company currently engages in.

Spotlights internal synchronization and consistency of effort. One of the hallmarks of strategic decisions discussed in Chapter 1 is that they significantly affect all parts of the organization. Coordination across departments and functional areas (marketing, finance, operations, etc.) is integral to effective strategic management. While many activities highlighted in a value chain analysis will occur within these functional areas, the value chain explicitly recognizes the need to coordinate with other departments. In this way the company accomplishes the required level of cross-department integration and consistency of effort in its competitive approach. Therefore identifying how activities are coordinated across the value chain becomes extremely important. This important dimension will be discussed further in the next section.

Provides more actionable information for managing strategy. With attention on the day-to-day activities as the means to understand how competitive strengths are developed, it should come as no surprise that value chain analysis can be very useful as a tool of management. Since the analysis has drilled down to the level of actions that departments and people take, decisions to enhance strengths or correct weaknesses can focus on specific activities. By breaking down a conceptual strength (such as "new product development capability") into specific sets of activities that lead to competitive advantage, management has more actionable information that can guide investments made to enhance the process.

Potential Value Chain Drawbacks

Depends on information systems to provide useful data. It is nice to be able to break down a company's overall strengths into sets of activities that in combination or in sequence produce a positive outcome. Yet the risk remains that these contributing activities are described in only general terms, and this does not go far enough to understand the company's approach relative to competition. Remember from Chapters 1 and 2 that the goal of strategic management is to be different from and better than competitors. The provision and use of objective information is required to draw informed conclusions.

One NASCAR team worked diligently to reduce the pit time for its driver, which contributes mightily to overall race standings. Yet by collecting metrics to evaluate their improvements relative to their competition, they discovered that competing teams had also reduced their pit times. Moreover, the team that thought it had achieved competitive superiority on this dimension employed a greater number of pit crew workers to accomplish the reduced time, and so the cost/benefit comparison with its competitor looked even worse. A company may conclude, for instance, that its new product development capability is strong because it moves through the R&D process quickly (from idea to finished product). However, more data is needed to have confidence that this conclusion is warranted. Is the development time, in fact, faster than what competitors have been able to engineer? Is the development time compressed because the company overspends on staff and resources in this area, relative to competition?

Even though competitive information may not always be easily available, the company must use data to develop metrics providing hard evidence to support preliminary conclusions. Activity-based costing, which students are exposed to in management accounting classes, can be helpful in developing internal cost and performance metrics.

More focus internally, less focus on market. One of the positive features of SWOT is that it explicitly recognizes market threats and opportunities as components of its analysis. With value chain analysis there could be a tendency to simply focus inwardly on activities and behaviors of the company, and not account for the nature of the marketplace. It is not uncommon to find that companies perform sets of activities in certain ways "because they have always done it this way," or because these activities have contributed to past successes and have therefore been reinforced over time. In the 1990s, the pigments manufacturing division of Ciba-Geigy had significantly reduced their costs per ton produced while maintaining product quality. Yet they later discovered that they were losing market share because competition had moved to more adeptly respond to escalating customer requirements by producing higher quality at even lower costs, leaving Ciba-Geigy behind.[14]

Value is defined in the marketplace, and the market is constantly shifting based on technological advances, changing customer preferences, and dynamic competition. When companies consider the activities they engage in as part of the "value chain," attention must remain focused on how the marketplace continues to shape the meaning of value.

VALUE CHAIN AND COMPETITIVE ADVANTAGE

Value Creation

What is value, and how is it created? This simple question is really at the very heart of effective strategic management. Value creation occurs when some other party appreciates something that we do for them and is willing to execute a profitable transaction with us as a result. Value is thus defined in the marketplace through transactions between willing buyers and willing sellers; it is not defined by either party in isolation from the other. In his California kitchen, Wally Amos created a special recipe for chocolate chip cookies that people loved and which he developed into the Famous Amos brand that has flourished for over 40 years. In contrast, Fortune 44 was a Colorado company that developed sensational tasting fortune cookies, only to discover that few people appreciated a great-tasting fortune cookie enough to buy them. The company went out of business very quickly.

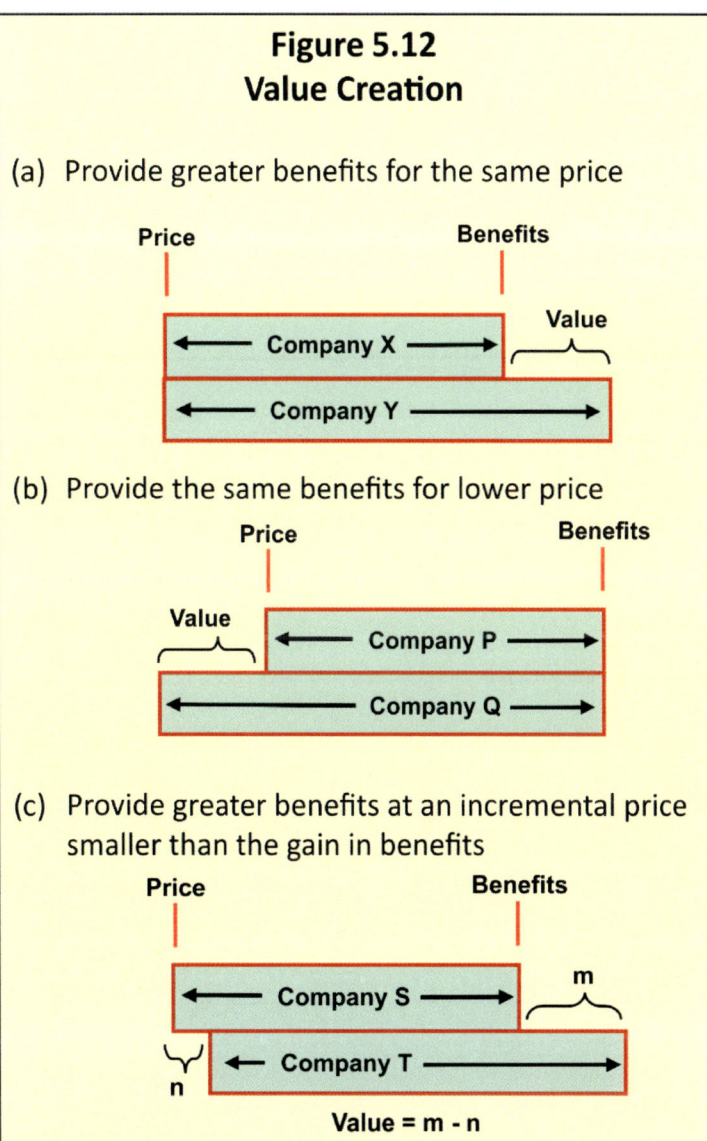

There are several basic ways in which value can be created. The most obvious way to create value appreciated by others is to provide greater benefits to them for the same price they have been accustomed to paying previously. Panel (a) in Figure 5.12 illustrates that Company Y has created value in this fashion, compared to Company X. For example, in 2005, for no extra annual fee The Wall Street Journal added a "weekend edition" delivered on Saturdays to its regular subscribers.

Another means to create value involves just the opposite of these examples, by providing exactly the same benefits as always but at a price that has been reduced below what is normally paid. In panel (b) of Figure 5.12 Company Q has somehow figured out how to deliver to its customers precisely the same benefits they have always received, but at a lower price than Company P still charges (presumably reflecting that Q has discovered ways to effect cost savings). At the dawn of the "browser wars" in the 1990s, Microsoft gave away Internet Explorer for free while Netscape continued to charge customers for its software.

Panel (c) of the figure combines elements of both these basic methods for creating value. In this case Company T has raised its prices over what is normally paid, but it delivers significantly greater benefits than does Company S; here the value created by T is the difference between m and n in the figure. For corporate customers Dell started preloading not only software but also inventory "tag" information on both its PCs and the customer's inventory database, charging $100 more for this service but also creating up to $200 savings in inventory tracking expenses per PC for the corporate customer. Apple's iPhones also fall into this category. They are certainly more expensive than other smartphones. Yet the Apple product is often the smartphone of choice because its design and capabilities deliver significantly greater benefits to customers (both real and perceived) that more than offset its higher price.

There is a fourth method of value creation that is not illustrated in the figure. It is also possible to create value by broadening access to benefits to a wider audience, without sacrificing the benefits delivered to existing customers. For many years Coors beer was not distributed east of the Mississippi River – a decision made by the company for both operational and marketing reasons. This created a sort of mystique about the brand on the east coast. In 1981 national distribution was initiated, spreading the highly desirable western brand to those in the east who had never before tried it. eBay and Craigslist become more valuable to existing customers when their networks of users expands, since this provides everyone a more efficient auction environment, through a greater selection of merchandise and a larger group of potential buyers. Often the value created by broadening access involves building a new type of customer base or reaching out to new geographic markets, such as was the case with the Coors expansion.

However, value can also be viewed as a social good, unrelated to products and services provided by companies. Several states have, over the years, managed to reduce unemployment and its associated governmental cost by connecting unemployment compensation applicants with a local jobs database. Value is created for taxpayers because government spending can then be redirected to other vital needs, and value is created for unemployed workers who get connected with potential employers.

Consider Dell Technologies. In 2013 the computer manufacturer established the 2020 Legacy of Good Plan, which promoted values important to customers, suppliers and employees.

These included recycling as well as advanced HR practices encouraging flexible work options, mitigating unconscious bias, and improving satisfaction. In 2019 the company updated and extended these value-creating efforts in its new 2030 Progress Made Real initiative. The new social impact programs are designed to advance sustainability, cultivate inclusion, transform lives, and uphold ethics and privacy. These values, which can only be fully articulated by people throughout the organization working across traditional department and functional silos (i.e. working across the value chain), will be appreciated by many stakeholders as well as the communities in which Dell locates.

As this example suggests, although ordinarily value creation is discussed in the context of what companies are able to do for their customers downstream in the industry, it is also appropriate to consider value creation possibilities upstream for suppliers. A company can create value for suppliers in several ways, and then capture that value to enhance its strategic position relative to its competitors. For example, research and development may identify a new manufacturing process that reduces costs previously borne by suppliers in providing highly specified raw material inputs. Another alternative may be that a company will outsource a particular function to a supplier that takes advantage of the supplier's own unique capabilities. Toshiba, for example, used United Parcel Service for pickups and redeliveries in its laptop warranty repair service. Finding that its laptop customers valued "speed" when needing repairs, Toshiba turned to UPS – where speed is a valued organizational process – to outsource the actual laptop repair operation. Laptop customers were pleased because repair time was reduced, and value was created for supplier UPS by delivering new business to them.[15] A new venture often confronts suppliers who are hesitant to do business with an unproven, risky enterprise. However the promise of providing access to entirely new end users is a significant value because it can accelerate supplier growth. Whole Foods provided precisely this type of broader market access to organic foods manufacturers, whose increased volume and greater efficiencies later resulted in cost savings for Whole Foods.

Value Capture, Imitation, and Competitive Advantage

For a company to gain competitive advantage it must be able to capture the value that is created. Assume that Company Y in Figure 5.12 (a) has, in fact, figured out a way to provide greater benefits than Company X or the rest of its competitors without charging a higher price. Building on the logic of perfect competition we explored in Chapter 4, we might expect that the other competitors will observe what Y is doing and then imitate it right away. Any kind of advantage gained from providing greater benefits will be competed away over some period of time. How, then, is value captured? To capture value a company must perform a set of activities that is superior to the way in which its competition acts. In addition, the company's set of activities must be idiosyncratic, meaning that they must be unique. To perform a set of activities in a unique fashion also means that competitors will not be able to *imitate* that set of activities, or cannot imitate them very easily or very inexpensively. Therefore, value capture occurs when a company creates value by acting in ways that its competitors cannot. Usually this means the company has created what we call barriers to imitation.

So what portions of a company's value chain activities are difficult or impossible for a competitor to imitate? Look back at the company value chain diagram in Figure 5.10. In most cases the primary activities associated with the actual production of a manufactured item or a service can be reproduced because they are more observable to outsiders. Although the Coca-Cola secret recipe has been the subject of much speculation and news over the years, any food technologist could easily identify its chemical makeup with commonly available analysis equipment. Knowing the formulation, an exact imitation of the product could be reproduced. With sufficient financial backing, an efficient canning line could also be installed that replicates the manufacturing process for the finished product. Indeed, Sam's Choice Cola was released to the market in 1991 and although sold only in the Walmart chain, has done exceedingly well as a private label brand.[16] Similarly, competitors in the coffee business can closely imitate the physical characteristics of a   typical Starbucks shop, the roast of its coffee, and its other beverage selections. These characteristics are more tangible, and can be reverse-engineered and reproduced fairly easily.

Value chain activities that are far less obvious to outsiders and competitors, and therefore far more difficult to imitate, are the support activities. These are unobservable to outsiders, so competitors can only surmise how the research and development operates, what kinds of human resource practices are employed, the nature of internal financial controls that provide for sound management, or the policies and procedures used by a purchasing department to ensure higher quality inputs and/or lower costs. If a company hires exceptional employees to staff these support domains, and if the company develops particularly effective ways of operating within each of these domains, then it increasingly insulates the company from competitive imitation.

Taking this line of reasoning one step further, the greatest source of value capture resides in the coordination and linkages that exist between and across elements of a company's value chain. Look once again at the coordination links depicted in the fast food company value chain in Figure 5.11. Consistent with the nature of strategy, to the extent that a company can tightly organize, coordinate, and orchestrate all of its value-creating activities into a unified, consistent approach to the marketplace, the more it ensures that its value chain is idiosyncratic and not subject to imitation. The intangible, unobservable nature of this sort of coordination – often embedded in routines and tacitly-understood ways of acting – means it is impossible for competitors to copy it. *This is really a critical point, and we urge you to thoughtfully re-read the last two paragraphs*!

Here are two illustrations. Hackensack University Hospital reduced the time it takes to treat heart attack patients by 30 percent and has a mortality rate for heart attacks 2 percent below the national average. It has further reduced readmission rates for heart patients. It achieved these results because of an intense effort to review and establish new cross-functional procedures and coordination.[17] In the $89 billion electronic manufacturing services industry, 77% of manufacturing is done outside the United States in order to take advantage of low-wage countries. However Plexus, a Neenah, Wisconsin, company, generates 69% of its revenue from components manufactured in the United States. The company uniquely specializes in low-volume production of a wide variety of items. To do so requires tremendous coordination across its internal and external value chains in order to achieve both flexibility to change quickly and inexpensively as well as maintain control over costs.[18]

Even if a competitor were to hire away a top executive and his or her staff (which has occasionally happened in various industries), it will be difficult for that individual or staff to be as successful in their new organization. The nature of their relationships with other people and departments will be new and take time to develop, and routines or procedures to work across functions will be different. The aspects that work toward coordination and consistency of approach throughout any organization – factors such as culture, communication systems, personal relationships established among employees, long-held cross-organizational routines – are impossible to objectively observe and extremely difficult for competitors to duplicate. We will talk more about these types of intangibles as critical "resources" in the next chapter.

Disney's Princesses: Working Across the Value Chain [19]

Disney employees have long debated how far the company should go in updating its heroines for newer times. The company has been criticized for promoting outdated notions of femininity and damsel-in-distress stories in which only a man can save the day. Parents wrestle with messages the stories send their children, especially in an age of female presidential candidates, women CEOs, and #MeToo. Popular stars have commented publicly on this situation:
- Kristen Bell (voice of Anna in "Frozen"): "Don't you think it's weird that the prince kisses Snow White without her permission?"
- Keira Knightley kept "The Little Mermaid" from her home because Ariel decided to

forfeit her voice to find love: "...do not give up your voice for a man. Hello?!"

How has Disney responded? Hundreds of employees work on a princess brand when a new movie is in production. They work across functions within the film group, such as creative development, animation, marketing, marketing research, and finance. And they must work across different groups, because major new movie releases are also timed to involve consumer products, theme parks, and pre-planned television extensions. Sharing ideas across platforms about colors, language, attitude, and personality of the new princess achieves the coordination and balance necessary to resonate with the largest number of fans. A modification in one area is only made if it is coordinated with and amplifies actions in other areas.

Have they been successful? Rey, the lightsaber-wielding protagonist in Star Wars, won over young girls. "Elena of Avalor" and "Sofia the First" portray more independent heroines. Elsa, the strong-willed "Frozen" star, embodied just the kind of message they wanted to send. The two "Frozen" movies have collected $2.7 billion in the worldwide box office. The 2017 live-action remake of "Beauty and the Beast" included a more confident Belle, and has collected $1.3 billion at the box office.

Value Creation and Capture Through Opportunity Recognition

In the first few pages of Chapter 1 we pointed out that *value creation* and *opportunity recognition* are strategic imperatives for competing in the 21st century. The value chain concept allows us to see how these can be accomplished simultaneously. Implicit in the notion of value creation and capture is that a company is able to identify an opportunity to provide greater benefits for customers or suppliers, or discover ways to reduce costs and prices. There are a great many ways in which new ideas and opportunities are brought to the surface in organizations.[20] Competitive advantage, however, arises to the extent that some company in an industry is more successful in this process than others, and to the extent that its methods for doing so cannot easily be imitated.

The sets of activities through which companies may excel in opportunity recognition include the following: 1) through internal coordination within the company value chain, 2) through external relations downstream with customers and upstream with suppliers, and 3) through other external relations and "boundary-spanning" activities that enhance the company's ability to anticipate emerging trends and industry/competitive dynamics.

The first approach – relying on internal activities and processes – is the traditional approach. Many companies have extremely vibrant and well-funded internal research and development efforts underway. Occasionally, centralized R&D efforts have been broken up into physically separated "skunk works" units in order to shed some corporate policy guidance and loosen up development teams. A trend through the 1990s was to increase the level of cross-departmental coordination on new developments, such as through cross-functional teams involving R&D, marketing, operations, and purchasing to simultaneously provide input rather than sequentially examine new ideas. These methods parallel value capture methods that focus on the linkages across internal company value chain activities.

Working upstream with suppliers and downstream with customers has proved successful for some companies. An investment in activities that regularly feeds back customer preferences and feeds forward supplier ideas can stimulate further internal development activity. Paralleling value-capture methods that work across the industry value chain, investments in these activities can work to combine customer needs identification, supplier research, and the company's own knowledge. Procter & Gamble's former CEO A. G. Lafley instituted a "connect and develop" program that produced over 35% of the company's innovations and billions of revenue dollars. Through this program they developed new ideas that arose from bringing together information from seventy "technology entrepreneurs" who identified emerging consumer needs with the 50,000 R&D workers employed by fifteen major suppliers.[21]

Procter & Gamble's "Connect & Develop" Program

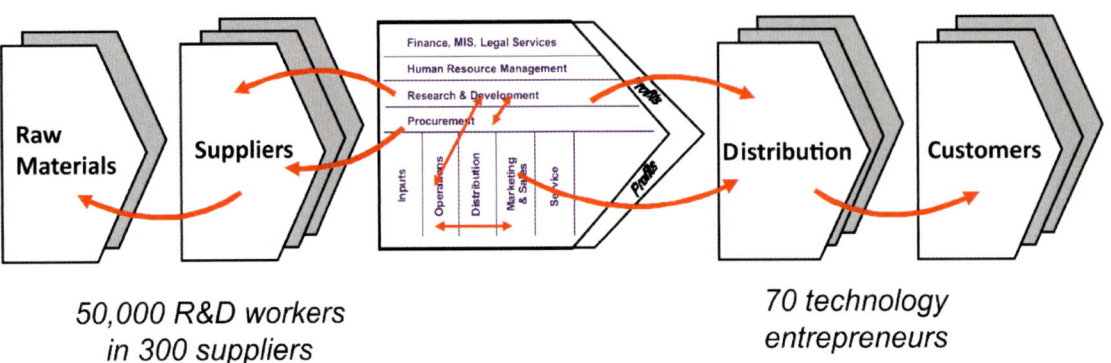

50,000 R&D workers in 300 suppliers

70 technology entrepreneurs

Just to be clear, working upstream with suppliers or downstream with customers is not a "one way street" where value is created only for the company. Wrigley Mars, for example, sources cocoa for its chocolate products in Côte d'Ivoire. In order to secure sufficient supply from the cocoa farmers, the company provides them with advanced farming knowledge, capital, and financing. Value for value is created in this exchange.

The third approach involves boundary-spanning outside the industry. In this fashion companies identify emerging competitive, technological, environmental, economic, and social trends (e.g. STEEPG) that are expected to have a significant impact on their business or industry. Ideas that spring from such broad, prospective activities may often result in small internal efforts to prototype new products or services that could respond to the emergent industry environment. Early prototyping activities enhance the potential for a company to better anticipate and successfully take advantage of significant changes. The types of activities associated with these efforts are often the most challenging to undertake in any organization. This is because they are intentionally focused on identifying opportunities that do not exist in the present, and on products or services for whom a customer base has not yet developed.[22] Yet as described in Chapter 1, the nature of industries and markets today suggests that these prospecting capabilities are of growing importance. The ability to create and capture value depends to an increasing extent on the activities that a company structures to develop prescience about their industries and to use such prescient knowledge productively. We will further discuss these ideas in Chapter 9 on innovation.

Millions Recycled, Zero Waste[23]

Refurbished phones represent the fastest growing segment of the global smartphone industry, accounting for 11% of devices sold and $50 billion global revenue in 2021. The Wireless Alliance specializes in recycling of smartphones, tablets, and other consumer recyclables. It is one of the industry's most trusted names in collection and buyback programs, recycling millions of cellular devices and over 3000 tons of peripheral material in a zero-waste fashion. For all incoming cellphones, the company deletes data and either refurbishes, reuses or recycles the materials – including plastics and copper – while the precious metals gold, silver and palladium are sent to smelters for recovery.

The company operates a tightly-integrated value chain to accomplish its goals. Collecting used phones from corporate clients and individual user recycling stations around the U.S., pallets containing thousands of devices arrive weekly at their main hub. Receiving crews sort phones into  lots according to manufacturer, style, internal technology, and condition. Staying on the cutting edge of advanced standards for safety and materials recycling, the data security department implements updated handling protocols for unlocking phones and erasing data. Investments in data testing and wiping technology enables teams to process over 250,000 phones monthly and ready them for repackaging and resale. Non-salable electronics are quickly shredded by other teams to recapture precious metals and plastics. Marketing and sales work closely with receiving and data security to submit bids to customers for the phones and recyclables that are in the system at any given moment. Used phones are then packed and shipped each week to customers at companies around the world. HR profit-sharing policies incentivize teams to work efficiently together to achieve monthly volume goals.

CONDUCTING A VALUE CHAIN ANALYSIS

There are five significant results of a value chain analysis. First, the company creates a better understanding of the complete set of value-creating activities it engages in – sort of a roadmap of all the steps it takes to manifest a product or service for its customers. Second, it helps clarify how activities in different functional areas of the company (marketing, purchasing, production, customer service, etc.) are either working in sync in support of a common strategic approach, or how they may be working at odds with each other. Third, a detailed analysis will identify how much contribution is made by intangible service activities performed in the company (the top half of the value chain diagram in Figure 5.10), and how important is the coordination of activities among departments. Fourth, this type of analysis can shed light on how and where value can be enhanced and/or where costs can be lowered without sacrificing value. Finally – reflecting the strategic imperatives mentioned in Chapter 1 – value chain analysis can reveal the extent to which the company engages in activities that recognize new opportunities emerging in the competitive environment. If we think about a company as an organization of activities designed to create and capture value, then this type of analysis focuses our attention on what the company actually does that makes a difference in achieving superior performance.

There are three primary steps in a value chain analysis:[24]

1. Identify the value chain activities.

2. Evaluate their value-creating properties and cost characteristics.

3. Identify improvements that allow the company to capture greater value.

Step 1: Identify Value Chain Activities

The first step is to identify key value-creating activities throughout the organization. Every functional area of the company should be part of this process since, as we have argued earlier, value is created through activities and there are important activities performed in all departments throughout the organization. Therefore a value chain analysis is one means for understanding how higher-level strategic goals and direction are translating to day-to-day behavior in each functional area.

We are not suggesting that we identify and analyze every single activity performed by every single employee! Looking at the millions of such activities goes way too far. There are some guidelines that help us focus on particular kinds or particular categories of activities. The important activities to pay attention to are those that exhibit any of the following characteristics:

- They represent a significant percentage of operating cost;

- What enables the activity to be performed or what it costs to perform the activity is different from what's involved in other activities in the company;

- The activities are performed by competitors in different ways (competitive analysis on key success factors, strengths and weaknesses is critical); or

- The activities appear to have great potential to create strategic differences from competition.

Occasionally, these guidelines may focus our attention on an entire department or function in a company. Usually this is because the function is a huge part of the operation, or because the company is regarded as being particularly good in a type of function. More often than not, however, simply considering an aggregation of activities at a summary functional or departmental level will be inadequate for achieving the understanding we seek from this analysis. There is just too much going on across an entire department or function; we need to drill down deeper inside. Just as we described earlier how "new product excellence" can be a result of a series of different activities, departmental or functional excellence in all likelihood comes from subsets of activities within its sphere.

**Figure 5.13
Activities Associated With Advertising**

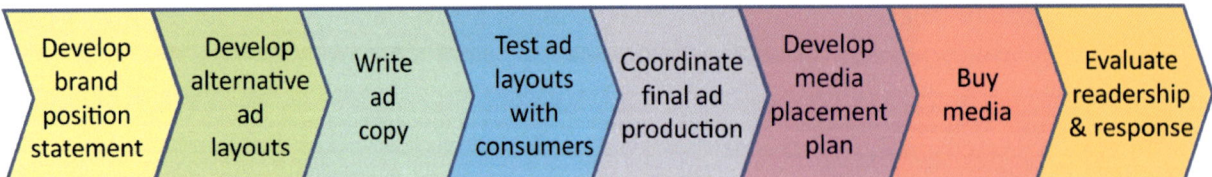

Let's say, for example, that we believe our company's excellence in its marketing actually springs specifically from the effectiveness of its advertising. We have evidence from our ad agency that our online ads are superior, that they generate high levels of click-throughs and readership, and that consumers access our digital coupons and use them at a higher rate than industry averages would suggest. Value chain analysis would then prompt us to break down the activities associated with advertising, in order to identify more precisely what we do and how we do it so well. Figure 5.13 provides a view of the chain of value-adding activities in this one area within the marketing function. With this more detailed articulation, now we are able to focus in more carefully on what steps contribute to great advertising.

Step 2: Evaluate Activities' Value Characteristics and Costs

In the earlier discussion of potential drawbacks to the value chain we mentioned that information systems are necessary to capture useful data. This is especially true when we seek to understand the cost- and value-creating characteristics of various activities. The typical company does not readily capture specific enough cost information, for example, on the activities in the advertising function outline in Figure 5.13. Yet this type of detail can be especially revealing.

Figure 5.14 shows how helpful it can be to identify important categories of activities as suggested in Step One, and to capture essential cost information about those categories. This information is from a manufacturing company whose key strategic position in the marketplace depends on custom manufacturing of unusually complicated electronics components and a very tight relationship between its sales force in the field and the customers. Before the company ever begins a custom production run of an item, there is a sort of a dance it engages in between the customer, sourcing possible suppliers, and buying the parts needed for the customer's special order, receiving the various parts, and testing and preparing them for use in production. The astute student will recognize that sales and purchasing are both functions that exist in the top half of value chain diagram (you can't "drop them on your foot"), while receiving and testing is on the lower half in the primary activities sector. So this is a company that has to coordinate well across value chain sectors in order to excel in its market.

Figure 5.14
Manufacturing Firm Value Chain Analysis

Traditional accounting		Value chain analysis		
Salaries	$177,400	Sales	Field sales purchase orders	$72,300
Benefits	56,325		Purchase order processing	24,500
Supplies	36,600		Expediting delayed orders	13,500
Fixed costs	11,275			
		Purchasing	Sourcing suppliers	68,000
	$281,600		Issuing supplier orders	36,000
			Tracking supplier order status	7,500
		Receiving	Receiving & handling	8,300
			Resolving supplier quality	24,300
			Reissuing supplier orders	10,700
			Preparation for production	16,500
				$281,600

The left side of Figure 5.14 shows the traditional accounting treatment for the personnel and minor supplies and overhead expenses that are involved in these efforts. These costs would usually get rolled up into a corporate income statement, but they do not tell us anything at all about the essential activities performed by the company. However, company management thought carefully about the categories of activities that were important in their business, and then used an activity-based costing system to produce the figures on the right side. The "Sales" category is really a combination of field sales and internal sales office activities (which themselves are a subset of the Marketing and Sales department). "Purchasing" is a subset of activities within the Procurement department that relate specifically to these types of custom orders, and "Receiving" is also a subset of activities within the entire warehousing function. None of these categories of activities would appear on any regular financial statement. Yet the combinations and categorizations reveal not only where the greatest costs lie but also where there may be opportunities to enhance value capture.

Each activity performed by a company presumably creates value and involves costs, and hopefully many activities will have value-capturing characteristics (meaning that they are unique and cannot be imitated very easily). To better understand how each activity creates value and what determines its cost, we can evaluate it by considering two different kinds of drivers: executional drivers and structural drivers (Figure 5.15). Executional drivers come from the execution of the business activities – involving people, systems, routines, culture, and coordination – and usually have a fairly important learning dimension to them (i.e., get better over time). Structural drivers are derived from the strategic choices made about the underlying economic logic and structure of the business - such as the scale and scope of its operations, the complexity of its products or services, and its use of technology. Executional and structural drivers can be sources of either value enhancement or cost reduction, and sometimes both simultaneously. In Chapter 7 when we more carefully describe business level strategies, which depend on the value chain ideas we're covering here, we will spend considerably more time discussing the nuances of these types of drivers.

Figure 5.15
Value Chain Activity Drivers

Executional Drivers
- Work force involvement
- Total quality management
- Plant layout
- Capacity utilization
- Routines & coordination
- Culture

Structural Drivers
- Scale & scope
- Experience curve
- Complexity of products & services
- Technology utilization
- Capital intensity

Step 3: Identify Improvements That Allow the Company to Capture Greater Value

The categorization and cost itemization of value chain activities in the previous step ordinarily make this final step much easier, and sometimes almost obvious. For example, in the company profiled in Figure 5.14, management learned that $24.3 million was spent annually in checking the quality of received parts from suppliers, and nearly $11 million on efforts to reorder from suppliers whose received material did not meet specification. Management realized that by investing a bit more in the effort to source quality suppliers to begin with, the company would save costs later on, orders could go into production sooner, and customers would be shipped final product more quickly. Management also realized that an investment in more sophisticated enterprise management software would lead to reduced costs in order processing and tracking, and again lead to smoother flow of orders to manufacturing.

There are five basic questions to ask during this step of value chain analysis. These reflect the ways in which value can be created, shown earlier in Figure 5.12 and its discussion:

1. Can we increase benefits in this activity (or subset of activity), holding costs constant?

2. Can we hold benefits constant while reducing costs?

3. Could we reduce assets required for this activity, while holding both benefits and costs constant?

4. Would a further investment in assets improve the company's ability to either create benefits or improve costs?

5. Can we expand the scale or scope of our activities to a broader audience without sacrificing benefits or costs to our current sets of stakeholders?

It may be that, through identifying sequences of value creating activities, we also realize that outsourcing is a possibility for some activities – that is, they could be handled more effectively by other companies. We need to be careful about the decisions used to determine whether even minor sets of activities are outsourced to others, since they could have important strategic consequences. We will return to the topic of outsourcing in Chapter 7, when we describe more carefully the types of strategies companies can follow and the key value chain activities choices they make for each.

Managing in Markets: Question for Class Discussion

Value creation and the value chain are usually considered as useful to businesses when they compete in the marketplace. How can the essential ideas about the value chain be applied to governments and their agencies? Think about your own experiences you have had dealing with a government agency (e.g. the driver's license bureau or the Internal Revenue Service). How can an agency like this put the value chain idea to use?

CHAPTER SUMMARY

Internal analysis can improve our understanding of why there are performance differences between companies in an industry. By examining carefully what a company does, what it fails to do, and how it operates, one can better identify the sources of strengths (and weaknesses) that enable it to occupy a leading (or lagging) position in an industry. SWOT tends to provide a perceptual snapshot of a company at a point in time. Value chain analysis is a more dynamic view because it exposes behavioral causes and effects, and draws our attention to the critical concepts of value creation and value capture. The value chain provides important insights on sources of competitive advantage by focusing on unique activities that cannot be imitated by competitors.

The value chain concentrates on activities conducted within a company. Primary activities are those we can easily observe, and are usually associated with the more tangible aspects of products and services that a company produces. Support activities involve the efforts of company employees and management behind the scenes, including functions such as human resources, research and development, finance and accounting, procurement, and administration. Coordinating activities are those that seek to ensure strategic consistency across the company by tightly linking activities across different functional areas of the value chain and making sure they are mutually reinforcing. The uniqueness that provides a foundation for competitive advantage often resides in support activities, and especially in how well coordination occurs across the entire value chain.

Companies may prosper by creating value for customers, for suppliers, and for broad stakeholder groups such as communities. Value can also be created through company processes that more effectively detect emerging opportunities and take advantage of them before competitors do. Sustained superior returns resulting from these efforts depend on whether a company's unique value-creating activities can be imitated.

Value chain analysis is a three-step process that helps management identify and understand the subsets of critically important activities in a company. By identifying and categorizing important sets of activities, and by understanding their value creation and cost characteristics, managers are in a better position to explore how to create and capture greater value and/or how to reduce costs and prices without sacrificing benefits.

Chapter 6 will further explore internal analysis by discussing the relationship of resources to sustainable competitive advantage. One of the principal characteristics of strategic resources is that they create value. We will return to value chain analysis in Chapter 7 on Business Level Strategies, which can be better understood as coordinated sets of value-adding activities.

Learning Objectives Review

1. *Explain the differences between internal analysis and external analysis.*

   - External analysis examines industry structure and driving forces, in order to assess the attractiveness of an industry and identify key success factors that every company must attend to. External analysis can explain roughly 20% of the variation of performance of firms.

   - Internal analysis can be conducted using SWOT analysis or value chain analysis. SWOT tends to present a static snapshot, while value chain tends to present a dynamic view. Internal analysis is intended to identify what a company is particularly adept at doing as well as possible points of weakness. Strengths and weaknesses usually arise because of activities and routines that companies engage in. Value chain analysis helps dig deeper to identify these activities and routines.

2. *Explain the benefits and drawbacks of using SWOT analysis.*

   - Benefits: 1) easy to understand and use; 2) helpful in seeing how strengths and weaknesses align with opportunities and threats; 3) provides simple overall direction; 4) enables competitive comparisons using objective data; 5) provides a strong starting point for further in-depth strategic planning.

   - Weaknesses: 1) often results in a long list of items, too many to effectively manage; 2) can over-simplify complex business processes; 3) possible confusion between strengths and weaknesses, and these can change over time; 4) may prompt companies to build on strengths that are less relevant to changing markets; 5) provides a static view without insight into the sources of strengths and weaknesses.

3. *Describe how value is created through a firm's internal sets of activities (value chain).*

   - There are four ways to create value: 1) provide greater benefits for the same price; 2) provide the same benefits for a lower price; 3) provide greater benefits at an incremental price smaller than the gain in benefits; 4) broadening access to benefits to a broader audience without sacrificing current customers.

- Value can be created for both customers downstream and suppliers upstream.

- Value is created through primary and support activities that companies engage in, and through the extent to which all these activities are internally consistent and well-coordinated.

4. *Assess how the value chain perspective provides insight on sources of competitive advantage.*

- Competitive advantage arises when competitors are unable to easily imitate a successful company. Such barriers to entry and barriers to mobility are often created through actions that a company engages in which its competitors cannot observe. In the value chain the support activities and the efforts to coordinate activities across the company are usually unobservable.

5. *Perform a value chain analysis.*

- There are three steps in conducting a value chain analysis: 1) identify value chain activities; 2) evaluate the value characteristics and costs of these activities; 3) identify activities that allow the company to capture greater value, and those where further improvements are desirable and possible.

Key Terms

Activity-based costing - A managerial accounting method used to assign all direct and indirect costs to a particular activity.

Executional drivers - Performance and cost dimensions of activities that are derived from the execution of the business activities - involving people, systems, routines, culture, and coordination - and usually have a fairly important learning dimension to them.

Idiosyncratic - Unique to the company and which cannot be reproduced by a competitor or imitated very easily.

Outsourcing - Activities that are part of producing a company's products or services which are provided by other companies on a contractual basis.

Structural drivers - Performance and cost dimensions of activities that are derived from the strategic choices made about the underlying economic logic and structure of the business - such as the scale and scope of its operations, the complexity of its products or services, and its use of technology.

SWOT analysis - A form of analysis, resulting in a listing of a company's strengths, weaknesses, opportunities, and threats. It is a static view of the company at a particular point in time.

TOWS matrix - A matrix that compares a company's strengths and weaknesses against its opportunities and threats, providing general direction.

Value capture - When a company creates value by acting in ways that its competitors cannot or will not act.

Value chain - A concept emphasizing that a company is an organization of interrelated activities designed to create value for stakeholders, and that the derivation of superior performance is better understood by focusing on what a company actually does.

Value chain analysis - A method that identifies value-creating activities in a company, categorizes them into important subsets, develops information to understand how the activities create value and what their costs are, and pinpoints opportunities for enhanced value creation and cost reduction. It is a dynamic view of a company's activities.

Value creation - When some other party appreciates something that is done for them and is willing to execute a profitable transaction as a result.

Short Answer Review Questions

1. What does SWOT stand for?
2. How can SWOT be effectively used in organizations?
3. What are some positive characteristics of SWOT?
4. What are some negative characteristics of SWOT?
5. What elements constitute a value chain?
6. What are the big differences between the primary and secondary activities?
7. Where is the best place to look for value in an organization? Why?
8. What can you reasonably expect to result from a value chain analysis?
9. How is a value chain analysis conducted?
10. How do you use a TOWS matrix?
11. What are some of the executional drivers?
12. What are some of the structural drivers?
13. How is opportunity recognition enhanced with the use of value chain analysis?

Group Exercises

1. Draw a value chain for a manufacturing company, such as Dell Technologies. Be sure to include industry value chain relationships as well as internal value chain activities. Highlight activities that you believe help insulate Dell from competitive threats.

2. Draw a value chain for an internet-based company such as Google. Who are the suppliers? Who are the customers? What activities do you imagine Google has engaged in to become the world's premier search engine, and what must they do to sustain this position?

3. Draw a value chain for your business school. Are students to be considered as part of the supply network or part of the customer network? What value chain activities does your business school engage in to develop competitive advantage?

Investor Relations Sites for Companies Mentioned in This Chapter

3M: https://investors.3m.com/ir-home/default.aspx
Apple: https://investor.apple.com/investor-relations/default.aspx
Canon: https://global.canon/en/ir/
Ciba-Geigy (BASF): https://www.basf.com/global/en/investors.html
Coca Cola: https://investors.coca-colacompany.com/
Dell Technologies: https://investors.delltechnologies.com/
Famous Amos (Ferrero SpA): https://www.ferrero.com/
General Electric: https://www.ge.com/investor-relations
Greenbrier Resort: https://www.greenbrier.com/about-us.aspx
Hackensack University Medical Center: https://www.hackensackmeridianhealth.org/en/About-Us
HP Inc.: https://investor.hp.com/home/default.aspx
Kodak: https://investor.kodak.com/
La Croix (National Beverage): https://ir.nationalbeverage.com/
Mars Wrigley: https://www.mars.com/about
Molson Coors: https://ir.molsoncoors.com/overview/default.aspx
Pepsico: https://www.pepsico.com/investors/investor-contacts
Pfizer: https://investors.pfizer.com/Investors/Overview/default.aspx
Plexus: https://plexus.gcs-web.com/
Procter & Gamble: https://pginvestor.com/
Roche Holdings: https://www.roche.com/investors.htm
Toshiba: http://www.toshiba.co.jp/about/ir/index.htm
Toyota Motor Corp.: https://global.toyota/en/ir/
UPS: https://investors.ups.com/
Walmart: https://stock.walmart.com/investors/default.aspx
Walt Disney Company: https://thewaltdisneycompany.com/investor-relations/
Wilmington DE: https://www.wilmingtonde.gov/
Wireless Alliance: https://www.thewirelessalliance.com/

References

[1] Barboza, David, 2016, "An iPhone's journey from the factory floor to the retail store," New York Times, December 29. Kubota, Yoko, 2018, "Apple to cut iPhone X output," Wall Street Journal, January 31, B1. Kubota, Y. & T. Mochizuki, 2018, "Apple supplier runs into trouble," Wall Street Journal, April 21, B4. Lombardo, Cara, 2017, "Apple awards $390 million to face ID tech company Finisair," Wall Street Journal, December 14, B11. Mickle, Tripp, 2017, "Among the iPhone's biggest transformations: Apple itself," Wall Street Journal, June 20, A1. Reisinger, Dan, 2017, "Apple iPhone X took years to develop—and it's just the beginning," Fortune, October 14.

Supply Chain 24/7, 2017, "Apple's iPhone X sells out – supply chain suggests only half can be delivered in 2017," October 27. Webb, Jonathan, 2017, "Apple's supply chain attracts criticism for performance but also praise for sustainability," Forbes, October 30.

[2] Bradley, C., M. Hirt, & S. Smit, 2018, "Strategy to beat the odds," *McKinsey Quarterly*, February. Rumelt, R. R., 1991, "How much does industry matter?" *Strategic Management Journal*, 12: 167 - 185.

[3] 3M Annual Report, 2016.

[4] Wadley-Donovan GrowthTech, 2014, "Wilmington Delaware SWOT Analysis."

[5] See https://www.columbusstate.edu/strategicplan/2018-23/data.php.

[6] For perspective on the capacity to manage in complex environments, see: Miller, George A., 1994, "The magical number seven, plus or minus two: Some limits in our capacity for processing information," *Psychological Review* (101)2: 343 - 352.

[7] Gryta T., J. S. Lublin, & D. Benoit. 2018. "How Jeffrey Immelt's 'success theater' masked the rot at GE," Wall Street Journal, February 21, A1.

[8] Cademartori, Lorraine. 2012. "Saving West Virginia's Greenbrier Resort, an American classic." Forbes, May 7.

[9] Porter, Michael E. 1980. *Competitive strategy*. New York: Free Press.

[10] Porter, Michael E. 1985. *Competitive advantage*. New York: Free Press.

[11] Porter. Michael E. 1980. *Competitive strategy*. New York: Free Press.

[12] Quinn, J. B., 1988, "Technology in services: Past myths and future challenges," In B. R. Guile and J. B. Quinn (eds.), *Technology in services: Policies for growth, trade, and employment.* Washington, D.C.: National Academies Press.

[13] There is considerable evidence that significant strategic value is added by support activities and the coordination that occurs between primary and support activities. For example, the Gartner Group recently reported that worldwide spending in 2018 on information technology was estimated to include $2.5 trillion for technology services, but only $1.3 trillion for manufactured hardware and software (which both include significant support activity components). In the strategy press over the last few years there has been significant attention paid to "knowledge" management and other intangible resources that underlie the manifestation of services and products by successful companies. See Blackler, F., 1993, "Knowledge and the theory of organizations: Organizations as activity systems and the reframing of management," *Journal of Management Studies* 30(6): 863 - 883; Grant, R., 1996, "Toward a knowledge based theory of the firm," *Strategic Management Journal* 17: 109 - 122; Winter, S. G., 1987, "Knowledge and competence as strategic assets," In D. J. Teece (ed.), *The Competitive Challenge,* 159 – 184, New York: Harper & Row. Quinn argues that the "manufacturing-services interface is now the key to most manufacturing organizations." See Quinn, J. B., 1992, *Intelligent enterprise*. New York: Free Press.

[14] Pascale, R. 1997. *Nothing fails like success*. Princeton, NJ: Films for the Humanities and Sciences.

[15] Friedman, Thomas. 2005. *The world is flat*. New York: Farrar, Straus and Giroux.

[16] Discount Store News. 1993. "Sam's Choice climbs beverage brand list - Walmart's Sam's American Choice beverage brand." October 4.

[17] Szabo, L. 2006. "Hallmark of quality care: Efficiency," USA Today, October 20: 3B.

[18] Bulkeley, W. 2005. "Plexus strategy: Smaller runs of more things," Wall Street Journal. October 8: A1.

[19] Schwartzel, E., 2018, "Beauty and the backlash: Disney's princess problem," Wall Street Journal, November 17, B8.

[20] Baron, R. 2006. "Opportunity recognition as pattern recognition: How entrepreneurs 'connect the dots' to identify new business opportunities." *Academy of Management Perspectives* 20(1): 104 - 119.

[21] Huston, L., and N. Sakkab. 2006. "Connect and develop." *Harvard Business Review*, March: 58 - 66.

[22] For a fuller discussion of this challenge, see Christensen, C. 1997. *The innovator's dilemma*. Boston: Harvard Business School Press.

[23] Martin, T. W. and D. FitzGerald, 2018, "Your love of your old smartphone is a problem for Apple and Samsung," Wall Street Journal, February 28, A1. Workman, M., 2015, "Unlocking value," Recycling Today, January 6, 1. http://www.thewirelessalliance.com/.

[24] This section draws on material from Shank, J. K., and V. Govindarajan. 1993. *Strategic cost management*. New York: Free Press. See also Hammer, M., and J. Champy, 1993, *Reengineering the Corporation*, HarperBusiness: New York. See also Grant, R. M., 2005, *Contemporary strategy analysis* (5th edition). Malden, MA: Blackwell.

Chapter 6: Resource-Based Competitive Advantage

LEARNING OBJECTIVES

1. Demonstrate how to compare the types of company resources, and show which can generate competitive advantage.

2. Explain the difference between resources and capabilities.

3. List the categories of resources that companies may draw upon to develop competitive advantage.

4. Outline a practical model for analyzing which resources and capabilities will work to deliver competitive advantage.

Popping the Cork[1]

Nomacorc Mission: "We help wineries and retailers ensure their wines present as intended, delight the consumer and succeed in the marketplace." Nomacorc Vision: "Be the most innovative, most sustainable and most trusted global supplier of complete wine closure solutions to the still and sparkling wine industry."

For over 300 years, since French Benedictine monk Dom Perignon first adapted it to close wine bottles, the wine industry has relied on cork to seal its products. And then along came Nomacorc LLC. Founded 23 years ago in Zebulon NC, synthetic corks made from Nomacorc's (and sister company) extruded plastics now seal 14% of full-sized bottles of wine sold worldwide. 56% of the top 200 best-selling wines in the U.S. are closed with Nomacorc.

Over-production of natural cork in the 1980s led to the prevalence in cork of the naturally occurring chemical TCA, which "tainted" up to 15% of fine wine and rendered it undrinkable. This opened the door for synthetic closures. Today natural cork closes only 11% of wine worldwide.

With previous experience in plastic extrusion, Nomacorc entered this industry in 1999. But the company took plastic closures to another level. Focusing on reverence for the tradition of winemaking, the company recognized early on that simple extruded closures do not provide the oxygen transfer properties that had made cork so central to fine wine. Nomacorc invented and patented a process for co-extruding two types of plastics into a single closure – a firm inner core to hold shape, and a spongy exterior creating better fit. They have partnered with wine research institutes and hired PhDs to study "oxygen management" issues related to types of plastic, extrusion methods, and even bottle neck design.

In 2010 the company introduced its Select Series closures to precisely control oxygen ingress into wine. Their research collaborations have explored not just closures, but a full spectrum of the winemaking processes and their relationship with oxygen. In 2017 they debuted Green Line, a new "category" of closures derived from sustainable, renewable sugarcane-based raw materials. With this knowledge in hand they are now designing co-extruded closures specifically for certain wineries and their varietals. In 2022 the company owns 90 patents (with 49 patents pending) related to closures for containers and the process predicting the oxidability of a wine or grape must. In 2014 the *Wine Enthusiast's* number 1 pick for the year (out of 17,500 reviewed) was Abbott Claim Vineyard Pinot Noir, sealed with a Nomacorc closure. In 2016 it won a *Wine Business* award for its new oxygen scanner technology, which for the first time enables this kind of analysis to be applied directly in the wine through the use of miniaturized disposable sensors.

By 2022 Nomacorc (now owned by Vinventions) has operations on eight continents. It serves 8,000 wineries in 50 countries.

QUESTIONS

1. What are the activities this company performs that create value? Are these unique? Could other companies imitate them easily? Why or why not?

2. Do the company's activities and accomplishments fulfill its mission statement?

In the previous two chapters we explored industry analysis technique for examining the external competitive environment, and value chain analysis for understanding the means by which a business can create a valuable position in its industry leading to competitive advantage. In this chapter we will extend both of these approaches by outlining a framework for understanding how the business can develop a *sustainable* competitive advantage. Now we drill down deeper into the nature of value creation in order to understand the reasons for how and why a particular strategy has the ability to be successful over time. Here we focus on resources that provide the foundation for the firm to succeed in the market. We will see that the careful identification and analysis of a *narrow* set of resources provides a business with the *broadest* possible opportunity to succeed in the marketplace and to sustain that success over time.

THE CHARACTERISTICS OF RESOURCES

Strategic resources of an organization are the foundation of the development of its sustainable competitive advantage. Originally suggested almost fifty years ago, the "resource-based" approach has been carefully and more fully developed over the last twenty-five years by strategic management scholars.[2] This approach contains a fairly well-developed theoretical framework, but it has often been difficult for people in business to implement the ideas in practice. So this chapter will lay out principles behind the approach, but most importantly will also provide a useful method for how to use it in practice.

Ordinary and Extraordinary Resources

At the outset we need to make a distinction between resources as contemplated by this approach and the way we might normally think about assets possessed by a firm. Whereas assets are typically thought of as items listed or accounted for in the firm's balance sheet, the resource-based approach contends that not all such "accounting" assets are strategically important to the firm. As an example, the office desks and power tools of any business are indeed assets of the firm accounted for in its financial statements; however, physical office furnishings and drill bits do not represent a foundation upon which the firm can develop and sustain a competitive advantage. Having the finest, most ergonomically correct Italian leather chairs and handcrafted desks may feel good, but few customers would buy from a company or pay more for its products because its back-office operation has those nice appointments.

In contrast, the resource-based approach concentrates on resources of the business that have the potential to be strategically important. There are two types of resources that have the potential to be strategically important: tangible resources and intangible resources. Tangible resources are physical assets such as equipment, buildings, land, furniture, money, and raw materials. Tangible assets are relatively easy to identify, and can usually be acquired in the marketplace. While many tangible assets may have no strategic value, in some instances physical assets do indeed provide the business with a strategic foundation. Highly-unique raw materials, special manufacturing equipment or facilities, and other customized operational asset investments[3] are the kinds of tangible resources with strategic importance. Championship Chili (mentioned in Chapter 4) was produced using highly-specialized food manufacturing equipment that other chili companies did not have and could not easily acquire. For the gas station located on the busy corner in your neighborhood at home, its property is of strategic value. No other competitor can now occupy the location that provides convenience for traffic coming from multiple directions.

Intangible resources are those assets that are not physical in nature but are often more critical to the success of the business. Intangible assets include such things as relationships with key suppliers and other businesses, the culture of the organization, processes or routines within the organization, patents and trademarks, as well as the knowledge and skills of the management team or other key employees. The skills and experience of founders, for instance, is often cited as a key intangible asset in the development of new ventures.[4]

Ways to Describe Resources	
Physical Nature	Strategic Value
Tangible	Ordinary
Intangible	Extraordinary

To this distinction between tangible and intangible resources, we also need to distinguish between ordinary resources and extraordinary resources. Some resources are necessary simply for the business to operate in an industry, while others may be truly unique to the business and can help set it apart from its competitors. Many of the resources possessed by a firm are ordinary resources, those that the firm must have on hand just to be a credible contender in the industry. If you operate a sit-down restaurant, then you must have refrigerators, food preparation equipment, food preparers, serving staff, utensils, plates, napkins, condiments, a cash register, a credit card transmitter, telephones, a building to operate within, computers, some office furniture, lighting, a payroll system, a business license, and so on. These constitute the minimum resources that must be in place for the restaurant to operate. Similarly, many of the capabilities of the business, such as serving safe food to customers that meets cleanliness standards, may be done very well. However, these resources provide no distinctive competitive advantage to the firm. The expectation of customers is that every restaurant possesses these capabilities. Thus, while necessary to compete in this industry, this set of resources is not sufficient to be a source of sustainable competitive advantage.

We don't mean to suggest that ordinary resources and capabilities are unimportant. Quite the contrary! They must be developed and they must be developed at least as well as the standard in the industry. A restaurant that barely clears its health inspection and receives a low grade may indeed operate. However, since the usual customer expectation is that restaurants should have an "A" rating from the health department, a lower rating is likely to negatively impact a restaurant's performance. Investment in ordinary resources required in a particular industry is a *necessary* condition to operate, but alone they are not *sufficient* to develop a competitive advantage.

To create a sustainable competitive advantage and the associated opportunity to earn superior returns, some of the resources that the business possesses must be extraordinary resources. These are resources that either individually or in combination with each other:

1. Provide the business with the opportunity to create value versus competitors;
2. Are unique in the industry;
3. Allow the business exclusive access – to either suppliers or customers – for some period of time;
4. Cannot be easily matched by another business in the short run; and
5. Cannot be easily transferred to or appropriated by another business.

There must be a reason why customers would consider giving their business to your company. For most people it is far more convenient to continue in their established patterns of behavior than it is to change those patterns. Customers are often not willing to switch unless there is a compelling reason to do so. A company's extraordinary resources can create exceptional value and become the source of that motivation to change.

Why would you choose one restaurant over another? Will the restaurant have a unique atmosphere, type of cuisine, level of service, or entertainment when compared to other restaurants? Will its cost structure allow for prices to be set significantly lower than those of the competitors, while still providing comparable value on other dimensions? Will access to its location be more convenient? If it is only going to do the same thing that other restaurants do, why would you switch? The strategic focus of every company, therefore, is to identify and develop extraordinary resources that enable the firm to offer *an improvement in value which cannot be easily copied by competitors*. Extraordinary resources are at the foundation of value creation and value capture; they offer the opportunity to achieve superior returns in a particular industry. Figure 6.1 presents characteristics that help distinguish between ordinary and extraordinary resources.

Figure 6.1
Differences Between Ordinary and Extraordinary Resources

	Tangible Hard assets; on balance sheet	Intangible Soft assets; not on balance sheet
Ordinary Necessary to compete, but not sufficient for advantage	Easily viewed Easily purchased	Easily recognized Well known routines Able to learn easily
Extraordinary Provide basis for sustainable competitive advantage	Difficult to acquire Uncommon in industry Possibly immobile	Difficult to identify or understand Difficult to evaluate Requires time to learn Requires experience to understand

The descriptions of extraordinary resources in Figure 6.1 prompt us to recall the discussions in Chapter 4 about imperfect markets and barriers to entry or imitation. Whether tangible or intangible, extraordinary resources are not readily available in competitive markets. Any industry in which firms have been able to develop and utilize extraordinary resources is one that will tend away from the perfectly competitive markets endpoint (Figure 4.1), because barriers to entry or barriers to imitation prevent others from operating similarly. Extraordinary resources also tend to take time to develop, and build further on value chain ideas from Chapter 5. As we shall see in the discussion below, the often-intangible nature of these resources emphasizes the importance of routines that enhance coordination across the value chain.

Five Key Dimensions of Extraordinary Resources

How can one determine if resources are ordinary in nature, or if they are extraordinary and provide a foundation for sustainable advantage? While various strategy textbooks and articles provide somewhat different names or approaches, in general five elements help answer this critical question. This is the VRIST framework. You might remember it more easily by thinking about the Latin word *verist*, meaning "truth," because any resource that exhibits all five characteristics is truly extraordinary. Truly extraordinary resources present a foundation for the business's strategy.

Strategy Acronym: VRIST
Extraordinary Resource Dimensions

V	Valuable	It is Valuable
R	Rare	It is Rare
I	Imitation	It is difficult to Imitate
S	Substitution	It cannot be Substituted for
T	Tradable	It cannot be Traded for

Is it valuable? Only those resources that have the ability to create value for the company might qualify as extraordinary. In assessing value creation, the truly extraordinary resource must help the company in at least one of several possible ways (Figure 6.2). These mirror the discussion we had in Chapter 5 about the value chain: 1) lower its cost structure relative to competitors for a particular product or service; 2) provide enhanced product or service benefits to customers while maintaining parity on costs and prices; 3) provide the ability to charge more for its products/services and more than offset any related cost increases; or 4) enhance the company's ability to reach target customers more effectively or attract additional customers more efficiently than competitors.

Johnson Controls (JCI) operates in the auto parts industry against hundreds of competitors. A major challenge in this industry is keeping track of thousands of auto parts while keeping costs low to remain price-competitive. In 2016 JCI was reaping the benefits of an earlier investment it made in RFID tags and tracking procedures for its reusable shipping boxes and parts storage racks. While maintaining its same level of service and pricing, it has lowered its costs.[5]

Figure 6.2
Ways to Create Value

Accomplish this	While providing this
Lower costs	Parity on product/service features
Add benefits	Parity on costs and prices
Increase revenue	Revenue increases more than cost increases
New customers	Undiminished value to existing customers

Buc-ee's, a 41-shop convenience store chain (in Texas, Alabama and Florida), was looking for a way to create greater value than its competitors. They decided to create the "World's Cleanest Bathrooms." They invested heavily in the design and maintenance system for their bathrooms, and then very slightly raised prices on many impulse purchase items in the store. Customers stop in because the clean bathrooms are "worth the wait" while driving. And once there they are inclined to pick up convenience items rather than loading the kids back in the car and heading to another store to save a few pennies. Now customers go long distances before stopping for a rest break,  just so they can enjoy Buc-ee's. The company's approach has resulted in a Facebook account with nearly half a million followers, and more ten million YouTube views of in-store videos shot by customers. Who shoots videos of convenience stores or follows their Facebook page? Customers adore Buc-ee's! Their sales volume and profits shot up during the following years, returning the investment for the upgrades and providing a continuing value proposition for the company that cannot be easily imitated by competitors.

Is it rare? Each potentially extraordinary resource must be evaluated for its uniqueness relative to the competitors in the industry. Krispy Kreme Doughnuts went public in April 2000 with a business based on a number of rare tangible and intangible resources. These included its brand name, its heritage in the southeastern United States, a unique recipe, and doughnut making system that utilized proprietary company-designed machinery. These resources were unique in the industry, providing potential for competitive advantage. Prior to the advent of high speed internet and video streaming possibilities, Blockbuster's retail store coverage (5800 U.S. stores at its peak) provided rare access to complete movie libraries for most neighborhoods in America.

One reason McDonald's restaurants are so popular is the general perception that they have cleaner food preparation operations and eating areas than other fast food chains. Cleaning standards are, in fact, incorporated into their franchise manual so that every McDonald's restaurant follows virtually identical procedures. Yet these standards are not actually rare, evidenced by the incorporation of similar procedures at Burger King, Wendy's, and other national fast food restaurants. But a resource that is *perceived* as rare can be just as powerful as a real resource that is rare. The cachet of a brand name is a perception by consumers, and yet may provide a significant resource-based advantage for the firm that simultaneously meets all five of the VRIST criteria.

Is the resource truly unique or rare for the company's industry? The question of rarity should be answered using research and objective data, although occasionally qualitative judgments may be necessary. If the management team finds that the resource or capability does not qualify as rare within the industry then it cannot be categorized as extraordinary.

Starbucks, Part 1

Starbucks is one of the great business success stories of our time. Taking a Seattle-based roasting and coffee bean operation as its base, Howard Schultz had a vision of opening Italian-style coffee houses around the world where people could enjoy great coffee in an atmosphere that would welcome them from the time they walked into the door. Seeking investor money for a business that was going to sell coffee at prices that had never been seen, using Italian names for sizes that no one understood, and encouraging people to hang out in the store: all seemed to be a recipe for disaster, and he was turned down by 95 percent of the investors he approached.

As if that weren't enough, he dramatically changed the model upon which employees would be treated. The company provided all employees (even part-timers) with health insurance coverage, paid living wages, and provided matching contributions for their retirement accounts. The baristas behind the counter were expected to know customers, know coffee, provide great service, and love their store.

QUESTIONS

1. Did these characteristics make the Starbucks model work? Why?
2. Why didn't other companies just imitate their model?
3. Should Starbucks leverage its resources to expand its store operations to serve sandwiches and burgers? Why or why not?

Is it difficult to imitate? If you have determined that a particular resource is valuable and rare, then the next step is to determine whether some other company might be able to easily imitate it. If it can be imitated, how perfectly can it be copied? One obvious means to prevent imitation is to obtain intellectual property protection for the resource, such as through a patent or trademark. Trademarks protect names and graphic designs associated with a company from being copied. Patents may be granted to unique, nonobvious products and business processes. These make it illegal for a competitor to "reverse engineer" a product and then turn around and produce exactly the same thing in exactly the same way. Qualcomm patented computer chips providing CDMA (code division multiple access) technology for digital cell phones, which became one of the two worldwide industry standards. No other company has been able to infringe on their rights, and every cell phone equipment provider that utilizes CDMA must pay Qualcomm a royalty.

More often than not, however, resources that cannot be imitated involve unobservable routines or processes within a company; they are "behind the scenes" from the physical product produced or service provided. Boeing re-engineered its aircraft design system in the 1990s, so that all its future commercial aircraft would be designed entirely using electronic methods with no paper blueprint drawings ever produced. This was an enormous undertaking because each of their airplanes incorporates 3 million parts and critical aerodynamic features with extremely small tolerances. In turn, this digital conversion made electronic sourcing with thousands of worldwide suppliers much easier. Competitors Airbus and Embraer, unable to observe this process, also began to move in this direction but had to invent the process for themselves. It took years to do so.

Consider the organ transplant "industry." By 2022 an average 3,951 Americans per year over the previous 5 years had actively waited for heart transplants but there had only been on average 3,557 procedures per year during the same period, performed in 144 heart transplant facilities nationwide.[6] Why don't more hospitals and their cardiac units get into this field? The answer is that "imitation" of successful practice here is incredibly difficult. These facilities must be pre-approved by hospital boards of directors as well as federal and state health care regulatory agencies, stocked with incredibly expensive diagnostic equipment and specially developed clean areas in a hospital, and staffed by transplant-trained doctors and medical staff, whose surgical techniques and skills cannot be imitated or easily learned.

Can it be substituted for? Every resource that a company determines to be potentially valuable, rare, and not subject to quick or easy imitation should be evaluated for close substitutes. Here substitution means other ways that competitors can provide comparable value-creating benefits. So a substitute is something that meets the same basic need being satisfied by a company's resource. As with the question of rarity, it is often the case that tangible resources can be easily substituted. Retail or corporate location, machinery, equipment, and raw materials are all usually substitutable. Amazon developed and patented its "One-Click" method for customers to use in buying books and merchandise; however, other online retailers have developed similar systems that allow customer information to be retained and called up easily at the time of purchase.

So substitution most often applies to intangible resources, like internal routines and coordinating efforts across the value chain. General Electric's Superabrasives Division competes with DeBeers in industrial diamonds and cutting tools. Some years ago GE discovered that DeBeers had invented a new process that yielded higher quantities of industrial diamonds, thus lowering their costs and allowing them to price more aggressively in the marketplace. There was no practical substitute for this process that GE could put into place. This is different from the airplane manufacturing example just above, since in that case a "paper and pen" process would still have allowed Airbus to design aircraft and compete with Boeing. But in the GE case they were being priced out of the market, losing business hand over fist. Their only hope was to imitate what DeBeers had already accomplished; developing this was an expensive undertaking and took a long time, giving DeBeers a significant timing advantage in the market.

Occasionally, it is possible to substitute for intangible resources. The "brand management" system of marketing was developed by Procter & Gamble in the 1960s, but other consumer packaged-goods companies (e.g., General Mills, Kraft, Clorox) developed their own "product management" systems that worked equally well in the marketing of consumer products.

From this discussion it should become clear that the questions of imitation and substitution begin to focus our attention on the *durability* of advantage that any developed resource might confer. We will return to the question of durability in the following section.

Can it be traded for? Once again, for those resources that are simultaneously valuable, rare, not subject to imitation, and not easily substitutable, the business must consider tradability (or transferability) of the resource. How mobile is it? Can it somehow be purchased by another company, and if so will there be a loss in the short- or long-term value-creating benefit of that resource? Is the resource most valuable only in a particular geographic location? A potentially extraordinary resource increases value to your company if it is also difficult to transfer.

In the early 1980s John Sculley was president of PepsiCo, after having been promoted up through the organization. He was well known for his marketing acumen; in fact he oversaw the initiation of the Pepsi Challenge, which enabled Pepsi to begin gaining market share from Coca-Cola in U.S. supermarkets. In 1984 Sculley was hired away from Pepsi to become chairman of Apple Computer, while founder Steve Jobs' responsibilities were stripped away. The Apple board believed that Sculley could bring the same kind of marketing success for their company that he had engineered in the soft drink business. However, his tenure at Apple was marked by suboptimal product development plans, failed market launches (e.g., the Newton PDA), and increasing division and dissension within the company. It appeared that the success at Pepsi had been a combination of Sculley and the team of individuals involved, the culture of the company, the cooperation they fostered, and the unique procedures and knowledge base of all the other employees at that company. The Apple board had deemed that this resource could be imported into their growing company, when in reality it was a nontransferable combination of people, culture, and systems. Steve Jobs ultimately returned to run Apple, and navigated the company to its next successful run of strong performance. For the same reasons that Sculley was successful at Pepsi but not at Apple, Jobs was successful at Apple.

Figure 6.3 summarizes these concepts and provides examples of each of the five VRIST dimensions. Whenever you discuss sources of competitive advantage and the potential for a sustainable position, you should always use the VRIST framework as an evaluative tool.

Figure 6.3
VRIST Extraordinary Resource Criteria

Criteria & Key Question	Illustrations
Valuable Does the resource lead to a product or service that creates value?	Your company has a staff of highly traveled and experienced agents who custom design premium vacation travel. Customers regularly pay a premium to have your company create the whole vacation package. Paul Newman created a non-profit organization, The Hole-in-the-Wall Gang, providing terminally ill children a no-cost camp experience. His reputation enabled the non-profit to attract a high level of philanthropic giving. Firm XYZ developed a targeted method to reach consumers very active in outdoor activities. Their consumers provide feedback information about camping equipment that XYZ shares with its suppliers to assist them in future new product development.
Rare How unique is the resource?	After years of research and investment, your organization has developed a new diagnostic process for detecting with 99% accuracy that your computer's hard drive is about to fail.
Imitation Is it difficult or costly to imitate?	Your programmers created an innovative new web site that relies on a novel, non-obvious method allowing users to access a public database. Although competitors will be able to view your approach immediately through the website, patent protection would prevent duplicating your method for a time.
Substitution How easily can competitors develop a strategically equivalent resource?	Your firm has an in-house staff of process engineers that enable you to take designs to production in a very efficient manner. However, there are process engineering consulting companies that can be hired by competitors to accomplish essentially the same task. Ride the Rockies Inc. worked out an exclusive agreement with the National Parks allowing them to run downhill bike tours in Rocky Mount National Park.
Tradable How mobile is the resource?	A restaurant whose business depends on drive-through traffic manages to snag the last remaining corner location on the busiest route in town.

Connecting Extraordinary Resources to Sustainable Advantage

The five criteria shown in Figure 6.3, used to determine whether or not resources are extraordinary, also help describe why extraordinary resources are the foundation of a competitive advantage that is *sustainable*. This is a critical point in strategic management; the question of sustainable advantage was the second question we asked in Chapter 1 that defines what strategy is about. It was earlier pointed out that there may be no unique strategic positions discernible as a result of conducting an industry analysis, because the information that feeds into such analyses is commonly available to all companies. A firm's competitive advantage thus depends on the development or possession of an idiosyncratic resource or set of resources that cannot be easily developed or acquired by other firms.

Three of the criteria discussed above – rare, non-tradable, non-substitutable – characterize a resource that is *unique* to the business and that cannot be appropriated by potential competitors. These characteristics confer the possibility to develop an *immediate* competitive advantage because no competitor has the resource nor can they buy it or substitute for it.

We understand, however, that – while no advantage lasts forever – all businesses wish for their advantage to last as long as possible. Practice suggests that there are two ways to examine and predict the *durability* of advantage. First, there can be an anticipated time lag between the development of a particular competitive advantage and the point where a competitor will be able to closely match that advantage. This lag creates a window where the business can earn extraordinary returns. Second, a competitor may be required make huge investments and devote great amounts of management attention in order to achieve the same result. If so, the competitor may not be able to earn an adequate return on its investment or may believe that too much attention would be diverted away from its existing business. Keeping competitors at bay increases the potential for durability and the ability to earn extraordinary returns in relation to the industry.

Because the question of durability is so central to sustainable competitive advantage, it is important to know about the three primary sources of durability:[7]

1. *Historical conditions*. The ability to develop unique resources can depend on historical conditions – the time and place in which businesses locate, begin, or grow. For example, real estate entrepreneurs Richard Peery and John Arrillaga began buying California farmland in the early 1960s, subsequently converting it into industrial use and office space. Their original plot of farmland is at the corner of Maude and Mathilda Avenues in downtown Sunnyvale, the very center of what became Silicon Valley. Peery-Arrillaga Properties is one of the largest commercial real estate firms in North America, leasing buildings to companies like Apple, Intel, and Google. The two founders are regularly listed among the world's wealthiest individuals.[8] By virtue of the time period in which they were acquiring in their specific location, Peery and Arrillaga were able to control vast resources, locking up the "supply" of land and preventing other would-be real estate developers from becoming involved.

2. *Causal ambiguity*. Causal ambiguity exists when the link between a business's resources and its competitive advantage is poorly understood by others. If the linkage is poorly understood, then potential competitors are likely to have a difficult time trying to imitate the "recipe" for success. We might think about causal ambiguity as what occurs when we try to teach people how to ride a bicycle when they have never done so before. We can describe the mechanics of peddling and steering but there is a tacit component that is impossible to describe,[9] such as the relationship between speed and turning or understanding how to ride safely on a gravel surface. Experience is necessary to understand how superior performance is attained, but what is

learned from the experience cannot be completely written down or easily communicated to others. For example, General Electric was widely-recognized for its ability to produce exceptional business leaders who went on to run other large corporations. It is something more that happens there than the GE experience or their system of rotating managers between businesses. Amazon has been hailed as a modern company producing effective leaders for new startup companies, because of the culture and aggressive approach they each learned within Amazon.[10] What creates this capability cannot be completely explained; so competitors have a very difficult time trying to reproduce it.

You should recognize that there is a sort of paradox about this notion of causal ambiguity.[11] Just as it makes it difficult for a competitor to understand the foundation of your company's strong competitive position, it may also be difficult for your own management team to identify why your company is doing so well. Resource positions are not always obvious, even to those who benefit from them. In fact, one of the challenges of growth and development is the accurate internal identification of the kinds of resources that your company can build upon effectively. We will return to the challenge of identifying resources in a few minutes.

3. *Social complexity.* Here the business's resources may result from social complexity, a phenomenon that cannot be systematically managed or influenced. For example, Apple's iPad resulted from a socially complex design/product development process. Highly trained engineers worked closely with designers in a culture that values the unique and exceptional. Other companies may be able to hire away the engineers for their technical or design skills, but the integrated combination of the team, culture, and environment cannot be easily reproduced elsewhere. Social complexity may also extend upstream or downstream to relationships that companies develop with their suppliers or customers, where the business relationship regarding product or service transactions is further cemented by other personal and social relations.

The astute student will recognize that strategic resources are seldom available in the external industry environment. If they are there, then other companies may also acquire them, thereby eliminating the important VRIST dimension of rarity. So rare resources are usually those developed internally.

You will also see that the criteria for assessing whether a resource is "valuable" ties back directly to the discussion in Chapter 5 about the value chain. Resources are *valuable* if they enable the company to implement an approach that achieves superior performance. If the company is unable to utilize a particular resource to earn above-average returns, then while it may be potentially interesting, that resource cannot be classified as extraordinary. It does not represent a foundation for competitive advantage. It is not uncommon to have a particular resource meet all four of the other criteria previously mentioned, and yet still be unable to create value by reducing costs relative to competitors, delivering added benefits for the exact same price, increasing revenues, or obtaining more customers. If a firm performs an activity that is rare, inimitable, non-tradable, and non-substitutable, but not valuable relative to competition, then no economic advantage can be garnered. Figure 6.4 illustrates that the five critical dimensions of extraordinary resources, if fulfilled, create conditions – *valuable, unique,* and *durable* – that together confer sustainable competitive advantage.

The identification and creation of value, in part, depends upon differences in expectations about how resources may be utilized. In the real estate example mentioned earlier, Peery and Arrillaga purchased land that was thought by most investors to be useful only for farming. The real estate entrepreneurs had a different concept in mind about possible uses for the land and the significantly higher revenue potential that the land appeared to present. Think about almost any successful new venture that you happen to follow or whose business you subscribe to. Their services and products likely originated from founders who saw new opportunities by assemble VRIST resources.

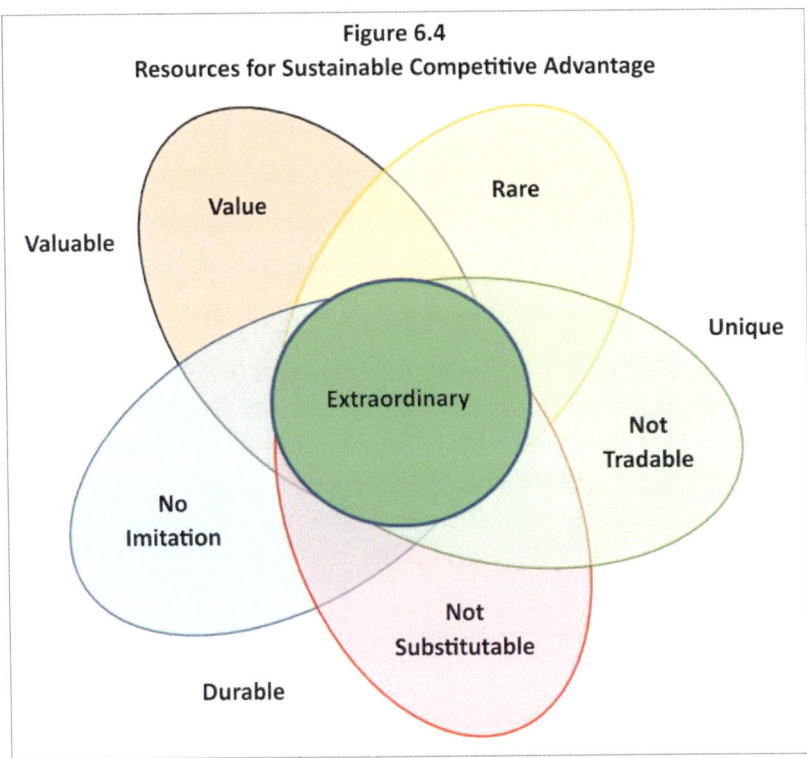

One of the central premises of this text is that both value creation and opportunity recognition are strategic imperatives for all companies in the twenty-first century (Chapter 1). The notion of differing expectations about value creation potential illustrates precisely where these two imperatives come together. Superior and sustainable performance requires more than luck in happening to come upon a new idea that builds on resources exhibiting the five VRIST criteria. Strategic management today involves anticipating markets, and then creatively using new and already developed resources to take advantage of emergent trends. The next step involves structuring the organization and its internal processes to regularly generate new business ideas and new resource possibilities that can create future value. Managing growth through innovation will be covered later on in Chapter 9, and structuring the organization will be covered in Chapter 13.

The identification of extraordinary resources should guide any business in its investments and strategic development. To reiterate, those resources and capabilities that are ordinary must be done well, but they need not be done any better than the average for the industry. Having stunning office chairs may be nice, but it is not going to create strategic value for the company. However, extraordinary resources should receive attention and investment by the management team. These become the core foundation upon which to develop competitive advantage. Over-investment in the ordinary dimensions of the business will distract attention needed at the critical strategic core, and have the potential to siphon much-needed funding and time into areas that are not capable of yielding superior economic returns. These ideas allow students and managers to see that strategic management is a balancing act: using the financial and human capital available to develop ordinary resources that must be in place just to conduct business, while dedicating as much funding and attention as possible to extraordinary resources that can deliver competitive advantage.

Types of Extraordinary Resources

Earlier writings in economics and strategy discussed three basic types of resources that firms might rely upon in their development of strategy: physical capital, financial capital, and human capital. The word "capital" in these categories was an extension of previous economic thinking about the "factors of production" used by manufacturing firms. Strategic management theory and analysis have since evolved considerably, increasingly recognizing service-based enterprises and the importance of knowledge in all types of business. Strategists now recognize an expanded list of resource categories (Figure 6.5). As we move forward into the analysis of resources, it is helpful to keep these categories in mind as a guide.

\multicolumn{2}{c}{**Figure 6.5**}
\multicolumn{2}{c}{**Categories of Resources**}
Resources	**Examples**
Knowledge	Unique knowledge about a potential opportunity Prior industry experience Prior new venture startup experience Entrepreneurial orientation
Social	Informal networks to gain business and startup knowledge Formal industry and value chain networks – industry leaders, suppliers, customers
Human	Prior relevant management experience Credibility, reputation Functional area expertise
Financial	Access to seed stage and growth capital Access to institutional capital for later stage development Relationships to support cash flow management
Organizational	Ability to organize complexity: administrative systems, task systems, policies Coordination expertise and combining expertise Methods to articulate complex resources and capabilities Ability to share and routinize capabilities in other parts of the new venture
Technology	Intellectual property claims Unique/special manufacturing process or physical equipment
Physical	Manufacturing facilities and location Unique access to suppliers Unique access to customers

Occasionally, a company's resource may be combinations of several of these descriptive categories. For example, TJX – the parent company of retailers TJ Maxx, Sierra Trading, and others – depends on its buyers to spot opportunity for fashion goods that can be priced to move quickly. Becoming an outstanding buyer demands curiosity and training. Training involves class experience, apprenticeship, learning about negotiating, vendor communication, financial responsibility, planning and more. Former TJX CEO Carol Meyrowitz believes it is at the core of the company's sustainable advantage.[12] It combines knowledge, social, human, and organizational categories of resources into a special competence.

RESOURCES AND CAPABILITIES

So far in this chapter we have referred solely to the idea of "resources." Many strategy professors and people in business, however, often refer to "capabilities" as well as resources. Having presented the five VRIST criteria that help determine if resources are extraordinary, we are now in a position to more carefully examine the difference between these two frequently used concepts. Extraordinary resources represent the raw materials of a business, a core foundation upon which the sustainable advantage of the business may be built. Capabilities may be thought of as sets of tightly integrated activities, organizational skills, and internally developed routines that rely on extraordinary resources and that allow the company to create value in a fashion superior to other companies.[13] As can be seen from the earlier Apple iPad example, exciting new products can result from intermediate level capabilities existing between extraordinary resources and the products actually sold in the marketplace. In the Apple case the intermediate level includes a new product development process that works extremely well. The new product development capability, however, is a result of extraordinary resources of the firm at a deeper foundational level – such as their recruiting process for engineers, a culture that emphasizes design and technical excellence, and the cross-functional coordination that occurs early on in the development process. Each of these extraordinary resources meets all of the VRIST criteria.

This development process capability might be leveraged in multiple ways, such as creating multiple types of new products (e.g., Apple TV, iPod Nano, MacPro, iWatch) or by working with various types of customers (consumers, schools, government, business). So we see that resources and combinations of resources lead to the development of firm capabilities, which in turn provide a platform from which multiple approaches to the marketplace may be pursued.[14] In this case Apple intends to leverage its resource-based capabilities to produce additional products and entertainment gadgets that will enable the company to "colonize rooms throughout the home."[15]

Figure 6.6 captures the sense of this relationship between resources, capabilities, and business performance. The figure shows that extraordinary resources are the foundation upon which capabilities are built. Together these enable the business to introduce products or services in order to generate superior performance. Interestingly, this perspective also reiterates that ordinary resources are important only if they are built on a proper strategic foundation of extraordinary resources and capabilities. This idea can be extended further by suggesting that the accumulation of ordinary resources and the development of products or services are often not even possible unless the proper strategic foundation has been laid. For example, investors and venture capital firms are often

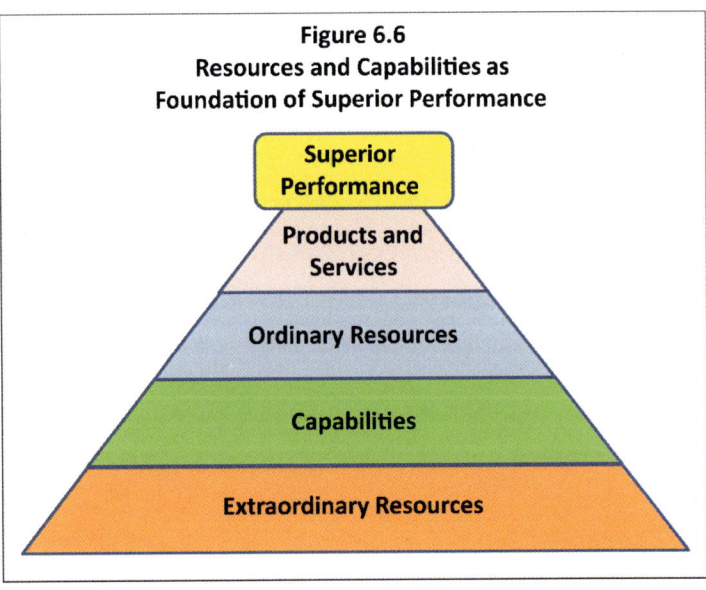

unwilling to support a new venture unless there has been some very clear thinking about the sources of sustainable competitive advantage. The foundational levels of extraordinary resources and capabilities are critical. Similarly, top management teams and boards of directors of established firms would be remiss in their shareholder responsibilities if they decided to embark on a major new direction without significant attention devoted to the question of sustainability and its foundation.

The combination of resources and capabilities at the base of a business again prompts us to return to the value chain model explored in Chapter 5. The value chain discussion highlighted the critical importance of the coordination of activities across both the internal and external value chains of the business. A product development process, such as that which existed for the iPod and iTunes, is a capability involving an entire coordinated set of value adding activities. In this instance, research and development worked closely with both procurement and operations internally, as well as with upstream suppliers of components. The legal staff developed relations with artists and music labels, and worked carefully with programmers to create digital music protocols that would protect copyrighted material. The marketing team developed plans for selling iPods through new channels of distribution. The ecosystem they created through these types of connections and coordination in the value chain are valuable, unique, and durable, giving rise to a sustainable competitive advantage. For this reason Apple dominates the paid music download market. Even more consequentially, the company leveraged these iPod development capability facets first into iPads and iPhones, and then into the Apple Music store for streaming content which replaced Spotify as market leader in the U.S. in 2019. Although the overall digital music industry in 2022 is small relative to Apple's total revenue, the coordinated activity sets created a foundational platform that will contribute substantively to the company's profits and shareholder returns over time. The ability to understand and manage these connections, once developed or learned, is also become a valuable capability.[16]

Starbucks, Part 2

Everywhere Starbucks looked in 2008, they were being attacked. McDonald's announced that it would be putting into its stores the same coffee drink machines that Starbucks had used. It would also be offering drinks for substantially lower prices. Neighborhood coffee shops were sprouting up nearby established Starbucks. And the economic recession had prompted consumers to think twice about high-priced goods. Starbucks was not growing as it wished.

Facing this situation, CEO Howard Schultz wrote a letter to the employees about the commoditization of coffee and the need to again make Starbucks unique in the market. He acknowledged that recent decisions the company had made to handle growth had been for the right reasons, in isolation, but that the sum of the decisions was a dilution of Starbucks cachet. They had moved to automated machines, vacuum-packed coffee, and cookie-cutter store designs. They had also started offering breakfast items, putting them squarely in competition with other chains.

He told the employees, "I have said for 20 years that our success is not an entitlement and now it's proving to be a reality. Let's be smarter about how we are spending our time, money and resources. Let's get back to the core. Push for innovation and do the things necessary to once again differentiate Starbucks from all others."

QUESTIONS

1. What did Starbucks do to counter the trend toward commoditization? Do you think they have succeeded?

2. What are their resources and capabilities, and based on these, what new avenues would you suggest for Starbucks?

Managing in Markets: Question for Class Discussion

Transparency is increasingly valued when public companies file their quarterly and annual reports. Shareholders, stakeholders, and the investment community seek to better understand the nature of a company's business, as well as its challenges and opportunities. In order to be more transparent, should public companies discuss in detail their value chain and resource-based foundations in these periodic reports?

CONDUCTING A RESOURCE ANALYSIS

Although a few company illustrations of the ideas about resources and capabilities in this chapter have been provided, the treatment of this important strategic concept often stays at a very conceptual level in most classroom discussions. And in the executive suite of most companies, talk about "resource-based advantage" seldom occurs. This is because many find it difficult to translate these important ideas into a practical guide. Theory is only great if it can be put into practice! So in the final section of this chapter we want to bring the ideas closer to practice. Here we discuss how they can be easily used by students of strategic management.

A resource-based analysis approach allows each resource or capability to be examined for its potential to provide the business with a competitive advantage. We seek to identify extraordinary resources or capabilities that will provide a focus for the business. Resource-based analysis is a tool providing management with a practical method for discerning the core foundation for sustainable competitive advantage. This methodology has five basic steps that should be proceeded through in sequence:

1. Develop a listing of all resources and capabilities, including those that are tangible and those that are intangible;

2. Divide those resources and capabilities into the categories of ordinary and extraordinary for the industry in which the company competes. Ordinary resources are those that must be developed, but no better than the standard for the industry.

3. For those resources and capabilities that appear to be extraordinary, use the VRIST framework to determine which are truly extraordinary:
    - Valuable
    - Rare
    - Difficult to imitate
    - Cannot be substituted for
    - Cannot be traded for

4. For those resources and capabilities that pass the VRIST test, develop the means to leverage these extraordinary positions.

5. Evaluate the relevance of extraordinary resources for the Key Success Factors required for success in the industry. If there is a mismatch, consider how to develop appropriate resources that address the KSFs.

The following discussion walks through each step of this process.

Develop a resource and capability list. The best process to accomplish this task involves gathering together the key decision makers in the organization. This group will develop a complete list of all the tangible and intangible resources that the company is believed to possess at that particular point in time.

While this inventory process may seem a bit mundane, it is absolutely critical to the identification of potential resources or capabilities that may provide a sustainable competitive advantage for the organization. As this is the first step in the process, it is important to develop as complete a list as possible encompassing the entire breadth of knowledge within the management team. The developed list may be quite long and should include everything that the company possesses now if it is already in business or, in the case of a new venture that it may possess at the time it begins to conduct business.

Identifying the intangibles often presents the greatest challenge for managers and their key advisors or employees. We tend to think of our companies in terms of the products or services they provide or the customers they serve. This is because this is what we experience on a day-to-day basis. On the one hand, this natural orientation is positive because it reflects a fundamental customer and value-creation orientation. On the other hand, we need to recognize that products, services, and satisfied customers are simply a manifestation of a set of underlying organizational resources and capabilities that the business is built upon (refer back to Figure 6.6). Remember also our Chapter 5 insights on the importance of support activities in the value chain and coordinating activities across the value chain. Together these argue for an examination that goes deeper than mere products or services.

In identifying the intangibles it is important to continue to ask questions that drill down to the essential core of what the company is really all about and what it does particularly well. In our experience by repeatedly asking a single penetrating question to probe deeper and deeper, the core resources of a firm can be revealed. That question is: "What is the cause of this outcome?"

Here's an example showing how to develop insight about intangible resources that may be extraordinary. In this example, a management team is exploring one facet that they collectively feel contributes to their success in the marketplace and thus to superior performance. They believe there are several facets they must explore, but in this illustration they are just exploring the derivation of one. They have identified it as how well their products fill important customer needs. Here they see that their capability (the routines created by the new product development team) depends fundamentally upon their recruiting network enabling them to hire strong managers, a knowledge database they have developed over time, a particular manager with knowledge about managing fast-cycle teams, and a culture that rewards ideation.

Figure 6.7 provides a straightforward illustration of the probing process to identify important intangible resources. Repeatedly asking the question "What is the cause of this outcome?" gets to the heart of critical intangibles.

Figure 6.7
Process to Identify Intangible Resources

Question	Management Response	
What is one of your competitive advantages?	Our products uniquely fill important needs of our customer.	
What is the cause of this outcome?	Our product development team is very good.	
What is the cause of this outcome?	The team is able to respond quickly to new customer needs we identify.	
What is the cause of this outcome?	They work extremely well together as a team.	
What is the cause of this outcome?	We recruited people who each had previous experience in high performing new product teams.	They have developed a system and protocols on what works in product development.
What is the cause of this outcome?	Our recruiting network is quite strong. We have HR expertise in hiring in this industry.	A knowledge database provides guidance on what we should pursue in new products. Senior manager with development team coordination experience and expertise. Culture that encourages ideas and experimentation.

These intangibles, then, might be added to the company's developing list, which might resemble the list in Figure 6.8.

Figure 6.8
List of Identified Resources

Tangible Resources	Intangible Resources
Building location Equipment Initial financing Inventory Patents and patents pending Software and systems for business Renovations and improvements to facility	Industry experience Contacts and networks Previous experience in same type of business Education Unique knowledge of the industry (from previous research) Skills sets of founder and managers (innovation, team coordination, presence with stakeholders, etc.) Name and branding Recruiting network New product development knowledge database Organizational culture

Identify potentially ordinary and extraordinary resources and capabilities. The lists of resources of the organization now serve as a foundation for the next step in the process. Management should further divide the list of tangible and intangible resources into what they believe are either ordinary or extraordinary resources. This usually results in a much smaller list of items believed to be extraordinary.

Use the VRIST framework. Each of the potentially extraordinary resources should be evaluated using the five-point VRIST framework to determine if it truly is extraordinary. Those that pass through all five steps are the unique resources and capabilities that the company should plan to leverage.

Those that fail to pass all five steps should be re-categorized as ordinary. Each of the ordinary resources or capabilities should be evaluated to determine if the company is meeting median expectations in the industry. Ordinary resources, which are normal in an industry and provide no basis for advantage or sustainability, need only the amount of effort and time necessary to achieve parity with other competitors in the industry.

Leverage extraordinary resources. The result of this effort is the creation of a short list of truly extraordinary characteristics for the business. This process moves beyond the question of "why would a customer purchase from us?" Now the business can narrow its strategic focus to those areas that are most important to creating a sustainable advantage. These areas should receive the time, investment, development attention, and focus of the firm. Leveraging the extraordinary resource positions may be accomplished in one of three ways, which include the following:

1. *Extending the current business model into additional products or customer segments.* After building its unique method for selling books online, Amazon leveraged its developed internet capabilities into other product segments. In 2013 it leveraged into fine art, and has since gone further into music, video, food and more. As it further developed its back end computing and database operations, it recognized that these capabilities provided a platform for additional segments of business. So by 2016 one of Amazon's biggest growth segments – and one of its most profitable – is "cloud computing" offered to other businesses. The AWS division of the company is now one of its largest revenue generators. In 2018 it started to extend its VRIST-based distribution infrastructure (e.g. warehouse sorting facilities, trucks, tracking systems, people organization) – into "bricks and mortar" retailing, through its 2017 acquisition of Whole Foods and expansion of its own Amazon-branded retail shops.

2. *Replicating the resource or capability elsewhere in the organization to enhance the performance of the business.* United Technologies was a multi-national diversified corporation. In its Otis Elevator subsidiary it developed a comprehensive training and assessment program designed to enhance productivity and quality simultaneously, nicknamed ACE for "achieving competitive excellence." Management replicated the ACE program in other divisions of the corporation, making a significant difference in their business and relationships with suppliers.[17]

3. *Developing complementary resources.* Inmar Enterprises came into existence as a manufacturers' coupon clearinghouse, processing millions of coupons received by retail stores for manufacturers' products. They processed payments for the retailers and billed the manufacturers. Originally organized using low-cost labor in other countries, Inmar has since made technology investments to economize on processing fees, and the technology now provides superior competitive market and user information reports and service to its retail and manufacturer clients.

Evaluate relevance of extraordinary resources for KSFs. Extraordinary resources should be relevant for the Key Success Factors that have previously been identified as important in the company's industry. If they are relevant and pivotal, then the company is well-positioned to succeed in the industry on a sustainable basis.

However, occasionally the previously developed extraordinary resources have become obsolete as an industry has evolved (for example, Blockbuster's retail presence when DVD-by-mail and video streaming became popular). Or perhaps through the resource-based analysis the company has discovered it does not have extraordinary resources that match well to industry demands. This will then prompt an effort to determine how to develop a resource base that will enable the company to compete more effectively. This could mean enhancing an existing ordinary resource so that it becomes extraordinary and a point of strategic differentiation. Or it could trigger the development of an entirely new resource.

The VRIST evaluation process may also yield insight on *other* industries that a company might consider entering. Consider, for example, Samsung's historical presence in flat screen TVs and cellphones. It was not a major leap for the company to redirect their resources and capabilities in these markets into tablets, as well. E*Trade started life as an online equities investment service. Yet their core strengths in backroom processing of electronic transactions prompted them to broaden their services into online banking.

An Illustration of the Process

A fairly high-end web design business was formed in the late 1990s around three very talented and personable individuals. In short order the company hired many more people and grew to thirty employees. They offered quality web design, hosting, and customer relationship tracking services at a premium price in an industry that was in its infancy. After five years in business the company hit a point where their business seemed to stall. During the next nine months they noticed a slow, gradual but steady decline in new business. Discussions with clients and others in the business failed to point out any particular problem with the operation.

They decided to take a break and held a two-day retreat to think through the business. They began by asking everyone to talk about aspects of their business that served as a resource enabling them to compete in the industry. After a slow start the ideas started to flow more rapidly and a very, very long list was developed. A small part of that list is recreated in Figure 6.9 as an example.

Figure 6.9
Web Page Design Company Resources and Capabilities

Nice office space, desks, chairs, telephones, cubicals	Customer relationship experts on staff
Computers for each employee	Internet marketing experts on staff
Computer servers for client hosting	Payroll system
Attractive reception area	Project management systems and staff expertise
Break area for employees with free soft drinks, coffee	Experienced account executives
Real-time web host tracking and reporting capability	Business cards, letterhead, logo
Web design expertise including creative designers	Strong web presence
Accounting, cost, budget and time management systems	

The shock in the meeting room was palpable as they realized that many of the areas listed, which had been unique to them just a few years earlier, were now just standard fare in the industry. This company had started out with three individuals working out of a rented house with two computers, one telephone, no letterhead, and just a plan for designing web pages. Creating and hosting websites had developed as a result of a client's request for the service. As is the case in many industries, this industry had benefited from upward trajectory and sophistication of readily available technology. So as the internet became increasingly ubiquitous into the 2000s, and as the barriers to entry to web designing became relatively inconsequential (a PC and widely available software), the supply of competing firms grew dramatically. Pricing for similar services dropped precipitously, as an increasing number of firms competed for what was essentially moving toward a commodity type of service. Figure 6.10 illustrates the changes occurring in this industry during a time when the supply of web design firms expanded significantly.

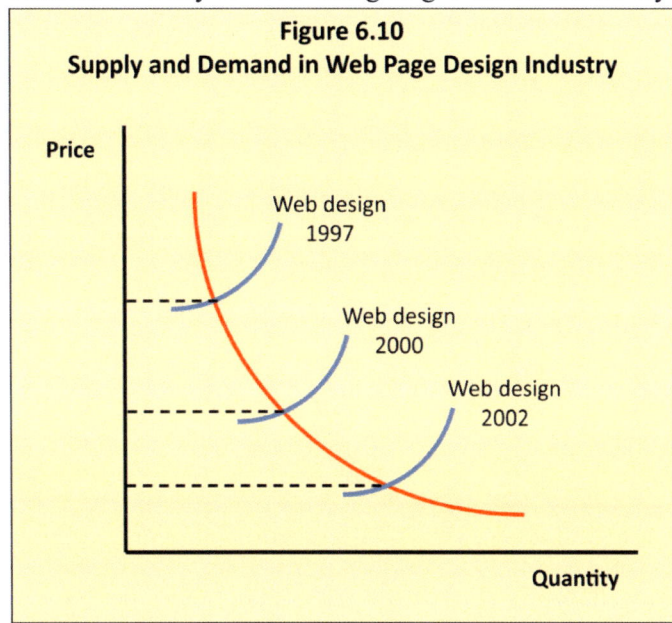

Careful examination found they were relying on resources or capabilities which had become commonplace and standard in the industry. This being the case, they had become simply average in their competitive space and were being outcompeted by new businesses offering comparable services at a lower price. This reflects the lesson that durability is not forever. What was extraordinary at one time will become ordinary at some point, as competitors continue efforts to imitate, substitute, and invent their own value-creating practices. As durable advantages dissipate, uniqueness declines, opening the door for competitors to create the same value in the same ways or equal value in different ways.

The most important list to create and regularly update is the list of extraordinary resources or capabilities at the foundation of the business. This list is usually quite small, but in it are the seeds of success. The web design management group carefully considered what was at the root of their ability to attract business, and developed the new list in Figure 6.11

Figure 6.11
Potentially Extraordinary Resources and Capabilities

Strong client base of fortune 500 firms
Well known brand name – winner of several national awards
Located in a very desirable location with relatively low cost of living
Unique web development system that saved 70% of the time needed when compared to standard web development
History of successful web page designs
Talented team that worked as a cohesive unit

Each of these potentially extraordinary resources or capabilities was then subjected to the resource-based analysis, using the VRIST framework. While one might disagree with their analysis, the important lesson here is that there is both art and science involved in determining key sources of competitive advantage. The science of the process involves: 1) understanding which resources are tangible and which are intangible; 2) using the VRIST framework to divide those resources and capabilities into ordinary and extraordinary for the industry in which the company competes; and 3) deciding to focus attention on extraordinary resources, and investing only as necessary in ordinary resources to maintain competitive parity. The art of the process involves judgment of degree, discretion, and experience. The company's final chart appears in Figure 6.12.

Figure 6.12
VRIST Evaluation of Resources

Resource	Valuable	Rare	Difficult to Imitate	Difficult to Substitute	Difficult to Trade
Strong client base of Fortune 500 firms	Yes	Yes	No	Yes	Yes
Well known brand name	**Yes**	**Yes**	**Yes**	**Yes**	**Yes**
Desirable location with low cost of living	Yes	Yes	No	No	Yes
Unique development system saving 70% of time	**Yes**	**Yes**	**Yes**	**Yes**	**Yes**
History of successful designs	Yes	No	No	No	Yes
Talented team that works as a cohesive unit	Yes	No	No	No	Yes

During this retreat the team decided that just two of their potentially extraordinary resources or capabilities were truly a foundation for developing competitive advantage. And so the company set about the process of developing a strategic approach that focused on these areas. In turn, this approach prompted them to redefine the industry segment they were targeting as client firms that required high-quality designs quickly. It also prompted a refocusing internally on advanced development of these targeted capabilities, and a shifting of time and investment away from practices that merely supported ordinary web design efforts.

CHAPTER SUMMARY

This chapter examined the nature of the resources and capabilities of businesses that provide the opportunity to earn superior returns on a sustainable basis. Resource-based analysis is an important supplement to value chain analysis because it enables any business to consider the uniqueness and the sustainability of its position. This perspective helps to answer one of the two key questions that define strategy: "How are competitive and performance differences *sustained*?" (You might recall that the subtitle for this textbook is "Value Creation, Sustainability, and Performance").

A process was described that incorporated the following items: 1) develop a listing of all resources and capabilities; 2) divide those resources and capabilities into categories of ordinary and potentially extraordinary for the industry in which the company competes; 3) evaluate those that appear to be extraordinary based upon the VRIST framework as follows:

- Valuable
- Rare
- Imitation
- Substitution
- Tradable

4) determine ways to leverage extraordinary resources that pass the VRIST test, and 5) assess the relevance of extraordinary resources for addressing key success factors in the industry.

The combination of these five characteristics confers value, uniqueness, and durability on a company's efforts. Thus extraordinary resources and capabilities provide the foundation for entering markets with products and services, and for earning superior returns versus competition on a sustainable basis.

Most typically, extraordinary resources will be comprised of intangible factors, such as the special coordination of routine activities within a company or the unique knowledge that company has developed about some aspect of its business. Value chain analysis can help identify these sorts of coordinating patterns of activities, which are difficult or impossible for competitors to see or imitate.

There are additional issues for businesses to consider in using the resource-based framework for developing its strategy. We highlight a few of these here:

1. How do businesses develop a resource position to begin with? Almost without exception, every new venture begins as merely an idea about a potential opportunity. The prospective entrepreneur possesses no assets or resources that can be claimed by the new venture he or she might start up. Thus a very real dilemma for the prospective entrepreneur is how to create something out of nothing.

2. What kinds of resources should be developed or invested in? At any stage of a business's development, managers face choices about the application of their time and the limited financial capital they may have backing their efforts. So what should be the priority of focus in the resource development process?

3. All businesses confront specific and identifiable types of strategic challenges over time as they develop through stages. Is there a resource development path that businesses should follow to respond to these widely experienced strategic challenges?

4. Like any kind of organizational asset, resources and capabilities can become obsolete over time. How should businesses respond in their resource development efforts to dynamic changes in industry conditions, evolving competition, and the general obsolescence of previously developed resource positions?

We will explore some of these critical issues in the chapters to come.

Learning Objectives Review

1. Demonstrate how to compare the types of company resources, and show which can generate competitive advantage.

- Two types of resources are used by companies in the design and execution of their strategy: ordinary and extraordinary.

- Ordinary resources are those which the company must possess and utilize roughly at parity with its competitors in an industry. Ordinary resources are not a source of competitive advantage. The lack of ordinary resources may put a company at a competitive disadvantage.

- Extraordinary resources are those which exhibit the VRIST dimensions: valuable, rare, cannot be imitated, cannot be substituted for, and cannot be traded for. These are the foundation of sustainable competitive advantage because they confer the qualities of value, uniqueness and durability.

2. *Explain the difference between resources and capabilities.*

- Extraordinary resources are the foundation of sustainable competitive advantage.

- Capabilities are sets of tightly integrated activities, organizational skills, and internally developed routines that are based on and configured out of extraordinary resources. Capabilities provide a platform from which a variety of new products or services may be developed and multiple customer types pursued.

3. *List the categories of resources that companies may draw upon to develop competitive advantage.*

- Knowledge; social; human; financial; organizational; technology; physical.

4. *Outline a practical model for analyzing which resources and capabilities will work to deliver competitive advantage.*

- Develop a list of all resources and capabilities, including those which are tangible and intangible.

- Divide the list into those you believe are ordinary resources and those you believe may be extraordinary resources.

- Use the 5-point VRIST framework to determine which are truly extraordinary resources.

- Leverage the identified extraordinary resources: 1) extend into new products, services and/or customer segments; 2) replicate the resource elsewhere in the company to enhance performance; or 3) develop complementary resources.

- Assess the relevance of extraordinary resources for the Key Success Factors important in the industry.

Key Terms

Capabilities - Sets of tightly integrated activities, organizational skills, and internally developed routines that build upon extraordinary resources and allow the company to create value in a fashion superior to other companies.

Casual ambiguity - A condition that exists when the link between a business's resources and its competitive advantage are poorly understood.

Extraordinary resources - Those resources or capabilities that simultaneously exhibit the characteristics of: valuable, rare, durable, relatively non-substitutable, and non-tradable.

Historical conditions - The ability to develop unique resources often depends on the time and place in which the business began operations.

Intangible resources - Those resources and capabilities that are not physical in nature. They including relationships with key suppliers/businesses, the culture of the organization, the history of the business to date, patents, the skills of the founders, and perhaps most importantly the tacit knowledge embedded in the organization's routines and systems.

Intellectual property protection - A legal means of protecting tangible and intangible assets that are unique to the organization. This is accomplished through patents, copyrights, trademarks, and trade secrets.

Ordinary resources - Those resources or capabilities that are necessary to operate in an industry, but which do not confer competitive advantage.

Resource-based analysis - A method that examines the extent to which a company possesses resources that will allow it to achieve sustainable competitive advantage.

Social complexity - Resources that may result from a socially complex phenomenon, something which cannot be systematically managed or influenced.

Tangible resources - Physical assets such as equipment, buildings, land, furniture, owned raw materials, the size and geographic scope of the work force, and financial assets.

Short Answer Review Questions

1. How are tangible resources used in business?
2. How do ordinary resources impact the competitive advantage of a business?
3. What are the ways that extraordinary resources can create value for a business?
4. Explain which resources should be processed through the lens of resource-based analysis.
5. How is the VRIST framework used to the advantage of a business?
6. Ordinary resources must meet what criteria for the organization to be successful?
7. Broadly defined, what are the types of resources that may be employed by a business?
8. What is your conclusion about a resource/capability that meets all five criteria in the VRIST framework?

Group Exercises

1. In 2021 Saks Fifth Avenue split out its Saks.com online business into a completely separate legal entity. In the same year department store goliath Macy's has come under pressure from investors to also separate its e-commerce business from its physical store business. There are pros and cons of this approach. What are the implications for extraordinary resource investments when a retailer spins out its online business? What extraordinary resources does each entity need to develop? What extraordinary resources might two such entities jointly share?

2. Your group has decided to start a new business. You see an opportunity to open up a drive-in movie theater. With the dramatic rise in gas prices, people are not traveling very far and they are looking for a great bargain. You plan to charge only $8 per car. What ordinary resources will you need? What might you add to this business that could be extraordinary?

3. Using the VRIST framework, evaluate the extraordinary resources and capabilities that you listed in Question # 1. Which resources and capabilities provide the company with a real opportunity for a sustainable competitive advantage? Why?

4. Have the group do an internet search on Walmart. What elements of the business does the group believe make Walmart unique? Process those items through the VRIST framework. Which ones hold up as potentially providing Walmart with a sustainable competitive advantage?

Investor Relations Sites for Companies Mentioned in This Chapter

Amazon: https://ir.aboutamazon.com/overview/default.aspx
Apple: https://investor.apple.com/investor-relations/default.aspx
Boeing: https://investors.boeing.com/investors/overview/default.aspx
Buc-ee's: https://buc-ees.com/about/
De Beers: https://www.debeersgroup.com/
E*Trade (Morgan Stanley): https://www.morganstanley.com/about-us-ir
General Electric: https://www.ge.com/investor-relations
Johnson Controls: https://investors.johnsoncontrols.com/
Krispy Kreme: https://investors.krispykreme.com/
McDonald's: https://corporate.mcdonalds.com/corpmcd/investors.html
Nomacorc (Vinventions): https://us.vinventions.com/vinventions
Peery-Arillaga Properties: https://www.peery-arrillaga.com/
Procter & Gamble: https://pginvestor.com/
Qualcomm: https://investor.qualcomm.com/
Starbucks: https://investor.starbucks.com/ir-home/default.aspx
TJX: https://investor.tjx.com/
United Technologies (Raytheon): http://investors.rtx.com/

References

[1] Green, J. H. 2015, "6 reasons why the future of wine is looking bright, Wall Street Journal," December 9, p. D1. Pierson, D. 2014, "Wine cork makers seek to put a stop to declining sales," Los Angeles Times, December 7, p. C1. Aeppel, T. 2010, "Show stopper: How plastic popped the cork monopoly," Wall Street Journal, May 1, p. A1. www.nomacorc.com.

[2] Alvarez, S. A., and Busenitz, L. W. 2001, "The entrepreneurship of resource-based theory," *Journal of Management* 27(6): 755–775. Barney, J. B. 1991, "Firm resources and sustained competitive advantage," *Journal of Management* 17(1): 99–120. Grant, R. M. 1991, "The resource-based theory of competitive advantage: Implications for strategy formulation," *California Management Review* 33: 114–135. Penrose, E. T. 1959, *The theory of the growth of the firm*, New York: John Wiley & Sons. Peteraf, M. A. 1993, "The cornerstones of competitive advantage: A resource-based view," *Strategic Management Journal* 14: 179–191.

[3] Ghemahat, P. 1991, *Commitment*. New York: Free Press.

[4] Hall, R. 1993, "A framework linking intangible resources and capabilities to sustainable competitive advantage," *Strategic Management Journal* 14(8): 607–619.

[5] Swedberg, C., 2016, "RFID prevents Johnson Controls' containers from being lost," RFID Journal, May 17.

[6] U.S. Department of Health & Human Services, 2022. https://optn.transplant.hrsa.gov/data/.

[7] Barney, J. B. 1991, "Firm resources and sustained competitive advantage," *Journal of Management* 17(1): 99–120.

[8] Mangalindan, J. P. 2014, "The secretive billionaire who built Silicon Valley," Fortune, July 7. http://www.forbes.com/2003/02/26/billionaireland.html.

[9] Polanyi, M. 1967, *The tacit dimension*, Garden City, NJ: Anchor Books.

[10] Mattioli, D. 2019, "Amazon takes over from GE as CEO incubator," Wall Street Journal, November 21, A1.

[11] Kogut, B., and Zander, U. 1992, "Knowledge of the firm, combinative capabilities, and the replication of technology," *Management Science* 3(3): 383–396.

[12] Meyrowits, C. 2014, "The CEO of TJX on how to train first-class buyers." *Harvard Business Review*, May, 45-48.

[13] Quinn, J. B. 2005, "Leveraging intellect," *Academy of Management Executive* 19(4): 78–94.

[14] There has been much discussion in the strategy literature about the relationship between resources, capabilities, and core competence. The definitions of these terms are somewhat different depending on the authors. The argument that resources lead to capabilities, which can be leveraged in multiple ways, captures the sense of the collection of authors. Coyne, K. P., S. J. D. Hall, and Clifford, P. G. 1997, "Is your core competence a mirage?" *McKinsey Quarterly* 1: 41–55. Porter, M. 1996, "What is strategy?" *Harvard Business Review* Nov–Dec: 61–78. Prahalad, C. K., and Hamel, G. 1990, "The core competence of the corporation," *Harvard Business Review* May–June: 79–91.

[15] Wingfield, N. 2008, "Apple daydreaming: Report predicts move toward home devices," Wall Street Journal, May 22: D1.

[16] Teece, D. J., Pisano G., and Shuen, A. 1997, "Dynamic capabilities and strategic management," *Strategic Management Journal* 18: 509–533.

[17] Roth, G. L. 2013, "An uncommonly-cohesive conglomerate," *Strategy+Business*, 72 (Autumn).

This page is intentionally left blank.

Chapter 7: Business-Level Strategy

LEARNING OBJECTIVES

1. Compare and contrast business-level strategies available to organizations, and describe how they create competitive advantage.

2. Examine the underlying drivers that enable a company's choice of business-level strategy to be successful.

3. Analyze when outsourcing makes strategic sense.

Cementing Its Position[1]

Eagle Materials is the 7th largest producer of construction cement in the U.S., competing against larger multinational public corporations. In this commodity business, where all cement pretty much looks and acts the same, having a cost structure to ensure competitive pricing is a key to success. Eagle is the low cost producer. They have gained this position by carefully managing all aspects of their operations, so they have cost advantages on multiple dimensions: raw materials, natural gas usage, production and construction waste, administrative overhead, inbound and outbound transportation expense. Because their operations use less energy and produce less waste, they are equally aligned with environmental sustainability goals. Since they charge competitive prices but their delivered cost to the market is lower, Eagle earns superior returns. In 2021 they reported an industry-leading 39% EBITDA. Their 5-year pretax margin is 16% higher than the nearest competitor, and their 5-year ROE of 15.7% exceeds all companies in the industry.

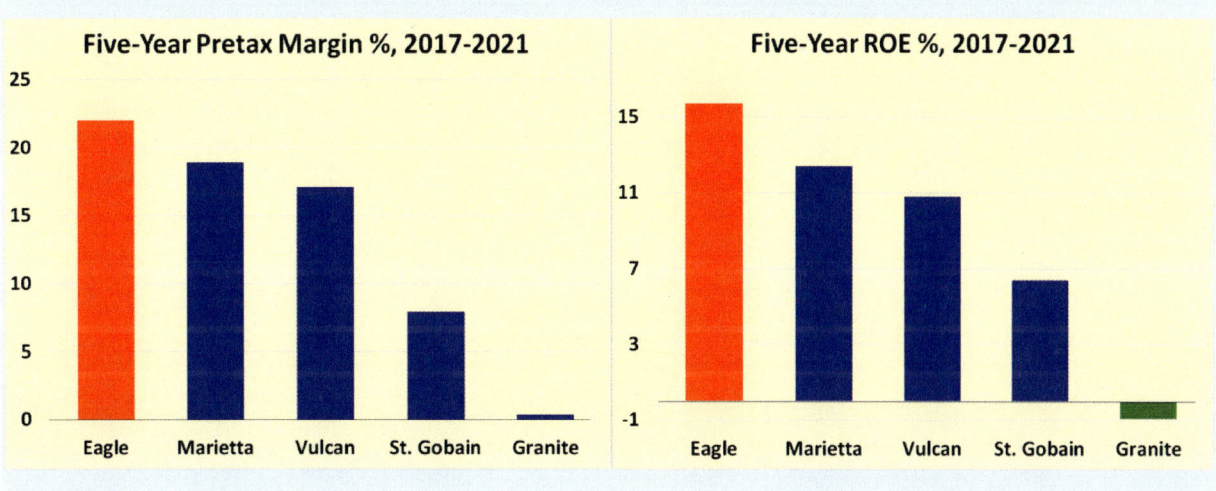

Bowing to the Masters

In a sun-drenched studio outside Boston, Benoit Rolland's personal touch and mastery of his craft has resulted in customers populating a who's who of the world's leading violin, viola and cello musicians. Rolland makes bows for the masters to use when they play their Stradivaria, Guarneri, and other remarkable stringed instruments. Before beginning a bow for any client, he listens to them play to get a feeling for their fingerings and style. "After a while, I'm able to guess their bowings. And then the fingerings. And the fingerings are very important, because they are linked to the bowings." He then creates a design to accommodate the strengths and the weaknesses specific to the musician. He uses a Brazilian wood called Pernambuco, which is celebrated for its tone, strength and longevity. The wood is now hard to come by, but years ago Rolland stockpiled it so he would have enough to last his lifetime. He then sculpts each bow, according to his design, by carving and shaving it. He taps each bow regularly as he progresses to listen to its tone. He determines precisely when it is complete by what he hears and what he feels with his hands. To see a video of the craftsman at work, click the following link: Benoit Rolland.

More than 450 musicians have collected Rolland bows. Because he only produces roughly 30 each year, selling for $15,000 each, a secondary market for the bows has been created. They are often auctioned by companies such as Sotheby's, and have appreciated in value over time.

QUESTIONS

1. How do sets of activities required for a low cost strategic approach differ from activities required for a differentiated approach that enhances benefits but costs more?
2. What is similar in these two approaches?

Danger Out There

On April 24th, 2013, an eight-story complex of clothing factories called Rana Plaza, near Dhaka, Bangladesh, collapsed. As the site was gradually cleared, the final toll counted over 1100 people killed, mainly young women. The building was not designed for industrial use and its owners had illegally added three floors. In the previous decade 800 more people have died in factories in Bangladesh, mainly through fires. It illustrates the dangerous nature of work in garment factories in low-wage nations.

Over the past decade major players in the clothing industry have flocked to Bangladesh, where an average wage of $38 per month has helped control costs in a global industry worth $1 trillion annually. But outsourcing production presents challenges that may offset cost benefits:

coordination and communication issues, quality control, factory safety procedures, warehousing and inventory complications, extended lead times, and more.

Clothing is made in Bangladesh for many famous world brands – including Benetton, Walt Disney, Walmart, German clothing company Kik. None of these companies had authorized factories in Rana Plaza for outsourced manufacturing, although remnants of their brands were discovered in the rubble. UK company Primark and Canada's Loblaw (owns Joe Fresh clothing line) acknowledged production at Rana Plaza and promised compensation to families of the victims.

QUESTIONS

1. Under what circumstances should a company outsource some parts of its value chain activities?
2. How would you organize an internal effort to monitor and control outsourced activity?
3. How can a company recover from the damage to its reputation through involvement in tragedies such as Rana Plaza?

LOGIC OF BUSINESS-LEVEL STRATEGIES

It is now time to step back a bit and look at strategy from a broader perspective. In this book so far we have developed a set of techniques for evaluating industry conditions and the value-creating foundations for creating sustainable competitive advantage. Starting with an examination of the external environment in which a business operates (Chapter 4), we used the five forces analysis, key success factors, and strategic maps to identify conditions in which the business operates. Next, two techniques for completing an internal analysis were examined – value chain (Chapter 5) and resource-based analysis (Chapter 6).

The part of the logic that has yet to be developed is the overarching question of *how* to coherently put all this together so a company can compete successfully. Over the years a popular framework has developed suggesting that successful companies must use one of five types of business-level strategy approaches. Any company not pursuing some form of these types of strategies is unlikely to develop competitive advantage or achieve above-average returns.

These five strategy types lay out a high level organizing approach to business. Each is extremely valuable for creating coherence in decisions and actions throughout the company. Nonetheless, they are rich, quite complex, and very much a challenge to manage effectively.

Basic business-level strategies are the bedrock component of successful companies. They are used as a rallying point for consistency and coordination among value chain activities and for evaluating sustainability using resource-based analysis. The decision to embrace a particular business-level strategy, in combination with a mission statement, enables management to get everyone in the organization moving in the same direction. Companies may be tempted to vary what they do from time to time in reaction to other competitors, the shifting environment, beliefs of new top management team members, stakeholders, or recent financial performance. However the consistent pursuit of a business-level strategy approach over a longer period of time is usually a recipe for strong performance. Strategic management research confirms that selecting and following a distinct, overarching business-level strategy improves company performance.[2] Your ability to understand and apply this framework, and also to be able to explain its optimal uses and limitations, will put you in a stronger position in whatever companies you work for.

In the 1980s through the work of Michael Porter our understanding of strategy was given a significant boost as a means for systematically enhancing performance. His initial description of a set of "generic" strategies is: "Competitive advantage grows fundamentally out of value a firm is able to create for its buyers that exceeds the firm's cost of creating it. Value is what buyers are willing to pay, and superior value stems from offering lower prices than competitors for equivalent benefits or providing unique benefits that more than offset a higher price."[3] These generic approaches have been applied at the business-unit level and have thus come to be referred to as business-level strategies.

Reflecting these ideas, the most prevalent framework used by strategists suggests that competitive advantage can be achieved when firms employ one of two basic approaches: low cost or differentiation. Ordinarily we think of these approaches as polar opposites from each other, such as what Figure 7.1 suggests. Either a company seeks to cut costs versus competitors while offering a competitive level of benefits to customers, or it seeks to enhance the benefits it provides to customers versus competitors while maintaining a competitive level of cost. Within many industries, however, we recognize that there are often several competitors appearing to pursue a low cost strategic approach. However, only one company will, in fact, occupy THE low cost leadership position, and there is usually intense competition among those seeking to own this position.

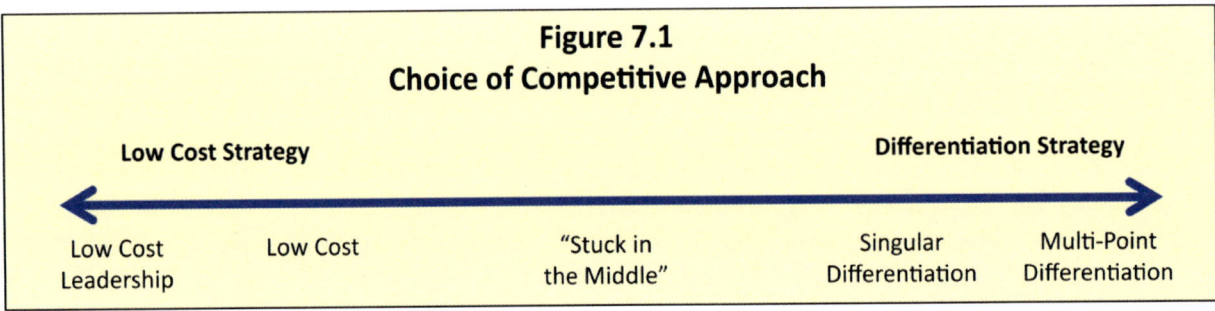

Dell Technologies, the computer giant headquartered in Texas, had developed a competitive advantage by focusing on being the low cost leader in their market space. After Michael Dell dropped out of college to start his company, he completely reinvented the value chain for personal computers and squeezed costs out of every conceivable area in the company. The most visible of these efforts to consumers was their direct sales model, which first used only telephone sales and then subsequently combined that approach with the internet to bypass the traditional retail distribution system. This not only had the advantage of enhanced personal contact and avoidance of retailer markups, but allowed Dell to change the flow of goods through the primary activities part of the value chain by allowing buyers to customize their computers rather than purchasing stock computers on the shelf at a store. Dell also pressed its suppliers of parts and components to locate and operate their own supply distribution centers adjacent to Dell's assembly facilities. This way Dell was not required to incur the costs of carrying parts inventories. Subsequently in 2002 Hewlett Packard acquired Compaq and sought a low cost leadership position based largely on manufacturing efficiency through large scale, which involved a very different set of activities and method compared to Dell. Then between 2008-2015 Asia-based manufacturers of PCs (e.g. Lenovo, Asus, Acer) have grown market share based on the use of inexpensive assembly labor costs abroad. You can see already in this story that there are different ways to pursue low cost as a strategic key success factor.

As these competitors developed lower cost positions for essentially-identical PC models, Dell first announced that they believed both their supply chain and manufacturing areas could be further improved. Michael Dell stated, "I think you are going to see a more streamlined organization, with a much clearer strategy."[4] Dell strayed from its direct sales focus during this period with a decision to begin selling PCs in Walmart and other retailers, just as its competitors enabled consumers to order online directly. Amidst this intense industry competition, Dell lost its mojo (i.e. its low cost leadership). Its market share declined, its stock price had declined by 31% by 2013, and in that year Michael Dell bought out the company to take it private. In 2018 Dell once again became a publicly-traded company. But it is really hard to capture (or re-capture a lost) low cost position; in 2021 it remains 2nd in U.S market share and 3rd in global share of units shipped, having years ago ceded the leadership position to other companies.

Just as low cost competition is fierce, there are usually several companies competing in the differentiation spectrum. Sometimes a competitor's success can be created by a single point of competitive differentiation, such as Qualcomm's targeted research and development resulting in its patented CDMA cell-phone transmission technology. Other competitors seek to develop multiple points of differentiated competitive advantage, in order to make competitive imitation less likely. Apple's i-devices product platform (iPod, iPad, iPhone, iWatch) combines elegant product design, proprietary copy protection software that inhibits piracy and file sharing, a slick Web interface for any type of computer, and an unparalleled digital music catalog. Any one of these features present significant challenges to competitors, while the combination affords Apple a huge advantage.

In Figure 7.1 we see a wide space between the low cost and differentiation approaches. This has long been believed to be a sort of strategic "no man's land." Companies that find themselves simultaneously doing a bit of low cost and a bit of differentiation have often been called "stuck in the middle"[5] This is because they seek to compete in multiple ways against companies that more single-mindedly dedicate resources and manage their value chains toward one of the "pure" strategic approaches. HP is the leading manufacturer of PCs in the U.S. in 2021 (Lenovo leads worldwide). Its revenue is 17% of Apple's but its R&D spending is only 9% of Apple's. If HP were to challenge Apple as an innovator (differentiator), for example, it would need to invest much larger sums in research and development. This would reduce its ability to compete for a low cost position. This type of change would be both difficult and expensive, possibly leading HP to a position of being stuck in the middle.[6]

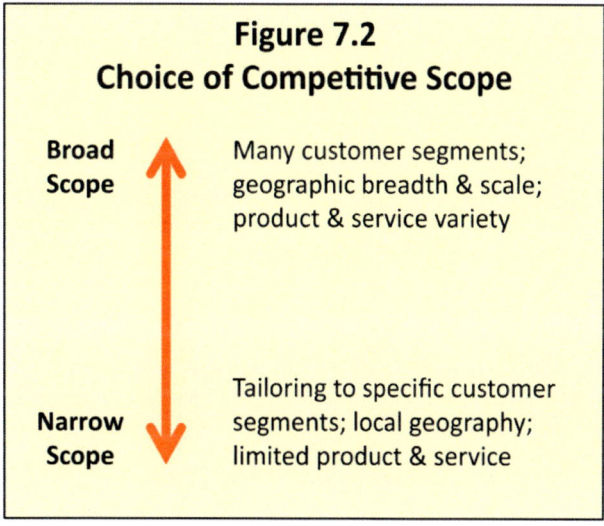

Another important decision that companies must make when they select their business-level strategic approach is about the scope that they intend to compete in. As suggested by Figure 7.2, a company can either compete broadly or narrowly.[7] Broad strategic approaches are pursued across multiple customer segments, broad geographical territories (even global; e.g., Staples in office supplies retailing and distribution or Arcelor-Mittal in steel), and often involve providing a variety of products or services to meet multiple needs or desires. In contrast, narrow strategic approaches tailor offerings of specific products or services to particular customer segments or limited geographic territories, and do so to the exclusion of a broader approach.[8] Regal Entertainment Group and Cinemark Holdings are national companies, operating theaters across the U.S. that show movies appealing to all ages and demographics. In contrast, Cinema Latino operates theaters in only three cities and focuses exclusively on Hispanic populations, showing first-run movies subtitled or dubbed in Spanish and serving Hispanic foods at the concession stands. Ryanair provides low cost passenger airline travel throughout Europe, while Wizz Air focuses on low cost air travel primarily in and out of eastern European countries.

When a choice about competitive approach is combined with a choice about competitive scope, the result is the array of business-level strategies illustrated in Figure 7.3. Across the top are the broad low cost and differentiation strategies. The approaches that pursue a narrow scope – whether low cost or differentiation – are commonly referred to as *focused* strategies.

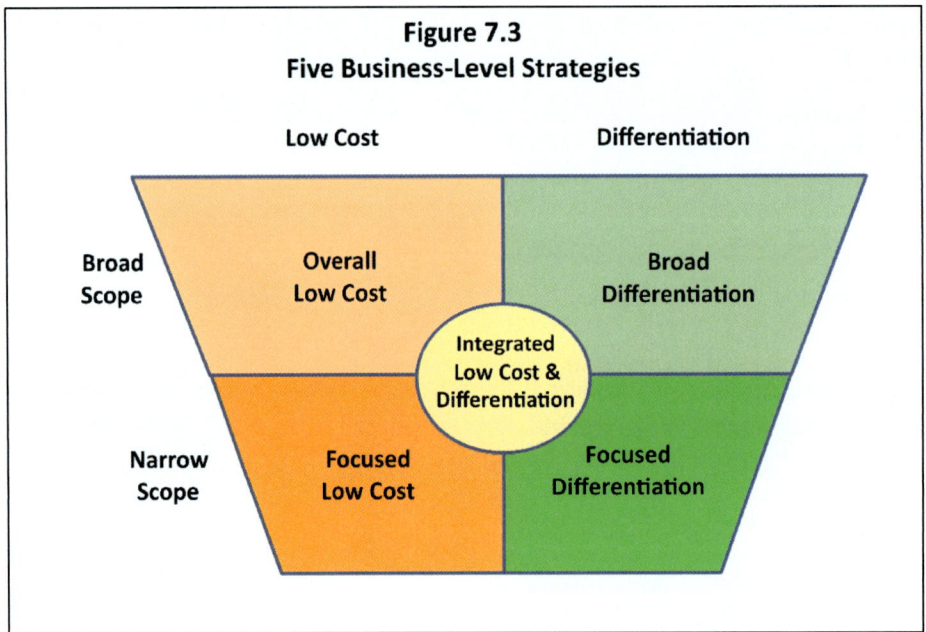

You will notice that a fifth business-level strategy, called the "integrated low cost and differentiation" strategy, has been added in the center of Figure 7.3. This approach is reflected in companies that seek to provide exceptional benefits while at the same time using a reasonably competitive cost structure. Though we mentioned the possibility of getting stuck in the middle when pursuing both low cost and differentiation simultaneously, there have been recent developments and evidence from industries suggesting that combinations are plausible under certain circumstances. It is a higher risk approach; we will return to discuss this later in this chapter.

Connecting Business-Level Strategies with Superior Performance

The point of employing a business-level strategy is that it can generate competitive advantage, and competitive advantage is supposed to result in above average returns or superior performance. We can see why this is the case by referring to Figure 7.4 and comparing each strategy to an average performing company in an industry. The average competitor in the industry earns a level of profits based upon an average cost structure and an average level of pricing charged for the benefits provided by its goods or services. The company pursuing the low cost strategy seeks to lower its costs while providing roughly the same level of benefits as the average competitor and charging roughly the same prices. In Figure 7.4 the low cost strategy (in red) shows that superior profitability is achieved when the company successfully reduces its cost structure. The company pursuing the differentiation strategy seeks to provide enhanced benefits to its customers while maintaining roughly the same cost structure as the average competitor. With enhanced benefits that are valued in the market, it should be able to charge higher prices than the average competitor, and thus earn higher profits (in blue). While not shown in the figure, the integrated low cost/ differentiation strategy seeks to earn higher profits by slightly lowering its costs while slightly elevating the benefits provided and its prices.

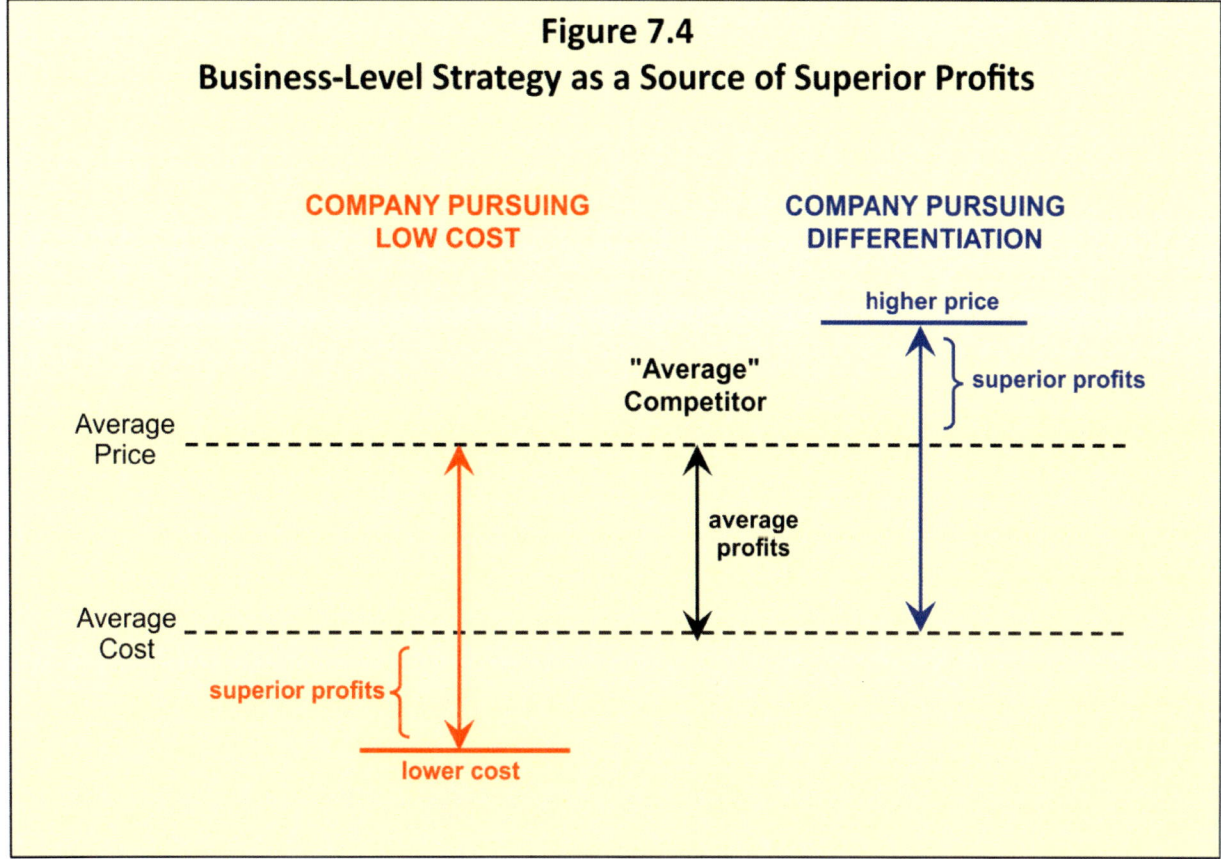

If the diagram in Figure 7.4 reminds you of Figure 5.12 on value creation in Chapter 5, it is not a coincidence. As we have already suggested, business-level strategies are closely tied to the value chain and value creation. Consistency of purpose across value chain activities can result in either the lowering of costs (and possibly prices) or the enhancement of benefits with the possibility of charging higher prices. Achieving this consistency of purpose requires strong understanding of the resources and integrated sets of value chain activities that contribute to cost reduction or value enhancement, so that they can be proactively managed.

A business-level strategy can best be thought of as the overarching philosophy of value creation within the company. Each element of the value chain displayed in Figure 7.5, along with each of the interrelationships between value chain elements will yield more value if they are coordinated toward a singular approach. Similarly, resource-based investments that are all geared toward one type of strategy allow the firm to take advantage of both the organizational learning

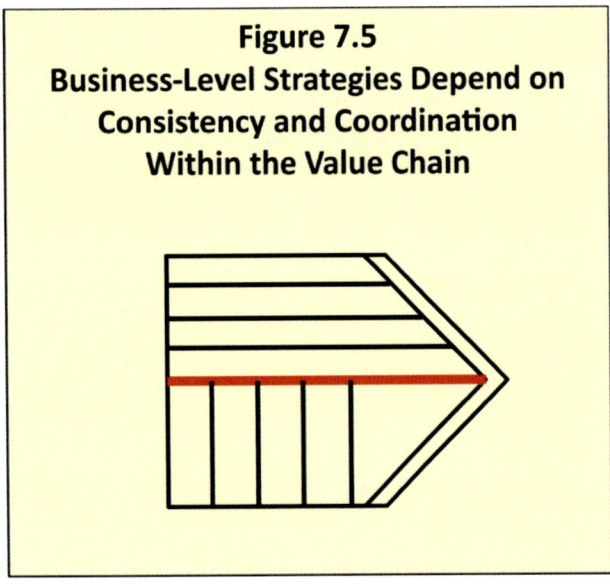

**Figure 7.5
Business-Level Strategies Depend on Consistency and Coordination Within the Value Chain**

cycle and consistent application approach that is possible with a steady message to all employees. In contrast, companies that are internally inconsistent within their value chains or resource-based investments will find themselves working at cross-purposes. They present themselves to the marketplace with conflicting approaches, and will likely find themselves moving toward a "stuck in the middle" position (doing neither one particularly well). Friendster was the first social networking site, starting up in 2002, predating both MySpace and Facebook, yet the business flamed out early in the United States due to internally inconsistent approaches to the marketplace. According to founder Jonathan Abrams, each of the top executives hired by the company "came to Friendster with strong ideas about how to make the company as big as possible as fast as possible... 'Everybody had their own agenda.' The result was a kind of corporate schizophrenia."[9] Management of the company lost sight of what values social networking site users sought and became involved in several competing initiatives that were based upon entirely different and incompatible strategic differentiation approaches. Competitors honed in carefully and consistently on these dimensions and succeeded wildly.

Business-level strategies rely on internal consistency in activities across the company's value chain, in order to successfully pursue a single approach. Once the decision on a strategic approach has been made, then it should be applied with rigor *all* across the organization. In the next sections we explore important drivers of each of the business-level strategies, and draw attention to the relationship between each strategy and the value chain.

Important Caveats!

There are three really important cautions that need to be understood before we go on to examine each of the business-level strategies in detail. Each of these cautions reflects crucial conditions upon which the success of a strategy rests.

1. **Parity conditions**. All of the efforts made to pursue a business-level strategy will be wasted if the company does not achieve parity on other conditions that are valued by the marketplace. Differentiation on some dimension is an advantage only if other expected values are also delivered, and only if costs are roughly equivalent with those of competitors. It is very difficult to claim that your business is a five-star restaurant if the health rating on your establishment is a "C." The expectation in the industry is an "A" rating. Diners at five-star restaurants appreciate excellent food and very nice surroundings. But these cannot be achieved by disregarding or eliminating something else they value.

    Cost leadership is an advantage only if there is reasonable parity on other values delivered by the products/services of competitors. Remember the old axiom "you get what you pay for." Many companies have come and gone over the years by providing a product or service at a significantly reduced price based on a low cost structure that resulted from skimping on essential features or quality. Packard Bell, a now-defunct manufacturing company that sold inexpensive PCs, was renowned for its poor customer service. In the 1990s "as the market moved from novice buyers to second-time buyers, many experienced consumers shied away from Packard Bell, citing its reputation for shoddy quality and indifferent service and support."[10] The effectiveness of each strategy assumes that all of the ordinary aspects expected by customers are adequately delivered by the company.

2. **Evolution of customer expectations**. Pursuing one business-level strategy does not mean ignoring the positive aspects of other approaches. Importantly, as time goes by, customer expectations about valued product or service characteristics will tend to escalate. Therefore, pursuit of a business-level strategy requires the company to continually refine its own approach as well as ensure it maintains parity on other evolving conditions. "A firm should always aggressively pursue all cost reduction opportunities that do not sacrifice differentiation. [Similarly] a firm should also pursue all differentiation opportunities that are not costly."[11]

3. **Evolution of competition**. Competition is always knocking at the door! A complacent business that is slow to react can thrive until competitors wake up or move to catch up. Unsophisticated industries – such as dry cleaning, lawn care, and veterinary services – left large openings for focused well-designed competitors. Banfield, The Pet Hospital, was founded in 1955 in Portland, Oregon, and developed a reputation for bringing human-quality medical practice to pets. In 1994 PetSmart, recognizing an opportunity to bring consistency of practice to a nationwide scale, asked Banfield to join with them to build veterinary clinics in its stores. Today there are 900 Banfield clinics in PetSmart stores.[12]

   In intensely competitive industries the efforts of other companies can cause obsolescence of a company's position more quickly, can push the envelope of customer expectations, and can escalate parity conditions. Netflix obsoleted the Blockbuster physical store model for video rental. But then along came Amazon's streaming services, Disney+, HBO Max, Starz and more, and of course movies on demand through local cable providers.

Parity conditions and their evolution – either through normal customer growth or through competitive dynamics – make the management of a business-level strategic approach more complex.

Wendy's International, Part 1[13]

Wendy's International was founded in 1969 and now has over 6,828 outlets in 31 countries worldwide. The company has always sought to differentiate itself in the fast food industry. With customization of sandwiches, unique offerings (the square hamburger made with fresh – never frozen meat, and the Frosty), and a stated focus on high-quality food products, they expanded rapidly. In the early 2000s the corporate office felt that Wendy's was suffering in sales growth because cash-strapped consumers were avoiding their stores. They then developed a 99¢ Super Value Menu and pushed franchisees to increase the number of such offerings on the menu to draw in traffic. One franchisee laid out the problem. "The differentiation of Wendy's from the other [fast-food] concepts was the fact that we were recognized as being the quality player," said Dave Norman, chief financial officer of Maryland-based DavCo Restaurants Inc., which operates 161 Wendy's. "For us to compete at that 99-cent threshold, we either have to give away food...or we have to damage our quality image because we cannot purchase the quality commodities."

QUESTIONS

1. Should Wendy's continue as a differentiator or try to pursue a low cost approach?
2. What would switching to a low cost approach mean for activities in the value chain and how they are coordinated?

LOW COST STRATEGY

Creating and maintaining a low cost position requires the organization to systematically lower its costs throughout its operations, such that the margins for that business exceed those of its competitors. The Vanguard Group was founded in 1974 as an investment company that single-mindedly focused on a low cost position. Founder John C. Bogle reasoned that if his asset managers matched market investment performance in the long term with the lowest costs and the lowest charges to his clients, then the company's returns would consistently exceed the market averages.

Their Vanguard Total Stock Market Index Fund has grown to become the largest mutual fund in the world with assets over $1.3 trillion. Vanguard runs 13 out of the 25 largest mutual funds with assets exceeding $100 billion. In every facet of the business, they concentrate on lowering costs: returns are distributed directly to individual investors rather than through intermediary brokers, they advertise very little, have pleasant but not elegant offices, and formalize cost containment as a key component of the annual bonus. In 2021 the company reports average annual fund expenses of 0.10%, compared with the industry average of 0.60%. Their competitors call this huge difference in fees the "Vanguard Effect."[14]

There are several conditions under which the pursuit of a low cost strategy may be more appropriate and hold a greater potential for success. One way to think about these conditions is to refer back to the five forces analysis (Chapter 4) to understand how each industry force might impact the low cost approach.

- **Rivalry**. When there are few opportunities to differentiate one's product or service offering (because such values are not appreciated by buyers), then standardization of product/service features is accompanied by highly competitive pricing. When there is standardization of products or services among competitive rivals, the low cost competitor will tend to fare better because the company with the low cost structure will enjoy a higher profit margin.

- **Buyers and Suppliers**. When buyers and suppliers have strong bargaining power and are able to exact economic concessions from competitors, the company with the lowest cost structure is able to fare better. In addition, if buyers experience low switching costs, the low cost competitor has the greatest flexibility to reduce pricing in order to keep and attract buyers.

- **New Entrants and Substitutes**. Other companies outside the industry may seek to offer products and services that provide a challenging price/value relationship. Given a set of values the company currently provides buyers, a low cost position offers flexibility to reduce prices and offset any perceived advantages that other companies may offer.

There are several factors that can lead to a low cost position. These include: 1) economies of scale; 2) capacity utilization; 3) experience curve; 4) product/service design; 5) process innovation (value chain design); and 6) internal value chain coordination. We discuss each of these below.

Economies of scale. Economies of scale are realized as unit costs drop while quantities produced each period grow larger, as illustrated in Figure 7.6. As firms increase their production (whether a product or service), many are able to attain cost savings as a result of being able to spread fixed and indirect costs over a greater number of units. This is especially important for companies competing in industries in which significant fixed investment is necessary, such as steel and automobile manufacturing or for a fuel refinery. Cost reductions through scale often occur because of the specialization of activities and the efficiency of assembly lines that are possible when seeking to produce large quantities in a given time frame.

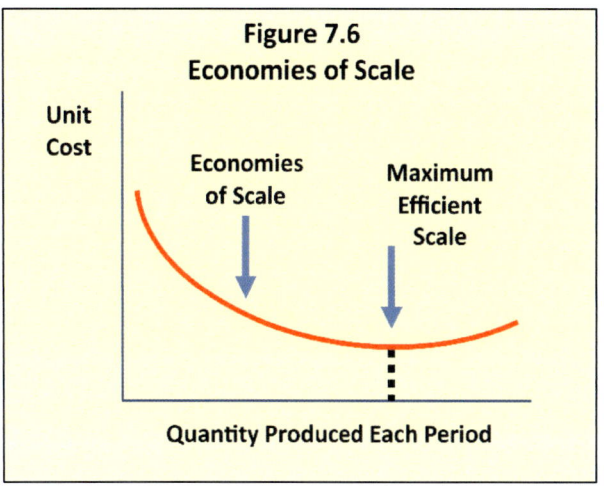

Capacity utilization. Capacity utilization is closely related to economies of scale. Scale economies result from the cost savings associated with production through large facilities. However, those costs are particularly sensitive to the ability of companies with large facilities to fully utilize them. If they are not fully utilized, then the fixed-cost burden of the facilities is spread across fewer units produced and any possible scale benefits are lost. It is difficult in the short run to exactly match capacity to projected sales. However, companies that pursue a low cost strategy as their overarching approach constantly evaluate this area in order to maximize their investment return. There are many industries where fixed costs are significant and profits are highly dependent upon small fluctuations in demand. The dramatic turnaround in the airline industry in 2012-2016 was a direct result of restraint in increasing the number of available seat miles (the standard measure of capacity in the industry) at the same time that airline passenger traffic was increasing. The result was much higher fleet utilization. Capacity of the big three domestic automobile manufacturers (GM, Ford, Stellantis) far exceeded demand for their vehicles during the 2008-2010 recession, creating significant cost and competitive pricing problems. Each sought to shed capacity in order to reduce unused fixed costs, while each also offered multi-year interest free loans on new cars in order to generate immediate sales and keep factories operating.

Experience curve. As organizations gain greater experience over the years in producing a product or a service, employees usually learn how to perform many functions quicker, cheaper, and with fewer mistakes. This is called the experience curve. A company that takes this tendency and translates it into a systematic approach to improvement can produce significant cost reductions. The Six-Sigma approach, for example, aims at systematically examining every facet of the organization, reducing redundancies, eliminating variation, and sharing best practices. It is one of a number of systems used to increase the capability and improve the quality within organizations. The experience curve, illustrated in Figure 7.7, has been observed in a wide variety of industries (e.g., bottle caps, refrigerators, long distance calls, insurance policies[15]). It is a well-understood process through which companies achieve cost savings associated with learning to do things better and better over time.

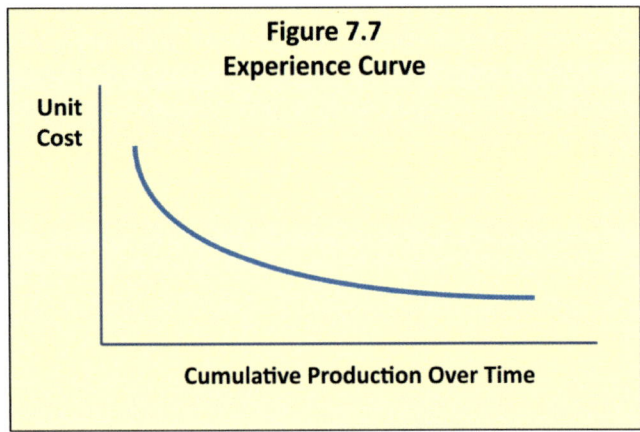

Product/service design. One of the most important areas in developing cost savings is the fundamental design of a product or service. Rather than looking for uniqueness from a customer perspective, a low cost strategic approach can also benefit from design simplicity, easy manufacturing, simple sourcing of raw materials, and inexpensive packaging. The product/service low cost approach must be both systematic and systemic. That is, the company must carefully examine every aspect of the product or service element, taking absolutely nothing as given and fixed. Simultaneously the company must engineer the process across the value chain, from input to delivery, in a manner that keeps costs as low as possible. Kodak entered the inkjet printer business some years ago, in competition with HP. HP's replacement ink cartridges are expensive because each contains a chip that determines how ink is dispensed onto the paper. Kodak re-engineered this product, putting the chip in the printer and eliminating this costly element from their cartridges. The cartridges were cheaper and faster to manufacture, and could be priced lower at office supply stores.

Process innovation (value chain design). A new process that radically speeds up assembly, design, or delivery can yield dramatic cost savings that are not enjoyed by competitors. The ability of an individual firm to change those processes in a manner creating new efficiencies can be a key to cutting costs. In its development of the long-range 777 aircraft, Boeing scrapped the traditional design/build process and completely reinvented it. Moving entirely to an electronic process, the 777 was designed digitally in virtual space, and all 3 million parts for each $150 million airplane were sourced electronically among 3,000 suppliers worldwide. Then-CEO Phil Condit claimed that they bet the company on this bold new initiative, which shaved eighteen months and more than $1 billion off the new plane's development, and which was then used in designing next-generation aircraft. By 2020 both Boeing and Airbus had introduced greater robotics and mechanization to their assembly lines to increase their annual output in the face of huge customer demand for aircraft.[16]

As a new entrant in the very tough airline business many years ago now, Southwest Airlines sought to provide a true low-price alternative to the major airlines. This approach demanded that they have the lowest cost operation in the business. Every aspect of the operation was examined for cost savings, and the entire organization was designed to ensure consistency across the value chain and uniform approach throughout the enterprise. The company purchased and flew only one style of Boeing aircraft. This, by itself, made gate operations and mechanical servicing more consistent and faster because ground crews had to deal with only one type of aircraft. Parts inventories were slimmer since they only serviced one plane type. Every pilot was capable of flying virtually every airplane, so scheduling and crew replacement was faster. Southwest avoided reserved seating in order to speed up passenger boarding. Pilots, flight attendants, and other employees accepted a lower wage to work at a fun organization that didn't lay people off, in part made possible because senior managers of the company did not collect obscene salaries or work in plush offices.[17] A low cost approach to design permeated the business. And amidst this all, the competitive parity condition of positive customer flying experience was not diminished.

The ability to outmaneuver competitors by the use of speed can provide significant cost savings while providing customers with something of value. France's automaker Renault determined it needed to rapidly produce a new car for a market that was demanding a compact, fuel-efficient car. The company put all the functions in automobile development under one roof, reporting to one leader, and slashed the development time in half. The Twingo was delivered in eighteen months, well ahead of their competition, at a sharply reduced developmental cost.[18]

Internal value chain coordination. Regardless of how costs are wrung out of the individual activities and functions within a company, the ability to reduce costs through the interrelationships between value chain activities is another crucial element in a low cost strategy. For example, when Human Resources is able to staff individual positions within activity areas that create best fit within those units, costs are reduced for the whole company because productivity is enhanced. Above we mentioned efforts made by Boeing to reduce costs. Boeing staffed "design-build" teams for the new 777 airplane, putting together pilots, mechanics, assembly plant supervisors, and computer designers with both customers and suppliers. Involving all parts of the organization in parallel improved the development of the plane, by identifying and avoiding technical problems in later stages that used to come up between different areas of the company. This approach sped up the whole process wringing costs out of the system in both the short and long run.

With recycling of products moving to center stage in society, some companies have utilized their R&D, production, distribution, and customer service operations to jointly develop easily-recycled products. This has actually led to significant cost savings and has put those companies well ahead of their competitors who might be forced into heavy investments to catch up. HP spent considerable effort redesigning the supply chain for their PCs and their ink cartridges for easier recycling and reuse. The result has been a dramatic lowering of production costs, which allowed them to offer another value appreciated by customers. "We're making it easier for customers to reduce waste by designing easily recyclable products. Where feasible, we use common fasteners and snap-in features to avoid applying glues, adhesives, or welds. This makes it easier for recyclers to dismantle, separate, and identify different plastics. Most HP PCs, printers, and servers are more than 90% recyclable by weight. Through our "closed loop" recycling process, Original HP ink and LaserJet toner cartridges are reduced to raw materials that can then be used to make new cartridges as well as other metal and plastic products."[19] Through 2020 HP has used over 125,000 tons of recycled plastic in printer cartridges.

Value Chain and Low Cost Strategy

The low cost business-level strategy can be an extremely effective means of achieving superior profits. How might it be put into place, and what are the interrelationships that are involved? Using the value chain, let's look at a detailed example. Ryanair is the dominant low cost carrier in Europe today. They enjoy the largest available seat mile (ASM) capacity among Europe's discount airlines. In 2019-2020, before the Covid-19 pandemic and consequent drop-off in customer volume, they earned 13.3% operating margins, the highest among all European airlines.[20] In 2021 they reported operating costs per passenger carried at 71% lower than EasyJet.

Founded in 1985, Ryanair almost died within the first five years by trying to provide a range of services, including business class and a frequent flyer program, using a variety of small aircraft flown to and from Ireland. The airline accumulated over £20 million in losses. The company was recapitalized in 1990 with a new mantra to be THE low cost airline and made no apologies for their rigorous approach to the new strategic direction. Figure 7.8 diagrams their value chain and highlights key low cost-producing activities in each cell.[21] Because of their efforts across the entire value chain, Ryanair enjoys a low cost advantage in Europe that is larger than the advantage that Southwest Airlines enjoys in the United States.[22]

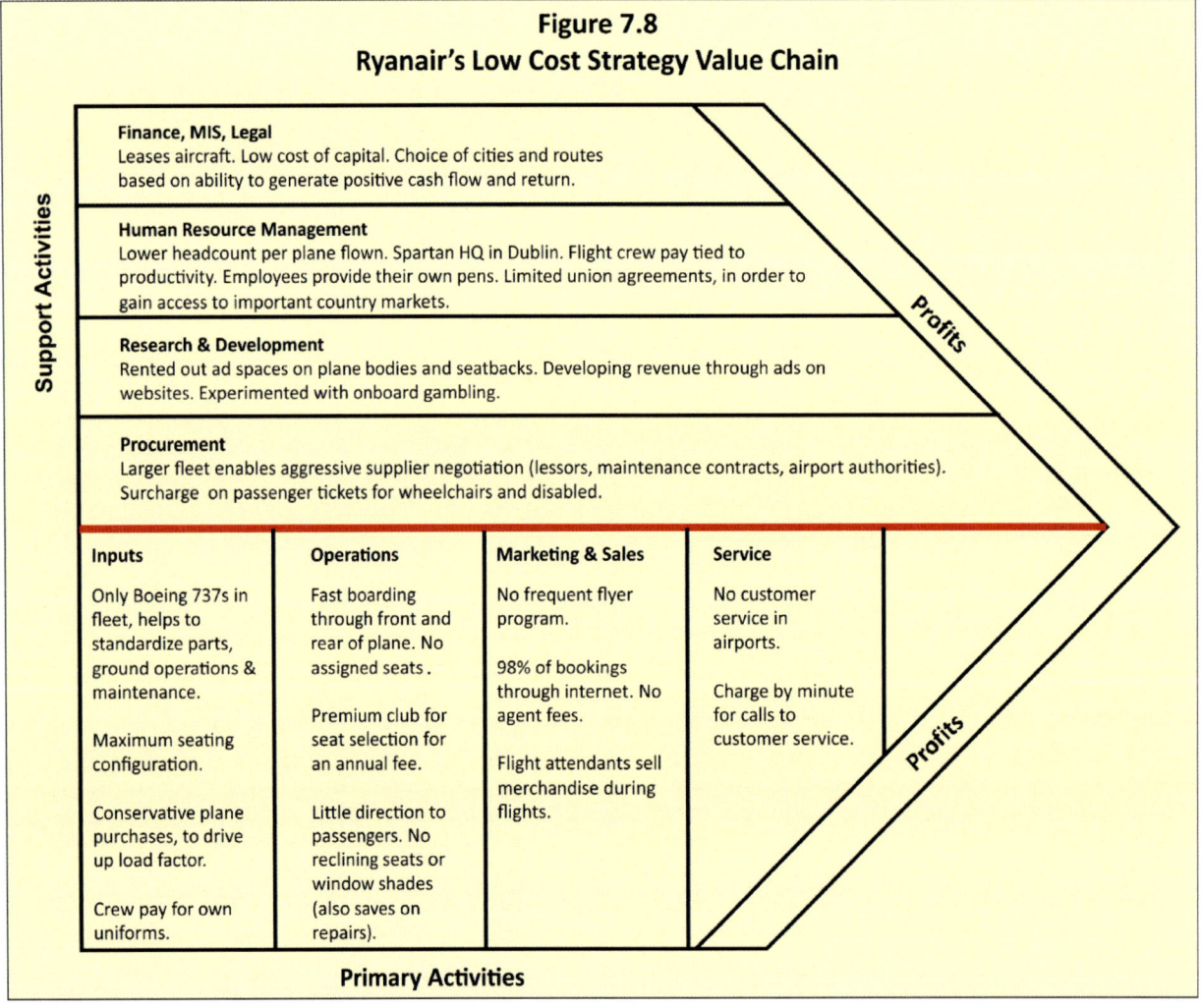

Risks Associated with Low Cost Strategy

No business-level strategy is without risks. This is because each involves significant investments, learning, development, and refinement across the company's entire value chain - a complex and time-consuming management undertaking. Here we outline several risks associated with the pursuit of a low cost strategy.

Low cost strategy versus low cost leadership. As suggested by Figure 7.1, in most industries there may be a number of companies pursuing a low cost leadership strategy. It may be that some companies pursuing this strategy can, in fact, generate returns that are superior to the industry averages because they have managed to create cost structures that are superior to average competition. However, in any market there can be one – and only one – low cost *leader*.

Low cost leadership is at the endpoint of the continuum in Figure 7.1 and represents the most powerful competitive position among companies pursuing a low cost approach. Every other business is simply a wannabe low cost leader, chasing the well-heeled, well-focused, low cost leader. This can be a recipe for failure over the long run. Witness the rise of Walmart in discount retailing during the 1980s. Its low cost structure often allowed it to *price* lower than Kmart's *costs*, so that in markets where the two companies were competing head-to-head, Walmart could price low and still earn profits while Kmart would lose money on every sale.[23] Walmart's low cost structure helped drive Kmart into bankruptcy in the 1990s.

Price is not a strategy. A low-price approach is often confused with a low cost strategic approach. Price by itself is not a strategic factor, since prices can be changed instantaneously without strategic investments. It is relatively easy for any competitor to try and use low price as way to attract customers, or to instantly match another company's price. Yet without actually having the low cost operation to back it up, low price is a sure means of achieving lower returns. Pricing is tactical, while managing to a low cost position is very strategic requiring investments in facilities, practices, and more.

Customers do not value the benefits derived from low costs. Often a company will use its low cost position to reduce prices in order to make its products or services more attractive and drive up sales volume. However, in some situations and at some points in time customers may not be interested in cost- and price-based benefits, but instead may have significantly greater appreciation for other product or service characteristics and the benefits they convey. Many low cost companies introduced MP3 players into the marketplace in the early 2000s, yet the market continued to embrace the Apple iPod despite its higher price.

Cost positions can be imitated over time. Technology, greater access to global markets, and the greater ease of forming alliances and joint ventures make it possible for competitors to more easily imitate the cost structure of low cost leaders. Companies pursuing a low cost position must be constantly on guard against the evolution of competitive positions, and must continue to reinvest resources to further protect low cost positions.

Wendy's International, Part 2[24]

Wendy's continued to push their value meal offerings. In an effort to further drive revenue growth, they then decided to roll out a breakfast offering to half their operating units within the next year. In addition they announced that they would strategically invest in four areas of the business; 1) stronger marketing; 2) more new products; 3) sharper store operations; and 4) better relationships with franchisees.

An activist investor on their board remained unconvinced that the value meal approach and their newly-announced investments made strategic sense. The board began to consider the idea of selling the company. The investor had little faith that the company executives had a coherent strategy for the firm, but were instead just using the same methods as their competitors.

QUESTIONS

1. How would selling the company improve its strategy?
2. Which strategic initiatives should Wendy's pursue and which should they drop?
3. What are the implications of offering a breakfast menu for a low cost generic strategy?

DIFFERENTIATION STRATEGY

Differentiation is perhaps the most widely utilized business-level strategic approach. This is because there are virtually unlimited methods by which a company can attempt to uniquely create value for customers. As with the low cost strategy, effective differentiation requires a company to systematically organize its activities throughout its value chain in order to deliver superior value and thus command higher prices. Ferrari has always held out a reputation for extraordinary performance vehicles that have a standard twelve-to-eighteen-month waiting list. While Porsche sold over 300,000 cars in 2021, Ferrari sold just over 10,000. The company

carefully manages its activities in order to create the value that customers prefer. In research and development the company applies Formula 1 technology to production cars, and has conducted advanced aerodynamic studies in its own wind tunnels. It does not rely on competitive market suppliers for key components such as aluminum, but instead operates its own specialist aluminum production arm. Every vehicle is assembled and customized by a staff that is required to spend years in training before being "allowed" to join the production line.[25] Employees are so dedicated to the company and its culture that it was named in 2007 as the best place to work in Europe, and it ranks in the top 60 companies in the world in 2019.[26] The price premium Ferrari commands is directly related to the operation of its value chain. Neither speed to market nor product standardization is a critical component at Ferrari, whereas in the industry both are valued on an almost religious level.

There are several conditions under which the pursuit of a differentiation strategy may be more appropriate and hold a greater potential for success. We again refer back to the five forces analysis to understand how each industry force might impact this strategic approach. The key point for each of these forces is that downstream customer markets must embrace variety within the industry for a differentiation strategy to be successful.

- **Rivalry**. When diversity and variety exists among customers and their needs, then strategic variety is possible within an industry. So long as all buyers do not uniformly demand a common or standardized set of features or benefits, differentiation is a realistic and practical option for competitors.

- **Buyers**. If buyer concentration does not exist and consequently buyers have little power, then cost/price relationships may become less influential in the buying process.

- **Suppliers**. Suppliers may still exert bargaining power on competitors, but as long as diversity of needs exists among buyers and there is no standardization or commoditization occurring within the industry, higher costs from suppliers may be offset by higher prices charged that support the kind of value chain investments in differentiation.

- **New entrants and substitutes**. Effective differentiation often shields competitors from new competition presented by new entrants and possible substitutes. Unique value chain and resource investments designed to create differentiated value should be difficult to imitate.

There are several drivers of an effective differentiation strategy. These include: 1) product and service features; 2) psychographic and cognitive benefits; 3) process innovation (value chain design); and 4) internal value chain coordination. Here we briefly explore each of these drivers.

Product and service features. Most products and services are clearly delineated by their unique features relative to the competition. These features create the opportunity to attract new customers, make existing customers more loyal, and provide the foundation for charging a premium price that offsets the costs of differentiation. There are three dimensions of product/service features that help create an effective differentiated strategic position:

1. **Characteristics that respond to customer needs**. People buy products and services to fulfill their needs and desires, and they will balance the "performance" of purchases against the prices they pay. This price/performance relationship between the higher prices paid for products or services and their level of performance – is the basis upon which customers will judge value and respond to company efforts to differentiate. Performance dimensions that are judged by customers tend to be the kinds listed in Figure 7.9.

    CarMax made the process of car buying and selling easy, allowing consumers to avoid the hated car salesman rat race at most car dealerships. Their no-haggle system allows consumers to buy and sell cars in a very objective process without having to negotiate. In 2020 Carvana took the car-buying process to a new level where, as the TV ads explain you can stay at home, binge watch your favorite episodes of The Office, buy your car online, and then have it delivered directly to you. Convenience to the max!

    Many travel agencies found their business plummeting as online reservation systems became convenient. Now some agencies not only book airlines and hotels, but also arrange tours, set up restaurant reservations, arrange for child sitters and guarantee an entire trip against unforeseen circumstances. The packaging of formerly separate services has allowed them to survive and charge a premium price compared to the single-function agencies.

Figure 7.9
Product & Service Performance Dimensions

- Effectiveness in intended use
- Physical characteristics (e.g. color, size, shape, etc.)
- Variety
- Quality
- Safety
- Consistency
- Convenience (location, ease of access)
- Immediacy
- Complementarity with other products (e.g. cellphone synching with computer)
- Speed
- On the cutting edge

In Chapter 1 we described how opportunity recognition and value creation imperatives drive today's strategy. Attempting to stay on the cutting edge of product and service characteristics is one manifestation of these imperatives that we regularly observe. For example, in 2006 Lexus designed a system that allowed a car to automatically perform a parallel park. In 2007 Microsoft introduced Surface, a 30-inch display in a table-like form factor, which uses cameras to sense objects, hand gestures, and touch to turn an ordinary tabletop into a vibrant, interactive computer screen. The 2010 Kinect for the Xbox for the first time cut the umbilical wire between the gamer and their machine, allowing free motion to dictate commands. Alexa and Siri have skyrocketed in popularity because Amazon and Apple, respectively, recognized an opportunity to deliver greater value to their customers.

2. **Integrity of the product or service.** Before they purchase, customers increasingly evaluate the prospects of long-term satisfaction with a company's product or service. Historical defect ratings and repair histories factor into automobile and other purchase decisions. Automobile manufacturers go to great lengths to assure prospective buyers about these important dimensions. Intuit guarantees the integrity of its TurboTax software, agreeing to pay for any tax bills resulting from errors in its program. Research firm Nielsen's 2015 report titled "*Global Trust in Advertising*" revealed that 2/3 of consumers act upon online reviews of products and services, and these are especially meaningful to Millennials.

3. **The use of quality inputs.** Many of the performance dimensions mentioned previously can be achieved, in part, through sourcing quality inputs from suppliers. This could mean the use of Intel chips in the assembly of laptops, or the staffing of biotech company R&D departments by hiring top Ph.D. candidates from premier university biochemistry programs. In contrast, inferior quality inputs can contribute to poor performance characteristics as well as loss of product integrity. The Samsung Note 7 smartphone caught fire because it used poorly-manufactured batteries from two suppliers. This was a major market setback for the world's leading smartphone supplier, giving Apple and other competitors a window of opportunity to capture smartphone buyers.[27] In 2007 pet food manufacturers in the United States discovered that Chinese suppliers of the ingredient wheat gluten were spiking its protein count by adding melamine, a poisonous chemical, which resulted in the deaths of hundreds of pets. Once reputation has been sullied, it can require heroic efforts to recover it.

Psychographic and cognitive benefits. Customers gain value from companies that go beyond physical or operational characteristics of the products and services they buy. Psychographic and cognitive identification with a company and its products or services is difficult to create, but can be extremely valuable once the connection is made. One of the reasons that Chrysler was so successful in its 1980s introduction of the first minivan was that it used psychographic consumer research to better understand the image that young mothers had of themselves and their needs. Traditional demographic research could not reveal the developing market for a new type of vehicle, nor could the usual trends in sedan or truck sales.[28] There appear to be three sources of this type of value creation:

1. **Marketing and advertising**. One of the significant means by which companies can differentiate themselves in a visible and unique manner is with an effective advertising campaign. There is perhaps no other single item of as much importance in differentiation as

that of brand. The ability to create a brand that has instant recognition and instant reference to the product/service sold allows the business to draw in customers more easily than their competitors as well as charge more. Google, Target, Outback Steakhouse, Apple, WD-40, and Sony are among the most recognized brands in the world. Each is embedded in customers' minds and triggers a clear identity as to what may be obtained. Earlier in its corporate life the famous Macintosh ad titled "1984," which aired only twice (during Super Bowls XVIII and LII), permanently established Apple as providing leading-edge, break-the-rules machines. Your professors in marketing and strategy will help you understand that the "cola wars" fought for years between Coca-Cola and Pepsi have hinged greatly on "lifestyle" advertising as a means of developing very different images about the two arch-competitors.

2. **Responsiveness to customers**. When you call a company's customer service for help, how often must you navigate your way through an extended "phone tree" to get (hopefully) to the right person? How many times have you been put on hold when you call a toll-free airline reservation number, or find that the customer service agent you finally reach is unable to help you because of "company policy"? George Gershwin's *Rhapsody in Blue*, which plays when you are on hold with United Airlines, has been described as "the worst hold music ever."[29] We can hum it from memory because we have heard it so many times while waiting for United agents. Responsiveness to customers can make or break a company's image, as well as the desirability of buying or recommending its products or services. Some companies have engineered the customer interface to actually enhance the perceived benefit, presenting alternatives and ideas in advance to customers before they are even requested. Amazon.com presents book and music recommendations to customers who return to their website, based upon their automated analysis of the customer's previous buying patterns. Target analyzes your shopping data, and then matches that with your store or credit card, mails flyers to your home with special deals personalized just for you.

3. **Corporate reputation** Beyond the immediate experiences that customers have with a company's products and services, advertising, and customer service, a company's corporate reputation can facilitate or impede the creation of differentiated value to the customer. Mentioned earlier in this book, Newman's Own enhances its relationship with customers who buy its food products through its sponsorship of camps for terminally ill children and its support of other charitable causes. Trust in a company can be an important factor for both suppliers and customers, and enables some organizations to outperform others in their industry. The Betty Ford Clinic has developed a powerful reputation as a premier facility not only for the breaking of addictions, but also for its ambiance and confidentiality. Reputations are built on skills and experience, and they can lead to extraordinary returns for the business. In contrast, when British Petroleum's oil spilled into the Gulf of Mexico and all over the world's TV screens, the company's reputation was badly damaged and many customers now refuse to buy gas through BP's branded gas stations.

Process innovation (value chain design). The drivers of differentiation mentioned previously demonstrate that this strategic approach, like the low cost approach, depends upon supportive activities within each cell of the value chain (see Figure 7.10). In addition, reconfiguring the value chain in a manner that differs from the competition has the ability to provide unique value. In confronting the growing trend to dine away from home at restaurants, grocery store chains have reconfigured their value chains to better meet the needs of their customers. This includes preparation of fully cooked meals in their deli operations, so that customers on their way home from work can conveniently pick up high-quality meals ready to just heat up and eat at home. During the Covid-19 pandemic chains also accentuated their online ordering systems, where store personnel select and bag the desired groceries and deliver them to the customer curbside at an appointed time. The extremely competitive child care business has usually been considered a commodity business where companies seek to drive down costs, provide basic services, and minimally meet state licensing requirements. Bright Horizons discovered gold when they forged relationships with Fortune 500 employers, set up child care centers in or next to corporate headquarter office buildings, paid higher salaries, and incorporated learning centers within their facilities.[30]

Figure 7.10
Differentiation Strategy

Differentiation based on	Requires value chain excellence in
Product or service characteristics	Marketing research, R&D, Operations
Product or service Integrity control	Operations, Manufacturing
Quality inputs	R & D, Procurement
Marketing & advertising	Marketing research, Creative marketing
Responsiveness to customers	Customer service, Administration
Corporate reputation	Administration

Internal value chain coordination. The ability to achieve effective differentiation relies not only on consistency of activities within the value chain toward the intended point(s) of differentiation, but also on continuous coordination of these activities across the company. Figure 7.10 demonstrates that many of the drivers of differentiation rely on combinations of value chain activities. This recognizes, as is the case with the low cost strategy, that an action taken in one department or function of a company can have a ripple effect throughout the company. A substitution of ingredients brought in by purchasing can dramatically effect whether consumers like the taste of a product. A change in package size by marketing to accommodate more information will impact production line machinery and how packages might fit into cases for shipping. A change in administrative policy about repairs and defects can reshape how customers view a company when they talk to customer service agents. We could go on with many such descriptions of coordination effects at a very detailed level. What examples can you think of that illustrate the critical connections between parts of the value chain?

On a grander scale, consistency and coordination of activities, in fact, define whether the differentiated approach that a company takes can succeed. Kodak fought for its life as the film industry moved to a largely digital environment. A company that traditionally earned returns through its imaging, photographic paper and processing businesses, Kodak had to dramatically remake itself and find a new approach that distinguished it from competitors who embraced digital media much earlier on. Kodak developed cameras, printers, and internet-based printing services for consumers. A tremendous effort in research and product development resulted in a new line of products, while the sales department needed to forge new relationships with electronics retailers and marketing needed to reshape what Kodak stood for in the minds of consumers. Unfortunately, there was resistance internally to moves toward all things digital among older, long term employees. This resulted in poor coordination across departments and activities. Where consistency of approach across the entire organization does not occur, chances of failure escalate. These internal inconsistency and coordination issues led to the demise of Kodak as we knew it.

Value Chain and Differentiation Strategy

For the differentiation strategy to succeed, we have again stressed the importance of the value chain perspective. Let's look at Starbucks, another comprehensive example to see how it might be put into place and the interrelationships that are involved. Figure 7.11 diagrams its value chain and highlights key differentiation activities in each cell.

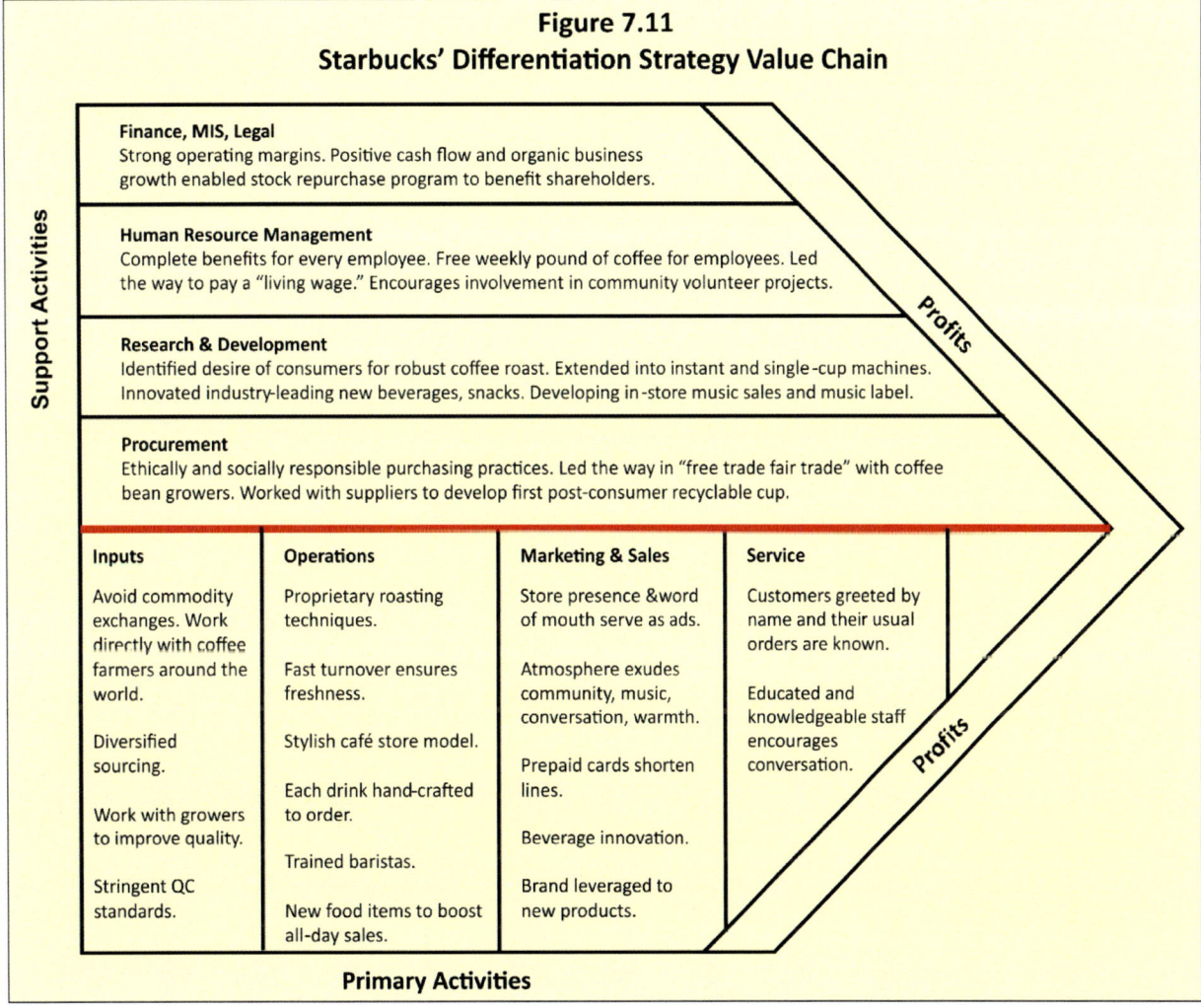

Starbucks started business in 1971 as a roaster and seller of whole coffee beans in the Pike Place Market in Seattle.[31] Purchased by one of their former employees, Howard Schultz re-imagined the business along the designs of the Italian coffee shops he visited. Selling premium coffee in a relaxing setting where the coffee barista would know your name and your preferences would allow the business to charge premium prices and differentiate it from the vast number of competitors (including at that time mostly home brewing). Their consistent approach to a differentiation strategy throughout the value chain becomes obvious when we look at what they have achieved. The company has over 15,000 U.S. locations in 2021, and another 17,000 stores in 76 countries. Its revenue of $29 billion in 2021 increased by 32% over five years earlier.

But these results are even more impressive when we consider how much Starbucks had walked away from its strategic differentiation just a few short years ago. After observing that lines and wait times had increased in their stores, the company began a systematic effort in the early 2000s to find ways to address growing demand. They installed machines capable of automatically grinding and brewing almost any coffee combination. This move made the process faster and more consistent, but at the cost of the sight, sound, and aroma (of grinding beans and working the knobs on the machine) so crucial to the original personalized Starbucks experience. The new machines were also so tall that they blocked the line of sight between the barista and the customer, cutting off conversation and loosening the bond between them. Other moves included the offering of hot lunch sandwiches and pre-packaging coffee beans in sealed bags. Microwaved breakfast sandwiches interfered with the coffee aromas floating around. These decisions to streamline operations and generate additional revenue negatively impacted the customer in-store experience, which had been so central to Starbucks' value creation efforts for years. Alignment between the functions of the organization is often much more critical than specific choices made in some departments of most organizations. Something that makes perfect sense in isolation may be a crushing hit to the armor of the company.

In the past two chapters we have talked extensively about extraordinary resources and the critical importance of intangible resources and capabilities. One of those crucial intangibles is the means by which organizations coordinate activities across the company. Another is the overall coherence and fit that the company achieves among all activities within the organization's value chain. Starbucks had begun losing this fit by failing to see the interrelationships. But it has since refocused on what is important.

Risks Associated with Differentiation Strategy
Like the low cost strategy, the differentiation strategy is subject to several risks. In addition to the parity caution offered earlier, several of the risks associated with a differentiation strategy are outlined as follows.

Product differentiation is not a strategy. In your marketing classes you have learned about product differentiation as an effective marketing tool – new sizes, flavors, colors, varieties, and so on. From the strategy point of view, however, mere product or service differences are not the sole basis for competitive advantage since these types of characteristics can generally be easily duplicated or imitated. Effective strategic differentiation has to do with the *activity* sets within and across the value chain. In this view product differentiation is a manifestation of something deeper within the organization. The *strategic* view of differentiation places a premium on processes that identify emerging customer needs and desires, and how a company organizes its activities in order to deliver the values that customers appreciate. Companies that focus their greatest attention on mere product differentiation may perform poorly over the long run.

Customers do not value the benefits derived from differentiation. Do you use all the functions that are embedded in your cell phone? In some situations and at some points in time customers may not be interested in differentiation activities that result in product and service features, but instead may have significantly greater appreciation for other dimensions. For example, in the desktop and laptop computer industry customers are most interested in standardization at a competitive price. Standardization is important for software compatibility, the use of "plug and play" peripheral devices, and ease of repair if a machine crashes. Price is important because the nature of technology trends have led customers to come to expect falling prices over time. While engineers and technical developers may value aesthetic and multifunctional designs, the technology-push capabilities of machines often exceed the desires and needs of customers.[32]

Differentiation positions can be imitated over time. When a company has developed a valued differentiation position that is insulated from competition, it enjoys an advantage over competitors and can earn superior profits. Competitors will not be unaware of what's going on, however, and will seek to imitate the value(s) that the company is creating and delivering to customers. Once again, with the advent of technology, greater access to global markets, greater access to financial capital, and the ability to more easily form alliances and joint ventures, in time competition will usually discover ways to become more competitive once again. Companies pursuing a differentiation approach must be constantly on guard against the evolution of competition, and must continue to invest resources to extend and deepen their positions.

Managing in Markets: Question for Class Discussion

In order to differentiate itself from other retailers, Target mines its shopper data to more adeptly deliver relevant ads and promotions to each customer. Target assigns each shopper a unique code, known as the Guest ID number, which keeps tabs on everything they buy. Using this data Target was able to identify about 25 products that, when analyzed together, enabled the company to assign to each shopper a "pregnancy prediction" score and an estimated due date for an impending birth. With this data Target could send coupons timed to very specific stages of a pregnancy.

After Target started mailing pregnancy product flyers to thousands of shoppers based on this model, a Minneapolis man demanded to see the local store manager. He was clutching coupons that had been sent to his daughter, and he was angry: "My daughter got this in the mail!" he said. "She's still in high school, and you're sending her coupons for baby clothes and cribs? Are you trying to encourage her to get pregnant?" Target knew that the girl was pregnant before she had announced it to her father.

What are the limits on how competitive advantage through differentiation may be created?

OTHER STRATEGIC APPROACHES

Focus Strategies

A variation on the two primary business-level strategies of low cost and differentiation is based on the breadth of the approach. Whereas a low cost or a differentiation approach is a broad market strategy, a focus strategy takes each into a unique segment of the market. Segmentation possibilities are virtually unlimited, but each is usually aimed at a very small part of a larger market. Within the focus approach, companies can pursue either a low cost or a differentiation strategy, thus in practice this is referred to as a cost focus or a differentiation focus. The obvious implication here is that by segmenting the market, a company is able to exploit an inconsistency between the needs of that particular market segment and the overall market.

In-N-Out Burger has longed reigned supreme in the burger market of the western United States, catering to a clientele that loves fast food but wants the highest quality product. At In-N-Out everything is made fresh to order. There are no microwaves or freezers. Customers can watch French fries being made from hand-diced, fresh, whole potatoes and the shakes being made from real ice cream.[33] They have narrowed their focus both geographically and by customer group. Their food is neither inexpensive nor fast when compared to the traditional fast food competitor.

Wireless audio speaker manufacturer Sonos is another example of focused differentiation. Even as Amazon's Echo has dominated the wireless speaker market since 2015, Sonos has maintained its focus on sound quality. The high-end customer segment has responded well, and in 2021 Sonos recorded a 73% increase in revenue on a 61% increase in units sold since 2017.[34]

Papa Murphy is a good example of a focused low cost competitor. With 1400 outlets, it is the largest "take and bake" shop in the country. Because it does not invest in baking equipment, its pizzas are inexpensive. In fact because they only sell food to be cooked at home, they can accept food stamps. This helps create value for a targeted segment that large pizza chains cannot address.

Have you ever heard of cellphone manufacturer Transsion? Probably not, even though it is the 4th largest phone maker in the world (measured by units shipped). Transsion focuses on people with low incomes and poor network coverage in Africa, selling low-priced "dumb phones" that gives them a 40% market share. Dumb phones cost a lot less to manufacture. In 2020 they sold 174 million phones![35]

Focus strategies are most appropriate under a limited set of circumstances. First, the segment in which the company seeks to focus is not as important to other companies pursuing broad strategic approaches. Pursuing a focused strategy is best accomplished by avoiding head-to-head competition with a larger company possessing deep pockets and great resolve to succeed. This can occur either because the segment is too small for the larger competitor to pay attention to, or the incremental investment by the large competitor to tailor its approach sufficiently to address the segment is greater than the estimated return it might earn. Second, the segment or niche is large enough and presents sufficient growth opportunity for the focused strategy company. The possibility for organic growth within a company's existing market niche is more attractive than having to leverage value-chain and resource investments into unfamiliar territory. Finally, the pursuit of a focus strategy is most appropriate for companies with constrained resources that cannot effectively operate on a broad-strategy scope.

It may not surprise you that start-up companies, young companies, and family businesses usually pursue focus strategies. Why do you suppose this is true? These types of companies ordinarily do not have the depth and breadth of resources that allow them to pursue broad markets. Instead, they rely on a very narrow set of resources, which in turn are the foundation for a relatively specific capability or set of value-creating activities. Broadening into different markets or segments usually requires access to fairly significant financial resources, which many of these types of companies do not enjoy. We will return to this topic of strategic challenges of growth and expansion that many companies experience in Chapter 8.

The biggest risk to the focus strategy is that competitors pursuing a broad strategy will drill down into this more narrow market space. Narrow markets or segments are places where larger, broad-strategy competitors can find additional sources of growth while at the same time leveraging their existing value chains and developed resources. In addition, the growth of the more-focused strategy company may entail ultimately confronting broader markets or segments more directly.

Integrated Low Cost/Differentiation Strategy

A great deal of attention has been paid lately to a variation on these business-level strategies where companies purport to borrow elements from both the low cost and differentiation approaches. This strategy runs a risk of leaving the company "stuck in the middle." Let's examine the approach in two ways.

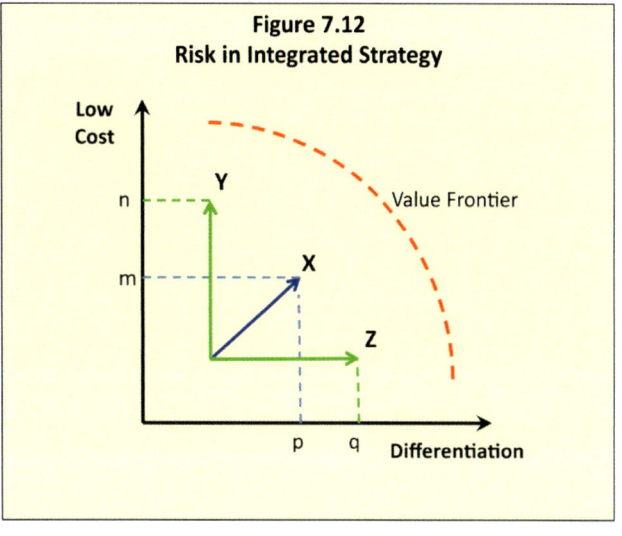

First, imagine three equally resource-endowed companies competing in an industry in which there exists strategic variety (i.e., in which both low cost and differentiation strategic approaches may succeed). In Figure 7.12 we plot the estimated trajectories of companies X, Y, and Z as they seek to reach the "value frontier" (the boundary of optimal possibilities combining both low cost and high differentiation). Company X, which pursues the integrated strategy, faithfully applies its resources and is able to accomplish level m in the low cost spectrum and level p in the differentiation spectrum. Yet company Y is single-mindedly focused on low cost, applies all its resources in that pursuit, and accomplishes level n in lowering its costs. This makes sense, because they are applying all of their resources and efforts against lowering costs. Similarly, company Z is pursuing differentiation with single-minded focus and accomplishes level q. Unless company X has somehow uniquely identified a special market that appreciates the combination of moderately low cost and moderate differentiation, all else being equal the company will be outcompeted by companies that pursue the pure business-level strategies. Management of X is following an integrated strategy right into a stuck-in-the-middle position, from which it may be difficult to recover.

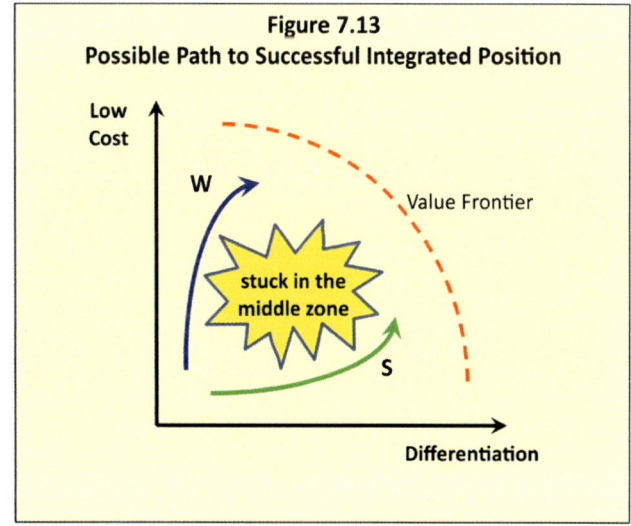

How is it possible for companies to successfully pursue an integrated strategy, then? One possibility is that a company single-mindedly pursues a pure business-level strategy, develops competitive advantage, generates superior returns, and then uses those superior returns to develop the integrated strategy with a secondary competitive position. This is illustrated in Figure 7.13, where a company avoids the zone of being stuck in the middle by moving away from a pure strategy only after it has sufficiently developed its position. Here company W has fully developed its low cost position, and is now using its superior returns to develop a differentiated position as well. Company S has moved out the differentiation path, and is now seeking to lower its costs as an added source of competitive advantage.

It looks simple on paper to move from one successful strategy into new terrain. However, the problem of developing competitive advantage based upon two different approaches simultaneously can be severe, even for highly successful companies. In 2006–2007, for example, Walmart sought to bring more fashionable clothing lines into its discount retail stores. The clothing lines did not sell well, causing huge inventory overstocks throughout the company's U.S. stores, and resulted in lower store sales growth than expected. This prompted write-offs from their income statement, and caused problems for suppliers upstream when the company cut subsequent orders. Walmart has long been known for its low cost strategy, which is supported throughout every activity in its value chain. To succeed in differentiating itself, in addition to low cost, the company would need to significantly enhance capabilities across its value chain that would support this new approach. The new approach requires: marketing research that identifies and understands fashion trends, buyers who can source goods on dimensions other than low cost and acceptable quality, new (usually more expensive) methods of display and merchandising in stores, the attraction of different types of customers who are interested in more fashionable clothing, and more. When a company has been consistently and successfully operating in one mind-set for decades, it is very difficult to begin operating differently throughout its value chain. Like any strategic initiative, embarking on a strategy takes time using appropriate resource development.

The same comments can be made about attempts to move from a highly differentiated position toward a position that also embraces lower costs – company S in Figure 7.13. As we mentioned earlier, during 2005–2006 Starbucks sought to increase the speed and efficiency of its store operations by moving away from handcrafted beverage preparations to machine-assisted preparations. In their stores machines were installed that automatically ground the beans and brewed the coffee for their lattés and other specialty coffees. On February 14, 2007, founder Howard Schultz wrote an impassioned letter to all Starbucks employees about their recent shift in strategy, titling the letter "The Commoditization of the Starbucks Experience," something which he claimed had resulted in declining performance and opened the door to competitive threats:

> "Over the past ten years, in order to achieve the growth, development, and scale necessary to go from less than 1,000 stores to 13,000 stores and beyond, we have had to make a series of decisions that, in retrospect, have led to the watering down of the Starbucks experience, and, what some might call the commoditization of our brand.
>
> Many of these decisions were probably right at the time, and on their own merit would not have created the dilution of the experience; but in this case, the sum is much greater and, unfortunately, much more damaging than the individual pieces. For example, when we went to automatic espresso machines, we solved a major problem in terms of speed of service and efficiency. At the same time, we overlooked the fact that we would remove much of the romance and theatre that was in play with the use of the La Marzocca machines. This specific decision became even more damaging when the height of the machines, which are now in thousands of stores, blocked the visual sight line the customer previously had to watch the drink being made, and for the intimate experience with the barista. This, coupled with the need for fresh roasted coffee in every North America city and every international market, moved us toward the decision and the need for flavor locked packaging. Again, the right decision at the right time, and once again I believe we overlooked the cause and the effect of flavor lock in our stores. We achieved

fresh roasted bagged coffee, but at what cost? The loss of aroma - perhaps the most powerful nonverbal signal we had in our stores; the loss of our people scooping fresh coffee from the bins and grinding it fresh in front of the customer, and once again stripping the store of tradition and our heritage?"

Having provided sufficient warning about the dangers of the integrated low cost/differentiation approach, we should also recognize that there are some shining examples of companies that have successfully gone down this path. Toyota is a company that readily comes to mind. It has not only achieved tremendous success through differentiation in design, development, and manufacturing of a range of vehicles that deliver value to customers. It has also achieved a singularly lower cost structure than its chief competitors, enabling the company to price lower and still earn healthy returns.

OUTSOURCING, STRATEGY, AND THE VALUE CHAIN

The connections we have made throughout this chapter between business-level strategies and the value chain allow us to gain further insight on the process of outsourcing, which has become prevalent among all kinds of businesses over the last twenty years. In Chapter 5, you will recall, we mentioned that outsourcing possibilities are occasionally identified through the value chain analysis. Outsourcing is a process through which a company depends on another organization to perform activities on its behalf. For example, Nike outsources manufacturing of its athletic shoes to production companies in the Far East that have lower labor costs and can produce shoes less expensively than in the United States. Walmart relies on other companies to manage the stocking and restocking of certain kinds of specialty merchandise within its own stores, instead of having that merchandise flow through its sophisticated distribution system. Why would a company outsource any of its activities? How does outsourcing work to improve a company's strategic approach to its industry? Under what conditions should a company refrain from outsourcing? We tackle these important questions in this section.

From a competitive strategy perspective there are two primary reasons that a company might decide to outsource some activity or set of activities: 1) to enhance strategic position in the marketplace, and 2) to offload activities in which they do not have any special competence and which do not contribute to its strategic position. Generally there are fairly straightforward situations that may fall into the first category. Small pharmaceutical companies often form joint ventures with larger companies in order to take advantage of their well-developed sales and marketing operations. In this case the outsourcing of marketing and sales can contribute to significantly greater buyer awareness and perceived legitimacy for the smaller company. Toshiba discovered that their customers value extremely fast turnaround times when their Toshiba computers break down and require authorized repairs. The company farmed out repair operations to trained UPS employees at the Kentucky hub of United Parcel Service, which also picked up and redelivered the machine. Avoiding the extra steps of delivery and pickup to Toshiba itself, Toshiba customers received repairs at least two days sooner and Toshiba's relationship with customers was strengthened.[36]

The second reason – offloading nonessential activities – is much more complicated for companies to determine. As we have illustrated in this chapter and in the earlier chapter on the value chain, management of the value chain to the internally consistent pursuit of a business-level strategic approach is a complex undertaking. If we simply look at the variety of activities occurring in each cell of the value chain, as well as the coordination required among cells and the connections made upstream and downstream with suppliers and customers (Figures 7.8 and 7.11), we begin to see how monumental a challenge this can be. For this reason, not every company is capable of managing and performing every one of the activities in its value chain. Our discussion in Chapter 6 on resource-based analysis helps us arrive at the same conclusion. Most companies develop and pursue unique resources and competitive excellence in a limited number of arenas; it is what they become especially good at, and what they become known for doing well. If in addition they attempt to manage and perform activities in which they have no unique capabilities or that do not leverage their resource positions, then they may be overextending themselves into activities that do not contribute to developing competitive advantage.

It is simple to see that this is the case in some examples, but more difficult in others. For example, every business generates volumes of garbage each day (even in this digital age). Part of conducting business effectively requires that they "take out the garbage;" however, few companies will actually haul their waste to the landfill. Instead, they outsource this to a local company. It makes sense, since hauling garbage is not central to what companies do. However when activities become more central to what a company does strategically, the challenge of deciding whether to outsource or not becomes much greater. On what basis does Nike decide to have other companies manufacture its shoes, and why would Walmart entertain having other companies manage what happens within their own retail stores?

It may be easier to tackle this question from the other side – that is, when is it *inappropriate* to outsource activities? There appear to be several conditions that describe when outsourcing may damage or hinder a company's strategic efforts:

Loss of control over costs or differentiation values. Having another organization perform important value chain activities can damage the company's strategic efforts if the company loses control over key values that are central to its strategy. In 2000 retailer Toys 'R' Us signed a ten-year agreement that made Amazon the exclusive online retail outlet for Toys 'R' Us toys, games, and baby products. Unfortunately, Toys 'R' Us was unable to control the "look" of its merchandise on the Amazon site, nor prevent the introduction of other toys through Amazon's zShops partners.[37] One might argue that allowing Amazon to enter the toy retailing sector so quickly and easily hastened the decline and exit of Toys 'R' Us. In 2017 it declared bankruptcy, and in 2018 it liquidated all of its stores worldwide.

In contrast, Ryanair has for years outsource much of its aircraft maintenance to other companies. When it started up as a low-cost airline, Ryanair did not possess an internal set of resources or capabilities to fully perform aircraft maintenance; the company's expertise is in managing route selection, flight operations, and customer-centric employee hiring on a low cost basis. Yet through long-term contracts they achieve low cost maintenance performed by other organizations, while still controlling and directing how maintenance is performed. So in this case outsourcing to third parties supports their strategy of low cost, but does so without the company having to relinquish control over that important dimension of the business.

Disruption of coordination and linkages in the value chain. Earlier we argued that the coordination and linkages that exist among elements in a company's value chain are the greatest sources of competitive advantage. This is because they are intangible and extremely difficult to imitate. When outsourcing breaks one of these important coordinating bonds, the company may be less well-insulated from competition.

Hollowing out the core. In the 1990s "business process reengineering" became the latest business fad to talk about in the classroom. Much of the reengineering had to do with outsourcing, and some companies were so enamored with the perceived benefits that they outsourced many of their activities. Individually, each activity may not seem strategically important. Yet often combinations of activities, and especially the coordinating linkages that exist between them, may be central to what a company does well. So any attempts to outsource should consider not only the activities by themselves, but the system and context in which those activities exist.

Competitive learning. In some instances, a competitor may gain greater insight into a company's internal value chain by observing which activities have been outsourced. Not only might the competitor learn more about the outsourced operation, because it will be more visible to outsiders, but they may be able to develop insights about what activities remain inside the company as constituting its strategic core.

Figure 7.14 presents a decision tree for outsourcing activity that summarizes the preceding discussion. In order to gain the benefits of outsourcing without incurring some of the problems that can accompany these efforts, companies will occasionally engage in either vertical or horizontal acquisitions in order to own another company that can perform an important set of activities. Acquiring another company can ensure control over the process and minimize competitive learning; however, acquisitions present their own sets of issues. We will cover mergers and acquisitions more completely in Chapter 10.

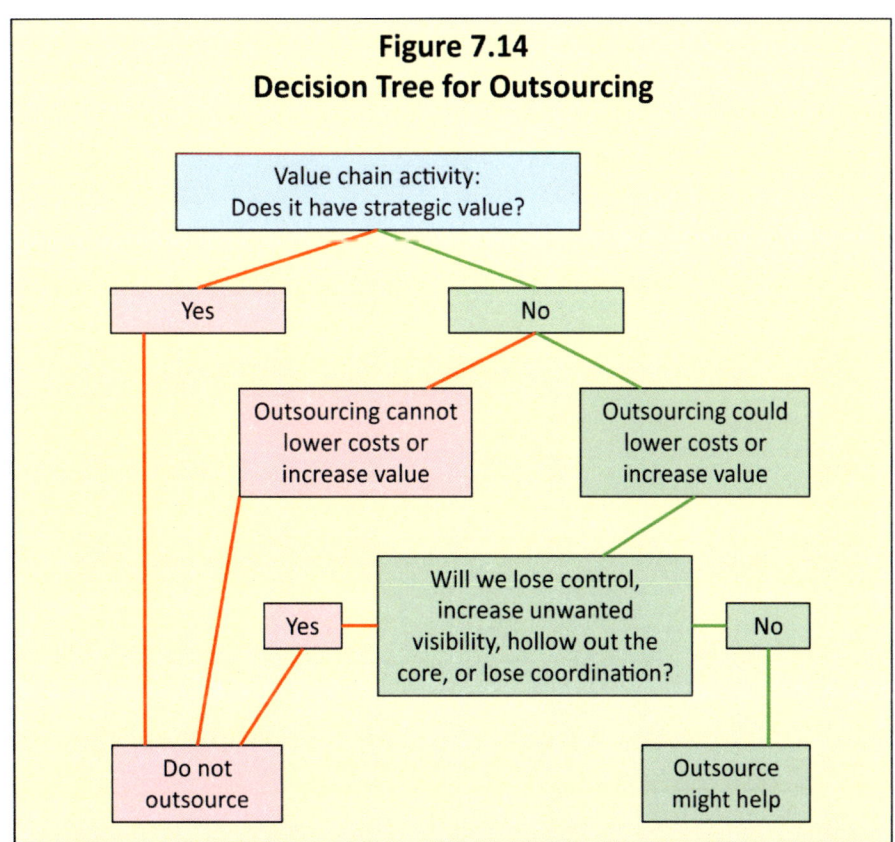

Managing in Markets: Question for Class Discussion

Your competition is lowering its costs by extending its value chain upstream and outsourcing production offshore. This has enabled them to lower prices so much that it will hurt your business. When you consider outsourcing your own production in response, though, two issues present themselves:
1. You find poor labor practices and low wages in other countries, and
2. You may need to lay off some of your own employees.

What should you do?

CHAPTER SUMMARY

In this chapter we have examined the business-level (sometimes referred to as generic) strategies of low cost and differentiation as well as the variations of both focus strategy and integrated cost/differentiation strategy. These archetypes lay out the highest-level approach to a business and are valuable as communication and coordination tools, making important decisions, and managing the business. They are used as a rallying point for organizations and as a means to evaluate consistency in various approaches when using value chain and resource-based analysis.

Although several companies in an industry may attempt a low cost approach, there can really be only one low cost leader in a market. The low cost leader has the opportunity to make significant returns by taking advantage of its relative cost structure. All others may find themselves undercut by the leader and discover that it is difficult to prosper when market circumstances are challenging. On the other hand, a differentiation strategy has virtually unlimited variations in approach. Multipoint differentiators inherently enjoy greater security in their strategic positions than do single-point differentiators. For both the low cost and differentiation approaches, it is essential for companies to achieve parity on other competitive dimensions that are valued in the market.

A focus strategy approach takes advantage of segmentation in the market or geographical differences that can lead to a low cost focus or a differentiation focus. The integrated low cost/differentiation strategy is intuitively appealing, yet it appears to be a risky approach that even very successful companies find difficult to balance. By attempting to compete against other companies that are more single-mindedly concentrating on a pure low cost or differentiation approach, the integrated strategy company risks getting stuck in the middle.

The value chain plays a central role in understanding how business-level strategies are put into practice. A business-level strategy represents a philosophy of competing that should translate to mutually supportive activities in every cell of the company's value chain, producing a consistent approach to the market across the company. Assessing whether or not a value chain activity is central to strategy, and whether third-party organizations can perform the activity at a lower cost or higher value-added, provides a guideline for companies on outsourcing.

Learning Objectives Review

1. *Compare and contrast business-level strategies available to organizations, and describe how they create competitive advantage.*

- There are two basic types of business-level strategy, low cost leadership and differentiation.

- Either of these types can be pursued on a broad scope or narrow scope. The combination of two types and two scopes results in four different business-level strategies.

- A fifth version, known as the "integrated low cost and differentiation" approach, combines elements of the basic two types (but can be especially risky).

- Competitive advantage is a position in which a company earns above-average profits in its industry. The low cost leader earns superior profits by increasing its profit margin as a function of having a lower cost structure. A successful differentiation strategy earns superior profits because the company is able to more than offset higher costs associated with value-creation through higher revenues charged.

- Each business-level strategy is subject to three critical conditions, upon which its success rests: parity conditions on other dimensions valued in the marketplace, the evolution of customer expectations, and the evolution of competition itself.

2. *Examine the underlying drivers that enable a company's choice of business-level strategy to be successful.*

- A business-level strategy can be successful to the extent that it addresses existing or emerging key success factors in an industry.

- A business-level strategy can be successful to the extent that the company's value chain achieves coordination and consistency of activities that individually and in combination support the adopted approach.

- Drivers of the low cost strategy include: economies of scale, capacity utilization, benefitting from the experience curve, supportive product/service design decisions, value chain design that affects internal process, and internal value chain coordination.

- Drivers of the differentiation strategy include: responsiveness to existing and emerging customer needs, integrity of products and services, quality, psychographics and cognitive benefits to customers, value chain design that affects internal process, and internal value chain coordination.

3. *Analyze when outsourcing makes strategic sense.*

- Outsourcing activity can make sense under the following conditions:
- The activity does not have strategic value.
- Outsourcing can lower costs or increase value.
- The company does not lose control, increase unwanted visibility to what is at its core, or lose coordination benefits in its internal value chain.

Key Terms

Business-level strategies - A term for strategic approaches at a high, overarching level. Often referred to as "generic strategies." Business-level strategy is appropriate for a single line of business with related products or services. It is not appropriate as a means of organizing a diversified corporation with many lines of business.

Differentiation - One type of business-level strategy. It implies a broad market approach where activities performed by the company provide sufficiently differentiated value to allow the company to generate superior economic returns, generally through higher pricing.

Experience curve - Reductions in cost per unit that are achieved through the learning that occurs in cumulative production over time (in contrast to economies of scale, in which unit cost reductions are associated with volume during a fixed time interval).

Focus - A narrow scope for either of the two types of business-level strategies of differentiation and low cost. The company pursues a narrow targeted market, geographic area, and/or particular customer group.

Low cost - One type of business-level strategy. It implies a broad market approach where a company can earn superior economic returns by rigorously reducing costs and expenses below its competitors, while simultaneously maintaining parity pricing.

Low cost leadership - Of the companies that pursue a low cost strategy, one company will enjoy the lowest cost structure. This company has the strongest competitive position among low cost seekers, since it enjoys greater pricing flexibility and can more easily weather industry conditions that compress profit margins.

Outsourcing - When another outside organization is contracted to perform a business process or service.

Parity - Though companies compete on cost or some dimensions of differentiation, they must maintain relative equality on other dimensions that are valued in the marketplace. Without reasonable parity on other valued conditions, the lowest-cost competitor or most-effective differentiator on some dimension may not succeed.

Scope - The degree to which a company competes broadly or narrowly within an industry. Differences in geography, customer segments, and user needs can describe broad versus narrow scope.

Stuck in the middle - A condition where a company simultaneously pursues both a differentiation and a low cost strategy. The result is often that such companies are out-competed by competitors which pursue "pure" business-level strategies more single-mindedly.

Short Answer Review Questions

1. What are the three important conditions that must be kept in mind when considering any of the business-level strategies?

2. What are the five business-level strategies that businesses might employ?

3. Under what circumstances would a low cost approach be most likely to allow a business to achieve extraordinary returns?

4. Under what circumstances would a differentiation approach be most likely to allow a business to achieve extraordinary returns?

5. Under what circumstances would a focused, low cost approach be most likely to allow a business to achieve extraordinary returns?

6. Under what circumstances would a focused, differentiation approach be most likely to allow a business to achieve extraordinary returns?

7. What issues must businesses keep in mind as they consider simultaneously pursuing an integrated low cost and differentiation position?

8. How does a firm become "stuck in the middle"?

9. How are business-level strategies put into practice in the day-to-day running of a business?

10. What strategy would you recommend for a new business being started by a small team of entrepreneurs?

11. Under what conditions would a company be at risk pursuing a focused business-level strategy

12. How does consistency of effort across the value chain play a role in achieving extraordinary returns?

Group Exercises

1. Take two companies in the same industry that compete with each other in seemingly different ways. For example, take Netflix and Redbox, or try Nordstrom and Kohl's. Using information from their annual reports and business stories that you can find on the internet, attempt to identify the type and scope of their business-level strategies and how their value chains support that approach.

    a. Do they appear to be consistent across their value chain activities?

    b. What unique resources do they seem to be using to separate themselves from their competitors?

2. Take a single industry such as the grocery store industry. Map out where the top ten competitors are using the five Business- Level Strategies chart shown in Figure 7.3.

    a. Are all five approaches being utilized in the industry?

    b. Compare each of these firms based upon their five-year ROE performance. How are they doing? Why?

3. Periodically companies attempt to change their business-level strategy (usually due to significant changes in the environment). What cautions would you advise a business contemplating such a move? Can you name a company that has done just such a thing in the past five years?

Investor Relations Sites for Companies Mentioned in This Chapter

Apple: https://investor.apple.com/investor-relations/default.aspx
Banfield: https://www.banfield.com/about-banfield/
Boeing: https://investors.boeing.com/investors/overview/default.aspx
Bright Horizons: https://investors.brighthorizons.com/
Carmax: https://investors.carmax.com/ir-home/default.aspx
Carvana: https://investors.carvana.com/
Dell Technologies: https://investors.delltechnologies.com/
Eagle Materials: http://ir.eaglematerials.com/
Easyjet: https://corporate.easyjet.com/investors
Ferrari: https://corporate.ferrari.com/en/investors
HP Inc: https://investor.hp.com/home/default.aspx
In N Out Burger: https://www.in-n-out.com/employment/corporate/home
Kodak: https://investor.kodak.com/
Papa Murphy (MTY Food Group): https://mtygroup.com/relation-avec-les-investisseurs/
PetSmart: https://www.petsmartcorporate.com/investors/
Qualcomm: https://investor.qualcomm.com/
Regal Entertainment (Cineworld Group): https://www.cineworldplc.com/en/investors
Ryanair: https://investor.ryanair.com/
Sonos: https://investors.sonos.com/reports-and-filings/default.aspx
Starbucks: https://investor.starbucks.com/ir-home/default.aspx
Toshiba: http://www.toshiba.co.jp/about/ir/index.htm
Transsion: http://www.transsion.com/profile
UPS: https://investors.ups.com/
Vanguard: https://about.vanguard.com/
Wendy's: https://www.irwendys.com/home/default.aspx

References

[1] www.eaglematerials.com. Rivera, M. 2002, "In a modern world, a violin bow maker keeps his craft alive," November 23, www.nbcnews.com/business/modern-world-violin-bow-maker-keeps-his-craft-alive-1C7206756. www.benoitrolland.com/. Taplin, I. M. 2013, "Who is to blame? A re-examination of fast fashion after the 2013 factory disaster in Bangladesh," in *Critical Perspectives on International Business*. Johnson, K. 2013, "Brands risk image in varying Bangladesh building collapse responses," *Concord Monitor*, May 7, www.concordmonitor.com.

[2] Porter, M. E. 1985, *Competitive advantage*, New York: Free Press. Porter, M. E. 1996, "What is strategy?" *Harvard Business Review* 74(6): 61–78. Veliyath, R., & E. Fitzgerald, 2000, "Firm capabilities, business strategies, customer preferences, and hypercompetitive arenas: The sustainability of competitive advantages with implications for firm competitiveness," *Competitiveness Review* 20(1): 56–83. Thornhill, S., & R. E. White, 2007, "Strategic purity: A multi-industry evaluation of a pure vs. hybrid business strategies," *Strategic Management Journal* 28(5): 553–561.

[3] Porter, M. E. 1980, *Competitive strategy*, New York: Free Press. Porter, M. E. 1985, *Competitive advantage*, New York: Free Press.

[4] Lee, L., & P. Burrows. 2007. "Is Dell too big for Michael Dell?" BusinessWeek. February 12: 33.

[5] Porter, M. E. 1985. *Competitive strategy*. New York: Free Press.
[6] Lee, L. 2006. "It's Dell vs. the Dell way." BusinessWeek Online. February 23, 17.
[7] Porter, M. E. 1985. *Competitive strategy*. New York: Free Press.
[8] Porter, M. E. 1996. "What is strategy?" Harvard Business Review 74(6): 61–78.
[9] Chafkin, M. 2007. "How to kill a great idea." Inc. June: 85–91.
[10] Armstrong, L. 1996. "The numbers are crunching Packard Bell." BusinessWeek. December 30: 46.
[11] Porter, M. E. 1985. *Competitive advantage*. New York: Free Press, 20.
[12] www.petsmart.com/banfield/index.shtml.
[13] Arndt, M. 2006, "Out, damned trans fats," BusinessWeek, July 31: 12. Adamy, J. 2007, "Why no. 3 Wendy's finds vanilla so exciting," Wall Street Journal, April 6: B1.
[14] Simple calculations can reveal how profound this difference in fees can be. A $250,000 initial fund portfolio would save over $100,000 in fund expenses over a thirty year time frame. Lim, P. 2007, "How the biggest funds fared," U.S. News & World Report, January 15, 142 (2): 73. Maiello, M. 2005, "The un-Vanguard," Forbes. September 19, 176(5): 182–186. Perold, A. F. 1998, "The Vanguard Group, Inc. – 1998," Boston: Harvard Business School Publishing, 9-299-002. https://investor.vanguard.com/expense-ratio/vanguard-effect. Whitler, K. A., 2018, "Insight into the Vanguard brand: A top brand of the year in the Harris Poll," Forbes, January 28.
[15] Grant, R. M. 2005. *Contemporary strategy analysis*. Malden: Blackwell Publishing.
[16] "The development of the Boeing 777," 1998, Public Broadcasting System. Wall, R. & J. Ostrower, 2016, "Jet makers step on the gas," Wall Street Journal, July 19, p. B4.
[17] Tully, S. 2015, "Why Southwest's pilots just rejected a massive pay raise," Fortune, November 5. https://www.careerbliss.com/. https://www.airlinepilotcentral.com/.
[18] Capell, K. 2007. "Glaxo mimics carmaker to speed vaccine." BusinessWeek Online. April 5: 16.
[19] HP 2012 Global Citizenship Report.
[20] https://investor.ryanair.com/.
[21] "Walmart with wings," BusinessWeek Online, November 17: 13. Sullivan, W. 2007, "Flying on the cheap," U.S. News and World Report, March 6: 47. Davy. 2004, "Fare wars: A history lesson," European Transport and Leisure, February 16, Davy: Dublin.
[22] Serpen, E. 2006. "Key performance measures." Presentation at 3rd annual Managing Airline Operating Costs Conference, London.
[23] Ghemwat, P. 1986. "Walmart stores' discount operations." Boston: Harvard Business School Publishing, 9-387-018.
[24] Arndt, M. 2006, "Out, damned trans fats," BusinessWeek, July 31: 12. Adamy, J. 2007, "Wendy's to discuss strategic review with investors," Wall Street Journal, May 16: B17. Adamy, J. 2007, "Wendy's considers possible sale," Wall Street Journal, April 26: A2.
[25] Kahn, G. 2007. "How to slow down a Ferrari: Buy it." Wall Street Journal. May 8.
[26] www.greatplacetowork-europe.com/best/lists. See also www.forbes.com/companies/ferrari/#6857da096a70.
[27] Moynihan, T. 2017. "Samsung finally reveals why the Note 7 kept exploding." Wired, January 22.
[28] West G. P., & J. O. DeCastro. 2001. "The Achilles heel of firm strategy." Journal of Management Studies, 38(3): 417–442.
[29] https://www.flyertalk.com/forum/travelbuzz/712639-worst-airline-hold-music-ever.html.
[30] Brown, R. 2001. "How we built a strong company in a weak industry." Harvard Business Review, 79(2): 51–57.
[31] Adamy, J. 2007, "Starbucks chairman says trouble may be brewing," Wall Street Journal, February 24: A4. "Text of Starbucks memo," 2007, Wall Street Journal Online, February 24.
[32] Christensen, C. M. *The innovator's dilemma*. Boston: Harvard Business School Publishing.
[33] www.in-n-out.com/history.aspx.
[34] Sonos 10-K 2021, https://investors.sonos.com/reports-and-filings/default.aspx. Gallagher, D., 2019, "Sonos finds its voice," Wall Street Journal, November 21, B12. "Sonic Switzerland," 2018, The Economist, October 20, 61.
[35] http://www.transsion.com/profile. Wong, J., 2019, "China's 'dumb phone' giant looks smart," Wall Street Journal, April 20, B12.
[36] Friedman, T. L. 2005. *The world is flat*. New York: Farrar, Straus, and Giroux.
[37] M. Wolk. 2006. "Toys R Us wins suit against Amazon.com." MSNBC, March 2.

This page is intentionally left blank.

Chapter 8: Adapting Strategy to Industry and Life Cycle Stages

LEARNING OBJECTIVES

1. Explain the stages of an industry life cycle and their impact on business strategy.
2. Analyze the strategy implications of competing in fragmented or consolidated industries.
3. Utilize organizational life cycle stages and the kinds of problems and resources issues that businesses experience in each to proactively recommend value creation activities.
4. Describe steps a company can take to extend its growth stage of the organizational life cycle.
5. Explain the risks associated with being a first mover.
6. Explain how a company might successfully navigate a crisis.

"When the Music's Over, Turn Out the Lights"[1]

On July 27, 1997, an event occurred that changed your life, and it dramatically changed the trajectories of several industries that you know so well. On that day Don Katz invented a gadget to play "Motion Picture Experts Group Audio Layer 3" files, now commonly known as MP3 music files. His company, Audible, sold a few thousand of the gadgets. By 2020 roughly 86% of U.S. households listened to digitized music files. Driven over the last few years by the smartphone revolution, millions easily carry or stream their music and listen to tunes everywhere. In 2021 streaming surpassed radio as the most popular way to listen to music; radio had dominated music listening for over 100 years.

The introduction of the MP3 changed the course of music history and the commercial music industry value chain. The advent of MP3 technology led to the start-up and rapid growth of an entirely new industry around digital music and players. Whereas Sony had long dominated portable music players with its Walkman franchise, new companies rapidly entered this market space. Samsung leveraged its capabilities in electronic entertainment devices, as did Diamond Multimedia with its Rio player. SanDisk introduced its Sansa line of players applying its flash drive technology. The iPod represented an elegant next step in the evolution of Apple's innovative approach to consumer digital technology. Microsoft introduced the Zune because the company wanted to occupy a central position in the digital home. Figure 8.1 shows the rise of digital music.[2]

Paralleling the start-up and growth of MP3 music has been the devastating decline of the recorded music industry. Compact disks replaced vinyl LPs way back in the 1980s as a consequence of new technology introduced at the time. CD sales peaked at over $13 billion annually in 2000, just after the first MP3 player was introduced. In 2021 vinyl LPs, making a comeback, outsold CDs for the first time in over 30 years.

Music labels such as Warner and Universal found it more difficult to support musicians, as the economics of producing and marketing a new CD grew worse. In the prosperous years it would not be uncommon for a number 1 CD to sell 500,000–600,000 copies weekly, but now the best

CDs sell only 15,000-20,000 per week, prompting agents for musicians to claim that "CDs have become little more than advertisements for more-lucrative goods like concert tickets and T-shirts."

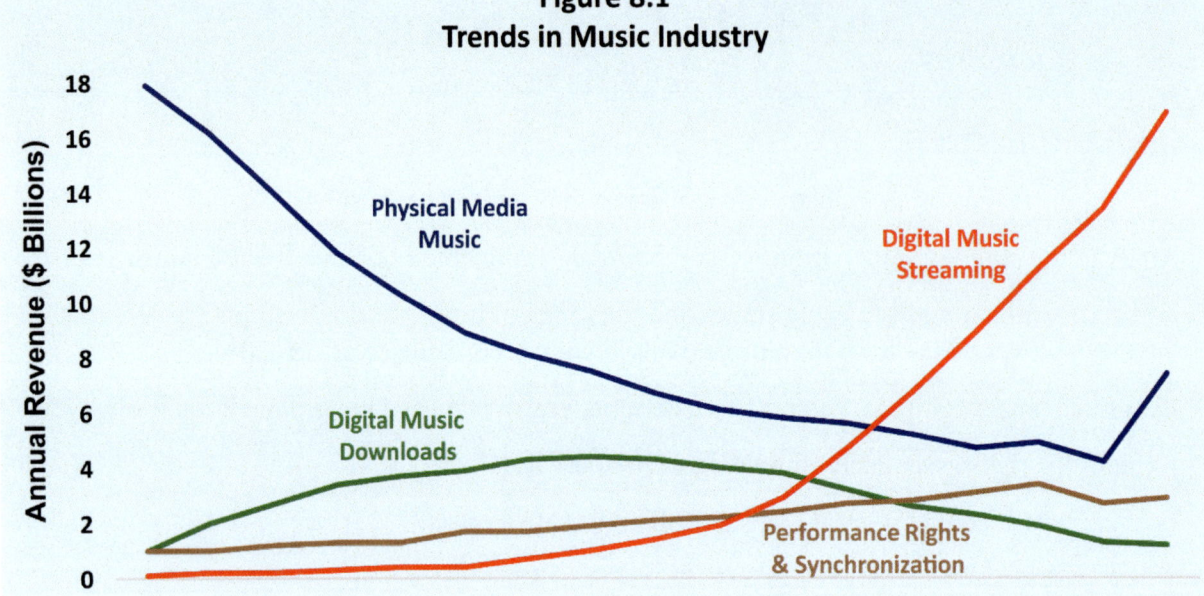

**Figure 8.1
Trends in Music Industry**

The decline in CDs has also had a cascading effect on other related industries, too. Longtime music retailer Tower Records, which had been in business for forty-six years and at one point had 800 stores nationwide, was liquidated in 2006. Because CDs were not selling quickly, Best Buy discontinued selling them in 2018. Now retailers like Walmart now represent roughly 65 percent of physical retail store music sales. But they focus on inexpensive $5 titles, not the new hits. Whereas Tower Records used to stock 100,000 titles, now only specialty stores carry CD titles. Walmart and Amazon started music download sites to participate in the increasingly-virtual market. Genres of music with narrower appeal – such as classical and jazz – now experience tremendous challenges in reaching consumers effectively.

Musical artists have also been impacted by the digital conversion. The reduced power of music labels in the industry value chain make direct connections with consumers more important. So concert tours have become central to the artists' ability to generate income. Performance rights (songs used at public venues and by broadcasters) and synchronization (songs used in advertising, games, and on TV) have grown in importance. Most artists receive royalties of between 10-20% on music sales, but since less costly single-song downloads and streaming now dominate the market their take has declined. Superstars like Adele and Taylor Swift have exerted star power by preventing streaming sales until CD sales are maximized, but this is unusual among artists.[3]

QUESTIONS

1. What steps would you take to address decline if you were in charge of strategy at a music label company such as Universal?
2. If you were a musician, what steps could you take to increase revenue for your music?
3. What do you expect the next big shakeup to be in the music industry, and how can your company prepare for this?

INDUSTRY LIFE CYCLES

One of the most exciting facets of the study of business and strategy is the nature of industry change. Many years ago the Austrian economist Joseph Schumpeter described "creative destruction" as a process that every industry experiences: they start up often based on some new entrepreneurial insight or innovation, attract new entrants, grow, begin to mature, and then a shakeup occurs that either launches renewed growth or thrusts the industry into decline. It's a "life cycle" that has been observed time and time again across dozens of types of industries.

Life Cycle Stages

An industry's evolution through a complete life cycle is fundamentally driven by two factors: new knowledge about how to create value and growth in demand (Figure 8.2). New knowledge about creating value forms the basis for any new industry to begin with – whether it be the application of modular manufacturing and assembly to democratize the automobile (Henry Ford), the use of durable-stitched material to sell the first pair of "blue jeans" (Levi Strauss), the creation of a new low-cost distribution method for retailing general merchandise (Sam Walton), or figuring out how to encode and play music digitally. However, new knowledge alone, without growth in underlying demand, would lead only to faddish products and services and short-lived industry categories such as Beanie Babies, Pet Rocks, Pogs, Cabbage Patch dolls, or disco music.

**Figure 8.2
Determinants of industry evolution**

New knowledge about value creation
Growth in demand

Growth in demand occurs because the sort of value creation resulting from an innovation is substantive and has long-lasting appeal to a wide audience of potential users. The potential for broad appeal attracts new entrants to the industry because they see the possibilities of earning profits, and they remain there to compete because of continued growth in demand. But the growth of companies and the entrance of new competitors eventually leads to saturation in supply. At this point an industry will experience one of two possible paths. Either there will be a renewed burst of growth because new, innovative knowledge developed within the industry provides the opportunity to create even greater value and attract new customers. Or new knowledge and innovation in some other economic sector will enhance the power of substitutes to draw off customers through compelling price/value propositions, leading to the industry's decline.

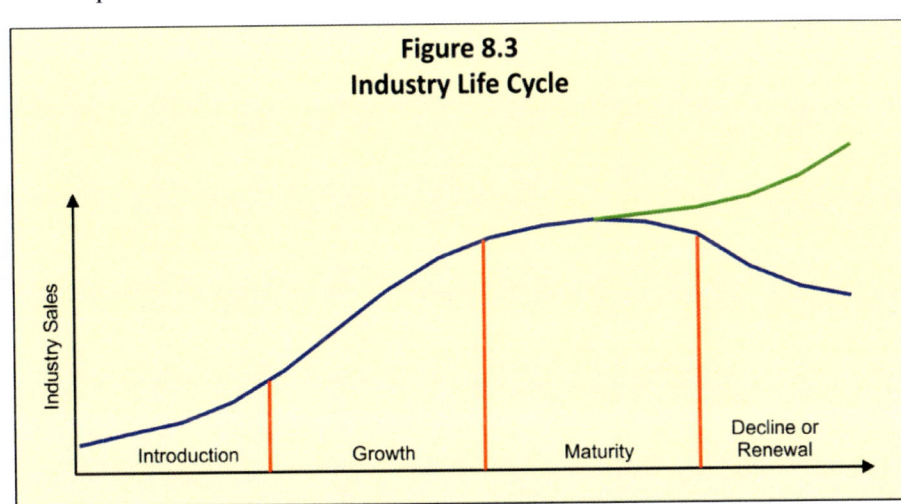

The evolution of most industries therefore follows a familiar pattern involving four stages, such as those illustrated in Figure 8.3. We typically describe the stages as the introduction, growth, maturity, and decline (or renewal). Each stage of the industry life exhibits its own defining characteristics with implications for the type of strategic approach that might be successful.

Introduction stage. You would not expect to see a lot of competitors populating an industry at its infancy. Almost by definition, in the introduction stage of an industry there will typically be a very small number of companies dipping their toes in the cold waters of a type of business that has never been tried before. Sometimes there is just one such "new entrant," often referred to as a first mover. First-mover advantage refers to a sustainable competitive advantage that is achieved by being the first company to enter a new industry or industry segment, and we'll address it in more depth later in this chapter. First mover companies have the widest latitude for strategic choice.

In this first stage early entrants are trying to determine which bundle of characteristics or approaches will create the greatest value for the customer, and so innovation efforts are widespread as firms try a variety of products or services. These companies are not only figuring out if customers will buy their offerings and which segments of customers might buy, but also which suppliers present the best opportunity for success. Consequently, value creation in the introduction stage is often occurring internally through product design as well as externally in relationship-building both upstream and downstream.

Growth stage. Industries move into a growth stage when the kind of value created begins to engender broader customer demand. Still experiencing the entrance of new companies seeking to profit from the potential, most industries will also begin to experience some corporate exiting by companies that are unable to successfully adapt to what is usually a growing degree of standardization of products or services. Although Sony essentially created the home VCR market in the 1980s with its Betamax technology, VHS technology became the industry standard and Sony finally withdrew the Betamax from the market. As demand continues to increase, competitors focus on achieving larger scale to more efficiently serve a broad swath of customers or markets while reliably and consistently delivering what they value. There is still an opportunity for innovation and an effective differentiation strategic approach during the growth stage. However, increasing standardization opens the door for a low-cost leadership strategic approach. Because of the focus on standardization and achieving scale and scope, value can be created internally through process as well as externally by working to develop broad downstream customer relationships. Some consolidation begins to occur among industry participants, enabling a small number of competitors to more rapidly increase size and scale.

Maturity stage. Industries mature when demand begins to slow down. In contrast to the 1970s and 1980s when soft drink per capita consumption grew by 50 percent in a fifteen year period, moving into the 1990s per capita consumption remained relatively flat. Maturity is also experienced when a high level of customer saturation is reached, meaning there are relatively few new customers to bring into the industry. The U.S. cell phone market is experiencing this now (Figure 8.4)[4] because the industry has 97 percent penetration among U.S. households. When these conditions occur, competition becomes fierce since one of the only routes to growth is to take market share away from other companies. Since 2017 there has been vicious competition among cellphone service providers in deals they offer to entice consumers to leave one and join another.

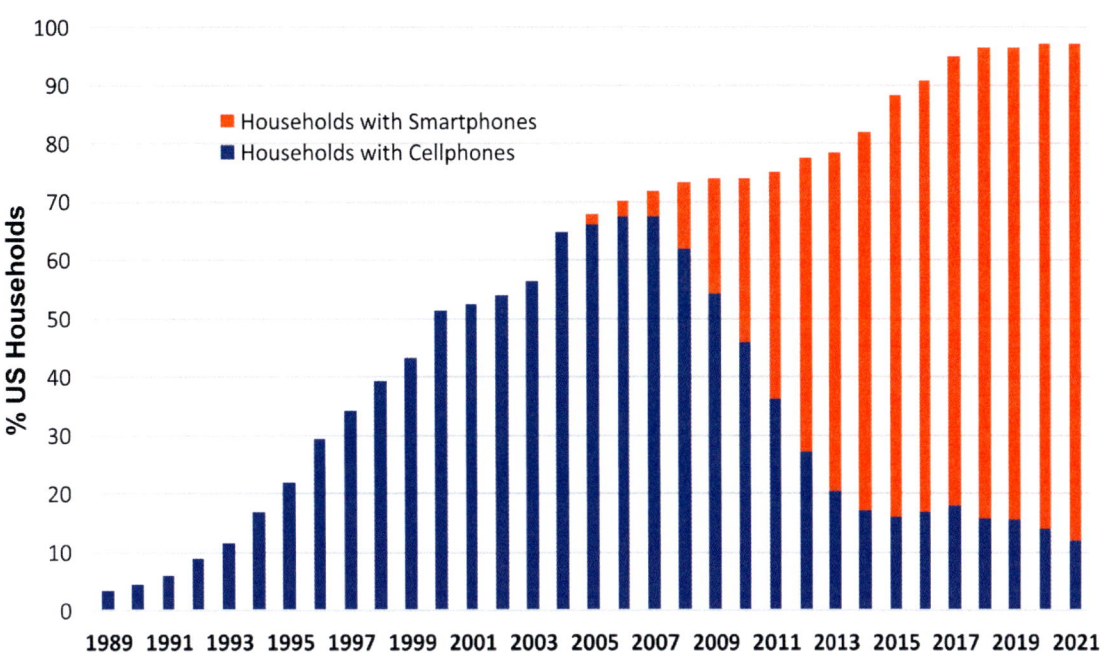

Figure 8.4
U.S. Cell Phone Penetration

Commoditization typically occurs in mature industries, when customers no longer value innovation and new doohickeys but instead expect a standard set of features that incorporates the best of market-tested capabilities. In turn this leads to less opportunity for differentiation-based advantage and more-intense cost competition among companies. Value creation at this stage is largely focused internally on cost efficiency. Companies without supporting low cost structures may be unable to compete effectively under such conditions, resulting in a shake-up among competitors and exits from the industry. The availability of low-cost labor in other countries has led others to outsource production in order to remain cost competitive; domestic employment in some industries such as furniture and textiles has suffered greatly. Many of the exits occur through mergers and acquisitions when businesses are sold to corporate buyers. The result is a smaller number of large industry powerhouses.[5] This occurred in 2018 when Sprint, unable to compete with its larger competitors, merged into T-Mobile. Now there are just three large telecom companies in the U.S.

Figure 8.5
Declining Industries and Their Causes

Declining Industry	Innovation Elsewhere
Passenger trains	Automobile, airplane
Photo finishing	Digital camera
Digital camera	Cellphone, Social media apps
Network television	Cable broadcasting
Cable broadcasting	Streaming TV
Public libraries	Online book sellers
Tobacco	Medical research
VHS tapes	DVDs
Rivets	Welding
Hard drives	The cloud

Decline stage. At some point an industry will evolve beyond the maturity stage, and one possible direction is decline. An industry may begin to decline because other substitute industries provide a more compelling combination of price and value. But ordinarily decline occurs because innovation in some other sector has made obsolete the value proposition that the industry had historically created. Figure 8.5 provides examples of industries thrust into decline because of innovations elsewhere. As end users flee to products and services offered in other industries, the competitors in the industry will experience overcapacity. Companies seek to shed assets and engage in cost cutting in order to survive. This often involves consolidation through horizontal acquisitions in order to gain control over remaining productive capacity, costs, and pricing. The value chain focus of companies in declining industries is primarily on internal operations in order to achieve cost control.

Renewal stage. The alternative to decline is renewal, where innovation *within* the mature industry leads to the opportunity to once again acquire new customers, new markets, and additional business from existing customers. Although one or two competitors in a mature industry might find ways to pump sales by courting niche arenas within the industry, renewal of the entire industry really depends on reconfiguring the industry value chain in one of several ways (Figure 8.6). Methods for reconfiguring the industry value chain include the following:

> **Figure 8.6**
> **Reconfiguring Industry Value Chain**
>
> Redefine industry boundaries
> Disaggregate blocks of industry activity
> Redefine value
> Shift to complements

- **Redefine industry boundaries**. Broadening the definition of the industry's boundaries enables its participants to conceive of new business opportunities by developing new sets of value-adding activities. In the 1950s the railroad freight industry was at a mature stage. Companies that survived the shakeout and participated in the industry's renewed growth broadened their industry definitions beyond purely "railroad freight" to "freight," which caused them to more carefully consider how trucking companies and barge freighters operated. The broader industry focus resulted in defining a new set of key success factors that the railroad companies paid attention to, which in turn prompted a reconfiguration of their value-adding activities.[6] You have probably noticed, for example, that freight trains often load detachable trailers from highway semi-trucks directly onto railcars, instead of using traditional freight cars.

   Approaching saturation in the cell phone services provider market (Figure 8.4), cell phone companies broadened their industry definition by enabling their users to surf the Web, take pictures, download music, instant message, check email and a variety of other services, no matter where they are. Recall from Chapter 4 that any redefinition of the industry will likely result in new sets of key success factors and new competitors! These kinds of efforts require companies to develop new supply-side relationships, develop or acquire new internal capabilities, and cultivate new customer user groups – essentially reconfiguring the industry value chain from end-to-end. In 2017 Verizon acquired Yahoo to drive additional search traffic volume through its network. In 2018 T-Mobile acquired Layer3 to enhance its video streaming capabilities. In 2019 AT&T acquired Time Warner, believing that the rich programming content owned by Time Warner and its HBO channel could generate additional revenue when it is streamed across AT&T's network.

- **Disaggregate blocks of value chain activity**. By considering how and where value is actually created in an industry value chain, companies may identify new opportunities by disaggregating sets of activities that are usually combined together in "how things are done." In the mature dry cleaning industry, for example, the typical retail store combines three value chain activities – management, operations, and customer service. New opportunities are being created, however, when dry cleaning chains unbundle this typical suite of activities. They now place customer service desks remotely in the lobbies of corporate office buildings, where customers can conveniently drop off and pick up their laundry. Placing the customer interface closer to the customer by separating it from cleaning operations helps change the usual configuration of value-creating activities. Similarly, supermarkets have unbundled their customary deli operations (mix, cook, serve) to allow customers to pick up fully assembled, prepackaged dinners made with fresh ingredients that need only be heated up at home. Instead of fully cooking meal items in advance and keeping them warm until the shopper is in the store, this new unbundling of activities captures customers who want freshly cooked meals without the guilt of going out to restaurants.

- **Redefine value.** Redefining industry boundaries leads to the identification of new key success factors and therefore to new value chain activities, and disaggregating blocks of activities can also lead to new ways to create value. A third possibility is to redefine an existing value that is at the heart of the industry, leading to a new configuration of activities. Locked in fierce competition with Coca-Cola in the 1990s, Pepsi embarked on a program that centrally redefined its low-cost approach; its "10X" program changed the focus of the business from "cost per can of soda produced" to "cost per satisfied customer." The new cost concept not only included the manufacturing cost of the product, but also its retail delivery truck schedules to ensure no out-of-stocks occurred, its vending machine technology to provide transmitted data alerts when cans in the machine were running low, enhancing its customer service center operations, and other activities that were part of the customer value creation effort.

    In 2022 many companies think about achieving enhanced value creation through the use of Net Promoter Scores (NPS). NPS is a measurement tool that indexes the willingness of customers to recommend a company's products or services to others. A score results from subtracting "Detractor" ratings from "Promoter" ratings (hence the term "net"). So value today can in part be redefined as not only creating exceptional value, but also eliminating negative value. Understanding the concerns of detractors can lead to the development of new internal practices that lower dissatisfaction.[7]

- **Shift to complements.** Complements are products or services that have a positive effect on the value of a company's own products or services. Apple's iTunes business complements its iPhones and iPad businesses. Video games developed for Microsoft, Nintendo, and Sony platforms all complement the value of the base game unit offered by each company, since the value of the base unit is zilch unless there are a variety of game applications that can be played on it. Disney became successful in theme parks, and then more recently in cruise vacations, because of its capabilities in providing entertainment value. As these examples suggest, generating renewal in a mature industry through a shift to complementary products or services relies on core characteristics of the companies involved. But it also requires new configurations of value chain activities to extend these core characteristics into related (but different) industries. Go back and look at Figure 6.6 in the chapter on resources and sustainability; the platform for new products and services is always extraordinary resources and the activity sets these encompass.

Figure 8.7 summarizes the characteristics of industry life cycle stages we have just discussed.

Stage	Introduction	Growth	Maturity	Decline	Renewal
Type of demand	Experimenters, early adopters	Broad penetration	Mass market	Traditionalists, loyal core	New customers, new segments
Competition	Few new entrants	Entrants & exits, consolidation	Shakeout, exits	Overcapacity, exits	
Strategy	Differentiation	Differentiation, low cost appearing	Low cost, focused differentiation	Low cost	New differentiation
Value creation	Innovation, variety	Scale & access to markets Process: standardization, consistency & reliability	Commoditization, cost efficiency	Cost cutting, asset reduction	Leverage core value chain capabilities
Value chain focus	Choices: internal & upstream or downstream	Extend & refine: internal, downstream	Survival: internal	Survival: internal	Reconfigure: redefine industry, redefine value, disaggregate, complements

Figure 8.7 Industry Life Cycle Stage Characteristics

Length of Industry Life Cycle Stages

Lately it appears as if the business world has sped up, suggesting that industries evolve through at least the earlier life cycle stages fairly rapidly. Rapid progress has been the norm for consumer technology-based industries that we're more familiar with, such as compact disks or video cassette recorders and tapes, each of which moved from inception to peak to significant decline within a period of less than twenty years. Yet this is not always the case. Figure 8.8 illustrates the time periods associated with the rise and maturity of four different technologies that are central to our lives today.[8] The internet and the personal computer are being adopted really quickly after each was invented, but not at a steeper rate than was television or even electricity in the home.

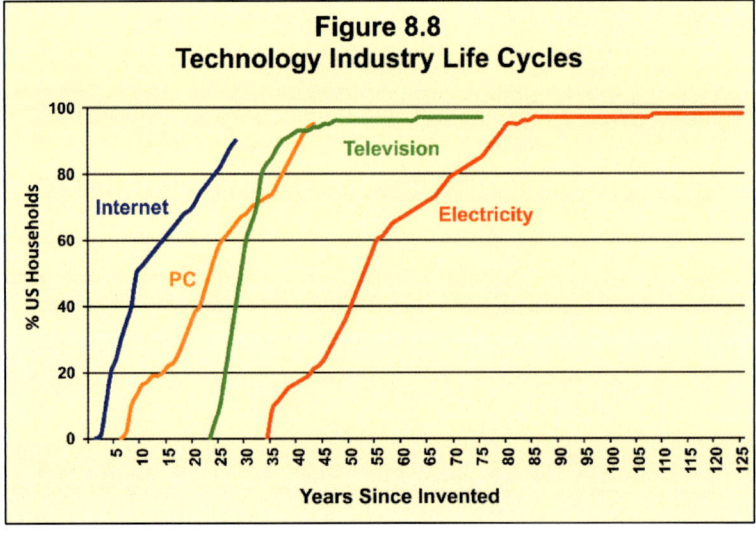

Figure 8.8 Technology Industry Life Cycles

It is still true that not all new industries grow up as quickly as some of these recent trends. Biotechnology, for example, has been around for nearly thirty years, has received considerable venture capital and corporate funding. Yet biotech industry sales are still considered in their infancy. Three factors work to stretch out the time it takes for a new industry to evolve beyond an introductory stage into growth. These include the speed of commercialization, affordability, and the existence of complementary infrastructures. Biotech is a case where commercialization takes a long time due to complex research and government regulation, and where each new biotech application can cost tens of millions of dollars to develop. Cable television was developed in the 1960s, but until the physical infrastructure of cable lines strung through communities was developed, there was no way to deliver the signal broadly.

Best Buy, Part 1

Best Buy's founder and long-time CEO, Richard Schulze, worked in the home electronics retailing business for over forty years. Following a tornado's destruction of one of his small audio components stores in Minnesota in 1981, he accidentally discovered that a larger market existed for electronics retailing when he ran a "tornado sale" that year to liquidate vast quantities of merchandise. Taking advantage of the increased disposable income of "baby boomers" who loved rock and roll and could now afford to buy stereo equipment, and of skyrocketing demand for home VCRs, in 1983 Schulz changed his chain's name to Best Buy. Commissioned sales people "took a more proactive role" in assisting shoppers in the store, and retail prices often reflected the desire of the sales staff to earn high commissions. The chain expanded to twenty-four stores by 1987 and generated $240 million in revenue. By 1989 Best Buy had grown to nearly 100 stores.

Expansion of the consumer electronics retailing industry continued to be driven by new technology coming to market, such as innovative waves of personal computers and peripherals, compact disks, and larger televisions. Like Best Buy, other chains were also growing larger. In 1989 Best Buy nearly went bankrupt after a price war initiated by one of its large competitors. Schulz decided to modify his retail store model by increasing its square footage to generate more floor selling space, providing wider aisles, displaying a wider variety of merchandise, ending commissioned sales to take pressure off the salesperson-shopper relationship, and focusing on a low-margin high-turnover economic model. As the first "big box" discount electronics retailer, the combination was a hit with consumers and suppliers.

QUESTIONS

1. Describe how Best Buy's moves reflected changes in the industry's developments.
2. How does a company know what stage of the industry life cycle it is in?
3. As the electronics industry matures and competition becomes fiercer, what methods of creating value would you recommend they pursue?

FRAGMENTED AND CONSOLIDATED INDUSTRIES

Industry life cycle models ordinarily portray consolidation beginning to occur during the growth stage and then gaining in prominence as an industry moves into and through the mature stage. This is because standardization – and then commoditization – become valued competitive dimensions as an industry evolves. It is often true that larger companies with scale can achieve better standardization of features at lower costs and therefore compete more successfully. This is not always how the story goes, however, and we briefly mention here two other strategic possibilities in industry evolution. The first is how to compete in consolidated industries without benefiting from scale and a low-cost structure. The second is how to compete when industries mature without consolidation ever occurring, that is, in fragmented industries.

Consolidated Industries

Focused differentiation is one strategic approach that can succeed in a consolidated industry where the values of standardization and low cost tend to prevail. The department store industry is in a mature or even declining phase, now dominated by a small number of national chains, for example when Federated and May merged in 2005 and then rebranded nearly all the combined stores as Macy's (Figure 8.9). The increased size of Macy's provided improved buying power across its dozens of suppliers, while achieving greater economy of scale in managing operations. It also resulted in greater consistency in retail execution from store to store across the chain – values on which most department stores competed. Yet Saks Fifth Avenue and Neiman Marcus each occupied highly focused differentiated positions in this same market, by carrying high-end merchandise, investing in expensive store fixtures, pampering customers, and (no fooling) charging higher prices to pay for these luxurious enhancements that create value for targeted segments of the shopping public.

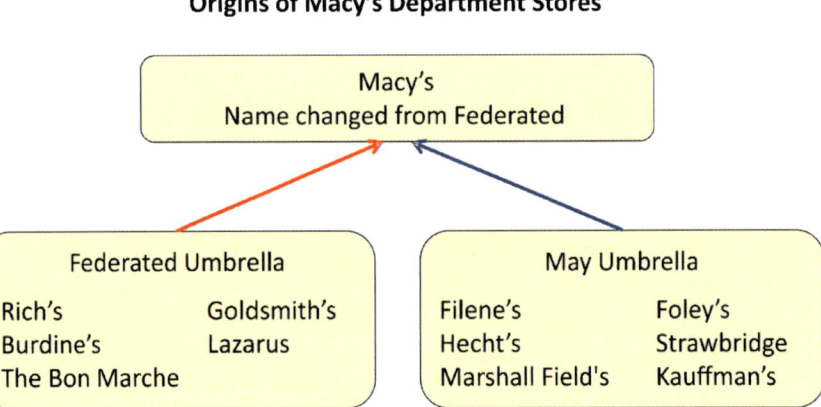

Figure 8.9
Origins of Macy's Department Stores

For competitors to succeed in consolidated industries without following the standardization and low-cost recipe, one of several conditions must exist (Figure 8.10). Although size confers the previously mentioned advantages of scale and efficiency, it also creates mobility barriers. For large companies with a portfolio of dedicated resources targeted at one type of competition, it is difficult to go after another business segment that would require a different set of resources and capabilities. Dedicated sets of resources and traditional ways of doing business also cause large competitors to be blind to new opportunities afforded by niche positions within

Figure 8.10
Consolidated Industry Conditions Allowing Nonstandard Competition

Mobility barriers of large companies
Anti-trust concerns
Blindness to niche opportunities
Financial resources access

their industries. This allows other companies to gain traction and develop defensible positions. IBM considered, but then rejected, the opportunity to get into the personal computer business in the 1970s. Its entire value creation system was designed for mainframes and customized corporate software applications. Management could not imagine computing occurring in any way other than how it had traditionally been done. Of course, this opened the door for Apple. Size may also present potential anti-trust concerns, since as we read in Chapter 4 the regulatory authorities are keen on preventing any one company from commanding too much market power. Finally, because consolidated industries are often characterized by cost/price competition, it suggests that many companies may be experiencing profit margin pressure along with low growth. This is especially the risk for those that do not in fact own the low-cost leadership position. Such companies can be short on financial resources (cash on hand, access to inexpensive capital), which can prevent them from going after another more differentiated competitor.

The brewing industry provides an interesting example of how to compete successfully in a consolidated industry. From the 1970s into the 2010s the beer industry experienced increasing  consolidation. Today the top breweries are global giants usually headquartered overseas. Only one major brewery is headquartered in the U.S., Molson Coors. Along the way, though, came the microbrews that have been so successful over the last twenty years (e.g., Sam Adams, Fat Tire, Saranac, Foothills), defined as breweries with less than 15,000 barrel brewing capacity per year. Microbrews involve higher-cost ingredients, shorter production runs, longer aging, more expensive packaging, lower sales volume unsuitable for mass distribution. These are all characteristics that the major breweries were ill equipped to operate because their business was big volume, with scale-efficient production and distribution. The big brewers were at first blind to this new niche market emerging within the industry. Their resource investments and capabilities prevented them from pursuing it. Since microbrews represented the biggest growth segment in the industry, however, they ultimately had to enter. So they began acquiring microbreweries. AB InBev has acquired Elysian, Breckenridge, Blue Point, 10 Barrel, Four Peaks, Wicked Weed, Karbach, and many others over the last seven years. In Chapter 10 we will discuss the challenges of making and managing acquisitions.

Fragmented Industries

Fragmented industries present an entirely different picture. These are industries in which few large companies have emerged, and consequently where the HHI index or concentration ratio (see Figure 4.13) is extremely low. In 2022, for example, there are nearly 40,000 retail stores offering dry cleaning services in the United States.[9] Yet the two largest companies in the industry have fewer than 1,000 stores, and represent only 9% of industry sales volume. Industries remain fragmented because either 1) there are no mobility or entry barriers to insulate a company from competitive duplication, enabling easy entrance to the industry, or 2) value creation is largely dependent on local labor or conditions for a significant portion of its cost and competitive market position. These two reasons illustrate that fragmentation is the antithesis of consolidation, which depends on barriers to forestall competition and on advantages gained through scalable dimensions of the value chain. Because they behave much more like perfectly competitive markets, in fragmented industries the opportunity to earn superior profits is very small.

A successful strategic approach will involve reconfiguring the industry value chain, usually by unbundling or disaggregating its normally combined parts, into a new system that creates added value and cannot be easily imitated. For example the day-care industry has long been characterized by small neighborhood facilities, low-wage staff, poor benefits, high turnover and thus "barely adequate" child care services.[10] Bright Horizons, which solved the fragmentation problem to become the world's leading provider of child care, hired quality employees and  developed rich experience programs, then used the quality care value to seek corporations as customers. By establishing child care centers in corporate office buildings and staffing them with quality staff, the company created value for corporations that are viewed as better supporting their own employees who have young children.

In the highly-fragmented office supplies market, previously populated by thousands of small independent shops across the country, the industry was reconfigured in an "industry roll-up" when lots of small stores were bought up by large players. Each larger chain unbundled the combined value chain activities at each individual store, and created new value through specialized investments at the corporate level in information systems, procurement expertise, large stores, and retail location modeling.

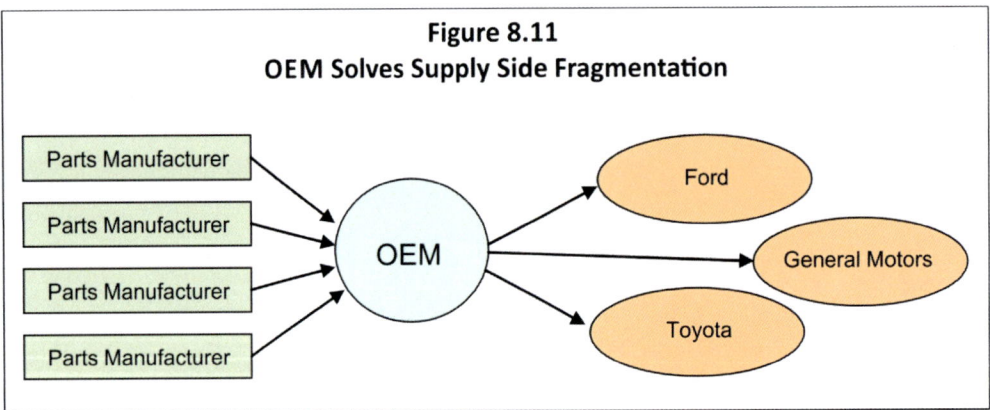

These examples might suggest that fragmented industries largely exist downstream at the "retail" level, but this is not always the case. Fragmentation can characterize the upstream supply side, as well. As the automobile manufacturing industry grew, for example, suppliers of parts and subsystems that were assembled into finished cars remained fairly fragmented (Figure 8.11). Other than minor design differences among competing automobile brands, a piston is a piston is a piston, and many machine shops manufactured pistons which were then incorporated into engines. An opportunity existed to create more consistent quality and provide better control and governance over the supply chain, and thus original equipment manufacturers (OEMs) came into being.[11] OEM companies acquired and consolidated many smaller contract manufacturers, as well as managed additional outsourced manufacturing, creating organizational and quality control values needed by the end users.

ORGANIZATIONAL LIFE CYCLES

In addition to the industry life cycles, firms also face challenges associated with what is known as the organizational life cycle. Like the industries in which they compete, companies also go through stages of development. As a company starts up, it first goes through a conception stage where the idea for the new business is further fleshed out and the strategic approach to the market is developed. Then the company actually "goes to market" in the commercialization stage, developing customers and achieving initial sales. If things go well, the company enters the growth stage as the customer base and geographic nature of the business expand. At some point a maturity stage will be reached, at which time the company's business growth rate begins to flatten out. The pattern of growth in sales that typically illustrates a company's stage of development (Figure 8.12) is familiar because it has been witnessed over and over again, so much so that venture capitalists often refer to it as the "hockey stick" curve.

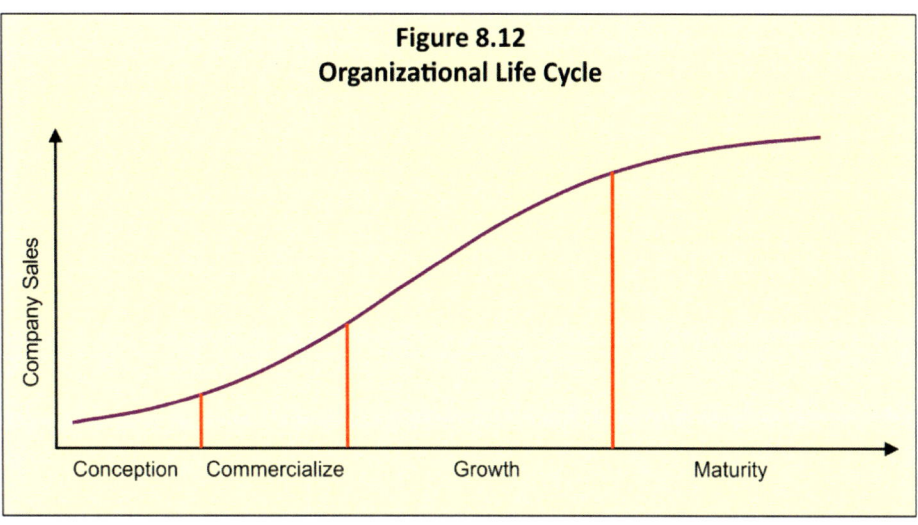

The organizational life cycle concept is useful because it highlights two separate but related issues. Each stage of the organizational life cycle exhibits its own characteristic problems and issues that have implications for the focus of management attention, the development of functional areas of the company, and the development of strategic resources appropriate for the problems encountered (review Figure 6.5 for types of resources). These are the more pressing, shorter-term dimensions that determine a company's success in its present circumstances. But there are also strategy issues that are crucial to the longer-term success of the company, and these manifest themselves at different parts of the cycle.

Life Cycle Stages and Functional Area Issues

Conception. This first stage of a company's development is marked by a focus by the founders on three important elements that the business will require to move forward. First they must have a product or service that works, and so an intense effort is put behind the research and development function. This is often informal and experimental, usually involving a small number of product developers or engineers who have been recruited specifically for this task. Second, the founders must develop a clear articulation of their market entry strategy. This is where some of the insight about both industry analysis and the previous discussion in this chapter about industry stages can come in handy. Entering a mature market populated by large incumbent competitors presents a considerably different strategic problem than entering an early-growth industry where strategic variety exists and no company has yet achieved a dominant position. The strategic approach selected can have an impact on the product/service development effort, for example including more bells and whistles if the industry analysis indicates these could be effective strategically. Third, the founders must seek financial capital so that they are able to support the business appropriately when they do enter the market. Raising capital depends on having both an effective product or service and a clearly articulated market entry strategy. Few sophisticated investors would support a new venture unless a clear understanding of the competitive set and the strategic positioning had been developed, even if the product or service was phenomenal.

The key problems for companies in the conception stage are putting the right people with the right knowledge in place. Completion of the product or service development requires specialized technical knowledge. Science-based companies (such as biotech or medical device manufacturers) must also develop scientific procedures and protocols at this stage, so some formalization of the research and development process may be required. The articulation of strategy requires bringing in people who understand the market and the type of business, and raising capital requires tapping into social networks through which knowledgeable financial partners can be recruited. From a strategic resources point of view, the success of the company at this stage depends on the extent to which the founders can leverage their own knowledge about a market opportunity into these kinds of technical knowledge, human, and social resources.

Commercialization. Having invented something, the company must figure out how to consistently make it or provide it in some quantity. New food product companies are often based on a recipe cooked on a stove, but translating the stovetop recipe to a manufacturing quantity of, say, 15,000 pounds at a time is a challenge that must be met. Then, it makes no sense to manufacture 15,000 pounds or more unless the company has customers to sell it to, so marketing and sales programs now need to be developed. Of course, these efforts should be consistent with the overall strategic approach that the company has previously developed. When manufacturing begins and sales are generated, a need develops for administrative systems of reporting and control.

The key problems that commercialization-stage companies confront have to do with these production and market start-up issues. Discrete organizational functions like manufacturing, marketing, sales, and finance ordinarily come into being at this point. The existence of "departments" containing these functions requires an organizational structure with lines of authority and the allocation of decision-making authority. Hiring the right people for the new functional areas becomes important, so that at this point a human resources position or department is also created. Greater complexity results from the combination of resources that have now been assembled to conduct business.

The company's performance at this stage depends on its ability to attend carefully to the myriad of organizational and operational details that make market entry efforts a success. Manufacturing procedures, marketing efforts, and effective selling approaches should be documented and reviewed, so that the company can make corrections that are needed or amplify on methods that are working. So in the face of greater organizational complexity at this early stage, it is important for companies to articulate carefully what works so that it can be reproduced.

Growth. With market acceptance and the existence of demand for the kind of value the company has created, it will experience a period of growth. The growth stage is an exciting time for any company; however, it can also be a time when great pains are experienced because growth exposes flaws in the system the business has so far developed. For example, to sell in vast quantities requires production in vast quantities. So the scale-up issue from the previous stage is compounded: instead of how to go from 0 to 15,000 pounds at a time, now the challenge is how to go from 15,000 to 150,000 pounds (or more). Often this type of scale-up requires significant investment in physical facilities. The addition of facilities generates derivative manufacturing process and efficiency issues, because the effective integration of large new production capacity does not magically happen overnight. Sales and marketing take on a much more central role in most organizations at this stage, since growth is often driven by the efforts of these functions. Internal conflict may arise, because sales and marketing are focused on selling more while manufacturing is having problems scaling up to produce more without sacrificing quality. Usually manufacturing wants to go slower, while sales and marketing have the pedal to the metal – often promising more than manufacturing can consistently produce and deliver.

This is precisely what occurred during late 2007 when Nintendo's manufacturing division could not keep up with the demand created by the company's marketing efforts for the new Wii. It resulted in significant out-of-stocks at retailers across the United States during the peak holiday sales period. Nintendo encouraged retailers to provide prospective buyers with "rain checks" for when manufacturing would have stock back in stores in February. One CNN news commentator noted, "There is nothing like the squeal on Christmas morning when the kid opens up the box and finds an IOU."[12]

Growth-stage companies are often challenged because they need to activate many types of strategic resources, even as they are constrained by financial resources. So organization and planning take on much greater importance. Growth can be developed through a number of ways – existing customers buying more frequently, new customers added, and new territories opened up for sale. Management needs to make decisions about focusing limited resources on the best opportunities, not fragmenting efforts across many directions simultaneously. The resource problem facing companies at this stage is how to coordinate what has become very complex very quickly. Whereas in the previous stage the advice for the company was to make all the steps and procedures explicit so that best practices could easily be repeated throughout the company, now companies need to routinize activities so that employees tacitly and intuitively understand what to do and can execute best practices without close direction or supervision. Now companies also need to achieve greater cross-department coordination that does not require constant senior management involvement. Figuring out how to achieve coherence across the value chain is critically important.

Maturity. At some point following tremendous growth, the maturity stage sets in. It happens to nearly every business. This is not necessarily connected with industry maturity; it may be that the particular products or services provided by the company have achieved customer saturation even though the industry is still growing, or that the kind of value appreciated by customers in an evolving industry no longer match the kind of value created by the company.

As growth in revenue slows down, growth in profitability will depend upon greater efficiencies and cost reduction. Internal controls become more important, and the roles of the accounting and finance functions become more central to managing for enhanced financial performance. The company at this stage must also find ways to maintain previous growth momentum and market position, which typically involves enhancing R&D to develop extensions to the product/service or introduce a second-generation line of products/services. This is a predicament Kraft experienced in 2019. Consumers had shown a willingness to pay more for innovative and healthy foods, foods that were not central to Kraft's portfolio. So Kraft had recently been cutting costs over two years, including a cut of 9% in R&D for new brands, in order for its traditional brands (Mac & Cheese, Heinz catsup) to compete on prices with other traditional mainstream packaged foods.[13] As its business matured, the cost cuts in R&D presented problems in extending their business further.

Most companies in the maturity stage have become organized using a traditional functional structure, and are characterized by established operating principles. A functional orientation and operating policies are useful for monitoring and exerting cost control over operations, in order to improve the profitability of the existing business.

\<td colspan=5>**Figure 8.13** **Organizational Life Cycle Stage Characteristics**				
Stage	**Conception**	**Commercialization**	**Growth**	**Maturity**
Dominant problems	Innovation effort Strategy design Raising capital	Startup production Hiring Systems	Scale-up production Marketing & sales Chaos & pace Loss of culture Organization	Profitability Internal controls Future growth
Functions important to address problems	R & D	Manufacturing Information Systems	Manufacturing Marketing Sales	Finance Accounting
Resources development challenge	Leveraging founders' knowledge to develop additional resources	Combining resources; Making explicit the processes that work so everyone understands	Coordinating resources; Making routine the processes that work so they can be performed without direction	Developing secondary or complementary resources
Important resources	Knowledge Human Social capital Technology	Human Organizational	Financial Organizational Physical	Knowledge Technology

Figure 8.13 summarizes the characteristics of organizational life cycle stages we have just discussed, including the problems encountered in each stage, the importance of functional areas of the company, and the resource challenges.

Is Maturity Inevitable? The maturity stage is probably a stage that every organization will inevitably experience. A company's "age and size are often perceived as vulnerabilities"[14] because they suggest the company is inflexible and cannot change its way to embrace new ideas. Thus even as products and services move toward obsolescence, the thinking goes, established companies are unable to change things up.

Yet there is some evidence that the transition from growth to maturity can be delayed, with the effect of lengthening the more productive growth stage. Reflecting the twin strategic imperatives of value creation and opportunity recognition that we have mentioned all along in this book, established companies moving through the growth stage can draw on three capabilities to extend their run:[15]
- Re-emphasizing coherence to create alignment across the internal value chain

- Leveraging relationships up and down the external value chain
- Balancing immediate demands with long term performance

Let's briefly describe each of these.

Recall that during the growth stage one of the increasing challenges is cross-department coordination. As companies grow, the usual emphasis is on doing "more of the same" and just doing it more and more efficiently. Decision spheres and activities become departmentalized to achieve that kind of efficiency, and thus become compartmentalized. People stop talking as much to each other across the organization, established supply chains are taken for granted, and customers are known by the values that are currently being satisfied. There is resistance to trying to change what has been working well for a while. This is a combination that does not lead to opportunity recognition or to new value creation.

The solution for management is to re-emphasize company values that led the organization into growth in the first place: mission, foundational strategic resources, and an emphasis on addressing values increasingly appreciated in the marketplace. Often this sort of effort is sparked by visible leadership communications, organization structure changes to ensure that decision making is decentralized, and alignment of incentives to ensure collaboration across the value chain. We will talk more about each of these later on in Chapters 13-14. Rebuilding coherence of this sort can generate greater cross-department coordination and a renewed orientation to ongoing value creation. Actively seeking opportunities for new value creation with suppliers and customers can help lengthen the company's trajectory in the growth phase.

At the same time management takes steps to re-emphasize internal coherence and value creation in the short run, steps should be taken to prepare for the future. This is accomplished by embedding longer-term opportunity recognition and value creation efforts in everyday company activities. These include efforts to move beyond customary methods of gathering market intelligence and to explore the potential for disruptive or even radical innovations. We will discuss these ideas in greater detail in Chapter 9.

Best Buy, Part 2

With the U.S. economy falling into a recession in 2001, Best Buy experienced a slowdown in its growth rate. In 2000 they reported that "same-store sales" (sales in stores open at least one year) had increased 11%, but in 2001 this had dropped to 5% and then to only 2% in 2002. In 2003 CEO Richard Schulz introduced a new strategy named "Customer-Centricity." The new approach involved: 1) customer segmentation research to better understand who were their most profitable customers and their purchasing behaviors; 2) geographic and demographic research to better understand customers living each store; and 3) creating store merchandise and marketing programs tailored at the local level to these specific customer targets. The merchandise stocked in stores therefore varied by location, and customers began to receive personalized promotional mailings. This was in contrast to their competitors, who stocked the same merchandise in every store while employing broad-based general advertising. These new efforts enabled Best Buy to increase same-store sales rates, and to enhance gross margins through opportunistically charging higher prices.

QUESTIONS

1. Do you think Best Buy's initiatives were in response to industry life cycle or organizational life cycle issues? Why?

2. Since Best Buy moved first into this new way of cultivating the customer, would there have been any advantage for Circuit City to try the same thing then?
3. Electronics retailing is now well into the maturity stage. Exits have occurred (Circuit City, HH Gregg), commoditization has developed, and cost/price competition is rampant. What should Best Buy do now in light of this industry's stage?

STRATEGY ISSUES IN STAGES

Some strategy approaches do not fit neatly into the box of generic business-level strategies (Chapter 7), but instead are more appropriately considered in the context of the organizational life cycle. Two of these are first-mover strategy in the earlier stage, and managing really fast growth within the growth stage. A third issue deals with strategic renewal, anticipating what might happen once a maturity stage is on the horizon. We will save this third issue of renewal for the upcoming Chapter 9 on managing innovation. Here we deal with first mover strategy and fast growth.

First-Mover Strategy

A first-mover strategy describes the decision to enter a new market or industry space before any other company has done so. It is about creating a brand new business in a brand new market. So it is really about executing a particular strategic approach for the earliest stage of a business at the earliest stage of an industry.

In our experience students believe there is a cachet associated with being first into a new market space, as if getting there first is always the ticket to a sustainable strategic position. Let's be clear that this is not always the case. There are plenty of examples illustrating that the company moving first into a new market was not the ultimate "winner" in the ensuing competition (Figure 8.14).[16] So we need to understand and balance both the advantages and disadvantages of pursuing a first-mover strategy.

Figure 8.14
First Mover Winners & Losers

Industry	First Mover	Winner
Disposable diaper	Procter & Gamble	Procter & Gamble
Instant camera	Polaroid	Kodak
Jet airline	De Haviland	Boeing
MP3 player	Diamond Multimedia	Apple
Personal computer	Xerox	Dell or HP
VCR	Sony	Matsushita
Web browser	Netscape	Microsoft
Meal kits	Blue Apron	to be determined!

There are two kinds of advantage that can accrue to first movers: timing advantage and size advantage. Any kind of sustainable competitive advantage rests on the ability of the company to use timing or size to create barriers to entry to the industry. Or they can use them to create barriers to mobility when other companies do finally enter the industry.

Possible advantages due to timing can be a consequence of any of the following four dimensions:

- **Standard setting**. The company hopes to be able to set an industry standard as a result of entering first, thereby requiring other companies to follow design specifications that are created by the company. This is risky, because user tastes and preferences are difficult to predict before they have had a chance to spend time with a product. What users ultimately desire is obscured by technological and market uncertainties. Superior quality products are not always the standard that emerges (e.g., Betamax versus VHS tapes).

- **Installed base and buyer switching costs**. By entering first, the company expects to develop a large base of users who become functionally and/or emotionally attached to their product or service. This can "lock them in" and make it difficult for them to switch to competitors. Sony and Microsoft each pursued this approach with their game platforms, which had installed user bases significantly exceeding Nintendo's DS system. Programmers want to write game software for the platform that will deliver the greatest economic rewards. This feeds back on consumers who want to buy game platforms that have the most (and coolest) games written for it.

- **Reputation**. Where product performance or quality is difficult to determine prior to buying and there are no major price differences, customers will defer to the company with the strongest reputation. The first mover has a chance to build reputation before others gain traction. This is an approach that E*Trade Securities adopted early in its entry into the discount online trading industry. The technological trading capabilities of competitors were perceived as being nearly identical, but in the infancy of online trading perceived trust in handling personal investments was paramount.

- **Preemption**. First movers can lock in sources of supply and thus lock out competitors. The clearest example is when McDonald's is first to locate on the busiest corner of a high-traffic intersection; once it owns the land, no other company can occupy that spot. For a period of time in the 1980s Pepsi had an exclusive supply relationship with the popular artificial sweetener NutraSweet, which enabled Pepsi to develop a consumer franchise for its diet soda before Coca-Cola was able to.

It is possible to develop competitive superiority due to size advantages that accrue to first movers. These include:

- **Scale**. When cost per unit declines with larger production volumes in each period, the company that generates a higher volume of business sooner can enjoy cost – and presumably pricing – advantages. See Figure 7.6 and our earlier discussion.

- **Experience curve**. The longer it has done something, the more efficient a company becomes because it has the chance to apply its learning to improve its methods of operation. See Figure 7.7 and our earlier discussion.

- **Scope**. If a first mover is able to broaden its procurement of goods and services faster than other competitors, it should be able to develop stronger bargaining power with suppliers and lower costs more quickly as a result.

- **Network**. When a company can more quickly achieve size, its buyers may derive greater value as a result of the presence of other buyers. Facebook is only as strong as its network of users (imagine how often you would visit Facebook if its network had only 1,000,000 active users instead of 2.5 billion in 2020).

This is a fairly compelling list of advantages. But there are also some significant disadvantages from pursuing a first-mover strategy. These challenge the conventional wisdom that first-mover status always confers sustainable advantage over the long run:

- **Pioneering costs.** It is expensive to carve out a new business in a new industry space. The costs of pioneering include the R&D, building new infrastructure, and educating customers about what the heck you're trying to do. After all, it is a new business in a new industry, so no one has seen it before. Competitors coming in to the market space later on can build on the knowledge gained from your company's efforts, and can generally effect a market entry at a lower cost. The economic benefits to being first must somehow overcome the economic costs of getting there first, and this usually cannot be evaluated up front. Therefore, there is greater risk involved for the first mover.

- **Technological uncertainty.** As is illustrated by the Betamax story and other examples from Figure 8.14, "it ain't over til it's over."[17] You may be first in to the market with sweet technology that is superior on many fronts, but customers are unpredictable. In fact, it is often the case that pioneers in a market are banking on advanced technology of some sort. However, the early consumers are usually the "innovators" and "early adopters," and are in many respects not comparable to the mass market that will follow (Figure 8.15).

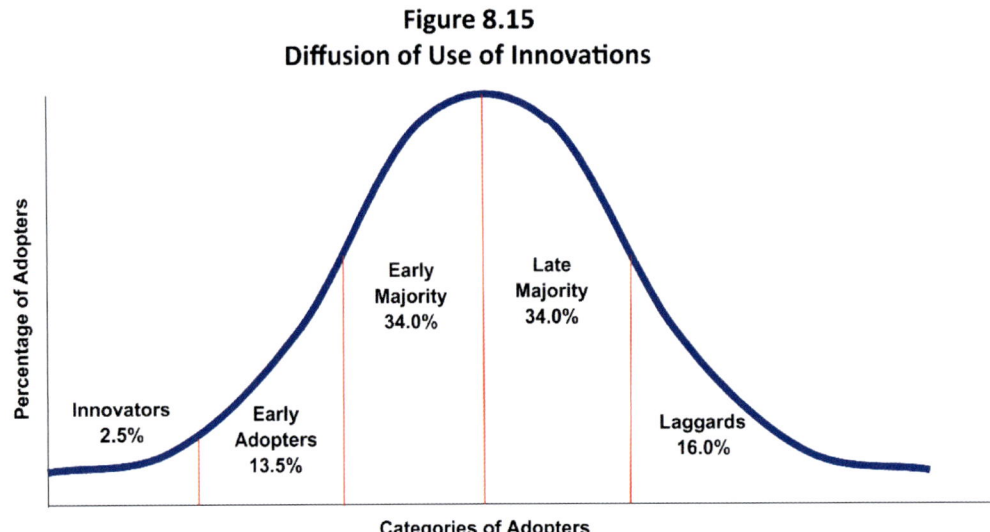

Figure 8.15
Diffusion of Use of Innovations

- **Demand uncertainty.** First movers typically have to make significant investments in specific manufacturing methods and other aspects of infrastructure, long before they know if sufficient demand will exist or even if the technology and standards are what will be preferred over the long run.

- **Reputation can be a slippery slope.** Strong reputation requires consistent investment over time to build, ensuring that products and services, internal process and external communications uniformly tell the story. One slip-up can damage a reputation. And even with best internal efforts, relative strength of reputation can be eroded by strong efforts of competitors. E*Trade's reputation diminished over time with the advent of TD Ameritrade, Schwab, and others.

- **Inertia.** Having entered the market first and then discovered that different standards or technologies are taking off, many companies are still reluctant to modify their approaches. Sometimes this is based on a "sunk cost" argument that extols continuing on because of past spending, and sometimes it is based on the naïve belief that things will get better if they simply "try harder" and do "more of the same." Managers and product developers are often emotionally attached to their ideas, resistant to change even in the face of evidence that other approaches are preferred.

Figure 8.16 summarizes the advantages and disadvantages around the "first mover" question:

Figure 8.16
First Mover Advantages & Disadvantages

Timing Advantages	Size Advantages	Disadvantages
Standard setting	Scale	Pioneering costs
Installed base & user switching costs	Experience curve	Technology uncertainty
	Scope	Demand uncertainty
Reputation	Network	Inertia
Pre-emption		

Fast Growth

Imagine the challenges you would face if your college workload (credit hours, amount of reading and homework) increased by 20 to 25 percent or more in every year! The volume and pace of activity picks up dramatically in any fast-growing organization. It is not uncommon to find middle level managers putting in sixty- to seventy-hour weeks just to keep on top of current activity. During fast growth the company experiences a dramatic increase in customer volume, requirements from suppliers, extended operations, and more internal paperwork flow. It also attracts attention from competitors who observe what is going on and who likely have vested interests in forestalling further growth. It is often tempting to "throw bodies" at the problems of work overload by hiring more, so that some of the chaos that typically reigns can be balanced across more people. Most organizations experience a loss of "culture" during this phase because in the midst of pressure to grow and frenetic activity, employees often lose sight of what it was that bound them together in the first place. The real possibility exists that employees will spend inordinate amounts of time putting out the most immediate "fires" as opposed to focusing on the best long-term moves for the company.

This is why fast-growth organizations need to ensure consistency with the original strategy, vision, and mission. Vision and mission – which we discussed in Chapter 3 – become critical during times when other forces are trying to pull the company in many different directions simultaneously. Refocusing on the business-level strategy that first propelled the fast-growth company into its current "predicament" is also called for. Here the importance of coordination across the value chain is absolutely critical. Despite frenetic activity, by doing so each functional area of the company can be pulling in the same direction and mutually supporting each other.

Fast-growth companies often find themselves challenged to implement the right kind of organizational structure to support their strategic approach. What works for companies that are mature or even growing at a normal rate, however, often does not work in fast-growth situations. Earthlink founder Sky Dayton had planned to sign up twenty to thirty new users a week to his new "dial-up" internet service back in 1995, but found their new internet service was so popular that his company was fielding calls from thousands of interested users a week. He claims it was impossible to create an organizational structure that worked effectively, since the structure created one day was inundated within weeks. Therefore, he cycled between organizing and coping, organizing and coping. But he made sure that he and his team kept reconsidering how to organize on a regular basis as the company continued to grow. We'll talk more about structure in Chapter 13, where we will emphasize the point that structure goes hand in hand with strategy.

STRATEGY DURING CRISIS

Before we move on, it is also important to discuss the unique challenges to strategic management presented by a crisis. Just in the last twenty-two years in the United States we have experienced the September 11, 2001, terrorist attacks, the Iraq war, the great recession from 2008 until 2012, vitriolic political strife with disruptive social movements, and most recently the 2020-2022 global coronavirus pandemic. These suggest that interruptions in the normal course of affairs, unique events, and even globally impactful crises have now become "normal" in the sense that something like this occurs regularly. Strategic managers have worried and wondered about how their organizations should respond. So this brief section provides some guidance.

First, let's be clear what we mean about "crisis." Here we are not referring to a sudden competitive move that has industry-wide implications. Nor are we referring to an industry-wide decline, which we discussed earlier in this chapter. Those occurrences are reasonably predictable, tend to be confined to a single industry, and can therefore be anticipated in strategic planning.

Crisis refers to an event or events that are unforeseen and are unpredictable. A crisis has macro-economic implications, usually for many industries simultaneously and the entire economy. It creates economic disruption. It has implications for both the supply side and the demand side of the business, and thus it will impact the internal operations of the business. Look back at the short list of events, mentioned just two paragraphs earlier. You can see that each of these affected multiple industries or the entire economy, created disruptions in supply and demand, and were usually accompanied by significant government responses.

Despite the regularity of their occurrences over the last quarter century, most companies remain unprepared to deal with crisis. In 2019 McKinsey conducted research among over 1000 global companies on their preparedness and performance during the 2008-2012 financial crisis. 45% of the companies produced negative total returns to shareholders, and the average return among all companies they examined was 0%.[18]

When a crisis occurs, both tactical and strategic responses are called for. Recall from Chapter 1 that tactics refer to how to match up resources and strengths in the short run with challenges and opportunities; strategy refers to the overall direction and organization of resources leading to longer term outcomes. Figure 8.17 portrays six tactical and strategic responses that companies might take when confronted with crisis.

**Figure 8.17
Responses in Crisis**

Type / Actions	Accelerated Decision Making	Interventions
Tactical	Establish crisis management team Simplify organization Value chain awareness	Unlock balance sheet
Strategic		Enhance digital value creation Vertical value chain control

Accelerated Decision Making

Any crisis will produce conditions that won't be completely understood or that normal business processes won't completely accommodate. A condition might affect one or several parts of the company directly, but not all parts immediately. Yet the immediate trouble in one part of the company can have cascading effects throughout the rest of the company in short order. A crisis usually calls for decisions to be made immediately, rather than waiting for the cascading effects to be experienced. But decisions made locally within one part of a company may themselves have ripple effects across the company, without some sort of oversight that takes into account the entire organization.

During the financial crisis, for example, bank credit froze and so loans for mortgages and new cars were hard to come by. For real estate developers the physical construction work was not immediately affected, nor was manufacturing on the automobile assembly lines by car companies. But continuing to manufacture automobiles or homes when credit was lacking would have compounded the problem. When the Covid-19 pandemic hit, Airbnb's rental business almost completely evaporated as travel was suddenly curtailed around the globe. The immediate drop in bookings revenue had cascading effects on cash flow that was funding marketing and other development initiatives.[19]

Crisis management team. So the first step during a crisis is to establish a crisis management team. Usually composed of senior managers from key functions across the organization, this team can consider the implications across the entire company for what might be happening in just one area at the moment. This team can also control all communications out to employees and stakeholders about how the company is planning to respond. In this way there is a consistent, unified message about the company's response.

Simplify organization. The crisis management team can only be effective insofar as its lines of communication with the rest of the organization are direct and rapid. Many organizations deeply affected by crises are large and bureaucratic, with many departments and multiple reporting layers of management. The crisis team must engineer and put in place a method for receiving new and compelling information quickly from all quarters of the company. It is especially important to receive rapid updates from those on the front lines who are experiencing the effects of a crisis immediately. And when it makes a decision to respond to some new condition associated with the crisis, its decision and implementation plans must be disseminated clearly, consistently and rapidly to all affected departments.

Typically a crisis will impact revenue fairly quickly, and in many cases may actually lead to a decline in revenue as well as increasing costs. This, then, puts pressure on margins. This has occurred during a number of the crises mentioned earlier. Therefore the crisis management team should look for immediate ways to trim unnecessary expenses. When we say "unnecessary," this means programs and initiatives that are unrelated to the core business and the company's central mission. Some have called for **zero-based budgeting** during times of crisis. This means no program is funded merely because it has been funded previously, but instead each and every program must justify its level of spending in the current environment.

Value chain awareness. An organizing framework for our entire discussion of strategic management in this book has been the value chain. In Chapters 5 through 7 we argued for the centrality of the strategic coherence that is achieved when activities in different parts of a company's value chain are connected, and better yet when they are supportive and amplifying of each other. These connections represent VRIST conditions that confer the potential for sustainably superior performance, and contribute to an effective business-level strategy.

But often as companies grow larger and more complex, such valuable connections are either taken for granted, or they are tacit because they have become so well embedded in the fabric of the organization. This is problematic during a crisis response. When a crisis management team makes a decision, it must be acutely aware of the cascading effects its decision will have throughout the value chain. Plans to temporarily scale back new product development efforts, for example, will have subsequent effects upstream on suppliers who were building capabilities to provide materials to the company. The decision by Inditex in 2021 to close 1200 of its Zara stores had implications not only for employees to be laid off, but also for customers who must now learn to shop for clothes online.[20] Decision making teams that can account for and anticipate rippling effects throughout the company's value chain will more successfully navigate through a crisis.

Interventions

The previous section discusses how the decision making environment in the company might be modified and accelerated during a crisis. The organizational steps here are all tactical, since they are taken in the here and now and are intended to have immediate effect. Now we turn to specific actions the team should take to intervene in the normal flow of operations. Here there is one action that is tactical and two that are of a more strategic nature.

Unlock balance sheet. Because revenue is apt to flatten out or even decline during a crisis, and because costs may rise, cash flow and cash reserves can become critical for any organization. Any organization seeking to weather a crisis will be more successful if it has financial flexibility. Cash is king. Beyond steps mentioned earlier to curtail expenses in non-core initiatives, the crisis management team should assess how to unlock financial flexibility from the balance sheet. This might include trimming inventories, advancing receivables and delaying payables to the extent possible without damaging customers or suppliers, deleveraging by reducing debt or retooling it with lower interest rates, and more. At the onset of the Covid-19 pandemic Airbnb CEO Brian Chesky went "line by line" through the company's statements looking for ways to unlock financial resources.

The team might also consider divesting under-performing assets of all varieties. This might include plant and equipment, and possibly even entire business units. We will have more to say about divesting business units in Chapter 10. Freeing up financial resources through these actions creates flexibility to act and react to newly-emerging circumstances.

Enhance digital value creation. Of a more strategic nature is the need to enhance value creation using digital technologies. Of course, many companies in 2022 have been marching down this path already. And yet over and over again since the Covid-19 crisis emerged, we have all seen new digital initiatives take a far more central role in the conduct of business. Think about online ordering from restaurants and supermarkets, the increase in online shopping while retail stores have suffered, the wholesale changeover in entertainment from major studios (Disney, Paramount) to streaming. But these were easily imagined efforts, and they were underway already when the crisis hit. These companies simply accelerated their rollout.

Yet the lessons learned here are not lost on other companies in other industries. When the normal conduct of business is interrupted, the flexibility to move to alternative methods can help a company to weather the storm. These sorts of initiatives, to be successful, are not just slapped together and introduced. Each requires a significant rethinking of how value is created and how digital initiatives can enhance – or even begin to replace – such efforts. This is why this action is more strategic in nature, less tactical.

Vertical value chain control. Another action of a more strategic nature involves exerting greater control over the external value chain, upstream toward suppliers and downstream toward customers. If a company has but one source of supply for key inputs, then during a crisis it may not survive if the crisis damages the supplier. Identifying and qualifying additional suppliers might be done quickly, but better off to have taken this action earlier during normal times.

Similar thinking can be applied downstream toward customers. Reliance on a small set of customers can be dangerous, so efforts to broaden the customer base can offset crisis effects. Locking in customers, for example with "rewards" programs or other incentives, can further insulate a business from a potential dropoff. And carefully thinking through how existing methods of value creation might be extended to other customer segments can pay off handsomely.

CHAPTER SUMMARY

In this chapter we have explored the defining characteristics of industry life cycle stages, and assessed their potential impact on company strategy. The five stages are introduction, growth, maturity, decline, and renewal. Strategic variety can exist in an industry in its earlier stages. But increasingly as the industry grows toward maturity, standardization and then commoditization privilege low-cost strategic approaches. When an industry enters decline, renewal efforts are largely focused on either redefining the boundaries of the industry, reconfiguring industry activities, or redefining values that have been important in the industry. All three directions prompt the creation of new value chain activity sets.

Strategy effectiveness is also dependent on the organizational life cycle context. Organizations experience four different stages of development: conception, commercialization, growth, and maturity. Companies experience different kinds of problems at each organizational life cycle stage. Consequently they need to build different strategic resources for each. It is possible that companies may extend their time in the growth stage, and delay the maturity stage, by renewing coherence and proactively working across their value chain to create new business.

Unique strategic issues are highlighted by considering the organizational life cycle. These include the nature of first-mover advantage in the early stage of an industry's development. There are both advantages and disadvantages from moving first into a market, and business history provides evidence of both successes and failures by companies adopting this approach. Fast growth presents another unique context that emphasizes the importance of vision, mission, and strong coordination across the internal value chain.

Crises occasionally occur, and these affect entire industries and economies. Accelerated decision making steps enables a company to be more responsive to newly-emerging conditions presented by a crisis. Interventions initiated by a company can release financial resources that confer flexibility. Digital initiatives and value chain related steps can cushion the effects of a crisis on revenue generation.

Learning Objectives Review

1. *Explain the stages of an industry life cycle and their impact on business strategy.*

    - There are four basic stages of an industry's life cycle. Every industry goes through its introduction, growth, and then maturity. In the fourth stage an industry can either enter into decline or be subject to renewal. Often renewal efforts occur after an industry has passed into early symptoms of decline, when industry participants finally recognize that change is called for.

- Differentiation strategies are particularly appropriate for industries in the introduction and growth stages. This is because standards have not yet been set in the industry and there are shades of variety that appear to be possible.

- Low cost strategies become more important in maturing and declining industries. Here standardization and commoditization of products and services often appear. Therefore cost efficiency, and cost-cutting to maintain profitability or have greater pricing flexibility, become paramount.

- Industry value chain reconfiguration is most appropriate for a renewal stage. This can involve redefining the industry's boundaries to focus on new key success factors, disaggregating blocks of value chain activity, redefining value itself, or shifting to complement products and services.

2. Analyze the strategy implications of competing in fragmented or consolidated industries.

- Consolidated industries often privilege scale and scope which confers cost efficiencies and the low cost strategy. However, large scale companies are slow to move because they are so complex, may be blind to new niche opportunities, must be careful about getting too large for antitrust reasons, and may have constrained financial resources because of their focus on efficient operations. These all present mobility barriers enabling smaller, more agile companies to do well.

- Fragmented industries are usually more perfectly competitive, experiencing a high level of new entry. Companies in these industries can be successful by reconfiguring the industry value chain, disaggregating usually-combined operations or finding ways to aggregate usually-fragmented operations.

3. Utilize organizational life cycle stages and the kinds of problems and resources issues that businesses experience in each to proactively recommend value creation activities.

- There are four organizational life cycle stages: conception, commercialization, growth, and maturity.

- Companies in the conception stage face innovation, strategy design, and raising capital as the key challenges. These require the development and use of knowledge, human, social capital, and technology resources.

- Commercialization stage companies face the problems of startup production, hiring, and systematizing production of what had been ad hoc experimentation in the R&D phase. This requires strong organizational and human resources.

- In the growth stage companies must scale up production, develop sophisticated marketing and sales, and deal with a frenetic pace of activity which can lead to loss of culture. Physical and financial resources assist in operations, and organizational resources can address the people and culture issues.

- Mature companies often experience profit pressures and worry about future growth. Developing a process to gain insight on emerging trends can be especially helpful, and technology resources can assist in providing information and internal controls on existing operations.

4. *Describe steps a company can take to extend its growth stage of the organizational life cycle.*

To extend the growth stage of its organizational life cycle and delay maturity, a company should consider:

- Re-emphasizing coherence to create alignment across the internal value chain
- Leveraging relationships up and down the external value chain
- Balancing immediate demands with long term performance

Rebuilding coherence by emphasizing mission, strategic resources, and value creation can generate greater cross-department coordination and a renewed orientation to ongoing value creation. Actively seeking opportunities for new value creation with suppliers and customers can help lengthen the company's trajectory in the growth phase. At the same steps should be taken to prepare for the future. This is accomplished by embedding longer-term opportunity recognition and value creation in regular company activities.

5. *Explain the risks associated with being a first mover.*

The first mover into a new industry or product category often receives great attention and becomes popular to the untrained eye. But there can be risks to this approach. These include:

- Pioneering costs, where it is very expensive to be first in. Others can come along later at a lower cost.
- Technological uncertainty, where it is unclear at the beginning what sort of standard will ultimately be most-highly valued by customers.
- Demand uncertainty, where it is unclear at the beginning whether a segment will grow sufficiently large.
- Inertia, where once in a new segment with a developed product or service, it is usually difficult for a company to make changes even when things are not going as expected. Here the mindset is to dig in and try harder doing more of the same.

6. *Explain how a company might successfully navigate a crisis.*

When a crisis occurs, a company must take both tactical and strategic actions that accelerate decision making and provide appropriate interventions to normal operations.

- Accelerated decision making
  - Establish crisis management team – to centrally collect emerging information, consider its organization-wide effects, and provide consistent communications.
  - Simplify organization – delayer reporting to ensure rapid communication; cut back on non-core spending programs and initiatives.
  - Value chain awareness – ensure understanding of how decisions will impact each area of the company.

- Interventions
    - Unlock balance sheet – create flexibility with actions to release financial resources.
    - Enhance digital value creation – seek opportunities to enhance revenue through digital initiatives.
    - Vertical value chain control – avoid over-reliance on sole suppliers or small groups of customers.

Key Terms

Commoditization - An industry condition in which a standard set of features and benefits is required for any serious competitor, and in which such features and benefits are readily available from a variety of suppliers. These conditions lead to low-cost competition.

Complements - Products or services that have a correlation relationship with, and can affect the value of, a company's own products or services. For example, iTunes and iPod.

First-mover advantage - The sustainable competitive advantage that is sought by being the first company to enter a new industry or industry segment.

Industry roll-up - The consolidation of an industry when many small fragmented competitors are combined into a larger company.

Mobility barriers - Strategic actions and resource investments that prevent competitors in the industry from imitating the company.

Perfect Competition – A marketplace in which there is perfect information, zero transactions costs and costless entry, so that all firms become virtually identical and no firm earns any profit.

Reconfiguring the industry value chain - A strategic approach that calls for changing the usual sets of relationships across the industry value chain.

Size advantage - One of the possible benefits of first-mover status when entering a new industry. Size advantages tend to produce favorable cost structures and network effects.

Standardization - An industry condition in which customers begin to appreciate a standard set of features and benefits or products or services.

Timing advantage - One of the possible benefits of first-mover status when entering a new industry. Timing advantages tend to build customer loyalty through setting standards, building reputation, and achieving customer lock-in.

Zero-based budgeting – A method of determining whether a program should receive funding. Even pre-existing programs would not continue to receive funding, simply because they have been funded in the past. Instead, programs are funded if they are perceived as necessary to the core strategy and central mission of the company.

Short Answer Questions

1. How do life cycle stages affect the decision process of businesses?
2. Explain why a new product tends to follow a life cycle.
3. Where are the value creation opportunities in a consolidating industry?
4. Why do industries consolidate?
5. How does a fragmented industry offer opportunities for expansion?
6. Explain why a first mover can be so successful.
7. How is being a first mover also dangerous for an organization?
8. How do companies initiate a pattern of continuous renewal?
9. Why is renewal so difficult to achieve for established organizations?
10. What unique issues does fast growth require management to address?
11. Explain how the organizational life cycle growth stage can be extended.
12. Does a crisis affect companies in different organizational life cycle stages in different ways?

Group Exercises

1. Using your knowledge of the latest and greatest gadgets to hit the market, map out the life cycle of a particular product. How fast will it traverse the entire cycle? How many competitors do you predict will enter the market and when? What would you recommend to management knowing that this cycle will most likely play out? What should the company do when the product moves into decline?

2. Over the years a number of formerly fragmented industries have gone through a rapid period of consolidation that changed the dynamics of the industry. Select at least two industries that you and your group believe are ripe for consolidation. What avenues do you think are available for the current players in this industry? How will consolidation change the business model they use? Will consolidation open other opportunities in the industry?

3. Choose a company that you believe has fared well during the Covid-19 pandemic. What steps did it take to achieve strong performance? In contrast, choose a company that has suffered during this time. Discuss both what it failed to do, as well as it what it might have done.

Investor Relations Sites for Companies Mentioned in This Chapter

AB InBev: https://www.ab-inbev.com/investors/
Airbnb: https://investors.airbnb.com/home/default.aspx
Apple: https://investor.apple.com/investor-relations/default.aspx
ArcelorMittal: https://corporate.arcelormittal.com/investors
Best Buy: https://investors.bestbuy.com/investor-relations/overview/default.aspx

Bright Horizons: https://investors.brighthorizons.com/
Earthlink (Windstream): https://investor.windstream.com/home/default.aspx
E*Trade (Morgan Stanley): https://about.etrade.com/investor-relations
Ford: https://shareholder.ford.com/investors/overview/default.aspx
General Mills: https://investors.generalmills.com/home/default.aspx
IBM: hhttps://www.ibm.com/investor
Ikea: https://www.inter.ikea.com/en/performance/download-financial-reports
John Deere: https://investor.deere.com/home/default.aspx
Kontoor Brands: https://www.kontoorbrands.com/investors
Kraft Heinz: https://ir.kraftheinzcompany.com/
Krispy Kreme: https://investors.krispykreme.com/
Macy's: https://www.macysinc.com/investors
McDonald's: https://corporate.mcdonalds.com/corpmcd/investors.html
Microsoft: https://www.microsoft.com/en-us/investor
Molson Coors: https://ir.molsoncoors.com/overview/default.aspx
Nintendo: https://www.nintendo.co.jp/ir/en/index.html
Pepsico: https://www.pepsico.com/investors/investor-contacts
Procter & Gamble: https://pginvestor.com/
Sony: https://www.sony.com/en/SonyInfo/IR/
Tata: https://www.tata.com/investors
T-Mobile: https://investor.t-mobile.com/investors/default.aspx
Toyota Motor Corp.: https://global.toyota/en/ir/
Walt Disney Company: https://thewaltdisneycompany.com/investor-relations/
Zara (Inditex): https://www.inditex.com/investors/investors-and-shareholders

References

[1] The Doors. 1967. "When the music's over." Strange Days. Elektra Records: New York.
[2] Data based on Mintel Reports, Recording Industry Association of America (RIAA), IFPI, Statista.com, U.S. Department of Commerce, and authors' estimates.
[3] Smith, E. 2007, "Sales of music, long in decline, plunge sharply," Wall Street Journal, March 21, A1. Karp, H. 2014, "Artists press for their share," Wall Street Journal, July 21, p. B4.
[4] Mintel Reports and authors' estimates.
[5] Deanes, G. K., F. Kroeger, and S. Zeisel, S. 2002. "The consolidation curve." Harvard Business Review. December: 20–21.
[6] Barr, P. S., J. L. Stimpert, and A. S. Huff. 1997. "Cognitive change, strategic action, and organization renewal." Strategic Management Journal, 13(5), 15–36.
[7] Markey, R. and F. Reichheld. 2012. "Net promoter system: Creating a reliable metric." Bain & Company Insights, February 14. http://www.bain.com/publications/articles/creating-a-reliable-metric-loyalty-insights.aspx.
[8] Cox, W. M., and R. Alm. 1996. "The economy at light speed: Technology and growth in the information age and beyond." 1996 Annual Report, Dallas Federal Reserve Bank. Dallas: Federal Reserve Bank.
[9] https://www.sec.gov/Archives/edgar/data/920317/0001019687070011141/usdry_sb2a3-041907.htm.
[10] U.S. Department of Labor. http://www.doleta.gov/SGA/sga/99-006sga.htm.
[11] Bitran, G. R., S. Gurumurthi, and S. L. Sam, 2006. "Emerging trends in supply chain governance." Massachusetts Institute of Technology working paper. Cambridge, MA.
[12] CNN Headline News. 2007. December 18.
[13] Stoll, J. D., 2019, "What's on Kraft's menu besides cuts?" Wall Street Journal, April 24, B6. http://ir.kraftheinzcompany.com/index.php/company-profile
[14] Malnight, T. W. and I. Buche, 2022, "The strategic advantage of incumbency," Harvard Business Review, January-February.

[15] Ibid.

[16] Teece, D. 1987. *The competitive challenge: Strategies for industrial innovation and renewal.* Ballainger: Cambridge, MA.

[17] Attributed to Yogi Berra.

[18] Laczkowski, K., M. Mysore, and S. Brown, 2019, "Stronger for longer: How top performers thrive through downturns," McKinsey Strategy and Corporate Finance, December 20, https://www.mckinsey.com/business-functions/strategy-and-corporate-finance/our-insights. These survey results and the subsequent outline of responses are from this article.

[19] Rana, P. and M. Farrell, 2020, "Airbnb's rapid response pulled it from the brink," Wall Street Journal, October 13, A10.

[20] Ryan, C., 2021, "Zara's owner bets crisis will speed up fashion's big trend," Wall Street Journal, June 11, B12.

This page is intentionally left blank.

Section C: Implementation – Growth Alternatives, and Competition

Many companies today view the growth challenge as one that necessitates moving beyond the existing business into other types of businesses. They can do this three ways: innovation to bring out new products and services, acquiring new business through diversification, and expanding internationally.

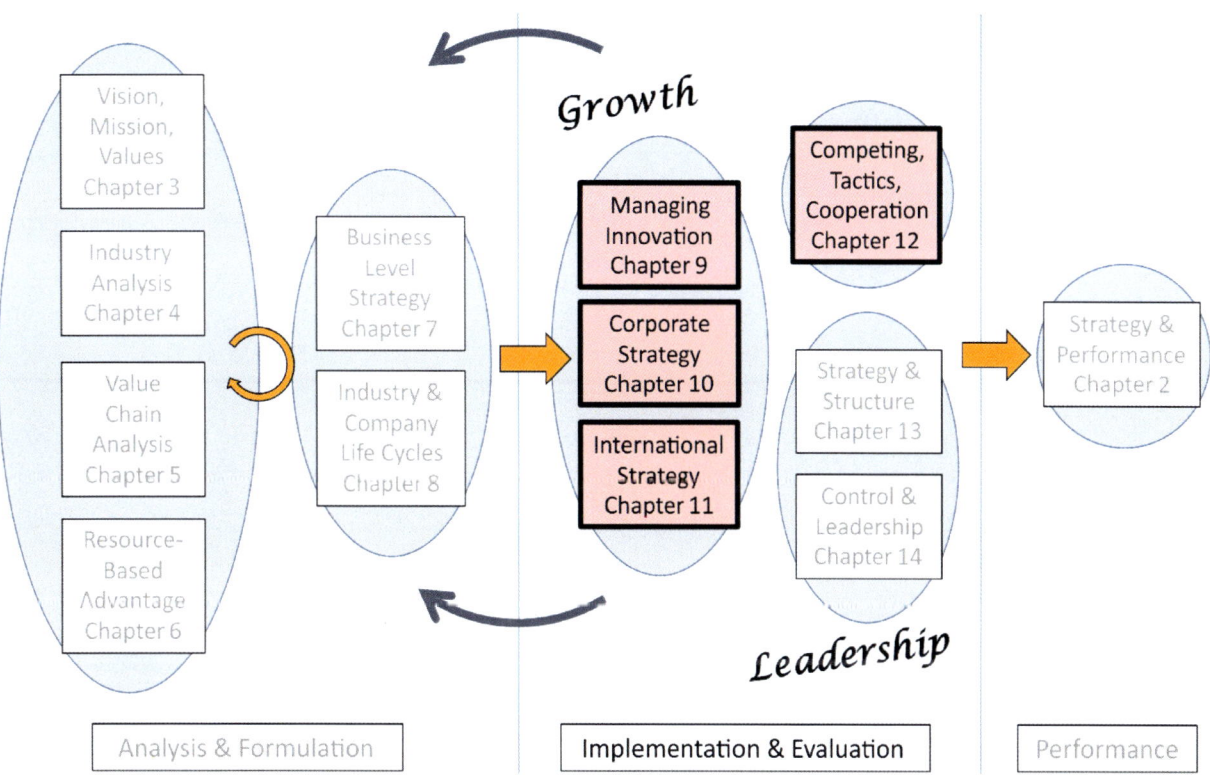

We tackle innovation in Chapter 9. There are different degrees of innovation. These range from incremental using existing value chains and resources, to radical which depends on new value creation routines and new resources. Trying to do anything new creates uncertainty and risk for the company, but there are techniques to use to manage the risk. These can improve the long term odds of success.

One of the key questions that defines strategic management has to do with corporate strategy, that is, the management of a diversified corporation that runs different businesses. Diversification is a major avenue taken to achieve growth. This is the subject of Chapter 10. The chapter provides perspective on why it is so difficult to engineer successful diversification, meaning why it is a challenge to provide positive returns to shareholders. Managing a diversified company that operates in multiple industries presents its own unique strategic management challenges and decisions. So this chapter considers the nature of strategic management from a different perspective, that of senior executives at corporate headquarters.

As companies evolve and seek growth, many inevitably confront the possibility of operating internationally. Chapter 11 explores dimensions of international strategy. There are several motivations for expanding internationally, and there are several types of international strategy. Each depends, again, on the nature of value creation needed. But as we say, expanding from Atlanta to Delhi presents a whole host of challenges that go far beyond expanding domestically from Philadelphia to Dallas. This chapter discusses frameworks to assess these risks, and offers practical advice about issues companies are likely to encounter as they move abroad.

Many executives refer to today's business climate as hypercompetition, which we will discuss in greater depth in Chapter 12. Here, competitive dynamics play a central role in the success of a company's chosen strategy. Competing successfully in markets today is akin to winning in the Fortnite game: it requires performing well on straightforward executional aspects, but also anticipating and responding appropriately to hostile moves and tactics that competitors employ. Here we profile how to assess competitors and identify those most likely to attack, as well as a range of tactical responses you can use if and when they do. Often hostile moves can be pre-empted, and potential competitors can become allies, by engaging cooperatively with other companies. So here we also outline how and when cooperation works best.

Chapter 9: Managing Innovation

LEARNING OBJECTIVES

1. Describe the differences between product and process innovation.

2. Explain the relationships between life cycle stage and resource use that are typical for the four degrees of innovation.

3. Compare methods for recognizing opportunities for each degree of innovation.

4. Describe ways to reduce risk and uncertainty for radical innovation efforts.

5. Detail steps companies should take to enhance overall innovation effectiveness.

Innovation Hotbed[1]

The *Wall Street Journal* annually ranks companies to be included in the "Management Top 250" based upon 33 indicators in 5 categories. One category is "innovation." Out of 886 companies examined in 11 industries the largest concentration of highly-innovative companies is in the consumer staples sector. This includes well-known consumer packaged goods companies such as Procter & Gamble and Colgate-Palmolive. These companies are perceived by customers at excelling in 7 attributes: usefulness, quality, simplicity, coolness, uniqueness, variety, and competence.

How do they accomplish this? One company in this sector – General Mills – has engineered a sophisticated model for developing new consumer food products. The company employs this model across different divisions of the company, including Big G cereals, Betty Crocker baked goods, Gold Medal flour, Green Giant frozen foods, Yoplait yogurt and more.

Ideas for new food products come from many sources. These include primary research with their own consumers, big data tools to gain unique insights into evolving needs, secondary research on emerging consumer trends, drawing on their advertising agencies for out-of-the-box ideas and trends, and talking to suppliers about new developments in ingredient technology.

Every new product idea is written up into a short, objective statement of the product that outlines values the product might deliver. The company tests every new product idea in a regularly-scheduled "concept testing" survey among consumers. In 2022 having now tested tens of thousands of concept statement ideas, the feedback on every new idea can then be compared to earlier ideas that were similarly tested and later became successful products.

Once a product concept is deemed strong enough, food development technicians create prototype products. These are then shared with consumers in "focus groups" to get qualitative feedback on how well an actual product matches up with the original concept statement. Operations evaluates a prototype for how it can be manufactured and its manufacturing cost. Purchasing examines ingredients and their costs. Then a preliminary brand P&L can be generated.

Packaging and advertising development proceed in parallel after preliminary consumer acceptance has been witnessed. Researchers expose prospective buyers to package designs and potential ads to get feedback on their effectiveness.

Manufacturing facilities pilot the production of a new product in small batches. Samples are compared with the original handmade prototypes from the technical laboratories. Produced samples are provided to consumers for "in-home" tests, where data is gathered about how the product is used and liked in everyday situations. In an occasional real world test, packaged samples are also placed on supermarket store shelves to observe how well they will sell.

If all continues to look positive through these steps, a full test market will be scheduled. Finance works out financial projections, manufacturing production runs are coordinated, and an advertising agency develops promotional plans. Marketing works with Sales to select 2-3 medium sized cities to test product performance in a limited area. Distribution is arranged with participating supermarkets, local ads on television and newspapers are scheduled, and targeted internet ads are purchased. The results of the test market are then projected to a national basis, to determine if there would be sufficient national volume to warrant fully moving forward.

This entire process, from idea generation through test market, can take as long as 3 years.

QUESTIONS

1. What are the key management decisions that must be made in this innovation process?
2. Can you make a list of value chain activities and coordination the company engages in?
3. Are you surprised the process can take 3 years? What might you cut to shorten it, and why?
4. This process seems to work well for developing products that are similar to what the company already does. What might the company have to do differently to create something that is radically different?

The previous chapter's discussion on organizational life cycles appears to make managing a business a bit linear, as if a company's only challenge is how to start up and grow a particular product or service. But throughout each stage of the life cycle the strategic imperatives of opportunity recognition and value creation are ever present. This is because, as we have earlier described, industries continuously evolve and competition does not stand still. Industry evolution opens up doors for new business. Competitors will not be waiting around until their product line matures before they engage in their own new business development. Customers' needs and desires continue to evolve. So the pressure is always present to be planning for what's next.

Throughout this book we have highlighted the tension that always exists between the opportunity recognition imperative and the value creation imperative. Think about a new venture starting up or an established company that is plugging along. They track along the organizational life cycle, passing from conception into commercialization and then growth. They make progress because they learn how to manage in each stage better and better, building resources and solving the problems associated with each stage. They seek to refine how they create value, enhancing the activities and resources that are working and jettisoning those that are not. Over time the tendency is to fine tune the business engine, making its past successes more repeatable and reliable.

But opportunity recognition and the consequent development of new business will often require doing things differently. This will usually involve new activity sets and building new resources and competencies, beyond those that led to past success. There is usually resistance to this sort of change across the value chain. Employees will say, "But wait! We just figured how to do this really well, and now you want us to change it all up?" And engaging in new activities that are untried and unproven subjects the company to higher levels of uncertainty and risk.

The tension brought on by the need for innovating becomes thick during the mature stage of a company's development. In today's dynamic markets it is seldom the case that a mature company can continue on indefinitely without its base business beginning to erode away. This type of erosion could be occurring – not because the entire industry is in a state of decline – but because other industry and competitive conditions are obsoleting the value the company's business was originally designed to create. At first the mature stage presents itself as a decelerating rate of growth, then growth flattens out, then finally it begins to actually decline year over year. Some kind of renewal effort is called for (and it likely should have started before the mature stage).

Under Armour provides a perfect illustration of precisely this situation. From 2008-2016 its North American sales grew from $700 million to $4 billion, achieving sales milestones faster than any other athletic apparel brand in history. But competition responded to its phenomenal growth: Nike, Adidas and others introduced performance wear products. As the total market size continued to grow by 36%, however, Under Armour sales declined 7%. Its net income turned negative in 2017-2018 and its return on invested capital (ROIC) dropped below 6%, lower than its weighted average cost of capital (WACC). What happened? Analysts believe that the company has no "moat" afforded by its brand name, no production cost  advantage, no ability to negotiate lower supply prices, no scale efficiency from its distribution system, and that switching costs for direct customers (retailers) and consumers are non-existent. Moreover, Nike initiated price competition in 2018 based on a cost structure that Under Armour could not match. "We think Under Armour has fallen behind on innovation and its product is not sufficiently differentiated…we do not have confidence it will generate economic profits for 10 years."[2] Three years later the problems remain. So what options does CEO Patrik Frisk now have?

Throughout the organizational life cycle, and then especially during maturity, innovation arising from opportunity recognition is critical to the long term growth of the company. Growth can happen in one of two ways: 1) expansion through the development and introduction of new businesses, or 2) expansion through the acquisition of other businesses. An entire chapter of this textbook is devoted to corporate strategy and the acquisitions of other companies (Chapter 10). We will wait until then to go down this path in detail. But research suggests that innovation-created "organic" growth typically generates greater value and shareholder wealth.[3] So we devote this chapter to the strategically-important dimension of managing innovation.

FORMS OF INNOVATION

Typically we think of innovation as something like a new product that is introduced to the market. This could be a new flavor of Cheerios or a completely new type of phone such as the iPhone when it was introduced in 2007. But we should remember the idea we presented when first introducing the value chain concept in Chapter 5. That is, products and services that we associate with companies or experience for ourselves are nothing more than the manifestation of *activities* within the companies that produce them.

This distinction leads us to define innovation as the commercialization of a new way of creating value. And then we can ask what different ways are there to newly create value? Of course, one of these would be to come up with a new product such as that new flavor of Cheerios. But we would also be inclined to include new ways of doing things. We mentioned Championship Chili at the beginning of Chapter 4. The company used the same ingredients as other chili companies, but used a different manufacturing method that resulted in a much higher  quality product. When Henry Ford installed the moving assembly line and started using interchangeable parts, he changed the process of auto manufacturing. He reduced the time to make a single car from 12 hours to 90 minutes, cutting costs and making cars affordable for the first time to mass markets. These examples illustrate that there are two basic forms of innovation that create new value: product innovation, and process innovation.

Product innovation is the commercialization of new value in the form of a new product or service offering. Usually this results from new product designs or the application of new technology. The new value created might be the new cereal flavor, the new giant size package, or perhaps an improvement to an existing cereal by only using non-GMO ingredients (i.e. "new and improved"). New services also embody innovation that creates value. Many banks have incorporated the Zelle payments platform into their online services, making it easier to pay bills electronically. Digital textbooks, such as this one you are reading, used to simply offer electronic text reproduction. But enhanced algorithms now enable students to highlight text, take notes, bookmark material, create flashcards, and share their ideas with their study team members. Product innovation is generally visible to the customer.

Product innovation is usually driven by escalating customer desires or requirements, outdated product design, technology advancements, or new developments upstream at suppliers. It tends to be more prevalent during the earlier stages of the organizational life cycle, and is more likely to be associated with companies engaging in a differentiation strategy.

Process innovation is the commercialization of new value that results from new activities or activity sets within a company, or from the development of new capabilities. In most cases process innovation is designed to either reduce costs through greater efficiency, enhance materials utilization, increase reliability and improve quality, or shorten production time. It can involve changes in the equipment used in manufacturing, the technology (such as computer-aided design software used in product design), modifications in the supply chain and delivery system, new methods used for accounting and customer service, or the new organization of responsible teams. In the 1980s, for example, Toyota became a world leader in automobiles and an exemplar for innovative practices. They excelled by putting into place "lean manufacturing" principles using team-based decision groups in production, total quality management, six-sigma techniques, flexible manufacturing systems, and just-in-time scheduling for car parts and components arriving at their plants.

Process innovation usually manifests itself in later stages of the organizational life cycle. Since standardization occurs increasingly at that time, companies are focusing greater attention on cost structures. The techniques described above can allow companies to not only reduce costs but also deliver enhanced reliability and quality.

As you might imagine, what goes into process innovation is much less visible to the customer. This is because it depends on new activities behind the scenes, and new coordination or reconfiguration of value chain activities. This is also far less visible to competitors, and therefore very difficult to imitate. A recent study concluded that two of the most effective ways to innovate without competitive imitation include the lack of transparency of the company's innovating activities and the extent to which production of the innovation draws on coordinated and integrated value chain activities.[4] So effective process innovation capabilities can present a VRIST-based foundation for sustainable advantage.

DEGREES OF INNOVATION

There is a huge difference between introducing yet another new flavor of Cheerios and introducing an iPhone for the first time. When General Mills concocts a new cereal, they build upon long-established internal capabilities, pre-existing and well-understood channels of supply and distribution, in an industry where they have been operating for a century. But in 2007 when Apple introduced the iPhone – the very first smartphone – it was completely different from anything they had done, and it entered an industry they had never before been in. In fact, since there had never before been any sort of smartphone, the uncertainty of whether customers would adopt this gadget *en masse* was very high. Apple was in the infancy of a new industry (Figure 8.3) going after innovators and early adopters (Figure 8.15).

These simple examples illustrate that there are degrees of innovation that companies can engage in. The range of innovation runs from incremental to radical (Figure 9.1).[5] The differences in degrees of innovation have to do mostly with the extent to which they build on existing value chain activities and VRIST resources, and the extent to which they are targeted at known markets or new markets. We explore each of these briefly below.

Figure 9.1
Degree of Innovation with Implications for Value Chain and Resources

	Use Existing Value Chain & Resources	Extend / Leverage Value Chain & Resources	Reconfigure Value Chain & Resources	Develop New Value Chain & Resources
Incremental	✓✓✓			
Amplifying		✓✓✓		
Disruptive			✓✓✓	
Radical				✓✓✓

Incremental innovation draws on existing value chain activities and strategic resources. Innovation of this sort often extends or expands an existing product or service line by tapping into developed organizational capabilities, supply relationships, and customer relationships. Incremental innovation can bring in new revenue by offering enhanced value to existing customers and by broadening the attractiveness of the established lines of business to new customer segments. In this sense incremental innovation is a sustaining effort, designed to modestly enhance and extend a company's business. Because it draws on existing activities and resources, there is lower uncertainty in the development effort. But at the same time there is likely to be a ceiling on potential gains to be made from only innovating incrementally.

Amplifying innovation is a bit more adventurous, involving a bit greater risk but also greater potential reward. Here the innovating company continues to utilize its existing value chain activities and strategic resources, but it extends or leverages them into a new market or new segment that is different from its established business. Coors beer used to be distributed only in the western states in the U.S. With a world-class brewing operation in Golden, Colorado, it had also developed a sophisticated distribution system across the west. This involved ensuring its beer was only shipped using refrigerated trucks, in order keep the beer cold all the way (no want wants "skunky" beer). When Coors opened up east coast distribution, it had to create an entirely new bottling plant and distribution network east of the Mississippi. But to do so, it leveraged its prior knowledge and experience in managing warehouses and trucking line relationships.

General Mills, the makers of Wheaties cereal and Betty Crocker desserts, leveraged their resources and value chain into the restaurant business when they acquired Darden Restaurants. Darden operated Red Lobster, Olive Garden, and other casual dining restaurants. The restaurant business is completely different from packaged foods sales to supermarkets. Yet at the core General Mills had refined capabilities in sourcing food ingredients through its supply chain, understanding changing consumer eating patterns through its marketing research, and effective marketing through its world-class brand management system. It leveraged and applied these very same activities and resources. This certainly entailed greater risk than simply adding on another cake mix flavor, yet it also offered the promise of much greater returns.

Both incremental innovation and amplifying innovation tend to occur in earlier stages of the organizational life cycle, up into the growth stage. This is when a differentiation strategy is apt to be more effective. It is when organizations internally are focused on manufacturing, marketing, and sales, and when they have achieved good coordination among and routinized their value chain activities. Typically the decision to move into new businesses are based upon traditional, established metrics – revenue and profit potential, and contributions to efficiency or overhead.

Disruptive innovation is quite different, because it is about disrupting an existing market with a different value network. The essence of disruptive innovation is "taking a product and making it simpler and more affordable, so many more people have access to it."[6] These sorts of innovations are typically less expensive than existing products serving the market, and often offer less value than existing "fully-loaded" options provide. They find a following among a customer segment that has been under-served all along, or not served at all. And then as they gain traction, they can lead to the erosion of the traditional market and the decline of companies serving the traditional market.

Figure 9.2 illustrates the usual disruptive innovation dynamic. Disruptive innovation is seen when smaller companies, endowed with fewer resources, successfully challenge existing companies. Existing companies ("incumbents") usually engage in incremental innovation, gradually improving their products and services by layering on additional features and benefits over time. As they do so, they overshoot the needs of customer segments that are not as demanding. Along comes the smaller company that targets those segments by providing something that is "good enough" – suitable functionality at a lower price. Incumbents don't

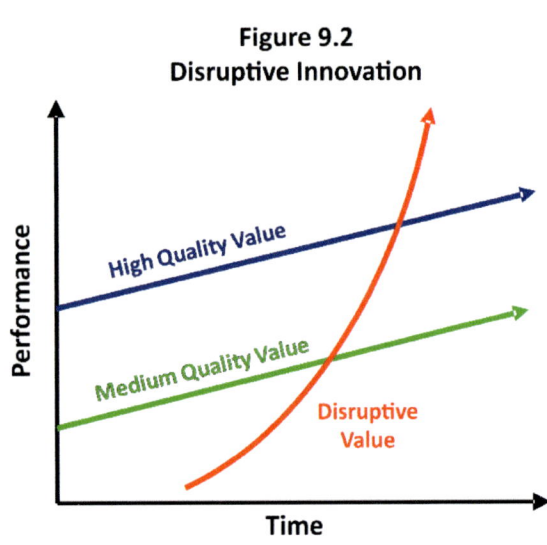

Figure 9.2
Disruptive Innovation

chase after this business because their more sophisticated products are thick with features, more expensive, and more profitable. In time, the disrupters will begin to move "upmarket" by adding quality and more desirable features. At this point the incumbents' customers then begin to switch, disrupting the market.

Strategy scholar Rita McGrath calls these "inflection points." An inflection point is "a time in the life of a business when its fundamentals are about to change…[that] upends the assumptions that a business is built on…They have the power to bring exponential change…10X larger, 10X cheaper, 10X more convenient, and so on."[7]

Disruptive innovation requires a company to reconfigure its value chain activities and resources. They must do this in order to deliver the combination of reduced functionality and lower price that appeals to the target customer segment. For established companies, trying to pare down or cut out learned and connected value-creating activities in the value chain to go after this downmarket segment can be problematic. This is the reason why this type of innovation usually comes from smaller companies.

If you were born after 2000, the odds are you may never have used (or even heard of) the Encyclopedia Britannica (EB). Founded in 1768 in Scotland, the company printed multiple volume sets until 2010, at which point it ceased print publishing. When CD-Roms became popular in the early 1990s, Microsoft introduced its EnCarta digital multimedia encyclopedia. With sufficient material for student use and a price low enough for parents and school libraries to buy, it completely disrupted the EB business. Upstarts Dollar Shave Club and Harry's did the same thing to Gillette in the razor business just a few years ago.

But disrupters need not only be upstarts. Netflix disrupted the video rental business in the 1990s and early 2000s, when they offered DVDs by mail to combat Blockbuster. But Netflix itself disrupted its own market when it introduced streaming video in 2007, at a time before internet bandwidth fully supported large file transfers. To engage in streaming Netflix had to reconfigure how it worked with studio suppliers, build out different internal capabilities for hosting and distributing content, and upgraded the front-facing customer interface. Same market, but it attacked using different capabilities that resulted in faster delivery of films.

Chemistry Beyond the Chemists[8]

Procter & Gambler (P&G) was interested in inventing a new household cleaning product for floors. Mopping is about using "a device (a sponge on a stick) to wet the floor. The dust (it's mostly dust, not ground-in dirt) is then transformed to…fine mud. Your wet stick-mop-thing then proceeds to smear the mud around. Plunging your mop head in a bucket of fresh water helps for a while…until the fresh water is transformed into a bucket of mud-dog-hair-gunk, and the whole process becomes an exercise in cleaning up the mop-smear…. For years, the chemists toiled in the lab, producing failed attempt after failed attempt. At the end of the day, they simply couldn't overcome the 'smear it around' paradigm of mopping."

Out of frustration P&G decided to run "consumer focus groups" and spend hours watching people mop floors. A studio was set up with a one-way glass so the chemists could discretely observe recruited consumers in action. Hours and hours went by. Finally, one elderly woman swept up spilt coffee grounds with a broom. Then she slightly damped a paper towel, stepped on it with her shoe, and rubbed the damp towel with her foot across the remaining grinds to pick them up.

The Swiffer mop idea was born. In 2022 Swiffer will sell well over $500 million.

QUESTIONS

1. Can qualitative consumer research lead to disruptive innovations?
2. Can big data techniques lead to incremental or adaptive innovations?

We turn finally to radical innovation. In contrast to the previous three degrees we have discussed, radical innovation is all about new value chains and resources applied to completely new markets. It entails the creation of new knowledge and the commercialization of completely novel ideas or products. That's why it is called "radical," because everything the company is doing is new and different. For these reasons there is much greater uncertainty, and consequently much greater risk, associated with radical innovation.

While disruptive innovation is linked to reconfiguring value chain activities and resources and to low-end market encroachment, radical innovation depends on creating knowledge of two types: new knowledge about a market, and knowledge about new organizational capabilities. Whereas incremental and amplifying innovation helps firms to stay competitive in the short-term, radical innovation has a much longer time horizon. It will likely involve cannibalizing current products, altering the relationship between customers and suppliers, and creating completely new product categories.

Radical innovation is usually initiated by changes in technology, and more often than not the technology comes from outside the industry. Companies that employ new cutting edge technology must not only determine how it can be used productively to engineer products and services, but must also invent new routines and capabilities that maximize the new possibilities. For over 100 years John Deere has sold basic farm equipment to middle America. But with the advent of big data and parallel technology capabilities, the company came to realize a new opportunity existed through radical innovation. Embedded hardware and software in tractors, combines, and other field equipment now collects data on crops, yields and fertilizer use. Connected wirelessly to the company's massive database which houses "the most encompassing eco-system for agricultural products,"[9] John Deere can help farmers solve problems they are experiencing locally by tapping into data collected from thousands of farms around the world. Farmers can now better manage each individual field for maximum productivity.

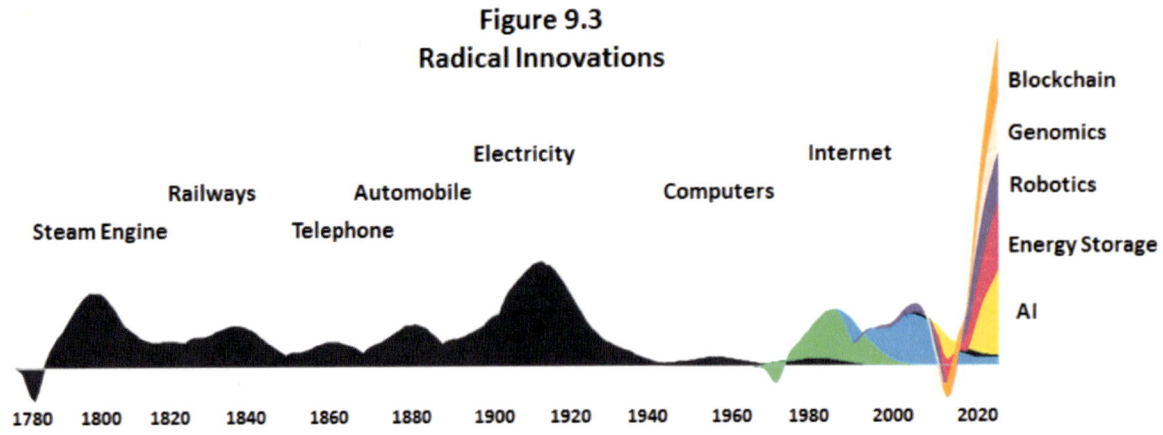

Figure 9.3
Radical Innovations

Figure 9.3 portrays a history of radical innovations over time.[10] In each case the technology developed elsewhere forever changed companies and industries in which it was then used. Looking at the now-emerging technologies on the right side of this depiction (e.g. blockchain, artificial intelligence, etc.), the future promises radical innovation in industry after industry as these are better understood and deployed. This is a heads-up for companies.

Both disruptive and radical innovation can occur at any time, but they are usually seen in the latter stages of the organizational life cycle. This is because they each in large part depend on the identification of new markets or segments. As companies commercialize and grow, they tend to be more internally-focused in getting things right, becoming better at what they do, and expanding their established lines of business. But as growth becomes more difficult due to industry and competitive forces, and especially as maturity is reached, they will be increasingly interested in identifying new opportunities for long term future growth.

Disruptive and radical innovation are also the most difficult kind of innovation to be successful at. They each require a significant effort to learn and develop new knowledge about emerging markets, evolving technology, and how the company might respond. The market, the product, and the strategy are all unknown at the outset. Disruptive and radical innovation each involve changing or creating new value chain activity sets and capabilities. They each challenge the existing culture and system of incentives that employees have come to know. All of these efforts will take time. It subjects the entire enterprise to greater uncertainty and therefore greater risk. Risk tends to cause people to resist, or at least to go slow.

For these reasons understanding *when* disruptive or radical innovation is appropriate, and *how* to manage the innovation development process, will become a critical VRIST-based capability in the future. We tackle these ideas next.

OPPORTUNITY RECOGNITION AND EVALUATION

There is an order of magnitude difference between opportunity recognition for incremental and amplifying innovation versus opportunity recognition for disruptive and radical innovation. Identifying incremental and amplifying innovation opportunities tends to involve an "inside-out" approach: begin with the existing set of resources and capabilities to identify ways in which they may be more broadly and productively put to use. Ideas for new business arise through identifying new combinations of existing products, processes, and technology, and from predictable changes and evolution of the industry and competition. It is usually a more "left brain" process to identify such opportunities: information gathering from known sources, analysis using established methods, and evaluation using traditional metrics. New business development efforts here usually seek to build on the company's existing mission.

Recognizing disruptive and radical innovation opportunities involves a fundamentally different process. Searching for opportunities for these degrees of innovation can best be described as an "outside-in" approach: look to novel external events and developments (especially outside the industry), use these to generate interesting ideas for new value creation, and then specify how much existing routines, resources, and capabilities might have to change. Since each breaks the mold of the existing business, they may serve to broaden the company's mission or be used to navigate toward a long-term event horizon (see Figure 3.4).

Since disruptive and radical innovations each address new markets that are as yet undeveloped and untapped, there is little market data that can directly point to or predict a new opportunity. Where do you go to look for such opportunities, then? Former Intel CEO Andy Grove used to say that "snow melts from the edges."[11] So if you want to see where and how the existing state of affairs (the snowfield) is about to change, and how fast, get out of its center. Go to its edges and look beyond the snow. By purposefully seeking out new and different perspectives compared to the customary view from inside a company or an industry, one can gather and better sense "weak signals" of impending inflection points (disruption) and better identify promising new technologies and their possible uses (radical).

Figure 9.4 provides some guidance for this sort of effort.[12] This is not just a guide for senior executives, but for all employees who are involved in strategy. The challenge to identify and recognize frame-breaking opportunities is not the province of just the executive suite. Here "right brain" skills can often be usefully employed at all levels of the organization. These include exploring in an unstructured way, generating multiple ideas out of a single reference point, looking for associations between unrelated fields, counterfactual thinking, and analogical reasoning.

Figure 9.4
How to Identify Disruption Inflections and Opportunities for Radical Innovation

1. Get out of the corner office, and listen to what employees on the firing line think and see.
2. Get out of the building, meet with customers to learn what they think and see.
3. Seek out and talk to representatives (and customers) of the future.
4. Seek diversity of thought, opinion, and experience.
5. Develop stories and scenarios of the future, then play them back to the present to identify when and how critical elements change.
6. Create incentives to locate and share new information, and to try new ideas.
7. Embrace and explore evidence contradicting current assumptions. Encourage counterfactual and analogical thinking, devil's advocacy.
8. Proactively solicit ideas from throughout the organization; make small investments to support their gestation.

OK, let's say that a company uses the above techniques and begins to identify a number of ideas that could present significant opportunity. Now what? How are such ideas evaluated? The problem for disruptive and radical innovation efforts is that traditional metrics used in established industries are often not very useful. By definition these degrees of innovation are going after target markets that do not yet exist. When Microsoft initiated its digital encyclopedia effort, nothing else existed that could provide insight on its odds of success. Historical sales of 22-volume printed sets would not have been useful at all. When John Deere went down the path of big data and embedded technology in tractors, there was nothing else like this anywhere and the techniques had never been tried. Part of the problem is that the disruption inflection points and the advent of game-changing technologies take time to come into view more clearly. At first there are only weak signals, or applications elsewhere that are difficult to understand.

The solution to this problem is four-fold: portfolios, small bets, options, and platforms.

- **Portfolios**. First, at any time companies should be managing a portfolio of new business development efforts. The portfolio should encompass a range of developmental projects that span the degrees of innovation, from incremental to radical. Such a portfolio balances great uncertainty with low uncertainty, and long time frame to fruition with shorter time frame. Since for disruptive and radical innovation efforts the opportunity will only reveal itself over time, as the weak signals become stronger and the emergent technologies become clearer, the portfolio approach provides the company the ability to continue to stage new business entries.

- **Small bets**. Second, the portfolio approach enables the company to make a series of small bets that "test the waters" across a variety of possible initiatives. A series of small bets to investigate a range of new ideas enables the company to learn without incurring great risk on any initial foray. Companies not only learn through small wins in such bets, but also in small losses. Small wins help confirm and validate emerging data and a new approach, and small losses help the company avoid going down unproductive paths.

- **Options**. Options involves establishing checkpoints or milestones for each small bet, and then evaluating whether continued funding is warranted for each. Since traditional evaluation metrics are not very useful at the beginning of disruptive and radical innovation efforts, interim checkpoints for these projects can be established based on currently-available data. As these opportunities are better revealed over time, more rigorous checkpoints can be developed. And when each project achieves its milestone, then further funding can be provided.

- **Platforms**. Instead of focusing on a series of discrete new business opportunities, many companies today – especially those in industries where research and development costs can skyrocket – seek to focus on platform innovations. A platform represents a base upon which several promising new lines of business can be developed. Refer back to Figure 6.6 and our discussion of resources and capabilities. For example one nanotechnology research group is focusing on the integration of nanostructures into devices for light gathering. This is a platform that can then be developed into high-performance lighting systems for different markets: the home, office, and transportation sector uses. When a company such as Microsoft introduces a "developer application toolkit" for its Xbox game hardware (specifications for developers to use in writing applications to work with the hardware), the toolkit essentially represents a kind of platform off of which dozens and dozens of new products can be developed. Platform development represents a more efficient way of making R&D investments, since it promises multiple possible outcomes from a singular direction.

MANAGING THE PROCESS

Successful innovation requires an entire, coordinated organizational effort. As we have seen, creating new value is accomplished by involving the company's value chain – either building on it, leveraging it, reconfiguring it, or changing it completely. To get to the desirable outcome of success and growth any innovation effort needs "all hands on deck" – up and down the hierarchy, and all across the value chain. Even though specific teams may be placed in charge of discrete innovation projects, as part of a portfolio of initiatives, managing innovation requires practical steps be taken that set the tone for the entire organization and provide proper company-wide support. These include the following

1. Establish a culture of innovation. Being innovative should be a company-wide value. It should be visible to all employees, and should be reinforced regularly in many ways.

    - The value of being innovative should be in the company's statement of principles – words and ideas that help guide every employee's behavior on a day to day basis.
    - Senior management and team leaders should lead by example, modeling these same behaviors.
    - Establish informal and formal mechanisms or channels to feed forward ideas, so that employee voices can be heard and their insights taken seriously.
    - Publicly celebrate small wins and small losses as learning opportunities. Acknowledging those who tried something new can have broad impact.

As companies move into the mature stage, bureaucracy and formalization often reign. These are characteristics that do not support a culture of innovation. Some time ago Rosabeth Moss Kanter described efforts that can stifle innovation efforts (Figure 9.5).[13]

Figure 9.5
Rules For Stifling Innovation Efforts Inside A Company

1. Regard any new idea from below with suspicion – because it's new, and because it's from below.
2. Insist that people who need your approval to act must first go through several other levels of management to get their signatures.
3. Ask departments or individuals to challenge and criticize each other's proposals. That saves you the job of deciding; you just pick the survivor.
4. Express your criticisms freely, and withhold your praise. Let them know they can be fired at any time.
5. Control everything carefully. Make sure people count anything that can be counted, frequently.
6. Assign to lower level managers, in the name of delegation and participation, responsibility for figuring out how to implement threatening decisions you have already made. Get them to do it quickly.
7. Above all, never forget that you (the higher ups) already know everything important about this business.

Management must reengineer the organizational structure and incentive systems to encourage experimentation and innovation and to avoid punishing such efforts that do not succeed. Chapter 13 will offer greater insight on structure and systems that provide the appropriate kind of environment for encouraging innovation.

2. Human resources support. As the gatekeepers for everyone who works in different parts of the company value chain, HR policies can have a significant positive impact.

    - Hiring new employees who are naturally curious and resourceful, non-linear thinkers, who embrace novelty, and who are connected.
    - Annual reviews should reward questioning, being observant, experimenting, and bridging across networks to source new ideas in a constructive way.

3. Creating innovation teams for success. Closest to the actual day-to-day management of innovation efforts, proper team composition can heighten the prospects for success.

- Team members with previous experience in successful innovation projects.
- Cross-functional representation, since any new business must be integrated into and coordinated across the internal value chain.
- Ensure the team members have access to suppliers, customers, and operational areas. This proximity keeps the team more connected with the marketplace.
- Authority and budget provided to the team to explore, experiment, play. Separate the budget request / approval process from the ordinary annual plan justification.
- Separate team member personal performance from the performance of the innovation itself. Since most new ideas do not succeed, this removes the stigma from failure.

4. Collaboration and cooperation with partners. Not every degree of innovation can always be successfully engineered from within the company. Consider strategic partnerships or joint venture agreements with other companies, to cooperate on developing new business. We return in Chapter 12 to a more detailed discussion of cooperation and its dimensions.

Managing in Markets: Question for Class Discussion

Remarks by Senator Amy Klobuchar (D, Minnesota) on December 15, 2021, at Senate Judiciary Subcommittee on Competition Policy, Antitrust, and Consumer Rights:

"Innovation is part of the American spirit. It is the core of the American spirit. Innovation generates new opportunities and new hopes for businesses, workers, and families. Breakthroughs in science and technology have given us the vaccines that are getting us through the pandemic and driving the development of clean energy solutions to take on the climate crisis that we see every day, as my state is getting a record heat wave and thunderstorms in the middle of December today. Emerging technologies like artificial intelligence are driving innovation across our economy. Of course, some of our economy's largest companies began as start-ups with new innovations and we continue to see innovations. But we also have to remember that innovation is all about competition and bringing in new players to innovate. That if we just simply have monopolies, over time, we do not get the innovations that we need….But in recent years, we have seen the growth of monopoly power across the American economy — from cat food to caskets. Dominant players are using their power to maintain monopoly positions and thwart competition….Why invest in innovation, why spend on research and development, why start a new business if the markets are controlled by a handful of dominant companies that control access to customers and have the power to suppress new businesses? Monopoly power threatens to choke off innovation."

Do you believe there is a monopoly problem in the economy that chokes off innovation?

CHAPTER SUMMARY

As companies move to the latter stages of growth and into maturity, innovation becomes increasingly important. Product and process innovation are the two types; process innovation by its nature can more easily confer advantage because it is less visible. Companies should manage a portfolio of innovation projects across four degrees of innovation – incremental, amplifying, disruptive, and radical. Each is characterized by the extent to which it uses the existing value chain and resource base, and the extent to which it targets existing or new markets.

Effective innovation depends on opportunity recognition capabilities. Incremental and amplifying innovations are ordinarily identified using existing sources of information and customer feedback, and are evaluated using customary and established performance criteria. Disruptive, and especially radical, innovations are often identified using non-traditional methods of gathering data about markets that do not yet exist. These are more risky ventures because there is greater uncertainty. Risk can be managed by relying on portfolios, small bets, options, and platform development efforts.

Managing innovation calls for appropriate structure, leadership and incentive systems to enhance the prospects for success. Culture plays a central role in a company embracing innovation on an ongoing basis, and HR can play a supportive role in its hiring qualifications and practices. Cross-functional teams help to bridge the value chain in development efforts. Collaboration and cooperation with external partners may occasionally be warranted.

Learning Objectives Review

1. *Describe the differences between product and process innovation.*

- Product innovation is the commercialization of new value in the form of a new product or service offering. It is usually driven by escalating customer desires or requirements, outdated product design, technology advancements, or new developments upstream at suppliers. It tends to be more prevalent during the earlier stages of the organizational life cycle, and is more likely to be associated with companies engaging in a differentiation strategy.

- Process innovation is the commercialization of new value that results from new activities or activity sets within a company, or from the development of new capabilities. It is usually designed to either reduce costs through greater efficiency, enhance materials utilization, increase reliability and improve quality, or shorten production time. It ordinarily manifests itself in later stages of the organizational life cycle.

2. *Explain the differences in life cycle stage and resource use that are typical for the four degrees of innovation.*

- Incremental innovation. Occurs in early life cycle stages. Targets known markets. Uses existing value chain activity sets and resources.

- Amplifying innovation. Occurs in middle life cycle stages. Targets known markets. Extends or leverages existing value chain activity sets and resources.

- Disruptive innovation. Can occur anytime, but usually seen in later life cycle stages. Targets unknown market segments. Reconfigures value chain activity sets and resources.

- Radical innovation. Can occur anytime, but usually seen in later life cycle stages. Targets new unknown market. Requires new value chain activity sets and resources.

3. *Compare methods for recognizing opportunities for each degree of innovation.*

- Incremental and amplifying innovations. Uses an "inside-out" approach seeking to identify ways to extend existing resources and capabilities in predictable ways. This is a "left brain" process that relies on gathering information using established sources.

- Disruptive and radical innovations. Uses an "outside-in" approach that begins with novel external developments, and then examines how existing resources and capabilities must be changed or newly-developed to address them. This is a "right brain" process that purposely seeks out different perspectives and challenges conventional thinking.

4. *Describe ways to reduce risk and uncertainty for radical innovation efforts.*

- Portfolios. Have a portfolio of innovation projects, from incremental to radical, in development at any one time.

- Small bets. Fund a range of new ideas with limited funding, generating small wins and small losses to facilitate learning.

- Options. Establish checkpoints and hurdles for each small bet. Continue to fund those that look promising. Discard those that do not.

- Platforms. Focus innovation on a base from which multiple new businesses may be created.

5. *Detail steps companies should take to enhance overall innovation effectiveness.*

- Establish a culture of innovation. Experimentation and the free flow of ideas should be visible, elevated, and rewarded.

- Support the culture and the efforts through human resources. Hire resourceful non-linear thinkers who are curious. Annual reviews should reward behaviors associated with innovation.

- Create cross-functional innovation teams. Teams with experienced and connected members should have the authority to explore and experiment. Annual reviews should separate personal performance from the success of a particular project.

- Collaborate and cooperate with external partners, as needed. Occasionally, innovation depends on resources and capabilities that a trusted partner can provide.

Key Terms

Amplifying innovation – Extends or leverages existing value chain and resources into a new market or new segment that is different from its established business.

Disruptive innovation - Reconfigure value chain activities and resources in order to deliver the combination of reduced functionality and lower price to a customer segment in an existing market that has been under-served all along or not served at all.

Incremental innovation – draws on existing value chain and resources. Extends or expands an existing product or service line by tapping into developed organizational capabilities, supply relationships, and customer relationships.

Innovation - The commercialization of a new way of creating value.

Options - An investment approach that places a small initial bet on an initiative, with the opportunity to invest further if the initiative makes favorable progress and reaches positive milestones.

Process innovation – The commercialization of new value that results from new activities or activity sets within a company, or from the development of new capabilities.

Product innovation – The commercialization of new value in the form of a new product or service offering.

Radical innovation – Creation of new knowledge and the commercialization of completely novel ideas or products in new markets. It entails creating new value chain, resources and capabilities.

Short Answer Questions

1. Which is more important, product innovation or process innovation?
2. Which degree of innovation should a company pursue, incremental innovation or radical innovation?
3. Give an example of a successful company effort for each degree of innovation: incremental, amplifying, disruptive, radical.
4. What are the greatest challenges for radical innovation, and how can these be overcome?

Group Exercises

1. The founder of Staples hatched the idea for the business by analogizing office supply retailing as a grocery store – broad selection, low prices, high volume. In 2022 what type of business opportunity in some other industry can you recognize by using supermarkets as an analogy?

2. Make a list of specific ways in which "big data" and "analytics" may be used to identify emerging trends and new business opportunities.

3. Read the most recent Microsoft annual report and 10-K filing. Make a list of each type of innovation that the company has engaged in over the last five years.

4. What company do you believe is the most innovative, and why? Discuss your choice and rationale with your group.

Investor Relations Sites for Companies Mentioned in This Chapter

Apple: https://investor.apple.com/investor-relations/default.aspx
Ford: https://shareholder.ford.com/investors/overview/default.aspx
General Mills: https://investors.generalmills.com/home/default.aspx
John Deere: https://investor.deere.com/home/default.aspx
Microsoft: https://www.microsoft.com/en-us/investor
Molson Coors: https://ir.molsoncoors.com/overview/default.aspx
Netflix: https://ir.netflix.net/ir-overview/profile/default.aspx
Procter & Gamble: https://pginvestor.com/
Under Armour: https://about.underarmour.com/investor-relations
Toyota Motor Corp.: https://global.toyota/en/ir/
Zelle (Early Warning Services): https://www.earlywarning.com/about

References

[1] Wartzman, R. and K. Tang, 2021, "Which industry excels at innovation? You'd be surprised," Wall Street Journal, February 22, R8.
[2] Sadfer, K., 2019, "Under Armour reports sales decline in North America," Wall Street Journal, July 30, B1. Swartz, D., 2019, "Under Armour lacks a competitive edge as it struggles to overcome self-inflicted wounds," Morningstar, August 2. Swartz, D. 2021, " Activewear sales have soared during the pandemic, but Under Armour lacks a competitive advantage," Morningstar, December12.
[3] Goedhart, M. and T. Koller, 2017, "The value premium of organic growth," McKinsey Quarterly, January. Ahuja, K., L. H. Segel and J. Perrey, 2017, "The roots of organic growth," McKinsey Quarterly, August.
[4] See Cohen W. M., Nelson R. R., and Walsh J. P., 2000, "Protecting their intellectual assets: Appropriability conditions and why US Manufacturing firms patent (or not)," NBER Working Paper No. W7552. Patents are generally regarded as quite important in protecting innovation, however this study finds that patents afford the least amount of protection.
[5] We note that many who write about strategy usually only discuss three types of innovation: incremental, disruptive, and radical. We add the fourth category of "amplifying" innovation here, recognizing that degree of innovation runs along a continuum. Some call this "architectural" innovation, which often refers to technologies and their reconfiguration. The key distinction we offer here is that each degree of innovation depends on how resources are used / developed, and whether the target market is known / unknown.
[6] Lagorio-Chafton, C., 2013, " Clay Christensen: The wrong kind of innovation," Inc., October 2.
[7] McGrath, R. G. 2019, *Seeing around corners*, Houghton Mifflin Harcourt: New York.
[8] Busse, S., 2012, "How spilt coffee created a billion dollar mop," Kinesis, April 11, https://www.kinesisinc.com/. Lehrer, J., 2012, "*Imagine: How creativity works*," Houghton Mifflin: New York.
[9] Hopp C., Antons D., Kaminski J., and Salge T. O., 2018, "What 40 years of research reveals about the difference between disruptive and radical innovation," Harvard Business Review, April.
[10] ARK Invest, 2019, "Big ideas 2019," https://research.ark-invest.com/big-ideas-2019.

[11] Cited by McGrath, 2019, op. cit.
[12] McGrath, R. G. 2019, *Seeing around corners*, Houghton Mifflin Harcourt: New York. Roundy, P.T., Harrison, D. A., Khavul, S., Perez-Nordtvedt, L., and McGee, J. E., 2018, "Entrepreneurial alertness as a pathway to strategic decisions and organizational performance," Strategic Organization, 16 (2), 192-226.
[13] Kanter, R. M. 1985. *The change masters*. New York: Free Press.

Chapter 10: Corporate Strategy

LEARNING OBJECTIVES

1. Compare and contrast corporate strategy decisions and business strategy decisions.
2. Appraise historical acquisition performance and the explanations behind it.
3. Create a map explaining why companies diversify.
4. Explain the two primary types of diversification: related and unrelated diversification.
5. Using the types of diversification methods available, support an argument for a conglomerate to utilize each one.
6. Apply tools for managing a diversified conglomerate effectively.

Deli Meat Slicers, Car Door Handles, and Six-Pack Carriers[1]

Illinois Tool Works was founded in 1912 in Chicago as a manufacturer of metal cutting tools. Over the years it branched out into completely unrelated enterprises such as electric switches, screws, fasteners, transmissions, and plastics. The company created and patented the plastic 6-pack can holder, among many other inventions. By the early 1980s the company had forty separate business units, each operating a different type of business in a variety of industries. After several of its business units came under competitive pressure from Japanese manufacturers and a troubled domestic auto industry, the company accelerated acquisitions. The blistering pace of acquisitions over 40 years results in a company that operates 800 businesses in 83 divisions in 52 countries. In the last 5 years it has acquired 49 businesses and divested 12 businesses. In 2022 its portfolio of businesses is organized into 7 SBUs (strategic business units). The ITW headquarter office extols its "portfolio management" capabilities for handling this kind of business diversity.

Cousins: Mickey Mouse, Princess Leia, and Iron Man[2]

Walt Disney acquired Marvel Studios in 2009, giving it access to a trove of iconic characters like Iron Man and The Avengers. Then it acquired Lucasfilm Ltd. in 2012 for $4.1 billion, with its Star Wars franchise. It paid half this acquisition price in cash, and half with Disney shares. Disney CEO Robert Iger had a clear vision that that Disney's future rested on enduring characters. Building on its previous acquisition of Pixar Animation, the Marvel and Star Wars portfolios gave Disney more material to appeal to a broader range of children and families, especially teenage boys. George Lucas, who produced Star Wars, had initially been worried about giving up control and oversight of the Star Wars franchise and details to another company. However, Disney and Lucasfilm had already collaborated on a Star Wars ride at Disney World, and this had given each company to a chance learn about how the other worked. Lucas commented on the sale of his company: "Disney's reach and experience give Lucasfilm the opportunity to blaze new trails in film, televisions, interactive media, theme parks, live entertainment and consumer products." By 2012 the seven Star Wars movies to date had generated $4.5 billion in worldwide theater revenues over a 30-year period. Iger defended its acquisition price: "We are confident we can earn a return on invested capital well in excess of our cost of capital."

In 2015 Disney released its first Lucasfilm collaboration, *Star Wars Episode VII: The Force Awakens*. The film achieved the highest domestic box office of all films ever, and 4th highest worldwide box office ever. In 2017 Disney followed with *Star Wars Episode VIII: The Last Jedi*, which outsold all movies domestically that year and is ranked 13th on the best-selling films worldwide. Under the Marvel Studios name in 2018 Disney released *Black Panther*, now 5th in domestic box office revenue ever, and in 2019 *Avengers Endgame* which is now 2nd in domestic box office among all films ever released. Thirteen of the top 20 movies in cumulative world box office revenues by 2022 are from Disney-owned businesses.

Breaking Up is Hard to Do[3]

Three years after she took over as CEO of Hewlett-Packard, Meg Whitman announced that the iconic company would rend itself into two separate entities – one selling PCs and printers (HP), and one selling enterprise hardware and systems (HPE). The dynamic of the two businesses were very different in 2014. PCs and printers were a mature industry, where large scale and thin profit margins prevailed amidst ever-increasing global competition. Enterprise hardware and systems (massive servers and cloud computing technology) were fast growth industry segments that required speed and agility. Although operating them as completely separate divisions was possible, markets tended to push down HP's stock and overall growth assessment because of the old, staid PC business. Splitting the company in two, HP's investors would continue to benefit from the cash flow produced by PCs, while allowing for greater management focus on the growth segment.

Breaking up is hard to do. The company planned to spend $1.3 billion in restructuring costs and another $950 million in taxes to accomplish the split. Leadership was reshuffled, and 80% of the company's headcount moved over to the spun-off enterprise business. Whitman herself became CEO of HPE, while retaining the position as non-executive chair at the PC and printer business.

Since the breakup in late 2015 investors have made out well. Each investor received one new share of the new HP and one share of the new HPE for each original share owned. By 2022 the combined value of the new shares was 245% of the value of the original spun-out shares. The market has responded favorably to this spinout, as each business has been able to focus its resources on its unique product lines.

Share Prices		
	Nov 2015	Feb 2022
HPQ (original shares)	$ 12.24	
HP Inc. (new shares)	$ 13.83	$ 38.01
HPE (new shares)	$ 8.57	$ 16.89

QUESTIONS

1. Although some companies bring together similar businesses, others operate businesses that are completely unrelated to each other. What does strategy mean for these highly diversified companies? How can corporate headquarters add value to related and unrelated divisions?
2. How is success measured when acquisitions are made?
3. On what basis should a corporation decide to divest itself of one of its businesses?

CORPORATE STRATEGY VERSUS BUSINESS STRATEGY

For most of this book we have focused on strategy as it relates to managing a single business. Industry analysis, value chain, business level strategy, life cycles, and innovation: all fundamentally relate to how a company formulates its strategy for a particular type of business and competes in an industry with its products or services. When a company operates in only one line of business, the discussion stays in the realm of business strategy. As the opening vignettes to this chapter illustrate, however, companies often move beyond a single business by acquiring other similar or related businesses or by acquiring completely unrelated businesses. When a company owns multiple companies and/or operates in multiple lines of business, then we move into the realm of corporate strategy. Here, senior executives must make decisions about managing sets of businesses. Recall from Chapter 1 that one of our five critical questions defining the field of strategy is: "What is the nature of strategy in a multi-business firm?"

Corporate strategy involves making decisions about issues that rise above – but also take into account – the decisions made at the business strategy level. Corporate strategy decision domains include the areas listed in Figure 10.1.

**Figure 10.1
Domain of Corporate Strategy**

Deciding which industries to enter and exit
Defining a strategic business unit
Establishing business unit investment priorities
Effecting resources and management transfers
Structuring the corporation

Deciding which industries to enter and exit. At the corporate strategy level executives contemplating growth through internally developed new businesses or acquisitions will evaluate the industries in which these new businesses would exist. Remember in Chapter 4 we concluded that industry structure can enhance or impede the ability of a participating company to earn above-average returns? It usually makes more sense to enter an industry where prospects for profits are strong. In addition, companies that have previously diversified will periodically reevaluate the wisdom of continuing in a particular industry. Diversified companies often decide to divest a business because they determine that its industry is no longer sufficiently attractive.

Defining a strategic business unit. When a company owns and operates many different lines of business, management must decide how to organize the portfolio of businesses. The concept of the strategic business unit (SBU) captures the idea that a set of businesses may share similar challenges and strategies, and can therefore be combined and managed as a single unit. General Electric has for decades encompassed hundreds of products and services across literally dozens of industries in countries all over the world. Until recently they were organized into nine important groups and within each group were SBUs. Within the GE Power group, for example, were nine SBUs (e.g. Gas, Steam, Nuclear, Grid), each of which combines multiple lines of business that are different from other SBUs but internally confront similar issues and challenges. Defining strategic business units and which lines of business should be within them can be an extraordinary challenge for corporate strategists, especially in organizations as diverse as GE or Illinois Tool Works that operate hundreds of businesses.

Establishing investment priorities. The diversified corporation usually engages in a budgeting process in which divisions or SBUs seek corporate investment to further develop their businesses. Corporate management must decide how to judge the merits of requests for additional capital investment in SBUs and how to allocate available capital among competing requests. The process effectively makes the corporate headquarters operate much like a bank, doling out resources based upon estimated output and return measures. Developing an effective set of evaluative criteria and creating a means of analyzing competing requests is a critical issue for corporate strategy decision makers.

Making resource and management transfers. Many corporations decide to acquire companies that are somewhat related to their existing lines of business. This is done to take advantage of anticipated synergies that might exist with the newly acquired company, or possibly to redeploy existing resources to more promising lines of business in an acquired company.[4] Acquiring a related business might also help the company establish a foothold in another promising area. When this happens, corporate management needs to determine how best to infuse the new company with the unique resources and learning from its existing business, as well as how to leverage back what is special about the acquired company into its other existing businesses. Facilitating this sharing of resources can be exceedingly difficult for a variety of reasons, which we will return to in a later discussion about capturing synergies. The corporate office must also implement appropriate management changes to align the new company with the corporation. Such moves may ultimately have the added benefit of developing managers with a broader experience across the entire organization.

How to structure the corporation. To accomplish all of this, corporate management must determine the type of structure that will be most effective for this complex set of businesses. Neither a traditional functional organization nor the hierarchy of a typical single-line business will generally work for a multiple-business corporation. For example, R&D, purchasing, HR and other functions within the commercial airline engine and military defense units (both business lines within GE Aviation) are worlds apart and each requires a completely different set of skills. Corporations employ a variety of structures to accomplish coordination, sharing, control, and management. This topic will be discussed in detail in Chapter 13, "Strategy and Structure."

HISTORICAL PERSPECTIVES

Developing a deep understanding of corporate strategy is important for students of strategy because diversified corporations are a significant part of the business landscape in the United

States and around the world. Rarely does a week go by that the *Wall Street Journal* does not report on yet another corporate merger or buyout. The diversified company has become increasingly important in the U.S. economy. Figure 10.2 illustrates merger and acquisition (M&A) activity over the last 30+ years in the United States. Until the mid-1980s, although the number of M&A deals rose and fell, the total value of such deals remained fairly constant. Since the early 1990s both the number of transactions and their value has grown dramatically; in 2021 the value of all U.S. mergers and acquisitions was $3.2 trillion.

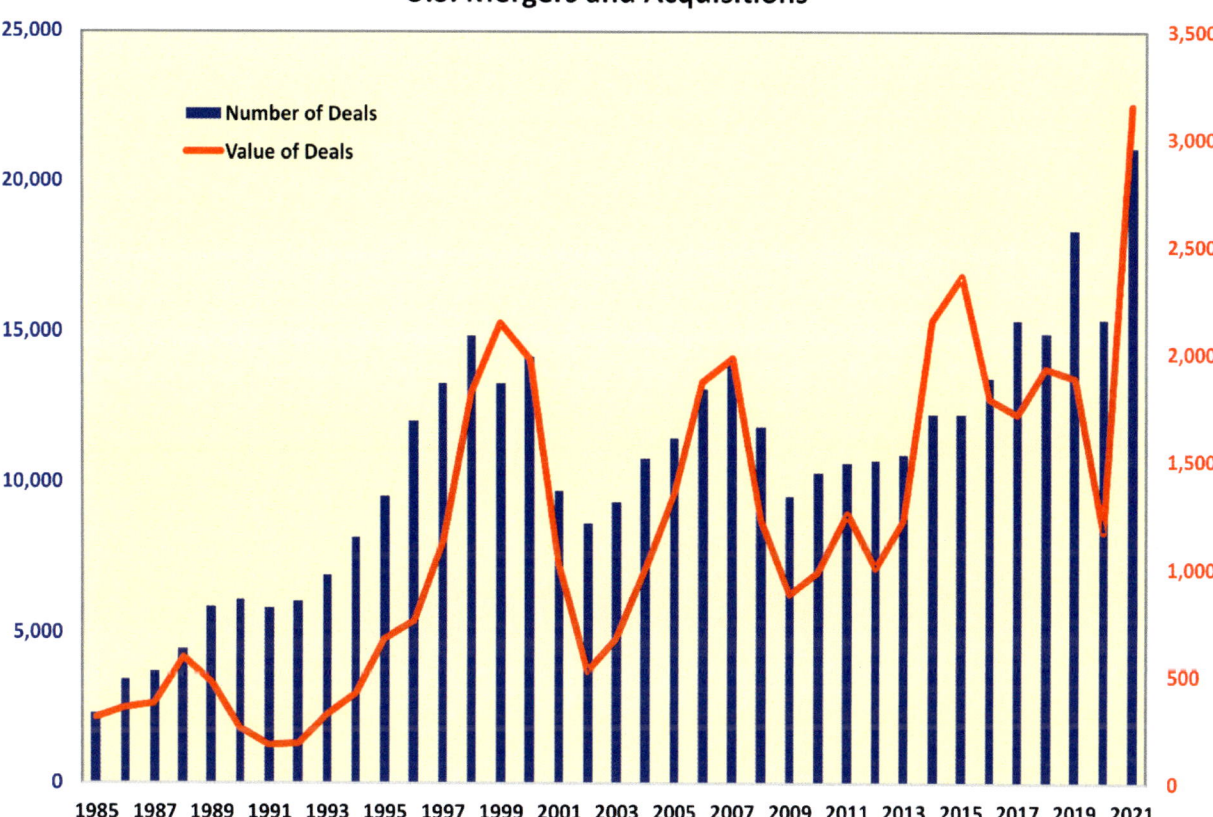

Figure 10.2
U.S. Mergers and Acquisitions

The reasons for M&A activity over the years have changed. Until the 1960s many corporations had grown through internally generated new business within their own industries, or had completed horizontal diversification in order to own and manage other companies that were very similar to their core business. However, by the late 1960s many U.S. corporations found it increasingly difficult to grow because of maturing domestic markets, greater foreign competition in the United States, and concerns about antitrust enforcement since industry concentration ratios had increased in many domestic industries (see discussion in Chapter 4).[5] Therefore they sought to fuel growth by getting into new industries outside their dominant business. The era of conglomerates took shape, during which corporations acquired many types of companies that were completely different from what had originally been their dominant business. If you think of a conglomerate in its usual definition – "rock composed of fragments varying from small pebbles to large boulders in a cement"[6] – then you have a picture of what conglomerate corporations were like. Textron, Gulf+Western, ITT, Litton Industries, and General Electric are corporate names often associated with conglomerates. In fact, during the 1960s GE competed in 23 of the 26 industries defined and tracked by the Commerce Department,[7] with 46 different operating divisions and 190 departments.

Conglomeration continued into the early 1970s as the largest corporations grew even larger. One business reporter, believing the trend toward monster-size corporations would not abate until virtually all companies were owned by only a few giant corporations, was prompted to write an article titled "The Day They Couldn't Fill the Fortune 500."[8] By 1974 the complexion of the U.S. economy had changed significantly from 25 years earlier. Figure 10.3 shows how diversified the Fortune 500 had become during this period of time. In 1949 over 40% of the largest corporations operated in only a single business, and 70% operated in a single business or were predominantly in a single industry. By 1974, in contrast, 64% of the largest companies were diversified and operating in multiple industries. But by 2014 this level had increased to 90%.[9]

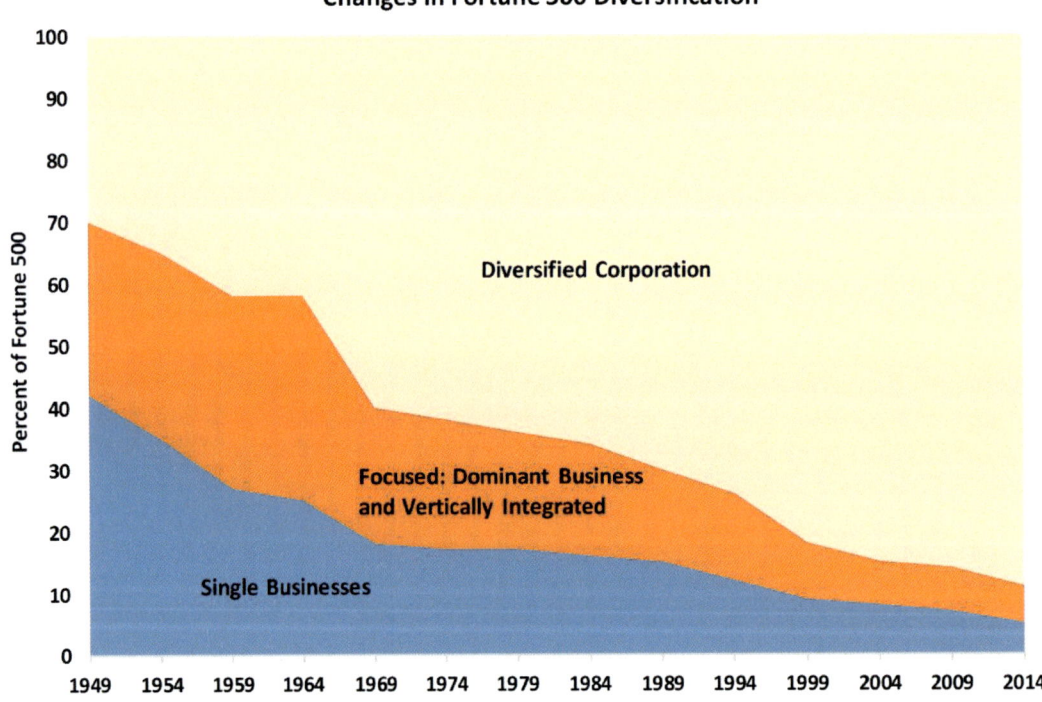

**Figure 10.3
Changes in Fortune 500 Diversification**

By the 1980s large, widely diversified firms were experiencing significant difficulties in the sound and profitable management of such a breadth of businesses. Conglomerate company stocks started trading in equity markets at a discount in PE ratio to more focused firms (the "conglomerate discount").[10] What goes up must come down – or so we are led to believe. Corporate activity during the 1980s was characterized by efforts to dismantle conglomerate firms in order to redeploy their assets more effectively and efficiently. With a more permissive antitrust environment under President Reagan's administration, and with financial innovations such as junk bonds and leveraged buyouts (LBOs), conglomerates began to shed unrelated businesses in order to become more focused in their portfolio of businesses.[11] By 1988, when the value of deals peaked during the decade (Figure 10.2), 63% of acquisitions involved cash or debt (as opposed to using equity). LBOs were the talk of the town on Wall Street; the most exciting deal was the frenzied $25 billion LBO of RJR Nabisco in 1988, subsequently chronicled in a popular book titled

Barbarians at the Gate.[12] If you enjoy corporate finance, backroom politics, soap opera, and drama, this book is a must-read page-turner!

The 1990s witnessed the escalation of M&A activity to a point never before experienced in the U.S. economy. Increasing globalization and more intense competition provided the impetus for firms to grow larger. The soaring stock market and a continuation of the restrained antitrust environment enabled firms to use their own highly valued shares of stock to acquire companies that were related to lines of business they were already in. The confluence of these factors led to a dollar volume of deals that exceeded 20% of the U.S. gross national product (Figure 10.4).

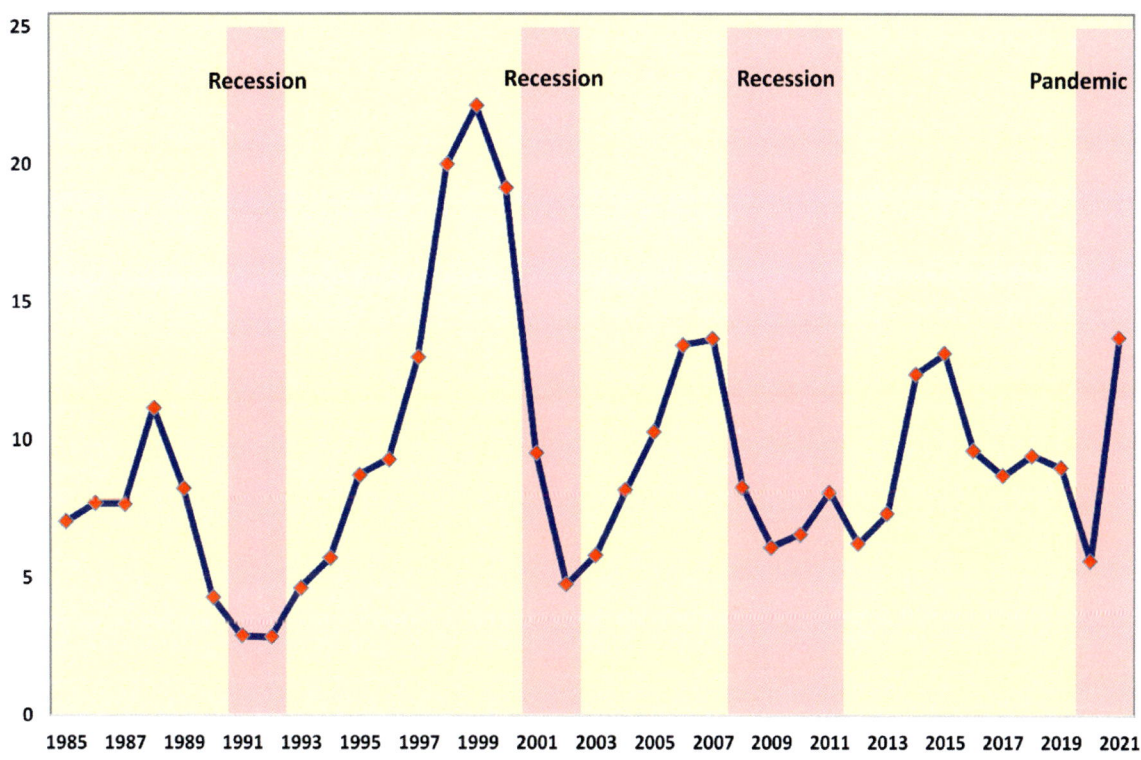

Figure 10.4
Value of U.S. M&A as Percentage of GDP

After the "dot-bomb"-led recession in the early 2000s and the corresponding decline in diversification activity, M&A activity resumed its rise once again. Before the 2008 financial crisis this activity was assisted by the growth of private equity firms and by the advent of innovative financing methods such as SPACs (special purpose acquisition companies) and CLOs (collateralized loan obligations).[13]

Since 2000 three aspects of M&A have become evident. First, within the United States and advanced economies, this sort of broad diversification is not just the province of traditional manufacturing and service companies. Technology firms have been very active in diversifying, led by the likes of Microsoft and Google. Since 2000 Alphabet (Google) has acquired nearly 250 companies, using the hoard of cash sitting on its balance sheet. Second, diversification appears to be prevalent in many emerging countries. Sometimes dominated by family ownership, diversified corporations can often perform well because their internal organization of management and finance can overcome the institutional voids and government influence that crimp market-based transactions in emerging nations. Finally, because of their size the largest companies are usually unable to achieve the rates of growth they need entirely through organic internally-developed growth. They must engage in programmatic mergers and acquisition. Corning, for example, maintains a steady pipeline of deals under evaluation, each year conducting due diligence on roughly 20 companies and submitting bids on roughly 5 in order to consummate 3 deals.[14]

One of the Worst Deals Ever? Part 1[15]

In 2006 Boston Scientific closed a deal to acquire Guidant. In an investigative *Fortune* story the deal was called "a roller-coaster tale of bet-the-franchise corporate brinkmanship, miscalculation, and overreaching. It is a stark lesson in how the single-minded pursuit of victory can blind even brilliant execs to the true costs of a deal." Boston's $80 per share bid for Guidant beat out Johnson & Johnson's $71 offer after multiple rounds of bidding in which the "bad blood" that had existed between Boston and J&J manifested itself in "gladiatorial" combat.

J&J had originally bid to acquire Guidant because it saw opportunities for significant growth through Guidant's pacemakers and defibrillators in the medical products industry. J&J already competed in this industry and wanted to broaden its product lines. Boston Scientific saw an opportunity for growth through related acquisition. The marriage of Boston's Taxus drug-coated stent business and Guidant's promising new stent products and proprietary stent implantation technology also made a potential merger quite attractive.

Boston's winning bid was the eighth bid entertained by Guidant's board of directors. After earlier J&J bids had been viewed favorably by the Guidant board, Boston's CFO Larry Best is claimed to have announced to his internal team, "We need to make a bid that ends this, to swing for the fences." Best was viewed as a "mercurial street fighter" who "doesn't like to lose." The final Boston bid was $27.2 billion, valuing Guidant at $80.03 per share, representing a PE ratio of 64.6 and a premium of 40+ percent over its share price before the first J&J bid. The bid was paid in part with newly issued Boston shares, which increased its share count by 80 percent and diluted Boston shareholders. Part of the bid price was paid with cash, requiring Boston to borrow $6.5 billion on which it was to pay in excess of $300 million annually in interest.

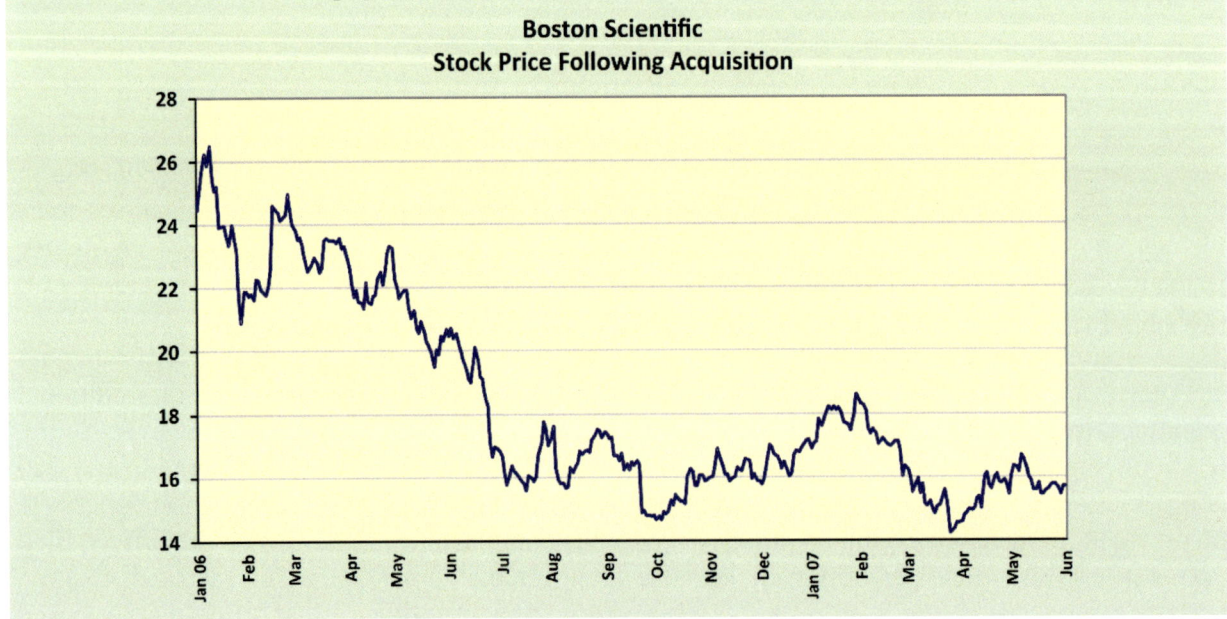

After the deal was done, Boston was plagued with poor performance. Guidant recalled stents due to poor quality control. The FDA warned Boston about its manufacturing facilities, preventing approval for new products. Drug-coated stents, in general, also received negative publicity from the health-care community. These factors interfered with Boston's efforts to increase Guidant sales. With the interest that Boston paid on the acquisition debt, the Guidant business was contributing nothing to the company's earnings. Boston's share price dropped 34 percent into the mid-teens. Larry Best insisted the acquisition would pay off and that success should be judged in three to four years, not based upon short-term hiccups. CEO Jim Tobin had "no doubt" that the company would eventually realize the deal's potential.

QUESTIONS

1. What would you recommend to the Boston Scientific board of directors that the company should do to improve its business?
2. What are the synergies in this combined business?

MOTIVATIONS FOR DIVERSIFICATION

We saw in Chapter 8 that companies experience different life cycle stages and strategic considerations in the course of their development. After a company has started up and then gone through the commercialization and growth stages, the challenges of managing a mature business set in. As a company matures and its sales growth starts to flatten out, the strategic option to diversify is often considered by senior management.

When a company diversifies by acquiring another company, there is usually a core logic that is operating. The company sees potential competitive advantage that might be attained with the combination. Through the application and sharing of corporate resources, the acquiring company believes that it will be able to assist the acquired company to become much more than it could have been if it had remained independent, or much more than it could have been if it had been acquired by another company. So the core logic of diversification through acquisition is usually that "we can do something special for them, and as a result our overall corporate performance will be significantly improved." It's also often the case that acquiring companies have something to gain from the acquired company, such as new technology or new capabilities. Here the logic is "they can also do something for us."

There tend to be four primary motivations for diversifying a company, which include:
    1) seeking growth,
    2) market entry,
    3) seeking market power, and
    4) spreading risk.

Within each of these primary motivations are sets of underlying reasons, and we briefly discuss each below.

Growth

The desire to continue growing a company generally heads the list of motivations to diversify, and this motivation to grow through diversification can occur for various offensive or competitively defensive reasons.

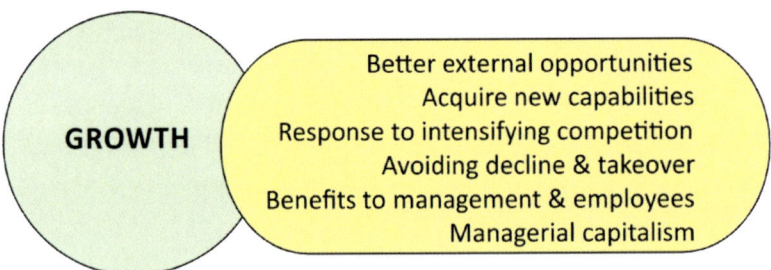

Better external opportunities. Corporate management will come to believe that they have exhausted their opportunities to sustain strong growth rates through their customary internal development process. They may not see any exciting new products in their development pipeline, they may believe that they have saturated their current channels of distribution, or they may have expanded geographically as far as they possibly can with existing products or services. It may be that large markets or segments no longer exist in their core business that can satisfy the level of growth a company desires. (Remember that as a company grows in size, it will require larger increments of new revenue in order to sustain a given percentage rate of growth). Or it may be that the cost of expanding further within an existing business domain appears to be prohibitively expensive. To try to change an established organization so that it can generate a significant number of innovative ideas can be difficult, time consuming, and fraught with uncertainties that appear overwhelming. In these cases companies will typically search for external opportunities to fuel growth, and will consider acquiring another business that meets their acquisition criteria.

Acquire new capabilities. Expansion into new products or industries may require new capabilities and resources that the company does not possess. A company may access new capabilities through alliances or joint ventures with other companies, which we will discuss in Chapter 12. Yet the outright acquisition of another business and its inherent capabilities allows the parent company to own and control new resources and capabilities, and prevent access to them by competitors.

Oracle is a prime example of these first two reasons for growth through acquisition. The company was known historically for its database software. However it was clear that the industry was maturing. So they began to acquire other companies in business application software, financial services, and telecommunications. Over a three-year time period Oracle acquired more than twenty-five software application companies, as well as major purchases of PeopleSoft and Siebel Systems. Acquisition represented a quick route to maintain Oracle's historical growth rates, but was also required because Oracle systems developers did not possess the skills or capabilities required to enter other software application categories.[16]

Response to intensifying competition. As competitors become larger and more powerful, companies are often prompted to acquire other businesses in order to maintain a competitive position. Acquiring another business can generate benefits of size, reduce the company's dependence on its limited array of products and services, and reduce dependence on specific geographic markets or customer segments. In 2007, organic grocer Whole Foods sought to acquire Wild Oats Markets, another organic grocer, in order to counter the growing competition in organic foods from conventional supermarkets such as Kroger, Supervalu, and Walmart. The argument was that the two organic grocers would save on overhead costs and would allow the combined company to more effectively compete for customers through advertising and retail location.

Avoiding decline and takeover. As internally generated growth of a company begins to slow down, management typically comes under pressure from investors and the stock market to continue generating attractive returns. This kind of slowing growth can occur for any number of reasons: the overall market is maturing, competitors are increasingly effective, the company's strategic approach is increasingly ineffective, or the overall complexity of the corporation makes it difficult to manage effectively. If revenue growth is slowing, improving returns can happen only through cutting costs, and cutting costs can only go so far before interfering with a company's competitive strategy in the marketplace.

Lackluster revenue growth and inadequate investor returns paint a target on the backs of senior management, since they are responsible for performance. If the problem of growth in returns is not resolved, the business may become ripe for a takeover, in which another company buys the business and replaces the management team to make necessary changes. Senior managers therefore look at acquisitions and other diversifying moves as an effort to arrest decline and forestall the possibility of any sort of takeover.

Benefits to management and employees. Attempts to grow through acquisition occur for reasons sometimes unrelated to what is actually best for the company itself. Employees and (especially) senior managers derive benefits from working in larger organizations. Compared to smaller companies, in larger organizations there are usually greater opportunities for advancement in position and responsibility while compensation also tends to be higher. For senior management, incentive programs that include bonuses and stock options tend to become more lucrative in larger companies, and can be a powerful inducement to create growth for growth's sake. In this sense, big is beautiful, and getting bigger may be more attractive to employees for personal reasons.

The idea that important strategic decisions for a company might be made in order to personally enhance members of management highlights what is known as the agency issue. Corporate officers and managers are duty bound to act in the interests of shareholders, yet personal incentives may corrupt this straightforward charge. This is one of the reasons that controls are put in place by boards of directors.

Managerial capitalism. The last two ideas suggest that something other than the basic economics of a business and its industry can affect whether and how managers pursue growth – that, in fact, managers may pursue growth based on their own personal needs, interests, and aspirations. Building on this idea, Robin Marris long ago suggested that managers trade their desire for growth against fear of takeover.[17] In his model of "managerial capitalism" corporate managers seek growth in ways that go beyond economic justification, until such time as they have assembled more than they can effectively and coherently manage. We will see further evidence of non-rational thinking about mergers and acquisitions in our following discussions.

Market Power

The quest for greater market power is a companion motivation to the quest for growth. Market power refers back to some of the dimensions of industry analysis that we covered in Chapter 4. Here a company seeks to attain a position in the industry that enables it to earn superior returns, through one of several ways.

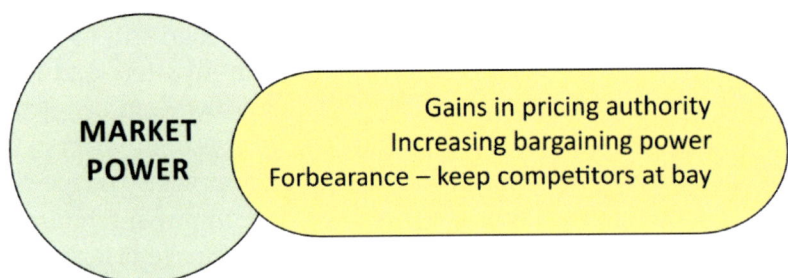

Gains in pricing authority. A company that grows larger in its industry by horizontally acquiring one of its competitors can develop size advantages it previously did not enjoy. These include greater economies of scale in its operations, as well as cost savings through the integration of identical support activities in its value chain (such as combining R&D, purchasing, and human resource functions). Together, these cost savings create greater flexibility in establishing prices for products and services. Most industries have price leaders and price followers; however, the price leaders tend to be the larger companies with the better cost structures.

Increased bargaining power. Because they command a greater percentage of sales in an industry, larger companies will often enjoy enhanced bargaining power when they deal with both suppliers and customers. Increasing bargaining power and consequent gains in pricing authority are one of the key reasons that the 2019 acquisition of Sprint by T-Mobile came under scrutiny. States' attorney generals worried that the consolidation of mobile service will result in higher prices to consumers. In 2022 Microsoft announced its intention to acquire gaming giant Activision Blizzard, and shortly thereafter the FTC announced that it would take a closer look to see if the deal would disadvantage customers or suppliers.[18]

Mutual forbearance – keeping competitors at bay. Mutual forbearance is defined as "the ceding of control of one product or geographic market to a competitor in exchange for that competitor's acquiescence in another market."[19] This means that, in order to keep a competitor out of its industry (or at least less aggressive) and maintain its competitive superiority, a company might acquire a company in another industry in which that same competitor is active. It is sort of a "tit for tat" approach: if you do this to me, I'll do it to you. For example, to slow down Gillette's entry into the disposable pen market which was BIC's primary market, BIC decided to enter the disposable razor blade market which was Gillette's hallowed ground. As was pointed out in Chapter 1, this type of "attack" is taken directly from Sun Tzu, who suggested that attacking something of value to the enemy will cause them to reconsider attacking you. Although in this example BIC entered razors through internal development, many examples of mutual forbearance exist through acquisitions into an industry. In 2008 Microsoft bid to acquire Yahoo! to compete more aggressively in the online advertising business. This move was in part designed to prompt Google to devote much greater attention and resources to this battle, since it is central to Google's revenue stream. By doing so it might draw Google's attention and resources away from its efforts to develop software applications that would compete with Microsoft.

Market Entry

Companies often seek to enter industries outside of where they currently operate. They plan to accomplish this type of diversification through acquisition, rather than through internal development, for a number of reasons that relate to cost and speed.

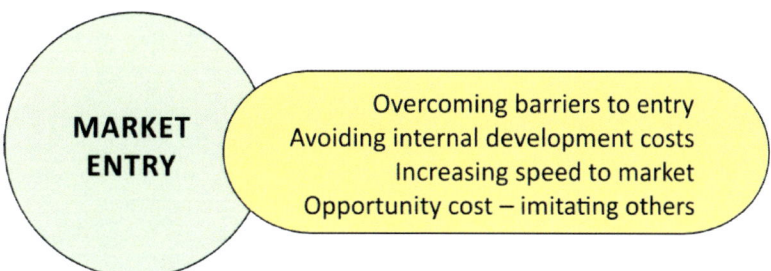

Overcoming barriers to entry. The competitors in most industries seek to raise entry barriers to keep the flow of new entrants to a minimum, thus better preserving their own stakes in the industry's profits. Barriers to entry can be both significant and expensive – whether they involve building scale-efficient manufacturing facilities, developing broad distribution, or creating brand awareness through advertising and promotion. Acquiring an existing company in a new industry does an end-run around the costs of breaking through the entry barriers because the company takes advantage of an existing industry player who already holds the resources needed to be a competitor. Breaking into the sports drink market with a new product line would have been a difficult and slow road for Quaker Oats to pursue; instead they purchased Gatorade (at a somewhat outrageous price) and immediately became an important player in the industry.

Avoiding internal development costs. Similarly, through the acquisition of a going concern in an industry, the acquiring company can avoid the costs and uncertainty of developing products or services internally. Buying a company means taking over an existing business with defined suppliers and a customer base. Therefore most of the uncertainty and risk that is usually associated with any type of innovation effort is also avoided.

Increasing speed to market. If analysis reveals that another industry is attractive, acquiring a company in that industry enables the acquiring firm to begin operating more quickly than would be the case if it developed its own products or services internally. Acquisitions often close within six to twelve months, whereas effective new product development efforts can take many years.

Opportunity cost. Finally, a "bandwagon" effect sometimes happens when a leading company in one industry makes an acquisition in another industry, encouraging competitors to make similar acquisitions. In the 1990s, pharmaceutical manufacturer Merck acquired generic drug distributor Medco, and shortly afterward a number of Merck's competitors also snatched up drug distribution companies. As this suggests we occasionally witness a flurry of similar types of acquisitions in an industry within a short period of time. In these cases the first acquisition prompts other firms to consider the opportunities they might be missing if they stayed on the sidelines. This kind of bandwagon effect usually occurs when the industries involved are undergoing dynamic changes, revealing possibilities for value creation through a new combination achieved by acquisition.

We can see an example of the bandwagon effect by looking quickly at the rapidly-evolving healthcare industry. This is an industry undergoing dynamic change, since great economic and political attention is being directed at health care and the cost of prescription drugs. Figure 10.5 shows recent merger activity in this industry. Here pharmacies and pharmacy benefit managers (PBMs) are combining with insurance companies, to achieve better scale and control over the industry value chain activity. Pharmacies are also moving into the provision of health care through clinics. Once one company engages in a merger, then others may follow so they are not left behind.

Figure 10.5
Mergers in Pharmaceuticals Management

	Amazon	Walgreens	CVS Health	IngenioRx	Meridian	Optum Rx	Express Scripts
Pharmacy Benefit Management							
Pharmacies	PillPack	Rite Aid					
Clinics and Home Health Care	One Medical	Village MD Care Centrix	Minute Clinic				
Insurance Providers			Aetna	Anthem	Well Care	United Health	Cigna
	2018-22	2018-21	2018	2017	2018	2011	2018

Spreading Risk

The final motivation for diversification has to do with spreading risk. Every company experiences two kinds of risk. There is the systematic risk that is associated with macro-economic

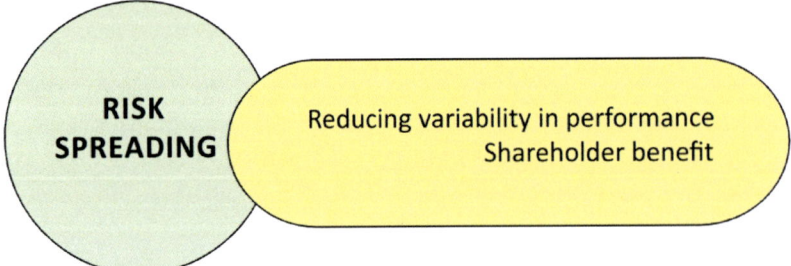

forces (forces that affect everyone in the economy), and the unsystematic risk that is associated with its particular line of business. You have no doubt run into these terms in finance classes you have taken previously, since both are used to calculate the beta (β) of a company's stock. Companies that diversify can reduce their unsystematic risk by acquiring other companies whose lines of business offset performance variations in the company's own business. In Figure 10.6 Company A's business fluctuates, such as might be the case when A manufactures hot chocolate mix primarily sold in colder months or in mostly northern states. During the warm months A must reduce employment because seasonal sales are low, but may still find that it loses money because of high fixed overhead costs associated with its underutilized plant during that time. So during the summer its revenue and profits decline, as suggested by curved line A. When it files its quarterly reports with the SEC, the investment community responds to unprofitable quarters by selling stock, and its stock price declines. So Company A decides to acquire Company B, which manufactures popsicles sold primarily in the warm months and the southern states. After the acquisition, A combines the two manufacturing operations so that consistent employment and better plant utilization can be maintained. Administrative, marketing and sales efficiencies work to lower other costs as a percentage of revenue. Since revenue and profits do not now fluctuate widely, the company may report more consistently profitable quarters throughout the year. Shareholders of A benefit from the smoothed-out revenues and earnings the company now achieves.

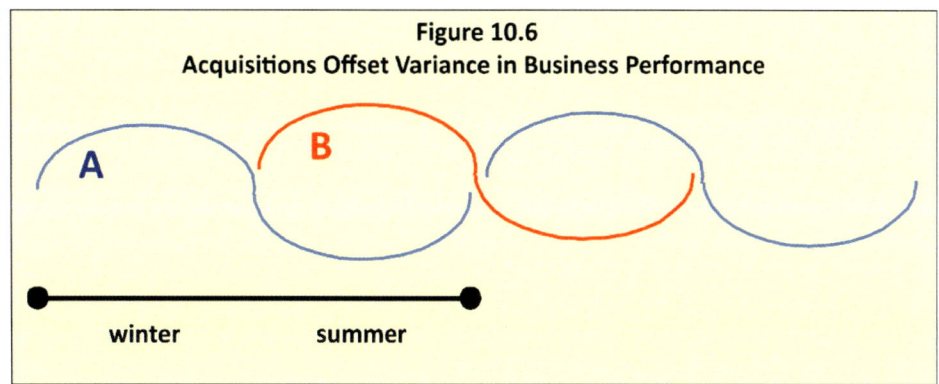

Why couldn't shareholders in Company A simply buy shares of Company B to accomplish the same level of risk spreading? In this case Company B's business also fluctuates considerably during a year and across geographies. So shareholders of A who also invest in B would simply be buying another company with a fair degree of unsystematic risk. However, by putting together the lines of business the fluctuations associated with the combined company are reduced[20] and shareholders thus benefit from a stock price that should be more stable over time.

Managing in Markets: Question for Class Discussion

The U.S. has a long heritage, from the days of Teddy Roosevelt, of protecting markets so other businesses can compete and innovate. But government regulation of free market transactions, such as mergers and acquisitions between companies, steps on traditional values of market freedom.

In 2020 the Federal Trade Commission sued to block a $1.4 billion deal in which the maker of Schick razors sought to buy upstart rival Harry's Inc. In 2022 the FTC will weigh in on whether Microsoft should be allowed to acquire Activision Blizzard. Should mergers and acquisitions be subject to government approval?

TYPES OF DIVERSIFICATION

In Chapter 9 we covered innovation options that companies have at their disposal for growing their businesses. They may also expand into new geographic regions or internationally (Chapter 11) or form alliances or joint ventures (Chapter 12). Because this chapter deals with corporate strategy (managing multiple lines of business), we have more or less focused on the acquisitions route at this point. We have to recognize, however, that companies may still diversify into new businesses through internal development efforts, international expansion or through joint ventures and alliances, in addition to acquisition. As discussed in the preceding section, diversifying through acquisition can offer some advantages over these other methods. These advantages relate to control of resources and capabilities, overcoming entry barriers avoiding internal development costs, and increasing speed of entry.

Regardless of why a company diversifies, there are distinctions in the type of diversification that a company engages in. These distinctions can be described in terms of the combinations of industry similarity and value chain similarity (Figure 10.7). The primary types of diversification fall into two well-known categories: related diversification and unrelated diversification.

Figure 10.7
Types of Diversification and Their Distinctions

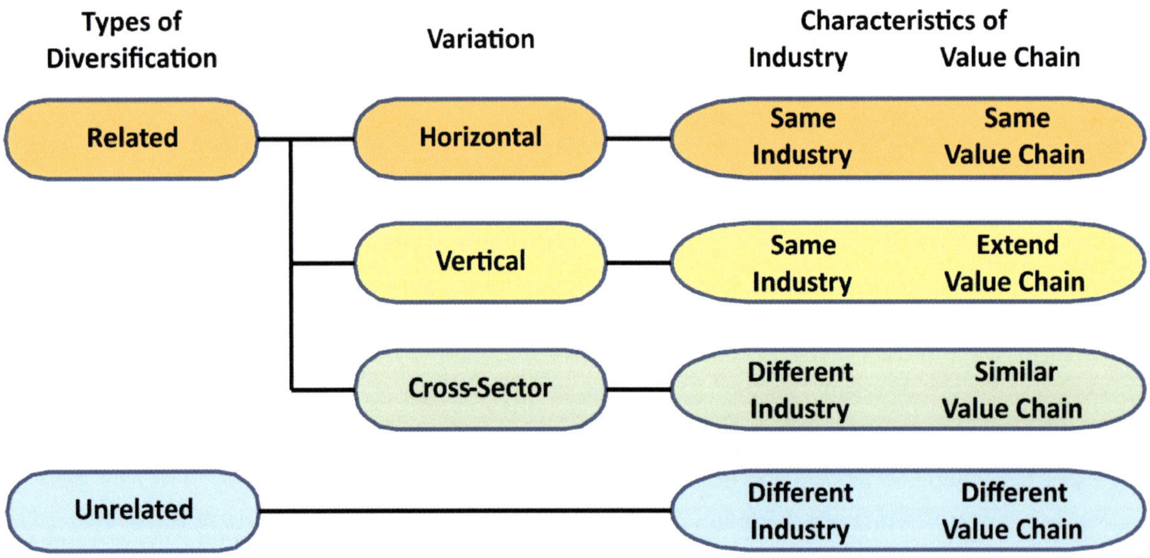

Types of Diversification	Variation	Characteristics of Industry	Value Chain
Related	Horizontal	Same Industry	Same Value Chain
	Vertical	Same Industry	Extend Value Chain
	Cross-Sector	Different Industry	Similar Value Chain
Unrelated		Different Industry	Different Value Chain

Related Diversification

As the phrase implies, related diversification means that there is some dimension of similarity between the corporation and the company it seeks to acquire. Related diversification can be divided into three variations: 1) horizontal, 2) vertical, and 3) cross-sector. Horizontal diversification occurs when a company enters another business in the same industry and essentially employs the exact same value chain as is used in its core business. Earlier we mentioned how Whole Foods sought to acquire Wild Oats Markets during 2007. These two organic foods grocery store chains drew upon the same suppliers, operated in the same fashion at retail, and sought to attract the same types of customers. Black & Decker, the 100-year-old manufacturer of power tools for homeowners and the construction trade, acquired Vector Products which manufactures battery chargers, jump-starters, and other equipment for the automotive market. Since many of the Vector products are sold in traditional hardware store channels of distribution, Black & Decker is able to leverage its resources and capabilities in tool manufacturing and sales distribution to significantly expand the presence and impact of the Vector line.

Because horizontal diversification extends a company's influence further into an industry in which it is already operating, acquisitions of this sort tend to draw the attention of regulatory authorities. Acquiring companies in the same industry may lead to significantly enhanced market power, through which they may exert undue influence upstream on suppliers or downstream on customers, in the form of pricing demands or other requirements. When InBev sought to acquire Anheuser-Busch, for investors it justified the move by announcing plans to cut $1.5 billion from AB's cost structure partly by reducing the number of independent distributors and reducing payments to those distributors that remain. Of course, this created angst downstream at distributor customers.[21] From our earlier discussion in Chapter 4 on industry analysis, we know that the Federal Trade Commission and the Department of Justice are interested in preventing combinations that lead to excessive market power for just these reasons.

Occasionally companies will engage in vertical diversification, in which they enter new businesses in the same industry but which occupy different positions up or down the value chain. Vertical acquisitions ordinarily occur when a company wants to continue operating in its own industry, where it has deep knowledge and capabilities, but wants to exert greater control over some part of the industry value chain. This usually occurs when companies seek to gain greater control over sources of supply in their value chains. You have probably been advised by your university, for example, to back up your files in case the hard drive on your computer fails. Professors really don't want you to lose those papers you have been working on. Before Dropbox and Google Drive came along, Western Digital was a leading player in the data backup industry. It manufactures internal and external hard drives used for this purpose, and their drives are often sold in electronic stores like Best Buy. In 2007 the company acquired Komag for nearly $1 billion. Komag manufactures the rotating disks that serve as the storage media inside the drive box. The acquisition was made so that Western Digital could better keep pace with technological developments and cost changes in the manufacturing of this important subcomponent. This allowed them to be more competitive with Seagate Technology and the evolving online backup services. Said John Coyne, CEO of Western Digital, "This acquisition puts us in a position to be in greater control of our own destiny."[22] In 2019 AT&T completed its acquisition of Time Warner. This vertical acquisition was designed to own studio movie content and programming shared directly to AT&T's cellphone and Direct-TV network users.

Cross-sector diversification describes the situation when a company enters a completely new industry but intends to utilize a value chain that is similar to that employed in their core business. When Disney decided to enter the cruise line business, it could have simply licensed its name and the use of its characters to another company that already operated in this business. Yet Disney believed that the quality of the customer experience is at the heart of the company and its value creation, and that delivering an exceptional experience

333

is a critical part of their strategy. Monitoring how another company accomplished this on their behalf would have been incredibly difficult. It might have subjected the company to a significant risk that the Disney image might be tarnished. So, in entering this business they decided to build and operate their own cruise ships and a cruise line reservation service. Now they can take their internal value chain capabilities related to reservations, vacation packages, entertainment and food scheduling and more, and apply it in this new business.

Other cross sector moves are familiar to us all. Long known for its razor blades, Gillette acquired Duracell in 1996 believing that its value chain capabilities in innovation, marketing, and retail sales management could be effectively brought to bear on the battery business. In a further twist of corporate combinations, Procter & Gamble subsequently acquired Gillette in 2005. Although P&G already operated in many different industries (paper products, personal care items, cleaning agents, etc.), acquiring the Gillette lines of business could also be considered cross-sector diversification because they expected to leverage their existing value chain capabilities by entering new industries. In discussing the acquisition, CEO A. G. Lafley claimed that Gillette was "one of our biggest growth opportunities, and served to provide… a balanced mix of businesses, brands, markets, and customers provide flexibility to deliver results reliably, in good times and challenging times alike."[23] It becomes apparent that P&G viewed the Gillette acquisition as a means of generating future growth, as a way to enter new markets, and as a means to spread risk – three of the motivations for diversification mentioned previously.

Why Related Diversification Is Supposed to Succeed

Corporate performance is expected to improve because diversification takes advantage of synergies that are believed to exist between the corporation and the company it will acquire. Each of the types of diversification discussed above illustrates how related diversification builds upon or leverages aspects of the corporation's existing value chain (Figure 10.8).

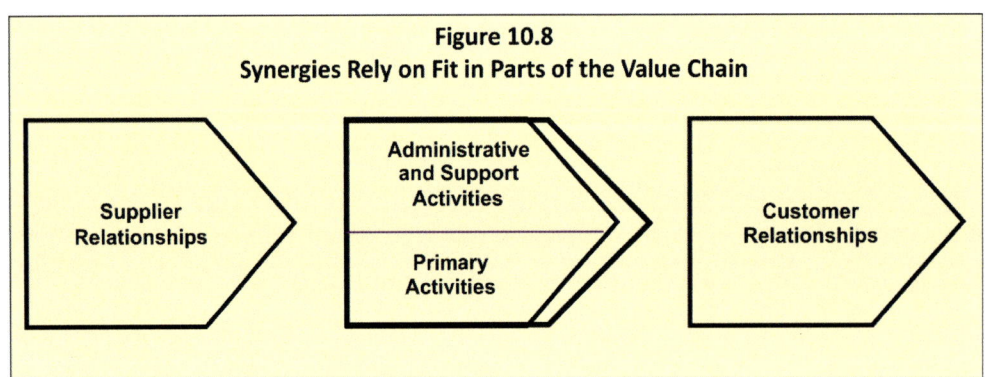

Three forms of "fit" offer the opportunity for synergistic gains from an acquisition: market fit, operational fit, and management fit. Synergies may spring from market fit, in which the corporation takes advantage of external value chain relationships with customers or suppliers in order to improve the competitive position and business of the acquired company. When Cisco Systems acquires another company, for example, advanced planning allows Cisco to add the acquired company's products onto its own price list the very first day the new company is officially part of the Cisco family. In this way the Cisco sales organization can immediately begin selling the new company's products on a much broader scale. Procter & Gamble expected to significantly expand the Duracell and Gillette product lines throughout their worldwide organizations, selling these products to wholesale and retail accounts that P&G already had relationships with.

Operational fit occurs where the corporation is able to combine similar primary value chain activities, such as manufacturing facilities, transportation systems, or warehousing operations. In 2007 XM Satellite Radio Holdings proposed a merger with Sirius Satellite Radio, its chief competitor. The two companies, competing aggressively with each other and both losing money as a result, combined very similar aspects of their nearly identical broadcasting operations and eliminate duplicate operational activities. E*Trade Financial and TD Ameritrade also engaged in merger talks during 2007, believing that "uniting both company's accounts on a single computer system" would eliminate duplicate computer operations and minimize the cost of adding new customers.[24]

The third type of fit is the kind of management fit that occurs when synergies might be realized in the administrative and support activities of the value chain. Combining procurement and purchasing functions can lead to increased bargaining power with suppliers and with the shippers who deliver raw materials and other inputs to the company's primary activities locations. Research and development efforts can be enhanced either through the streamlining that can occur when redundancies are eliminated or through the access to new types of technical knowledge, processes, or patents that result from combining two companies. Other corporate support functions, such as finance and legal, can also be made available to acquired companies and thereby further reduce redundancies. Perhaps most importantly, the more sophisticated knowledge possessed by management about how to successfully build a business and compete can be leveraged into a newly-acquired division.

Just as there are three fit sources of synergies in related diversification, there are three types of synergistic benefits that related diversification efforts can lead to: scope, economizing, and leverage (Figure 10.9). Scope is created when the corporation is able to broaden its product line or broaden its customer base by virtue of an acquisition. Scope provides immediate performance benefits in the form of higher sales revenue. It also provides immediate opportunity for sales revenue growth, such as the type that Procter & Gamble or Cisco count on, by expanding distribution into existing channels of distribution.

Figure 10.9
Sources and Results of Synergies

Sources of Synergies	Results of Synergies
Market fit	Scope
Operational fit	Economizing
Management fit	Economizing; Resources Leverage

Many of the merger and acquisition deals announced in the newspapers trumpet the synergies to be gained from economizing. Economizing refers to the cost savings accomplished by operating the combined companies more efficiently. Occasionally efficiencies are created by combining separate manufacturing operations into a large, scale-efficient plant. More often than not, however, the efficiencies they talk about are those realized through layoffs and workforce reduction of redundant and duplicate jobs. This kind of economizing strikes white collar workers in support and administrative activities as often as it does blue collar workers in manufacturing and service in the primary activities sector of the value chain. Arguments

Fortune Magazine euphemisms for synergy

- Corporate "catch and release" program
- Fueling demand for lottery tickets & malt liquor
- Dissing the gruntled
- Hiring a bunch of people, only backwards

for economizing have become so prevalent as justification for acquisitions that *Fortune* magazine offered a wry view about the real meaning of synergies.

Both scope and economizing present more objective, more obvious benefits of related diversification. Consequently, corporate announcements and actions following an acquisition tend to focus on these more visible economic benefits. However, the cost of making an acquisition is seldom paid back through these types of benefits alone. The return on investment in related diversification will usually occur when the corporation develops the benefits of resources leverage. Leverage does not occur through merely combining; it occurs through the extension and application of corporate resources to the newly acquired company. If we think back to the discussion of resources and the value chain in Chapters 5 and 6, we will recall that the dimensions of the value chain that are most valuable are those that have to do with "the coordination and linkages that exist between and across elements of a company's value chain." This is because they are unobservable to competition and extremely difficult to reproduce. The resource-based arguments of Chapter 6 would call these "extraordinary" resources, ones that provide the opportunity for sustainable advantage. Other intangible resources include management knowledge. The greatest performance benefits that accrue to corporations that diversify relatedly through acquisitions should therefore come from the extension, or leverage, of these extraordinary resources into the newly acquired company. Because coordinating mechanisms within a corporation are often tacit and buried in routines or culture, they are less obvious and more complex. And therefore it can be extremely difficult to leverage them effectively. We will return to this point when we discuss the evidence on diversification performance.

Figure 10.10
United Technologies Synergy Fits

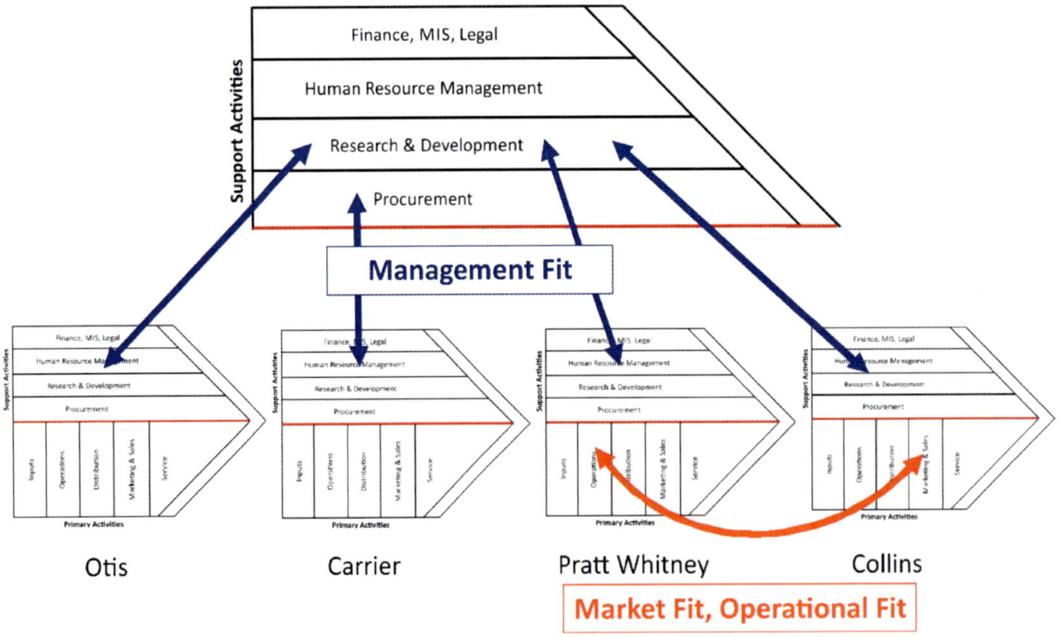

United Technologies, now a part of Raytheon, was a leading industrial firm with four SBUs operating in three different sectors: elevators (Otis), climate control systems (Carrier), and aerospace (Pratt & Whitney, Collins). Figure 10.10 illustrates how the primary and support value chain activities connections achieve fit either between SBUs or between the headquarters and the

SBUs. In the aerospace sector they appear to achieve all three forms of fit, where market and operational fit occur between the two different companies. They appear to have achieved only management fit in their corporate ownership of Otis and Carrier. So in 2020 they spun off these two SBUs in order to focus on aerospace. We will discuss spinoffs later in this chapter.

Unrelated Diversification

Unrelated diversification occurs when a corporation enters a new business in a different industry from that in which it currently operates *and* does not expect to achieve any value chain synergies through the combination. Unrelated diversifiers are usually referred to as either *conglomerates* or as holding companies. Conglomerates such as GE operate multiple lines of business under one corporate name. In contrast, holding companies own other companies, or at least own the majority of the voting shares of other companies so that they may control management and operations by influencing or electing their board of directors. Holding companies often allow their portfolio companies to operate as relatively independent entities. In 2022 Warren Buffet's holding company Berkshire Hathaway owned 42 subsidiary operating companies that compete in five major industry segments, and the company continues to aggressively manage its portfolio of companies. The company's 2017 annual report states:

> "Berkshire's operating businesses are managed on an unusually decentralized basis. There are essentially no centralized or integrated functions (such as sales, marketing, purchasing, legal or human resources) and there is minimal involvement by Berkshire's corporate headquarters in the day-to-day business activities of the operating businesses."[25]

Kohlberg Kravis Roberts and other private equity firms also operate as holding companies, owning shares and controlling the companies but not actually participating in the active management of the business of these companies.

If unrelated diversification is not intended to improve corporate performance through capturing synergies, then what is the reason for this type of corporate acquisition behavior? Unrelated diversification is supposed to succeed because of the exceptional financial expertise that the acquiring corporation brings to the table. The senior management in these organizations usually excel in identifying undervalued companies, financially distressed firms with strong business fundamentals, and companies that have significant growth prospects if they can gain access to financial capital. With the injection of corporate financial capital, as well as a strong corporate governance system to ensure effective monitoring of the performance of acquired companies, unrelated diversifiers expect that corporate performance will be buoyed by above-average performance of their acquisitions.

Berkshire Hathaway is an exemplar of this sort of exceptional expertise. With a core capability in prudent investment of capital, "few companies are better at allocating capital than capital markets, but Berkshire Hathaway is one of them." Warren Buffet uses the zero-cost cash flow from its insurance company portfolio as capital to invest in its other businesses.[26]

The astute student will recognize that these types of unrelated diversification transactions are apt to occur primarily when there are certain types of financial market imperfections. In some cases financial markets may look unfavorably at an entire industry, in which case the stock price of a company that has particularly strong fundamentals or prospects may get "unfairly" beat down. Corporations that identify these "diamonds in the rough" can provide the financial capital that the companies cannot gain access to through financial markets. Another issue may be that the costs of raising either equity or debt capital is prohibitively expensive in financial markets, whereas the corporate holding company's transactions costs for providing capital are significantly lower.

Parenting Advantage

The above discussion of related and unrelated diversification ordinarily focuses on the extent to which the resources and capabilities that exist within the current portfolio of companies might be applied to a newly-acquired company. A "parenting advantage" framework can offer some additional insight and utility in thinking about how well a newly-acquired company might fare under the corporate umbrella.[27] The idea here is that the headquarters of the corporation has its own capabilities and can influence the outcome of an acquisition simply by virtue of the "parent-child" relationship. Value can be created when the Parent's skills and resources fit well with the needs and opportunities of the company targeted for acquisition.

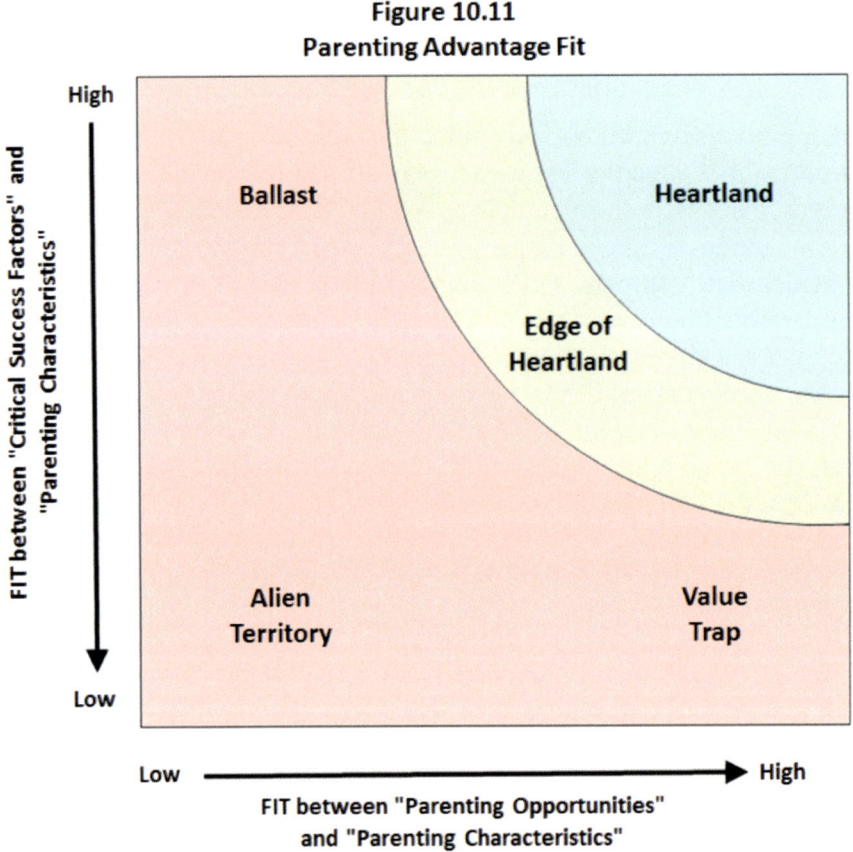

Figure 10.11 provides a matrix to use to assess the parenting advantage fit.[28] Fit is assessed along two axes, and each depends on understanding important characteristics of the parent company. These "parenting characteristics" include the overarching philosophy HQ management regularly uses, the corporate structure, central functions and services the parent is particularly good at, the experience set of senior management, and the degree of decentralization the HQ office allows. Is there a fit between these characteristics and the sort of headquarter support that is needed by the target acquisition (horizontal axis)? If the fit is high, then this may bode well for the acquisition. But the vertical axis helps us understand if there is also fit between parenting characteristics and the specific key success factors the target company must address in its industry. If there is high fit on this dimension, then the business is seen as falling into the "heartland" where value can be created by the parent company. This might be the case, for example, when an acquired company wants to expand internationally, and it can take advantage of the corporate parent's

structure that is organized with country-level subsidiaries. Often parent companies can provide needed corporate services to acquisitions but are unable to help acquisitions with key success factors that are critical in the target company's industry. These fall into the "value trap" segment in the matrix, where the parent really cannot help the acquired company on factors that are critical to its success.

By a similar logic, it may be the case that the parent company has relevant experience through its other divisions in the target company's industry that are useful for key success factors, but has low fit between what HQ does well and what the target might need from HQ. Perhaps the parent company is a holding company of independently-operating retailers. In this case, although the acquired company may benefit from resources and learning from within the other subsidiaries, the parent itself has little value it can offer. These potential acquisitions would represent "ballast," something that just weighs the corporate parent down. And then there is "alien territory," where nothing about the target company matches up well with the corporate parent HQ.

DIVERSIFICATION PERFORMANCE

Even though mergers and acquisition activity is a huge economic force, the evidence is *mixed* as to whether these diversification efforts actually enhance the performance of corporations. Corporations engage in diversification in order to derive corporate benefits from bringing a new business into the corporate family. Ultimately, these moves should provide enhanced returns to shareholders of the corporation.[29] Yet a variety of sophisticated studies over the years conclude that diversification is nearly as likely to destroy shareholder value as it is to create shareholder value. One popular study from the 1990s examined 150 deals that exceeded $500 million, finding that shareholder value was eroded 50% of the time, while shareholder value was only created 17% of the time. In the rest of the cases (33%) there was little change in shareholder value.[30] Recently, "meta-analysis" research examined dozens of sophisticated studies and arrived at a similar conclusion. Here they find that shareholders of acquired firms make out exceedingly well. However they find the benchmark-adjusted return to shareholders of corporations that do the acquiring "is close to zero… 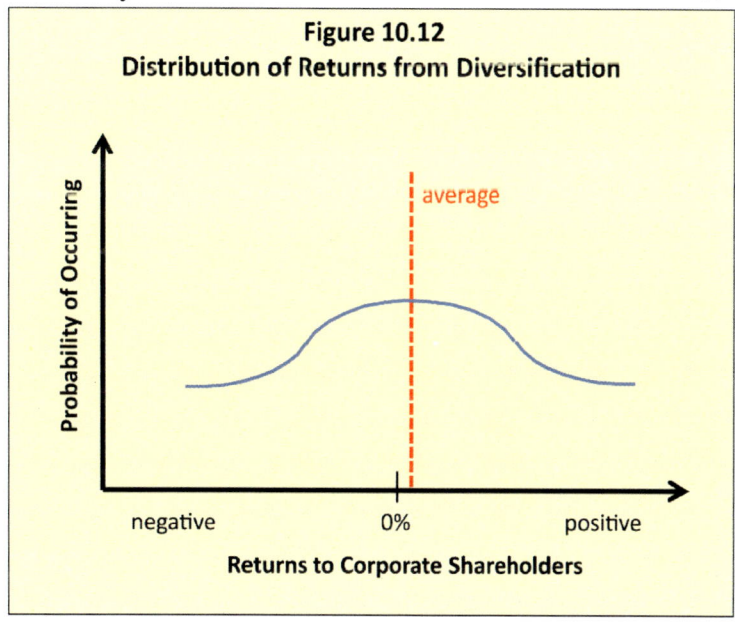 [and] the distribution of corporate returns is wide – which means that many buyers in M&A transactions should prepare to be disappointed."[31] Figure 10.12 illustrates this conclusion: a relatively flat distribution curve shows negative returns to shareholders are nearly as likely as are positive returns, and the average level of returns is marginally above zero. The conclusion, then, is that acquisitions on average produce slightly positive returns but those efforts subject shareholders to high volatility.

There is some evidence that management teams with previous acquisition experience tend to produce better corporate returns. For corporations that have been down the acquisition path at least six times, positive shareholder returns are created 72% of the time; zero or negative returns occur only 28% of the time.[32] We suppose this is a better story than the 50/50 chance of enhanced performance mentioned previously. However the ability to accomplish even this modest feat may come only over time after the expense of multiple costly business mistakes one out of four times.

What type of diversification do you think would produce better returns for corporations: related or unrelated? Once more, the story is somewhat mixed. You might think that corporations that diversify relatedly, capturing synergies by taking advantage of similarities in industries and value chains, would tend to perform better than would corporations that acquire completely unrelated companies. One study reports that moderate related diversification can enhance performance versus single-business firms, but that moving into unrelated businesses leads to poor performance.[33] Corporations that move beyond a single-business can better utilize assets through scale and scope advantages, and through economizing by combining value chain activities. Yet the ability to effectively manage many different types of businesses becomes increasingly difficult as a corporation moves further into related businesses. That kind of complexity can contribute to poor performance. The effectiveness of diversification efforts depends on a number of critical factors.

Factors Affecting Acquisition Performance

In speaking about successful diversification through acquisition, someone once declared that it is like having a baby: "easy to conceive, but hard to deliver." It is pretty easy for corporate managers to imagine how great a combination of companies can be. Unfortunately, there are a number of factors that are critical to engineering successful acquisitions, both individually and collectively. Figure 10.11 lists the range of factors that corporate managers must pay attention to if they want to increase the likelihood that their diversification moves will produce positive shareholder returns. Some of these are relatively obvious but deserve brief mentioning anyway; some of them are not so obvious.

**Figure 10.13
Acquisition Performance Depends On**

- Selecting attractive industries
- Strategic rationale
- Due diligence
- Capturing synergies
- Acquisition premiums
- Loss of focus of acquiring company
- Accelerating growth of acquired company
- Post-acquisition integration efforts

Attractive industries. In Chapter 4 we learned how various forces can cause a particular industry to be more or less competitively attractive. Less attractive industries are those in which competition begins to resemble perfect competition – where standardization of products or services is highly valued, growth has slowed, profit margins are razor thin, rivalry is intense, and companies that do well are those that have truly superior cost positions. These conditions often characterize mature industries, as we read about in Chapter 8, and they present tough environments for any company. Some industries may involve onerous conditions like significant government regulation, as in health care or medical products and services. In contrast, more attractive industries are those that are experiencing growth, and where strategic variety can exist. Since industry attractiveness impacts the opportunity to earn above-average returns, it stands to reason that diversification efforts should take advantage of industry context.

Strategic rationale. The more successful acquisitions are those that spring from well-defined acquisition target criteria that relate to the strategy of the corporation or its existing business units. Acquisitions are occasionally pursued because corporate managers concentrate more on the opportunity that a target company presents, rather than its consistency with existing strategy. Establishing criteria for acquisitions that mirror the corporation's strategy narrows the field of potential target companies to those that offer the greatest possibilities for economizing, scope, and leverage.

Cisco Systems, a leading supplier of networking equipment and network management for the internet, has been particularly successful in its string of acquisitions because it specifies strategic criteria before it ever engages in a search for target companies. These criteria include:
- Must be complementary technology,
- That can be sold using Cisco's existing sales force,
- And serviced by Cisco's existing customer support organization,
- And which leverage Cisco's resource base.

Establishing strategic criteria up front such as Cisco has done, can avoid costly acquisitions based on speculation about synergies.

Examples abound of companies that did not follow the Cisco advice, resulting in very poor acquisition outcomes. eBay acquired PayPal in 2002 for $1.5 billion, and then Skype in 2005 for $2.6 billion at a time when Skype was only generating $7 million in annual revenue. eBay then-CEO Meg Whitman claimed this move was central to its strategy of developing significant presence in the three related internet commerce domains of "buy, pay, communicate" (Figure 10.14). Skype was designed to enhance communication in the auction environment between sellers and buyers, just as PayPal had made financial transactions smoother. Yet eBay could bring no particular strategic resources to bear to either of these acquisitions. They each had to stand on their own. Few ended up using Skype, though, as early adopters of eBay began defaulting back to huge online retailers like Amazon.com. The hoped-for synergies never materialized. Four money-losing years later eBay, having never integrated the service into its auction business, sold 70% of Skype to a group of private investors for $2.8 billion.[34]

Figure 10.14
Strategic Rationale for eBay's Acquisitions

| Find | Buy | Pay | Communicate | Entertain |

eBay — #1 in eCommerce
PayPal — #1 in online payments
Skype — #1 in voice communications

In 2022 AT&T completed the unloading of its WarnerMedia group, which it had acquired in 2018 for $85 billion. AT&T had tried to put together a studio and media content company with its 5G network cellular phone business. Smart strategic thinking did not drive this deal to begin with. There was very little fit between these businesses. Paralleling the disaster 20 years earlier when AOL acquired Time Warner, it became evident very quickly that the management, resources and operational fit between the two companies was sorely lacking and could never be engineered.

Occasionally a corporation discovers an acquired company needs to employ a different strategy in the marketplace. This is what occurred when Gillette purchased the Duracell business. Gillette's core razors and blades business was built on a differentiated approach, and they believed they could leverage their differentiation capabilities into the battery business. However, the battery market was in transition, where what was becoming increasingly valued in the marketplace was low cost and price – a set of strategic management disciplines that Gillette did not possess. Shouldn't they have realized this was where the battery market was going? See the next point!

Do the due. Corporate acquisition teams often fail to complete a thorough due diligence process. In due diligence every aspect of a targeted company's external and internal dimensions, as well as its potential fit with the corporation, should be exhaustively investigated. This includes the target company's markets, customers, suppliers and competitors, its internal operations, its people, its culture, and more. Due diligence includes analysis that carefully identifies where and how opportunities for scope and economizing exist through the acquisition, and how the management and cultural fits between the two companies can leverage the corporation's resources and competencies.

Acquisitions are plagued by poor due diligence, which manifests itself in two important ways. First, many acquisition efforts fail to rigorously research the deal. This leads to statements such as the following by QVC's chairman Barry Diller when he contemplated acquiring CBS in 1994: "Sure there are some (synergies) here for sure. I don't know where they are yet. To say that now would be an idiot's game."[35] When there is poor due diligence, acquiring companies make the mistake of simply assuming that synergies exist and can be easily captured.

Second, even when the due diligence process is followed, some acquisition analysis teams focus on the more obvious of the potential economic benefits – scope and economizing – while devoting significantly less effort to the more difficult and complex area of leverage through management, administrative systems, resources, and culture. GE Capital's John Lanier commented on this failure, claiming that errors during the due diligence process are rarely due to faulty technical analysis: "The reason why the prognosticated value fails to appear in many cases is that people fail to pay enough attention to cultural factors. That is why many acquisitions flounder – because of the people side, the soft side. That is the reason for failure in three out of five cases."[36]

Capturing synergies. Identifying potential synergies leading to scope, economizing, and leverage is one thing; actually capturing them is quite another. Combining sales organizations and operations to accomplish scope and economizing is difficult enough. It is often unclear how to leverage the intangibles of the corporation – value creation routines, resources, capabilities – to the advantage of the acquired company.

Integrating cultures usually leads the list of reasons why synergy is so difficult to achieve. Corporations that acquire companies try to avoid a "winners and losers" or "conquerors and conquered" mentality, but often these feelings persist in the post-acquisition phase anyway. In addition, the clashing of very different cultures can make any synergistic effort fail miserably. The best known clash of cultures occurred when America Online (AOL) acquired Time Warner in 2001 for $103.5 billion. AOL was a hip, knowledge-based internet company run by freewheeling young people tuned in to the new digital age. Time Warner was a traditional asset-based media company (magazines, books, studios, cable television) run by old school managers who made money the "old-fashioned way." After five years management of the combined company finally gave up trying to push synergy across two such different enterprises.[37]

In an effort to exert control over newly acquired companies, corporations often install new rules and regulations, routines, procedures, and corporate managers in the acquisition. Inadequately communicated as to why these actions are taken, they are either misunderstood by employees of the acquired company or serve to reinforce the "conquered" feeling. It is also difficult to start changing the ways one acts on a day-to-day basis, so the implementation of new systems and procedures often requires the "new" employees to take time away from the business itself in order to attend to the "administrivia" forced on them from the new corporate owners.

In 2021 French retailer LVMH took over Tiffany's, the famed but faded jewelry retailer. The acquisition "started with insults, lawsuits, and accusations of mismanagement…employees joked that French lessons were a prerequisite for job security…a group of Tiffany staffers circulated an unsanctioned memo offering tips on Franco-American nuances and etiquette…[including] 'expect less warm and fuzzy.' "[38] These attitudes will be tough to overcome.

In combination, the clash between cultures and the installation of new systems leads to serious problems in achieving the synergies that the corporation had hoped for. One study quantified the negative impact of acquisitions on employees in acquired companies (Figure 10.15).[39] When Charter Communications acquired Time Warner Cable in 2016, the corporate office reorganized territories for field workers and changed their compensation plans. With wider territories requiring more travel time and fewer bonuses, the "acquired" Time Warner employees were very unhappy with their new owner.[40] Presumably a corporation acquires a company because it believes the employees of the company have accomplished something worthwhile that the corporation can build upon. When employee morale and productivity suffer, and when employees resign, it is difficult at best to achieve the hoped-for leverage.

Figure 10.15
Workforce Impact of Acquisitions

Decrease in employee productivity	17%
Decrease in employee morale	41%
Increase in unwanted turnover	25%
Increase in retirements	25%

Acquisition premiums. Due to the synergistic opportunities for scope, economizing, and resources leverage in an acquisition target, corporate executives generally believe a target company is worth more than how financial markets value that company. They are therefore willing to pay more than the current stock price for the target company. Between 1978 and 1990 the average premium paid over a company's stock price immediately preceding an acquisition announcement was 34%.[41] After the excesses of the late 1990s stock market internet bubble, one would think sanity might return to the corporate suite, but in fact in the 2000s acquisition premiums increased to an average of almost 40% over a target company's stock price three months prior to acquisition. In 2021 median takeover premiums were down to 29% across all size deals, but were at 34% for middle market deals between up to $500 million.[42]

Huge premiums over the market value of the stock of the target acquisition make it very difficult to produce a positive return for their shareholders. Use a spreadsheet to calculate this very simply: to break even on a 35% premium would require the corporation to increase the acquired company's ROE by 10 percentage points (say, from 14% to 24%) in the second year, and then to maintain that increase for the next seven years. Such increases would call for significant short-term improvement in some combination of the ratios that make up ROE (profitability, asset productivity, or financial leverage – see Chapter 2), all very difficult to pull off.

Why are corporate executives willing to pay so much to acquire other companies? Figure 10.16 lists the most compelling reasons behind this behavior. Poor due diligence is right at the top of the list (literally). Poor due diligence leads to what is known as the "synergy trap," in which executives justify ever-higher prices because of synergies they think they will be able to find and capture. Then we witness bidding wars occurring with some regularity, such as what happened between Boston Scientific and J&J profiled earlier in this chapter. In 2007 Tom Tom and Garmin, the two leading manufacturers of GPS tracking devices, engaged in a bidding war for electronic mapmaker Tele Atlas. Tom Tom finally bid 41% higher than its initial bid earlier in the year, at a level representing an 81% premium to Tele Atlas's shares before the initial bid.[43]

Figure 10.16
Reasons for Acquisition Premiums

Poor due diligence
Synergy trap
Bidding wars
Hubris & ego of CEO
Bandwagon effects

Executives can become emotionally tied to acquiring a particular company, so that in the face of competitive bidding they are willing to increase the stakes. Often the egotistic personalities of corporate executives play a hand in this. Supreme self-confidence – some call it hubris – leads executives to believe that they can accomplish nearly anything.[44] "Almost all of us believe ourselves to be in the top 20% of the population when it comes to...managing a business."[45] This tendency is also evident in the Boston Scientific–Guidant acquisition, where CFO Larry Best didn't want to lose and believed that the management team could make the acquisition work at even higher prices. Occasionally, we observe a bandwagon effect happening, where an acquisition is made "because everyone else is doing it" and because "we don't want to get left behind." A rash of internet advertising firm acquisitions during 2007 is an example of this type of corporate behavior, and the herd behavior can easily lead to over-bidding.

Loss of focus. It is not uncommon to find corporate management so caught up in trying to effectively integrate two businesses to capture synergies that they pay less attention to the core business of both the corporation and the acquired company. In 1997, for example, Boeing and McDonnell Douglas merged to create a larger commercial aircraft manufacturer and the largest defense contractor. Unfortunately, the problems of integrating McDonnell Douglas into Boeing led Boeing executives to "take their eyes off the ball," and Boeing soon experienced serious problems in managing its own aircraft assembly operations. In turn this led to a dramatic management shake-up, but more importantly it led to an opportunity for Airbus to gain additional business and challenge Boeing's status as the worldwide leader in the commercial aircraft industry. That ultimately led to today's situation where Airbus often leads Boeing in the market. There can be a long-lasting effect for having lost strategic focus and discipline!

Accelerating growth is tough. The evidence shows that most acquiring companies fail to accelerate their growth (Figure 10.17).[46] When companies spend so much energy trying to attain synergies, when they spend so much effort seeking to combine different cultures, when they lose focus on their core businesses,

Figure 10.17
Success in Accelerating Growth

Change in Revenue Growth	%
Slowed down	19
No change	64
Accelerated	12

it becomes difficult to accelerate the growth of the acquired company. Employees worry about their jobs and new procedures, suppliers worry about their contracts, and customers become unsettled. Accelerating revenue growth under ordinary conditions is difficult because of competition, but under these circumstances accelerating growth becomes an extraordinary challenge.

Accelerating growth of the acquired company is one of the most important challenges that management of the corporation faces, since the economic success of acquisitions ordinarily depends more on revenue growth than it does on cost savings. Where there is little revenue growth, then management is under tremendous pressure to cut costs drastically in order to achieve the desired return on the premium price it paid for the acquisition. This became an issue of significance in 2018 for Kraft, which was acquired by 3G Capital three years earlier. 3G had a "cost-cutting formula" which it put into play immediately, resulting in huge costs savings by shuttering outdated factories, shedding thousands of jobs, and consolidating food manufacturing operations. This resulted in earnings increases despite declines in sales. Now opportunities to improve earnings further through cost cuts have run out.[47] And in the meantime, the cost cuts across the board have damaged Kraft's ability to respond to changes in the market and keep up with competitors.

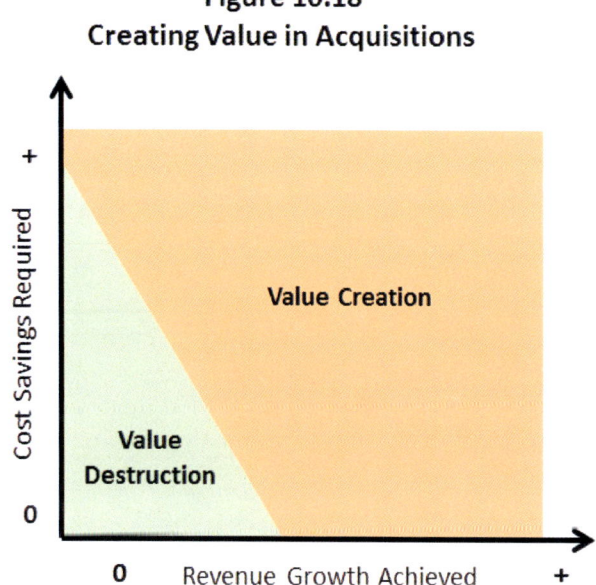

Figure 10.18
Creating Value in Acquisitions

On the other hand, the pressure to cut costs is significantly reduced where revenue growth has been accelerated, as is suggested in Figure 10.18.[48] While holding costs constant, accelerating revenue growth of the acquired company will deliver enhanced cash flows to the corporation. The most successful acquisitions are those which economize, create scope, and leverage resources in order to both accelerate growth and cut costs. These are companies that operate in the upper right corner of Figure 10.18, creating value for their shareholders through the acquisition.

Post-acquisition efforts. A few lessons have been learned about post-acquisition efforts by observing companies that have an enviable track record, such as Cisco. Although every acquisition situation offers a unique context, the following steps enhance the odds of success:

- **Immediately establish an integration team**. The team should be jointly formed with members from both the acquiring and the acquired company.

- **Ensure that senior management of both companies are visibly involved**. Involvement by senior management of the corporation signals that the acquisition is important, while involvement by senior management of the acquired company signals that the perspective of the acquired is critical.

- **Give accountability to the integration team, and also provide them authority and resources to effect changes**. Nothing is worse than constituting a team that can only advise and wait for a decision to be rendered. This slows the integration process down, and signals that senior corporate management really holds all the cards after all.

- **Have a human resources transition plan and team in place before the acquisition becomes official.** In order to avoid the kind of turnover mentioned earlier, it is helpful to make HR resources available to employees of the acquired company to answer questions and calm concerns.

- **Implement a system that provides financial controls and operational indicators.** While strategic responsibility for the integration is shifted to the integration team, it must be clear that financial performance is the overarching goal of the corporation. A system of operational indicators will provide valuable feedback to both the integration team and corporate management if problems are cropping up.

- **Communicate early and often.** Employees of both the acquired company and the corporate parent don't want to be left in the dark about what is going on or how things are going. Building on the discussion in Chapter 3 on vision and mission, communicating with employees helps to align their day-to-day actions with the goals of the company. The corporation should also have a proactive plan to communicate with suppliers and customers.

One of the Worst Deals Ever? Part 2[49]

Two-and-a-half years after completing the Guidant acquisition, Boston Scientific continued to suffer from the deal. On top of massive cuts and continuing restructuring charges related to the deal, the company was also impacted by the entry of a new, very powerful competitor. Medtronic received approval from the FDA to sell its coated stent in the U.S. market starting in 2008. In the first quarter of its release to the market, Medtronic's share went from zero to 26%.

In April 2008, Boston Scientific announced that it was going to divest itself of what it referred to as "noncore" businesses and lay off 2,300 employees in an effort to cut expenses by over $500 million a year. They also announced that the integration of Guidant was complete and the company was poised to move forward.

What has happened since? Boston Scientific faced a major controversy relating to the concealment of a defibrillator design flaw by Guidant. By 2011 it had paid $234 million in settlements to affected patients and $296 million in fines. This raises concerns about the quality of Boston Scientific's due diligence process to begin with. In 2015, nine years after the acquisition, Boston finally settled a lawsuit filed by its original bidding competitor – Johnson & Johnson. J&J had sued because it claimed Guidant had breached a prior merger agreement. In addition to this $600 million settlement Boston has written off nearly $9 billion in assets since 2006, mostly related to Guidant. In 2017 Boston's stock price returned to where it had been when it originally bid for Guidant 11 years earlier. Its highest stock price ever of $44.92 occurred two years before the Guidant acquisition. The stock closed out 2021 at $42.48. Finally back…whew!

QUESTION

1. Given the discussion in the earlier section, what pre-acquisition advice would you have given to the Boston Scientific senior managers before they acquired another company?

2. With Guidant completely absorbed into Boston Scientific, how can you determine whether or not the acquisition was a success? For Boston shareholders? For Guidant shareholders?

MANAGING THE CORPORATE PORTFOLIO

The advent of highly diversified companies created a new management problem that had not been experienced previously. How do you manage such a variety of different types of businesses? How does corporate management establish investment priorities among subsidiary operations? On what basis does corporate management decide to prune the portfolio, weeding out companies that no longer seem to have real promise to contribute to corporate performance?

Portfolios Management Tools

In response to these evolving challenges, two consulting firms developed methods of evaluation that became popular tools used by diversified corporations. These include the GE Business Development Matrix developed by McKinsey, and the BCG Growth Share Matrix developed by the Boston Consulting Group. We'll discuss each briefly because you will undoubtedly run into these at some point. However we'll also mention a few of the limitations of portfolio tools, because they do not fully reflect more contemporary thinking about corporate strategic management.

**Figure 10.19
GE Business Development Matrix**

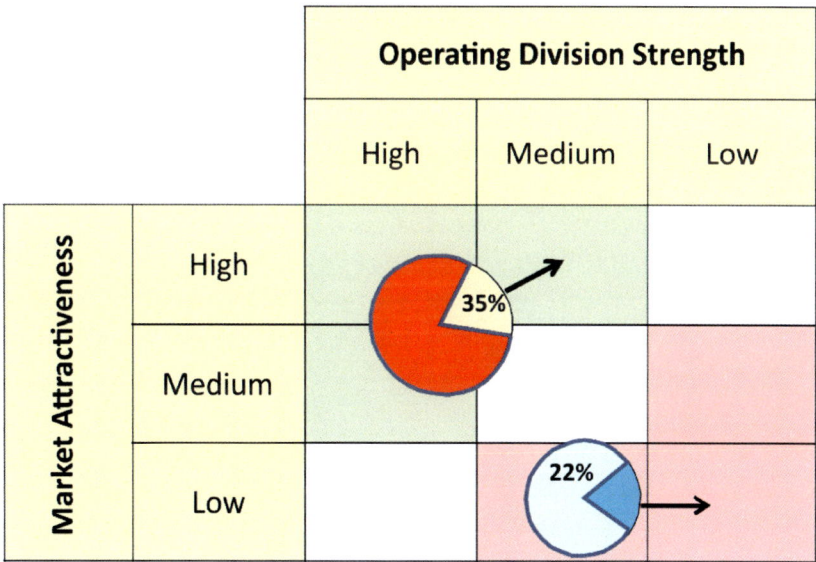

GE business development matrix. Figure 10.19 presents an example of this matrix developed originally for General Electric but now more widely used. Every operating division is plotted on the chart using metrics that assess the attractiveness of its industry (vertical scale) and the operating division's strength (horizontal scale). Market attractiveness is determined by many of the same factors we discussed in Chapter 4 on Industry Analysis. A rating for the strength of the division is developed after assessing factors such as brand strength, market share and market share growth, cost position and margins relative to competitors, innovation strength and technological capability, quality, management strength, and other dimensions. As in measuring key success factors and creating strategic groups maps in Chapter 4, one needs to carefully quantify factors to avoid pure judgment or "guesstimates." Doing so provides an objective picture of the operating divisions. By convention, the size of a circle around each plotted division represents the size of the industry in which the business unit operates. The "pie slice" within each circle represents the market share of the business unit. The arrows represent the direction the business unit is expected to move in the future.

The green shaded cells in the figure represent areas of opportunity for the corporation because divisions in these cells or headed into these cells are strong business units operating in attractive industries. These are divisions that the corporation would want to invest in. On the other hand, the divisions in or headed into the pink shaded cells are those with weaker business strength operating in less attractive markets. These divisions might be candidates for divestiture, since continued investment in them might not pay off.

BCG growth share matrix. By far the most popular tool for assessing portfolios of companies under a corporate umbrella is Boston Consulting Group's Growth Share Matrix (Figure 10.20). The BCG matrix contains only four cells, but here the operating divisions are measured and plotted along the dimensions of industry growth rate (vertical scale) and relative market share (share relative to largest competitor – horizontal scale). One of the reasons the BCG matrix is so well known is because each cell is labeled according to its cash flow characteristics and needs.

**Figure 10.20
BCG Growth Share Matrix**

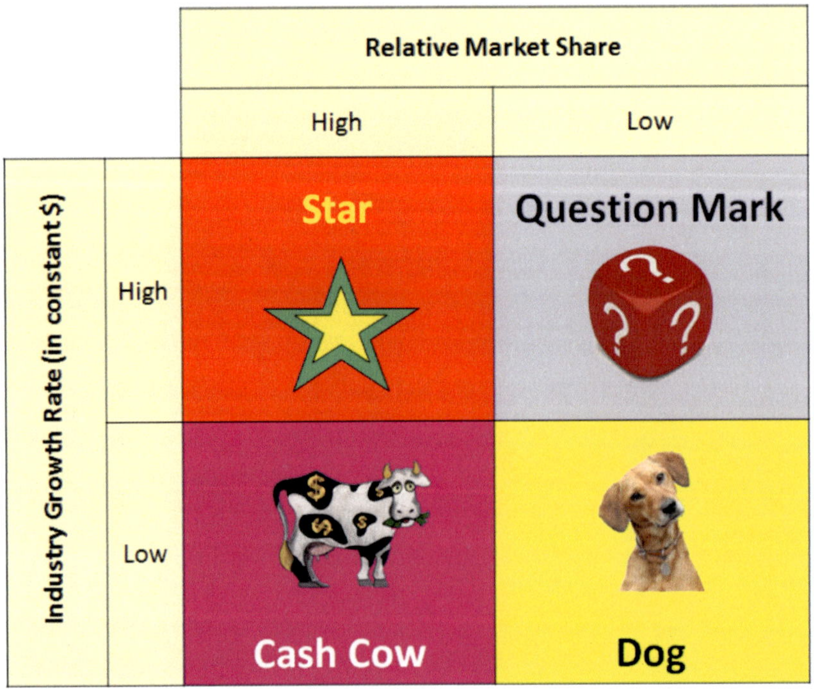

		Relative Market Share	
		High	Low
Industry Growth Rate (in constant $)	High	Star	Question Mark
	Low	Cash Cow	Dog

Where the division has a high relative market share in a growing industry, it is a "star" and merits investment by the corporation. Where the division has a high market share but is in a low-growth industry, it is called a "cash cow"; it should not receive major corporate investment. Instead the corporation should "milk the cash cow," using cash the division generates to fund other more promising divisions. A "dog" is a division that is a candidate for divestiture: low share in a low-growth industry. The only way to grow that kind of a business would be to steal share from stronger rivals, which would require a huge investment – typically a risky move. In the upper right corner is the "question mark," because it is unclear what to do with businesses that fall in this low share-high industry growth quadrant. To gain market share in a growth industry would require growth faster than the rest of the industry, which means taking market share from competitors. Divisions that exist in this quadrant are thus likely to require large injections of capital from the corporation.

Here is an example of the BCG matrix in action. In 2018 publishing giant Meredith Corporation acquired Time and its magazine brands. A BCG matrix of the various brands then owned by Meredith provided guidance on which brands to invest in, and which to consider divesting. Four of the magazine titles acquired – Time, Money, Fortune, and Sports Illustrated – are all located in the Dog quadrant. They have unattractive market positions relative to other news providers, because of the relative ease of finding this sort of content elsewhere. The news magazine industry segment is not growing, in fact it is declining in both newsstand revenue and advertising pages. So after having acquired these assets as part of the bundle of magazines from Time, Meredith believed it was in their best interest to sell off these brands. And in fact from 2018-2019 it sold off all four magazines. But People magazine presented a different situation. It has unparalleled access to celebrities and its unique content cannot be easily sourced through other news outlets. So Meredith believed that opportunity existed to invest in the brand and turn it into a Star. Meredith's other lifestyle brands (Fixer Upper, Hungry Girl) shared similar market position and industry growth characteristics.[50] Meredith's performance was so improved by their M&A moves that in 2021 the entire company was profitably sold to IAC in a $2.7 billion deal.

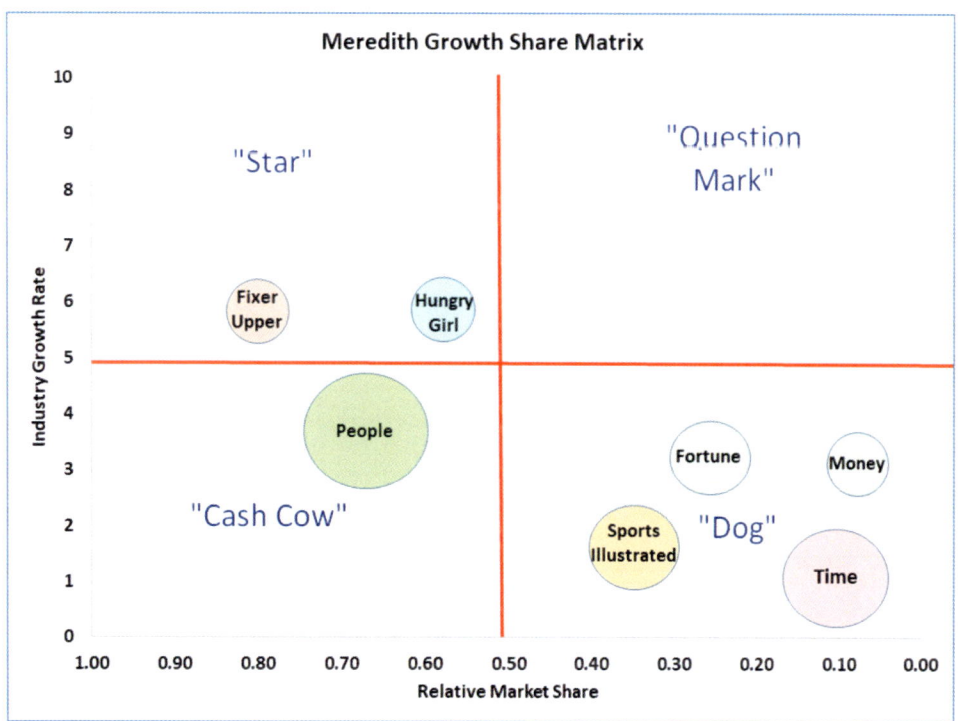

Drawbacks of portfolio techniques. While these two methods for arraying a corporation's businesses do provide a comprehensive picture and are relatively easy to understand, there are a number of drawbacks that users of the tools should be aware of. Most importantly, neither method draws upon the dimensions of competitive advantage that have been emphasized throughout this book: value chain, extraordinary resources, or capabilities. Earlier in this chapter we described how GE organizes its multiple lines of business into strategic business units, since they acknowledge that there are strategic characteristics that are shared across businesses. The GE and BCG matrices are static, not necessarily accounting for whether or how strategically important resources in one business could be leveraged into others. In addition, if an operating division is in one of the uncolored cells in the GE matrix, or is a cash cow or question mark in the BCG matrix, there is no straightforward advice that corporate managers may take from the analysis. It is not clear whether investment in the question mark businesses will result in market share growth. Even cash cows may be costly to fortify and defend if competition grows more intense (which often happens in low-growth industries).

Finally, the BCG matrix critically depends on an underlying assumption that high market share is always related to superior profitability. Following this assumption, BCG advice has usually been to expand product lines and sales territories in order to develop experience curve economies (see Chapter 7), which would result in lower unit costs and presumably higher profits. We now know that enhanced profitability is *sometimes* related to higher market share, but this relationship is certainly not *always* the case. Market share can be "bought," such as when companies invest in a business at a rate higher than makes economic sense for long periods of time. Additionally, efforts to support larger market shares, such as building additional manufacturing capacity to achieve scale efficiency – especially if at the same time pursued by competitors – may result in industry overcapacity, leading to poor asset utilization, higher unit costs, and lower profitability. The domestic automobile manufacturing industry in the first decade of the 2000s is a dramatic, striking example of the economic dilemma that occurs when a number of competitors build more capacity than they can productively use. Overcapacity, combined with stiff competition from foreign-owned manufacturers, left each of Detroit's "Big 3" struggling for their very survival.

Restructuring

The waves of conglomeration and acquisitions seen in the United States and global economies over the last few decades have ordinarily been followed by periods of restructuring. As in baseball, amusement parks, and life, "what goes up often comes down." Corporations that have diversified too much or too broadly through acquisitions often find they have difficulty managing the resulting complexity and experience performance declines. They then engage in restructuring, through which they seek to improve performance by divesting undesirable businesses.

Typically, restructuring efforts will involve what is known as downscoping.[51] Through downscoping a corporation reduces its level of diversification and strategically refocuses on core businesses where the synergies of scope economizing, and leverage are more evident and more easily realized.[52] In 2007, for example, VeriSign announced that it would sell off ten of its fifteen business units. The financial community on Wall Street had criticized the company for poor financial performance due to over-acquiring into fields unrelated to its core internet name registry and e-commerce security businesses. Analysts had seen little synergy among its wide array of technology businesses, beat down the company's share price, and forced the resignation of the CEO who had acquired all these businesses between 2004 and 2006. William Roper Jr., the new CEO, indicated that "with so many divergent businesses and teams fighting for resources, the company had lacked a coherent focus."[53] Pruning out these less-related divisions allowed the company to focus.

Downscoping can also involve unloading part of a company in order to achieve better strategic focus. In 2018-2019 VF Corporation announced it would divest its Nautica brand, and spin off jeans brands Wrangler and Lee into Kontoor Brands as a separate company. This was part of a broad effort by the company to focus its attention on "edgier" brands that have youth appeal (for example Vanns, The North Face, Timberland). Nautica's target base were older folks, often jeans-wearing parents of the young people the company is more interested in for its core brands. By focusing down VF believes it can achieve greater economies and performance through sourcing, manufacturing, distribution, marketing and more.

This trend continues into 2022 with major downscoping initiatives announced. After decades as the exemplar of conglomerate, General Electric is splitting itself up into three separate public companies with each focused on its own segment – aviation, healthcare, and energy. Toshiba announced it will split up into three companies – one focused on infrastructure, one on semiconductors, and one on flash memory. Johnson & Johnson is splitting out its consumer business from its pharmaceutical and medical devices business. The essential point of all these moves is to achieve far greater strategic focus in each resulting company.

Restructuring the corporate portfolio can also simply reflect the fact that divisions within the corporate portfolio no longer present the same opportunities for returns through leverage that they once did. It may not be that the corporation needs to be refocused. It may be that the capital released from divesting a division can be put to much more productive use within another division, or through a different acquisition. In fact, recent research among 2,300 of the world's largest public companies reveals that companies which regularly reallocate capital, in part through divestiture, stand a better chance of moving into the ranks of the highest-performing companies.[54]

Another cause for restructuring is when *some* of the parts are worth more than the whole (which is in contrast to the usual synergistic argument that the *sum* of the parts are worth more than the whole). In 1994 Ralston Purina spun off its breakfast cereals business into a new company named RalCorp. Management of the new company could pay attention strictly to the cereal business and not be distracted by the much larger pet food business, which was Ralston Purina's core focus. Consequently, the RalCorp cereal business performed much better, and the new company's stock price rose from $15 per share to $23 per share in a little over a year.[55] Ralston Purina shareholders who received shares of RalCorp would never have seen this kind of rise with the cereal business buried inside a pet food company.

Other similar restructuring stories abound. The breakup of HP into two separate companies, profiled in the beginning of this chapter, is one high profile recent example. We mentioned above how eBay sold off Skype, but they also spun out PayPal because the market placed a higher value on PayPal as a stand-alone company. In 2007 General Electric discovered that financial markets placed a significantly higher value on the Saudi Basic Industries plastics business it divested than had GE's own management. It realized $11.6 billion in the sale of the business, 45 percent higher than internal valuations placed on the business. In 2019 United Technologies spun off the Otis and Carrier divisions for similar reasons.[56]

Often restructuring efforts such as those described here are undertaken not only to improve the corporation's performance, but also to smooth relations with large activist shareholders. Activist shareholders or equity funds accumulate large blocks of corporate stock and then command management and board attention when they point out the need to do something about underperforming businesses or divisions. If existing management does not improve the performance of the underperforming business or sell it off, the possibility exists that the large shareholders will persuade other shareholders to join them in an attempt to take over control of the company. In 2019 Elliott Management disclosed a $3.2 billion stake in AT&T. It criticized management of the company for having diversified too much and lost its focus, especially after it had moved into media content with its acquisition of Time Warner. Elliott used its shareholder position to press for divesting some divisions, changing management itself, and getting seats on the board of directors. Voila! In 2022 AT&T is spinning out the media content business.

Deciding What and How to Unload

The idea of gaining more strategic focus through restructuring begs the question of what businesses to divest. Referring back to the BCG Growth Share Matrix (Figure 10.18), we could simply sell off the "dogs." However, as we described in that earlier section, this tool provides insight only on the market share characteristics of businesses and not on their strategic importance. It is also silent on possible beneficial relationships between business units. So management needs to develop another set of criteria to help guide decision making on divestitures.

Divestiture, of course, is simply the reverse of acquisition. This simple insight suggests that management can use many of the same decision criteria for divesting that guide their thinking about acquiring:

- Is the industry still attractive?
- Is there a strategic rationale for holding onto a particular business?
- Are there scope, economizing, and leverage synergies that are possible with other businesses in the corporate portfolio?
- Do opportunities still exist to grow the business?
- Will the invested capital that the business requires enhance the corporate ROE?
- Is the value of the business greater as part of the corporate family, as an independent business enterprise, or as part of some other corporation's portfolio of businesses?

If the answer to any of these questions is "No," then the business under scrutiny is a candidate for divestiture.

There are generally three ways to divest a company (Figure 10.21). As HP did in 2015 with its HPE enterprise hardware and systems division, the corporation can spin off the business into a new independent company. Corporate shareholders receive shares in the newly formed enterprise, and a new board of directors is created. Spin-offs will generally favor corporate shareholders when the new company has a strong competitive position in its industry and the industry environment is attractive.

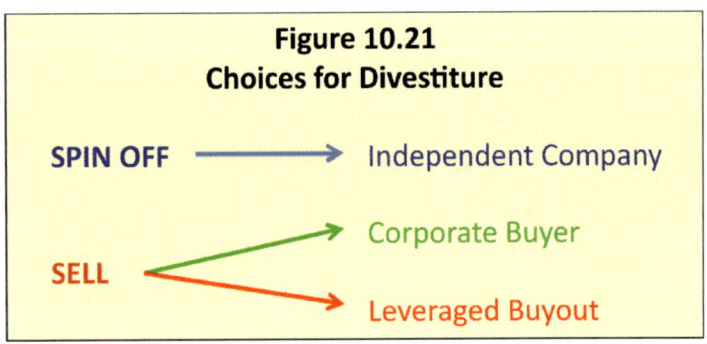

The other two ways of divesting are by selling a business, either to another corporate buyer or through a leveraged buyout. Most typically, another corporation will be the buyer for a business that is being sold, and that corporation will entertain the same set of acquisition criteria that we discussed earlier (Figure 10.13). During 2007 Kraft Foods downscoped by selling off its Post Cereals business, which allowed Kraft to focus its management attention and resources on faster growing brands. The buyer for Post Cereals was RalCorp, earlier spun out of Ralston Purina; the acquisition increased RalCorp's sales by 50 percent, making it a larger player in the cereal business.

Leveraged buyouts occur when the management of a company uses debt financing to buy the company from its corporate parent, and then continues to run the company. LBOs occur when management of the business sees greater potential in the business than does the corporate parent, or when the corporate parent is unable or unwilling to provide corporate financial resources that would be necessary to take advantage of the potential that exists. Extremely popular in the United States in the 1980s, LBOs surged in Europe in 2007–08, fed by well-functioning capital markets abroad and the rising purchasing power of the euro. Yet the success of LBOs depends on interest rates, since the "leverage" in the phrase indicates that the companies are purchased using large amounts of debt. High interest rates tend to depress LBO activity and make consummated transactions very risky. The success of LBOs also depends critically on both cutting costs and accelerating revenue growth (Figure 10.16), since interest payments on the debt create onerous conditions for management if the business does not improve.

CHAPTER SUMMARY

Whereas business strategy concerns itself with management of a single business, corporate strategy involves the management of sets of businesses. Corporate strategists must make decisions about which industries to enter and exit, how to combine businesses that are strategically related, how to establish investment priorities among a portfolio of businesses, how to achieve synergies among related businesses, and whether to acquire or divest businesses. These are important decision domains because the economic landscape of the United States has been dominated by diversified corporations for nearly fifty years.

Corporations diversify beyond a single business for a variety of reasons. They seek to grow, to develop market power, to enter new markets more rapidly, and to spread risk – all in an effort to enhance corporate financial performance.

Diversification is either related or unrelated. Unrelated diversification depends on financial market imperfections, in which case corporate financial expertise presents an advantage over market-based transactions. Related diversification depends on similarities in industry and value chain conditions between the corporation and its intended acquisition. Synergies that take advantage of these similarities are of three types: market fit, operational fit, and management fit. The benefits of synergies can be scope, economizing, and leverage. Leverage is the most challenging to achieve, but also the most rewarding if achieved. The parenting advantage matrix can help assess the degree of fit between headquarter capabilities and the needs of the business being considered for acquisition.

Successful acquisitions hinge on the following factors:

- Selecting attractive industries

- Being guided by a well-articulated strategic rationale

- Conducting due diligence, examining in very specific terms where synergies can be captured

- Not paying a huge premium to acquire a company

- Post-acquisition steps that enhance the integration of the companies

Due diligence and a well-articulated plan to capture synergies will help corporations avoid the loss of focus and the difficulty in accelerating growth that often occurs after the acquisition is completed. Refusing to pay outrageous premiums reduces the urgency to cut costs that management often feels is necessary, and instead leads to concentration on creating scope and leverage synergies that accelerate revenue growth.

Corporate strategists also make divestiture decisions in efforts to restructure the corporate portfolio. Downscoping involves divesting a business in order to focus more carefully on the strategically related businesses at the core or the corporation. Divestiture may also unlock economic potential of businesses that might fare better under different ownership.

Portfolio management techniques can help corporate managers decide which business divisions to invest in, which to milk, and which may be ripe for divestiture. The GE Business Development Matrix and the BCG Growth Share matrix are tools that have been popular for decades, although each has limitations.

Learning Objectives Review

1. *Compare and contrast corporate strategy decisions and business strategy decisions.*

    - Business strategy ideas and frameworks – e.g. value chain, resource based analysis, low cost leadership or differentiation strategy – are appropriate to use when a company operates largely in in only one line of business.

    - Corporate strategy decisions encompass a wider array of issues:

        - Which industries to enter and exit.

        - Defining a strategic business unit (SBU).

        - Establishing SBU investment priorities.

        - Effecting resource and management transfers among SBUs.

        - Structuring the corporation.

2. *Appraise historical acquisition performance and the explanations behind it.*

    - Research provides evidence that acquisitions on average produce low positive returns, but that there is wide variance in performance results. Many companies destroy shareholder value through their acquisition efforts.

    - Acquisitions are more successful when they involve:

        - entering attractive industries

        - a well-thought out strategic rationale that guides which companies to consider acquiring

        - when strong due diligence is performed in the courtship phase of negotiations.

    - Acquisitions are difficult to pull off because:

        - they usually depend on capturing synergies in culture and the softer parts of the value chain.

- acquirers pay premium prices to buy companies.
- there is a loss of focus on the core business, and accelerating growth is difficult.
- post-acquisition efforts are not well-organized.

3. *Create a map explaining why companies diversify.*

- Growth
- Market power
- Market entry
- Spreading risk

4. *Explain the two primary types of diversification: related and unrelated diversification.*

- Related diversification means that there is some dimension of similarity between the corporation and the company it seeks to acquire.
- Variations in the similarities of the industry and value chain determine whether the style of related diversification is horizontal, vertical, or cross-sector.
- Unrelated diversification occurs when a corporation enters a new business in a different industry and does not expect to achieve any value chain synergies through the combination.

5. *Using the types of diversification methods available, support an argument for a conglomerate to utilize each one.*

- A supermarket chain decides to expand the territory in which it operates by acquiring another supermarket chain in a different part of the country. This horizontal acquisition is designed to increase scale and result in cost savings throughout the company's primary value chain.
- The same company acquires a manufacturer of private label food products. This vertical acquisition enables the supermarket to gain control over the supply and costs of products it then sells in its stores.
- The supermarket chain itself is then acquired by a holding company, which also owns other businesses such as insurance services and veterinary clinics. The holding company provides an infusion of cash to the supermarket so it can upgrade its back end technology to become more competitive in the industry.

6. *Apply tools for managing a diversified conglomerate effectively.*

- The GE Business Development Matrix provides a method for evaluating which SBUs to invest in further and which to consider divesting. SBUs with strong market shares in attractive industries deserve further management attention and investment.
- The BCG Growth Share Matrix is a popular tool with four easy-to-understand dimensions based on industry growth rate and relative market share of the SBU. The usual advice is to invest in the Stars, milk the Cash Cows, and get rid of the Dogs.

- There are some important caveats for each of these matrices, since neither fundamentally considers possible strategic resource sharing across SBUS, and each presumes that high market share is associated with strong financial performance.

Key Terms

Agency – Where an individual (such as a corporate officer) acts on behalf of someone else (such as a shareholder).

Business strategy – The types of decisions made and direction created for a single business.

CLO Collateralized Loan Obligation – Large pool of bank loans bundled together by financial services firms and sold off to investors in slices, with the goal to spread default risk "an inch deep and a mile wide."

Conglomerates – A corporation that owns a large number of businesses that are different sizes and operate in different industry sectors.

Corporate strategy – The types of decisions made and direction created for a corporation that operates multiple lines of business.

Cross-sector diversification – Acquisition of a company in a different industry, but which employs a similar value chain.

Dominant business – A company in which 70–95 percent of revenue comes from a single business.

Downscoping – When a corporation reduces its level of diversification and strategically refocuses on core businesses where the synergies of scope, economizing, and leverage are more evident and more easily realized.

Economizing – Cost savings accomplished by operating combined companies more efficiently.

Holding company – Corporation that owns the majority of voting shares of other companies, but that allows the other companies to operate as independent entities.

Horizontal diversification – Acquisition of a company that operates in the same industry using the same value chain.

Junk bond – High-yield debt that is rated below investment grade at the time of purchase. These bonds have a higher risk of default, but typically pay higher yields than better quality bonds in order to make them attractive to investors. Typically issued by businesses that are unable to secure investment grade financing.

Leveraged buyout (LBO) – A process where a company is bought primarily using debt. Typically engineered by management of the company, or by private equity firms.

Management fit – When a corporation can take synergistic advantage of administrative and support activities of the value chain in making an acquisition.

Market fit – When a corporation can take synergistic advantage of relationships with suppliers and/or customers in making an acquisition.

Operational fit – When a corporation is able to combine similar primary value chain activities.

Private equity firm – Private (nonpublic) corporations or partnerships that use their financial resources to engineer buyouts and acquisitions of other companies.

Related diversification – A merger or acquisition where there is some similarity of industry and/or value chain between the corporation and the company it seeks to acquire.

Resources leverage – The benefits that develop through the extension and application of corporate resources to a newly acquired company.

Scope – Ability to broaden a product line or a customer base achieved through an acquisition.

SPAC Special Purpose Acquisition Company – Empty-shell firms that promise to buy businesses with the proceeds of their initial public stock offerings.

Spin-off – Divestiture in which a corporation creates a new company out of one of its businesses. The new company has its own shares of stock and shareholders, and its own board of directors. Typically, shareholders of the corporation will receive newly issued shares out of the spin-off company at its organization.

Strategic business unit (SBU) – The organization of a set of businesses that share identical or very similar strategies or strategic challenges.

Systematic risk – Risk associated with macro-economic forces.

Takeover – A process where a large group of shareholders vote in new members to the board of directors, with the result that the new board can make changes in the company's management.

Unrelated diversification – When a corporation enters a new business in a different industry from that in which it currently operates and does not expect to achieve any value chain synergies through the combination.

Unsystematic risk – Risk associated with a particular business.

Vertical diversification – Acquisition of another company upstream (supplier) or downstream (buyer) in the value chain of the same industry in which the corporation operates.

Short Answer Review Questions

1. Why do companies choose to diversify?
2. What are the critical questions that each company should ask itself before embarking on a course of diversification?
3. How do diversified companies decide which business areas to divest?
4. What issues would you discuss if you were approached about an opportunity to buy a related company?
5. How about an unrelated company?
6. What can management do to improve the odds of success in an acquisition?
7. What information does the BCG Growth Share Matrix provide?
8. How would you use the GE Business Development Matrix?
9. What considerations should a business make prior to divesting a business entity?
10. Discuss the different types of diversification.

Group Exercises

1. Take a look at the Wall Street Journal for the past week. What merger or acquisition has just been announced? Based on your analysis, how successful will this M&A be? What would you recommend they do in the short term?

2. In 2022 Microsoft announced its plan to acquire gaming company Activision Blizzrd. Using Microsoft's recent 10k statements, review the performance of their divisions. Use the BCG or GE matrices to determine how Activision will fit into its portfolio.

3. Activision Blizzard has been one of the most successful gaming companies over the last decade. Entrepreneurial in spirit, it is home to hundreds of young people who just love gaming programming. How should Microsoft manage the integration of Activision into its corporate portfolio, in a way that ensures the valuable programmers at Activision will want to stay put and really become part of a Microsoft team?

3. One of the more significant functions in a company that is an active acquirer is the analysis of which companies to acquire. Pick a company that actively acquires other companies (e.g., 3M, Alphabet, Intel) and develop a short list of potential target companies for them to approach. How much would you pay for such an acquisition? Why? Where are the opportunities for the acquiring firm?

Investor Relations Sites for Companies Mentioned in This Chapter

AB InBev: https://www.ab-inbev.com/investors/
AT&T: https://investors.att.com/

Berkshire Hathaway: https://www.berkshirehathaway.com/
Black & Decker (Stanley Black & Decker): https://www.stanleyblackanddecker.com/investors
Boeing: https://investors.boeing.com/investors/overview/default.aspx
Boston Consulting Group: https://www.bcg.com/en-us/
Boston Scientific: https://investors.bostonscientific.com/
Cisco: https://investor.cisco.com/home/default.aspx
eBay: https://investors.ebayinc.com/overview/default.aspx
General Electric: https://www.ge.com/investor-relations
HP: https://investor.hp.com/home/default.aspx
HPE: https://investors.hpe.com/
IAC: https://ir.iac.com/
Illinois Tool Works: https://investor.itw.com/investor-relations/default.aspx
Johnson & Johnson: https://www.investor.jnj.com/
Kontoor Brands: https://www.kontoorbrands.com/investors
LVHM: https://www.lvmh.com/investors/
McKinsey & Co.: hhttps://www.mckinsey.com/about-us/overview
Merck: https://www.merck.com/investor-relations/
Microsoft: https://www.microsoft.com/en-us/investor
Oracle: https://investor.oracle.com/home/default.aspx
Paypal: https://investor.pypl.com/home/default.aspx
Procter & Gamble: https://pginvestor.com/
Ralcorp (Conagra): https://www.conagrabrands.com/investor-relations
Sirius XM: https://investor.siriusxm.com/investor-overview/default.aspx
T-Mobile: https://investor.t-mobile.com/investors/default.aspx
Toshiba: http://www.toshiba.co.jp/about/ir/indcx.htm
United Technologies (Raytheon): http://investors.rtx.com/
VF Corporation: https://www.vfc.com/investors
Walt Disney Company: https://thewaltdisneycompany.com/investor-relations/
Western Digital: https://investor.wdc.com/
Whole Foods (Amazon): https://ir.aboutamazon.com/overview/default.aspx

References

[1] Brat, I. 2007. "Turning managers into takeover artists." Wall Street Journal. April 6: A1. http://www.itw.com/about-itw/investor-day-2017/. https://www.the-numbers.com/movies/#tab=year.

[2] Smith, E. and Orden, E., 2012, "Mickey, Darth Vader to join forces," Wall Street Journal, October 31. B1. Leonard, D., 2013, "The inside story of how Disney bought Lucasfilm – and its plans for Star Wars," Bloomberg, March 7, www.bloomberg.com/news.

[3] Ovide, S., Lublin, J. S, & Mattioli, D., 2014, "Hewlett-Packard set to break up 75-year-old company," Wall Street Journal, October 6, B1. Bort, J., 2015, "The HP breakup will happen for real in November," Business Insider, March 19, 1. Anders, G., 2015, "After a costly breakup, HP Inc. is ready to have some fun," Forbes, October 14.

[4] Sakhartov, A. V. and T. B. Folta, 2014, "Resource relatedness, redeployability, and firm value," Strategic Management Journal, 35, 1781-1797.

[5] Nissan, E., and J. Caveny, 2005, "Aggregate concentration in corporate America: The case of the Fortune 500," International Journal of Applied Economics 21(1): 132. Yellen, J. L., 1998, Testimony before Senate Judiciary Committee. June 16, Washington, DC: http://clinton2.nara.gov/WH/EOP/CEA/html/19980616.html.

[6] Definition from *Webster's New Collegiate Dictionary*. 1974. Springfield, MA: G. and C. Merriam Company.

[7] Using 2-digit industry codes under the Standard Industrial Classification (SIC) system.

[8] Tobias, A, 1976, "March 3, 1998: The day they couldn't fill the Fortune 500," New York, December 20: 63. Three weeks after this article was published, New York was acquired by media mogul Rupert Murdoch.
[9] Rumelt, R. P. 1982. "Diversification strategy and profitability." *Strategic Management Journal* 3: 359. The data presented in this article are from a sample of the largest firms listed annually by Fortune. In addition, the author's own research on the Fortune 500 provides update data into 2014.
[10] Ramachandran J., Manikandan K. and Pant A., 2013, "Why conglomerates thrive (outside the U.S.)," Harvard Business Review, 91 (12), 110-119.
[11] Markides, C. 1992. "The economics of de-diversifying firms." *British Journal of Management* 3: 91.
[12] Burrough, B., and J. Helyar. 1990. *Barbarians at the gate*. New York: HarperCollins.
[13] Ng, S., and H. Sender, 2007, "Behind buyout surge, a debt market booms," Wall Street Journal, June 26: A1. More than half the loans behind buyouts in 2006 were resold to investors as CLOs. The Economist, 2014, "From dodo to phoenix," January 11, 58. The Economist, 2014, "The new GE: Google everywhere," January 18, 63.
[14] Bradley, C., M. Hirt, & S. Smit. 2018. "Strategy to beat the odds." *McKinsey Quarterly*, February.
[15] Burton, T. M., 2006, "Boston Scientific faces pivotal test after victory in fight for Guidant," Wall Street Journal, January 26: A1. Hensley, S., 2006, "How Boston Scientific beat J&J," Wall Street Journal, January 26: C1. Rappaport, M., 2006, "After Guidant deal, a case of seller's remorse," Wall Street Journal, October 23: C3. Tully, S., 2006, "The [second] worst deal ever," Fortune, October 16: 102.
[16] Vara, V., 2007, "Oracle results reflect successful acquisitions," Wall Street Journal, March 21: B3. Vara, V., 2007, "Oracle's profit shows acquisition spree is paying off," Wall Street Journal, June 27: A3.
[17] Marris, R. 1999. *Managerial capitalism in retrospect*. New York: Palgrave Macmillan.
[18] Tracy, R. and B. Kendall, 2022, "FTC to review Activision acquisition," Wall Street Journal, February 2, B5.
[19] Golden, B., and H. Ma. 2003. "Mutual forbearance: The role of intrafirm integration and rewards." *Academy of Management Review* 28(3): 479.
[20] Technically, the covariance between the company's returns and market returns would be reduced, leading to a lower beta.
[21] Foust, D. 2008. "Looks like a beer brawl." BusinessWeek. July 28: 52–53.
[22] Clark, D. 2007. "Western Digital purchase shows disk-drive dilemma." Wall Street Journal. June 29: B5.
[23] Procter & Gamble 2005 Annual Report.
[24] Craig, S., and D. K. Berman. 2007. "TD Ameritrade in merger talks with E*Trade." Wall Street Journal. August 22: A1.
[25] Berkshire Hathaway, 2017 Annual Report, p. K-1.
[26] Favaro, K. 2014. "How IKEA, Disney, and Berkshire Hathway succeed with adjacencies." *Strategy+Business*, March 11.
[27] Campbell, A., Goold, M. & M. Alexander. 1995. "Corporate strategy: The quest for parenting advantage." *Harvard Business Review*, March-April, 120.
[28] Please note that this illustration differs from the one used by Campbell, Goold, and Alexander in their seminal article, ibid. Here the vertical axis is reversed, so that the axis measures FIT, not MISFIT. The axis rises from Low to High, and consequently Ballast is in the northwest quadrant. This layout is easier for students of strategy to understand and use.
[29] Returns or the investors in the corporation can be measured in several ways, including the following in increasing order of rigor: 1) Did the share price of the corporation rise after the acquisition? 2) Did the corporation's return exceed a comparable benchmark in which they might otherwise have invested, for example an S&P 500 index? 3) Are corporate shareholders better off after the acquisition than they would have been if it had not occurred? This third test is difficult to assess in practice because there is no way to know what might have happened if a deal was not struck.
[30] Sirower, M. 1997. *The synergy trap*. New York: Free Press.
[31] Bruner, R. 2004. "Where M&A pays and where it strays: A survey of the research." *Journal of Applied Corporate Finance* 16(4): 63–76. King, D. R., G. Wang, M. Samimi, and A. F. Cortes, 2021, "A meta-analytic integration of acquisition performance," Journal of Management Studies, 58 (5), 1198-1233.
[32] M. Sirower, op. cit.
[33] Palich, L. E., L. B. Cardinal, and C. C. Miller. 2000. "Curvilinearity in the diversification- performance linkage: An examination of over three decades of research." *Strategic Management Journal* 21(2): 155–174.
[34] Fowler, G. A., 2009, "eBay retreats in web retailing," Wall Street Journal, March 12. A1. Mitchell, D., 2011, "Skype's long history of owners and also-rans: At an end?" Fortune, May 11.
[35] Quoted in Mueller, D. C., and M. L. Sirower. 2003. "The causes of mergers: Tests based on the gains to acquiring firms' shareholder and the size of premia." *Managerial and Decision Economics* 24(5): 373–391.

[36] Knowledge@Wharton, 2001, "The right way—and some wrong ways—to make an acquisition." General Electric Corporation, http://www.ge-cef.com.

[37] Karnitschnig, M. 2006. "After years of pushing synergy, Time Warner Inc. says enough." Wall Street Journal. June 2: A1.

[38] Kapner, S., 2021, "French takeover unsettles Tiffany," Wall Street Journal, December 24, B3.

[39] Towers Perrin. 2004. "HR rises to challenge: Unlocking the value of M&A." http://www.towersperrin.com/tp/getwebcachedoc?webc=HRS/USA/2004/200412/TPTrack_MA.pdf.

[40] Based upon field interviews conducted by author, 2017.

[41] Mueller and Sirower, op. cit.

[42] https://www.factset.com/. William Blair & Company, 2004, Presentation to the board of directors of Johnson Outdoors, http://www.secinfo.com/d14D5a.166Mw.d.htm. Monga, V., 2013, "M&A mystery: Why are takeover price plummeting," Wall Street Journal, November 26, B1.

[43] Singer, J., and A. Ewing. 2007. "Tom Tom escalates bid war for digital mapper." Wall Street Journal. November 8: B4.

[44] Hayward, M. L. A and D. C. Hambrick, 1997, "Explaining the premiums paid for large acquisitions: Evidence of CEO hubris," *Administrative Science Quarterly* 42 (1), 103-127. Malhotra, S., T. H. Reus, P. Zhu, and E. M. Roelofsen, 2017, "The acquisitive nature of extraverted CEOs," Administrative Science Quarterly, published online http://journals.sagepub.com/doi/full/10.1177/0001839217712240.

[45] Lovallo, D. P., and O. Sibony. 2006. "Distortions and deceptions in strategic decisions." *McKinsey Quarterly*. February: 19–29.

[46] Bekier, M. M., A. J. Bogardus, and T. Oldham. 2001. "Why mergers fail." *McKinsey Quarterly* 4: 6–10. Based on a sample of more than 160 acquisitions made during 1995–1996.

[47] Baskin, B. and A. Gasparro. 2018. "Kraft Heinz fixed factories. Now it has to sell bologna." Wall Street Journal, February 12, A1.

[48] Bekier, M. M., A. J. Bogardus, and T. Oldham, op. cit.

[49] Kamp, J., 2008, "Boston Scientific net falls hurt by charges, stent sales," Wall Street Journal, July 22: B6. Twitchell, E., 2008, "Recovering from heart failure," Smart Money, April: 29. Barron's, 2012, "Boston Scientific's Guidant acquisition led to fines, settlements and penalties," March 2. Farrell, M., 2015, "Can Boston Scientific finally move on from its Guidant mistake?" Wall Street Journal, February 18, B1.

[50] Trachtenberg, J. A., 2019, "In lousy market, magazine giant axes nostalgia," Wall Street Journal, May 24, A9.

[51] Hoskisson, R. E., and M. A. Hitt. 1994. *Downscoping: How to tame the diversified firm*. New York: Oxford University Press.

[52] Vidal, E. and W. Mitchell, 2018, "Virtuous or vicious cycles? The role of divestitures as a complementary Penrose effect within resource-based theory." *Strategic Management Journal*, 39, 131-154.

[53] White, B. 2007. "VeriSign to slim down, sharpen its focus." Wall Street Journal. November 14: A12.

[54] Bradley et al., op. cit.

[55] Forest, S. A., G. Burns, and G. DeGeorge. 1995. "The whirlwind of breaking up companies." BusinessWeek. August 14: 44.

[56] Cox, R., and D. Cass. 2007. "Placing value on GE's Parts." Wall Street Journal. May 22: C14.

This page is intentionally left blank.

Chapter 11: Developing an International Strategy

LEARNING OBJECTIVES

1. Explain when and why a company should expand internationally.

2. Compare and contrast the different types of international strategy and how value chain considerations relate to each.

3. Describe the ways in which Distance can impact a decision to expand internationally.

4. List and describe the essential differences in modes of international expansion.

Going Global, or Not[1]

"I don't believe that retail is a global business."
Hubert Joly, Chairman, Best Buy

"Walmart Inc. helps people around the world save money and live better....Each week, we serve over 240 million customers who visit approximately 11,400 stores and numerous eCommerce websites under 54 banners in 26 countries....Walmart International had net sales of $121.4 billion for fiscal 2021, representing 22% of our fiscal 2021 consolidated net sales...."
Walmart 10-K, 2021

Beijing's Global Cancel Culture[2]

"Xi Jinping has become something of a master at flexing China's commercial muscle in political disputes with foreign critics. The Chinese President's latest targets are Swedish t-shirts and American sports shoes....Fast-fashion retailer H&M and Nike came in for a Chinese social-media bruising this week. H&M saw its products removed from several major e-commerce retailers...as netizens rained scorn on the brands on sites such as Weibo....The companies' offense is to have issued statements last year decrying forced labor in the concentration camps Beijing operates to imprison Uighurs in Xinjiang....Those statements are becoming grist for the Communist Party's outrage mill....Beijing has imposed sanctions on several European officials....The Communist Party strategy is to use China's market power as leverage to shut down critics anywhere in the world."
Wall Street Journal editorial, March 26, 2021

The Ripples of Streaming[3]

Nearly 14% of the world's population have paid subscriptions for video streaming services in 2022. Netflix is the global leader with 214 million subscribers, 65% of whom live outside the

United States. Amazon occupies 2nd place, and rapidly-rising Disney+ is now 3rd. Crunchyroll actually has more subscribers than Disney+, however most are not paid.

Moving overseas has not been simply a matter of opening up new servers for overseas digital file transfers. Disney launched Star+ to better tailor content to Latin America. In Europe the U.S. streaming companies are encountering rules and regulations. Local governments in Europe require streaming companies to reveal which shows generate wide viewership, with benefits to unions whose members have worked on the shows. Under European Union regulations 30% of the content offered on streaming platforms in the EU must qualify as European content. In France streaming companies must reinvest a percentage of revenues back into more local content. To address these sorts of rules streaming companies are now locking in European video production companies and professionals for help. This is driving up video production prices abroad, and reducing the availability of production companies for locally-developed content.

QUESTIONS

1. Under what conditions would it make sense for a retailer to expand internationally?
2. Besides politics, what other non-economic factors can play into success or failure in expanding internationally?
3. How do VRIST resources and value creation factor in to where and how to expand internationally?

Throughout this textbook we have regularly referenced how globalization impacts the kind of dynamic competitive environment that companies face in the twenty-first century. Globalization affects companies in many ways, some positively and some negatively. The fact that we live in a "global village" makes it easier for foreign competitors to compete against us, since they now have significantly better access to information, technology, financial capital, and alliance partners. This makes nearly every industry more perfectly competitive, since barriers to entry are more easily skirted and new entrants make themselves known and felt. These conditions also create more varied competition. The type of "strategic space" that we evaluate when using strategy maps (Chapter 4) is populated with many companies competing on a variety of strategic dimensions.

But globalization can also work in our favor, too, since this dynamic presents opportunities for our business to expand internationally. Domestic companies with deep pockets can also more easily form alliances abroad, resulting in enhanced selling opportunities or reduced cost structure. In addition, companies can more easily outsource to save costs or focus on core activities, and can more easily manage remote outsourced efforts using advanced technologies. So competition has thus become more complex, and it has become increasingly difficult to "own" or control a sustainable space on the playing board.

For these reasons the potential for growth through an international strategy draws significant attention from management, and from strategy professors. It looks exciting, but the complexity and challenges are great:

"Leaders often see themselves as explorers embarking on a mission to conquer far-off, unexplored lands. They salivate at the potential for double-digit sales growth and are seduced by opportunities that promise to slash costs by half or more, simply by shifting operations overseas...Executives often make dangerous assumptions about what it takes to succeed in global markets."[4]

We want to be very clear that international expansion does not automatically follow from the fact that the world is now a global marketplace. International expansion is but *one* method of growth or renewal for a company, among others we have already discussed (innovation, acquisition). As with any new strategic initiative the decision to expand internationally must be made for the right reasons, at the right stage of development. It must account for the value creation capabilities and resources that a company has developed and can leverage, and it must fit with conditions present in the targeted countries.

There are entire courses in business schools that are devoted to international strategy or management, and we could devote many pages to this broad topic. We will focus our discussion of international strategy mainly on the following important dimensions in this chapter: motivations for international expansion, leveraging resources and the value chain, assessing fit and risk, and practicalities any company confronts in such expansion. But first we take a few minutes to lay out how we arrived here.

HISTORICAL PERSPECTIVES ON GLOBAL TRADE

A millennia ago global commerce really began. In the 1100s Marco Polo ventured to China from Venice, where he established trading relationships and partners. These efforts led to the famous "silk road" that connected the east with the west. Consequently, Venice thrived as the center of world trade for two hundred years.

Our globally connected world today builds on ideas and developments that came to light two centuries ago. In the 1800s economist David Ricardo proposed the theory of comparative advantage; this attributed the causes and benefits of international trade to the differences in the relative opportunity costs (costs in terms of other goods given up) of producing the same commodities among countries. Together with foreign relationships created through the previous century of European colonization around the globe, this idea led to increases in global commerce. The industrial revolution added to the dynamic: large factories, mechanized transportation to ports, steamships and greater security in global navigation. By 1913 the annual volume of goods moving across borders was 30 times greater than it had been when Ricardo was writing.[5]

Two world wars and the Great Depression intervened. But following World War II forty-four countries signed the Bretton Woods agreement. This agreement established fixed currency exchange rates based on the gold standard, eliminating exchange rate risk. It thus provided a stable platform for international transactions, and led to the creation of the International Monetary Fund and the World Bank. In 1951 the European Common Market was established, presaging the eventual creation of the European Union. In 1965 an agreement was struck to standardize the size of shipping containers used to transport goods globally, making it far easier for shipped goods to take advantage of common shipping and receiving infrastructures. By the 1960s both European countries and Japan had rebuilt industrial infrastructures and were expanding beyond their borders. "Made in Japan" was an often-seen mark on inexpensive goods popular in America.

In 1971 the United States for the first time imported more goods and services than it exported; in only two years since then has the U.S. exported more than it imported. U.S. consumers and businesses have a thirst for (or depend upon) foreign-made products and services! This trend has continued, and grown, ever since. In 2021 the annual U.S. trade deficit grew to a whopping $859 billion (Figure 11.1).

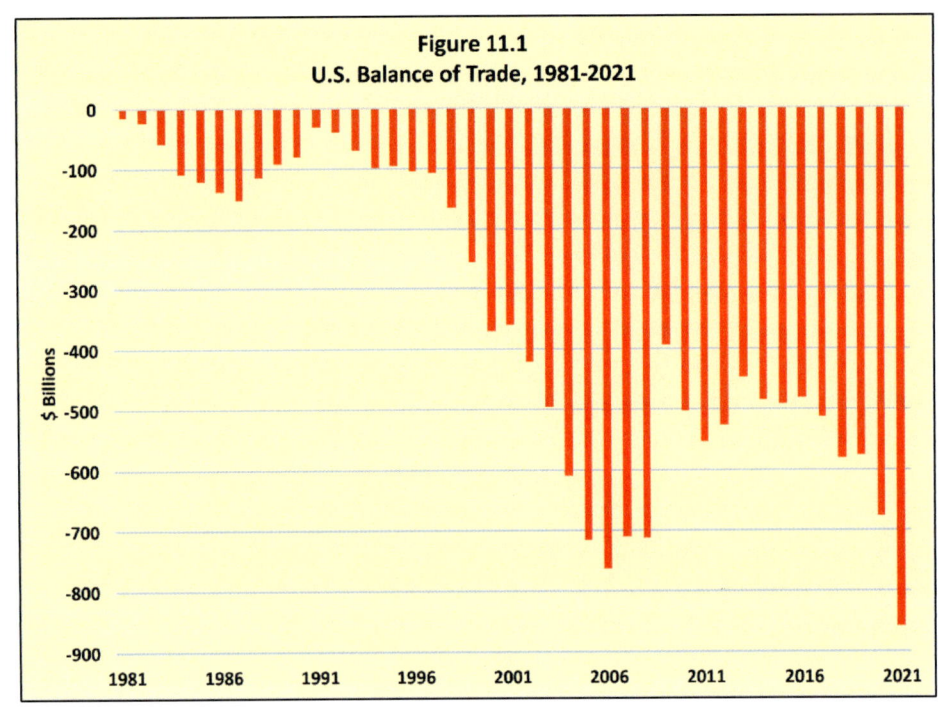

With the world at peace for 50 years, with generally reduced tariffs, and with the advent of technology and advanced communications, from 1990-2021 the level of global commerce has

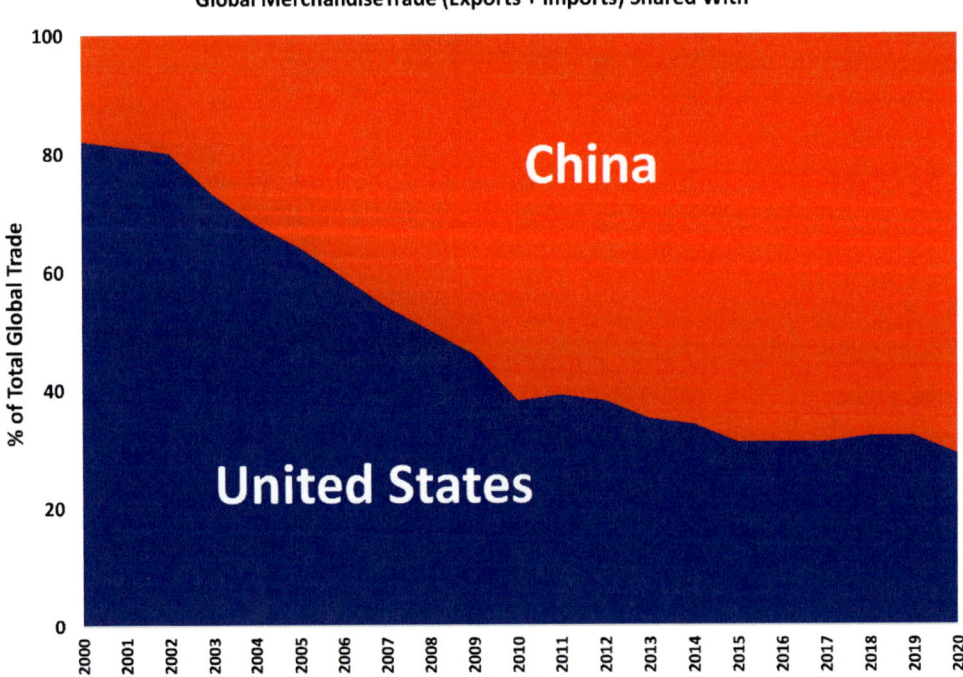

skyrocketed. Since it had begun to open up to the west in the 1970s, China's economy had been rapidly advancing. In 2001 China was admitted as a member to the World Trade Organization (WTO). WTO membership is supposed to increase competitiveness by reducing trade barriers, eliminating unfair domestic practices, and providing equal access to member states. Figure 11.2

shows that of total global merchandise trade shared by other countries with the U.S. and China in 2020, over 60% is now shared with China.[6]

> ## *Managing in Markets: Question for Class Discussion*
>
> The Belt and Road initiative is a global infrastructure development strategy adopted by the Chinese government in 2013 to invest in nearly 70 countries and international organizations. It is considered a centerpiece of the Chinese leader Xi Jinping's foreign policy. The program in part calls for lending money to other countries to complete massive trade infrastructure improvement projects (e.g. harbors, ports, roads, railroad hubs). In return, China often receives a long term contract to manage a facility once completed, and/or special consideration for Chinese companies using the facilities. For the next 40-50 years Chinese companies may gain better access and preferential terms in their international trade activities.
>
> Western countries – such as the United States, Mexico, United Kingdom – generally refrain from government investments in infrastructure to aid private companies.
>
> Does the Belt and Road initiative put western companies at a relative disadvantage? Should governments invest in facilities to aid private businesses?

MOTIVATIONS TO EXPAND INTERNATIONALLY

Among the many reasons for companies deciding to expand internationally, five stand out as the most traditional from a strategic point of view (Figure 11.3). Seeking new revenue growth, or achieving synergies with existing value chain and capabilities, reflect the kind of rationale discussed in Chapter 8 about growth and progress during stages of a company's organizational life cycle. Seeking revenue growth is usually the most obvious reason suggested. But the decision to expand into international markets must be compared to expanding the existing business in domestic markets, and to introducing new products or services into existing or new domestic markets, which we discussed in Chapter 9. The unique challenges presented by international markets – for example political, economic, and cultural risks – make this type of expansion more uncertain than simple domestic expansion or internal innovation.

**Figure 11.3
Reasons for International Expansion**

Traditional Motivations
- New geographic revenue opportunities
- Leveraging existing value chain & resources
- Spreading risk
- Overcoming trade barriers
- Achieving location advantages

Emerging Motivations
- Financial pressure for global integration
- Technology facilitates achieving greater scale
- Competitive counter-response

Yet it is often the case that international markets experience more favorable economic conditions than domestic – such as higher growth rates, very large potential customer base, and stronger economies with better customer purchasing power. See Figure 11.4 for international market key comparisons. These are very good reasons for considering such expansion, and are central to why so many companies today are especially evaluating the growing BRICS markets, whose share of world GDP grew by more than ten percentage points between 2008 and 2021.

Figure 11.4
2021 Regional Economic Comparisons

	United States	European Union	BRICS*
Population (millions)	332	450	3,278
Share of Population	4.2%	5.6%	41.2%
GDP ($ trillions)	23.0	17.1	23.8
Share of World GDP	24.2%	18.0%	24.8%

* Brazil, Russia, India, China, South Africa

Growth is easier to come by, similarly, if the methods used to generate it are identical to existing methods. If expansion into foreign markets takes advantage of a company's internal value chain, or builds upon its foundation of extraordinary resources and capabilities, then the risks of such expansion are reduced. Leveraging the value chain and capabilities may lead to greater efficiencies through increased manufacturing scale or market scope, or may simply extend a proven differentiated strategic position from the domestic market, such as quality or reputation, with minimal risk. Nomacorc, which we profiled at the beginning of Chapter 6, moved from the United States domestic market into other countries that presented a large untapped market. The move built on the company's resource foundation (of technical knowledge about wine enclosures). In contrast, in its international expansion plans Walmart has repeatedly discovered that the local conditions encountered in other countries (e.g., Brazil, China, Germany, Japan) do not always allow the company to perfectly translate its successful U.S. business model elsewhere.

A third traditional reason to consider expanding internationally is to spread risk. When a company's revenue base is largely tied in to the status of the domestic economy, then its entire business is subject to a systematic country risk that it cannot affect. So when there is a recession within a country and consumer spending declines, a company that depends on that market will feel the pain. If a company that sells only domestically procures its raw materials or other inputs from abroad, then it could fall prey to exchange rate fluctuations when its home market currency declines on the international exchange. Different countries experience different economic conditions, rates of growth and cycles, and currency fluctuations. So expansion abroad can help smooth out the effects of any one country's economic situation.

The first three reasons have essentially dealt with reasons to expand revenue-generating efforts into other international markets. But it is sometimes the case that such efforts encounter trade barriers of various sorts. Multi-lateral agreements, such as the USMCA (trade pact between Mexico, Canada, and the U.S.), are intended to promote more open borders and freer flow of goods and services. But foreign governments often place other trade restrictions and tariffs on companies with no physical presence in country. In 2018-2019 the tariff war between the U.S. and other countries severely impacted U.S. companies that sell overseas. By locating new offices or production facilities in another country, companies can sometimes navigate around such burdens.

The final traditional reason listed in Figure 11.3 has to do with the process of value creation, that is, where and how should a company produce its products or services? Establishing production operations in international markets can make sense when such efforts take advantage of local conditions that enhance a company's value creation efforts. For this reason apparel and shoe companies establish facilities or outsource manufacturing in countries in which wage rates are much lower than those paid domestically. They hopefully do this without sacrificing either quality or company image, since it is critical to maintain parity on other competitive dimensions that are valued. The Maytag division of Whirlpool Corporation sources standardized motors from China and Mexican-manufactured wiring harnesses for its dishwashers, but then assembles the final products in Tennessee. They say they want to build cost-competitive machines but also "stay as close as possible to the end market and avoid shedding American jobs."[7] Some steel companies mine iron ore in Brazil and then ship it to Trinidad to convert to iron carbide, since Trinidad has inexpensive natural gas to run blast furnaces.

More recently an emerging set of motivations have played a more prominent role in why companies extend their international presence. Any company with a globally-integrated presence will have better access to financial resources worldwide. Financial markets often view globally-active companies that mitigate country-specific risks as lower risk and deserving of favorable terms. Advanced technologies also encourage a more global approach. This is because technologies today have overcome what used to be the challenges of managing far-flung enterprises. Both of these dimensions also reflect the third emergent motivation for expanding internationally, that competition is driving it. Competitors are taking advantage of global financial resources and of advancing technology, so often companies believe they cannot afford to be left behind. More importantly, competition from around the world increasingly shows up on your company's doorstep. According to a UPS strategy vice president speaking about his retailing clients, "if they stay only within their country boundaries, other merchants will compete from outside their country boundaries."[8] Taking the battle to another country may prompt competitors to defend their turf at home rather than expand. Recall the Sun Tzu advice from Chapter 1 on "vacuity and substance," where the recommendation was to show them potential harm in order to keep them from coming forth!

Best Buy

By 2001 Best Buy achieved $15 billion in revenue and net income of $396 million through 419 stores open in the United States. Over the next few years CEO Richard Schulze took the company into international markets through a combination of acquisitions and opening new stores abroad. The first market the company entered outside the United States was Canada, where they acquired an existing chain (Future Shop) and began opening Best Buy stores. Future Shop gave the company an immediate presence in the Canadian market and allowed them to leverage their U.S.-based capabilities such as their supply chain and administrative functions. The new Best Buy Canada stores they built then took advantage of their proven merchandising techniques and advertising prowess.

In 2007 Best Buy acquired a 75 percent interest in Five Star, one of China's largest appliance and electronics retailers, with a contractual option to acquire the remaining 25 percent in several years (subject to Chinese government approval). This initial foray into a very different consumer market was designed "to increase our knowledge of Chinese customers and obtain immediate retail presence" in the market. The company opened its first Best Buy store in Shanghai in 2007, and planned to open eight more by 2009.

But China is a very tough market to break into. By 2013 the company had shuttered its own Best Buy branded stores in the country because of significant competition from entrenched

Chinese retailers. Instead, it was focusing on expanding its business through Five Star's 184 stores in 20 Chinese cities. Nevertheless, in 2014 Best Buy sold out its interests in Five Star to its minority Chinese partner, and completely exited the country. During the same year it also divested its interests in its European partners.

QUESTIONS

1. With overall company sales continuing to grow so quickly, why did Best Buy decide to expand into international markets?
2. Why did they choose Canada, China, Mexico, and Turkey as markets to expand into?
3. What are the challenges in gaining acceptance and creating a successful business in other countries?

LEVERAGING VALUE CHAIN AND RESOURCES

As suggested by the preceding discussion and the Best Buy vignette, a central consideration in international strategy is if and how the company's value chain and resource position might be leveraged. This issue becomes of increasing importance as companies seek to expand further and further into international markets. Should the company adopt the same approach in South Africa as in Brazil? Should the company establish new manufacturing facilities abroad at the same time it establishes new sales offices? How much coordination is needed between operations in different countries? How does senior management ensure that such coordination is occurring? As we can see, the decision to expand abroad raises a number of questions that are materially different from the decision to expand our reach from Baltimore to Denver.

To answer these fundamental questions we can refer back to value creation once again. Here we ask two value chain questions that are related to the two basic business-level strategies of differentiation and low cost:

1. Where is value created in the value chain?
2. Is there pressure for efficiency in the value chain?

The answers to these questions help us determine the type of international strategy the company should seek to develop, and there are four types that are revealed. Figure 11.5 provides a useful visual guide for this discussion.

We will start at the upper right of Figure 11.5, and move counterclockwise looking at each type. When value is created upstream, closer to manufacturing or the supply side of a business, it is far less

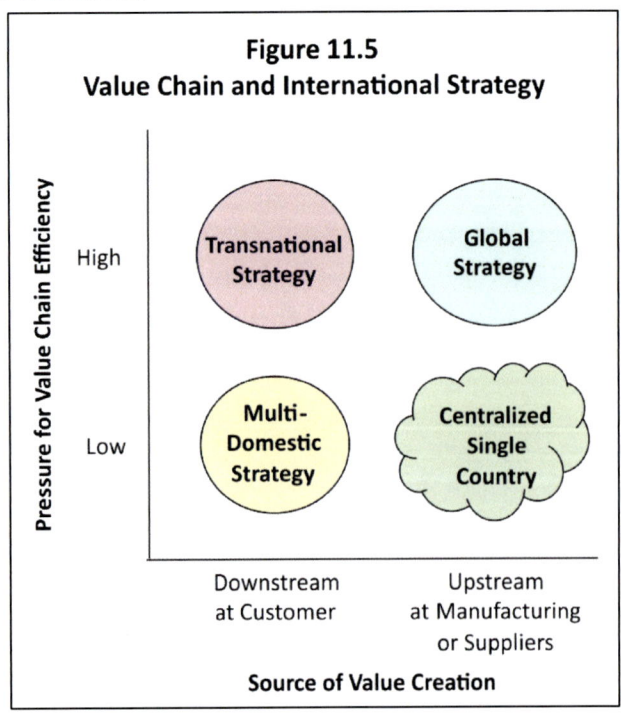

Figure 11.5
Value Chain and International Strategy

important for companies to make a series of discrete investments in each country in which it seeks to do business. Those types of in-country investments are not necessary, since they do not dramatically impact value creation. When there is significant pressure in the competitive market for efficiency, such as when pricing is competitive and low costs can be generated by manufacturing scale or scope, then the company should pursue a *global strategy*. Here the company produces a similar product or service for all international markets, and seeks to do so through a combination of facilities investments that optimize costs. Steel is a marvelous example of this type of approach. Steel companies locate their plants to optimize the inbound transportation costs of raw materials and the outbound transportation costs of finished products. Arcelor-Mittal and other global steel companies have created networks of strategically located facilities to accomplish this goal in a cost-competitive commodity industry. A global strategy approach of this sort requires significant and complex integration and coordination capabilities by the corporation. Many automobile manufacturers have been searching for decades for a "world car," one that could be sold in all nations without being modified to local conditions. Ford has been going after this for decades, first with the Taurus and then later in 2008 with the Fiesta. Hope springs eternal! Unfortunately, automobile manufacturing is quite unlike steel or other commodities; consumer variation in preferences across countries and cultures is significant.

Where there is significant pressure on value chain efficiency, but where value creation must also account for local contexts, then a company is apt to follow a *transnational strategy*. This is the top-left position in Figure 11.5. As the name implies, the company's efforts are geared toward producing in a way that bridges across national boundaries in order to gain the efficiencies dictated by the competitive market. However, the pressure to deliver values that are appreciated differentially by local market customers necessitates flexible manufacturing or production – the kind that can tailor aspects of the product or service to local cultures. Many food manufacturing firms follow this type of approach: basic brand research and development is centralized at headquarters, but then brand flavor and size adjustments, packages printed in foreign languages, production, and specialized distribution arrangements are tailored to local countries and cultures. Most automobile manufacturers are actually closer to this type of strategic approach today, seeking as much efficiency and low cost as possible by centralized R&D, along with scale-efficient manufacturing facilities. But such facilities are still able to respond to local, or at least regional, differences around the world.

A *multi-domestic strategy*, lower-left position in Figure 11.5, is appropriate when there is little pressure for efficiency in value creation and where value creation occurs very close to the customer. In this approach a company sets up an operation in each country it enters, so that it can respond directly to the specific needs of customers in that country. While there will always exist competitive pressure to reduce costs and garner efficiencies, these conditions do not represent critical facets for successfully competing. There is little strategic coordination needed across borders with this type of strategic approach, since each country places its own unique demands on the company. Any type of strategic decision authority centralized at headquarters may in fact hinder quick response to emerging in-market situations. Therefore you would ordinarily find that companies pursuing a multi domestic approach would set up offices in each country with fully staffed functions across the board. Multi-domestic strategy has historically emerged where there are significant differences in countries presented by culture or government regulation. This used to be the case across Western Europe, but with the advent of the European Union and the euro currency, such barriers to transnational or global approaches have been somewhat dissipated.

The three types of international strategic approaches we have discussed are the most prevalent. The fourth type – what we call *centralized single country strategy* in the lower-right position in Figure 11.5 – does not occur very often anymore in the twenty-first century. Here a company essentially produces and sells out of just one centralized operation for the entire world. It would make sense when there is little need to respond to local conditions and when there is little competitive pressure to wring efficiencies out of the value chain. Although these conditions may have described global competition in the 1950s and 1960s, before modern globalization and global competitive dynamics took hold, there are few instances today when this approach can make sense. Specialized pharmaceutical drug manufacturing is one example, where a company's small niche product is patent protected. Both Pfizer and Moderna fit this profile in 2021 with their Covid-19 vaccine businesses. Here there is no need to set up more than one manufacturing facility and competition is effectively eliminated because of the patent. French wine used to represent this type of approach, but now we can buy very high-quality cabernets and merlots from California, Australia, and many other wine-growing regions. Moreover, customers today are typically demanding greater customization, and competitors are always putting pressure on efficiency. It is for this reason that we put this type in a cloud in the figure; today it is only a type of international situation that companies could dream about encountering!

Figure 11.6 provides a summary of these four international strategy approaches.

Figure 11.6
Four International Strategy Approaches

Strategy	Characteristics	Example
Global	Value added in upstream activities Efficiency through scale and scope is competitively important Only minor country-to-country variations Requires strong integration and coordination Location decisions important	Arcelor-Mittal steel
Transnational	Value added downstream near customer or user Efficiency through scale and scope is competitively important Variations across countries are meaningful Headquarters involved in strategy formulation, country offices in implementation and tactics	Kellogg's cereals McDonald's
Multi-Domestic	Value added downstream near customer or user Little or no pressure on efficiency Variations across countries are significant Country offices responsible for strategy formulation, implementation, and tactics	MTV in Europe
Centralized Single Country	Value added in upstream activities Little or no pressure on efficiency Occurs mainly where markets are protected or government controlled	Specialized pharmaceuticals Hollywood movie studios

ASSESSING STRATEGIC FIT WITH COUNTRY

It may well be that the motivations are sound for a company to expand internationally, and that the company has determined that a particular international strategy approach makes the most sense. But before embarking on a cruise to another country, an assessment of the fit with that country must be made. To move into another country is brutally expensive, time consuming, and a distraction from the company's existing business. Examples mentioned above – such as Best Buy in China, Walmart in Germany – show that much time and valuable resources can be wasted if the fit with a country is not right.

The first method is to evaluate the potential fit between the target country, the industry environment, and the company's endowments of resources and capabilities. In earlier chapters we showed that when resources and capabilities match up well with the key success factors (KSFs) demanded by an industry, the potential is strong to develop competitive advantage and earn superior returns. But to this pairing we must also compare the unique conditions that characterize the target country into which the company contemplates moving. Our friend Michael Porter (value chain, business-level strategies) also wrote about factors affecting national competitiveness, which are important to consider here (Figure 11.7).[9]

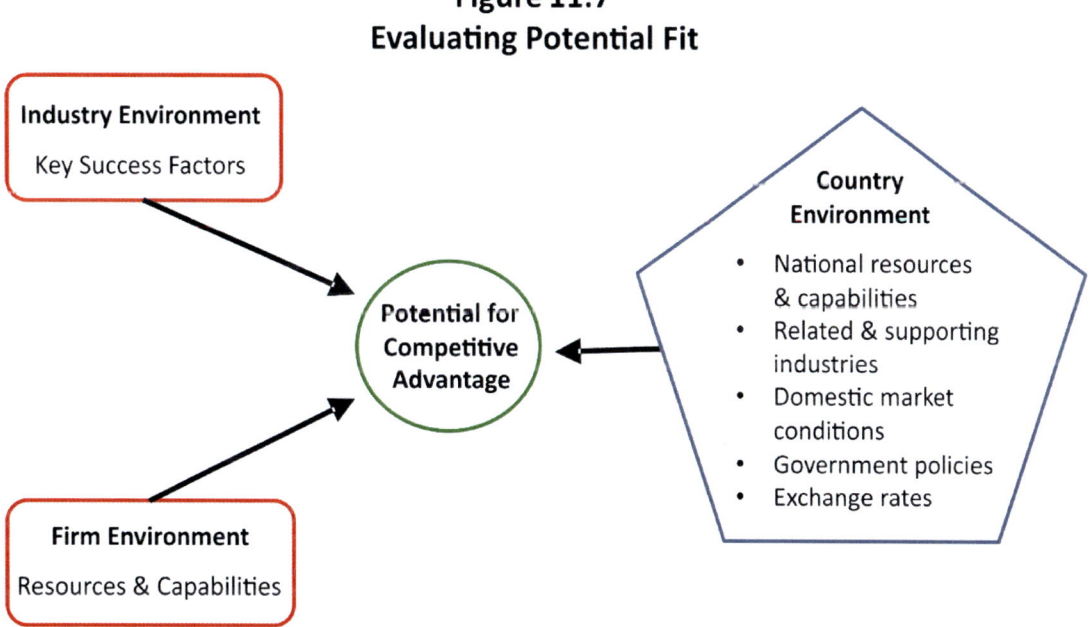

Figure 11.7
Evaluating Potential Fit

In each country its national resources and capabilities can dramatically impact the potential for successful expansion. These include facets such as the availability of appropriate human resources for needed labor, the transportation and communication infrastructures, the availability of or access to suitable raw materials for manufacturing, and whether the legal system provides protections and the rule of law to ensure that credible commitments can be made. The presence of other local industries that complement the company's business may be important, for example shoe producers and leather manufacturers near each other in Northern Italy. Their proximity and resource sharing has been shown to improve innovation and competitive performance. The domestic economy and the country's market conditions can impact growth, just as the interaction between a country's economy and the rest of the world can affect exchange rates, interest rates and other factors.

A second fit assessment considers the risks involved in doing business that is distant from the company's headquarters. Typically, we would think of distance in physical terms: how many thousands of miles away is this new country? This is certainly one important dimension. But here we refer to the CAGE distance framework used to assess the risk of distance along a number of dimensions (Figure 11.8).[10] These dimensions include cultural, administrative and political, geographic, and economic. We offer examples to illustrate each distance dimension:

- **Cultural distance**. Culturally, how different is the local company from the sort of culture in which the company's business does well? Cultural distance arises because there are different languages, ethnicities, religions, and/or social norms at play in the country you wish to move into, compared to your home base. Krispy Kreme has done exceedingly well in the United Kingdom with its yeast-raised doughnuts. However, the prospects of success just a few miles away across the channel in France would be remote because French culture embraces fresh-baked breads in local shops.

Figure 11.8
CAGE Distance Framework

	Evaluative Dimension	Characteristics	Contemporary Example
C	Cultural distance	Different languages Different religions Different ethnicities Different social norms	Krispy Kreme in France
A	Administrative and Political distance	Political differences Government laws & policies Institutional voids Different monetary systems	Ikea in India
G	Geographic distance	Remoteness Poor transportation systems Difficult access Different climate & time zone	Jaguar Land Rover in China
E	Economic distance	Different income levels Availability of human resources Education & training Intermediate supplies	Procter & Gamble in Bangladesh

- **Administrative and political distance**. Often the institutions and policies in another country are remarkably different from what we are used to. Political hostility to non-domestic companies, government policies that protect the domestic economy, and the lack of institutions and infrastructures (like efficient and transparent financial institutions, or highway networks), can hamper efforts to get established or grow a business there. Sweden's Ikea wants to sell its products in India, since their inexpensive design and manufacturing matches up well with a growing Indian middle class. Yet their inability to identify local sources of supply has run afoul of Indian law about requisite levels of domestic manufacturing. Trying to administer procurement and supply chain relationships in a new territory has proven very complicated.

- **Geographic distance**. Here we are talking about pure physical distance and the challenges it creates. Remoteness from your company's home country operations, poor transportation access, differences in climate and time zones – these can all interfere significantly in doing business in another part of the world. JLR, the Tata division that manufactures Jaguar automobiles, has established a production facility in China. Thousands of miles from the UK where superior-quality manufacturing can be easily observed and tweaked, it is proving a challenge to reproduce the same dynamic so far away.

We should note here that geographic distance is less troublesome for large companies with deep pockets. They feel they can afford to play a long ways away. But recent research shows that since these firms are more bureaucratic and set in their ways, they are less adaptable to novel circumstances. So they find the cultural distance more problematic.[11]

- **Economic distance**. The economic distance between east and west, or between north and south, can be a huge barrier to developing business abroad. Annual per capita GDP in the U.S. in 2020 was over $63,000, but in Vietnam it was only $2,800. Differences of this order of magnitude make it very difficult to take what we do well here and duplicate it over there. Local resources that companies usually count on when they establish a presence in another country – for example the quality of human resources, training and education levels, or supplies of intermediate parts needed for manufacturing – are often far less developed than what may be needed. Like many U.S.-based multi-nationals, Procter & Gamble seeks to develop its business in new markets. But the maker of Tide detergent finds this a challenge in parts of the world where tap water is uncommon and the wash cycle is less frequent than in the west. Developing a robust business is a challenge where the economic distance between existing customers and new customers is so vast.

PRACTICAL DIMENSIONS OF INTERNATIONAL EXPANSION

Finally we mention practical considerations in expanding to countries. We first draw attention to the different ways in which such efforts might take shape.[12] These range from more transactional relationships with little commitment and risk, to heavy resource commitments and risk through significant foreign direct investment. Paralleling this dimension is the level of ownership and control a company will have over its business in another country.

Figure 11.9 illustrates the variety of modes that a company may employ to expand internationally. Many companies move internationally at first through pure export. With minimal commitment other than lining up sales channels of distribution (through local agents in the country), this approach entails the least risk. It provides an opportunity to "test the waters," although it may not be a true test of the ultimate potential in the country since the investment into the market has been limited by choice. Agents often handle multiple lines, including competitors, so less attention is devoted to the company's business in this very hands-off approach.

Licensing or franchising represent a greater investment and commitment by the expanding company. Typically licenses or franchises are relationships created to last for some time, and thus the company will make an investment in identifying the best partners in the country with which to do business.

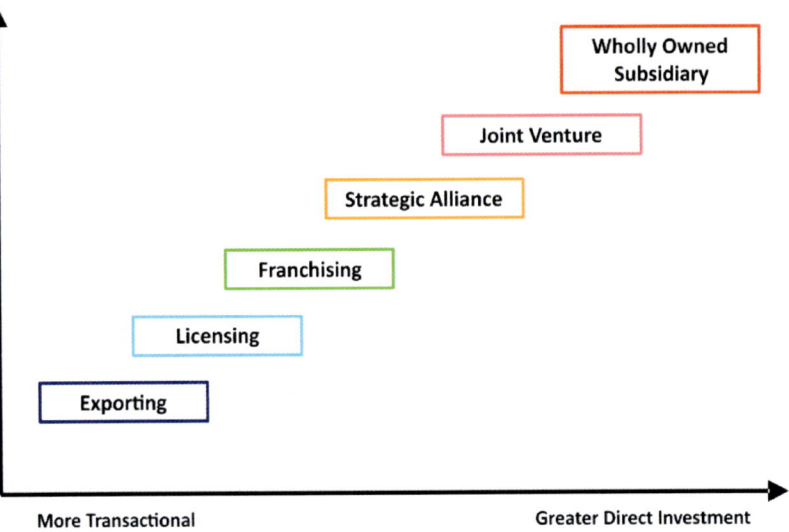

Agreements will usually specify ways in which licensees and franchisees must conduct business, in order to protect the reputation of the company. Through both methods the company is able to exert greater control over its business in the country. On the other hand, such efforts require efforts to monitor the behavior of foreign licensees and franchisees. So the greater dedicated attention one receives through this mode of entry is offset by the greater costs involved in setting it up and managing it.

Strategic alliances and joint ventures can solidify stronger, more compelling long term relationships with foreign entities, and enable the company to exert greater ownership and control over what happens. These sorts of partnerships go beyond arms-length licensing and franchising arrangements. Here the company and its foreign partner both make strategic commitments designed to accomplish goals over the long run that are of mutual interest. Kontoor Brands – the North Carolina based corporate parent of jeans brands Wrangler and Lee – has engineered joint venture  manufacturing relationships with clothing manufacturers in the Far East. Here Kontoor invests its own patented technology in foreign-owned plants, enabling them to make top quality clothing while at the same time enjoying the benefits of low wage labor. The foreign entities are able to learn about new manufacturing techniques invented by Kontoor, and to apply these to businesses that do not compete with Kontoor.

The mode of foreign entry which retains the greatest ownership and control is establishing a wholly-owned subsidiary in the country. This also entails the greatest investment of strategic resources. Usually this step is taken after the company has already conducted business in the country, learned about its market, culture, and government, and has developed a deep knowledge base about how to compete there successfully. Minimizing the risk of this approach also usually entails the hiring of managers from within the country. In Chapter 13 we will provide further discussion of how a foreign subsidiary might be organized within the structure of the corporation.

Of course instead of building its own facilities abroad, a company may acquire a foreign business that is already up and running. Netflix and Amazon are seeking to build their own video streaming businesses in India from the ground up. In contrast, Disney acquired the assets of Hotstar, which dominates the Indian market with decades of inventory of popular TV shows in eight Indian dialects, rights to cricket matches, and more.[13] This is a faster means of entry, but as we will discuss in Chapter 10 making acquisitions successful is fraught with its own challenges.

Ethical and Political Considerations

No discussion of international strategy is complete without mentioning at least briefly the political and ethical risks that become more prevalent when moving offshore. Political risks occur in both western cultures and emerging nations. One of our former colleagues was involved with Pepsico's international sales in the 1970s, and was setting up agreements in Nigeria that would allow the company to begin selling soft drinks there. On the morning of his meeting with country's president, he received a call in his hotel room that a coup had occurred removing the president from office, and that his meeting had been cancelled. It was not until the late 1990s that an era of military coups in the country ceased to regularly occur. The United Kingdom's "Brexit" decision, where UK citizens voted for their country leave the European Union, resulted in the rapid decline of the British pound in foreign exchange markets and much greater volatility across European markets. For those companies doing business in Europe, and especially those with UK-based subsidiaries where their revenue was denominated in pounds, this had clear effects on annual performance. In 2018 Walmart acquired Indian e-commerce firm Flipkart, as part of its global strategy to enter the Indian retail market. But shortly thereafter, the Indian government passed laws putting restrictions on supply chains for foreign-owned businesses, and making deep discounting illegal. What an unexpected development!

There may also be domestic political issues that arise out of corporate efforts to start doing business overseas. Figure 11.9 shows the modes of expanding revenue generation internationally. But many domestic companies dip their toes in international waters by first manufacturing overseas for domestic consumption back home. Usually the reasons for establishing foreign manufacturing for domestic consumption, of course, is for cost reduction or tax savings.[14] Overseas labor is far less expensive in many countries. Corporate tax rates abroad are often lower than domestic rates. Yet this can provoke political turbulence at home. Labor unions and residents of communities in which the company has a presence may bitterly complain about loss of jobs and loss of income to the communities. Politicians may elevate such corporate efforts into the public consciousness, such as candidate Donald Trump did with Ford and Carrier during the 2016 presidential campaign. Corporate inversions to escape paying taxes was so prevalent during the Obama administration that the President signed executive orders laying penalties on companies that made these moves. On the other hand, establishing at least a manufacturing presence in another country enables the company to learn more about that country and possibly overcoming some of the CAGE distances over time. Such efforts could then lead to efforts to sell to customers overseas.

We also encourage interested students to think carefully about ethical issues which manifest themselves as companies expand internationally.[15] Cultural norms of business conduct can be extremely different in other countries, compared to what we are used to. It is not unusual in many countries for company executives to be discretely encouraged – or forthrightly asked – to make "contributions" to indigenous officials in order to accomplish an important business goal for the company. Be forewarned! In 1977 the United States passed the Foreign Corrupt Practices Act (FCPA), which makes this sort of behavior illegal under U.S. law. The law applies to both individuals and companies, and can result in significant fines or imprisonment. In 2014 Alcoa paid more than $200 million in fines and was forced to give up $175 million in revenue previously-booked, because the company was found to have bribed Australian officials. Walmart underwent an exhaustive 3-year investigation by the Department of Justice for its activities in Mexico; DOJ found little in the way of major offenses, but the investigation was a drain on executive resources and a public relations nightmare for years. Other countries have passed laws similar to FCPA.

So what advice can be offered when ethically-challenging situations arise, as they inevitably will? The easiest and clearest advice is to be aware of company policy, be aware of the laws (both domestic and foreign), and – though it sounds corny – "do the right thing." More practically, international managers might view these sorts of situations as opportunities for negotiating better ways to deliver value to local interests and economies. In the U.S., for example, it is not uncommon for companies to seek economic incentives from local authorities in order to establish a new office or manufacturing facility. Local authorities ask for and usually receive some promise about future employment to be generated by the business. So a "win-win" arrangement is created. Created is the right word to use here, since the creativity involved in opportunity recognition and value creation can help companies wend their way through such situations.

Managing in Markets: Question for Class Discussion

In 2019 unrest in Hong Kong over mainland China's policies boiled over into street demonstrations, violent clashes between citizens and police, injuries and arrests. Under pressure from the Chinese government both Apple and Google barred apps from their devices which would identify police locations or allow users to role-play as protesters.

Boston Celtics basketball center Enes Freedom was an outspoken critic of China's alleged suppressive policies in Hong Kong, Tibet, and the Xinjiang region. China immediately banned all Celtics game broadcasts there. The NBA League warned him about speaking out. In 2022 he was traded away by the Celtics and then cut from the Houston Rockets roster.

The NBA waffled on its response to a coach who voiced support for democracy and free speech in Hong Kong. The NBA has a significant economic interest in its basketball presence in China.

How should U.S. companies respond when countries they seek to do business in challenge or suppress dearly-held values of freedom?

Managing in Markets: Question for Class Discussion

In 2022 the Russian army violently invaded Ukraine. In response, many companies decided to cease operations in or cease doing business with Russia.

How is this different from the situation in China? How much violence does there need to be before making the decision to refrain from doing business?

CHAPTER SUMMARY

In this chapter we have considered important dimensions of international strategy. Moving into international markets is not a foregone conclusion; it is a decision to grow or expand that should be considered against other alternatives for growth. Often there are good reasons to expand internationally, especially if foreign markets present significant revenue enhancing possibilities or opportunities to leverage the company's value chain and the resources. Four types of international strategy are described, where each depends on where value is actually created in the value chain and the extent to which there is competitive pressure on the value chain to be efficient. These four types include global strategy, transnational strategy, multi-domestic strategy, and centralized single-country strategy.

Companies contemplating international expansion should assess their fit to do so. There are two ways to assess fit. The first method assesses how well the country conditions match up with the company's own resources and capabilities and with the key success factors demanded by the industry. The second method uses the CAGE distance framework to assess cultural, administrative and political, geographic, and economic distance of the target country from the company's home country.

Companies must also carefully plan their mode of entry into other countries. A continuum of choices, from pure export to wholly owned subsidiary, requires increasing resources investment but also promises greater ownership and control over foreign operations. Company representative may encounter ethical challenges when doing business abroad, usually resulting from differences in norms and culture. The laws are very clear that bribery is illegal. Creative approaches to negotiating value creation may present ways to more easily open up new markets.

Learning Objectives Review

1. *Explain when and why a company should expand internationally..*

   - The decision to expand internationally should be made after careful evaluation of other growth opportunities (domestic expansion, innovation, and acquisition). International expansion raises added sets of complexities for companies, including legal and cultural issues, which do not exist in domestic growth initiatives.

   - Companies expand internationally for a variety of reasons. These include:
     - New geographic revenue opportunities
     - Ways to leverage existing value chain and resources
     - Spreading risk
     - Overcoming trade barriers
     - Achieving location advantages
     - Pressure for global integration or from encroaching competition

2. Compare and contrast the different types of international strategy and how value chain considerations relate to each.

The four types of international strategy should be determined by two questions:

- Where in the value chain is value created? A different approach is called for if value is created downstream close to the customer versus upstream in manufacturing.
- What is the pressure for efficiency in the value chain? Where efficiency is prized, the strategy will usually call for some sort of centralized manufacturing or production that affords scale.
- Global strategy: value creation upstream, high pressure for efficiency
- Transnational strategy: value creation downstream, high pressure for efficiency
- Multi-domestic strategy: value creation downstream, low pressure for efficiency
- Centralized single company strategy: value creation upstream, low pressure for efficiency

3. Describe the ways in which Distance can impact a decision to expand internationally.

Distance refers to cultural, administrative and political, geographic, and economic distance of the foreign country from the home country.

- Cultural – arises from different languages, ethnicities, religions, social norms and customs.
- Administrative and political – arises from remarkably different institutions, political hostility, government policies, infrastructures.
- Geographic – arises from physical distance, differences in times zones, and climates.
- Economic – arises from differences in income, education, training, and development levels of supporting industries.

4. List and describe the essential differences in modes of international expansion.

- Exporting – generate sales through local agents.
- Licensing and franchising – short duration relationships that specify how business is to be conducted, requires monitoring for compliance.
- Strategic alliance and joint venture – longer term relationships, often made with mutual commitments and jointly-articulated goals.
- Wholly-owned subsidiary – fully owned operation, based upon having learned deep local knowledge and usually employing in-country managers.

Short Answer Questions

1. Why do companies seek to grow internationally?

2. International value creation opportunities are best under what circumstances?

3. What are the biggest challenges in operating in an international location? How can these be minimized?

Group Exercises

1. You have recently been hired as the head of strategy for a rapidly growing chain of computer repair shops. The company provides on-site service for all laptop and desktop computers, guaranteeing all repairs within a twenty-four-hour period. The CEO has announced a decision to expand internationally and has asked you to develop a detailed plan for making this a reality. How will you organize the effort to develop the plan? What do you need to research? What critical issues seem to have the highest potential for derailing the expansion? What country(ies) will you expand to, and what is the best mode for entering?

2. Which CAGE distance is the most challenging, and why? Discuss this in your team, providing examples that you have read about outside this book.

Investor Relations Sites for Companies Mentioned in This Chapter

Amazon: https://ir.aboutamazon.com/overview/default.aspx
ArcelorMittal: https://corporate.arcelormittal.com/investors
Best Buy: https://investors.bestbuy.com/investor-relations/overview/default.aspx
Ikea: https://www.inter.ikea.com/en/performance/download-financial-reports
Kontoor Brands: https://www.kontoorbrands.com/investors
Krispy Kreme: https://investors.krispykreme.com/
Netflix: https://ir.netflix.net/ir-overview/profile/default.aspx
Nomacorc (Vinventions): https://us.vinventions.com/vinventions
Pfizer: https://investors.pfizer.com/Investors/Overview/default.aspx
Procter & Gamble: https://pginvestor.com/
Tata: https://www.tata.com/investors
UPS: https://investors.ups.com/
Walmart: https://stock.walmart.com/investors/default.aspx
Walt Disney Company: https://thewaltdisneycompany.com/investor-relations/
Whirlpool: https://investors.whirlpoolcorp.com/home/default.aspx

References

[1] Coggins, B., 2020, "Transofrmation and resilience: An interview with Best Buy's executive chairman Hubert Joly," Mckinsey, July, https://www.mckinsey.com. Walmart 10-K, 2021 .
[2] "Beijing's global cancel culture," Wall Street Journal editorial, March 26, 2021, A14..
[3] Watson, R. T., 2021, "U.S. streaming services take bigger overseas role," Wall Street Journal, May 13, B4..
[4] Salomon, R., 2016, "Globalization: A cautionary tale," Rotman Management Magazine, Spring.
[5] Levinson, M., 2021, *Outside the box: How globalization changed from moving stuff to spreading ideas* Princeton: Princeton University Press. Other data from this source are cited in this section.
[6] Based on IMF Direction of Trade Statistics and author's calculations.
[7] Aeppel, T. 2003. "Three countries, one dishwasher." Wall Street Journal. October 6, C5.
[8] Berman, D. K. 2014, "My jacket from China and what it portends," Wall Street Journal, December 19, p. B1.
[9] Porter, Michael E. 1990, *The competitive advantage of nations*. New York: Free Press. Bartlett, C. A., and S. Ghosal, 1998, *Managing across borders: The transnational solution*. Boston: Harvard Business School Press.
[10] Ghemawat, P. 2001. "Distance still matters." Harvard Business Review, September.
[11] Li, Y., Zhang, Y. A., and Shi, W., 2019, "Navigating geographic and cultural distances in international expansion: The paradoxical roles of firms size, age, and ownership," Strategic Management Journal, doi 10.1002/smj.3098.

[12] Westhead, P., M. Wright, and D. Ucbasaran, 2001, "The internationalization of new and small firms," Journal of Business Venturing, 16, 333–358. Jacques, L. L., and P. M. Vaaler, 2001, "The international control conundrum with exchange risk: An EVA approach," Journal of International Business Studies, 32, 813–832. Arnold, D. J., and J. A. Quelch, 1998, "New strategies in emerging markets," Sloan Management Review, 40(1), 7–20. Prahalad, C. K., 2005, *The fortune at the bottom of the pyramid*, Wharton: Upper Saddle River, NJ.

[13] Purnell, N., 2019, "Netflix and Amazon trail a local video rival in India that's now Disney-owned," Wall Street Journal, June 4, B1.

[14] Frazier, K. C., 2017, "The Senate tax bill has a cure for corporate inversions," Wall Street Journal, November 27. Michelle, M. A., 2017, "For Kangol hats, a costly move to the U.S." Wall Street Journal, September 29, B5.

[15] Kolk, A., and R. V. Tulder, 2004, "Ethics in international business: Multinational approaches to child labor," Journal of World Business, 39, 49–60. Rodriguez, P., K. Uhlenbruck, and L. Eden, 2005, "Government corruption and entry strategies of multinationals," Academy of Management Review, 30(2), 383–396.

Chapter 12: Competitive Dynamics, Tactics, and Cooperation

> LEARNING OBJECTIVES
>
> 1. Describe how to use industry and company trajectories to evaluate an industry environment.
> 2. Select and evaluate the appropriate techniques for producing competitor intelligence.
> 3. Describe the differences between tactical and strategic methods for responding to competitors.
> 4. Discuss the conditions under which cooperation can be an effective competitive approach.

Will You Switch Games?[1]

Nearly fifty years old, the video gaming is a $180 billion dollar industry globally dominated by three main competitors: Sony, Nintendo, and Microsoft. Over the years these competitors have released system after system aimed at the same hard-core gaming market of boys and young men.

The pace of competition has intensified in this industry. Game console manufacturers have stepped up the frequency with which they introduce new consoles that take advantage of newer technology such as memory, chipsets, and networked computing. In the first fifteen years following the 1972 introduction of the first console game system, 6 major new consoles were introduced by a handful of competitors. But in the last fifteen years, 14 new consoles have come out as the industry moved from 4th to 8th generation platforms using more advanced technology.

The three major competitors each jockey for the privileged position of coming to market first and trying to lock in consumers. In 2012 Nintendo led with its Wii U, then Microsoft and Sony followed in 2014 with their new Xbox One and PS4 upgraded systems. In 2016 Nintendo's partner companies introduced the new Pokemon Go mobile game app, downloaded over 15 million times worldwide in the first few days. In 2017 Nintendo again led first by introducing Switch, the fastest selling platform of all time in the U.S. That year Microsoft brought out the Xbox One S and X platforms. In 2020 Sony's updated PS5 platform came out. Within a few days Microsoft also released the Xbox Series upgrades. Game on!

Each generation of platform pushes the technology envelope in its updated hardware. The Switch married tabletop and mobile capabilities, connected with other mobile devices, and employed controllers that simulated Wii gaming. Microsoft's Xbox One X built in native 4K HDR gaming with triple the graphics core speeds, a built-in Blu-ray player and huge terabyte memory to handle large games. PS5 and Xbox Series consoles have enhanced graphics processing, but cheaper models come with no hard drive since they can now rely on cloud computing.

The competitive focus in the industry is also on the suppliers of game software. History shows having robust software development is crucial for a console to be successful. Strong software sales encourages publishers and developers to release new games for the console. A highly successful console launch can net hundreds of millions for the successful video game producer. And so when competitors introduce new game consoles, they also introduce new games to take advantage of the technology. Accompanying Nintendo's Switch were new versions of classic Nintendo titles loved by millions: Super Mario Odyssey, Zelda, Mario Kart 8, Sonic Forces. With the XBox One X came favorites such as Halo 5 and Star Wars Battlefront. In 2022 Microsoft announced it will acquire Activision Blizzard, a leading game developer.

QUESTIONS

1. How can any of these companies predict what its competitors will do next, and when?
2. How should Sony and Microsoft respond to the advent of mobile games?
3. How should Sony respond to Microsoft's acquisition of Activision Blizzard?

A Galaxy Far From Google[2]

Samsung introduced its Galaxy phone in 2009. The phone utilized the Android operating system, which was developed by Google. By the end of 2012 Samsung had the leading worldwide market share of smart phone unit sales, with a 30% share compared to only 19% for Apple's popular iPhone.

In 2013 Samsung introduced its S4 smart phone, but significantly downplayed its involvement with Google and its reliance on the Android operating system. The Android "ecosystem" is similar to the PC ecosystem, which combined Windows and Intel chips into what was known as the "Wintel" standard. Samsung needed the system. So it cooperated with Google in the development of its phones, in order to ensure that the hardware and OS software were compatible. But Samsung did not want to rely exclusively on Google, so it developed its own apps in a way that reinforced Android but provided competitive product benefits for its users.

Cooperation presents an interesting dilemma for both parties. Google developed Android as an alternative to Apple's iOS systems. They were right: by 2022 over 70% of devices shipped relied on a version of Android. But Samsung is the 500-pound canary, leading in worldwide unit sales and the largest user of an Android OS.

Google worried that Samsung would eventually develop its own version of Android relying much less on other Google services like maps and search. This is what Amazon had done with its Android-powered Kindle Fire. So in 2012 Google acquired the cell phone division of Motorola, solidifying patents and an installed base of its phones that utilized Android. Then in 2014 Google sold the Motorola phone business to Lenovo, and it worked with other manufacturers to create its own Google-branded Pixel phones which were introduced in 2016. Google's efforts over the years have helped establish a balance among competing manufacturers and mobile operating systems.

QUESTIONS

1. What are the benefits and risks of cooperation?
2. Why would Google play one company off another and seek "balance" in this industry?

COMPETITOR INTELLIGENCE

Through this text we have so far focused on understanding the foundation for strategy, and how to grow the business. That includes: 1) knowledge of the relationship between strategy and performance; 2) recognition of the need for vision and mission for the organization; 3) analyzing the competitive environment; and 4) appreciating how to use value chain and resource-based analysis to develop a sustainable competitive advantage. In addition we have discussed how these relate to the choice of a fundamental business level strategy approach, and how strategies might be modified given varying industry and company life cycle conditions. We then detailed three methods to achieve growth: innovation, acquisition, and international expansion.

But strategy cannot be developed and growth does not occur in a vacuum, since conditions are always changing. It is incumbent for strategy thinkers to not only react to competitors, but to anticipate how competitors might react to moves that their business makes. The dynamic of competition creates tremendous uncertainty, which amplifies the importance of thinking through the intentions and estimated moves of competitors. This chapter is about competitive dynamics and the application of techniques to predict, respond to, and even preempt competitor moves.

This chapter is much more about tactics than about strategy. Recall from Chapter 1 that strategy is about longer-term moves, significant resource investments that play out and pay out over time, a focus on sustainability and long-term performance. Subsequently in Chapters 2 and 4 we explored how financial statement analysis and industry analysis can reveal patterns of financial resource investments, strategic positions, and intentions of competitors. In contrast when we take up the topic of competitive dynamics, we are interested in the more immediate moves, countermoves, and responses of competitors to both changes in the industry environment as well as our own company's initiatives. Grand master chess players are known to think strategically about how their opponents will move eight to ten turns from now; in this chapter we want to think tactically about how they will move over the next one to three turns. Short-term tactics will (or should) be consistent with long-term strategy, so the previous work we have done in understanding strategy and competition is certainly helpful here.

INDUSTRY CHARACTERISTICS AND TRAJECTORIES

Before examining the individual attributes of companies, we should recognize that competitive dynamics fundamentally relate to the types of conclusions we draw from industry analysis (Chapter 4). One important characteristic of an industry is how benign or hostile it is. A benign environment provides companies with potential because of less intense competition. However many companies operate in intensely competitive environments and must therefore figure out how to prosper in hostile conditions. We will briefly examine the characteristics of each and then tie that analysis to approaches that provide the best opportunity for sustainable advantage.

Benign Environments

Benign environments are usually characterized by conditions such as: 1) market demand exceeds market supply; 2) high gross profit margins; 3) low competitive intensity, meaning no one competitor controls a high proportion of the market; 4) strong customer loyalty; and 5) customer tolerance of occasional management miscues.

Studies have suggested that benign environments reward differentiators. As you may remember from our discussion in Chapter 7, differentiation exists on one end of the business level strategy continuum. In benign environments customers are looking for unique product or service characteristics, high levels of product or service quality, and often rely on a substantial amount of informative or lifestyle advertising in order to make purchase decisions.[3] Once a company secures a customer base in this type of industry environment, customers tend to remain loyal, and competitors do not vigorously attack established positions. In this type of environment, therefore, we would not expect competition to directly assail our company's product or market position.

But stop for a minute, before reading on, and try to think of an industry today which could be characterized as operating in a benign environment. It is tough to think of many (any?). Competition in the 21st century often occurs in more hostile environments.

Hostile Environments

Hostile environments are usually characterized by conditions such as: 1) slow growth, flat or even declining revenue; 2) frequent price wars; 3) strong competitive intensity, meaning that one or a few competitors control a substantial portion of the market; 4) low barriers to entry or imitation; 5) rapid pace of product or service obsolescence; or 6) active efforts targeted at cost containment by competitors. Hostile environments also occur where technological change is rapid, coming either from developments outside the industry or from suppliers or internal R&D. This is certainly the case in video gaming, where advances in memory, chip design, and software programming have led to increasingly more frequent introductions of new platforms and games.

Whereas benign environments tend to exist at the earlier stages in an industry life cycle, hostile environments seem to emerge once an industry approaches maturity. Referring back to Chapter 8, a low cost strategic approach seems to provide organizations the best opportunity for a sustaining sales and profits in maturing situations. In hostile environments, companies that seem to perform best have product lines that leverage a core set of resources and capabilities, a broad market approach to maximize their geographic reach, sophisticated process technology, and purchasing advantages relative to their competitors.[4] These factors tend to support the low cost management dimension that is important under these conditions.

The term "hypercompetition" was coined to describe a perceived new reality in competitive dynamics. This view of the competitive environment argues that traditional competitive responses are insufficient when the new realities of the marketplace – better information, global reach, access to technology and capital – mean that the dynamic of competition is accelerating. It suggests that the only real competitive advantage is that of speed. The rapid creation of new competitive advantages that either neutralize or obsolete the advantages of competitors is the new core capability of successful organizations.[5] Sun Tzu would have certainly agreed with this approach to dealing with competitors. He found virtually no advantage to measured responses and saw only positive consequences to the use of speed. Apple released the iPod in October 2001, and it rapidly became the gold standard for audio players. As industry competitors scrambled to match the capability of the original iPod, Apple successively released various versions aimed at specific points in the consumer market. iPod Nano, iPod Mini, iPod Touch, and iPod Shuffle all crushed the competitors' ability to respond, because before competitors could match the existing product, Apple had released its next version. Then came the iPhone, and now mp3 players hardly exist. In hypercompetitive markets companies seek to stay ahead of their competitors by constantly disrupting the old fabric (including their own products) and creating new rules of the game.

In hostile or hypercompetitive environments we might therefore predict that competitors will make a couple different types of moves. First, we can expect them to continue working on their cost structures in order to be price-competitive, to offensively engage in price wars, and to attempt disruption (Chapter 9). This means our company must continue its efforts to manage to lower costs, and we will need to carefully benchmark how we are doing relative to competitors on this dimension. Second, we might anticipate that competitors will introduce new products and services into larger customer and geographic segments in order to gain efficiencies and disrupt the status quo, and to engineer different sets of value combinations to redefine market segments.

Industry Trajectories

We learned in Chapter 4 how strategy maps can be useful in bringing together information about competitors in a compelling visual format. Competitive maps take a variety of forms, but the most popular strategy maps compare primary competitors on each of the key success factors in an industry. A rigorously maintained set of maps showing current relative positions as well as historical trends for each company can be especially useful for analyzing competitive moves. In that discussion we noted how historical trajectories in "strategic space" on a strategy map are an excellent indicator of future intention. Referring back to Figure 4.22, for example, if we were to predict the kinds of competitive moves that Dell might make in the future – based purely upon its past positions using maps that compare innovation and unit cost – we would expect the company to continue making investments that would lower its unit costs further (and not work so much on an innovation agenda). This was the trajectory the company had historically followed, and its capabilities were tied into this approach. So its future efforts might include pressing suppliers further, reorganizing its assembly operations, and possibly seeking additional distribution outlets for its existing products in order to increase scale. It comes as no surprise, then, that Dell's PC business level strategy involved exactly these steps.[6]

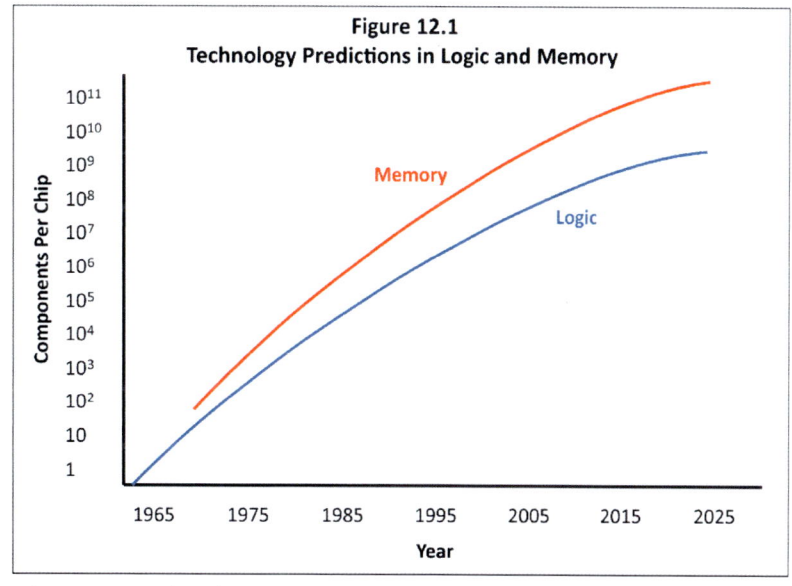

A second kind of industry trajectory prediction can also be useful in anticipating possible new moves by competitors. In this case what we are interested in is not so much what any one competitor might do based upon past historical trends, but what *all* competitors must do based on evolving supplier technologies and customer preferences. In 1965 Intel co-founder Gordon Moore predicted that every two years the number of transistors that could be inexpensively placed on a circuit board would double. Figure 12.1 shows a Moore's Law projection for memory and logic technologies. From that prediction, which has actually been observed in practice to occur about every eighteen months, many have been able to anticipate the advent of new devices utilizing advancing technology. StorageTek was started up by three IBM employers who followed "Moore's Law" in the tape disk storage industry; it rapidly became a Fortune 500 company. Some of the StorageTek people, relying on the same Moore prediction, subsequently founded two additional companies – Exabyte and Ecrix Systems – to take advantage of predictable new technology. The prediction was used by many technology companies to assess when they (and their competitors) would be in a position to introduce new products incorporating advanced technology. More recently tech industry observers have reported on how silicon performance has doubled every year since 2012.[7] This has led to predictions about how and when AI will be used in various fields including autonomous vehicles, surveillance, shopping, and more.

General predictions can also be made by carefully evaluating the evolution of customer preferences and demands. A better understanding of what sort of value will be needed in the future provides a company with an important roadmap of areas it might invest in. It can likely presage what competitors will also be thinking about. Figure 12.2 shows the evolution of technology models and value in the cell phone handset market.[8] This type of mapping enabled competitors to predict when premium segments would emerge. Competitors could likely anticipate how advanced Apple's newer models might be, based upon projections using the historically-descending value curve. Models in Samsung's and Apple's lines accurately follow this trajectory.

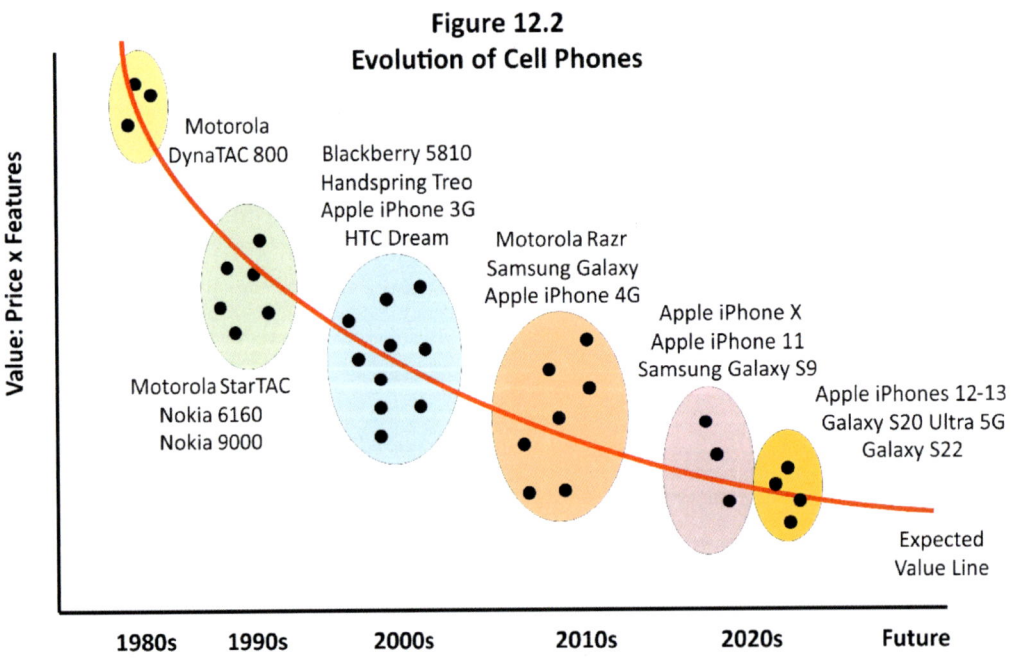

**Figure 12.2
Evolution of Cell Phones**

Scenario Analysis

The previous sections help companies appraise the industry as it exists today and in the near-term future. A final consideration for dealing with the competitive nature of an industry is the utilization of longer-range planning tools. These can be helpful to weather unanticipated crises as well as unfolding industry changes.

A very interesting approach developed over the past forty years is scenario analysis. The technique requires an organization to consider potentially dramatic or disruptive shifts in the business environment over a longer time frame, and to then map out a set of actions that it can begin to take if the warning signs of those shifts start to appear.

Crisis can trigger turmoil in the life of any organization. In his 2007 book *The Age of Turbulence* former Fed chairman Alan Greenspan recalled his concerns for the stability of the banking system in the hours after September 11, 2001. Stuck on an airplane being forced to return to Zurich as all U.S. airspace was closed to civilian air traffic, he knew there were well-developed plans in place that would be triggered if a scenario like this one played out. Arriving back in Zurich, he was relieved to hear that all the emergency plans had already been enacted and the Federal Reserve banking system was stabilized.[9]

Crisis scenarios about singular events should certainly be a part of any longer term planning process. But so is consideration of changes of significance unfolding over years. Indeed, scenario planning usually uses a time frame that can go from ten to twenty-five years. Not yet knowing exactly how an industry will reach the next plateau does not mean that planning will be useless.

Consider Figure 12.3, which shows oil price increases over the previous decades. To the shock of many organizations, in the first decade of the 2000s oil skyrocketed from $25 per barrel to over $125 per barrel. Just five year ago, who could have predicted that oil prices would then suddenly drop by over $50 per barrel? In 2020 a reduction in travel demand during the spread of Covid-19 caused oil to suddenly drop below $50. But in 2021 the new Biden administration unexpectedly took steps to curtail domestic oil production, and then the 2022 crisis with Russia invading Ukraine cast doubt on energy supplies for world needs. The result: oil prices leapt up once again. What if oil were to zoom to $200 per barrel? What would the impact of $200 oil have on an organization's transportation infrastructure, cost of goods, and the ability of customers to travel or buy a product? For companies dependent on oil, what could might they do to anticipate how such changes would affect their business?

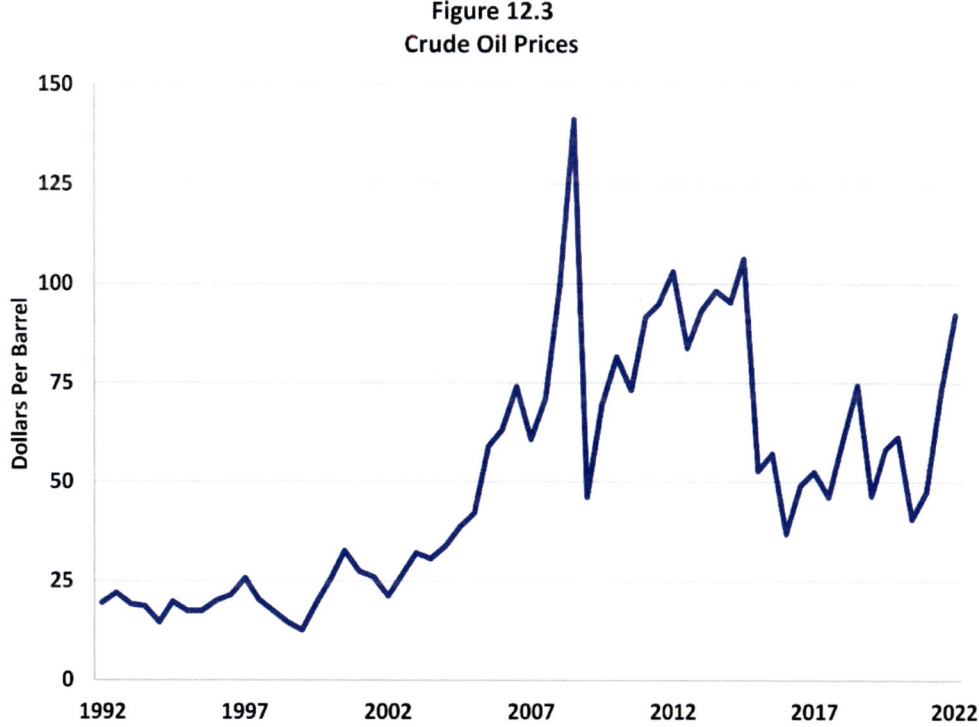

**Figure 12.3
Crude Oil Prices**

Scenario analysis enables companies to plan out potential responses for their organization as the environment changes, to have considered those actions long before they arrive, and to identify markers along the way which signal that a particular path is coming. Response effectiveness is dramatically improved if organizations have had the opportunity to consider and prepare for potential futures.

We mentioned earlier in this book how Netflix disrupted its own business model of DVDs through the mail, by gearing up for streaming. They had looked ahead into the future, and made predictions about how and when new streaming technologies would become central to our lives. In part they relied on the sort of technology prediction curves we discussed above. As the weak signals of evolving technology and consumer demand grew stronger, Netflix pulled the trigger on a host of internal infrastructure investments. They adeptly anticipated what was to be, and were ready to move when things started to change.

Scenario analysis is a multi-step process, and involves the following:
1. Imagine a hypothetical industry environment or state in the future that is dramatically different from the current state.
2. Identify what are the drivers and key success factors that would dictate success at that time.
3. Evaluate your current resources, capabilities, and value chain to identify what would need to be changed to address the hypothesized new reality. This identifies the "gap" between where you are now and where you would need to be.
4. Identify an actions plan to build new capabilities to close the gap.
5. Identify external events that signal the new reality is beginning to unfold. These would trigger initiation of the action plan to build new capabilities.

Most companies that engage in scenario analysis will typically generate 2-3 hypothetical scenarios, and go through this type of evaluation for each.

The result of this type of thoughtful analysis is a holistic look at the environment, competitors, and potential paths that might appear. Within each path, the company should consider how to apply its unique resources – or what new resources may be necessary to develop – in order to take action to ensure its sustainable position.

PREDICTING COMPETITIVE MOVES

As we can gather from the previous discussion, general characterizations about the industry environment can help us make general predictions about what competitors might be contemplating. We can, however, develop more specific and detailed information about key competitors in our industry. Competitive intelligence and the knowledge that such intelligence provides is the first step available for dealing with the competitive dynamic inherent in a hostile industry environment. Fortunately, we have a number of tools available that allow for effective classification and use for competitor prediction. These include: 1) classifying organizations based upon their behavioral styles; 2) examining internal competitor characteristics; and 3) assessing what companies are most likely to become rivals.

Classifying Organizations

The first technique available for examining potential competitor moves is to classify organizations based on their styles of behavior. In many ways past behavior is one the best predictors of future actions and reactions, whether we are talking about organizations or individuals in our own lives. There are many techniques available to classify organizations such that we can better understand and predict their intentions and likely reactions to moves by other companies. One of the more popular techniques is a classification system developed some years ago by Raymond Miles and Charles Snow.[10] They suggest that each company in an industry can be classified in one of four ways, as: 1) Prospector, 2) Defender, 3) Analyzer, or 4) Reactor (Figure 12.4). The first three are each sustainable and viable postures for a company to take in an industry. The fourth type (Reactor) is not sustainable, and companies that do not move from a reactor position are likely to under-perform or even fail. It is generally acknowledged that each type is present in most industries.

**Figure 12.4
Four Ways to Classify Companies**

Prospector
Defender
Analyzer
Reactor

Most companies do not fall cleanly into any one category, but are most likely to predominantly fall within one category. The lines between the categories are a bit fuzzy, so we look for overarching patterns in behavior to assist us in classifying the company's style. Let's take a look at each position.

Prospector. A prospector organization is one that tends to view the industry from its own internal perspective and that of its customer base rather than being concerned with the competition. Prospectors are usually leaders of change in the industry with little concern for the effects or impacts of other organizations. They are generally willing to cannibalize their own market position with something new, and they are thorough collectors of detailed information about customers and customer needs. A prospector organization is relatively inefficient primarily because it views control and cost-cutting efforts as counter to its primary objectives of organic growth and the opportunity to change the industry.

Apple is the epitome of the frame-breaking prospector organization, especially during the times that Steve Jobs served as its CEO. The introduction of the Apple II PC, the Macintosh, the iPod, iTunes, the MacAir and the iPhone, just to name a few groundbreaking products and services, virtually changed the nature of each industry that the company entered. Google created a platform that was simple to use and very intuitive for the user by means of a new algorithm for ranking website importance. Their approach to this segment of the internet fundamentally changed the way in which internet searches occurred and forced other companies to develop better methods.

We mention these two well-regarded companies here as exemplars of prospector organizations. However, it is important to recognize that it is not technology or technology-based businesses alone that occupy these positions. Prospector organizations are those which have embedded behaviors internally – across their value chains – that enable them to identify new opportunities and move on them with dispatch. Recall the two strategic imperatives we mentioned way back in Chapter 1.

Prospector businesses pursue an aggressive stance aimed at identifying new ways to satisfy customers, new means to extend their reach, and a creative desire to lead rather than follow. A prospector organization is unlikely to directly react to a move by a competitor. It will release its latest product or service on its own schedule and simply presume that it is what the market was looking for. These organizations rarely lower prices or make new market entries as a result of moves by a competitor.

Defender. At the opposite end of the continuum is a defender organization. Defender organizations are intensive rather than extensive. That is, they usually focus on a limited number of key criteria, analyze their costs, and rigorously defend their competitive position against all competitors or potential competitors. A defender is geared toward protecting its current position and maximizing market share. This type of organization spends very little on new product or service development, is highly efficient, and is structured in its policies and procedures.

The retailing icon Sears was once a prospector as it spread across the United States and became a one-stop shop for middle America. However, with the advent of other large specialized retailers it changed into a defender model as it sought to focus its efforts and protect what it perceived as its turf. Cereal companies, such as Kellogg's and General Mills, while exhibiting vital new business development behavior, are at their core defender organizations. Everything they do works to protect a brand's franchise, shelf position and presence in supermarkets, and market share. When competitors introduce similar products or flavors into new markets, consumer products companies will often flood those markets with high levels of promotional coupons or spot TV buys in order to wreck the results of the newcomers. Defender organizations will react swiftly and with an intensive attack to any move by a competitor that it deems threatening or even potentially threatening. They will lower prices, offer coupons, change formulas, add new extensions to existing product lines, pressure suppliers, run attack ads, and more to counter the move by a competitor. Recall that one of the attributes within the threat of new entrant dimension of the five forces analysis (Chapter 4) was potential competitive retaliation.

Analyzer. Somewhere in between these two more extreme forms of organizations are analyzers. In analyzer organizations parts of the company behave like a defender while other parts of the company behave like a prospector. Usually an artifact of the way the organization formed and grew over time, this two-part stance within a company is quite difficult to manage and maintain. While one part of the company performs the sophisticated customer analysis and develops products or services that will directly address the customer regardless of whether it cannibalizes its current product offering, another part of the organization is intensively examining competitors and trying to milk every dollar out of its current product or service portfolio. The risk for analyzer organizations, of course, is that they may become stuck in the middle from a business-level strategy perspective.

It is more difficult to predict exactly how analyzer organizations will respond to significant changes in the market. Because they have in the past demonstrated dual propensities, to both step out innovatively but also defend their turf vigorously, they deserve due attention by the strategist.

Reactor. Reactor organizations perform as the name implies, by essentially reacting (often very slowly) to emerging conditions in the competitive environment. This is usually an unstable form of organization and one that is not destined to last very long, because it tends to be buffeted by the forces in the environment rather than making proactive moves. It then has a choice: either to adapt and move to one of the other three models, or collapse as an independent entity. Defunct organizations such as Eastern Airlines, Montgomery Ward, and Gino's are classic examples of what happens to reactor organizations that refuse to change. Who are these companies, you may ask? Exactly!

Starting in the late 1990s McDonald's (a company often praised for its incredible strategy execution capability) had fallen into this mode. They were under attack from health groups, suffering from the consequences of a film documentary called *Super Size Me* (where one man ate super-sized meals at McDonalds every meal for a month), were ineffectively responding to growth by their competitors, and had lost perspective on their own competitive resources and capabilities. Same-store sales were dropping. But to the company's credit they sensed that they might soon be in a precarious strategic position. A new management team shook up the organization and moved them into a more defined analyzer role, where utilizing the combination of prospector and defender they flourished once again. Portions of the company had always exhibited prospector aspects – the first fast food operation to serve breakfast, the introduction of the Happy Meal for children, and the creation and funding of the Ronald McDonald House charity. More recently, though, they have exhibited defender characteristics – for example, the move into premium coffee service to bring back customers lost to Starbucks, a rigorous value meal selection, advertising aggressively, and seeking to buy up and hold potential real estate sites for future store growth.

It is important to understand the value and use of this Prospector, Defender, Analyzer, Reactor classification system as a means to gain important insight into competitive dynamics. The ability to classify organizations allows us to make relatively accurate predictions about how specific companies will respond to changes in the industry. This system also provides insight into how competitors view the industry. This systemization can augment the general kinds of predictions we make based upon industry characteristics, discussed previously. As an example, we might be preparing to release a brand new product that we believe has the potential to change the market. In the competitive analysis we would not be very concerned about the reactions to our new product release from prospector organizations, since they are usually focused on their own initiatives. Defender competitors are a significant concern, since they might view a new introduction as a competitive threat and therefore may actively work to defeat it. The company should then consider devising effective tactics to deal with anticipated competitor response. Analyzer companies are a bit of a wild card; each must be examined for its history and current position. We would be far less concerned about a potential response from reactor organizations, which have previously demonstrated non-threatening responsive behavior in the market.

The Four Walls Are Porous[11]

Access to technology, global reach, better information: these present hypercompetitive challenges to today's retailers - in the form of "showrooming." Four years ago a 25-year old shopper in Best Buy spotted the perfect gift for his girlfriend, a $185 Garmin GPS. But he first took out his Android phone and used Amazon's price comparison app, only to discover the same item for only $107 online (plus no shipping). He bought it from Amazon right on the spot. Last holiday season another shopper at Walmart considered buying a 2 Gb memory stick for $11.99, but her shopping app found it elsewhere for $2 less.

In 2009 mobile devices accounted for just 0.1% of visits to retail sites. One year later they accounted for 5.6%, a fifty-fold increase. By 2022 95% of shoppers use mobile devices for doing research for shopping, and 80% use them for comparison shopping at the same time they are in stores. During the Covid-19 pandemic mobile commerce grew 54% over just two years.

QUESTION

1. How should traditional "bricks and mortar" retailers respond to mobile shopping?

Internal Characteristics of Competitors

Classifying organizations as Prospector, Defender, Analyzer, or Reactor allows us to narrow the list of organizations that need closer scrutiny. A more detailed means of evaluating competitor moves is now in order. In this analysis we will consider a number of internal competitor characteristics and how they might impact our organization. These include: 1) understanding their management outlook and patterns; 2) conducting our own internal strategy analysis of competitors; 3) analyzing their financial situation; and 4) gathering competitor intelligence.

Understanding management patterns. One effective technique in the analysis of competitive dynamics is the observation and evaluation of patterns by competitor CEOs and their top management teams. Sun Tzu would argue that the general who never changes his pattern of battle is highly susceptible to a crushing defeat. All of us have patterns in our behavior. In fact, much research demonstrates that in times of challenging circumstances or crisis, people tend to rely on "automatic" behaviors as a response and coping mechanism. When those patterns become predictable, management exposes its company to potential harm. Some CEOs are aware of this problem and work diligently to address it by changing up approaches and seeking new solutions. However, when times get tough, there is a tendency to return to base patterns of behavior. Those patterns, when accurately observed, provide useful competitive insight.

"Chainsaw" Al Dunlap became famous as a CEO for his single-minded approach to corporate profit. He took the helm at several troubled companies with the same approach each time: fire thousands of employees, dramatically cut back on new spending and rigorously attack all current spending. This was his system at companies including Scott Paper, Crown-Zellerbach, and Sunbeam. Knowing his approach to business and his universal "game plan" for success, competitors were able to take advantage of the turmoil it created within his companies. Some top management teams have been observed using standardized "recipes" to respond to competitive threats. When this occurs, it makes it easier to predict them and therefore easier to work around.

On the other hand, companies that find themselves in a strong competitive position in a market will often ignore widely available information and miss opportunities that end up costing them their business. DEC was the king of minicomputers in the late 1970s and early 1980s, posting astounding returns in their industry. They held so strongly to the notion that minicomputers were their competitive advantage that they simply missed the PC revolution. The CEO at the time (Ken Olsen) noted the failure later when he observed that "we had 6 PCs in-house that we could have launched in the late '70s. But we were selling so many [minicomputers], it would have been immoral to chase a new market."[12]

The difference we see between these two examples has to do with the attitude of management of the company about the kind of business it is in, its "ownership" of a market, or its beliefs about effective ways of managing its business.

Strategy analysis of competition. Although much of this textbook has so far been devoted to tools and frameworks that you can use to develop strategy for your own company, the same tools and frameworks can be useful for understanding your competitors' strategies. Having your most recent industry analysis results in hand, and having identified current and emerging key success factors, now you might conduct a value chain analysis and a resource analysis of each competitor. What are their value chains, and how are these fundamentally different from your company's? Use the resource analysis method to deconstruct the sources and causes of capabilities that your competitors are particularly good at.

A colleague of ours was a brand manager for one of the major cereal companies. Her brand was being seriously challenged by a competitor's brand, and her brand's market share was sliding slightly. In 2022 the breakfast cereal market will generate over $75 billion sales globally and $21 billion in sales in the U.S. Slipping just *one* percentage point of U.S. market share would represent a loss of nearly $210 million in revenue! So she spent nearly three months digging deep into her competitor's business: understanding its supply chain, its marketing tendencies, the history of the decisions that the managers behind the business had made, and more. What resulted was an in-depth, highly detailed view of what her competition was very good at, and where there were holes in their armor. She used this information to exploit the weaknesses, effectively restaged her brand and reversed the trend in market share. She was subsequently promoted to marketing director. Her work was good for the company, and good for her career path.

The Baltimore Orioles baseball team won six division titles, 3 pennants and the World Series under the leadership of its successful manager Earl Weaver. The organization developed  resources and a process to assiduously study the tendencies of opposing managers. Weaver pored over this data and committed their tendencies to memory so that he could rely on it tactically in everyday game situations. He knew in advance when they would steal bases, put on hit and run plays, substitute pinch hitters, and employ other facets of the game. He was then able to preempt such actions with his own moves on the field. There are only nineteen managers who have ever been inducted into the Baseball Hall of Fame, and Earl Weaver is among them.

Many organizations maintain business analysis units that have as their task the job of developing competitor profiles. For some companies, these units have in fact become a resource exhibiting the VRIST characteristics, helping to confer sustainable advantage. Changes in the market and competitor responses are regularly tracked, to build an effective "map" of past and predicted moves. Much like playing chess with someone over and over, it then becomes much easier to predict his or her response to certain moves and therefore to use that information to beat that person in the game.

Financial analysis. As long as a company is growing and making reasonable returns or better, it is likely to maintain its current competitive approach, believing that it will continue to deliver results. Where its performance and returns are not as anticipated, it is more likely to react in unpredictable ways. And if its returns go really negative, then predicting its actions becomes more difficult. Sun Tzu reminds us that an army with no retreat available will fight to the last and fight with everything available. Competitors in this situation need to be closely watched for industry-damaging behaviors. The sort of financial analysis we did in Chapter 2 – connecting strategy to patterns of financial investments – can again be very revealing about what competitors are doing and the financial strengths of their organizations.

We can observe interesting behavior occurring periodically in industries with heavy financial investment in fixed assets. The "big three" automobile manufacturers each lose money during recessions. Their initial reaction to declining sales is to cut prices in order to move unsold cars off dealer lots and keep assembly operations going. Unfortunately, it is the rare organization that can cut its way to success. Price wars generally damage the market by removing future customers, generating the need for even greater cost savings, and opening the door for better-organized foreign competitors who have lower cost structures. The prudent strategist would have looked at this damaged economy, examined the financial situation of its key competitors, and been able to predict with probably great accuracy just what sorts of promotional tactics they would soon be engaging in.

Gathering competitive intelligence. Having classified each competitor as Prospector, Defender, Analyzer, or Reactor and having dug deeper into these organizations by evaluating their internal processes, we should also mention other methods for how detailed competitor information can be gathered. Sun Tzu wrote more than 2,000 years ago that "The means by which enlightened rulers and sagacious generals moved and conquered others, that their achievements surpassed the masses, was advance knowledge."[13] Foresight can be an extraordinary resource, because there are fewer ways to improve performance than knowing in advance what a competitor is planning to do. In virtually every sport or competitive activity, being able to predict how a competitor might react or how they will act can dramatically change the outcome. General George Patton was a prolific reader of military history and military strategy. He understood not only that there were patterns to success, but that particular generals had their own approach to victory. Having studied the tactical battle books written by General Rommel and used by most German tank commanders, Patton would set up his battle plans to take advantage of the patterns laid out in Rommel's books. The same type of intelligence is often just as easily available in business.

In 2001 Hewlett Packard announced its intention to acquire Compaq Computer, and at the time then-CEO Carly Fiorini acknowledged that combining the two companies into a single organization would take at least three years. Knowing this, other computer companies took advantage of HP's distraction to profit from their relative positions in the PC industry. HP performance suffered during this time period.

It is relatively rare to have available such a clear announcement of distraction as that made by HP to suggest direction for your company. Even official documents are not very telling. Annual reports are often characterized by what is termed "impression management," designed to glowingly discuss a company's past year; 10K

**Figure 12.5
Methods of Gathering Competitive Intelligence**

Media stories evaluation
Research among suppliers
Conferences and speeches

reports filed with the SEC reveal little of strategic substance. Fortunately, there are a number of other techniques for gathering competitive intelligence (Figure 12.5). Among many techniques are included: 1) using media evaluation services; 2) conducting research among suppliers; and 3) examining competitor comments from public conferences and speeches.

Each of these techniques allows us to drill down from the higher-level analysis performed in Chapters 2 and 4 as well as the overarching classifications we have talked about earlier in this chapter. For instance, utilizing our STEEPG approach we may have already drawn conclusions about the nature of an industry we wish to enter. The five forces analysis provided us with insight into the key characteristics of that industry, and an analysis of a specific competitor's financial statements allowed us to reconcile their actual strategy with their stated strategy. We then classified each competitor into its strategic posture (Prospector, Defender, Analyzer, or Reactor) and determined its patterns of behavior. We now wish to delve more deeply into those competitors that seem most likely to impact any new strategic move we would make.

1. Media evaluation services. For as long as news has been reported, there have been businesses that accumulate and report on that information. Competitive intelligence consulting organizations, known as clipping services, can provide a complete, detailed record of all available public information about any particular company, area, person, or situation. Much of this information is publicly available and could therefore be collected by anyone. In a few short years since the advent of the internet, the sheer volume of such material is beyond the scope of the typical company manager to deal with. For example, if you are interested in the fashion business a recent Google search turns up 25 million hits for Zara news and 8 million news hits for Ralph Lauren! So news gathering and evaluation service companies, which have developed their own capabilities to sift through and synthesize such a volume of information, will provide a more complete examination of a particular subject or company.

Hiring a service to maintain information on a particular competitor is a common practice. The costs of these services are usually based upon the level of detail that the client desires, the breadth of outlets that need to be researched, and the type of media that the client would like to review. In the not-too-distant past, these services would develop binders full of newspaper articles, magazine reference, videotapes from local news reports, audio tapes of speeches or radio broadcasts, and any press releases from the target company. Today this is all provided online with a secure website provided to the client.

2. Suppliers. A tremendous source of information is often available from suppliers that would like to conduct business with your company. Just as the supply chain is often a great source of information and inspiration for new ideas and materials, suppliers will often discuss what competitors are doing. They can possess unique perspective and insight into the industry and competition. There may be many reasons for providing information on what competitors may be up to, and these can include: 1) share cutting-edge technology or raw materials that can be useful to buying companies, 2) demonstrate a willingness to work with a customer, or 3) create a more competitive group of customers seeking to buy so that combined demand exceeds supply.

Start-up company Championship Foods, mentioned earlier in Chapter 4, learned how to reduce its cost of putting chili into glass jars by engaging in lengthy conversations with one of the country's major glass manufacturers. In the quest to seek glass jar cost reductions, the company learned that Anchor Glass supplied jars for Ragu spaghetti sauce. They then worked out an accord to incrementally add their glass requirements on to Ragu jar production runs. In this case Ragu was not a direct competitor, and the glass company found a way to increase its own production volume. But during the same conversation the company had learned that its chief canned product competitor had previously explored, but rejected, getting into a glass jarred product. Good news for investors in Championship Foods!

We should be careful to note here that competitive intelligence with a supplier may be a two-way street. Just as your company learns about competition from your suppliers, so too can they learn about you through the same channels.

It is equally as important to note that there can be significant ethical considerations in seeking competitor information through suppliers. On the one hand merely discussing publicly-available information seems well within the framework of acceptable corporate behavior. But careful discussion should occur internally before asking a supplier (or anyone else) to "look into" the nature of another company's business.

3. Conferences, speeches, earnings calls. There are occasions when senior managers of competition are engaged in unscripted events. This is where they must go beyond the printed statement or "talking points," and often respond to open-ended questions about their business. One of these occasions is during earnings calls (every quarter for most public companies). Here, after making a presentation update on financials, CEOs or their designated stand-ins will field questions from the financial analyst community. We know one CEO who assiduously reads transcripts of every earnings call of every one of his competitors. Over time a statement here and a mention there can arguably be revealing about future intent.

CEOs and senior managers are regularly asked to give speeches at various events and will often participate in presentations at conferences. While the text of a speech can be viewed with the assistance of a good news gathering service, the context, the Q&A session that typically follows a talk, and any other interaction or interviews after a speech can be particularly revealing. The value of conferences is much the same. Senior managers present new ideas, serve on panels, and provide comments on developments within their companies or on how their companies view markets and emerging opportunities. Even though these are generally open forums, the level and detail of thought provided can sometimes be quite insightful.

Dumpster Diving for Diamonds

DeBeers is renowned for its beautiful diamonds. But it also competes in industrial markets where diamonds are used as cutting tools. One of their chief competitors is the abrasives division of General Electric. Recently the General Electric division general manager scratched his head and wondered how DeBeers was managing to price its industrial diamonds so low. GE's manufacturing *cost* exceeded the DeBeers *price*. They needed to figure this out. One day some folks from the GE plant followed a trash truck leaving a nearby DeBeers plant to the local public landfill. They paid the customary fee for anyone to enter the landfill and searched through the debris left by the DeBeers truck, discovering pieces of molds used by DeBeers in its manufacturing. The molds were of a completely different size and material than anything GE had possibly imagined, and provided significant insight on the sources of DeBeers cost and pricing advantage.

QUESTIONS

1. What ethical considerations are raised by this story?
2. What are the ethical limits to gathering competitive intelligence?

Awareness, Motivation, Capabilities

The preceding discussion is intended to help the strategy manager to understand how to develop greater awareness of competitors. But we need to go beyond these tools to gain insight on which competitors will have a greater propensity to attack our business, and what parts of our business may be most susceptible to attack.

The "awareness-motivation-capabilities" (AMC) framework provides further insight. This model describes how we develop greater awareness of our rivals, their motivations and capabilities. When we have carefully assessed their motivations and capabilities, it allows us to better anticipate their intended moves.

But it is a two-way street. Our rivals also conduct the same assessments of our company. So if they develop awareness of our business, intentions, and trajectories, where might they attack? Evidence suggests that the most successful competitive attacks are those which go after "more peripheral markets…or require more cost and disruption to respond to."[14] These attacks are successful because we pay less attention to "peripheral" markets, and because we are less motivated to retaliate since they are not central to our business.

The astute strategist can turn this around, suggesting that our company's attacks on competition might be similarly situated in order to be successful.

The AMC framework has in the past typically looked at the direct relationship between two companies at a time, and usually these two are both rivals in the same industry. More recent work has helped us expand beyond this paired approach, to help us develop awareness about other companies who are not currently our rivals as potential attackers.[15] Potential competitors, who are indirect rivals, can be identified using three markers: proximity to the industry, blurring of industry boundaries, and diversification activity.

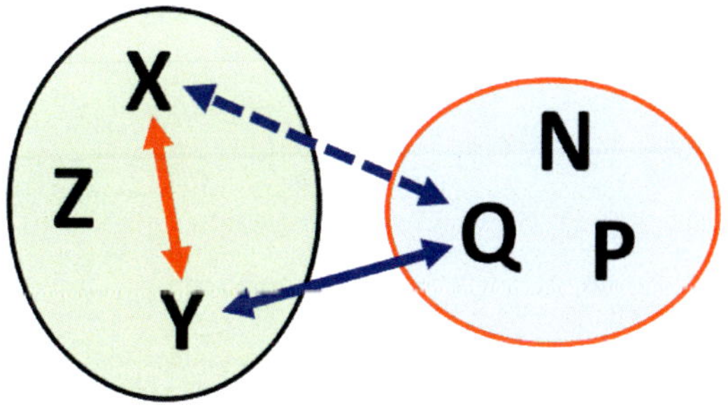

Industry proximity. A company that is not currently a rival, but which is "close" to the industry, is a potential rival. Using Figure 12.6 as a reference point, companies X, Y, and Z are direct rivals in their industry. In fact, the rivalry between X and Y is intense since they compete in many of the same ways as they address the industry's key success factors. But company Y also has some competition going with Q, a company in another industry. Q might be a supplier to Y, or perhaps it manufactures substitutes that more directly compete with some of Y's products, or Q may produce complements to some of Y's products. The point is that Q is already close to the X-Y-Z industry. As Q views its own options for expansion and growth, it may look for additional opportunities in this industry. Therefore, X should view Q as a potentially hostile company.

**Figure 12.6
Indirect Competition**

Industry boundaries blurring. When industry boundaries have over time become fuzzier and less distinct, then potential rivals exist just outside what were the traditional industry boundaries. This is called convergence – when technologies, capabilities, firms, and industries coalesce. We have to think no further than the cellphone industry: phones, phone service, cameras, browsers, gaming, digital books, and on and on. Imagine that X above was Kodak competing in film and cameras against Fuji, Minolta, Canon and others. Q was Apple or Samsung, embedding cameras into their devices.

Diversification activity. Highly-diversified companies are by their nature expansionary, always looking outside their current markets and industries for new opportunities. They move upstream and downstream in vertical moves, and they move horizontally into related businesses where "adjacencies" are present providing synergies. Referring once again to Figure 12.6, if Q has a history of diversifying, especially into related acquisitions, along with the previous two markers it must be considered as a potential rival.

TACTICAL RESPONSES

Companies establish their *strategic* position by considering long run performance through the value chains and unique resources they employ relative to the industry in which they compete. We must also recognize that there are a set of *tactical* actions that may be appropriate when taking into account the hostile moves of a competitor. Think of tactics as something that is "tactile:" it is more immediate, you can touch it. This is altogether different from the longer term perspective that strategy encompasses. Competitors will react to our company's activities, and we need to be prepared to react tactically in the short run to their behavior.

Figure 12.7 profiles response styles to hostile actions.[16] A company can respond to competitor moves with varying degrees of aggression. These degrees may be determined by a combination of the company's history, the collective personality of its current management, the nature of its position in the market, and most importantly the level of threat presented by the hostile move. Responses can vary from the most passive Acquiesce, to the most aggressive Absorb or Leapfrog. You can see that the increasingly aggressive moves are also increasingly strategic, meaning that the ability to respond this way will depend upon previously-developed capabilities. More aggressive responses blend both tactics and strategy. We discuss each response style below.

Figure 12.7
Tactical Response Styles

Tempo	Response Styles	Tactics	Descriptions
Passive	Acquiesce	Habit Imitate Comply	Following taken-for granted norms Mimicking accepted business models Obeying rules and accepting norms
Passive	Compromise	Balance Pacify Bargain	Balancing the expectations of multiple constituents Placating and accommodating stakeholders Negotiating with stakeholders
Increasingly Aggressive / Increasingly Strategic	Shape & Manipulate	Co-opt Influence Control	Importing influential constituents Shaping values and criteria Dominating constituents and processes
Increasingly Aggressive / Increasingly Strategic	Defy	Dismiss Challenge Attack	Ignoring emerging norms and values Contesting rules and requirements Assaulting the sources of pressure
Increasingly Aggressive / Increasingly Strategic	Neutralize	Contest Renew	Use legal actions to stall Redefine and deliver greater value
Increasingly Aggressive / Increasingly Strategic	Absorb	Takeout	Acquire the competition
Increasingly Aggressive / Increasingly Strategic	Leapfrog	Obsolete	Move beyond competitor with new offerings

Acquiesce. The Acquiesce style is the most passive approach to the advent of some competitive challenge. Where an industry or market has become known and accepted for operating in a certain fashion, a minimalist response that leverages the company's well-known and appreciated conduct can be followed. Continuing to follow rules and norms of conduct in the industry, continuing to act like other companies, and doubling down on efforts to comply with accepted standards – all might diminish the standing of a competitor which is trying to shake things up.

Compromise. Compromise styles are sort of the "jujitsu" approach. Here the goal of the company is to avoid direct confrontation against an aggressive opponent, but to still be proactive in some way. The force of the competitor is redirected, or at least deflected, so as not to damage the company's position and strength. Placating and accommodating affected stakeholders can be a particularly effective way of dealing with a competitive thrust. For example, investors may view a new competitor's effort as interesting and possibly valuable. The company's response might be to step up R&D and put greater weight on new business options it has been pursuing, while continuing its primary emphasis on its existing business.

It might also step up external communications to inform its stakeholders of its intentions to address their growing desires. If relationships with suppliers or buyers are potentially affected, the opportunity to bargain and renegotiate with them to reach new accommodations is in order. These approaches draw from the company's existing strengths and probably cost less to put into practice immediately.

Shape and Manipulate. Shaping and Manipulation is undertaken as the competitive threat develops and passive tactics cannot provide sufficient protection. This response style is associated with broad moves to coopt, influence and control other stakeholders, and to proactively shape industry values. Here a threatened company can pre-empt the threat by using its incumbent power and presence to organize a group to influence the market through setting broad standards and creating acceptable industry practices. These can disfavor the competitor. For example, Allied Steel organized steel tube producers to press for an industry standard that allowed only steel to be used for electrical conduit. When this was passed by the National Fire Prevention Association, Indian Head and other plastics tube manufacturers were closed out of this sector.[17]

It might seek to hire key employees from the competitor. In this way it seeks to degrade the capabilities of the hostile company while also injecting special knowledge about the competitor's new business into the company.

Another method is to actually become involved with the competing organization, such as through a strategic alliance, in order to have influence over its direction. Shaping has also been called competitive cooperation, which we will address in the final section below.

This it is a tactic that seeks to overwhelm without actually doing battle: overwhelm the competitor, the stakeholders, the market itself. Stepping up marketing, community, and investor efforts, the company attempts to dominate the market and its position. It is usually the case that shaping and manipulation is maximally effective when the competitor is newly-emergent, possibly local, and has not itself accumulated deep enough resources with which to fight a protracted battle.

Defy. Some hostile moves can just not be disregarded, even in the short run. Companies tend to be tactically aggressive when a key business segment that is central to its market position is threatened. Under these circumstances a company engages in activities directed specifically at the competitor.

Usually, defiance will draw on the company's well-developed functional capabilities in marketing, sales, operations, finance, its relationships with vendors, customer service, etc. When a new consumer product is test-marketed, it is not uncommon for an incumbent firm to flood the test market location with additional advertising and promotional activity. In this way the new firm is unable to accurately determine how well its product really fared. In confronting the onslaught of Netscape in the late 1990s Microsoft drew upon its excellence in R&D, married with its strong financial position, to develop and give away its Internet Explorer browser software at no charge. Why buy Netscape when you could get another browser for free? Netscape Communications did not last long as an independent company.

Occasionally, the advent of a new competitor to a region will trigger what is known as "mutual forbearance." Here the incumbent firm organizes a targeted attack back in the new competitor's own region, causing it to devote resources to its defense back there.

Neutralize. This response is employed when the competitive threat had not been fully appreciated earlier on, and it has now spread too widely to be shaped or fully defied. Here threatened companies turn to more aggressive means of attack. But the attack is not a frontal attack on the business, such as we would see under Defy. Instead, the efforts here are to make the competitor's entire business proposition ineffective and irrelevant.

One way of doing this is on the legal front. When Amazon first started selling books online, Barnes & Noble contested that they did not collect sales tax through internet sales. Or a company may challenge a new competitor's patent, prompting it to slow down and expend resources on a defense. Sattler Tech designs, manufactures and supplies high quality monitor brackets, TV and desk mounts. Competitor Humancentrics introduced a new line of stands that targeted the same market. Sattler was successful in blocking this product line by showing that the patent claimed by Humancentrics was invalid. The Recording Industry Association of America used the courts to shut down the renegade Napster, which was seriously impacting industry sales. This successful effort forced other Napster-like companies to cease operations or to stay so small that the RIAA would not seek sanctions against them.

The second means of neutralizing is of a much more strategic nature. One effective way of neutralizing an opposing business is to make it of lesser value in the market. This can be accomplished by redefining how value is defined in the marketplace, and making adjustments in the company's own value creation process to deliver on such renewed values. We mentioned this earlier in Chapter 8 in the discussion about the renewal stage of an industry life cycle. Redefining value and reconfiguring internal resources to deliver against redefined values, of course, cannot be accomplished instantaneously. Strategic investment is required in order to go down this path.

The final two response styles we mention fall clearly into the strategic realm. Here we have moved out of pure tactics. But though these final two response styles are strategic in nature, the decision to use them is a tactical decision based upon more immediate circumstances. So this is where tactics and strategy also come together.

Absorb. Absorption comes into play when it is clear that the competitive threat is likely to succeed and the prior approaches have not been as effective as desired. Threatened companies in this situation may often turn to acquisition of the new competitor as the response. This has the dual effect of taking the competitor out of the market, while conferring control over the threatening business to the incumbent. As discussed in Chapter 10, the incumbent can thus learn about new capabilities and possibly achieve synergies by leveraging them back into its traditional business. Microsoft has engaged this approach on numerous occasions, as the control of the desktop and the development of applications software moved increasingly to mobile computing and the internet.

In this sector (desktop control and mobile apps), as well as in other sectors in which they compete, Microsoft has had dozens of companies – both small and large – nipping at their heels and trying to make inroads. So in addition to massive internal R&D for devices and software, the company has also turned aggressively to acquiring companies in many areas related to mobile communications, digital marketing, video gaming and more. Since 2000 they have acquired or made investments in over 225 companies such as Powerset, YaData, Danger, GitHub, Skype Communications, Yammer, LinkedIn and more, spending in excess of $160 billion.[18]

Leapfrog. The final competitive response, and one which is absolutely strategic to the core, is what we call leapfrogging. Here the intent of the response is to completely obsolete a competitor's hostile attack. This is accomplished by moving well beyond the competitor with new products and service offerings. This involves bringing to market either disruptive or radical innovations (Chapter 9) that would completely reshape the competitive landscape and render the hostile company's move completely ineffective. Gillette has a long history of leapfrogging its competition with the release of newer and more technologically advanced razors. Apple has acted the same way in the smartphone sector. In both these cases, the strategic initiative leading to leapfrogging has been the significant investment in research and development designed to produce leading edge products. As with both neutralizing and absorption efforts, having a leapfrog response available requires significant strategic investment long before the immediate situation presents itself.

COOPERATION

A final category of competitive response that has recently received a lot of attention is cooperation with competitors. There are a number of reasons why a company might engage in cooperation, and these are listed in Figure 12.8. When companies decide to cooperate, they do so by making commitments to work together and to each bring something to the effort. Each party to a cooperative arrangement might bring its own VRIST resources to the effort, such as knowledge or relationships or management talent. Or the two companies might pool their similar resources to achieve greater economies or effectiveness through their pooled use.

**Figure 12.8
Reasons for Cooperation**

Hedge against uncertainty
Strengthen competitive position
Enter new markets
Access complementary resources
Learn new capabilities

The outcomes usually expected from cooperation are either to lower various costs of doing business, to create a new type of VRIST resource (e.g. new product or process), or to simply help a company overcome learning barriers in developing new capabilities. The fundamental reason for cooperating is that neither party could accomplish any of these goals on its own, or could not get them done as quickly as they would like. Cooperation success may strengthen their positions and open up new market possibilities.

Tacit Cooperation

We usually think of cooperation as some formal relationship that is established between two companies, and all the reasons listed in the figure could be relevant. But cooperation may also be tacit, meaning that companies do not formally strike a deal but they implicitly act cooperatively. Companies tacitly cooperating do so to reduce uncertainty associated with vicious competition.

Tacit cooperation can manifest itself when competition can be unusually destructive. We mentioned earlier the very destructive price wars that are often in vogue in the automobile industry. This has been experienced many times before in many different industries: prices are lowered by one manufacturer, triggering the lowering of prices by other competitors, resulting in the same volume of business for each competitor but now at a lower price (and lower profits). Fare wars in the airline industry have been rampant for the years following deregulation of the industry. The problem for competitors is that it is illegal to collude on competitive tactics such as pricing and markets. This is the classic Prisoner's Dilemma problem you have probably heard about in other courses. If all companies refrain from engaging in destructive tactics, then all companies are better off; but if one company fails to refrain, then all must jump into the fray.

The real solution to this type of problem where cooperation is desired is not easy, though. In some cases it never occurs, and competitors continue on in their mutually destructive ways. In some cases the competitors intuitively try to adopt a "multiple period" perspective, which deflects attention from the immediate need to generate added business volume through short-term tactics. Where industries are populated by companies that adopt this latter approach, there tends to emerge one or two companies who become "price leaders" or leaders in some other tactical dimension. Their behavior then "signals" what is acceptable to the rest of the industry.

Signaling is not just important in making tactical moves that other competitors will then follow. It also represents a means through which a company can *prevent* competitors from initiating destructive tactics. When a company repeatedly matches its competitor's tactics, action for action, time and time again, it sends a signal to the competitor and the rest of the industry that destructive hostile behavior will always be met with opposing force. This is otherwise known as making a credible commitment. In this way a company tacitly creates a cooperative situation in an industry, without formally cooperating.

Formal Cooperation

As the name suggests, formal cooperation occurs when two (or more) companies execute a formal agreement to work together. There are three basic structural choices for formal cooperative agreements (Figure 12.9): non-equity, equity, and joint venture.

Figure 12.9 Structural Choices for Formal Cooperation			
Structure	**Governance Form**	**Typical Use or Goals**	**Rationale for Using**
Non-Equity	Contract	Supply, distribution, or licensing	Interdependence between partners is low; easy to write a contract specifying required actions and measured results.
Equity	Equity investment in partner	Early exposure to new knowledge or process; possible option to fully acquire at a later date	Interdependence between partners is moderate; partners act separately but collaborate to produce outcomes that are difficult to measure.
Joint Venture	Create 3rd organization	Collaboration and coordination to develop new knowledge	Interdependence between partners is reciprocal on a continuous basis; partners contribute knowledge and process through activities that are hard to specify contractually to produce targeted outcomes.

Non-equity cooperation essentially takes the form of a contract between companies. The contract can fairly easily specify precisely what actions each company must undertake, and often targets specific and measurable outcomes as a means for evaluating whether each company lives up to its end of the bargain. This contractual form of cooperation is often used when companies want to work closely with suppliers or customers to accomplish goals that normal arms-length market transactions may not lead to. Licensing or franchising is another form of contractual cooperation that obligates each company to the other in very specific ways, leading to mutually-beneficial outcomes.

In late 2019 Microsoft and Team Ninja inked a multi-year deal that obligated Tyler Ninja Blevins, the "zero to hero" super-gamer, to play exclusively on Microsoft's Mixer streaming platform.[19] Mixer gains broad new visibility for its multi-function capabilities for online players, in its competition against Amazon's Twitch service. Ninja affiliates himself with a growth brand backed by deep financial and technical resources.

Equity-based cooperation occurs when one company becomes a part owner in another (and there are occasionally situations where both partners invest in each other). The goals leading to this sort of structure may be ill-defined at the outset, or the goals may be defined but the timeline to completion poorly-understood. Typically, the investing partner believes that the other company has great potential in the development of new technology, equipment or a process that one day might be really valuable. They want to participate by partnering, but the uncertainty of the development effort presents too much risk in the present for acquiring the other company outright. And it would be very difficult to write a contract that specifies definitive actions and definitive outcomes. Here the investing company can "watch and wait" until the uncertainty is diminished. Equity-based cooperative agreements often contain provisions allowing the investing company to increase its equity stake or buy out the partner at a fixed point in the future.

The joint venture is the third structural form of cooperation, and it is the most complicated. Like the non-equity form, joint ventures are usually started up with a specific target goal to accomplish. But like equity forms, the path to get to the goal or the timeline is unclear at the outset. And therefore it would be difficult to write a contract which specifies precisely the sorts of activities each party will have to engage in. The structure that joint ventures often taken is, in fact, a new independent organization with shares owned by the companies who are part of the venture. Typically joint ventures are created to collaborate on sophisticated research and development projects, where each party brings unique knowledge or practices to the interactions. These are projects where the risk of failure would be much higher if one company tried to go it alone, and/or where one company does not possess all the resources required to move successfully through the path of development.

Volkswagen and Ford, along with other automobile companies, are intensely interested in developing autonomous (self-driving) vehicles. Yet the technology is not fully developed, and the effort to do so alone would be monstrously expensive. GM is working with Honda, and Daimler (Benz) is working with BMW. In 2019 Ford and VW announced a joint venture for their combined effort.[20] In this deal VW will invest $1.6 billion in Ford's equity partner Argo AI, and will contribute the develop expertise of its autonomous driving unit of 200 engineers. Argo AI is far ahead of others in new technology development, and VW will now have access to their work. So Ford gains significant funding and enhanced expertise, while VW gains access to more-developed technology.

Joint ventures are also referred to as strategic alliances. Some time ago the automobile makers foresaw the need to have truly revolutionary battery technology. They did not want to leave this effort to chance, they did not want to embark on a development path where their direction would not become the accepted industry standard, and they did not want to deal with one powerful supplier that could control one of the most significant cost items in a car of the future. So they formed the Advanced Battery Consortium to cooperatively develop this critical component. New opportunity recognition in many industries will therefore involve the use of cooperation for the development of new technologies or new capabilities that can be beneficial to all competitors.

Types of Cooperation

There are essentially two types of formal cooperation among companies (Figure 12.10). We can think about these as different ways a company involves and extends its own value chain. Vertical cooperation seeks to extend value creation either upstream by working with suppliers or downstream by working with customers. No matter what governance form the cooperation takes (equity, non-equity, or joint venture), the company makes a strategic investment with industry value chain partners to accomplish goals it would be unable to achieve on its own. Horizontal cooperation is where one company works with another across similar value chain activities that they each perform, e. g. marketing with marketing or R&D with R&D. In some circumstances horizontal cooperation can become extremely difficult to manage. In the automobile industry, for example, Toyota and General Motors participated in a decades-long cooperative effort focused on educating American workers about Japanese lean manufacturing techniques. But at the same time the two companies were competing both strategically and tactically across a range of fronts include model design, dealer network development, pricing, and more.

Figure 12.10
Types of Formal Cooperation

Type	Value Chain relations	Examples
Vertical	Upstream with suppliers, or downstream with buyers	Clothing manufacturer installs its proprietary knitting technology in outsourced supplier factories, resulting in higher quality goods made inexpensively. High-end audio equipment manufacturer provides exclusive geographic territory distribution rights to a retailer.
Horizontal	Across similar functions of partners	Small pharmaceutical company with expertise in genetics R&D teams up with larger pharma company with expertise in chemistry R&D, to target new solutions for treating lymphoma. Large commercial airline sells "code-share" tickets on smaller regional airline, to provide point-to-point access through one airline for passengers. Two non-profits which both target aid to the homeless combine financial and fundraising operations, to achieve larger voice in the community and avoid redundant administrative expenses.

Cooperation Process

Cooperative alliances should not be entered into lightly. Each party must have a clear understanding of what its obligations to the alliance are to be (activities and investments), as well as what its estimated benefit will be. In this way, it can more accurately assess whether participation in the alliance makes sense, i.e. will the benefits exceed the costs. Far too many alliances have been entered into over the years where participating companies have not fully appreciated what their investments would need to be or what they would get out of the allied effort. Four steps can be taken to enhance the chances for success for cooperation: 1) define the goals, 2) identify and vet potential partners carefully, 3) choose the proper governance structure, and 4) soundly manage the cooperation effort.[21]

Define the goals. Any form of cooperation should be consistent with the overall mission, vision and strategy of the company. Like other activities designed to create value in unique and sustainable ways, a cooperation effort should be viewed similarly. How will such an effort extend or deepen the value-creating capabilities of the company? Rather than approach cooperation possibilities opportunistically, management should clearly articulate how a cooperative effort will support and further the company's strategic goals. As part of the regular strategic planning process, a "gap analysis" can reveal where the company needs to make investments that will bridge between what it does well presently and what it wants to be able to do well in the future. This sort of analysis can expose areas where existing resources and capabilities may be unable to bridge the gap. Thus, management can thoughtfully develop a strong case for how a cooperative arrangement with the right partner can further the company's strategic agenda.

Due diligence on partners. Defining the strategic goals of a cooperative effort makes the identification of the right partner easier. A number of other firms may present possibilities. Careful analysis and vetting of each potential partner will enhance the odds for success. What your company seeks to get out of cooperation will likely be quite different from what a partner company seeks. Performing due diligence on possible partners can reveal how mutual goals are aligned, or how differences may be too far apart to manage effectively. This effort can also shed light on how different partners may require different levels of investment and active involvement, because partners will themselves have varying strengths and capabilities. The attitudes, beliefs, transparency, and perceived trustworthiness of potential partners must also be assessed.

Proper governance structure. The first two steps above help determine whether the cooperative arrangement should be governed as a non-equity (contract), equity, or joint venture. If the actions that need to be taken by both companies are abundantly clear and can be carefully specified up front, and if the expected outcomes are clearly definable and easy to measure, then a contract presents the best governance structure. But in many instances contracts would be incomplete because partners enter into cooperation in order to discover and learn, and thus they cannot know up front exactly what they will do or exactly what the outcomes will be. In these cases either an equity investment or a joint venture is called for. The difference between the two will likely hinge on the extent to which your company would be actively involved in collaborating with the partner. Active collaboration in exploration typically calls for a joint venture arrangement.

Managing the cooperation. An effective alliance involves more than simply treating the effort as if it is the same as an internally managed department or project. Typically, the fullest value of an alliance is realized when multiple functions within a company are involved. We discovered earlier that achieving consistency and coordination across the internal value chain is one of the most difficult facets of strategic management. As with any effort that crosses functions, this makes effective alliance management a real challenge. Management must therefore carefully consider the time and commitment that such efforts will inevitably involve. A dedicated senior manager endowed with resources and staff is usually required for success.

Cooperative efforts will normally require the development of a new relationship-specific methods and practices. Then, too, the new knowledge or learning that results from cooperation must be productively used back within and across functions in the partnering company. So new routines and procedures must be created to accomplish this. Together, chapters 5 and 6 on value chain and strategic resources concluded that routines and procedures of this sort exhibit VRIST characteristics and can serve as a foundation for sustainable competitive advantage.

Effective management like this can usually only be developed if there is a high level of inter-firm trust between the partnering companies. Trust supplements contractual governance relationships, and is essential for equity and joint venture relationships. Trusting partners act fairly toward each other and behave in good faith consistent with both expressed and implied obligations and commitments.

Managing in Markets: Question for Class Discussion

Governments periodically provide funding support for their domestic companies, in order that they can out-compete foreign companies. In the 1980s the US government funded Sematech, a consortium of US chip manufacturers cooperating to build their capabilities so they could compete effectively with Far East companies, notably those in Japan. In 2000 the European Aeronautic Defense and Space Company (EADS) was formed, with support from the German and French governments. EADS companies cooperated together, with funding aid from their governments, to develop Airbus aircraft to compete more effectively with US-based Boeing.

Do you think it is proper for private companies to receive developmental aid from governments so they can compete more effectively?

CHAPTER SUMMARY

This chapter aimed to examine the intricacies of strategy in the context of real competitors and the environment in which they operate. The ability to understand competitors, track their efforts and predict competitive moves (both proactively and reactively) are essential capabilities in the running of a successful business. We first examined the industry conditions under which companies must make their strategic moves. Industries may generally be classified as either benign or hostile, and today can often be characterized as hypercompetitive. We looked at the conditions that describe each characterization, and the unique approaches that research has suggested are successful in these circumstances. Scenario analysis presents another tool for companies to map out strategic moves over a very long period of time based on alternative possible scenarios for the future.

Predicting competitive moves relies upon our ability to more carefully understand the nature of specific organizations. We can classify organizations into one of four categories: Prospectors, Defenders, Analyzers, or Reactors. We also looked at internal competitive company characteristics that offer insights into their potential actions and reactions. These included: management team behavior patterns, relative market positions, and financial conditions. Information sources of competitive intelligence include: 1) media reports through evaluation services, 2) suppliers, and 3) conferences or speeches by key executives of competitors.

We examined competitive responses and actions based upon immediate and strategic threats to the organization. Immediate threats are traditionally addressed with an array of possible tactical responses. These include: 1) Acquiesce; 2) Compromise; 3) Shape and Manipulate; 4) Defy; 5) Neutralize; 6) Absorb; and 7) Leapfrog. This array of response styles moves from passive to increasingly aggressive and strategic.

Finally, we took a look at cooperation as an increasingly important component of strategy in the twenty-first century. Informal cooperation among competitors can occur through signaling or credible commitments made by a particular competitor. Formal cooperation can be based on non-equity (contract), equity investment, or joint venture arrangements. Each has its distinctive advantages and challenges, and depend on the outcomes desired through cooperation. Cooperation with other companies can be very challenging. Following a process ensures greater success by engaging in cooperation: define goals, identify and vet possible partners, establish the right governance structure, actively manage the cooperation effort.

Learning Objectives Review

1. *Describe how to use industry and company trajectories to evaluate an industry environment.*

    - Examine whether the industry is benign or hostile, and analyze its trajectories using strategy maps and historical industry information.

    - Classify competitors according to their behavioral patterns as Prospectors, Defenders, Analyzers, or Reactors.

2. *Select and evaluate the appropriate techniques for producing competitor intelligence.*

    - Examine patterns of CEO and senior management's previous decision making.

    - Conduct an "internal" value chain and resource analysis of the competitor.

    - Analyze the competitor's financial statements.

    - Synthesize publically-available information about the competitor using a clipping services consulting organization.

    - Discuss industry and competitor developments with suppliers, with ethical considerations in mind.

    - Examine public speeches given by competitor employees.

3. *Describe the differences between tactical and strategic methods for responding to competitors.*

    - Tactical responses to competitors are appropriate for dealing with immediate challenges that might compromise short-term position of business.

    - Strategic responses to competitors are appropriate for dealing with emerging challenges that could impact the long term position and viability of the business.

4. Discuss the conditions under which cooperation can be an effective competitive approach.

- Cooperation is appropriate when passive agreement avoids destructive competitive behavior. This is usually a Prisoner's Dilemma type of situation, and often appears when it is illegal for companies to strike active agreements with one another.
- Active cooperation between companies takes the form of non-equity contractual efforts, equity investments, or joint ventures. Such efforts are beneficial when the challenges are greater than any one company can afford, or when mutually beneficial industry standards can be developed.

Key Terms

Analyzer - A company that combines both Prospector and Defender behaviors. Parts of the company behave like a defender and parts behave like a prospector.

Benchmark - A process through which a company compares its own process and structure to that of other organizations. Companies most often benchmark directly against competitors. Occasionally, benchmarking will be done against other unrelated companies that have a "best in class" process. For example, General Mills examined how NASCAR pit crews organize for pit stops in order to better understand how to implement rapid cereal production line changes.

Benign environment - Characterized by: 1) market demand exceeds market supply; 2) generally high gross profit margins; 3) low competitive intensity - meaning no one competitor controls a high proportion of the market; 4) strong customer loyalty; and 5) a tolerance for occasional management miscues.

Clipping service - Provides a detailed, synthesized analysis of all available public information about any particular company, area, person, or situation.

Credible commitment – When a company demonstrates repeatedly through its behavior and pronouncements that it will react strongly and appropriately if a competitor initiates an attack.

Defender - A company that is intensive rather than extensive. That is, they usually focus on a limited number of key criteria, analyze their costs, and rigorously defend their competitive position against all competitors.

Hostile environment - Characterized by: 1) slow growth; 2) continuous price wars; 3) high competitive intensity - meaning that one or a few competitors control a substantial portion of the market; and 4) a focus on cost containment by competitors.

Prospector - A company that tends to view the industry from their own perspective and that of the customer rather, and less concerned with the actions of competition. They are usually leaders of change in the industry.

Reactor - A company that reacts (often slowly) to conditions in the competitive environment. This is an unstable form of organization.

Scenario analysis - A technique allowing organizations to consider dramatic shifts in their business model. The organization maps out a set of actions that it can start to take if warning signs begin to appear along the path of a particular scenario.

Strategic alliance - A joint venture or partnership formed with other companies (sometimes competitors) in order to develop a new technology, process, or other type of strategically important resource.

Tactics - Dealing with short-term competitive moves and countermoves, as opposed to long-term direction, investments, and performance.

Short Answer Review Questions

1. How would a benign environment impact the strategic choices of an organization?

2. How would you characterize a hostile environment?

3. Provide an example of a Prospector organization (separate from the examples in the text) and explain how it reacts to its competitors.

4. Why can't a company remain in a Reactor mode and still be a profit generator?

5. How would you collect competitive intelligence on a group of competitors?

6. How would a scenario analysis assist the airline industry going into 2030?

7. What competitive tactics should Starbucks employ with the encroachment of McDonald's into the premium coffee business?

8. How should absorption be used as a response to an innovative new entry?

9. How does a company's financial position impact its strategic choices?

Group Exercises

1. Select a well-known company in the Fortune 500. Using publicly available information, put together an analysis of the CEO who runs that organization. What are his or her strategic tendencies? Has this CEO been consistent in his or her behavior over time, at this and other companies? How might he or she react to an encroachment by a competitor?

2. Using the same company that you selected in #1, create a strategy map based upon industry key success factors (see Chapter 4). Based upon its past trajectories, what are its probable paths forward? If you are one of its competitors, what actions can you take that would compromise its intended direction?

3. How can analytics and "big data" be used to identify emerging trends and new opportunities in an industry?

4. Select an example company from the past week in the Wall Street Journal that is under attack from a substantial new competitor or new process. Using the tactical responses defined in the chapter, what would you recommend for that company?

Investor Relations Sites for Companies Mentioned in This Chapter

Advanced Battery Consortium: https://uscar.org/usabc/
Allied Steel Industries: https://www.alliedsteelco.com/
Alphabet: https://abc.xyz/investor/
Apple: https://investor.apple.com/investor-relations/default.aspx
Baltimore Orioles: https://www.mlb.com/orioles/
De Beers: https://www.debeersgroup.com/
Ford: hhttps://shareholder.ford.com/investors/overview/default.aspx
HP Inc: https://investor.hp.com/home/default.aspx
Kellogg's: https://investor.kelloggs.com/overview/default.aspx
McDonald's: https://corporate.mcdonalds.com/corpmcd/investors.html
Microsoft: https://www.microsoft.com/en-us/investor
Netflix: https://ir.netflix.net/ir-overview/profile/default.aspx
Nintendo: https://www.nintendo.co.jp/ir/en/index.html
Samsung: tps://www.samsung.com/global/ir/
Sattler Tech: http://sattlertech.com/about.html
Sony: https://www.sony.com/en/SonyInfo/IR/
Volkswagen: https://www.volkswagenag.com/en/InvestorRelations.html

References

[1] Bremner, B. 2007, "Nintendo storms the gaming world," BusinessWeek Online, January 29, 21. D'Angelo, W., 2018, "PS4 vs Xbox One vs Switch global lifetime sales," vgchartz.com, January 3. The Economist, 2005, "Way beyond the PC," November 26, 83. Edwards, C., 2006, "Game definitely not over," BusinessWeek Online, November 16, 11. Edwards, C., 2006, "Nintendo Wii: One ferocious underdog," BusinessWeek Online, November 26, 10. Hall, K., 2007, "Nintendo: Calling all players," BusinessWeek Online, October 11, 24. Needleman, S., 2017, "Microsoft gears up for videogame turnaround," Wall Street Journal, November 7, B4. Sharma, R., 2014, "Four reasons why PS4 is outselling XBox One," Forbes, April 18. Sherr, I., 2013, "Microsoft's New Xbox girds for its smartphone battle," Wall Street Journal, May 20, B1. Wingfield, N., 2009, "Xbox chief's next play," Wall Street Journal, June 2, B4. Wong, J., 2017, "Nintendo powers up its results," Wall Street Journal, October 31, B11.
[2] Winkler, R., 2013, "A Galaxy far, far away from Google," Wall Street Journal, March 16, B16. Winkler, R., 2014, "Google's costly Motorola maneuver may pay dividends," Wall Street Journal, January 31, B6.
[3] Covin, J., D. Slevin, and M. Heeley. 1999. Pioneers and followers: Competitive tactics, environment, and firm growth. Journal of Business Venturing 15: 175–210.
[4] Ibid.
[5] D'Aveni, R. 1994. *Hypercompetition: Managing the dynamics of strategic maneuvering*. New York: Free Press.
[6] Worthen, B. and Sherr, I., 2012, "PC sales show steep decline," Wall Street Journal, October 11, B1. Moorhead, P., 2013, "Dell's PC growth strategy - in it to win it," Forbes, June 21.
[7] Mims, C., 2020, " Moore's law is dead, long live Huang's law," Wall Street Journal, September 19, B1.
[8] See D'Aveni, R. 2007. "Mapping your competitive position." Harvard Business Review. November: 1–10. D'Aveni uses slightly different competitor maps to predict the evolution of cell phone functionality and benefits. See also Christensen, C. M., 1997, *The innovator's dilemma*, Cambridge: Harvard Business School Press.
[9] Greenspan, Alan. 2007. *The age of turbulence*. New York: Penguin.

[10] Miles, R. E., and C. C. Snow. 1978. *Organizational strategy, structure and processes*. New York: McGraw-Hill Book Company.

[11] Bustillo, M and Zimmerman, A. 2010. "Phone-wielding shoppers strike fear into retailers." Wall Street Journal, December 15, B1.

[12] BusinessWeek, 1984, "The dark side of DEC's rebound, January 30, 51–53.

[13] Sun Tzu. *The art of war*. 1983 edited translation by James Clavell. New York: Delta.

[14] Chen, M-J. and D. Miller, 2012, "Competitive dynamics:Themes, trends, and a prospective research platform," The Academy of Management Annals: 19.

[15] Downing, S.T., J-S. Kang, and G.D. Markman, 2019, "What you don't see can hurt you: Awareness cues to profile indirect cmpetitors," Academy of Management Journal, 62 (6): 1872-1900.

[16] This continuum of response styles is developed from several sources. D'Aveni, R. 2002, "The empire strikes back: Counterrevolutionary strategies for industry leaders," Harvard Business Review, November, 5–12. Oliver, C., 1990, "Determinants of inter-organizational relationships: Integrations and future directions," Academy of Management Review 15, 241–26. Oliver, C., 1991, "Strategic responses to institutional processes," Academy of Management Review 16, 145–179.

[17] Gilbert, R., 2014, "Competition policy for industry standards," in R.D. Blair and D.D. Sokol (eds.), *The Oxford handbook of international antitrust economics*, Vol. 2, 554-585.

[18] www.microsoft.com.

[19] Needleman, S. E., 2019, "Microsoft aims to reset videogame-streaming market with 'Ninja' pact," Wall Street Journal, August 11, B1.

[20] Colias, M. and Germano, S., 2019, "VW ups its investment in Ford's self-driving car unit," Wall Street Journal, July 12, B1. Wilmot, S., 2019, "Ford-VW learns from Renault-Nissan's mistakes," Wall Street Journal, July 12, B5.

[21] Dyer, J. H. and H. Singh, 1998, "The relational view: Cooperative strategy and the sources of inter-organizational advantage," Academy of Management Review 23, 660-679.

This page is intentionally left blank.

Section D: Implementation – Structure, Control, and Strategic Leadership

In this final section of this book we will examine one of the most crucial and yet most difficult areas of the field – managing implementation. In the previous three sections we have laid out the foundations of strategy and its importance to organizations, developed a means for analyzing the competitive landscape and developing a strategic approach, and discussed a number of contextual situations for putting strategy into practice. This included a review of life cycles and organizational stages of development, management of innovation, international strategy, competitive dynamics, and corporate strategy for running multi-divisional companies. The chapters in Section D tackle areas that have to be addressed for the organization to successfully implement all of this great effort that has been formulated. A well-developed strategy that is right for the market and provides a competitive advantage is of little value if it is not effectively implemented. In fact, evidence suggests that many failures to achieve competitive advantage are the result of good strategy that is just implemented poorly.

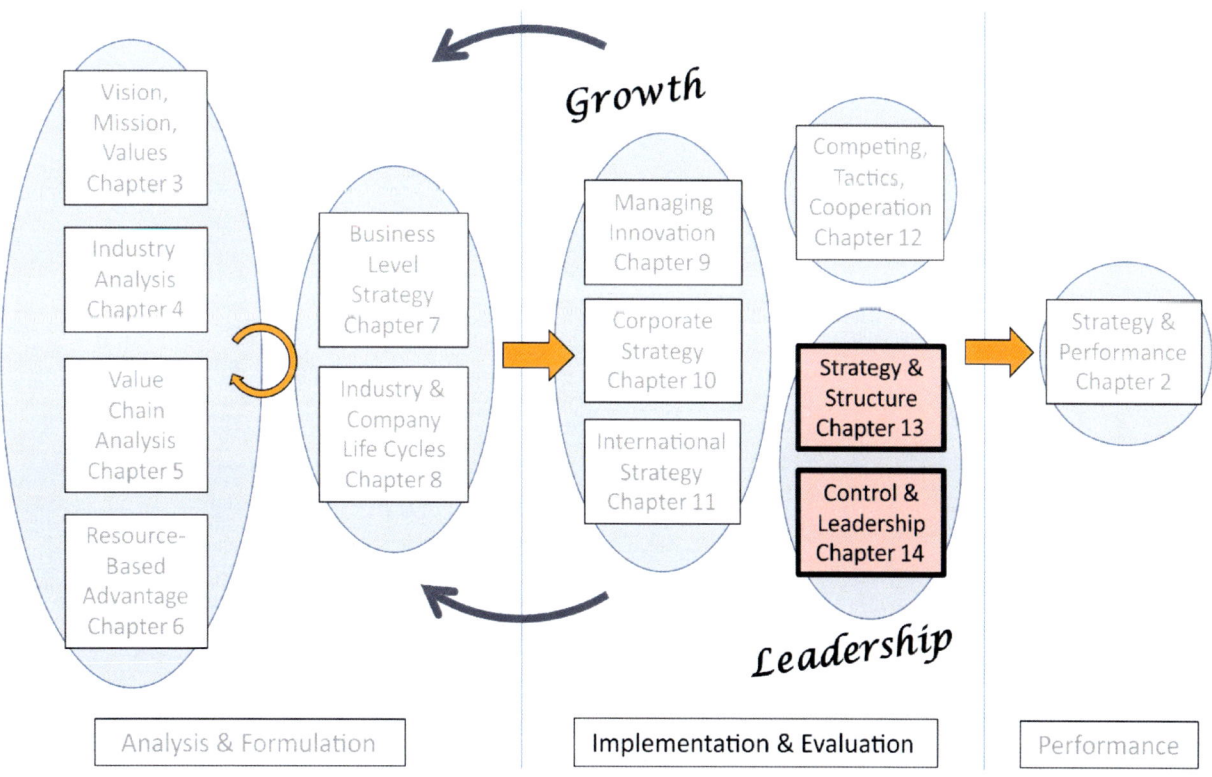

Strategic Management Model

In Chapter 13 we will examine how to structure the organization for success. There is a reason that organizations exist – to accomplish what cannot be accomplished by a single individual. When we have more than one person doing the work, questions immediately arise about who does what, who reports to whom, who makes decisions, who should be getting certain kinds of information, how people elsewhere in the company are to know what is going on, how we know that others are doing what they are supposed to do, and more. Structuring the organization in response to these types of questions is not only critical to our strategy, it is the means by which we accomplish it. The more effectively the company is organized, the more likely it is that we will meet expectations for superior performance. As we have done in previous chapters, we will look at this first from a broad level and then dig down deeper into the details. We incorporate some of the best thinking in consulting practices and solid academic research to provide you with a practical understanding and some very useful techniques.

In Chapter 14, we examine how to translate the ideas and practices from the preceding chapters into management tools and methods so that important strategic activities can be monitored and controlled and adjusted as necessary. Effective monitoring methods rely upon clear thinking about important value-creating activities, and on developing metrics that enable us to assess what's going on. These ideas again connect implementation to the value chain, and help the company to become a learning organization. We conclude our discussion of implementation with summary comments on strategic leadership.

Chapter 13: Strategy and Structure

LEARNING OBJECTIVES

1. Explain how strategy is implemented through a company's structure.

2. Construct a map of the types, characteristics, and outcomes of the most common means of structuring organizations.

3. Analyze and explain the type of mechanisms used to coordinate the activities in an organization.

4. Evaluate whether the structure of an organization aligns effectively with its strategy.

Breaking From The Past[1]

From: Satya Nadella, CEO Microsoft
Sent: March 29, 2018
To: Microsoft – All Employees
Subject: Embracing Our Future: Our Reorganization

Team,

Today, I'm announcing the formation of two new engineering teams to accelerate our innovation and better serve the needs of our customers and partners long into the future.

Over the past year, we have shared our vision for how the cloud and artificial intelligence (AI) will shape the next phase of innovation. First, computing is more powerful and ubiquitous from the cloud to the edge. Second, AI capabilities are rapidly advancing across perception and cognition fueled by data and knowledge of the world. Third, physical and virtual worlds are coming together to create richer experiences that understand the context surrounding people, the things they use, the places they go, and their activities and relationships.

These technological changes represent a tremendous opportunity for our customers, our partners – everyone. With all this new technology and opportunity comes a responsibility to ensure technology's benefits reach people more broadly across society. It also requires that the technologies we create are trusted by the individuals and organizations that use them.

Moving forward, Rajesh Jha will expand his existing responsibilities to lead a new team focused on *Experiences & Devices*. The purpose of this team is to instill a unifying product ethos across our end-user experiences and devices. Computing experiences are evolving to include multiple senses and are no longer bound to one device at a time but increasingly spanning many as we move from home to work and on the go. These modern needs, habits and expectations of our customers are motivating us to bring Windows, Office, and third-party applications and devices into a more cohesive Microsoft 365 experience.

Second, Scott Guthrie will expand his existing responsibilities to lead a new team focused on *Cloud + AI Platform*. The purpose of this team is to drive platform coherence and compelling value across all layers of tech starting with distributed computing (cloud and edge) to AI (infrastructure, runtimes, frameworks, tools and higher-level services around perception, knowledge and cognition).

Harry Shum will continue to lead our third engineering team, *AI + Research*, which is instrumental in the key technology advances required across all our product teams. Our primary goal is to accelerate the adoption of AI innovations from research into product, and the changes we are making today reflect our strong progress.

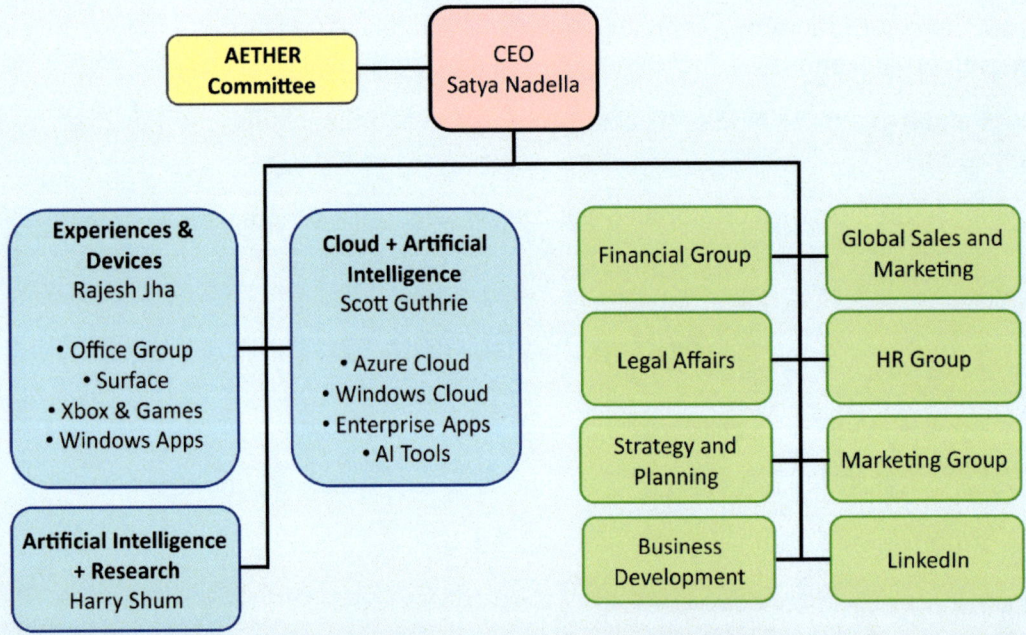

As we make technological progress we need to ensure that we are doing so responsibly. To this end, we have established the AI and Ethics in Engineering and Research (AETHER) Committee, bringing together senior leaders from across the company to ensure our AI platform and experience efforts are deeply grounded in Microsoft's core values and principles and benefit the broader society. Ensuring we always act responsibly will continue to be a hallmark of our work.

To truly get the best impact from our efforts, we will have to push ourselves to transcend Conway's law. We can't let any organizational boundaries get in the way of innovation for our customers. This is why a growth mindset culture matters. It will take courage to keep learning and growing together and collaborating as One Microsoft. It's amazing what we have been able to accomplish together, and yet I still believe we are in the very early days of what is possible.

Satya

QUESTIONS

1. How does the new organization reflect changes in the market and evolving customer needs?
2. Windows was "demoted" from its own engineering group, and separated into two separate divisions. Why?
3. Why does the new AETHER ethics and responsibility group report directly to Satya?
4. What is "Conway's Law?" Google this. How does this relate to organizational structure?

ALIGNING STRATEGY AND STRUCTURE

We have spent a considerable portion of this text learning how to create the optimal strategy for an organization. This has included analyzing the competitive environment, developing the resource base and value chain foundation for business level strategy advantage, and examining what types of businesses we should be involved with. We now turn our attention to implementing our strategy. The topic of structuring an organization is as old as the study of business itself. At its most fundamental level we are faced with an absolutely pivotal question: How do we orchestrate ten people in an organization, or ten thousand people, so that they are all moving in the same direction and that this direction is consistent with the company's strategy? Coordinating the activities of even a few people is challenging. You have probably experienced this on a small scale in team projects in school. However, it gets increasingly difficult as three impactful factors work against the organization. Those are: 1) the number of employees working in the company increases; 2) employees are increasingly dispersed geographically; and 3) the business becomes more multidimensional with different products, services, and operating divisions.

Let's actually consider the case of an orchestra as an example of coordination. Each musician has an instrument and a specific role to play in providing the audience with the finest performance. The conductor provides the overall coordination, but cannot and does not play the individual instruments. Instead, each musician is expected to be an expert in playing their instrument, reading the music, reacting to the musicians around them, as well as being able to

follow the direction of the conductor. The structure employed by a typical orchestra is referred to as a simple structure: there is one person to whom all the players "report." Yet there is effective coordination because all the musicians can see the conductor and simultaneously hear all the notes being played by the other musicians. By convention the coordinating mechanism for everyone has been distilled down to a universally understood metric – the musical note on a sheet of paper. What if the conductor was not present, or what would happen if the sheet music was lost by the airline when the orchestra traveled to its next concert site? What if there was a pandemic and musicians were dispersed and live-streamed their audio in as a broadcast that was then somehow mixed on stage in real time? What if the musical composition called for improvisational playing by certain instruments located in different places? How would you structure an orchestra to accommodate these innovative and eclectic approaches, and what kinds of systems would you need to coordinate geographically distant – and sometimes innovative and improvisational – efforts?

These are not just idle questions from a strategy textbook author. In 2023 Amazon will open a second headquarter office in Arlington, Virginia, far from its main campus in Seattle. Boeing's HQ is in Chicago, but they source and assemble parts all over the world and assemble planes in Seattle. The challenges these companies experience reflect the orchestra questions just asked: thousands of employees, remote location, communication challenges across different time zones, innovative work married to existing lines of business – and all without any sheet music to guide. How will this work? These are the kinds of challenges that strategic leaders in every organization face.

UNDERSTANDING THE STRUCTURING IMPERATIVE

Deciding how to structure an organization is perhaps one of the most visible components in effectively implementing strategy. It is much more than deciding who works for whom, although that is a crucial element. Structuring the company formalizes who is responsible and accountable for decision making, how important information is channeled within the company (and where channels may impede information flows), how budgets and resources are provided, how procedures and controls will be implemented, and how the company believes its organization of activities can enable it to outcompete its competition. Together, these characteristics of structure describe how the company's strategy will be shaped and implemented.

The answers to these questions become increasingly complicated as organizations expand and grow. Alfred Chandler, who first described "strategy" as it relates to companies, observed this complexity in his study of four large U.S. companies.[2] Expansion through new products and new markets pushes organizations to grow larger, with the usual result that individuals with strategic responsibility tend to become increasingly removed from day-to-day operations. At the same time field units and people on the operating level tend to become increasingly specialized and therefore separated from other functions and other operational units. This creates a new set of problems: coordinating disparate departments and workgroups, communication between the groups, creating the understanding of a common set of goals across the entire organization, and ensuring that day-to-day operations are actually consistent with overall direction. This is one reason we have emphasized value chain coordination throughout this book.

The complexity observed in aligning strategy and structure can be described by three structural facets of organizations: specialization, centralization, and formalization (Figure 13.1). Specialization occurs as companies grow, hire more people for functional areas such as marketing or production, and need to create greater efficiency or effectiveness of activities within these areas. Adam Smith first described this over two hundred years ago when he observed work in a pin factory![3] When departmental specialization occurs, then issues of centralization come up – whether important decisions are made centrally by the head office or by others in the newly formed specialized departments. Additionally, the more companies rely upon departments and divisions, the more formalization of rules and procedures takes the place of informal "seat of the pants" methods for making sure everyone is on the same page.

**Figure 13.1
Structural Facets of Organizations**

Specialization
Centralization
Formalization

The conflicts created by specialization, centralization, and formalization are a major issue in both large and small organizations. When growth necessitates the formation of departments or groups, removed as they are from easily interacting with each other, it is unfortunately not uncommon for individual departments to come to believe that their own activities are the *raison d'être* of the company. They begin to create their functional-level plans and goals in isolation from the rest of the organization. But the accounting department's goal in a manufacturing company is not to create a world-class audit and accounting operation (however laudable that effort may seem); it is to accurately track and report on the internal activities of the company. Human Resources' goal is not to demand every employee's participation in semiannual benefit program information sessions; it is to effectively support the hiring, retention, and growth needs of the employees and the company. Sometimes this may require progressive new systems, sometimes not. Engineering's goal is not to create a world-class R&D lab with every cutting-edge device available; it is more likely to be the development of functional products that meet the needs of the company's customers in the most desirable manner possible. Fragmentation such as this, and the variety of goals it can create, requires attention from management in order to achieve coherence.

So with the advent of departments, divisions, and groups that specialize come both varying degrees of centralization and formalization. Strategic decision making becomes the province of management in the central office to ensure that there is one consistent approach throughout the company, and formal rules and procedures are instituted to make sure all the departments are coordinated with that approach. This sounds good in the sense that the complexities created by growth and expansion may be resolved. Yet the combination of these three facets makes it exceedingly difficult for companies to excel at the two strategic imperatives we have discussed throughout this book: value creation and opportunity recognition. Value creation occurs more easily when various parts of the value chain are more aligned, where their respective activities are well-integrated with the rest of the company. When separate departments are created and formal rules and procedures are instituted, this type of synthesis is more difficult to achieve. Similarly, opportunity recognition capabilities often depend on cross-functional efforts, which also become more difficult with separation, centralization, and formalization. When centralization and formalization are prevalent, the kind of experimentation and flexibility that is important in trying to take advantage of new opportunities is reduced.

Communication, Coordination, Control

These ideas lead us to the fundamental issues that lie at the heart of the alignment of organizational structure with strategy – which are communication, coordination, and control. As we earlier described in Chapter 5 on the Value Chain, a business is nothing more than an organized system of activities that creates value. The structure of the business should be aligned with the strategy in order to support the system of activities. So the core structure question is how it can be used to facilitate communication, coordination, and control. By working to facilitate and improve these three Cs (Figure 13.2), the structure can enhance the system of value-creating activities.

Figure 13.2
Three C's of Systems

Communication
Coordination
Control

Communication. Effective communication is central to any organization structure. Think about how often it seems that one part of a company has absolutely no idea what another part is doing. Have you ever called an airline to get a fare quote, and then called back again later only to receive a completely different quote? How often have you heard someone say "I didn't get that email"? What's the effect on a company whose differentiation strategy involves new product introductions, if the manufacturing plant manager is only interested in producing the existing products 24/7? What do you suppose employees think and talk about when a new CEO or vice president is hired, someone who is hired because they have some new ideas about the business? How long does it take someone in management to approve a budget request for a new development project, or to OK a special price reduction for an important customer who has been enticed by an aggressive competitor? These questions point out that communication must be effective up, down, and across the organization.

The business strategy lays out the logic for how value will be created (e.g., through low cost or a specific type of differentiation). This logic must be communicated throughout the company, so that employees understand it and their efforts can be coordinated. This is accomplished partly through ongoing efforts to embed the vision and mission (Chapter 3), but this is also accomplished through everyday communications and information that flow through the formal channels created by structure. It is difficult to strike the right balance with information. We are ensuring that they are kept well-informed, keeping them in tune with their areas of specialization, and reinforcing the overall direction that the senior management wants to go. But because communication systems are even more sophisticated than they have ever been and we are in an instantaneous information-rich society (memos, reports, e-mails, text messages, blogs, Twitter, Zoom conferencing, Facebook, etc.), the danger of overwhelming individuals is huge. That they may ignore or tune out important information is a much greater risk now than it ever was in the past.

Organizational communication is more than just downloads from senior management up high. In addition, the organization needs a system through which employees can pass critical information back up to senior decision makers, and across departmental boundaries. Upward flows of information can provide better perspective on the sources of core competence within the company, and how activities supporting the strategic logic can be improved upon. In Chapter 9 we also saw how connected upward communication can be to effective innovation. Lateral flows between departments or divisions, without having to go up a chain of command and back down again, can improve organizational response to competitive threats and new opportunities.

Coordination. Central to effective strategy is the coordination of activities across the value chain, which achieves consistency of effort throughout the organization. We know pretty quickly when organizations have failed to coordinate their activities. The Boeing 737 Max, we now know, suffered deadly crashes and had its sales suspended in 2019 because the company failed to properly coordinate between designers, software engineers, pilots, and the inspectors at the Federal Aviation Administration. And even when it suspected there may be problems, it failed to properly coordinate with customers and their pilots on modified in-flight procedures. Disaster relief for Hurricane Katrina victims was delayed so long because of inept coordination by the U.S. government's FEMA office that George W. Bush's presidential standing and effectiveness was significantly damaged. We have also witnessed examples of coordination excellence. Recall from the chapter on diversification, for example, how Cisco Systems makes sure that an acquired company's products are listed on the Cisco's price list the day the deal closes so that its salespeople can immediately start selling them.

Control. Creating, maintaining, and managing an effective system of control allows senior management to implement the vision, mission, and strategy as designed. While we will discuss control in significantly more detail in Chapter 14, it is important to note here that structure performs one of the key control functions for strategy implementation. Structure not only provides the means to share certain information in an organized fashion. It also provides the opportunity to identify areas where there are problems, so that corrective action can be taken.

We can see that the issues of coordination, communication, and control are highly related to the decision about structuring a company. We want to be careful that any structure we put into place provides formal recognition to the kinds of coordination and communication that are most important for the company's strategy to be successful, and to the ways in which control must be exercised. We will see in a few minutes that there are a variety of ways to be thinking about this.

Prior to moving to structure, however, we think that managers should develop a better understanding of what type of activities need to be structured and how they might be coordinated to most effectively support strategy. There are three critical aspects to examine:

1. What are the key organizational components of the company's business?

2. What coordinating mechanisms are available for use with these components?

3. What types of structures might work best for a company's chosen strategy?

KEY ORGANIZATIONAL COMPONENTS

Every part of a business must be coordinated to some extent. However, as much as some people may not want to admit it, there are parts of an organization that are simply more critical to the overall success of a company than others. Understanding the elements of an organization is a crucial first step to structuring. Excluding senior management, in general the parts of any organization may be divided into three components: 1) Core, 2) Techno Structure, and 3) Staff Support.[4] We want to emphasize the universal nature of this part of structuring. Regardless of the type of organization (public or private, profit or nonprofit, domestic or international), the size of the organization or its age, these three parts of the company are central to any structuring or restructuring effort (Figure 13.3).

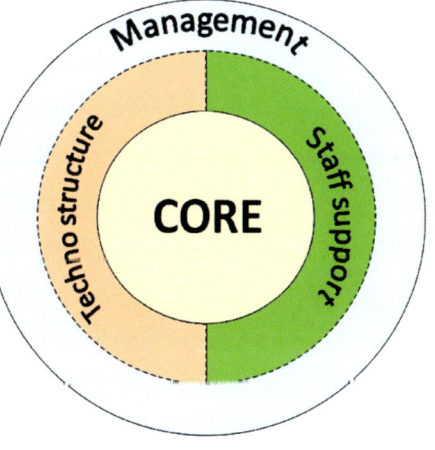

**Figure 13.3
Key Organizational Components**

The Core

What part of the business is most crucial to its success with customers? What area or areas of the company are therefore at the strategic core of the business? The core group or groups are those most central to generating the competitive advantage that the firm enjoys. Developed in our earlier chapters on value chain and resource based analyses, the areas of the business that are most critical for the competitive advantage of the business are the areas that should receive the lion's share of management time, attention, resources, and focus. The activities in other parts of the business, while still important, are then viewed as providing support to and servicing the strategic core of the company.

An example can illustrate what we mean by the core. If we were running an upscale restaurant known for its top-rated cuisine, it is pretty clear that the chefs would be the core of the business. This is the primary reason that customers come to eat here. If we mistakenly placed primary focus on the wait staff, then critical decisions might be made in support of the wait function – such as about when the food would be delivered and how it would be presented – that may compromise efforts of the chefs. This may seem a bit obvious, but it is also a central aspect of competitive advantage.

Some years back Bennigan's restaurant introduced a lunch deal where your meal was free if it took longer than 10 minutes to deliver it to your table from the time of your order. In this case, it's probably obvious that customers were not coming to the restaurant because of its superior quality food; they were coming because of the service promise. Bennigan's placed its order and wait staff at the strategic core: the table-serving process provided the advantage for the firm. It was the wait staff that had to deliver on the customer promise, both by getting the order to the kitchen and by getting it back to the table. Everything the company did was oriented around the facilitation of rapid order-taking, rapid food preparation, and rapid table-waiting. An acceptable quality of food was assumed to be an orthodox feature, and simply had to meet normal expectations.

Don't assume from this example that other areas of the company are not important – they are. They are just not the core reason that customers give the company their business. Reflecting our previous discussion on ordinary resources (Chapter 6) and competitive parity (Chapter 7), all other functions within the organization must be done well, but the company need not perform those tasks any better than at parity for its industry. That is, all the other jobs – like the chefs, hostess, table cleaners, dishwashers at Bennigan's – need to be done for the business to function. The dishes must be clean, the food must be satisfactory, and the host or hostess must be pleasant and efficient. They must perform in a manner that does not negatively impact the customer or the core. But there is no strategic benefit in outperforming the rest of the industry. Since resource allocation is a fundamental decision to make in strategic management, companies must decide where to concentrate their limited resources. Resources not applied to the core are missed opportunities for developing and sustaining competitive advantage.

The Noncore

Noncore functions of the business can be classified into two distinct areas: techno structure and staff support. The techno structure consists of those groups whose activities provide advice and policy input to the core, while the staff support consists of all other groups (other than the core and the techno structure) who carry out work of the organization. In the example of Bennigan's, where the wait staff was core, the chefs would be categorized as techno structure since their advice and food preparation policies must still be considered crucial to the operation. For instance, the wait staff may want the burgers put on the plate immediately to meet the 10-minute deadline, but the chefs are required to cook the burgers to a standard temperature prior to serving the customers. The chefs have bounds to their policy making and advice giving. They are bounded by the scope of their operational responsibility; however, their positions put them in a higher "orthodox" category as they have influence on the core.

In contrast, we might categorize the table cleaning crews as staff support because they neither provide advice nor establish any policy that might affect the core. Their job is to efficiently bus and clean so that the tables can be reset for the next customer. Staff are not in a position to advise the core on how plates should be arranged to make their work easier or set a policy for how long it is before they clean a newly abandoned table.

The relationship between the core and either techno structure or staff support is not a two-way street. While input and advice from the techno structure and staff may establish boundaries within which core activities occur, the demands of the strategic core exert a profound influence that completely shapes both the techno structure and the staff support. In the case of a fast-service restaurant like Bennigan's, the core premise of the business may demand that the kinds of meals prepared by the kitchen are only those that can be prepared quickly. Food ingredients and other supplies may be purchased and delivered in premeasured quantities that facilitate rapid preparation. Fast service also requires a certain amount of support staffing at the lunch hour to ensure that tables are turned around and dirty dishes are washed quickly in order to be ready for the next customers.

This division of activities allows any organization to function more smoothly as everyone more explicitly understands their relative contributions in a system that is focused on a specific method and process of value creation. Effectively developed and communicated, it allows for far fewer disputes that must be resolved by senior management. The operation is more focused on the sustainable competitive advantage of the organization.

Commercial Airlines in the United States

Think about the groups that make up a typical commercial airline: pilots, flight attendants, gate agents, maintenance workers, baggage handlers, reservation specialists, not to mention the back office operations of accounting, payroll, IT, policies and procedures, purchasing, human resources, training, etc.

What group do you think is the core at a typical airline?

What difference might it make if we defined different parts of an airline as the core? Remembering that the core group is primarily responsible for the areas of the company in which value creation occurs, what if we define the pilots as core? Do you know who your pilots are on a commercial flight? Would it make a difference if you knew in advance who your pilots would be for a flight? Would you choose your airline or flight based upon the pilots for that flight? Would you pay more for a particular pilot team?

The pilots of commercial airlines in the United States are typically in the techno structure of the company. In many ways they personify what it means to be techno structure. They must do their job and do it well; furthermore, they provide advice to the core and help set policies. Pilots can and do decide whether the planes are flight-worthy, and they make hundreds of decisions about how the flight proceeds. However, they make no decisions about the type of plane flown, what gate it will fly out of, what the scheduled departure time is, and what city the flight is headed to. If you make no decisions about which airline to fly based upon who the pilots are, if suppliers provide resources regardless of who the pilots are, and if management plans flights assuming that they will be able to staff the plane, then the pilots cannot be core to the function of the airline.

QUESTIONS

1. A similar analysis could be applied to every group that was mentioned at the beginning of this vignette. So, what group is responsible for the core in commercial aviation?
2. Why do you fly a particular airline?

COORDINATING MECHANISMS

Once the organization has been divided into the groups of activities that comprise the core, techno structure, and staff support, then decisions must be made about how to coordinate the work of each group. In other words, the first step is to distinguish among critical value adding activities and the next is to decide the most appropriate means of coordinating these activities. Outlined by Henry Mintzberg some years ago, there are five relatively common and effective methods for coordinating work.[5] They are:

1. Mutual Adjustment
2. Standardization of Work Processes
3. Standardization of Work Skills
4. Standardization of Work Output
5. Direct Supervision

These five mechanisms really represent a continuum from self-direction of the activities of a group to total direction of all aspects of the activities by a single authority within the company (Figure 13.4). Some units are best coordinated by mutual adjustment, while others by work skills. Even within smaller departments, there is sometimes the need to use multiple techniques, as for instance when we have technicians and administrative staff within the same unit.

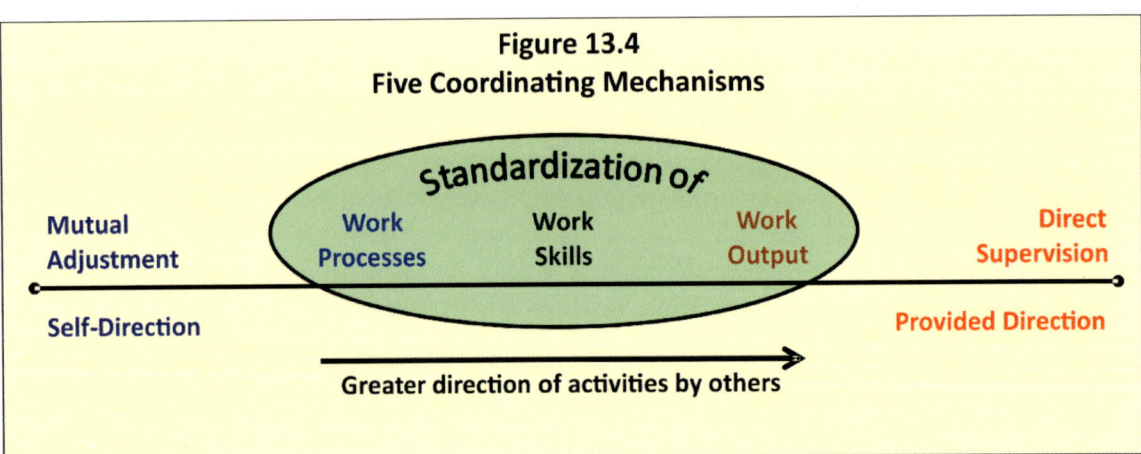

Within most organizations we typically find all five in use. Using a combination of coordinating mechanisms gives the organization an opportunity for the best fit for the actual work being done. But using a combination may interfere with one of the goals of effective structure design, which is reducing layers of hierarchy to the minimum necessary. Fewer layers in a company usually translates into swifter and more accurate transmission of important information both to and from the apex of the business (CEO and top management team), and thus generally leads to higher quality strategic outcomes. So there is a balance that is need between structure and coordinating mechanisms.

We should point out here that coordinating is not the same as evaluating. Virtually everyone within an organization will have their performance measured and evaluated in some form, and that form usually takes place as some type of output measure. Here we are talking about how to structure and coordinate activities, not how to measure the effectiveness of those efforts.

None of these coordination methods negate the need for effective performance measures that are tied to the overall performance of the organization.

Mutual Adjustment

The best possible coordination method is mutual adjustment because virtually 100 percent of each employee's effort is devoted to moving the company forward. Under mutual adjustment, each person knows everything that is happening in the organization and simply adjusts her or his work patterns for the conditions at hand. When used within departments these groups require a relatively small number of folks, because they all understand the goals and work collaboratively to accomplish those goals.

In a small organization where everyone works within the same room, this type of coordination method can be easily used. Take the packing operation at a typical UPS retail store. Various packages arrive during the day and must all be boxed correctly and prepared for shipping. A group of employees, each of whom is trained in all aspects of the operation, can mutually adjust to one another in order to handle the flow of customer traffic, counter operations, and packaging in the back room, and get what needs to be completed prior to the shipping time. Many entrepreneurial firms use mutual adjustment as their operations start up, where every member of the team is expected to do what needs to be done without a "supervisor" to coordinate their movements.

NASA mission control during Apollo 13, 1970

In class we occasionally use the example from the movie Apollo 13, where a dozen or so engineers were isolated in a room and had to design a carbon dioxide filter using the same spare equipment that was in the damaged space capsule. There were no supervisors and each person knew if they didn't get it designed within the next three hours that the astronauts would die in space. They did not have the time to establish a supervisor to coordinate their efforts, nor were they sure exactly how they would even design the filter. They had to experiment and innovate. These are perfect conditions for using mutual adjustment as a coordination method.

With mutual adjustment, almost no time is wasted in meetings, preparing status reports, or duplicating others' efforts. This coordination method provides the highest percentage of time devoted to work effort available. It seems to work best in the following situations:

1. Where there is a small group of people,

2. Where the tasks are either well-known so that everyone is cross-trained on all the jobs, or

3. Where the means to success is uncertain and a strong degree of innovation will be required.

Standardization of Work Processes

As the number of employees grows and mutual adjustment is no longer viable as a means of coordination, companies will look to one of three standardization criteria. Using these criteria, literally hundreds or more employees can be effectively managed without reverting all the way to direct supervision. Using standardization of work processes requires a deep understanding of the work involved so that a supervisor can manage the processes. To a certain extent employees are seen as somewhat interchangeable when this coordination method is employed. In an automobile manufacturing plant, engineers have meticulously designed the system so that a frame enters at one end of the plant and a car emerges from the other end. Each work station along the assembly line has been placed in a particular order with work done there in a particular manner for the finished product to be a success. Supervisors walk the line looking to see if the processes are being followed and trying to improve the processes along the way. The actual employee is evaluated on his or her ability to perform the process as designed.

In almost every organization of any size, there are parts of the business that can be designed into a process. For those areas, the process itself becomes the focus and the employees are measured against the process. Using this system, the number of employees reporting to a single supervisor can be dramatically increased. Each supervisor can manage larger numbers when the processes are well designed and implemented. Furthermore, this coordination method works for both manufacturing as well as service companies. In most banking operations tellers are expected to follow a very strict protocol for taking deposits and distributing money. Tellers are measured upon their ability to follow the procedures that have been set, and deviation from those procedures constitutes negative performance.

Blackjack dealers at a casino are another prime example of standardized work processes. Each dealer is required to shuffle in a particular manner, pay the winners in a particular order, make change with a standard process, and so on. Dealers are evaluated on their adherence to process. Same thing is true for most customer call center operations. If it is occasionally frustrating that a customer service rep on the phone can't solve your problem and appears to following some script for what she says, it is because she is closely following a dictated work process. She is evaluated in part on how well she adheres to the process.

Standardization of Work Skills

As we move away from our ability to use mutual adjustment there are groups within the company where it is inappropriate to attempt using process as a coordinating mechanism. Instead, we can use standardization of work skills as a basis for coordination. This is especially so for groups whose skill sets are well understood in the wider market. Traditionally, this was only done for groups of employees who held well-recognized state, national, or international certifications. These might include, for example, CPA (Certified Public Accountant), CFA (Certified Financial Analyst), state-issued Barber or Cosmetology license, JD (Law, usually with bar exam passage as an additional criteria), MD (Medicine, usually with Board certification), PE (Professional Engineer), Plumber and Electrician (requiring completion of both the exam and journeyman work time), CLU (Chartered Life Underwriter in the insurance industry), among others. Through their organizations and professional associations these groups tend to self-police and typically require ongoing maintenance of education in their professions. These groups of people can be managed in large numbers with the expectation that they have certain fundamental skills.

In practice, this coordination technique has been extended by a number of companies to include detailed training and certification within their organizations. For example, General Electric encouraged employees to gain Six Sigma certification (an efficiency and management control system), which became an important criterion for promotion within the company. The level, complexity, and importance to the organization elevated GE's training efforts well above the typical quick-hit training session so prevalent at most organizations. United Technologies had a less data-intensive ACE certification for its employees, but its company-wide implementation bolstered its reputation for quality and its standing with customers.[6]

The value of standardized skills includes a common nomenclature among the members, a common base knowledge set, and an understanding of the responsibilities expected by someone who holds that particular designation. Using this method of coordination, the manager hires only those individuals with the requisite qualifications and leans on the expectations of the certifying organization to provide a baseline for performance. Performance beyond that baseline is what is measured and evaluated within individual company human resources systems.

Standardization of Work Output

For those groups where standardization of work processes or work skills is not applicable, and yet when the group is too large or scattered to utilize mutual adjustment, one other means of coordination exists prior to reverting to fully direct supervision. Here employees can be coordinated via standardization of work output. There are many groups where the other coordinating techniques are simply not appropriate. How do you coordinate the activities of a sales staff? What makes a great salesperson? There is no standard set of skills, nor any outside society that can certify a salesperson as having achieved a requisite level of sophistication within the profession. Furthermore, there is simply no one best way to sell something. Companies that have tried to apply a rigorous methodology to a sales call or sales cycle have found themselves marginalized by other players in the market who discover more effective methods.

Working with a large automobile dealer operation on the east coast, we were struck by the complete dissimilarity of the three top salespeople. One was an outgoing, loud, bear of a person  who knew very little about cars but loved to talk with people. He turned many people off, but his manner was really loved by others and his sales numbers were the best in the entire multistate operation. The next person (with sales just barely behind the first person) was a quiet, professional woman who would wait and watch potential car buyers looking for clues as to their real needs. The third salesperson (again with numbers barely below the first two) was a bit of a slob who simply knew everything there was to know about cars. He was a classic "car guy." There were no processes that were the same between them and no common background on which to hang a skill set. They each worked in their own manner toward the objective of selling as many cars as possible in a month for as much money as could be made on each sale. The company used a variety of output measures to measure their performance. Output measures that are well crafted allow a manager the ability to easily track many people who might go about their jobs using different methods or techniques.

Care in developing the output measures is critical so that they include the balanced nature of the business. You want to sell a lot of cars, but you also want satisfied customers and a reasonable profit margin on each sale. Furthermore, when employees are coordinated through output measures, it is important to have a well-established ethical code of conduct. In this way the company explicitly jettisons any kind of "ends justify the means" mentality. We will further discuss the establishment of important output measures in Chapter 14 on control and performance.

Direct Supervision

Some situations move organizations toward direct supervision as a coordination method. Classic symptoms of this problem situation include products that are miss-shipped, a production line missing its targets, a backlog created in the operation, or employees voicing complaints regularly about lack of coordination. Poor coordination among employees demands that a more directed coordination approach be adopted.

Direct supervision is necessary when standardization of work processes, skills, and outputs are ineffective in achieving the kind of coordination that is necessary. Direct supervision is called for when an organization's strategic approach requires that work 1) be done in a certain way, 2) be done by employees with specific skills sets, and 3) result in a highly predictable and consistent output. Under these circumstances none of the standardization methods, by themselves, would be sufficient for what the company needs. For example, Johnson & Johnson's Alza pharmaceutical division manufactures implantable and transdermal drug delivery systems for personal use. Manufacturing these devices must follow FDA-approved methods, must be done by certified technicians, and absolutely must result in a consistently safe and effective final product since patients' lives are at risk. This type of business leaves no room for flexibility, and must be subject to direct supervision.

Another situation that may call for direct supervision is when cost control is of paramount competitive concern. The risk in striving to become the low-cost leader is that a company may not actually achieve the leadership position; a lower cost rival may then undercut it through aggressive pricing. In the early 2000s Dell achieved the low-cost leadership position in the personal computer business through a variety of value chain activities, including direct supervision of its PC assembly operations. In these types of assembly operations where strict control is required in order to drive down unit costs, information flows and coordination typically run through a supervisor or manager who is able to see the whole picture at once and immediately take any corrective actions needed in case a problem comes up.

These examples illustrate that there are very appropriate times and places for using this traditional method of coordination. In general, this is a default pattern of coordination that should be used as a last resort. In other words, it should be used only if one of the other four coordination methods cannot be effective.

Strategy and Coordination

The previous discussion implies that a certain type of coordination is appropriate for a certain type of strategic approach. A deep understanding of the core areas of a company and what methods might work best for its coordination provides good insight into an organizational structure that can enhance and support strategy. There are many ways to define the core by combining up groups of employees and then deciding on a set of coordination methods. Remember we stated earlier that a company uses a variety of different forms of coordination for the various groups it has identified. So there is simply no "perfect answer" to this process; it is at least as much art as it is science.

**Figure 13.5
Coordination and Generic Strategies**

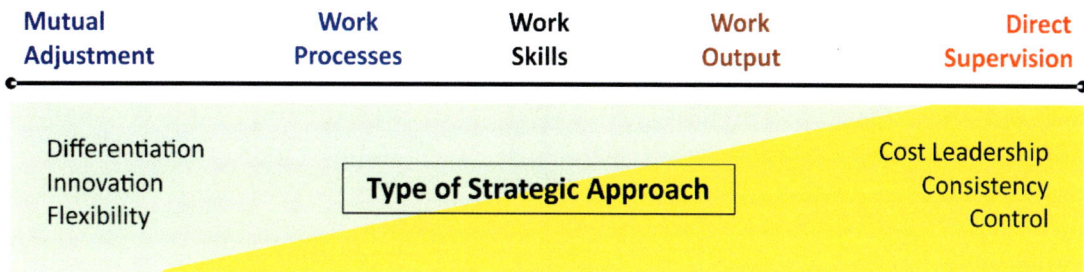

Yet we can offer some general guidelines for the mixture of strategy and coordination (Figure 13.5). Where a company's strategy depends increasingly on cost leadership, consistency of output, or significant control over aspects of the product or service production process, the method of coordination will tend toward the direct supervision end of the spectrum. The company values a strict, disciplined approach to the conduct of its business and discourages employees from acting independently. This is an organization that is more machine-like, with all the parts working tightly in synch. In contrast, where innovation and flexibility are desirable – often hallmarks of a company seeking a differentiation approach – coordination will tend toward the mutual adjustment end of the spectrum. Here employees are increasingly able to investigate new information they receive and respond to new ideas, making decisions on their own for the benefit of the company.

Occasionally we witness instances in which a company fails to achieve a good match between its strategy and its coordinating methods. In 2017 United Airlines had police drag a screaming customer, who had already been seated on a flight, off the airplane because he had been "bumped" due to over-booking. United should have had a customer-focused culture and privileged employee flexibility in dealing with frontline issues; instead, it had a rules-based culture that privileged operational efficiency. Its focus on a combination of getting planes out of the gate as soon as possible and written rules to control every employee action, resulted in a public relations disaster. An apology from then-CEO Oscar Munoz, placed in the *Wall Street Journal* a few days later, stated "procedures got in the way of employees doing what they know is right."[7]

TYPES OF ORGANIZATIONAL STRUCTURE

Understanding the key organizational components (core, techno structure, staff) and the possible coordinating mechanisms, we are now in a position to determine the best means of structuring the organization. Usually when we consider the key organization components, we think about them in the context of the company's functions (e.g. marketing, marketing research, customer service, sales, purchasing, etc.). This way of thinking about the components often parallels the layout of a value chain diagram with its primary and support activities categories. But we need to remember that VRIST sources of sustainable advantage often derive from how well the company coordinates and connects activities across the value chain that are performed by different functions.

Now we must now examine exactly how to apply our understanding of components and coordination using structure. It is one thing to be able to state with some clarity which groups are which and how you will coordinate the activity of each. It is quite another to develop that into an effective structure that facilitates communication, coordination and control across the value chain. That is the focus of this section.

While there are many variations on organizational structure, most evolve from four basic types. We consider how each of these builds on our understanding of the core and the appropriate methods for coordination. But we should also remember to pay attention to the two strategic imperatives of value creation and opportunity recognition within organizations.

The four basic structures we will discuss below are 1) Simple; 2) Functional; 3) Divisional or Multidivisional; and 4) Matrix.[8] We will also spend a few minutes on newly-emerging structure types that are designed to respond more flexibly to dynamic markets and the need to innovate.

Simple Structure

The simple structure appears just as its name implies. In a simple structure all areas of the company report to a single person. It usually develops organically as an organization has grown larger, with many of its "legs" being created originally as individuals or small groups. Each group has now become larger, and the company has reached the stage where it requires more formal coordination. The pure form of the simple structure is referred to as a flat organization structure such as the one in Figure 13.6.

A simple organizational structure provides most of its value in rapid response, but leans heavily on the capability of the singular head of the organization. The company's business is not really organized by functions, by products, or by geography; as Figure 13.6 illustrates, multiple individuals from the same functional area report to the leader. There is little to filter information, while coordination is clear and straightforward. It usually depends on good person-to-person managerial abilities. While this structure requires the leader to be

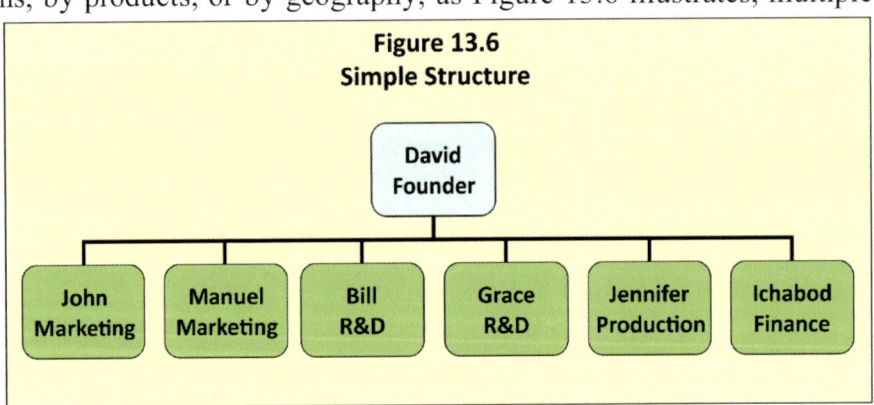

knowledgeable about a variety of functions, the structure is nonetheless easily understood. Since the "distance" is short between operating managers and the location of decision making at the leadership level, this structure allows for rapid opportunity recognition and quick changes to adapt to the market conditions.

On the other hand, the company is limited by the capability of the person in charge as well as by the resource constraints of having to manage an increasing number of people and issues. Increasing complexity makes it more difficult to maximize each employee's contribution, since the time the manager can spend with each employee is reduced. When a manager has six managers reporting to him or her, there are twenty-one different person-to-person relationships that exist within the group, and well over 100,000 possible paths through which information could be communicated between and among group members!

A simple structure is usually best under one of four situations: 1) single product (or function) organization; 2) a new organization; 3) one trying to maintain an entrepreneurial orientation; and 4) an organization in crisis.

The first situation where a simple structure works very effectively is a company that is a single product (or function) organization dealing in a relatively dynamic environment where reaction time is at a premium. The ability to make a quick decision to please a customer or react to changing conditions is a hallmark of the simple structure. Value is created in these organizations by having almost instant access to a decision maker. A simple structure allows the company to maximize this responsiveness. A small game development company is a great example. With a small team reporting to a single company owner, this structure enables them to mutually adjust and respond quickly to new trends emerging among gamers, to new mobile platform capabilities and competitor moves.

A second situation is a new organization. New organizations start with one person or a small number of people and as new people are hired they report directly to the founders. There is no need to complicate the communication system with a structure that negatively impacts the ability of the founders to make quick decisions.

In the third case a firm is trying to maintain an entrepreneurial orientation tied to the founder or leader of the organization. By flattening the organization, the company is able to rely on the entrepreneurial approach of the founder and his or her unique skills/insights. There are some individuals who possess an amazing capability in this regard, and a simple structure allows this person to use these talents to direct the actions of the organization.

A final situation is when confronting a crisis. At various times in the life of an organization a crisis may develop that demands swift attention and the focused efforts of everyone in the company. Just such a condition has been faced by companies like BP (Gulf oil spill), Tylenol (the tampering and poisoning of their products), Coors (an investigation by CBS News' *60 Minutes* reporters), and others. A crisis is best handled with a swift response, with few or no layers of hierarchy. The structure confers the ability to quickly respond to the slightest change, and to ensure that clear, consistent communications come from one central point in the organization.

Tying this back to the earlier discussion in this chapter, in a simple structure there is likely to be little difference between the core and the techno-structure. It is the nature of such small organizations that "all hands are on deck" and thoroughly involved. Typically, these organizations employ mutual adjustment for this reason.

Functional Structure

As organizations grow particular functions become either quite large, quite important to the mission of the organization, and perhaps operated some are operated at remote locations. One means for bringing a measure of control to this situation is to form the organization into functions. The functional structure usually divides the company based upon its departments or functional areas of expertise such as procurement, accounting/finance, marketing, production, and IT. Often a functional structure will include groupings similar to those areas in the basic value chain diagram (Chapter 5). This can be advantageous when applying various coordination methods, since a functional group can often have its work coordinated with straightforward methods. For example, managing the legal department with standardization of work skills is relatively easy. The company can require every employee to have a law degree and to have passed the bar exam in that state. As staff, the non-lawyers in the department can be coordinated by standardization of work outputs or processes. An R&D department can be coordinated using mutual adjustment for the scientists doing research, and standardization of work processes for the technicians in the testing center. Functional structures are effective organizational forms under one of the following three situations:

1) growing business activity or volume; 2) public or governmental organization; 3) large, mass-production organization.

Businesses tend to grow because they have developed a unique and inimitable method for creating value. Often this method will rely upon sets of specialized functional activities, as well as coordination across functions. At some point the company realizes that they need to have a structure that supports the type of specialization that will lead to an improving strategic position, and management also realizes the need to exert greater control over related processes and procedures that are evolving. As it grows, a company also tends to add employees simply because of the higher volume of transactions and activity. The growth in size and the need to better manage specialization often companies to adopt a functional structure.

High-speed internet service provider EarthLink is a marvelous example of just this process of growth and organization. Started up by Sky Dayton in 1994, EarthLink experienced phenomenal growth in the mid-1990s after Netscape's Internet browser software was introduced and consumers became aware that this thing called the internet existed "out there" somewhere. Dayton started off with a simple structure in his company – just himself and three other managers working together. However, as subscriptions to the service skyrocketed, he learned he needed to move from the chaos of the growing business to greater control using a functional structure including customer service, marketing, engineering, and finance.

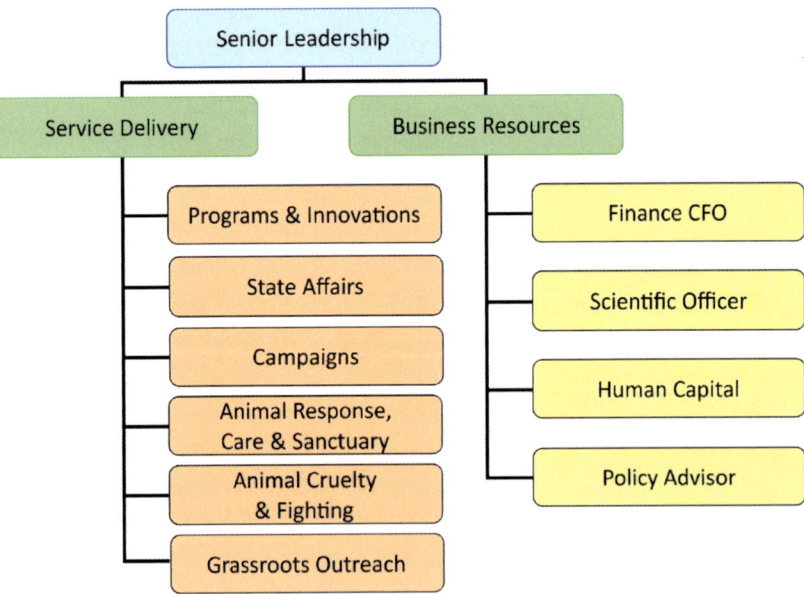

Figure 13.7
Functional Structure of the Humane Society of the United States

The Humane Society of the U.S. is the nationwide not-for-profit affiliated with local humane society offices throughout the country.[9] This quality organization provides resources for local offices. But it also runs its own nationwide programs beyond the scope of local offices, and develops scientific and policy initiatives for lobbying and fundraising efforts. Its functional structure appears in Figure 13.7. In this case the structure is split between two types of functions: traditional business functions like finance and HR, and the program functions it runs itself. Notice that the right side of the chart under Business Resources consists of the support value chain functions (Finance, HR, and R&D). The left side of the chart under Service Delivery consists of the primary value chain functions for this organization's activities that are evident in communities. This organization structure creates focus on the strategic direction of the organization. The structure formally elevates services as constituting the core, ensuring that greater attention is placed on each of these as well as the flow of important information and resources to support them.

A second situation in which a functional organization is particularly effective is in a government agency service operation. Since policy from legislators or senior officials guides how people act, such agencies need not be concerned as much with customer responsiveness. Control and rules-based decision making is paramount, more important than efficiency. These organizations tend to be molded along lines of specialization. Here people are adept at what they do because they their work is singularly focused in just one area. The negative to the functional structure becomes increasingly clear in this scenario, that of communication. Communication between functions, such as that necessary when conflicts need to be resolved, then may require many meetings or ad hoc groups specifically designed to achieve coordination between the different groups.

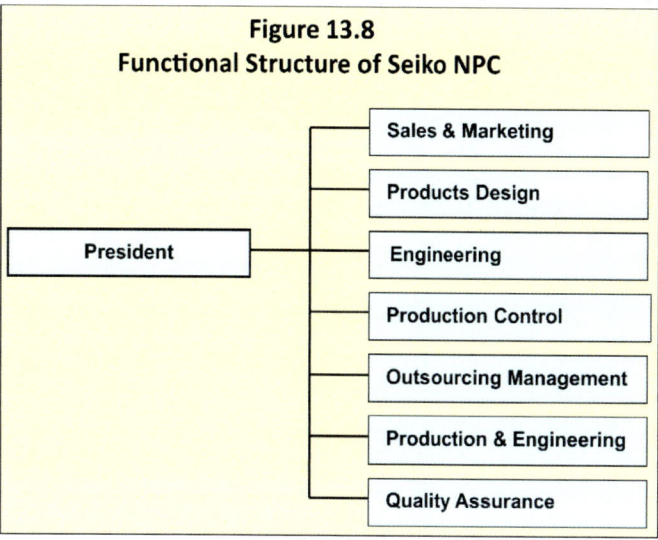

Functional structure also makes sense is in a large scale production organization. Developed for efficiency in manufacturing, these organizations tend to form functional specialties in order to tightly manage available skills and resources. Whenever production companies reach maturity, the functional organization makes it easier to focus efforts on efficiency and cost reduction. As long as the company is in a single line of business or a dominant business, then the functional structure provides it a better opportunity to wring efficiencies out of the system, while simultaneously endowing the organization with a level of sophistication in the development of its functional area expertise. A classic type of functional organization chart is that of the integrated circuit developer Seiko NPC Corporation (Figure 13.8).[10] Each segment is comprised of functional specialists who report to a department head. Each of these department heads reports directly to the president.

Divisional Structure (Multidivisional)

The divisional structure, also known as the multidivisional structure or "M-form," is traditionally used as companies develop and/or acquire completely separate lines of business. That is, as the company diversifies it establishes different operating divisions within the overall company. While it is common for many organizations to initially accommodate diversification through an existing functional structure, as diversification continues and greater complexity arises, most corporations move to some form of a multidivisional structure.[11]

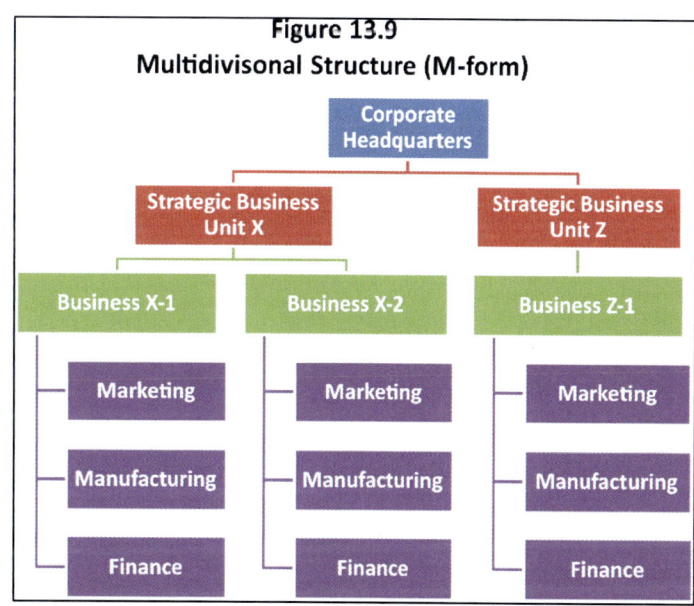

M-Form corporations can be structured in a variety of ways. Figure 13.9 shows one that is organized by SBU lines of business. Quite unlike the functional structure, each operating division is a fully functioning entity in which every area of its value chain is contained within. In turn, the divisions then set up their individual operations using a functional structure. In most diversified corporations there are also sets of staff functions at the headquarters level. Those are usually responsible for setting overarching company policies and initiatives, for performing financial and accounting analysis for the divisions, and for managing the flow of resources and information between the divisions. The headquarters office of the corporation usually exercises control over divisions using financial performance output measures, and comparing each division to the others for resource allocation purposes. Under this structure the headquarters operation continues to exercise considerable strategic input to decisions at the divisional or SBU level.

Divisional structure is also helpful when a company pursues a multi-domestic international strategy. Here value is created upstream in manufacturing and supply networks (Chapter 11), yet the divisional structure is organized geographically by region so that sales and marketing can be handled locally. Here the regional division offices are clearly important, yet the primary strategic value creation occurs through arrangement and activities orchestrated through the corporate office.

In the M-form organization value creation occurs in part because of the structure itself. The individual divisions need capital in order to pursue their markets. This capital is more easily and more cheaply obtained internally through corporate headquarters than through external financial markets. Furthermore, as an individual profit center each division is focused on the returns for that division and is in a better position to seek out new opportunities and pursue them with vigor. Communication between the divisions is usually problematic, since they will usually pay little attention to other parts of the corporation. An attempted solution to this problem is the creation of strategic business units (SBUs) that combine groups of related divisions or companies under a single office. If interactions between divisions is crucial for success and yet the organization wishes to have each division be nimble within its own market, then an SBU structure improves that coordination with another layer of management. Figure 13.9 illustrates this concept with Strategic Business Unit X. in which exist two separate but related businesses.

Other versions of the M-form are possible. Divisions of Boeing are organized by a combination of product line and customer segment (Figure 13.10). Other companies organize by geographic region. Coca-Cola is largely organized by geographic regions (Africa, Eurasia, European Union, Latin America, North America, Pacific), and within each region are complete capabilities for production of soft drinks, marketing, and sales that can respond adeptly to the region's unique culture and conditions.

**Figure 13.10
Boeing M-Form Divisions**

Customer
    Commercial Aircraft
    Integrated Defense Systems
    Phantom Works (aerospace)

Product Line
    Boeing Capital (financial services)
    Shared Services (design services)

Hitachi is a classic multidivisional organization displaying a mix of functional divisions, geographic offices and SBUs.[12] Developed to effectively handle a broad array of businesses, this M-form structure (Figure 13.11) has functioned well for this company for many years. We are excited to see that in 2022 one of its Corporate Administration sections is focused on Value Chain Integration! Now that's progressive thinking!

**Figure 13.11
Hitachi Organization Structure**

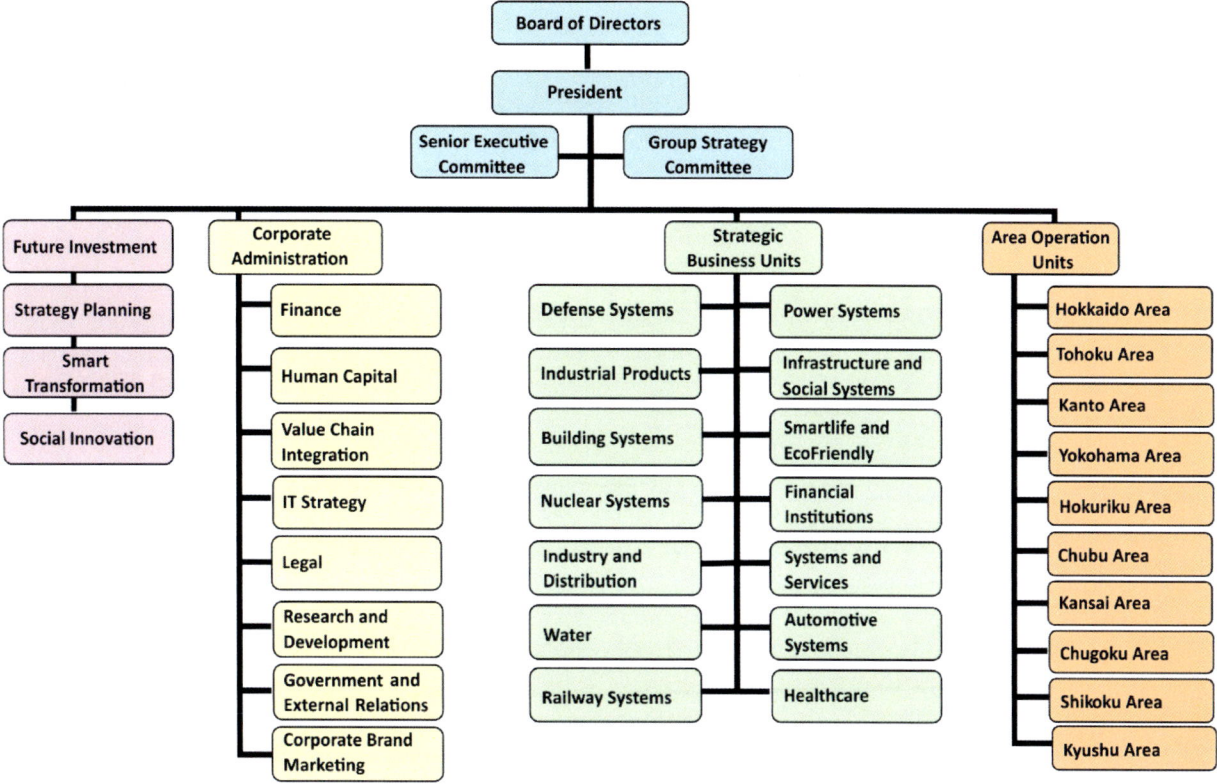

It is important to remind ourselves, however, that "structure follows strategy." So when strategy must change, due to new competitive threats or market-wide changes, then structure may need to change. Structures should evolve with the times. In the case of Hitachi, though quite large and complex, its structure continues to evolve.

Matrix Structure

Dissatisfied with the ineffectiveness of the functional structure for multiple lines of business, but frustrated with decentralization and the dispersion of control in the divisional structure, the matrix structure was developed to attempt to address both efficiency and effectiveness across diverse businesses. This form is no longer quite as fashionable as it once was, and yet there are a number of organizations that continue to use it despite its numerous negatives. The matrix organization has a dual structure where each employee in the organization has both a functional home as well as a divisional home. The functional home is their area of specialization and their divisional home is the business P&L (profit & loss) focus of their work flow.

As organizations grow they tend to add functional specialists to handle the increasing volume, complexity, and information needs of the company. In the normal ebb and flow of business, some lines of business end up with functional groups that are too large for the volume of business in that division, while others have significant needs that can't be quickly met through hiring. Existing employees develop a knowledge base about a company that helps make them effective more quickly than brand new employees hired from the outside. Furthermore, knowledge developed in one scientific area might be usefully applied in another line of business. All of this combines to suggest the matrix organization, in which functional specialists could be more easily reassigned across lines of business where the work was most needed.

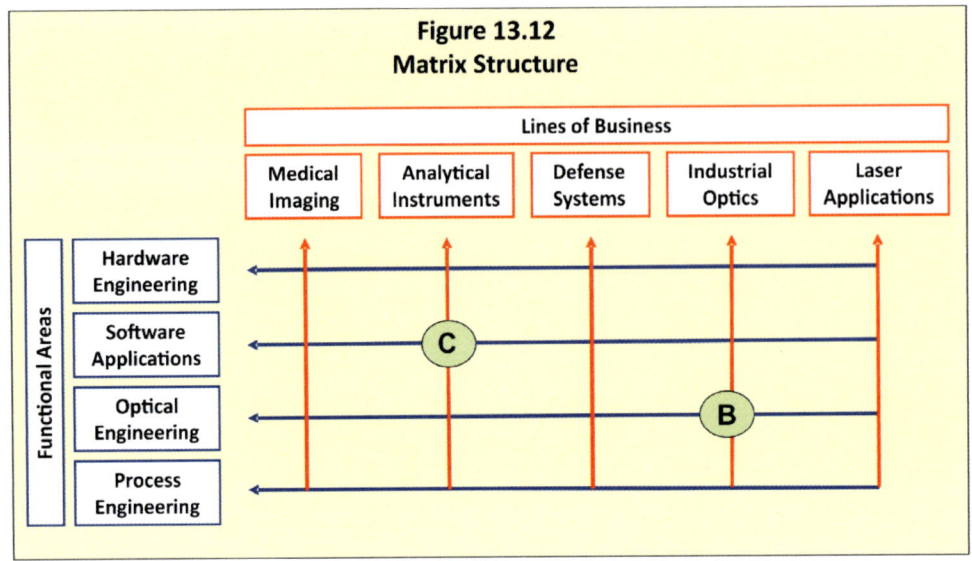

Perkin Elmer was founded in the 1930s based on the interests of its two founders in astronomy and precision optics. Over the years its core optics research led the company into a variety of different lines of businesses, including optical systems for defense applications, lasers, and medical imaging technologies. The company's most famous endeavor was grinding and polishing the primary mirror that is central to the operation of the Hubble telescope. In the 1970s the new leadership of the company implemented a matrix structure, such as that illustrated in Figure 13.12, in order to better manage the portfolio of scientific applications across multiple lines of science-based businesses. In this organization employee B had a reporting relationship to both the manager of Industrial Optics and the head of Optical Engineering, while employee C was responsible to the Analytical Instruments line of business manager as well as the scientist who oversaw software application development.

In theory, the matrix structure would provide a diversified organization with the best of both the functional and divisional forms. But resource allocations and trying to establish annual budgets between lines of business and functions can become a politicized process, with negotiated solutions developed through ongoing meetings involving heads of divisions, functions, and senior management. More importantly, the reality of the structure is that reporting to two bosses (their functional head and their line of business head) proves problematic for many people. The conflict that inevitably arises in devoting time to the requirements of each boss reduces an individual's effectiveness. The difficulties in planning and budgeting, together with the natural tendency of employees to please a particular boss or to choose between the wishes of competing bosses, have led to a drastic reduction in the number of companies that use this type of organization structure.

In 2019 Boeing announced it was partially adopting a form of a matrix structure in order to address huge problems that had cropped up in the development and introduction of its new 737 Max jet. In that process, which had largely been controlled by the line of business management, important aspects of engineering and systems development had taken a back seat. Systems failed in flight, and two deadly crashes brought these deficiencies to light. CEO Dennis Mullenberg announced that "top engineers throughout Boeing's sprawling commercial and defense units will also report directly to the company's chief engineer rather than the division chiefs."[13]

Emergent Structures

Companies confront facets of markets today that prompt them to rethink traditional structure. These facets include the dynamism and hypercompetitive environment, which puts a premium on flexibility, adaptation, and innovation. In addition, new work trends such as tele-work and new physical infrastructures such as shared work spaces (e.g. WeWork) place more emphasis on structures that can accommodate "cellular" organizations and individuals working remotely.

These circumstances lead to the creation (or recognition) of organizational forms with less formal structure that can take advantage of mutual adjustment as a coordinating mechanism. Two new structural forms have recently emerged: adhocracy, and helix.

In business organizations that can utilize an adhocracy there are no true supervisors and everyone in these groups function with a single goal in mind (Figure 13.13). You may have read about the online shoe retailer Zappos, which started up in 1999 but was acquired in 2009 by Amazon. Amazon pretty much lets it operate as an autonomous subsidiary. Former Zappos CEO Tony Hsieh instituted a "Holacracy" structure in 2015, writing a 41-page "constitution" to explain to employees how it would work. There are no managers, no one has titles, and there are no teams. Employees self-organize into "circles" and collectively decide on roles, responsibilities, and business issues. The basic idea is to let employees in their own self-formed groups make key decisions about how reliability and adaptability should be achieved. Organizations need reliable results which often come from standardization or supervision. But as we also know, organizations must also be adaptable to changes in competitive circumstances and the marketplace. Zappos is a large organization, with 1400 employees, a complicated online retail business model, that integrates its software onto Amazon's cloud platform. There has been much criticism of this non-traditional model, but after 7 years it is still in place.[14]

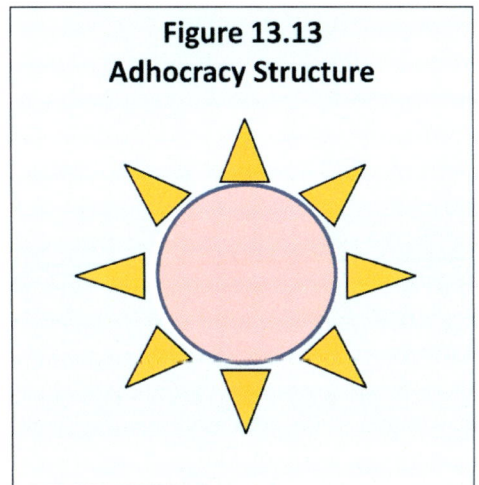

Figure 13.13
Adhocracy Structure

A second emergent form is the helix structure (Figure 13.14). Companies that use this structure are populated by small self-forming teams, occasionally referred to as "micro-enterprises" (MEs). Existing within functions (marketing, sales, R&D, design, operations, etc.), MEs work as they need to on different customer segments, tapping as needed into capabilities and value creation routines that flow across the entire organization and are relevant for those customers. This design is very fluid, encouraging small teams to reach out across the enterprise – or even outside the firm – to

Figure 13.14
Helix Structure

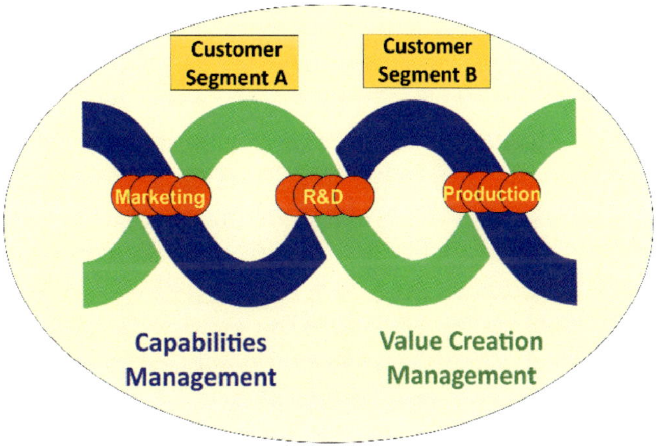

find what they need to work quickly and effectively. Haier, a huge Chinese appliance manufacturer, uses this structure to overcome the bureaucracy that it viewed as interfering with its efforts to innovate and stay relevant. In this system, their 4,000 MEs are all ultimately accountable to the customer.[15] It appears to be working: from 2015 through 2020 its revenue grew at greater than 18% per year.[16]

The adhocracy or helix forms are most effective and yield the best results under the following conditions: 1) when the means to task accomplishment is unknown, but the goal is well understood; 2) when the duration of the task is well defined; or 3) when creativity and flexibility are the most desired outcomes.

Means of task accomplishment is unknown. When the methods and outcomes are well known and repeatable, then a process can be developed and taught. In situations that are new to the organization, however, an adhocracy may provide the best structural solution. In this structure there are no supervisors and every person on the team mutually adjusts off of each other in order to attain the goal. Many small project teams are formed to find a way to accomplish some new need of the organization. For instance, a well-known shirt manufacturing company had to decide whether to accept a new order that would double the number of shirts produced during a year, but did not want to sharply increase its staff because they were uncertain as to whether they would get a reorder the following year. The company put together a small team to devise a means of accommodating the order while maintaining staffing at the current levels and not unduly taxing the current staff. They determined that a bonus system dramatically rewarding those employees who could increase their output and were willing to work extra hours in the short term would be a viable solution. The pay system solution, the communication approach to the employees, its impact on the organization, and the schedule for the implementation plan were put together over a two-day period by a team of six people.

Special effects teams that work on a movie are another classic example. The script may call for visuals that have never been previously filmed, and it is the special effects team's charge to bring those visuals to life for the director. These folks are not effectively managed in the same manner as a programmer; instead they are told what the outcome should look like and given free rein to find a means to create the scene for filming.

Duration of task is well defined. A second situation when an adhocracy structure works well is when the amount of time available prior to a decision is very well defined and usually very short. When groups have a very short time frame to accomplish their task, then an adhocracy structure helps to facilitate the best returns for the company. There is an old saying that the task will expand to the time allotted for its completion. Task success can be greatly enhanced with the use of an adhocracy.

Creativity and flexibility is desired. When the creativity of the solution is the most important outcome need of a group effort, then the use of an adhocracy structure is most likely to yield the best result. Not relying on any one individual to filter the solutions and having everyone understand the need for a speedy solution lends itself to an approach that eschews bureaucracy.

The most critical components of an these structures are to: 1) maintain the equality in the group; 2) ensure that all have a complete understanding of the goal and any relevant time frames; 3) isolate the group from the rest of the company to minimize interference from normal structural effects; and 4) free the group from any formal reporting criteria. All four of these criteria can be easily seen in the making of a large budget movie (providing the director and producer are sufficiently accommodating). The Apollo 13 example from earlier in this chapter is an excellent example of an adhocracy in practice.

The astute student will also recognize the challenges embedded in these more flexible forms. The idea of self-created and self-managed teams sounds wonderful and resonates with all of us who desire both responsibility and authority. But the success of these fluid forms also depends on clear strategic priorities that are set at the corporate level, based on a well-articulated mission, vision, and statement of principles or values. Senior management in the company must also direct and invest in the capabilities that smaller independent teams may draw upon.

CHAPTER SUMMARY

In this chapter we looked at the very sensitive and yet critical process of structuring an organization. "Structure follows strategy." Structure can either help or hinder the implementation of strategy, so strategic managers must carefully think through the type of structure that helps the most.

Three facets of structure include specialization, centralization, and formalization. These may present inherent conflicts in effective strategy implementation, and may be especially troublesome for companies seeking to address the two strategic imperatives of opportunity recognition and value creation. The goal of structure is to ensure that communication, coordination, and control help align the organization with its strategy.

We looked at the three components of any company's organization:
- The Core: the group or groups primarily responsible for the company's sustainable competitive advantage.
- The Techno Structure: those groups that are advice givers and policy makers.
- The Staff Support: those groups that are not core, and not advice givers or policy makers. These groups are responsible for the common aspects of running a company.

Typically the way we think about the components often parallels the layout of a value chain diagram with its primary and support activities designations. But we need to remember that VRIST sources of sustainable advantage often derive from how well the company coordinates and connects activities across the value chain that are performed in different departments.

Once these areas have been identified, then each group of employees needs to be organized by the most appropriate and effective means of coordinating work. The five coordinating methods, which generally exist in every organization, are:
- Mutual Adjustment
- Direct Supervision
- Standardizing Processes
- Standardizing Skills
- Standardizing Outputs

We then examined the different types of structures that organizations can use, and how the coordinating mechanisms aligned with those overarching structures. The four most prevalent types of organizational structure are:
- Simple
- Functional

- Divisional or Multidivisional
- Matrix

Two newly-emergent forms of structure include Adhocracy and Helix. Each values small work teams working autonomously in order to be flexible and innovative.

Learning Objectives Review

1. Explain how strategy is implemented through a company's structure.

- The structure of a company should follow, reflect, and support its strategy.

- Strategies oriented toward cost leadership, consistency and control are more likely to implement structures that call for more direct supervision of employees. Strategies oriented toward differentiation, innovation and flexibility are more likely to implement structures that call for greater mutual adjustment by employees. These represent the ends of a continuum of mechanisms to coordinate work.

- Management should define the key organizational components of the core, techno structure, and staff support. Together with mechanisms to coordinate work, identifying these parts will help influence how groups are formed and the resulting structure.

2. Construct a map of the types, characteristics, and outcomes of the most common means of structuring organizations.

- Simple structure. Provides the advantage of rapid response. Depends on responsive leader at the helm.

- Functional structure. Sound structure for growing or geographically-dispersed organizations, and where a particular function is at the core. Cross-functional coordination becomes an issue.

- Multidivisional structure (M-form). Often used by conglomerates and diversified corporations, and can result in strategic business units of related operating divisions. Needs to evolve as markets and competition evolve.

- Matrix structure. A solution for functional deployment across a multi-line business, without the decentralization associated with M-form structure. Very complicated to manage, and subject to internal politics.

- Adhocracy and Helix. Little formal structure, appropriate for projects requiring creativity, short time frames to complete a project, or where the means to complete the project is unknown at the outset.

3. Analyze and explain the type of mechanisms used to coordinate the activities in an organization.

- Mutual adjustment. Each individual understand strategy and adjusts their behavior accordingly.

- Standardization of work process. A mechanism to manage large numbers of employees based on the extent to which they follow prescribed process guidelines for doing work.

- Standardization of work skills. Relying upon sets of externally developed professional criteria to ensure that appropriate quality work will be performed.
- Standardization of work output. Mechanism that focuses exclusively on the output of work, because the work process cannot be standardized nor are there validated external criteria available to assess employees.
- Direct supervision. Every employee is directly supervised by another individual.

4. *Evaluate whether the structure of an organization aligns effectively with its strategy.*

- The structure should include groups formed to emphasize the strategic core.
- The structure should include groups formed to provide consistency between the business level strategy and the work coordinating mechanism most appropriate for that type of strategy.
- The structure should facilitate the two strategic imperatives of value creation and opportunity recognition.

Key Terms

Adhocracy – A method of organizing usually used within portions of the organization rather than the entire organization. There are no supervisors, and everyone in the group operates organically toward a well-defined goal.

Core – The group or groups that are directly responsible for competitive advantages that the firm enjoys.

Direct supervision – Every person is coordinated via a direct supervisor and coordination flows into and from that supervisor.

Divisional (multidivisional, M-form) structure – A method of organizing a company that divides up the organization into discrete companies (or semiautonomous divisions) within the overall company. These divisions generally contain all the elements of an independent company.

Functional structure – A method of organizing a company that divides up the company based upon their functional areas of expertise.

Helix - Structure populated by autonomous small self-forming teams, which work as they need to on different customer segments, tapping into capabilities and value creation routines as needed that are relevant for those customers.

Matrix structure – A method of organizing a company that utilizes a dual structure such that everybody in the organization has both a functional home as well as a divisional home.

Mutual adjustment – A method of coordination where every individual knows everything that is happening in the organization and adjusts his or her work pattern for the conditions at hand.

Simple structure – A method of organizing a company in which all areas of the company report to a single person. The pure form of the simple structure is referred to as a flat organization.

Staff support – All other groups who are not core and not advice givers/policy makers.

Standardization of work output – A method of managing large numbers of employees based upon a well-developed set of output measures that in combination provides insight into the performance of the employee.

Standardization of work processes – A method of managing large numbers of employees based upon the processes that they perform.

Standardization of work skills – A method of managing large numbers of employees based upon their skill sets as established by some externally validated means.

Techno structure – Those groups who are advice givers and policy makers to the core.

Short Answer Review Questions

1. How does structure affect strategy?
2. What groups are core to a company?
3. List what groups might constitute the techno structure of a bank.
4. Under what conditions would mutual adjustment be the best system to apply to a particular group?
5. Provide several examples where standardization of work processes might work the best in an organization.
6. Why is direct supervision a structure of last resort?
7. Explain how output measures are used to direct employee efforts.
8. What type of coordination method might you suggest for the payroll group of a large insurance company?
9. Under what circumstances would you suggest that an organization consider a divisional or multidivisional structure?
10. How does a functional structure assist an organization that has grown from an entrepreneurial venture?
11. Faced with a crisis in your organization, what structure might you suggest the company employ? Why?
12. What must you keep in mind if you wish to utilize an adhocracy?
13. What would you suggest to a manager who wants to increase the effectiveness of the communication within the company?

Group Exercises

1. Select a Fortune 500 company and, using its website, annual reports, and available public material, attempt to piece together its organizational structure.

    a. What do you think of the design that is in place?

    b. Does the structure align with their mission/vision/strategy?

    c. Pick a particular area within the company that you believe needs a change. What would you change and why?

2. Assume that a company manufacturing consumer products excels in opportunity recognition and value creation, resulting in a continuous flow of successful new products into the marketplace.

    a. Does the Core reside in one function, or is it shared across functions?

    b. What is the optimal structure for this company?

    c. What coordinating mechanisms would be best to use for the Core?

    d. What are the potential issues you see in the three C's – communication, coordination, and control?

3. Grocery stores are quite varied in their approach to the customer. Select two competitor grocery stores in your area.

    a. What are the differences in their competitive approach?

    b. Given your answer in "a," how would you structure each company?

    c. Create a chart with the grocery stores across the top and the following categories down the side—Core, Techno Structure, Staff, primary organizational form as it exists, suggested organizational form. Evaluate each.

Investor Relations Sites for Companies Mentioned in This Chapter

Bennigan's: https://bennigans.com/bennigans-history/
Boeing: https://investors.boeing.com/investors/overview/default.aspx
Dell Technologies: https://investors.delltechnologies.com/
Earthlink (Windstream): https://investor.windstream.com/home/default.aspx
Haier: https://www.haier.com/global/investor-relationship/
Hitachi: https://www.hitachi.com/IR-e/
Humane Society of the United States: https://www.humanesociety.org/
Microsoft: https://www.microsoft.com/en-us/investor
Perkin Elmer: https://www.perkinelmer.com/corporate/investors/
Seiko NPC: https://www.seiko.co.jp/en/ir/
United Airline Holdings: https://ir.united.com/
United Technologies: http://investors.rtx.com/
Zappos (Amazon): https://www.zappos.com/about/

References

[1] Greene, J., 2018, "Microsoft downgrades Windows' role in cloud-focused reorganization," Wall Street Journal, March 29, B1. Nadella, S., 2018, "Embracing our future," Microsoft News Center, March 29. 2017 Microsoft 10K.

[2] Chandler, A. D. 1962. *Strategy and Structure*. Cambridge, MA: MIT Press.

[3] Smith, A. 1776. *An inquiry into the nature and causes of the wealth of nations*.

[4] Adapted from Mintzberg, H. 1979. *The structuring of organizations*. Englewood, NJ: Prentice Hall.

[5] Ibid.

[6] Roth, George L. 2013. "An uncommonly cohesive conglomerate." Strategy+Business, 72.

[7] Carey, S., 2017, "Behind United Airlines' fateful decision to call police," Wall Street Journal, April 17, A1. Munoz, O., 2017, "Actions speak louder than words," Wall Street Journal, April 27, A18.

[8] Mintzberg, H., op. cit.

[9] www.cheltborohomes.org/.

[10] www.npc.co.jp/en/general/chart.html.

[11] Chandler, A. D. 1962. *Strategy and structure*. Cambridge, MA: MIT Press.

[12] www.hitachi.com/about/corporate/organization/index.html.

[13] Tangel, A., 2019, "Boeing CEO will take reins on safety," Wall Street Journal, September 26, B3.

[14] Groth, A., 2016, "Zappos is struggling with holacracy because humans aren't designed to operate like software," Quartz, December 21, https://qz.com/849980/zappos-is-struggling-with-holacracy-because-humans-arent-designed-to-operate-like-software/. Kinni, T., 2015, "The audacity of holacracy," Strategy+Business, August 19. Reingold, J., 2016, "The Zappos experiment," Fortune, March 15.Silverman, R. E., 2015, "Going bossless backfires at Zappos," Wall Street Journal, May 21, A1.

[15] De Smet A., Kleinman S., and Weerda K., 2019, "The helix organization," McKinsey Quarterly, October, 1-10. Hamel G. and Zanini M., 2018, "The end of bureaucracy," Harvard Business Review, November-December, 51-59.

[16] De Smet, A., C. Hewes, M. Luo, J.R. Maxwell and P. Simon, 2022, "If we're all so busy, why isn't anything getting done?" McKinsey, January, https://www.mckinsey.com/.

Chapter 14: Implementation, Internal Control, and Strategic Leadership

LEARNING OBJECTIVES

1. Translate strategy into functional area goals and activities using the keys to implementation control.

2. Develop effective metrics for the control and growth of the organization.

3. Describe the differences between the models used for implementing a strategic plan.

4. List and describe the core responsibilities of strategic leadership.

McDonald's[1]

McDonald's was a one-store business in San Bernardino, California, run by brothers Dick and Mac McDonald. In 1954 Ray Kroc convinced them to let him open several more restaurants based on their process-based business formula. The astounding success of the company is a testament to tenacity and a striving for perfection.

During the subsequent sixty-eight years, McDonald's has grown into a worldwide organization employing over 200,000 in its corporate-owned operations and another 2 million at franchisees in over 39,000 restaurants in 119 countries. The company was the first fast food chain to have a drive-thru window (1975), offer breakfast (1977), and create whole product categories such as the Happy Meal (1979) and the Chicken McNugget (1983).

The elimination of a corporate program for the evaluation of domestic stores, a focus on international expansion and a loss of focus on the nuts and bolts of its core business set off a terrible decline in performance in the mid to late 1990s. This was accelerated by rapid growth in the number and type of competitors, dramatic improvements in competitors' processes, a set of international crises, the parallel onset of interest in healthy eating, and the release of the film *Super Size Me* (2004) that took direct aim at McDonald's as the purveyor of an unhealthy lifestyle.

In January 2003, McDonald's reported their first-ever quarterly loss of –$343 million. Same-store sales (a critical metric for retail store health), stagnant for the past ten years, fell for fourteen straight months through the first quarter of 2003. The company's ranking amongst consumers was last among seventy fast food chains that same year. McDonald's was in trouble.

Jim Cantalupo (newly re-minted as CEO in 2003) came out of retirement to fix the company, after having been with it in various capacities over a twenty-eight year span. He developed an approach that was back to basics.

He focused on the McDonald's brand by systematically divesting businesses and reducing the importance of other brands the company had acquired during the years. These included: Chipotle, Boston Market, Fazoli's, Donato Pizzeria, and Pret a Manger. He cancelled big IT initiatives started by his predecessor and virtually halted the new store building program.

His next step was to determine what the key value drivers were for the company (elements that provide a foundation for success). The company looked back to ideas originating with founder Ray Kroc: "The basis of McDonald's success is serving low-priced value oriented product fast and efficiently in clean and pleasant surroundings." Cantalupo said "Those are the greens fees; unless you execute (those basics) you go nowhere." So McDonald's had its marching orders. The only question left was would they be able to execute this approach? Many analysts were skeptical and openly predicted his ouster in the next eighteen months.

QUESTIONS

1. In your experience what are the "key value drivers" for McDonald's?
2. What would you do to implement these back to basics facets?
3. How would you suggest they measure progress in an implementation plan?

KEYS TO IMPLEMENTATION

Having worked through the process of strategy design and development, it is then time to execute all that has been decided and planned. Far too much time, money, effort, and goodwill is devoted to the formulation of an effective strategy for its implementation to be ignored. In fact, recent research suggests that 90% of companies fail to execute strategy successfully.[2] Planning is one thing, but implementing the strategy brings it home. This can best be done by approaching the issue as a process that: provides direction for activities throughout the organization, provides monitoring and control, enables feedback and corrective actions, and ensures that the performance of the organization is tied to the mission.

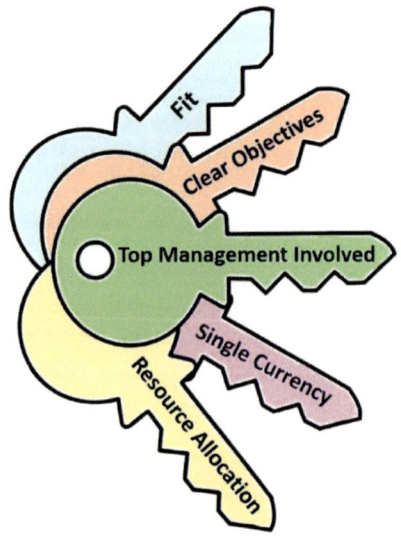

There are a number of methods that exist for coordinating the implementation of strategy. However, coordinating, monitoring and control begin with metrics. In this chapter we will examine the development of metrics that are helpful in gauging strategy progress, and then discuss three of the most popular implementation approaches: 1) the balanced scorecard, 2) the value-driver-action model, and 3) the 7-S framework.

Prior to that discussion it is important to highlight five overall keys to successful implementation. You should keep these in mind as you read on, and they should be the criteria by which implementation efforts are considered.

Key #1 – Top-Management Involvement

Implementation has been regarded by some as the messy part of business that is "operational" not "strategic," and therefore beneath the role of senior management. Nothing could be further from the truth. A well-designed strategy that is not effectively executed is useless. In fact, a recent study found that strategies deliver only 63% of expected financial performance because of inconsistent or nonexistent senior management involvement.[3] One of the most important functions of the executive is seeing that strategy is executed well. Larry Bossidy (retired CEO of Honeywell) and management advisor Ram Charan stated that execution is: ".... a central part of a company's strategy and its goals and the major job of any leader in business...."[4] There is no more important concept to keep in mind than how essential it is for leaders to be integrally involved in the implementation and execution of strategy.

Key #2 – Fit

OK, well there is another equally important concept to keep in mind, that of fit. The complete alignment of the company's strategy, structure, resources and value chain is crucial to success. Imagine a Google where every employee was required to be in his or her cubicle by 8 A.M. and the dress code was a business suit. Or you walk into a bank branch where there is trash on the floor and the tellers don't seem to have a handle on how to do simple math to give you the correct change. Have you recently called the 800-number for a company that distinguished itself in the marketplace through its customer service – only to find that you are kept on hold for eight minutes waiting for an agent who ultimately does not have the authority to correct an error the company originally made? How might a company such as Apple perform if it was led by a rigid, bureaucratic leader whose entire goal was organizational efficiency? These simple examples point out the most elementary aspects of the need for fit in everything a company does, from end to end. Companies are difficult to align and there are both formal and informal aspects that need to be dealt with in order to attain fit. The implementation process must ensure that the fit designed into the value chain and strategy is, in fact, happening during the execution phase.

Key #3 – Clear and Compelling Objectives

Implementation is a process that depends on everyone in the organization moving in the same direction. This is far easier to do if the objectives are not only clear to all the employees of the company, but also if every employee feels that he or she has the ability to truly contribute to that achievement. Far too often companies have a very general objective to grow sales or to increase profitability. These are both uninspiring and pretty remote to most employees down the line. People who not only understand a compelling set of objectives, but also see how they can contribute to success and make a difference themselves, will pour out their energy and ability. Therefore we should break down every high-level objective into definable goals and metrics that are relevant and important to employees.

Key #4 – A Single Currency

One of the quickest ways to dismantle an effective plan is to provide different employees with different types of performance incentives. Doing so can result in internal conflicts and inconsistent actions. Most reward systems are based upon some financial metric that is a proxy for strong performance, but companies often use different kinds of rewards for different groups of employees – such as bonuses, merit pay increases, stock options, stock grants, extra days off, and more. We call these rewards and incentives "currency" because they are "paid" to stellar employees. Virtually every type of currency has been tried. However, one factor that helps ensure effective strategy implementation is for companies to reward as many people as possible using the very same incentive. This keeps everyone focused on the same idea. Jack Welch talked endlessly about his success at General Electric as he shifted more and more people over to a system where they were rewarded with GE stock. Individual and departmental bonuses still existed, but they became a smaller part of the overall compensation package.[5] The financial rewards were primarily tied to the success of the parent company stock, and it was this single system that helped focus employees in a widely diversified conglomerate on the overarching corporate financial performance goal.

Key #5 – Resource Allocation

Strategy implementation is about action and the commitment of resources. A strategic plan that does not include a commitment of resources is doomed from the start. The concept of resources is broad and includes people, finances, plant and equipment, knowledge, time, and support, among others. One of the best ways to see if a company is truly committed to its stated strategic plans is to look at its resource allocations. A mismatch suggests either inconsistent follow-through in the management of the strategy, or alternative and competing priorities that are not aligned with the stated direction. Both situations are a recipe for disaster.

Keep these five keys in mind as you read through this chapter. These principles should help in organizing what is inherently a challenging part of strategic management.

Turning strategy into a workable program is a process of continuous improvement and of iteration. Refer back to Figure 1.6 in the very first chapter in which we discussed the "feedback" arrows. These suggest that what managers observe and learn about implementation efforts through structuring and internal control provides guidance for how to go back and modify the strategic approach. Separating Strategy Formulation from Strategy Implementation and Evaluation in this figure is something of an artifact arising from how strategy concepts have historically been taught using a linear and sequential approach. In practice, though, they are combined and continuous, constituting what many refer to as the "learning organization."

CONTROL LEADS TO PERFORMANCE

A company's strategy is usually quite complex, involving many ideas and moving parts all across the organization. This is why we have made the case throughout this book that the combination of vision, mission, value, and value chain integration are essential to bringing coherence to the effort on a day-to-day basis. But the added complexity is that most strategic initiatives involve the commitment of resources and practice over long periods of time, and will only begin to bear fruit at some point in the future. We talked about this in the very first chapter when we described "the nature of strategic decisions."

So strategy implementation presents a real conundrum: we must act here and now in the present, but we may not see desired results and outcomes for some period of time yet. There are a couple significant issues that this conundrum presents to senior management. First, because it requires this significant commitment of resources over time, an overall strategy or a particular strategic initiative can be seen as uncertain and risky. Big ideas in the executive suite are inert unless and until they begin to bear fruit. So both senior managers and members of the board of directors are likely to want to "prove it" that the plan will ultimately achieve targeted goals. On the surface, this is difficult to do. Just saying "Trust me" is not a viable solution.

Second, and this is especially true for public companies, there is usually heightened attention paid to short term financial performance. Public companies often provide "guidance" to financial markets regarding expected quarterly and annual revenue and earnings. Failure to "make the numbers" can result in unpleasant market reactions. So where longer term strategic investments do not have a clear short term financial benefit, senior management comes under increased pressure to explain what the heck is going on.

"The debate is a key concern for chief executives trying to justify many capital investments that can take years to pay off. Long range strategies can be hard to pull off in an era when Wall Street is fixated on three-month reporting periods...Bahram Akradi, founder of Life Time Fitness, [said] 'we were operating quarter by quarter as a public company...but the public market zeroed in on little things that weren't relevant.' "[6]

These realities have led to increasing attention on the use of control systems regarding strategy and strategic initiatives. Strategic control systems or methods seek to connect short term actions to long term financial results. They "tell a story" of strategy in a logical, cause-effect fashion. As we have long argued in this book such systems basically present the story that summary financial performance is a result of activities and practices within the organization: "If we do this and this and this, then we expect to achieve that result." And so these systems prompt us to identify the key contributing activities in the strategic approach, and to set targets for what we expect each activity or activity set to achieve. This helps organization distill the big strategic ideas down into day-to-day activities, and to use various metrics to track progress from these activities as time goes by. We turn now to a brief discussion of how metrics are critical in this process.

METRICS

Strategy implementation is focused on defining what constitutes success, and how to measure its progress and ultimate achievement. The development of metrics is a key to this process, but at the same time it can be difficult to do. Metrics should be tied to the overall goals of the organization and then translated by management down to all of the departmental, functional and individual levels within the company. All of the work effort should be tied in to a system of corporate metrics. So the development of metrics can also help identify work effort that is not directly related to the goals of the organization. These can then be minimized, outsourced, or eliminated.

Every company should have a unique mission and means of competing. The metrics developed for the company should be tied to that mission. ROE is a good general outcome measure of performance, but says little about *how* a company is achieving its individual mission internally. The mission articulates how the company competes today and provides guidance for the day-to-day value creation activities of employees (Chapter 3). When a system of metrics is developed to monitor progress on strategy implementation, then, it should resonate with what the mission states.

Of course one of the key challenges in strategic management is that effectiveness depends upon the execution of the wide variety of activities that fulfill the mission and constitute the essential value chain. So the development of metrics must account for a balance of simultaneous and coordinated activities across multiple departments. A company that merely focuses its metrics on high-level, highly-visible outcomes is apt to distort the actions of some of its employees. A "whatever yields financial returns must be good" approach can lead to ethical lapses and debilitating scandals like those at Tyco and Enron. A single focus upon market share can produce excesses that lead to unprofitable distortions where sales are maintained by cannibalizing profit, quality, or other critical areas.

In Chapter 2 we pointed out that companies deal with a multitude of stakeholders who have complex and diverse wants. Although shareholders are interested in stock price appreciation and dividend payout, customers may be interested in perceived quality, and communities are interested in corporate citizenship in the local areas. So not everything can be distilled down into a single number. Measures of performance that can resonate with varying stakeholders may be qualitative as well as quantitative. We also want to consider how to extend this performance measurement perspective and apply it *inside* the company as a means of focusing employee effort.

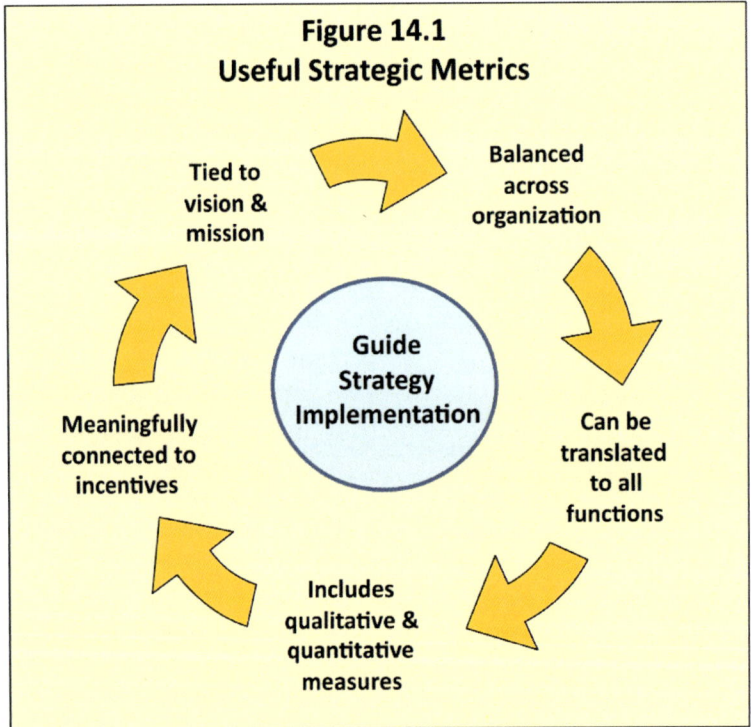

With these ideas in mind, implementation metrics should meet the following criteria (Figure 14.1):

1. Are tied to the overall mission/vision of the organization.
2. Are balanced across the organization so that all areas are covered.
3. Can be translated to all value chain functional activities and levels of employees.
4. Are composed of both quantitative and qualitative measures of performance.
5. Can be meaningfully connected to incentives on individual and group behavior.

Metrics Tied to the Mission/Vision

The most fundamental issue regarding the creation of useful metrics is ensuring that they are tied to the mission and vision of the company. It is relatively easy for a company to get caught up in the development of easily measured, but generally unhelpful measures of activity or performance. The mission statement for the organization should provide the guidance for how the company seeks to create value, and therefore the types of metrics that will show whether or not it is doing so successfully.

Consider the following points in the mission statement for the Coca-Cola Company:[7]

- Refresh the World . . . in body and spirit.
- Make a Difference . . . in people's lives, communities and our planet.

The Coca-Cola Company

This mission statement suggests there is a set of values that the company seeks to create in its business. These include the psychological and physical benefits of consuming its beverage products, the creation of a relationship with stakeholders that transcends mere consumption of food products, and a substantive contribution to communities and populations with which the company engages. If these values indeed reflect the mission of Coca-Cola as a company, then it is incumbent upon senior management to initiate activities that directly support the accomplishment of these values. In turn, management will need to develop metrics enabling them to track how well these activities are making progress toward achieving the value they envision.

The point here is that the metrics a company decides to employ should reflect its mission and the strategic approach it is taking. If the company is pursuing a differentiation approach, then capturing information about efforts to reduce costs can be unproductive in understanding whether progress is being made on the true strategic agenda. Unless "brand image" is a key success factor that must accompany "low cost" in being able to effectively compete in an industry, then precious management time, attention, and resources might be wasted by gathering up data on the effectiveness of a company's advertising campaign or the reputational effect of its product logo. So the kinds of metrics we refer to for implementation are those that guide the internal activities of the business in order to maintain strategic consistency.

Recall that strategic management has to do with making substantive decisions affecting every area of the company, the results of which may not be apparent for a long period of time. Between the time an important strategic decision is made and the time when the results of that decision are clearly apparent in the form of enhanced economic returns, senior management must somehow gain insight as to whether the company is actually making progress. Creating insightful performance metrics allows senior management to assess progress along the way, to enhance initiatives that are working well, and to change those that are not. Thus a set of metrics provides a means for senior management to gauge what is happening and exert strategic control.

Metrics that are Balanced

Effective implementation calls for distilling down overall mission statement goals and activities into a set of metrics that is relevant for every department and every employee. These guide daily activities in their domains, because they can understand how their activities directly relate to the overall organizational value creation objectives. To maximize their usefulness, therefore, metrics must have balance. What is needed is the right metric for the right level of the organization.

Important metrics must be developed for production operations, sales effectiveness, employee training, marketing and advertising, and other activities in the company. This is a key element in implementation as strategy involves coordinated and consistent effort across every area of the value chain. If a differentiation advantage based on "quality" is sought, this might translate not only to lower defect rates in manufacturing operations, but also the use of raw materials from

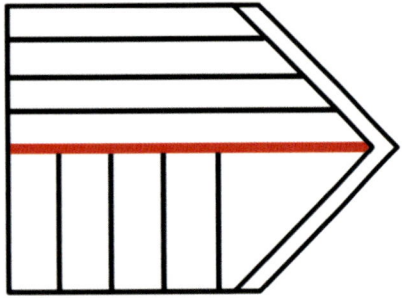

top-notch suppliers, the creation of superior packaging, the development of a unique advertising campaign, and the cultivation of a special customer segment. For a company to truly succeed in its differentiation strategy, we want to know how well the various areas or departments responsible for these efforts are coordinating on and amplifying each other's work in support for this approach. As we discussed in earlier chapters on the value chain and business level strategies, the coordination, consistency of approach within and across an organization, and fit is often at the heart of superior performance. Balanced metrics can clue us in to whether this is occurring or not.

Appropriate for the Functional Level

Distilling down strategic-level value creation goals into activity-level metrics at the functional, group, or individual level is a challenge. It requires management to develop a causal logic about how and why things work the way they do. For example, one manager might believe that quality, defined as minimizing defective products shipped, can be best achieved by ensuring that assembly line workers have undergone training to enhance their production skills and capabilities (standardization of work skills, see Chapter 13). But another manager believes that quality is enhanced when employees are evaluated at their individual stations at a certain piece rate per minute (standardization of work output) in combination with placing personal signatures on products to certify their adherence to quality standards (mutual adjustment). Here are two competing causal logics, so how do we determine which is accurate? We develop measures to evaluate each logic, and go with the one that works best (or some combination). The same kind of causal logic development can be applied to every area of the company that is mission-critical in pursuing a particular strategic approach.

Establishing appropriate metrics for each functional level fosters greater control over strategy outcomes by creating the opportunity for organizational learning. This means we can understand when and where to take corrective actions if something is not working out as planned. This is because the company can more closely monitor progress on the critical activities that are tied directly to the strategy, and can make changes more adeptly if progress is not apparent. In Figure 14.2 a company believes that the cause-effect logic of A holds, where a certain activity taken in one of its departments will lead to an expected outcome that supports the company's strategic approach. Yet what the company actually experiences is B, where that activity results in a less than stellar outcome. By collecting outcome metrics on this important activity-effect relationship, the company learns that its original causal logic is flawed. The

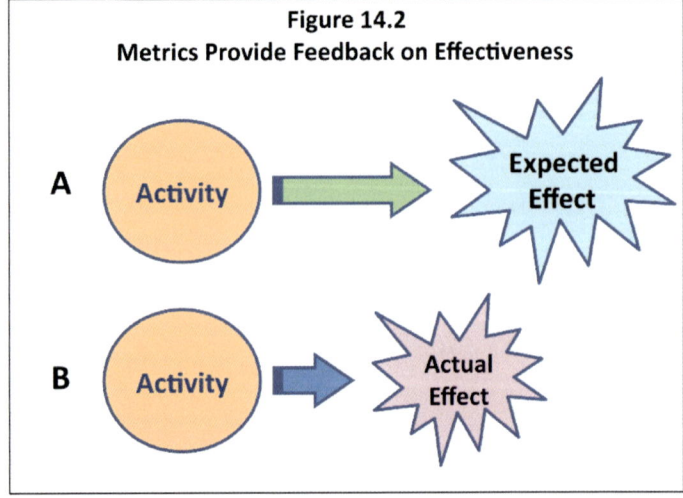

company responds in one of two ways. Either it strengthens the activity in order to achieve the desired outcome, by doing it more intensively or more frequently. Or it decides that the activity actually doesn't work, and it engages in a different activity to achieve the outcome. Either way, the early insight the company gains on this very specific activity increases the likelihood that the company can make necessary changes in order to enhance its strategy. Developing metrics distilled down to individuals and functions is fundamental in the creation of a learning organization.

This is exactly the process that Panera Bread went through a few short years ago. Having become incredibly popular for lunches, they found customers had to stand in line for up to eight minutes just to place an order. CEO Ron Shaich called it a "mosh pit." And because they were so busy, the orders were wrong 10% of the time. So they experimented with new order-taking and kitchen organization procedures, including online ordering. "It was literally hundreds of little things that we did." But they learned what did not work and what did. Lines decreased, orders were more accurate, online sales generated 26% of revenue, and by 2017 Panera's same-store sales growth of 5.3% beat the restaurant industry average of -1.6%.[8]

Metrics that are Quantitative and Qualitative

Companies should develop a list of performance metrics that are a mix of both quantitative metrics and qualitative metrics. As students of business we are most familiar with the quantitative dimensions – collecting and analyzing the hard, objective data. We are prone to relying on numbers because our ability to use sophisticated programs for statistical analysis makes us feel less uncertain about what's going on.

But qualitative measures are just as important as quantitative measures. Qualitative data collection requires that the management team resist the temptation to distill everything down to a number or to discount any "data" that cannot be distilled. Results from surveys, focus groups, call reports from the sales force, input from the customer service lines, trends in complaints or compliments are all ripe for quantification, losing valuable perspective and context that cannot be captured numerically. Qualitative metrics involve reading between the lines of numerical response data that are gathered, asking open-ended questions, and interpreting responses for which there are no clearly defined categories.

For example, although field sales reports may indicate that physicians are seeing pharmaceutical company representatives on a timely basis, they believe that the sales calls are not particularly helpful. Further interviews may reveal that physicians feel they are not receiving as much technical detail on new products as they would like. This suggests better training of the salespeople, the provision of more technically oriented literature, or possibly the creation of a company website strictly for physician use. This should lead the company to consider a measure of performance that is not a quantified number, but a perception from a physician's point of view. After changes are made at the pharmaceutical company, follow-up interviews yield fewer negative, and even positive, comments about the information received in sales calls.

Consumer products companies often use focus group research, engaging small groups of consumers in deep conversations, to better understand how consumers think about and use their products. The results from these explorations provide a much deeper insight into new advertising messages and possible new product extensions. A qualitative evaluation would include the impressions the focus group leaders had while observing the group rather than the number of times that X was said. The "sense" of customers is a key means of guiding a company's actions.

Whether qualitative or quantitative, all performance measures need to account for two aspects: 1) its current state, and 2) its comparability across time and to competitors. The current state establishes where things stand at the present moment, so that we can assess its change going forward. Both absolute increases and relative change calculations can impart valuable insight. If for example, the organization has determined that an important criteria for the success of the company is high quality, then it might measure defect rates. This gives the organization three important issues to deal with. The first is the establishment of the current defect rate. Taking a random sample of products over some period of time, the firm can establish the current average defect rate as well as the range of defects it experiences. Secondly the firm must decide by what denominator it will divide the defect rate, such that it can compare its performance to the industry. Comparing the absolute number of defects produced by a small shop versus those in a multinational business is not of much value unless the measure is somehow equalized or "common-sized." Defects per thousand products produced, defects per employee, defects per number shipped are among those that will provide valuable insight into what's really going on and how it changes over time in response to company actions. Finally, the same method should be used to research, estimate, or calculate comparable rates for each of the direct competitors.

Averages are usually reported with quantitative performance metrics, however they are not nearly as revealing without the range or variance also assessed. Assume that the defect rate is 10 for every thousand products produced. After significant efforts at reducing this rate the company is pleased to announce a 30 percent improvement to 7 per thousand. What those averages don't show is the range of defects, which might better represent what customers experience over time and what will matter to them. If the range per thousand moves from 7 to 50 defects beforehand but now runs from 3 defects to 100 defects, it shows that nominal improvements in the average defect rate have come at the expense of greater volatility (Figure 14.3). This subjects the customer as well as the company's reputation to higher risk. A narrowing of the range without an improvement in the average is arguably better because consistency is the expectation of most customers. The variation in a metric is therefore

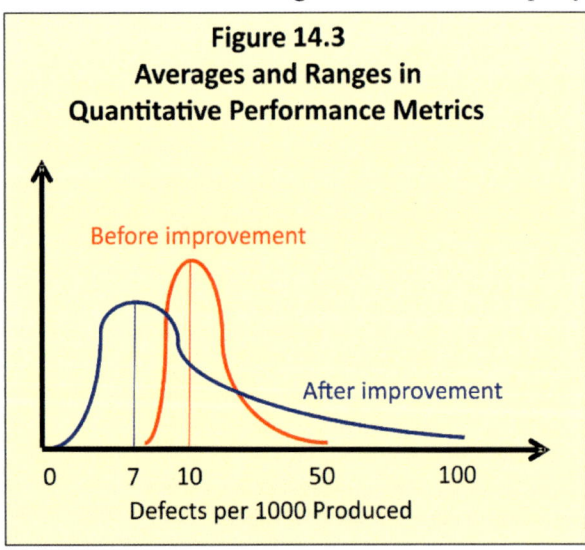

an extraordinarily powerful signal about performance, since it highlights the compelling issue of consistency of effort. Strategy execution is all about coherence and consistency!

Quantitative metrics that reveal progress toward strategic performance need not only be those which measure operations and capture hard, observable activities. Rather than a specific quantified measure of quality such as the defect rate, the business decides that an important measure to keep track of is the customer's perception of quality. Their causal logic is that *perceptions* of quality lead to repeat purchase behavior. Utilizing a survey methodology, the company contacts its customers periodically and asks them to rank the quality of the products it produces as well as those of its competitors. A relatively simple set of questions will allow a company to create a comparative chart of perceived quality. This sort of data can then be collected on a regular schedule, so that progress toward particular quality goals can be assessed. Figure 14.4 illustrates precisely these sorts of measures collected by automobile companies.

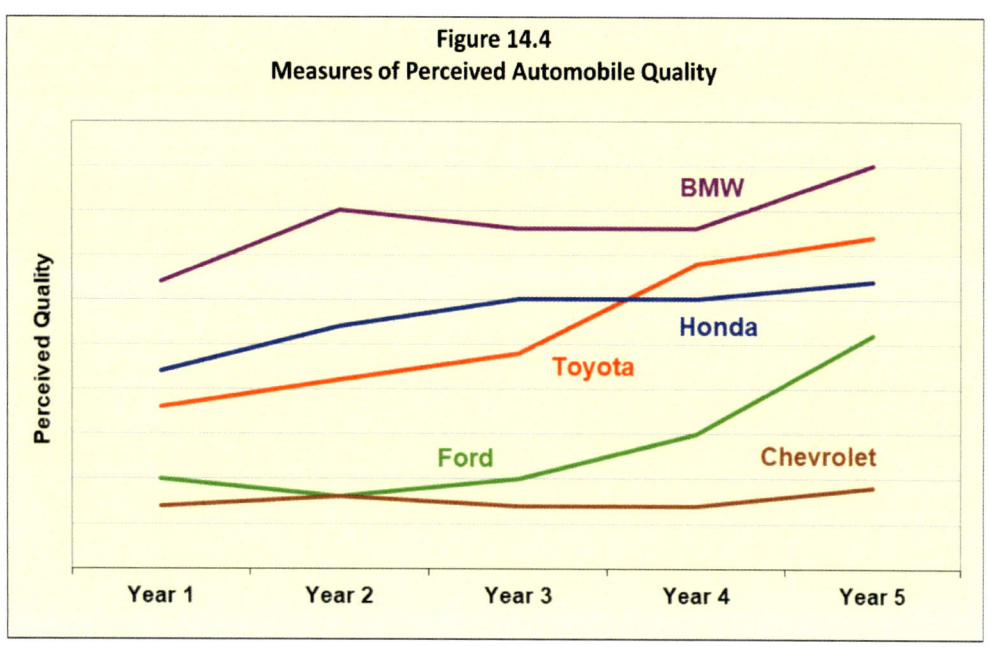

Figure 14.4
Measures of Perceived Automobile Quality

Metrics Connected to Incentives

Implementation is most successful if the organization can connect everyone's pay, bonuses, and incentive rewards to the same overall corporate strategic goal through metrics they are personally responsible for. Sun Tzu advised leaders to distribute the profits of war to everyone involved in order to incentivize their continued efforts. The "currency" of the business should be available to everyone in the company, not just the senior management team.

One of the most traditional means for public companies to forge this connection has been to use stock options (the option to purchase x number of shares of stock at a pre-set price with the hope that the stock will be worth substantially more over time). The theory is that this will focus attention on profitability and ROE (which will drive up stock prices), and thereby encourage employees to execute in ways that will increase the stock price. Even as some companies have increased the participation in stock option programs to include lower levels of management, its connection with what lower level managers actually do and can control is suspect at best. Stock prices rise and fall for a variety of reasons that may or may not have anything to do with individual actions. Furthermore when stock options are underwater (when option shares are priced substantially above the current market price), there is little to motivate performance.

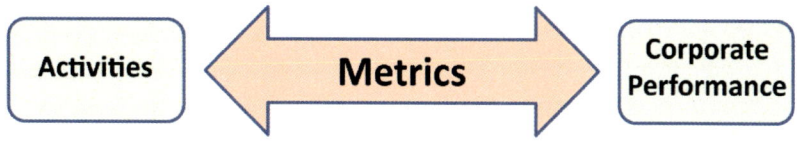

Since the metrics that are developed to monitor and control performance have a clear connection with the company's strategy, they should also have a clear and discernible effect on the company's financial performance. When metrics are developed, therefore, it should be made clear to employees exactly how their own individual efforts contribute to both strategic objectives and financial performance goals. The best performing organizations are those that connect the efforts of employees to these overarching objectives and goals.

Of course one way to accomplish this is to periodically re-communicate the company's vision and mission to all employees, to keep it centrally in mind. But here we are suggesting the need to put the connection into more daily practice, making sure that when employees perform everyday activities that are mission-critical, they can see how their actions help contribute to strategy and the rewards that accrue from executional excellence. If the focus of the company is on quality, then achieving certain stretch quality standards should result in economic rewards for everyone. If corporate success is tied to the simultaneous achievement of two values (as in Coca-Cola), then success in those areas as measured by stretch metrics should enable contributing employees to share in the rewards that result.

Unfortunately, this is not always the case. A 2022 PwC survey of global companies[9] revealed that in many cases the incentives that are used for individual employees do not match up well at all with corporate strategy performance goals (Figure 14.5).

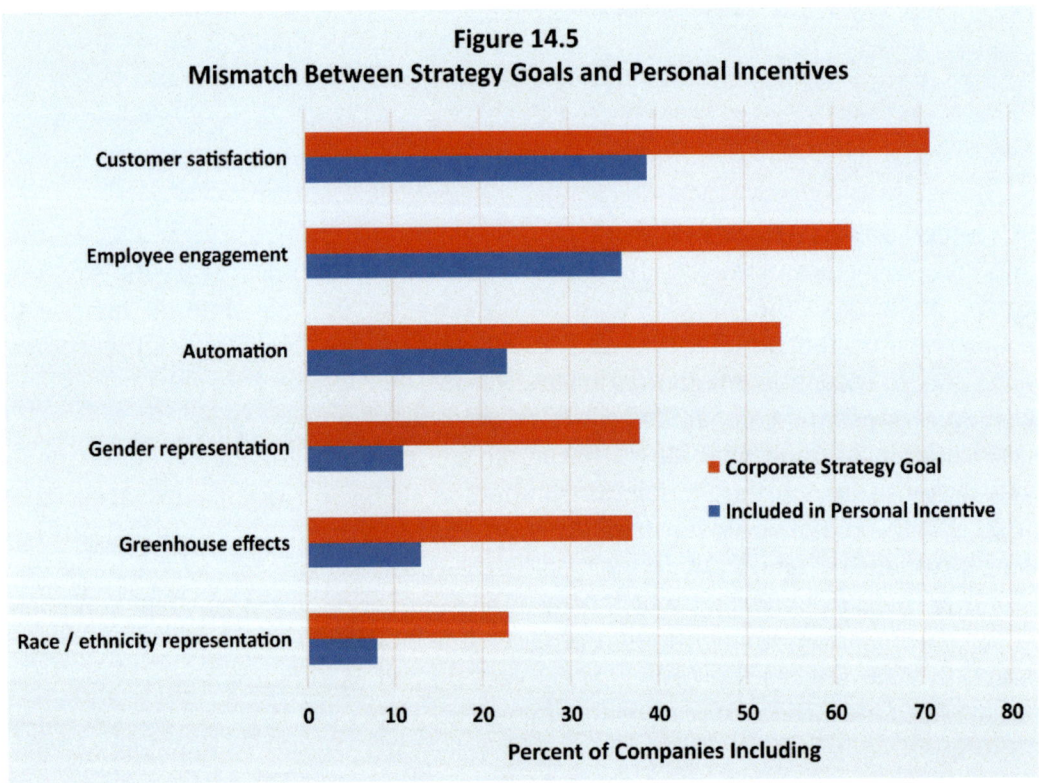

This is not always the case, though. In the 1980s startup herbal tea manufacturer Celestial Seasonings found itself in a pitched battle against Lipton, the world's leading tea company. Celestial Seasonings' mission included making people healthier by drinking non-caffeinated tea, and its stated values embraced "truth, beauty, and goodness." These ideas were regularly shared during frequent "all company meetings." The company's offerings embodied the values with exceptional tasting products in beautiful packaging that included wit, wisdom and snippets of philosophy for its consumers. The founders of the company started an employee stock ownership plan, through which every single employee – including janitors, truckers, warehouse staff, and all others – had an equity stake. Every department's goal was tied in

to the corporate goal of broader awareness of the company's products, and sales volume increases of high quality, healthy products that tasted better than competitors. Every department's activities (marketing, sales, purchasing, production, blending, shipping, etc.) tied in to the corporate goals, and every employee knew clearly how their daily work contributed and made a difference. Small Celestial Seasonings beat Lipton at its own game.

Causal logic, which we discussed earlier, forms the basis for the selection of metrics and is the key to making this practical connection for each and every employee. It is helpful if employees can become involved in developing the causal logic to begin with, although we recognize this is not always possible. But sharing the rationale for the selection of metrics by which employees will be incentivized, and making the connection to mission and strategy well known, helps to complete this process. We will see an example of how this connection is made in the next section, where we discuss the balanced scorecard.

Ford Motor Company[10]

Founded by Henry Ford and eleven business associates in 1903, Ford Motor Company pioneered the moving assembly line where workers remained in place, repetitively performing the same job on every automobile that moved down the line. Henry Ford's vision was to produce automobiles that everyone could afford. Over the next 100-plus years, Ford grew its line of automotive labels to include Ford, Jaguar, Lincoln, Mercury, Mazda, and Volvo.

Despite this proud heritage, by 2005 Ford was struggling with multiple issues. The U.S. auto industry had been challenging for several years. Arch-rival General Motors lost over $10 billion that year. Ford also lost $4 billion in the automobile sector. Its problems included enormous legacy costs (retirement benefits to former employees), high labor costs (fostered by decades of contentious labor relations with unions), a slow response to changes in the environment (gas price increases and changing consumer desires), and slow responses to new competitive challenges from foreign automakers.

In 2006 Chairman Bill Ford announced a new strategic plan dubbed The Way Forward. "Ford Motor Company stands for a far-sighted commitment to growth. We stand for a renewed focus on the customer. We stand for boundless innovation in every aspect of our business – from design, to safety, to fuel-efficiency, to efficiency on the factory floor. We stand for the distinctive look, feel, quality, toughness, boldness and fun of automobiles that are unmistakably Ford. And we stand for the hard-working men and women of Ford Motor Company and their families. Here is what we will not stand for: incremental change, avoiding risks, thinking short-term, blocking innovation, tying our people's hands, defending procedures that don't make sense, and selling what we have instead of what the customer wants. In short, we will not stand for business as usual….Today, I am announcing that Ford Motor Company will no longer publish annual earnings guidance... we cannot succeed in the long run if we're focused only on the short term."

The Way Forward plan called for dropping models, shutting down some assembly plants, reducing factory jobs, and innovating. "Our goal is simple – to build more of the products that people really want and value. Exciting new products that reflect the needs of today's and tomorrow's customers, with striking designs that are safer, more fuel efficient, and offer even greater value. That includes an expanded commitment to small cars, more crossovers, and more capable and fuel efficient trucks." With this, they spelled out exactly where they wanted to go. But these strategic initiatives would take years to pan out. So an important first task would be developing a set of strategic metrics enabling Ford to evaluate progress on the initiatives and to make changes along "the way" if things were not going in the right direction.

QUESTIONS

1. What metrics would you suggest?
2. If you had to keep it to seven or fewer metrics, which would be most important?
3. Focusing on the qualitative side, how might you measure "exciting new products" or "needs for tomorrow's customers"?
4. Why did Ford decide to stop publishing annual earnings guidance?

DEVELOPING AN IMPLEMENTATION PLAN

This next section describes practical approaches for creating an implementation plan. Translating strategy into action is at the core of strategy implementation. We will examine three models used for this process: 1) Balanced Scorecard; 2) Value-Driver-Action Model; and 3) the McKinsey 7-S Framework. Each of these bridges the divide between lofty strategic objectives and the day-to-day activities of employees.

Balanced Scorecard Model

Introduced in the 1990s, the balanced scorecard[11] is perhaps the most widely-discussed practical approach to connecting strategy to action. One of the top ten management tools used worldwide, in 2022 more than 50% of large companies employed this technique.[12] 80% of companies using it report improvements in operating performance.[13] This model allows top management to monitor progress toward overarching organization objectives and to identify those areas that are not meeting expectations. At the same time it affords the opportunity to connect and measure how individual and departmental activities work toward higher level goals.

The central notion of the balanced scorecard is that financial measures of performance are the *result* of a variety of activities that people engage in within the company. This central idea is entirely consistent with the nature of the value chain. That is, strategy has to do with the coherence of activity sets within and across the value chain. Such coherence, married with VRIST-based investments, generates sustainable competitive advantage and superior financial performance. Similarly, the balanced scorecard model focuses on activities and behaviors that generate superior financial results.

There are four important dimensions of the balanced scorecard model. This model:

1) Emphasizes balance, measuring progress across four different levels;
2) Examines how achievements in one level contribute to positive results in another level;
3) Examines the cause-and-effect logic operating within each level using a combination of "lead" and "lag" metrics; and
4) Is driven by strategy coherence overall.

Let's talk about balance first. Imagine you must pilot an airplane from Salt Lake City to Atlanta. The flight time is about three hours. Now imagine that in the cockpit of the plane there is no instrumentation to look at. You have only the throttle, steering columns, and your flaps to use. How would you actually get to Atlanta successfully? To do so you need to track your progress along the way. You need an altimeter (altitude), the pitot static tube (speed), GPS (position), communications (for other traffic and weather), on-board environment gauge (oxygen, humidity), and much more. The simple fact is that the accomplishment of a goal in a complex system requires using  a variety of instruments to assess progress along the way. Same thing with companies: a balance of measures is necessary to know that the company is going in the right direction.

The balanced scorecard model incorporates four different levels of any organization, which are connected in a cause-and-effect fashion:

- Learning & Growth Perspective
- Internal Process Perspective
- Customer Perspective
- Financial Perspective

Success in one perspective leads to success in the next perspective (Figure 14.6). In the Learning & Growth Perspective, management considers the skills and competencies that the company develops in its employees, as well as the facilitating systems, structure, and culture in which employees do their work. This calls attention to hiring practices – who do we hire, what are their qualifications, what are our source networks for prospective employees? What training and development programs does the company put in place to make sure that all employees have the potential to grow both personally and professionally? Are employees properly incentivized in ways that they understand how their actions help contribute to company results? Does management create a structure and communication system that appropriately balances coordinating mechanisms with the strategic approach? Does senior management work to build culture, and regularly renew its commitment to values and principles, espouse vision and mission that bring people together?

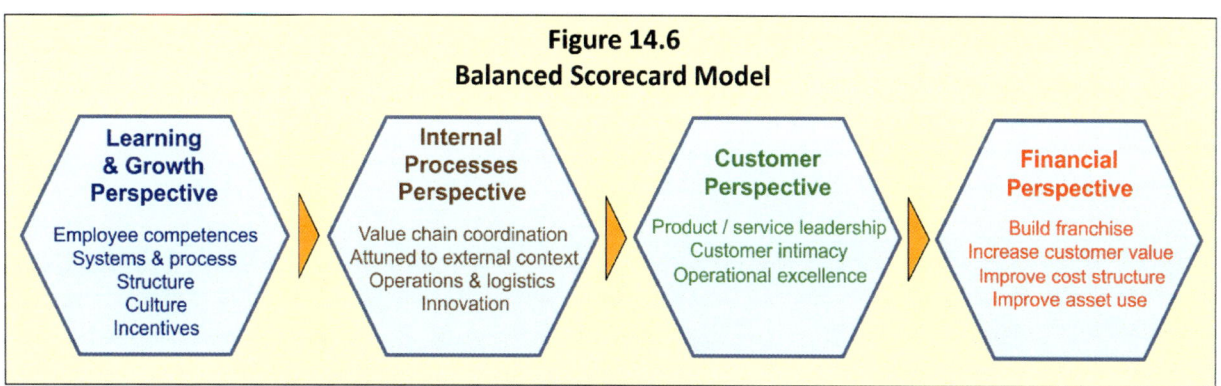

This comprehensive set of activities in the Learning and Growth Perspective lays a strong foundation for success in the Internal Processes Perspective. Here excellence in internal processes regarding innovation, production, and logistics are essential for developing and delivering new and better products or services to customers. But as we have discussed all along, coordination throughout the value chain is essential to pull this off. This means ensuring that internal activities are orchestrated and hopefully have amplifying effects with each other. It also requires stretching out across the industry value chain, in order to forge vibrant relationships both upstream and downstream. Attunement to external stakeholders also allows the company to become aware early on of newly-emerging trends, and to respond with programs and initiatives that are of growing concern to communities and regulatory authorities.

Excellence in the Internal Process Perspective lays the foundation for creating superior value in the Customer Perspective. Here customers are willing to try and repeat purchase the company's offerings when the company delivers attractive attributes such as quality, functionality, prices, and selection on a timely basis. Customer intimacy develops when customers trust the company's brand and view its offerings as best in class. When strong customer values such as these are delivered, in fact customers may come to think of themselves as "smart shoppers" for having chosen the company to do business with.

Finally, the successes achieved in the Customer Perspective should roll up into strong performance in the Financial Perspective. Because of strong performance in lower levels financial performance is enhanced through revenue growth, increased profitability by adding value to customers, improved cost structures, and greater asset productivity. Together, these may combine to increase return on equity and shareholder value.

Figure 14.7
Balanced Scorecard for Pharmaceutical Company

Financial Perspective	Revenue growth from existing customers	Revenue growth from new customers	Improve operating margins	Optimize risk on R&D investment
Customer Perspective	Retain customers	New customers	Partner of choice for meds supply	Build lasting relationships
Internal Process Perspective	Innovative New offerings	Efficiency and quality	Understand customer & markets	Anticipate regulatory concerns
Learning & Growth Perspective	Leverage R&D with technology	Attract & retain top scientists	Performance team culture	Rewarding work environment

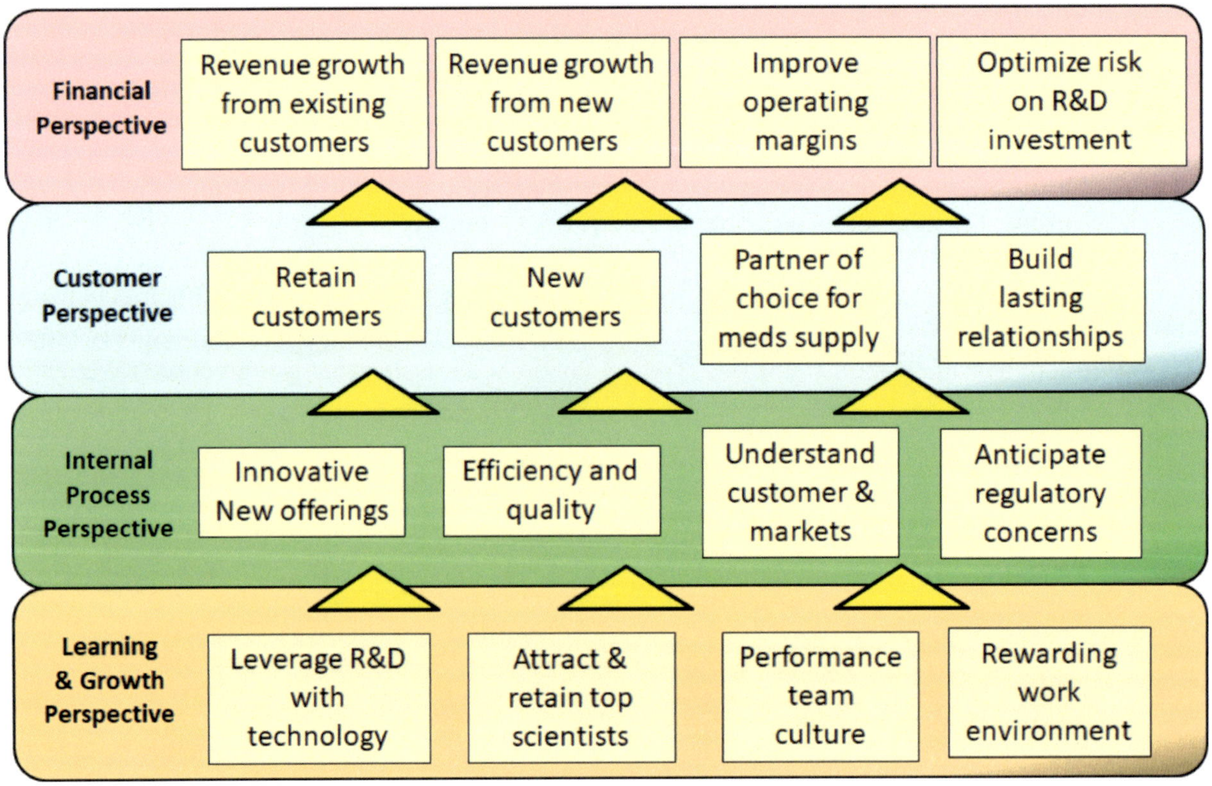

Figure 14.7 provides an example of a balanced scorecard developed for a pharmaceutical company. The company expects to recruit exceptional scientists who work with advanced technology to create new drugs for patient care. Typically you would begin at the bottom with the Learning and Growth Perspective, since employees, competencies, culture and incentives are foundational to organizations. Here the right kind of recruitment and proper development of organization-specific competencies at this level are believed to result in successes at the next level up. The Internal Process is targeted at innovation, lowering costs while maintaining quality, carefully understanding their markets, and working successfully with regulators in the government. These internal practices result in achievements in the Customer Perspective, where the company develops new and loyal customers and is seen by customers as a valued supplier. The consequence

of this strong customer effort in the Financial Perspective is growing revenue, improving margins, and more efficient utilization of capital. This example illustrates the causal logic that runs from bottom to top, connecting initiatives taken in the short run with longer term strategic objectives.

The challenge for management is to create a set of metrics that provides insight on whether the company is making positive progress on each of the key initiatives within the four perspectives. Similar to the cause-effect logic illustrated vertically from bottom to top in Figure 14.7, close attention to each initiative within each level enables management to monitor progress and make changes when necessary.

This brings us to the third pivotal dimension of the balanced scorecard model: the need to develop "lead" and "lag" metrics *within* each level. Figure 14.8 provides examples of lead and lag metrics of this sort in the Customer Perspective. For example, we may have a goal to acquire new customers. But the decision to buy from our company is up to the customer, not us. We act in ways that influence customers, but we cannot actually make their decisions. So we set a goal for customer acquisition, such as x new customers per month or z % increase per quarter. This is called a lag metric, because it follows from the actions we take. But there are actions our company can take that will impact this metric: increasing the visit frequency with buyers, increasing the training of our salespeople, or increasing how often we send out new products literature and information. These actions that we take directly are the lead metrics that we measure.

Figure 14.8
Examples of Lead and Lag Metrics in the Customer Perspective

LEAD: we can directly affect these	**LAG**: we can only indirectly affect these
% orders filled immediately	Customer acquisition
% on-time delivery	Customer retention
Customer survey feedback	Share of customer's total purchases
Number of sales calls per period	Ranking by customers vs. competition
Hours of training per sales person	% of sales from new products
Number of special customer requests filled	% of product line carried

This process boils down overall strategy into sets of related lead and lag metrics for each initiative, within each level of the balanced scorecard. Consequently, it effectively outlines a detailed cause-effect model for how actions create results. Take a look back at Figure 14.2 and our discussion there about the "learning organization." With well-articulated lead and lag metrics, now managers can properly assess whether the company is making progress on each initiative within each level, and also how well success at one level contributes to success at the next level up.

The fourth and last pivotal dimension of the balanced scorecard model is that it is completely driven by strategic coherence. The objectives within each of the four levels should consistently reflect the strategic approach that the company intends to take in the marketplace. The initiatives within each level should follow suit, and each initiative should work to coordinate with and amplify the effects of other initiatives. Then even further down the actions that employees take within each initiative should also be internally consistent with the strategy. This is, in fact, one of the distinct advantages of adopting the balanced scorecard method. In the process of designing and articulating the initiatives and the contributing employee activities (lead metrics), it forces management to evaluate 1) what are the most important activities to engage in, and 2) whether each activity is wholly consistent with the adopted strategic approach.

You might recognize that the balanced scorecard fundamentally reflects an important theme of strategic management that is carried throughout this textbook. Competitive advantage has to do with creating value through sets of well-coordinated activities across the company's entire value chain. Similarly, the balanced scorecard focuses attention on strategically important activity sets and how these, in combination, work toward superior financial performance.

Figure 14.9
Balanced Scorecard for Low Cost Airline

	Objectives	Metrics	Targets	Strategic Initiatives
Financial	Profitability Fewer planes Increase revenue	Market value Plane lease cost Seat revenue	25% per year 5% per year 20% per year	Optimize routes Standardize planes
Customer	Satisfaction Lowest prices Reputation	FAA rank: on time, bags lost Competitive ranking Passenger appreciation Gate agent/crew friendliness	# 1 in industry 90% of time 85% 95%	On demand crew Weekly comparison Customer survey Passenger survey
Internal	Fast ground turnaround Shorter downtime for maintenance	On-ground time On time departure % parts 10-year durability % suppliers with A+ rating	< 25 minutes 93% 65% 75%	Real time scheduling R&D joint venture Annual assessment
Learning	Ground crew capabilities & coordination Technology-assisted just in time (JIT) capability	% ground crew JIT certified % of pay based on JIT % ground crew who are stockholders # of JIT engineers hired % increase in IT spending	60% 25% 100% 50 25%	JIT training Stock ownership plan JIT recruiting plan Upgrade data systems

Figure 14.9 illustrates another example of a balanced scorecard, in this case a simplified version of a scorecard for a low cost airline.[14] In this example the overall strategy has been broken down into strategic objectives within each of the four levels. Specific lag metrics have been laid out – both the description and the quantified targets. And strategic initiatives identified with the accomplishment of each lag metric are indicated. Management needs to take one more step in this example, and further break down each strategic initiative into specific activities engaged in regularly by employees. For example, for just-in-time (JIT) training for ground crew employees the lead metric may be established initially at 60% annual participation. If this level of training fails to accomplish certification goals and the objective of ground crew coordination, then the airline can adjust the lead metric up, re-establishing it at 75%.

Value-Driver-Action Model

It is important to recognize the contribution that the balanced scorecard makes to the ability of organizations to implement their strategies. Forcing companies to simultaneously consider multiple facets of the company and to codify those into measurable outcomes has made a significant impact in the ways in which some companies manage and perform. On the other hand, the balanced scorecard model requires management to think about its organization using the four perspectives. These four perspectives do not resemble the way most organizations are structured (e.g functionally), or the ways in which managers might think about their value chain activities. So for many managers, the balanced scorecard may be like asking a right-handed baseball player to bat left-handed: you know what to do, but you are definitely not practiced at it and it therefore is difficult to put into use. In fact, most consultants claim that it can take 18-24 months to develop a really effective scorecard. So to get there requires great organizational commitment, involving people at all levels for extended periods of time.

An alternative to the balanced scorecard is the value-driver-action model. This model builds more directly off the key ideas that managers use all along when they are formulating strategy. Where strategy implementation can more transparently take advantage of strategy formulation ideas and perspectives, the effort can be more easily comprehended and developed. This enables its use across a variety of situations, such as global expansion (Nestle), acquisitions (IDEX), non-profit sustainability efforts (United Nations), and more. Like the balanced scorecard, this model also focuses on the needs of the individual company and its unique resource-based advantages.

An effective value-driver-action plan has five components:

1) Identifying key value drivers that will lead to a competitive advantage for the business;
2) Outlining the position the company wants to occupy from the perspective of how customers, suppliers, employees, and other stakeholders experience the company;
3) Translating desired stakeholder experience to business/market position;
4) Creating a list of actions to be taken, both short-term and long-term, that answer the question "what must we do now to ensure success?"
5) Developing metrics that measure progress toward the accomplishment of each value driver.

Key value drivers. The first and most critical element is the identification of the key value drivers for the organization. These can be identified from four sources:
- The list of key success factors (KSFs) identified through industry analysis (Chapter 4)
- Analysis and diagram of company's value chain (Chapter 5)
- The resource-based analysis that pinpoints extraordinary resources (Chapter 6)
- The vision and mission statements (Chapter 3)

One of the goals of industry analysis that we discussed in Chapter 4 was the identification of key success factors – those few competitive dimensions that are critical to succeeding in an industry. Through value chain (Chapter 5) and resource-based analysis (Chapter 6) managers can draw conclusions about extraordinary, advantage-producing resources that the company possesses. These are often embedded intangibly in sets of value chain activities and knowledge-producing routines. Finally, the aspirations of the company may extend beyond the immediate industry environment and immediate resource endowments. So critical dimensions for creating value over the long run might be identified by referring to the company's vision statement (Chapter 3).

The key value drivers for the company therefore arise out of some combination of current industry demands, current company activities and capabilities, and future company aspirations. It is usually the case that current demands and current organizational capabilities dominate the list of value drivers that management decides upon. There is no absolute "right answer" when it comes to establishing the drivers, but the choice of drivers will make a significant difference in the results of the overall implementation plan.

Earlier in this chapter we noted that the mission elements of Coca-Cola were: 1) to refresh the world in body and spirit; and 2) to make a difference everywhere they engage. Coca-Cola, which competes in an industry where scale, innovation, and global presence are critical, also has significant and extraordinary resources in brand marketing, international management, and bottler relations, among others. Together this combination of mission elements, industry requirements, and company capabilities should form the basis for identifying the value drivers for the business.

Desired stakeholder experiences. Articulating desired statements from the point of view of stakeholders anchors the second section of the value-driver-action model. Within each key value driver there will be a set of statements that the company aspires to hear from its stakeholders. These would indicate that the company has met its goals. It is relatively easy to develop a set of statements relating to a particular value. These might include statements such as "I really like drinking Dasani water because it tastes so clean" (retail customer), or "I get the best prices without ever going out of stock on a product that sells quickly through my stores" (store owner), or "We love investing in Coca-Cola because of their environmental efforts" (shareholders). These statements are a reflection of the way we believe we can create value for our stakeholders. In effect, they tell a story that we want to hear about our company, product, or service.

Translating experience to position. Having established the statements we are looking to hear from our stakeholders, each statement must be translated into a particular business or market position. These translations identify what the company must work toward achieving with respect to each value. In 2007 research was published that revealed how all bottled water is not the same. The research found that "potassium...may give water a sweet taste. Silica may impart silkiness. Calcium can give the water a lactic taste some people find refreshing. Others enjoy the cleansing quality of water with high sodium content."[15] If Coca-Cola would like to achieve the desired stakeholder statement "I really like drinking Dasani water because it tastes so clean," then its laboratory scientists may need to develop new techniques for purifying and fortifying bottled water, which in fact they did. Similarly, the desired shareholder experience of wanting to invest in the company because of its environmental efforts might prompt management to establish a goal of becoming the leading beverage company in the recycling of plastic containers.

This latter example points out a possible disconnect between a targeted business or market position (based upon desired stakeholder experiences) and a company's existing resources and capabilities. Accomplishing the business or market positions prompts us to evaluate which resources, capabilities, structures, or programs we must have. Of course, it is not possible for a company to instantly become a leader in recycling, because of significant investments required in science, infrastructure, manufacturing, customer relations, and other important value chain dimensions. Thus, the benefit of translating desired experiences to targeted business positions is examining what can be done immediately and also what will require longer-term investment.

Actions list. Implementation is often driven by the most pressing and immediate stakeholder values. The third piece of the value-driver-actions model consists of distilling the desired stakeholder perspective goals down into specific sets of actions. Starting with each statement listed in the stakeholder experience section, the next step is to develop a list of actions that must be undertaken. There are two time frames for actions identified in this phase: 1) actions that immediately address stakeholder experiences taking advantage of existing resources, and 2) actions to build new resources to address long-term aspirations and values.

If Coca-Cola wishes to develop water that has a "clean, refreshing taste," then a plausible immediate action might consist of an enhanced R&D budget for its lab to develop a series of test products that might fulfill the desired value, along with consumer research to test and verify the best formulations. In 2017 Ford announced new initiatives related to "disruptive" mobility trends that were advancing in the automobile industry. Anticipating that electrification, autonomous vehicles and ride-sharing will be values increasingly appreciated over time, the company formed "Team Edison" to research battery technology and develop an electric vehicle strategy. It established a joint ventured with Lyft, and another with Chinese company Zotye to gain a toehold in the huge all-electric vehicle segment in that country. These are all long term initiatives targeted at aspirations and emerging values.

Metrics. Finally, we return to the need to develop metrics for monitoring and controlling progress toward strategic goals. Each metric should tie directly to the stakeholder statement made for that value driver. The initial development effort will most likely lead to a long list of metrics. Prior to publishing a chart for widespread use in the company, the list needs to be consolidated to make it internally consistent, properly targeted and universally understandable. The goal of the plan is to focus everyone in the organization coherently to the same set of outcomes. Putting all of this together is the final step. Ideally, this entire plan can be seen on a single page that can be shared with everyone in the company. The chart might look something like the one in Figure 14.10.

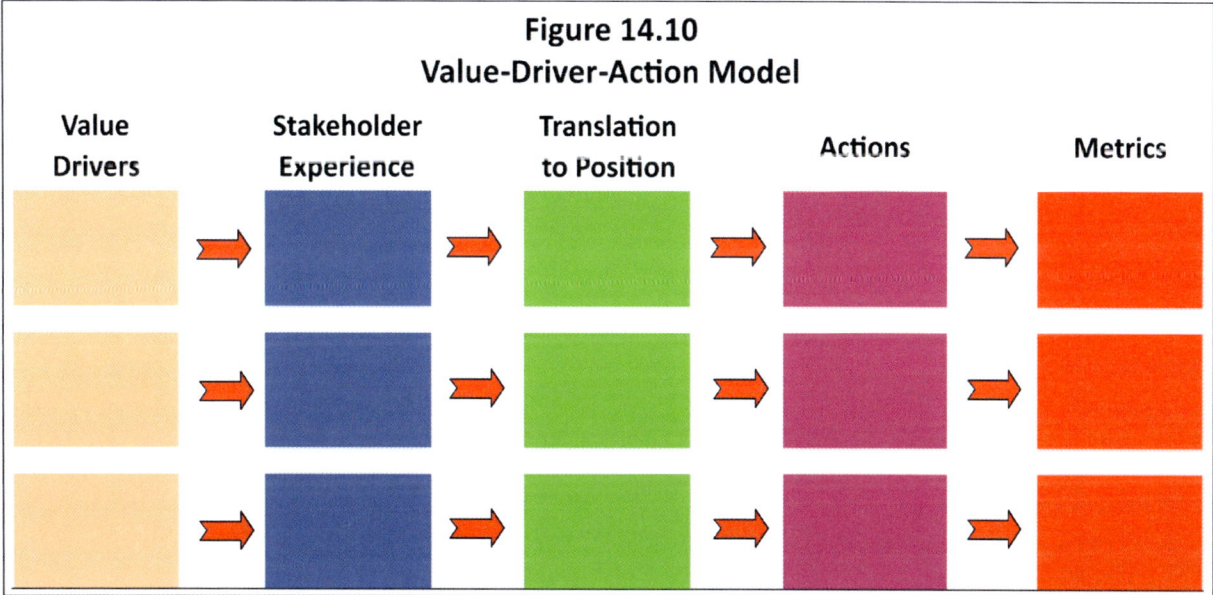

Earlier in this chapter was presented a vignette about Ford Motor Company's travails in the mid-2000s, leading to their plan "The Way Forward." Figures 14.11 (a) and (b) present a partial picture of the value-driver-action model for Ford, based upon two of its core value drivers of consumer economic value and brand focus. For consumer economic value the desired stakeholder experiences translated to business positions regarding the sales process and the underlying cost / design /quality dimensions of the vehicles. Classic designs manufactured at competitive costs would yield durable perceived value and strong resell prices. Revamping the dealer sales process and incentives would help remove the unpleasant "car haggling" that goes on when customers shop for cars. Metrics to be collected would measure the progress of the company on these actions.

Figure 14.11 (a)
Ford Motor Company Value-Driver-Action Model

Value Drivers	Stakeholder Experience	Translation to Position	Actions To Take Now	Metrics
Consumer Economic Value	1. I always feel like I'm getting most bang for my buck with Ford. 2. Buying is no haggling, straightforward, no cash on the hood rebates. 3. When I sell my Ford, it feels like I'm getting a good return.	1. List price = sales price. 2. No haggle sales process. 3. Develop classic popular designs to ensure high retained value. 4. Reduce cost structure to best in class.	1. Change incentive structure & sales process. 2. Reduce overhead thru efficiencies below to achieve best in class cost. 3. Revamp designs where needed to classic timeless designs.	1. # of rebates lowest in industry 2. Avg Ford discount /Industry avg discount 3. Residual prices highest in peer group 4. # Consumers Choice awards for value 5. Production cost/model compared to peer group

Figure 14.11 (b)
Ford Motor Company Value-Driver-Action Model

Value Drivers	Stakeholder Experience	Translation to Position	Actions To Take Now	Metrics
Brand Focus	1. My family has always owned Fords and we believe in buying American Ford vehicles…it's a tradition. 2. My job is to produce the best new Ford truck or car on the road. 3. Ford's repositioning strategy has combined the best of brand loyalty and preference. 4. People understand what we stand for – simply a Ford with focus on "Way Forward" consistency & reliability.	1. The Company divests other competing or distracting brands (Lincoln & Mercury). 2. Narrow Ford's selection to typify its heritage: Ford F-Series, mid-sized SUV (combining the best of the Explorer and Expedition), sporty Mustang and smaller, entry-level sedan (combining the best of the Escape and the Fusion). 3. Ford offers four colors: Ford Black, Ford Blue, Ford Red, Ford White. Develop each of the four colors as a distinct new color only offered on Fords. 4. Develop a unique integrated marketing "Way Forward" campaign that creates the 'buzz' and 'call to action' to compel consumers to buy a new Ford!	1. Locate a buyer for non-Ford brands. 2. Develop a timeline for selling down the existing Ford inventory. 3. Hire a new advertising and public relations firm to begin developing the message and planning the marketing & advertising campaign. 4. Plan an Analysts' Day to introduce Wall Street analysts to the new "Way Forward" strategy.	1. Survey consumers to determine the expected & unexpected for a new Ford vehicle, interior and exterior. 2. Ratio of customer complaints to total customer touch points (i.e. online feedback, service questionnaires, post-purchase surveys, car show visitors). 3. Market share of units sold in U.S. – both cars & trucks.

Brand focus as a value driver resulted in a number of stakeholder experience statements for various stakeholders – both customers and employees. For employees desiring to produce the best on the road, focusing on manufacturing fewer brands would have benefits across the manufacturing operation: fewer suppliers, fewer plants, fewer model changeovers, greater efficiency. Divesting certain brands (e.g. Jaguar) would help focus procurement, design, marketing and other departments on Ford. Greater attention to Ford brands should result in enhanced manufacturing quality and market share.

McDonald's – The Continuing Story[16]

McDonald's illustrates excellence in strategy implementation, utilizing many ideas discussed in this chapter to create their "Plan to Win." The plan put the implementation effort onto a single page, in a format allowing every employee to understand the keys to success and how they will be measured. First, they established their Key Value Drivers and what those drivers meant:

Key Value Driver	Meaning
Our People	Well-trained, friendly people are key to providing I'm Loving It Service
Our Products	Our menu features the choice and variety that consumers enjoy eating often
Our Places	The comfort and convenience of our restaurants attract customers
Our Prices	Through our products and restaurant experience, we deliver value to customers
Our Promotions	"Forever Young" and engaging, our Brand connects with people around the world

Each of these drivers was then converted into stakeholder statements such as:

Key Value Driver	Stakeholder Statement
Our People	"A simple smile makes me feel welcome... it's the perfect start to my meal... it's the reason I love McDonalds."
Our Products	"What do I want from a Restaurant? Good food and good choices. That's why I go to McDonalds."
Our Places	"McDonald's is a cool place where everyone can relax. I'm comfortable here, and my friends and I know we're always welcome."
Our Prices	"Whether I have a lot or a little to spend, McDonald's always offers great taste at a great value."
Our Promotions	"I love McDonald's. I can eat great food, play and get a fun toy. I guess that's why my mom loves McDonald's too."

The company listed critical success factors and "must do now" actions before designing a set of metrics. We illustrate metrics from one value driver as an example:

Key Value Driver	Metrics
Our People	Training & Development - $$ Investment, number of graduates from Hamburger University, New platforms for career development.
	Great Place to Work – Rated in 100 Best companies to work for.
	Diversity Initiatives – McDonald's trains more minorities and women than any other U.S. employer. 40% of Owner/Operators and more than 50% of workforce is women and minorities.
	McPassport – a program of employee training and certification that allows free movement throughout the E.U.

Overarching metrics included items such as return to shareholders, new product launches, store growth, dividend growth, etc. By virtually any measure available – whether sales, same-store sales, stock price, returns, etc. – McDonald's has executed with precision.

The 7-S Framework

The third tool available for turning strategy into action is one of the most popular and consistently-used frameworks over time. The 7-S framework was developed four decades ago by McKinsey.[17] Intentionally using alliteration to help aid memory, the technique helps us align the functions of an organization. Most strategists split the seven S's into the hard S's (so called because they are relatively easy to identify and articulate in a written document) and the soft S's (named because they are more difficult to pin down in a precise manner). The entire framework (Figure 14.12) is oriented around the concept of fit. The better each of the seven fit together, the better the organization performs.

Figure 14.12
McKinsey 7-S Framework

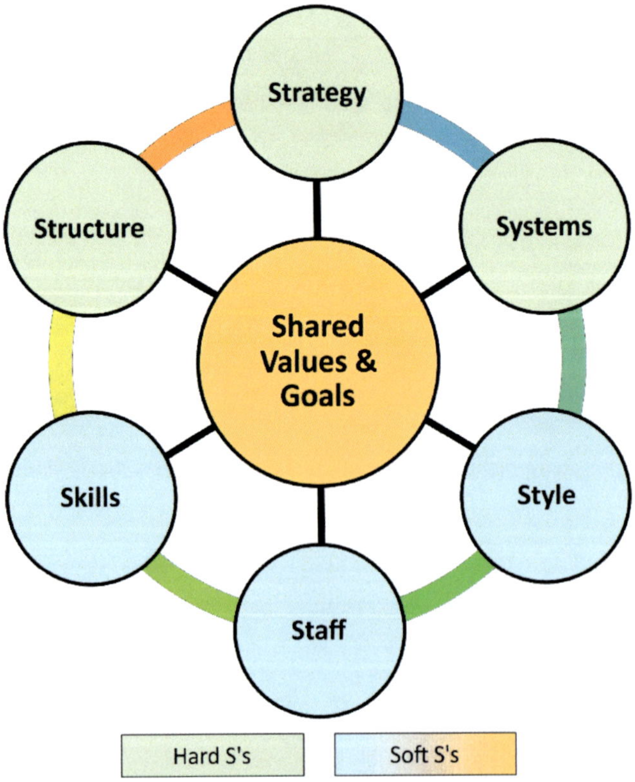

Strategy. This is the written set of statements that constitutes the strategic direction of the company. This formulation is the compilation of most of what we have discussed in this text. It is the examination of the value chain, capabilities, resource-based advantages, and business level strategy of the organization such that it can compete effectively. The strategy is the means by which the company intends to be successful.

Structure. Most people often seen this as the written organization chart, but readers of this text should view this as the *design* of the organization, which was discussed in detail in Chapter 13. That design is a combination of knowing: 1) what constitutes the core, techno structure, and support staff of the organization; 2) how activities will be coordinated consistent with strategy; and 3) what organizational structures you will use. The structure should be designed to support the strategy, because "structure follows strategy."

Systems. While often thought of as the information technology systems of the company, this just scratches the surface of what constitutes the systems of the company. Having designed an effective strategy and aligned the structure so it supports the strategy, it is incumbent upon senior management to align the systems of the company so they support both the strategy and the structure. Quality control systems, performance review systems, human resources systems, and policies and procedures are all amongst the systems that need to be considered. Aligning the systems so they support the new structure is a critical step in implementation. Little will happen if the systems do not provide the information needs of the company. Changing the systems of an organization can be quite traumatic as they have usually been developed over a long period of time, and employees are accustomed to them. That said, a new strategy and structure demands a reevaluation of all the systems of the organization. What can be eliminated? What needs to be done to support the new core functions? What new metrics must be gathered? Systems support the organization and its goals, providing the critical link between a strategy that is desired and a structure that is trying to implement that strategy.

Style. The symbolic behavior of the organization starts at the top of the organization. The way that employees treat each other, the balance between formal and informal behavior, and the approach to the work day are all elements of the organization's style. The CEO and the top management team of the company set the style that constitutes acceptable behavior. This element is based in action and often has little to do with what is actually said. An organization that is fundamentally built upon freedom of expression, creativity, and taking chances can be enhanced by a CEO like Steve Jobs who embodied those style elements and can be crushed by a CEO like John Scully whose style was corporate control and formality-oriented. In the previous chapter we mentioned the free-wheeling company Zappos, which has implemented an adhocracy structure. How strange it would be if they also instituted a coat-and-tie dress rule or required people to communicate through written memoranda! The alignment of style with the desired strategy, structure, and systems of a company has the ability to propel the organization forward because of its unifying effect.

Staff. Staffing is an examination of the means and processes for bringing in new employees as well as the processes inherent in getting them to be productive for the company. New employees take time to start really providing value to the organization. Staffing is about shortening that time and aligning the process with the rest of the company.

Too often employees are brought in with no formal means of incorporating their efforts into the organization. They learn the nomenclature, practices, and people via an informal, ad hoc system that makes early contribution to success almost impossible. Arthur Andersen & Co. was the storied accounting firm that had this process down to a science. Every employee started their career at the Andersen school in Illinois. They learned about the processes, practices, and expectations in a high-pressure, fast-paced program that made them quickly valuable to the organization.

Skills. These are the dominant skills of the organization, and dictate what is most important in creating value for that particular organization. These are similar to what we referred to as capabilities in Chapter 6 or the Core in Chapter 13. Within the same industry, we often see a wide variety of skill sets depending upon the overarching goals of the company. One insurance company might determine that deep knowledge of insurance is a core skill for their company. They might require everyone to study insurance and be certified in the area. Another insurance company might decide that the core set of skills is customer service. They would set their training program up to establish customer service skills as those that should permeate the entire organization. Another insurance company, such as Geico, might decide it is all about sales and marketing skills. They would organize around the salespeople and emphasize sales and marketing skills as the critical capabilities set of the organization.

Superordinate Goal (Shared Values). These are the overarching goals of the organization. In practice this is usually manifested in the vision, mission and principles of the company, representing the focus of the company and its reason for existence. Aligning the vision and mission of the company with the strategy would seem to be obvious. As we discussed extensively in Chapter 3, this is an important element in guiding the practices of every employee, every day of the week.

Art, Science, Balance, Continuity

Putting together the balanced scorecard, the value-driver-action model, or the 7-S framework for a company is as much art as it is science. With any of these implementation frameworks it is important to consider all of the elements when designing the plan and the appropriate metrics.

Balance across the company is always important. One interesting approach for incorporating the 7-S framework into the implementation plan is to require that at least several metrics touch each of the seven areas of the company. The other significant advantage of a balanced implementation effort is the benefit that it has on the speed with which the business can move in new directions. Well-designed metrics essentially create an early warning system. This enhances agility to meet emerging challenges, and can provide a key source of competitive advantage in dynamic markets. The strategic management model that we outlined in Chapter 1 (Figure 1.6) is a dynamic model that should provide continual feedback for the decision makers in an organization. Designing and implementing strategy is an ongoing process, not an event.

The effort at aligning the organization provides the information flow necessary to create a learning organization. Company-designed metrics can provide information on the resource-based advantages of the business and feedback to initiate a review of the process all over again with new insight. Insight is provided not only on the true capabilities of the company, but also exposes new opportunities for the organization. And as we have emphasized, opportunity recognition is critical for achieving sustainable competitive advantage.

Managing in Markets: Question for Class Discussion

Leaders cannot assume that everyone in a company agrees with the public stands the company may take, or with the direction the company is taking. Hidden conflicts with espoused corporate values and direction may drain away commitment. What should a leader do?

STRATEGIC LEADERSHIP

As a conclusion to our discussion of effective strategy implementation, we briefly mention the critical role played by strategic leadership. In fact, every step along the way in this textbook we have been highlighting points where strategic leadership is important. It is the responsibility of the senior management team to bring together all of the strategic management functions so that the business can develop sustainable competitive advantages and earn superior returns. These core responsibilities of strategic leadership can be summed up in the following list:

- **Establish vision, mission, goals.** Leadership is at its core about guiding the total business forward in a manner that has the potential to be extraordinary. Designing an appropriate vision and mission is at the heart of this effort.

- **Espouse principles and a code of ethics for behavior and decision making.** Establishing this moral framework and continuing to emphasize it regularly brings it alive throughout the organization.

- **Establish a match between the culture and personal leadership style.** The most effective CEOs find time to reflect, are relentless questioners, and seek to make sense of what is happening now and what changes are on the horizon. A culture that matches the values of the leader and is in harmony with the leader's actions will prove to be a powerful driving force for the organization. Sometimes this means the culture might change to reflect a leader's style, and in other cases it may mean the leader's style must match the existing culture.

- **Build management team.** Identifying, recruiting, and hiring the best people to lead a particular company at a particular point in time is crucial for success. But hiring for transformation is also critical. The strategic imperative of opportunity recognition is put into practice through innovation efforts that proactively seek out and embrace new ideas, encourage experimentation, and precipitate learning. The team needs to possess experience and capabilities for managing these efforts.

- **Establish management team process that challenges assumptions, surfaces alternatives.** This follows on from leadership experienced in innovation. The visibility of this process sends an important signal to the rest of the organization about desirable behavior.

- **Establish structure for communication, coordination, and control.** The structure of the organization is wholly dependent upon the strategy that has been designed.

- **Install a strategy implementation progress evaluation system.** Using a performance monitoring system ensures effective strategy implementation.

- **Evaluate, decide, act.** Decision making about value chain, resources allocation, type of strategy, growth, and implementation are the province of successful leaders. Commitment of resources to follow through on decisions is crucial.

- **Rational decision making.** Strategic moves are not decided on a whim or based upon personal egos or desires. Effective strategy requires excellence in deep, revealing analysis. This can then be married to intuition and perspective that comes from personal experience.
- **Motivate through incentives and rewards aligned with goals.** Establish a system that rewards employees when their individual accomplishments contribute to organizational goals.
- **Establish a leadership development program.** This could not only be for senior management, but also for employees throughout the company who are seeking to advance their careers and make greater contributions. Provide opportunities to meet and work with peers across the company. Find ways to expose managers throughout the company to cutting edge thinking emanating from other companies and consultancies.

Strategic leadership is most often the province of senior management, as the preceding list of bullet point ideas attests. But let us return to the initial idea about strategic leadership that we presented in the very first chapter of this book. Since strategy by definition involves all functions in a company and crosses all levels, everyone in the organization is exposed to it, affects its success, and can offer critical input on its formulation and its implementation. This includes you. Some of the ideas and frameworks you have read about in this book are newer ideas that others in your future companies won't be aware of. Not only do frameworks like value chain and VRIST analysis present you with your own potential for competitive advantage in your career, they also present your own opportunity to serve as a strategic leader within your sphere of influence!

Guiding an organization through the combination of dynamic challenges from the general environment, aggressive competitors, demanding customers, and other stakeholders is a complex process. It is a process that demands the application of both science and art. A deep understanding of the science of strategy and its application has been the goal of this book. Intuition married with an appreciation of the intangibles of leading and guiding is the art of strategic leadership. You will become the strategic leaders of tomorrow, and we hope this book helps you to succeed.

CHAPTER SUMMARY

This chapter focused on the issues involved in internal control and performance, which is a challenging part of strategy implementation. We began the chapter by discussing five keys to control and performance systems:

1. Top-Management Involvement
2. Fit
3. Clear and Compelling Objectives
4. A Single Company Currency
5. Resource Allocation

We reviewed the development of different types of metrics, because any system of control and performance must be based on definable dimensions that can be measured. The set of metrics must exhibit five conditions:

1. Are tied to the overall mission/vision of the organization.
2. Are translated appropriately to all functions and levels of employees.
3. Are balanced across all functions.
4. Are composed of both quantitative and qualitative measures.
5. Are connected to a unifying incentives system.

Next we reviewed three frameworks for monitoring and evaluating performance. These systems allow management to evaluate whether short-term progress toward long-term strategic goals is positive, or if corrective actions are called for:

1. Balanced scorecard model, which examines execution through four perspectives:
   - Learning and Growth
   - Internal Process
   - Customer
   - Financial

2. Value-driver-action model, which is directly translatable to an individual organization's strategic direction and consists of five parts:
   - Value Drivers
   - Stakeholder Experience
   - Translation to Position
   - Action
   - Metrics

3. The McKinsey 7-S framework, which consists of three hard S's and four soft S's:
   - Strategy
   - Structure
   - Systems
   - Skills
   - Style
   - Staff
   - Superordinate Goals (shared values)

Learning Objectives Review

1. Translate strategy into functional area goals and activities using the keys to implementation control.

- There are five keys to success against which strategy implementation should be evaluated: Fit; Clear and compelling objectives; Single company currency for incentives; Top management involvement; Resource allocations to support direction and commitments.

- Implementation begins with mission and vision. The strategic approach which will accomplish the mission leads to specific strategic initiatives. Value chain activities relevant to these initiatives are conducted. Metrics evaluating value-creating activities can monitor progress on the accomplishment of strategy.

2. *Develop effective metrics for the control and growth of the organization.*
   - Are tied to the overall mission/vision of the organization.
   - Are translated appropriately to all functions and levels of employees.
   - Are balanced across all functions.
   - Are composed of both quantitative and qualitative measures.
   - Are connected to a unifying incentives system.

3. *Describe the differences between the models used for implementing a strategic plan.*
   - The balanced scorecard connects long term competitive and financial performance to short term actions. It relies on a cause-effect logic that requires lead and lag metrics on activities engaged in by a wide variety of stakeholders.
   - The value-drive-action model builds more directly on strategy formulation efforts. Value creation goals drive actions to enable the company to move from its present position to a desired future position.
   - The 7-S framework seeks to align seven important dimensions of the organization.

4. *List and describe the core responsibilities of strategic leadership.*
   - Establish vision, mission, goals.
   - Build senior management team.
   - Establish structure for communication, coordination, and control.
   - Exert control over direction.
   - Establish a code of ethics for conduct and decision making.
   - Evaluate, decide, act.
   - Rational decision making.
   - Establish top-management team process that challenges assumptions, surfaces alternatives.
   - Establish a match between the culture and personal leadership style.
   - Motivate through incentives and rewards aligned with goals.

Key Terms

7-S framework – A method for examining the various aspects of the organization in such a way that alignment can be achieved. Elements include strategy, structure, systems, style, skills, staff and superordinate goals (shared values).

Balanced scorecard – An implementation method that considers a wide variety of stakeholders in the performance of the company.

Casual logic – A cause-effect statement of belief about how and why things work the way they do.

Characteristics of effective metrics – There are five elements to high-quality metrics. They are: 1) tied to the mission and vision; 2) appropriate for the function or level; 3) balanced across functions; 4) both quantitative and qualitative; and 5) connected to incentives.

Key value drivers – A small number of factors that epitomize the most critical ways in which value is created and appreciated. These are derived from a combination of current industry demands (KSFs), current company activities and VRIST-based capabilities, and future company aspirations.

Lag metrics – Represent the results that we expect to observe for each sub-dimension in a balanced scorecard.

Lead metrics – Represent the observable actions of employees that will lead to the results we are trying to achieve.

Qualitative metrics – Measures of success that are descriptive and relative rather than analytic.

Quantitative metrics – Numerically based measures of firm success.

Short Answer Review Questions

1. Why is strategy implementation so important to a company?
2. What elements would you consider to be critical for effective implementation?
3. What is a balanced scorecard?
4. How do the elements in the balanced scorecard work with each other?
5. Why do we start with the learning and growth part of the model?
6. How does the value-driver-action method differ from the balanced scorecard method?
7. How do we determine the key value drivers for an organization?
8. What types of statements constitute good stakeholder statements?
9. What criteria should you use when designing good metrics?
10. How do metrics guide the organization?
11. How would you recommend corporate metrics be translated to individual employee metrics?
12. What is a qualitative metric and how should it be used in the organization?

13. How are key stakeholder statements translated into action plans?

14. What issues should be addressed in the alignment of style?

Group Exercises

1. In 2022 McDonald's – a company profiled in this chapter for its use of the value-driver-action model – is undergoing a rethinking of their strategic approaches. This is because the marketplace and competition have changed over the years. They believe their products feel outdated to many young consumers. American's dining habits have shifted, with an inundation of restaurant alternatives and the advent of home delivery services. At the same time during the Covid-19 pandemic their more focused menu around burgers, chicken and coffee did extremely well. Their promotional tie-ins with Korean pop group BTS was very successful. A new loyalty program has begun to gain traction.

   a. What are the key value drivers for this company today?

   b. Given those drivers, what statements would you like to hear from stakeholders for each of the value drivers?

   c. How might you measure whether the company was successfully achieving those stakeholder statements?

2. Take a look at one of the package delivery companies such as FedEx, UPS, or the U.S. Postal Service. They each need a balanced scorecard for their organization and each of those scorecards should be quite different. Select one of those organizations and develop a balanced scorecard for the company based upon publicly available information.

3. A new salon has approached you about their business. The mission of this organization is: "Everything for the body." They plan to be the largest salon in the state of Colorado, with hairstylists, manicurists, massage therapists, tanning facilities, a huge 50 foot by 120 foot saltwater warm bathing area, sauna facilities, yoga facilitation, meditation classes, and Pilates. There will be a personal attendant for each customer and the customer will be truly pampered. A large office staff will be required, a day care facility for the children, a high-end artsy restaurant will be on-site for the patrons, and everything will be cutting edge with each patron only having to press their thumbprint to gain access to an area or pay for their purchases! The owner would like help in designing a 7-S framework for this new business idea. Design a 7-S for this business.

Investor Relations Sites for Companies Mentioned in This Chapter

Celestial Seasonings (Hain Celestial): https://ir.hain.com/
Coca Cola Company: https://investors.coca-colacompany.com/
Ford Motor Company: https://shareholder.ford.com/investors/overview/default.aspx
General Electric: https://www.ge.com/investor-relations
McDonald's: https://corporate.mcdonalds.com/corpmcd/investors.html

Panera Bread (JAB Holdings): https://www.jabholco.com/

References

[1] Grainger, David. 2003, "Can McDonald's cook again?" Fortune, April 14, 147(7): 40–47. Horovitz, Bruce, 2003, "It's back to basics for McDonald's," USA Today, May 20.

[2] See https://bscdesigner.com/balanced-scorecard-fact-sheet.htm.

[3] Mankins, M. C. and Steele, R. 2005. "Turning great strategy into great performance." *Harvard Business Review*, July-August, 123-131.

[4] Bossidy, L., and R. Charan. 2002. *Execution: The discipline of getting things done*. New York: Crown Business.

[5] Welch, Jack, and John Byrne. 2001. *Jack: Straight from the gut*. Warner Books. New York.

[6] Stoll J. D., 2018, "It's really hard to think long term," Wall Street Journal, December 4, R11.

[7] www.thecoca-colacompany.com

[8] Jargon, J. 2017. "Panera slices lines with mobile." Wall Street Journal, June 3, B1.

[9] PwC, 2022, "Reimagining the outcomes that matter," www.ceosurvey.pwc.

[10] Economist, 2005, "Changing gear," September 15. Economist, 2006, "Shrink to fit," January 5. Ford, W., 2006, "The way forward," speech given at Ford Motor Company Business Review, January 23. Ford Company 2006 and 2007 Annual Reports. White, J. B. & J. McCracken, 2006, "How U.S. auto industry finds itself stalled by its own history," Wall Street Journal, January 7.

[11] Kaplan, R. S., and D. P. Norton, 1992, "Balanced scorecard: Measures that drive performance," *Harvard Business Review* 70(1): 71–80. Kaplan, R. S., and D. P. Norton, 1996, "Linking the balanced scorecard to strategy," *California Management Review* 39(1): 53–79.

[12] Balanced Scorecard Institute, https://balancedscorecard.org/bsc-basics-overview/.

[13] Rigby, D. & B. Bilodeau, 2015, "Management tools and trends," Bain & Company, http://www.bain.com/. See also https://bscdesigner.com/balanced-scorecard-fact-sheet.htm.

[14] Adapted from Balanced Scorecard Institute, www.balancedscorecard.org.

[15] Kayal, Michele. 2007. Top beverage. The Winston-Salem Journal. November 5: D1.

[16] McDonald's Corporation – 2006 Annual Report.

[17] Waterman, Robert H., Thomas J. Peters, and Julien R. Phillips, 1980, "Structure is not organization," *Business Horizons*, June: 14–26. Waterman, Robert H., 1982, "The seven elements of strategic fit," *Journal of Business Strategy* 2(3): 69–73.

This page is intentionally left blank.

Index

3M, 30, 54, 175
7-S framework, 470, 472
AB InBev, 275
Absolute cost advantage, 139
Access to distribution, 140
Access to inputs, 139
Activision Blizzard, 108, 328
Activity-based costing, 184, 193
Adhocracy structure, 440
Advanced Battery Consortium, 406
Agency issue, 327
Airbus Industries, 33, 207, 208, 240, 344
Airline industry, 57
Alliances, strategic, 401, 406, 407
Alphabet, 89
Amazon, 21, 73, 96, 219
Analyzer organization, 392
Apple, 156, 169, 199, 200, 208, 384
Arab oil embargo, 39
Asset productivity (see Return on equity), 66
AT&T, 270, 333, 341, 352
Autoliv, 104
Automobile industry, 155
Awareness-motivation-capabilities, 398
Backward integration, 146
Balanced scorecard, 460, 461, 462, 463, 464, 472, 477
Baltimore Orioles, 395
Bandwagon effect, 329
Banfield, 237
Bargaining power, 143, 145, 146, 238, 245, 283, 328
BCG Growth Share Matrix, 347, 348
Berkshire Hathaway, 337
Best Buy, 273, 281, 369
Bidding wars, 344
Big hairy audacious goal (BHAG), 96
Boeing, 32, 207, 208, 240, 241, 344
Boston Consulting Group, 347, 348
Boston Scientific, 171, 324, 344, 346
Bright Horizons, 248, 276
Buc-ee's, 206

Business-level strategy, 231, 234, 235
CAGE distance framework, 374
Canon, 180
Capital requirements, 138
Carvana, 245
Cash cow, 348
Caterpillar, 100
Causal ambiguity, 210
Causal logic, 454
Celestial Seasonings (Hain Celestial), 458
Centralized single country strategy, 372
Ciba-Geigy (BASF), 184
Cisco, 334, 341, 345
Clipping service, 397
Collateralized Loan Obligation (CLO), 323
Commercialization, 278
Common stock returns, 68
Common-sized statements, 71
Competitive dynamics, 189, 385, 393, 394
Competitive Strategy, 40
Complements, 271
Concentration ratio, 144, 275
Conception, 277
Conglomerates, 321
Cooperation, 311, 401, 403, 404, 406, 407
Coordinating mechanisms, 336, 426
Corporate strategy, 30, 319
Costco, 75
Crisis, response to, 28, 286, 389, 433
Cross-sector diversification, 334
CVS Health, 73
De Beers, 140
Decline stage, 269
Defender organization, 392
Dell Technologies, 110, 186, 232
Delta, 57, 64
Differentiation strategy, 235, 244, 249, 250, 302
Direct supervision, 427, 430, 431
Divestiture, 348, 349, 351
Divisional structure, 435
Dominant business, 321, 435
Downscoping, 350

Due diligence, 342, 344, 407
E*Trade, 76, 283
Eagle Materials, 229
Earthlink (Windstream), 285
Economic logic, 75, 76
Economies of scale, 139, 239
Entry barriers, 138, 329
Ernst & Young, 109
Ethics, 41, 473
Executional drivers, 194
Exit barriers, 149
Experience curve, 139, 239, 350
Facebook (Meta Platforms), 106
Famous Amos (Kellogg's), 185
FASB, 136
Feeding America, 64
Ferrari, 244
Financial leverage (see Return on equity), 66
First mover strategy, 268, 282, 285
Five forces analysis, 137
Focus strategy, 251, 252
Ford, 405, 459, 467, 479
Forward integration, threat of, 147
Functional structure, 280, 433, 434, 435
Gas prices, shortages, 39, 82
GE Business Development Matrix, 347
General Electric, 208, 211, 347, 351
General Mills, 111, 208, 299, 304
GM Financial, 103
Good to Great, 68
Government regulation, 141, 331, 340, 371
Greenbrier Resort, 178
Growth stage, 268, 277, 278, 280, 282
Haier, 440
Halliburton, 101
Helix structure, 439
Herfindahl-Hirschman Index (HHI), 144, 275
Hewlett Packard, 232, 396
Hewlett Packard Enterprises (HPE), 318, 352
Hitachi, 436
Holding companies, 337
Horizontal diversification, 321, 333
HP Inc., 76, 156, 241, 318, 351, 352

Hypercompetition, 24, 386
IBM, 275
Ikea, 374
Illinois Tool Works, 317
Industry definition, 131, 160, 270
Ingersoll Rand, 63
Innovation
    Amplifying innovation, 304, 307
    Disruptive innovation, 304
    Incremental innovation, 303, 304
    Innovation, 34, 240, 295, 301, 314
    Process innovation, 302
    Product innovation, 302
    Radical innovation, 281, 306, 307, 308, 403
Installed base, of users, 76
Integrated strategy, 253
Intellectual property protection, 207
international strategy, 364, 365, 370, 372, 379, 436
Introduction stage, 268
JetBlue, 66, 142
John Deere, 306
Johnson & Johnson, 324, 351
Johnson Controls, 205
Key success factors, 128, 129, 151, 155, 338, 348
Key value drivers, 465
Kodak, 180, 248
Kontoor Brands, 351, 376
Krispy Kreme, 206, 374
Kroger, 32, 72
La Croix (National Beverage), 179
Lag metrics, 463, 464
Lead metrics, 463
Lenovo, 156, 232
Leveraged buyouts (LBO), 322
Life cycle, 267, 271, 272, 277, 280
Long-range planning, 39
Low cost strategy, 234, 238, 242
Managerial capitalism, 327
Marriott International, 63
Matrix structure, 437, 438
Maturity stage, 268
McDonald's, 392, 447, 469
McKinsey & Co., 286

Medtronic, 111
Merck, 171, 329
Merger and acquisition (M&A), 317, 321, 325
Metrics, 448, 451, 452, 455, 463
Microsoft, 61, 83, 246, 283, 305, 383
Mission statement, 91, 98, 112, 453
Mobility barriers, 274
Molson Coors, 275
Monopoly, 126
Multidivisional structure, 435
Multidomestic strategy, 371
Music industry, 215, 265
Mutual adjustment, 427, 428, 429, 431, 433
Mutual forbearance, 328, 402
NAICS code, 132, 164
Netflix, 305, 390
New entrants, 138, 238, 245
New York Times, 105
Nintendo, 279, 283, 383
NOAA, 89
Nomacorc (Vinventions), 201
Office Depot, 123
Offline Media, 98
Opportunity recognition imperative, 25, 300
Options, 309
Oracle, 326
Original equipment manufacturers (OEM), 276
Outsourcing, 230, 255, 256
Panera Bread (JAB Holdings), 455
Papa Murphy (MTY Food Group), 252
Parenting advantage, 338
Parity conditions, 236, 237, 241
Parker Hannifin, 102
Partners in Health, 65
Peery-Arrillaga Properties, 210
Pepsico, 111, 377
Perfect competition, 28, 126, 340
Perkin Elmer, 438
PetSmart, 237
Pfizer, 171, 372
Platforms, 166, 189, 308, 309
Plexus, 188
Portfolios, 308, 348
Post-acquisition efforts, 345

Pricing authority, gains in, 328
Primary activities, in value chain, 181, 187, 193, 335
Private equity firm, 323
Procter & Gamble, 189, 208, 305, 334, 375
Product differentiation, 141, 149, 250
Prospector organization, 391
Publix, 32
Qualcomm, 207
Qualitative metrics, 455
Quantitative metrics, 455
Reactor organization, 392
Recycling, 186, 190, 241
Regal Entertainment, 234
Related diversification, 332, 334, 335, 336
Renewal stage, 270
Reputation, 140, 141, 237, 246, 247, 283, 284
Residual income, 66
Resource-based analysis, 216
Resources
  extraordinary resources, 203, 204, 210, 211, 214, 250, 336
  intangible resources, 203
  ordinary resources, 203, 214
  tangible resources, 203
Restructuring, 350, 352
Retaliation, 142
Return on equity (ROE), 66
Revenue growth, 68, 345
Rivalry, 147, 238, 244, 399
Roche Holdings, 171
Rubbermaid (Newell Brands), 95
Ryanair, 234, 241, 256
Saks Fifth Avenue (Hudson's Bay Company), 75, 274
Samsung, 169, 384
Sarbanes-Oxley Act (SOX), 136
Scenario analysis, 388
Scope, 233, 234
Seiko NPC, 435
Signaling, in industry, 409
Simple structure, 419, 432, 433
Size advantage, 282, 283, 328
Social complexity, and resources, 211
Sonos, 252, 263

Sony, 110, 265, 283, 383
Southwest Airlines, 76, 104, 240
SQM, 140
Stakeholders, 62, 103, 452, 469, 474
Standard Industry Classification Code (SIC), 132
Standardization, 238, 251, 268, 274, 433
Staples, 123
Starbucks, 206, 215, 249, 254
Steelcase, 105
STEEPG forces, 133
Strategic alliances, 376, 405
Strategic business unit (SBU), 319
Strategic decisions, 34
Strategic group, 157
Strategic leadership, 42, 473, 474
Strategic management process, 43
Strategy map, 157, 158, 160
Structural drivers, 194
Structure-conduct-performance (SCP), 130
Stuck in the middle, 233, 234, 236, 253, 392
Substitutes, threat of, 142, 245
Supplier concentration, 146
Support activities, in value chain, 181, 187, 328, 335
Switching costs, 140, 145, 147, 149, 238, 283
SWOT analysis, 173
Synergy
    Management fit, 334, 335, 337
    Market fit, 334
    Operational fit, 334
    Synergy, 334, 342, 343, 357
Sysco, 63
Systematic risk, 330
Tactics, 286, 385, 400, 401, 402
Tata, 375
Techno structure, 424, 425, 426

The Art of War, 36
Thyssenkrupp, 110
Timing advantage, 208, 282
TJX, 213
Toshiba, 187, 255, 351
TOWS matrix, 175
Toyota Motor Corp., 255, 302
Toys 'R' Us, 256
Trajectories, industry, 158, 387
Transnational strategy, 371
Transsion, 252
Triple bottom line, 64
Truist Financial, 28, 109
Under Armour, 301
United Technologies, 219, 336, 351
Unrelated diversification, 332, 337
Unsystematic risk, 330
UPS, 146, 187, 255
Value capture, 187, 188, 204
Value creation imperative, 25, 300
Value-driver-action model, 465, 466, 467, 472
Vanguard, 238
Vertical diversification, 333
VF Corporation, 351
Vision statement, 91, 94, 110
Volkswagen, 90, 405
VRIST framework, 205, 209
Walmart, 21, 63, 254, 377
Walt Disney Company, 317
Waste Management, 101
Wealth of Nations, 125
Western Digital, 333
Whirlpool, 96, 369
Whole Foods (Amazon), 23, 111, 327
Wireless Alliance, 190
Zappos (Amazon), 439, 471
Zelle (Early Warning Services), 302

Made in the USA
Monee, IL
30 January 2024